CHRIST CHURCH CATHEDRAL, DUBLIN: A HISTORY

Christ Church Cathedral, Dublin
A History

EDITED BY
Kenneth Milne

FOUR COURTS PRESS

Set in 10.5 on 12.5 Ehrhardt for
FOUR COURTS PRESS LTD
Fumbally Lane, Dublin 8, Ireland
e-mail: info@four-courts-press.ie
and in North America by
FOUR COURTS PRESS
c/o ISBS, 5804 N.E. Hassalo Street, Portland, OR 97213.

A catalogue record for this title
is available from the British Library.

ISBN 1–85182–487–1

Printed in Great Britain
by MPG Books, Bodmin, Cornwall

Foreword

For the first time in its life of almost one thousand years the publication of this book gives Christ Church cathedral a major academic history. It is a story of its life and times, and of its witness to the gospel of our Lord Jesus Christ, through medieval, reformation and modern periods. It is also at times a story of human intrigue and of human folly. Any cathedral, after all, is an institution staffed by fallible men and women – though the men must accept the blame as well as the praise until as recently as the late 1960s.

On behalf of the chapter and the board of the cathedral it is not only my duty but also my pleasure to thank all who have contributed to this magnificent production in any way. Those named below have not only been hardworking within their own spheres, they have also met together, sometimes monthly, over some five years to listen to and comment on each author's draft chapters.

Dr Kenneth Milne has been the inspiration and general editor of the project as well as writing on the modern period. The other writers – each expert in his own sphere – are Dr Barra Boydell, Dr Alan Fletcher, Dr Raymond Gillespie, Mr Stuart Kinsella, Professor James Lydon, Dr Raymond Refaussé and Professor Roger Stalley. Professor Geoffrey Hand has given invaluable help throughout the project.

A feature of this publication is that it is not just words with some illustrations. A CD of music associated with the cathedral, or written by former organists, has been made possible through the dedication of the cathedral choir under their director of music, Mr Mark Duley.

Our thanks could not conclude without particular mention of Dr Michael Adams and the Four Courts Press. Not only have they undertaken the publication of this splendidly produced volume but also of the entire Christ Church documents series. Few cathedrals have been as well or generously served by their publishers.

Here within these pages is our past. Christ Church is now entering the third millennium. It is the hope of the present chapter and board of the cathedral that, capitalising on the work of our predecessors, and learning from their mistakes, we may the better attempt to serve the people of Dublin and beyond who come here either as pilgrims or visitors.

John Paterson
Dean of Christ Church
December 1999

Contents

Foreword *by the Very Revd John Paterson*   v

List of illustrations   ix

Preface and acknowledgments   xi

Abbreviations   xiii

Contributors   xxi

I   Introduction   1
Raymond Refaussé

THE MEDIEVAL CATHEDRAL

II   From Hiberno-Norse to Anglo-Norman, *c.*1030–1300   25
Stuart Kinsella

III   The construction of the medieval cathedral, *c.*1030–1250   53
Roger Stalley

IV   Christ Church in the later medieval Irish world, 1300–1500   75
James Lydon

V   The architecture of the cathedral and priory buildings,
1250–1530   95
Roger Stalley

VI   Liturgy in the late medieval cathedral priory   129
Alan J. Fletcher

VII   Music in the medieval cathedral priory   142
Barra Boydell

THE EARLY MODERN CATHEDRAL

VIII   The coming of reform, 1500–58   151
Raymond Gillespie

IX The shaping of reform, 1558–1625   174
    Raymond Gillespie

X   The crisis of reform, 1625–60   195
    Raymond Gillespie

XI The 1562 collapse of the nave and its aftermath   218
    Roger Stalley

XII The establishment of the choral tradition, 1480–1647   237
    Barra Boydell

THE MODERN CATHEDRAL

XIII Restoration and reorganisation, 1660–1830   255
     Kenneth Milne

XIV The flourishing of music, 1660–1800   298
     Barra Boydell

XV   The stripping of the assets, 1830–1960   315
     Kenneth Milne

XVI Music in the nineteenth-century cathedral, 1800–70   339
     Barra Boydell

XVII George Edmund Street and the restoration of the
     cathedral, 1868–78   353
     Roger Stalley

XVIII Optimism and decline: music, 1870–c.1970   374
      Barra Boydell

     Postscript   386

     Priors and deans   391

     Index   393

List of illustrations

Plates between pp 234 and 235

1		The cathedral from the south-east, showing the choir as rebuilt by George Edmund Street in 1871–8
2		The interior of the cathedral looking east
3		The interior of the nave in 1835
4		Plan of the cathedral as it existed in 1882
5		Plan of the cathedral drawn by William Butler in 1870–1
6		Interior of the quire
7	(a)	Three Romanesque capitals recovered from the walls in 1871–8
	(b)	The east end of the crypt as drawn by H.W. Brewer, *c*.1882
8		The exterior of the south transept
9	(a)	The interior of the south transept
	(b)	Section through the transepts depicting the east elevation
10	(a)	Roof over south transept as drawn by J. Dewhurst in the 1920s
	(b)	The interior of the south transept
11		The interior of the south transept, west wall, prior to 1871
12		Romanesque capitals from the transepts and choir carved about 1200
	(a)	a troupe of 'entertainers'
	(b)	griffons
	(c)	a group of fruitpickers
	(d)	affronted beasts
	(e)	foliate capital with berries (north transept)
	(f)	foliate capital with nailhead ornament
13		A view of the north elevation of the nave
14		The interior of the nave
15 (a & b)		sculptured capitals with protruding heads
	(c)	capital in similar style, perhaps carved by the same craftsman, at Overbury (Worcestershire)
16		Capitals from the nave
	(a)	moulded capitals
	(b)	foliate capitals
	(c)	capital from the triforium of the nave
	(d)	capital from St Patrick's cathedral
17		The interior of the nave
18		The Christ Church psalter
	(a)	Initial E to psalm 80 (*Exultate Deo*)

　　(b) Initial C to psalm 97 (*Cantate Domine*)
19 (a) The Kildare chantry chapel established by 1512
　　(b) The 'tomb of Strongbow'
20　　　The thirteenth-century chapter house
　　(a) the responds which supported the vault
　　(b) the doorway, with its cluster of moulded shafts
21 (a) The cathedral from the north as engraved in 1739
　　(b) The entrance to the tower
22 The interior of the long quire looking west, prior to 1871
23 (a) The exterior of the long quire in 1824, prior to restoration
　　(b) The cathedral from the south-east, *c.*1795
24 (a) The cathedral from the south, *c.*1826
　　(b) The cathedral from the south, prior to 1871
25 (a) The exterior of the cathedral from the west, *c.*1820
　　(b) A similar view today, which reveals the extent of Street's reconstruction
26 The interior of the nave looking west (south side), prior to 1871
27 The interior of the nave looking west (north side), prior to 1871
28 Furnishings ancient and modern
　　(a) an evangelist, detail from the pulpit
　　(b) detail of the brass gates at the entrance to the chancel
　　(c) the ancient lectern, thought to date from the later middle ages
29　　　Portrait of Henry Roe, as published in the commemorative volume of 1882
30 (a) The nave during the course of the restoration of 1871–8
　　(b) one page from the book of mouldings prepared during the restoration
　　　　of 1871–8
　　(c) a thirteenth-century capital, one of several removed from the fabric in
　　　　1871–8
31 Photograph of George Edmund Street
32 Street's original design for the synod hall

FIGURES

1 Christ Church cathedral: plan of the crypt (after Drew)   64
2 Winchester cathedral: plan of the late eleventh-century crypt
   (after Clapham)   66
3 Christ Church cathedral: the mouldings of the main arcade of
   the nave   71
4 Christ Church cathedral: plan of the cathedral precincts originally
   surveyed by Thomas Reading in October 1761 (after Seymour)   110
5 Fifteenth-century cloister arcade as reconstructed from the
   Cook Street fragments (after P. Ó hÉailidhe)   114
6 Christ Church cathedral: chapter house: suggested reconstruction
   of the east window (after Stuart Harrison)   117
7 Christ Church cathedral: chapter house: suggested reconstruction
   of the west facade (Stuart Harrison)   118
8 Map of Dublin and its hinterland, showing the source of building
   materials supplied to Christ Church   230

Preface and acknowledgments

To describe my fellow authors as 'contributors' is to do them less than justice. As well as researching and writing their several chapters they have all worked hard for the project in many ways, sharing willingly in the administrative chores that inevitably attend such an undertaking and bringing their expertise and experience to bear on what has been a major voluntary effort. My profound gratitude is due to them, and of greater significance, so is the gratitude of Christ Church cathedral which, I can assure them, is warmly accorded.

I know that the authors would also like me to say how much we owe to the labours of our honorary secretary, Stuart Kinsella, whose facility with modern information technology has served us well, and who, in addition to contributing to the text, has unselfishly assisted the rest of us not least by servicing over forty meetings since the project began.

The editor and the contributors would also like to acknowledge the help of Lesley Abrams, John Bartlett, Marie Betts, Roger Bowers, Ann Buckley, Howard Clarke, Brian Crosbie, Bernadette Cunningham, Carol Cunningham, Brendan Dempsey, Eithne Donnelly, Caitriona Doran, Seán Duffy, Máire Egan-Buffet, Geoffrey Hand, Stuart Harrison, Vivienne Hassell, Sue Hemmens, Lawrence Hoey, Martin Holland, Kerry Houston, Roy Johnston, Andrew Johnstone, Paul Joyce, Colm Lennon, Ailbhe MacShamhráin, Dept of Music, NUI Maynooth, Edward McParland, Richard Morris, Rachel Moss, Denise Neary, John O'Callaghan, Freddie O'Dwyer, Mark Philpott, James Roscoe, Ann Martha Rowan, Peter Scott, Christopher Shiell, Leo Swan, Malcolm Thurlby and, for the sections on the bells and bell ringing, Leslie Taylor.

For permission to quote from manuscript and other primary sources in their care the contributors are grateful to the National Library of Ireland, the National Archives of Ireland, the Board of Trinity College, Dublin, the Royal Irish Academy, Oriel College, Oxford, the Diocesan Councils of Dublin and Glendalough and Mr Hugh Cobbe. The earl of Longford most kindly allowed us to see the papers of Dean Pakenham and Dr Anthony Malcomson arranged for us to have access to them at the Public Record Office of Northern Ireland. Due acknowledgment of permission to use illustrations is recorded elsewhere in the book. Particular reference must be made to the facilities afforded us by Dr Raymond Refaussé, the librarian and archivist of the library of the Representative Body of the Church of Ireland and his colleagues there, Dr Susan Hood, Mrs Heather Smith and Mrs Mary Furlong. We would also like to express our appreciation of financial support for the project from the Church of Ireland General Synod Royalties Fund. The Dean, Chapter and Board of the cathedral have been unfailingly supportive, as have the Friends of Christ Church and the director of music, Mr Mark Duley and the ladies and gentlemen of the choir, and the administrative staff of the cathedral.

All photographs are by Roger Stalley except where indicated otherwise.

An especial word of appreciation is due to our publisher, Dr Michael Adams, and the staff of Four Courts Press. It is five years since a group of us first met at the Deanery to discuss the possibility of publishing a history of Christ Church. Michael encouraged us from the start, and undertook not only the publication of this present volume, but also of the accompanying series of documents, 'A HISTORY OF CHRIST CHURCH, DUBLIN'. Modesty almost (but not quite) prevents us from quoting a distinguished Irish historian who has described the Christ Church history project as one of the most important events in Irish historiography of the century. Without Four Courts Press it is unlikely to have happened.

Kenneth Milne
Dublin, December 1999

Abbreviations

We have followed the editorial conventions set by *A new history of Ireland* (Oxford, 1976-). These include using the term 'Catholics' to denote members of the Roman Catholic Church.

Until 1752 the new year in England and Ireland began on 25 March. However, in this volume it is taken to begin on 1 January each year, and therefore entries in chapter act books, for instance, dated 3 February 1722 or 3 February 1722/3 are given as 3 February 1723. Other dates are given old style.

The location of manuscript sources is given except in the case of material in the Christ Church archive in the library of the Representative Church Body, which is designated C6.

The following abbreviations are used in the case of ancillary volumes published by Four Courts Press in the 'History of Christ Church, Dublin' series:

Gillespie, *Proctor's accounts*	*The proctor's accounts of Peter Lewis 1564–1565*, ed. Raymond Gillespie (Dublin, 1996)
Lydon & Fletcher, *Account roll*	*Account roll of the priory of the Holy Trinity, Dublin 1337–1346*, ed. James Mills, introduced by James Lydon and A.J. Fletcher (Dublin, 1996)
Gillespie, *Chapter act book*	*The first chapter act book of Christ Church cathedral, Dublin 1574–1634*, ed. Raymond Gillespie (Dublin, 1997)
Refaussé & Lennon, *Registers*	*The registers of Christ Church cathedral, Dublin*, ed. Raymond Refaussé with Colm Lennon (Dublin, 1998)
Boydell, *Music*	*Music at Christ Church before 1800: documents and selected anthems*, ed. Barra Boydell (Dublin, 1998)
Sing *(CD)*	*Sing O ye heavens: historic anthems from Christ Church cathedral Dublin*, CCD1 (Dublin, 1999)
McEnery & Refaussé, *Deeds*	*Christ Church deeds*, ed. M.J. McEnery and Raymond Refaussé (Dublin, 2000)

OTHER ABBREVIATIONS

A.F.M.	*Annala ríoghachta Éireann: annals of the kingdom of Ireland by the Four Masters from the earliest period to the year 1616*, ed. and trans. John O'Donovan (7 vols, Dublin, 1851; reprint, New York, 1966)

Alen's reg.	*Calendar of Archbishop Alen's register*, ed. Charles McNeill (Dublin, 1950)
Anal. Hib.	*Analecta Hibernica, including the reports of the Irish Manuscripts Commission* (Dublin, 1930–)
Anc. rec. Dublin	*Calendar of ancient records of Dublin in the possession of the municipal corporation*, ed. Sir J.T. and Lady Gilbert (19 vols, Dublin, 1889–1944)
Archdall, *Mon. Hib.*	Mervyn Archdall, *Monasticon Hibernicum* (Dublin, 1786)
Atherton *et al.*, *Norwich*	Ian Atherton, Eric Fernie, Christopher Harper-Bill and Hassell Smith (ed.), *Norwich cathedral: church, city and diocese, 1096–1996* (London, 1996)
B.L.	British Library, London
B.L., Add. MSS	British Library, Additional MSS
B.L., Eg. MSS	British Library, Egerton MSS
B.L., Harl. MSS	British Library, Harleian MSS
B.L., Lansd. MSS	British Library, Lansdowne MSS
Bernard, *Ussher*	Nicholas Bernard, *The life and death of the most reverend and learned father of our church, Dr James Ussher* (London, 1656)
Bernard, *St Patrick's*	J.H. Bernard, *The cathedral church of St Patrick: a history and description of the building, with a short account of the deans* (London, 1903)
Berry, 'Records'	H.F. Berry, 'The records of the Dublin gild merchant, known as the Gild of the Holy Trinity, 1438–1671' in *R.S.A.I. Jn.*, xxx (1900), pp 44–68
Berry, *Register*	*Register of wills and inventories of the diocese of Dublin ... 1147–83*, ed. H.F. Berry (Dublin, 1898)
Berry, *Statutes*	*Statutes and ordinances and acts of parliament of Ireland, King John to Henry V*, ed. H.F. Berry (Dublin, 1910)
Bodl.	Bodleian Library, Oxford
Bodl., Rawl.	Bodleian Library, Rawlinson MSS
Bolton, *Caroline tradition*	F.R. Bolton, *The Caroline tradition in the Church of Ireland, with particular reference to Bishop Jeremy Taylor* (London, 1958)
Boydell, 'Cathedral music, city and state'	Barra Boydell, 'Cathedral music, city and state: music in Reformation and political change at Christ Church cathedral, Dublin' in Fiona Kisby (ed.), *Music and musicians in urban communities c.1350 to c.1650* (Cambridge, forthcoming)
Brannon, 'Celtic rite'	Patrick Brannon, 'The search for the Celtic rite' in Gerald Gillen and Harry White (ed.), *Irish musical studies, ii, music and the church* (Dublin, 1993)

Brereton, *Travels*

William Brereton, *Travels in Holland and the United Provinces, England, Scotland and Ireland*, ed. Edward Hawkins (London, 1844)

Bumpus, 'Composers'

John Bumpus, 'Irish church composers and the Irish cathedrals' in *Proceedings of the Musical Association*, xxvi (1899–1900), pp 79–159

Bumpus, *Stevenson*

John Bumpus, *Sir John Stevenson: a biographical sketch* (London, 1893)

Butler, *Christ Church*

William Butler, *The cathedral church of the Holy Trinity Dublin (Christ Church): a description of its fabric, and a brief history of the foundation, and subsequent changes* (London, 1901)

Butler, *Measured drawings*

William Butler, *Measured drawings of Christ Church prior to the restoration* (Dublin, 1874)

C.U.L.

Cambridge University Library, Cambridge

Cal. Carew MSS, 1515–74 [etc.]

Calendar of the Carew manuscripts preserved in the archiepiscopal library at Lambeth, 1515–74 [etc.] (6 vols, London, 1867–73)

Cal. doc. Ire., 1171–1251 [etc.]

Calendar of documents relating to Ireland, 1171–1251 [etc.] (5 vols, London, 1875–86)

Cal. justic. rolls Ire., 1295–1303 [etc.]

Calendar of the judiciary rolls, or proceedings in the court of the justiciar of Ireland ..., 1295–1303 [etc.], ed. James Mills (2 vols, Dublin, 1905, 1914)

Cal. pat. rolls Ire., Hen. VIII– Eliz.

Calendar of patent and close rolls of chancery in Ireland, Henry VIII to 18th Elizabeth, ed. James Morrin (Dublin, 1861)

Cal. S.P. Ire., 1509–73 [etc.]

Calendar of the state papers relating to Ireland, 1509–73 [etc.] (24 vols, London, 1860–1911)

Clarke, *Medieval Dublin: living city*

H.B. Clarke (ed.), *Medieval Dublin: the living city* (Dublin, 1990)

Clarke, *Medieval Dublin: metropolis*

H.B. Clarke (ed.), *Medieval Dublin: the making of a metropolis* (Dublin, 1990)

Close rolls, 1227–31 [etc.]

Close rolls of the reign of Henry III, 1227–31 [etc.] (14 vols, London, 1902–38)

Collinson *et al.*, *Canterbury*

Patrick Collinson, Nigel Ramsey, Margaret Sparks (ed.), *A history of Canterbury cathedral* (Oxford, 1995)

Commons' jn. Ire.

Journals of the house of commons of the kingdom of Ireland ... (19 vols, Dublin, 1796–1800)

Cotton, *Fasti*

Henry Cotton, *Fasti ecclesiae Hibernicae* (6 vols, Dublin, 1848–78)

Crosthwaite & Todd, *Obits*

The book of obits and martyrology of the cathedral church of the Holy Trinity commonly called Christ Church, Dublin, ed. J.C. Crosthwaite and J.H. Todd (Dublin, 1844)

Drew, 'Ancient chapter house'

Thomas Drew, 'The ancient chapter house of the priory of Holy Trinity, Dublin' in Clarke, *Medieval Dublin: metropolis*, pp 173–82

Drew, 'Christchurch'   Thomas Drew, 'Christchurch or cathedral of the
                        Holy Trinity, Dublin' in *R.S.A.I. Jn.*, xxiv (1894),
                        pp 73–4
Drew, 'Cloister garth' Thomas Drew, 'On evidence of the plan of the clois-
                        ter garth and monastic buildings of the priory of
                        Holy Trinity, now known as Christ Church cathe-
                        dral, Dublin' in *R.I.A. Proc.*, xvi (1879–86), pp 214–8
Dunton, *Teague land*   John Dunton, 'Teague land or a merry ramble to
                        the wild Irish', Bodl., Rawl. MS D. 71; printed in
                        Edward MacLysaght, *Irish life in the seventeenth
                        century* (1st ed., Cork, 1939), appendix B
Fiants Ire., Hen. VIII [etc.] 'Calendar to fiants of the reign of Henry VIII ...'
                        [etc.] in *P.R.I.rep.D.K.* 7–22 (Dublin, 1875–90)
Finlayson, *Inscriptions* John Finlayson, *Inscriptions on the monuments, mural
                        tablets etc., at present existing in Christ Church cathe-
                        dral, Dublin* (Dublin, 1878)
Gilbert, *Chart. St Mary's* *Chartularies of St Mary's abbey, Dublin*, ed. J.T.
                        Gilbert (2 vols, London, 1884)
Gilbert, *Dublin*   J.T. Gilbert, *A history of the city of Dublin* (3 vols,
                        Dublin, 1854–9)
Gillespie, 'Archives'   Raymond Gillespie, 'The archives of Christ
                        Church cathedral, Dublin' in *Irish Archives*, n.s.,
                        v, no. 2 (Winter 1998), pp 3–12
Gillespie, 'Borrowing' Raymond Gillespie, 'Borrowing books from Christ
                        Church cathedral, Dublin, 1607' in *Long Room*,
                        xliii, no. 43 (1998), pp 15–19
Gillespie, 'Champion'   Raymond Gillespie, 'The murder of Arthur
                        Champion' in *Clogher Record*, xiv (1990–4), pp 52–66
Gillespie, *Thomas Howell* Raymond Gillespie, *Thomas Howell and his friends:
                        serving Christ Church cathedral, Dublin, 1500–1700*
                        (Dublin, 1997)
Gir. Camb. op.   *Giraldi Cambrensis opera*, ed. J.S. Brewer, J.F.
                        Dimock and G.F. Warner (8 vols, London, 1861–91)
Graves & Prim, *St Canice's* James Graves and J.G. Prim, *The history, architec-
                        ture and antiquities of the cathedral church of St
                        Canice, Kilkenny* (Dublin, 1857)
Grindle, *Cathedral music* W.H. Grindle, *Irish cathedral music* (Belfast, 1989)
Gwynn & Hadcock,   Aubrey Gwynn and R.N. Hadcock, *Medieval
  Religious houses   religious houses: Ireland* (London, 1970; reprint 1988)
Gwynn, 'Cumin'   Aubrey Gwynn, 'Archbishop John Cumin', in
                        Reportorium Novum, i, no. 2 (1956), pp 301–10
Gwynn, 'First bishops' Aubrey Gwynn, 'The first bishops of Dublin' in
                        Clarke, *Medieval Dublin: living city*, pp 37–61
Gwynn, 'Origins'   Aubrey Gwynn, 'The origins of the see of Dublin'
                        in *Irish Ecclesiastical Record*, lvii (1941), pp 40–55,
                        97–112

Gwynn, 'Unpublished texts'   'Some unpublished texts from the Black Book of Christ Church, Dublin', ed. Aubrey Gwynn in *Anal. Hib.*, no. 16 (1946), pp 281–337

Gwynn, *Irish church*   Aubrey Gwynn, *The Irish church in the eleventh and twelfth centuries*, ed. Gerard O'Brien (Dublin, 1992)

H.M.C.   Historical Manuscripts Commission

Hand, 'Camb. MS'   G.J. Hand, 'Cambridge University MS 710' in *Reportorium Novum*, ii, no.1 (1958), pp 17–32

Hand, 'Psalter'   G.J. Hand, 'The psalter of Christ Church, Dublin (Bodl. Rawl. G. 185)' in *Reportorium Novum*, i, no. 2 (1956), pp 311–22

Hand, 'Rivalry'   G.J. Hand, 'Rivalry of the cathedral chapters in medieval Dublin' in Clarke, *Medieval Dublin: living city*, pp 100–11.

Hand, 'Chapter of St Patrick's'   G.J. Hand, 'The medieval chapter of St Patrick's cathedral, Dublin: the early period (*c.*1219–*c.*1270)' in *Reportorium Novum*, iii, no. 2 (1963–4), pp 229–48

Hand, 'Two cathedrals'   G.J Hand, 'The two cathedrals of Dublin: internal organisation and mutual relations, to the middle of the fourteenth century' (M.A. and Travelling Studentship in History thesis, National University of Ireland, 1954)

Hardiman, *Galway*   James Hardiman, *The history of the town and county of the town of Galway* (Dublin, 1820)

Harrison, *Music*   F.L. Harrison, *Music in medieval Britain* (4th ed., Buren, 1980)

Hastings MSS   *Report on the manuscripts of the late Reginald Rawdon Hastings, esq.* (H.M.C., 4 vols, London, 1928–47)

Hawkes, 'Liturgy'   William Hawkes, 'The liturgy in Dublin, 1200–1500: the manuscript sources' in *Reportorium Novum*, ii, no. 1 (1958), pp 33–67

Hist. & mun. doc. Ire.   *Historic and municipal documents of Ireland, 1172–1320*, ed. J.T. Gilbert (London, 1870)

I.H.S.   *Irish Historical Studies*

Irish mon. deeds   *Irish monastic and episcopal deeds, A.D. 1200–1600, transcribed from the originals preserved at Kilkenny castle, with an appendix of documents of the sixteenth and seventeenth centuries relating to monastic property after the dissolution*, ed. N.B. White (Irish Manuscripts Commission, Dublin, 1936)

L. & P. Rich. III & Hen. VII   *Letters and papers illustrative of the reigns of Richard III and Henry VII*, ed. James Gairdner (2 vols, London, 1861–3)

L. & P. Hen. VIII   *Letters and papers, foreign and domestic, Henry VIII* (21 vols, London, 1862–1932)

Laud, *Works*	*The works of ... William Laud*, ed. William Scott and James Bliss (7 vols, Oxford, 1847–60)
Lawlor, 'Chapel of Dublin castle'	H.J. Lawlor, 'The chapel of Dublin castle' in *R.S.A.I. Jn.*, liii (1923), pp 34–73
Lawlor, 'Diary of William King'	H.J. Lawlor, 'The diary of William King, D.D., archbishop of Dublin, during his imprisonment in Dublin castle' in *R.S.A.I. Jn.*, xxxiii (1903), pp 119–52, 255–83, 389–416
Lawlor, 'Liber niger'	H.J. Lawlor, 'A calendar of the Liber Niger and Liber Albus of Christ Church, Dublin' in *R.I.A. Proc.*, xxvii, C (1908), pp 1–93
Lawlor, *Fasti*	H.J. Lawlor, *The fasti of St Patrick's, Dublin* (Dundalk, 1930)
Leask, *Irish churches*, i [etc.]	H.G. Leask, *Irish churches and monastic buildings* (3 vols, Dundalk, 1955–60)
Lehmberg, *Reformation*	Stanford Lehmberg, *The reformation of cathedrals* (Princeton, 1988)
Leslie, 'Fasti'	J.B. Leslie, 'Fasti of Christ Church cathedral, Dublin', R.C.B., MS 61/2/2
Lords' jn. Ire.	*Journal of the house of lords [of Ireland], 1634–1800* (8 vols, Dublin, 1779–1800)
Lords' jn.	*Journals of the house of lords of the United Kingdom*
Mant, *Ch. of Ire.*	Richard Mant, *History of the Church of Ireland* (2 vols, London, 1840)
Marsh's Lib.	Marsh's Library, Dublin
Martin, *Crowning of a king*	F.X. Martin, *The crowning of a king at Dublin, 24 May 1487* (Dublin, [1988])
Mason, *St Patrick's*	W.M. Mason, *The history and antiquities of the collegiate and cathedral church of St Patrick near Dublin* (Dublin, 1820)
McVittie, *Restoration*	R.B. McVittie, *Details of the restoration of Christ Church cathedral, Dublin with a brief history of its preceding condition from the date of its supposed foundation (AD 1038) to the present time* (Dublin, 1878)
Miller & Power, *Holinshed*	*Holinshed's Irish chronicle*, ed. Liam Miller and Eileen Power (Dublin, 1979)
Mills, 'Notices'	James Mills, 'Sixteenth century notices of the chapels and crypts of the church of the Holy Trinity, Dublin' in *R.S.A.I. Jn.*, xxx (1900), pp 195–203
Murphy & Taylor, *Bells*	David Murphy and Leslie Taylor, *The bells of Christ Church, Dublin* (Dublin, 1994)
Murray, 'Tudor diocese'	James Murray, 'The Tudor diocese of Dublin', Ph.D. thesis, T.C.D., 1997
N.A.I.	National Archives of Ireland, Dublin
N.L.I.	National Library of Ireland, Dublin

New Grove	*The New Grove dictionary of music and musicians,* ed. Stanley Sadie (20 vols, London, 1980)
Otway-Ruthven, 'Church lands'	A.J. Otway-Ruthven, 'The medieval church lands in County Dublin' in J.A. Watt, J.B. Morrall and F.X. Martin (ed.), *Medieval studies presented to Aubrey Gwynn* (Dublin, 1961), pp 54–73
Owen, *Lincoln*	Dorothy Owen (ed.), *A history of Lincoln minster* (Cambridge, 1994)
P.R.I.rep.D.K. 1 [etc.]	*First* [etc.] *report of the deputy keeper of the public records in Ireland* (Dublin, 1869-)
P.R.O.	Public Record Office, London
P.R.O.N.I	Public Record Office of Northern Ireland, Belfast
Payne, *Sacred music*	Iain Payne, The *provision and practice of sacred music at Cambridge colleges and selected cathedrals c.1547–c.1646* (New York and London, 1993)
Phillips, *Ch. of Ire.*	W.A. Phillips (ed.), *History of the Church of Ireland* (3 vols, Oxford, 1933)
Rainbow, *Choral revival*	Bernarr Rainbow, *The choral tradition in the Anglican church, 1839–1872* (London, 1970)
R.C.B.	Representative Church Body Library, Dublin
R.I.A. Proc.	*Proceedings of the Royal Irish Academy*
R.S.A.I. Jn.	*Journal of the Royal Society of Antiquaries of Ireland*
Richardson & Sayles, *Admin. Ire.*	H.G. Richardson and G.O. Sayles, *The administration of Ireland, 1172–1377* (Irish Manuscripts Commission, Dublin, 1963)
Richardson & Sayles, *Ir. parl.*	H.G. Richardson and G.O. Sayles, *The Irish parliament in the middle ages* (Philadelphia, 1952; reissue 1964)
Richardson & Sayles, *Parl. & councils*	H.G. Richardson and G.O. Sayles, *Parliaments and councils of mediaevel Ireland*, vol. i (Irish Manuscripts Commission, Dublin, 1947)
Robinson, 'Bells'	J.L. Robinson, 'Dublin cathedral bells, 1670' in *R.S.A.I. Jn.*, xlii (1912), pp 155–62
S.P. Hen. VIII	*State papers, Henry VIII* (11 vols, London, 1869–85)
Seymour, *Christ Church*	Edward Seymour, *Christ Church cathedral, Dublin* (Dublin, 1869)
Shaw, *Organists*	Watkins Shaw, *The succession of organists* (Oxford, 1991)
Shuckburgh, *Bedell*	E.S. Shuckburgh (ed.), *Two biographies of William Bedell, bishop of Kilmore* (Cambridge, 1902)
Spink, *Cathedral music*	Ian Spink, *Restoration cathedral music 1660–1714* (Oxford, 1995)
Stalley, 'Buildings'	R.A. Stalley, 'Three Irish buildings with west country origins' in Nicola Coldstream and Peter Draper (ed.), *Medieval art and architecture at Wells and Glastonbury* (London, 1981), pp 62–80

Stalley, 'Sculpture'   R.A. Stalley, 'The medieval sculpture of Christ
                                    Church cathedral, Dublin' in Clarke, *Medieval
                                    Dublin: metropolis*, pp 202–26

Stalley, *Cistercian monasteries* Roger Stalley, *The Cistercian monasteries of Ireland*
                                    (London and New Haven, 1987)

Stat. Ire., 12–22 Edw. IV   *Statute rolls of the parliament of Ireland, 12th and
                                    13th to the 21st and 22nd years of the reign of King
                                    Edward IV*, ed. James Morrissey (Dublin, 1939)

Stokes, *Worthies*   G.T. Stokes, *Some worthies of the Irish church*, ed.
                                    H.J. Lawlor (London, 1900)

Street & Seymour   G.E. Street and Edward Seymour, *The cathedral
                                    of the Holy Trinity commonly called Christ Church
                                    cathedral, Dublin. An account of the restoration of the
                                    fabric ... with an historical sketch of the cathedral by
                                    Edward Seymour* (London, 1882)

Street, *Report, 1868*   G.E. Street, *Report to the dean and chapter of Christ
                                    Church cathedral, Dublin on the restoration of the
                                    cathedral church* (Dublin, 1868).

Street, *Report, 1871*   G.E. Street, *Report on the proposed rebuilding of the
                                    choir of Christ Church cathedral, Dublin and on the
                                    erection of a synod hall in connection with the cathe-
                                    dral* (Dublin, 1871)

T.C.D.   Trinity College, Dublin

Ussher, *Works*   C.R. Elrington and J.H. Todd (ed.), *The whole
                                    works of ... James Ussher* (17 vols, Dublin,
                                    1847–64)

Vignoles, *Memoir*   O.J. Vignoles, *Memoir of Sir Robert P. Stewart*
                                    (London and Dublin, 1899)

Ware, *Works*   *The whole works of Sir James Ware*, ed. Walter
                                    Harris (2 vols, Dublin, 1746)

Wetenhall, *Of gifts and offices* Edward Wetenhall, *Of gifts and offices in the public
                                    worship of God* (Dublin, 1676, 2nd ed., 1678)

Contributors

BARRA BOYDELL is a senior lecturer in music at the National University of Ireland, Maynooth.

ALAN J. FLETCHER lectures in old and middle English at University College, Dublin.

RAYMOND GILLESPIE lectures in modern history, National University of Ireland, Maynooth.

STUART KINSELLA is a postgraduate student in the History of Art department at Trinity College, Dublin.

JAMES LYDON is a former Lecky Professor of History at Trinity College, Dublin.

KENNETH MILNE is the historiographer of the Church of Ireland.

RAYMOND REFAUSSÉ is the librarian and archivist of the Church of Ireland.

ROGER STALLEY is Professor of the History of Art at Trinity College, Dublin.

Introduction

Raymond Refaussé

The cathedral church of the Holy Trinity, commonly called Christ Church, crowns the city of Dublin. Set on a hill above the River Liffey, it looks out over the site of Áth Cliath (the ford of the hurdles) and Duiblinn (the black pool) from which the city derived its names; gazes south-east across Christchurch Place towards Dublin castle, for long the seat of temporal power in Ireland; and stares defiantly southwards down St Nicholas Street towards its one time rival for ecclesiastical hegemony in the city and the diocese, St Patrick's cathedral.

Like the city, immortalised by the son of a Church of Ireland bishop as

> Fort of the Dane
> Garrison of the Saxon,
> Augustan capital
> Of a gaelic nation[1]

Christ Church reflects in its architecture, administration and worship, and in the people who made those things possible, the changing face of Ireland. Founded in *c.*1030[2] by a Hiberno-Norse king, Sitriuc 'Silkbeard' (Norse, *Sigtryggr Silkiskegg*), and an Irish bishop, Dúnán (Donatus), the cathedral was developed by Archbishop Lorcán Ua Tuathail (Laurence O'Toole) as a priory of Arrouasian canons, and later Anglo-Norman colonists gave it a distinctive physical appearance which subsequent restorations have not entirely obliterated. By the late middle ages it had become the church of the Anglo-Norman community of the Pale while remaining the church of the citizens of Dublin who viewed it with the same affection as Londoners regarded St Paul's. However, following the Reformation, the links with the civic and gentry families of the Dublin area diminished and Christ Church, as a sec-

---

1 Louis MacNeice, 'Dublin' in Philip Larkin (ed.), *The Oxford book of twentieth century verse* (Oxford, 1973), p. 399. 2 For the complexities of dating the foundation, see pp 27–9.

ular, Protestant, cathedral, became the place of worship of the colonial administrators and their retinue whose wealth and sophistication created an eighteenth-century city of style and elegance which is still apparent in many striking streetscapes and richly decorated domestic interiors. The flight of wealth
and influence following the Act of Union in 1800 left Christ Church to the
plainer Protestant people of Dublin and its environs, and in the wake of the
disestablishment of the Church of Ireland, in 1871, the cathedral, without a
formal role in city or state, became a small, rather close, middle class community dominated by the clergy and laity who worked there. This diminished role was exacerbated by the political events of the early twentieth century. Irish independence, and the markedly anti-British atmosphere which it
engendered, was profoundly foreign to the majority of Irish Anglicans who
reacted largely by keeping to themselves and taking little part in public life.
This low profile was echoed in Christ Church where little of remark happened in the early decades of the century. However, by 1940 there was sufficient confidence to begin the slow process of building a new relationship
with the cathedral's most immediate constituency, the city. In that year the
inauguration of a Citizenship Service provided a focus for the return of the
lord mayor and corporation to the cathedral on an annual basis, just as the
ringing in of the New Year on the Christ Church bells offered an opportunity for the less prominent of the inhabitants who thronged Christchurch
Place to join their first citizen in associating themselves, however sublimi-
nally, with the cathedral. During the second half of the twentieth century
Christ Church gradually re-established a significant place in the hearts and
minds of Dubliners, evidenced by the ready public support for a major
restoration programme in the 1980s. So at the beginning of the third millennium since Christ, the Dublin cathedral which bears his name is again an
integral part of the life of the city. A vibrant liturgy, inspirational music and
the openness of anglicanism in an age when old certainties are less defensible, have combined to attract to Christ Church a working and worshipping
community which transcends traditional denominational differences and which
offers Ireland a glimpse of that which can be its future. This is a remarkable
story but one which has been slow to be told. Inadequacies, both real and
imagined, in the sources, and the absence of a tradition of cathedral history
in Ireland seem to be the principal reasons for this surprising lacuna.

The early Irish church was monastic rather than diocesan and monasteries rather than parish churches were the centres of Christian life. Bishops,
although part of the ecclesiastical polity, generally lived in monasteries and
so the development of diocesan life based on the cathedral as the administrative seat of the bishop was slow to emerge in Ireland. It was not until the
synod of Ráith Bressail in 1111 that Ireland was divided into dioceses and
this administrative innovation was not regularised until 1152 when the papal

legate conferred pallia on four archbishops. The subsequent development of
cathedral life owed much to the influence of the Anglo-Normans who introduced the administrative arrangements and architectural styles of England
and western Europe. Christ Church was re-built in the 1180s, probably by
masons from the west of England, and similar influences are apparent in the
cathedrals of Cashel, Kilkenny and St Patrick's, Dublin, which, together with
those of Kildare, Down, Killaloe, Waterford and Ardfert, were built in the
thirteenth century. Yet although cathedral life was, in essence, an interpolation into the Irish ecclesiastical polity this was not initially a bar to its success and by the late middle ages cathedrals, such as Christ Church, were frequent places of individual and institutional devotion and were much visited
on pilgrimage. Chapels and chaplains of religious guilds and confraternities
abounded while relics, such as the *baculus Ihesu* and the miraculous speaking crucifix, drew the faithful from a wide area. It was the emergence of
protestantism following the Reformation which decisively divided cathedral
life from the majority of Irish men and women and which, by associating it
with a religious settlement imposed from England, emphasised its basic for-
eignness. The Henrician Reformation and the suppression of the religious
houses had little initial effect on the relationship of the citizens of Dublin
with their diocesan cathedral and their regard for it was evident in the successful popular opposition to proposals to suppress Christ Church in 1539.
Continuity rather than disruption was the norm both administratively and
liturgically. The prior and canons were converted to a secular dean and chapter while the mass remained as the central act of worship, although the significance of the cathedral as a site of pilgrimage largely disappeared with the
removal of the relics. However, the emergence of a more Protestant character in the Church of Ireland, initially in the reign of Edward VI and later
under Elizabeth, alienated the native population who, unlike the European
model by which the citizens followed the religious lead of their ruler, clung
to catholicism. Civic religious life moved from Christ Church to the parish
church of St Audoen where the religious guild of St Anne provided a focus
for Catholic expression, and by the end of the sixteenth century Christ
Church had become a Protestant cathedral for the Protestant officials from
Dublin Castle and those of the native population, always a minority, who
chose to conform. Christ Church and Dublin castle became two sides of the
one coin – and foreign currency at that.

The identification of Christ Church, and the other Irish cathedrals, with
the English presence in Ireland gathered pace in the seventeenth and eighteenth centuries as such places increasingly became foci for the Protestant
élite in Ireland. Christ Church was frequently visited by the lord lieutenant,
its congregation was largely made up of the colonial administration and its
followers, both immigrant and native, its deans were almost invariably

Englishmen, and its pulpit was a resort of preachers who sought to defend the English interest in Ireland by memorialising the great deliverance from the 1641 rebellion, giving thanks for the life of Charles I, king and martyr, or celebrating the anniversary of the 'happy accession' of English monarchs.[3] In such activity there was little place for the native Irish. Their alienation reached its apogee in the nineteenth century with the final rejection by the Roman Catholic Church of the cathedral structure in Ireland. In the late sixteenth and seventeenth centuries the papacy had continued to make titular appointments to Irish cathedrals in the expectation of eventually recovering these places of worship and there remained through the eighteenth century a residual belief that such a settlement might be effected. However, there was a fundamental change in attitude in the nineteenth century as the Roman Catholic Church, freed from the trammels of restrictive legislation and increasingly associated with the movement for Irish home rule, became more confident and assertive. In the face of a bright new future the past became less significant and it abandoned its interest in the old cathedral sites and created its own diocesan administration. In some places the new buildings were contiguous to existing cathedrals such as in Armagh, Derry or Dublin but often diocesan cathedrals were erected in new locations such as Mullingar, Longford, Cobh and Enniscorthy. These edifices, often on imposing sites and built and decorated to the highest specifications, became the centres of cathedral life for the majority of the people of Ireland and the older sites were left as places of worship for a declining Protestant population and as objects of curiosity for a small body of antiquarians.

With such a pedigree it is scarcely surprising that the cathedrals of the Church of Ireland attracted little serious historical attention, and the great flowering of historical enquiry in the second half of the nineteenth century largely passed them by. For the Catholic historians, many of whom were in holy orders, they existed only as a prelude to the chronicling of the history of the post-Reformation church or as objects of occasional controversy. Catholic studies, not suprisingly given the recent origins of their cathedrals, concentrated on diocesan histories and in the work of, for example, Comerford on Kildare and Leighlin, Power on Waterford and Lismore and O'Laverty on Down and Connor,[4] there was little about cathedral life after the Reformation.

---

3 For example, A *sermon preach'd in Christ-Church, Dublin on ... 23d of October, 1735 being the anniversary of the Irish rebellion, before ... Lionel, duke of Dorset, lord lieutenant ... of Ireland ... by Thomas, lord bishop of Derry* (Dublin, 1735); *A sermon preached in Christ-Church, Dublin ... on ... 30th of January, 1745, being the anniversary of the martyrdom of King Charles I by William, lord bishop of Raphoe* (Dublin, 1745). 4 Michael Comerford, *Collections relating to the dioceses of Kildare and Leighlin* (3 vols, Dublin, 1884); Patrick Power, *Waterford and Lismore: a compendious history of the united dioceses* (Cork, 1937);

For later controversialists, like Myles Ronan, 'Dublin's Catholic cathedrals' provided little more than an opportunity, under the guise of historical enquiry, to rehearse old Catholic claims.[5]

Nor did the Irish cathedrals prove particularly attractive as objects of study to those relics of the Protestant ascendancy who were moved to record for posterity the activities of their forefathers. There was some interest in aspects of Irish cathedral life among those who haunted the corridors of the Royal Society of Antiquaries of Ireland and among the historians who populated the universities and the Royal Irish Academy in the late nineteenth and early twentieth centuries but there seemed little inclination to attempt sustained institutional studies. Only Monck Mason's and Bernard's published histories of St Patrick's cathedral, Dublin, Graves's and Pim's investigation of St Canice's cathedral, Kilkenny, Butler's history of Christ Church, and the slimmer studies by Dowd, Carmody and Rogers of the cathedrals in Limerick, Lisburn and Armagh respectively could be deemed in any meaningful sense to be cathedral histories.[6] It might have beeen supposed that distinguished churchmen such as Cotton in Cashel, Reeves in Down, or Dwyer in Killaloe, all historians or antiquarians of standing, would have produced substantial studies of their diocesan cathedrals but this was not the case. Not that Protestant institutional histories were unfashionable – studies of Trinity College by Stubbs, the Royal Dublin Society by Berry and the Freemasons by Leeper and Crosslé[7] suggested that there was a willingness to chronicle at least some of the Protestant institutions and their contribution to Irish life but those at the very centre, whether due to the contempt of supposed familiarity, the fear of raising controversy, or the more familiar themes of apathy and indolence, were ignored.

There was, of course, a certain amount of investigation of particular aspects of Irish cathedral life. H.J. Lawlor, professor of ecclesiastical history at Trinity College, Dublin from 1898 and dean of St Patrick's, Dublin from 1924, was, as his offices might suggest, to the fore in this activity. He wrote on the deanery of St Patrick's, both the building and the office, compiled a *fasti* for the cathedral, and published some 'jottings' on its history.[8] Other

James O'Laverty, *An historical account of the diocese of Down and Connor, ancient and modern* (5 vols, Dublin, 1878–95). **5** M.V. Ronan, *Dublin's Catholic cathedrals: Christ Church* (Dublin, 1934). **6** Mason, *St Patrick's*; Bernard, *St Patrick's*; Graves and Prim, *St Canice's*; Butler, *Christ Church*; James Dowd, *History of St Mary's cathedral, Limerick* (Limerick, 1899); W.P. Carmody, *Lisburn cathedral and its past rectors* (Belfast, 1926); Edward Rogers, *Memoir of Armagh cathedral* (Belfast, n.d. [*c*.1882]). **7** J.W. Stubbs, *The history of the university of Dublin* (Dublin, 1889); H.F. Berry, *A history of the Royal Dublin Society* (Dublin, 1915); J.H. Leeper and Philip Crosslé, *History of the Grand Lodge of Free and Accepted Masons of Ireland* (Dublin, 1925). **8** H.J. Lawlor, 'The deaneries of St Patrick's' in *R.S.A.I. Jn.*, lxii (1932), pp 103–13; *The form and manner of making a dean,*

workers in the field included the Cork antiquarian, Richard Caulfield, who produced a number of short studies of aspects of St Fin Barre's cathedral, Cork and St Colman's cathedral, Cloyne; Richard Hayes who edited the register of Derry cathedral and J.R. Garstin who investigated the inscriptions in St Lasarian's cathedral, Leighlin.[9] As well, as the twentieth century progressed and the tourist potential of cathedrals became apparent, a growing number of brief historical sketches and guides was published. However, these, for the most part, contributed nothing new to cathedral historiography, providing little more than outline chronologies and basic descriptions of particular features of the buildings and the leading personalities associated with them. Short histories of, for example, the cathedrals of Armagh, Ross and Waterford were typical of the genre and its limitations.[10] However, if such studies did not lead to the ideal syntheses, that is, the writing of full scale cathedral histories, they probably contributed in some part to the succession of publications on the cathedrals of Ireland. These contained within the covers of a single volume potted histories of all the Church of Ireland cathedrals. T.M. Fallow's *The cathedral churches of Ireland*, which appeared in 1894, was the first of such anthologies, followed by similar offerings by Day and Patton, Wyse Jackson, and Galloway.[11]

The historiography of Christ Church largely followed this model with few attempts at sustained investigation, a weakness for recycled potted histories, and occasional outbursts of creativity on aspects of cathedral life, especially the fabric and muniments. Little of substance, with one important exception, was written about the cathedral before the late nineteenth century and the physical decay of the building seemed like an outward and visible sign of this disinterest. The situation was well summed up by Edward Seymour, prebendary of St Michael's in Christ Church, in the introduction to his account of the cathedral which appeared in 1869. He wrote 'It is not a little singular that, associated as Christ Church cathedral is with the

and other forms used in the cathedral ... of St Patrick (Dublin, 1912); 'Jottings on the history of St Patrick's cathedral' in *Irish Church Quarterly*, v (1912), pp 328–45; Lawlor, *Fasti*.   9 Richard Caulfield, *Annals of St Fin Barre's cathedral, Cork* (Cork, 1871); *Lecture on the history of the bishops of Cork and cathedral of St Fin Barre ...* (Cork, 1864); *Annals of the cathedral of St Colman, Cloyne* (Cork, 1882); Richard Hayes, *The register of Derry cathedral ... 1642–1703* (Dublin, 1910); J.R. Garstin, 'On some sixteenth century inscriptions in Leighlin cathedral, Co. Carlow' in *R.I.A. Proc.*, 2nd ser., ii (1884), pp 424–35. 10 Forde Tichborne, *St Patrick's cathedral, Armagh* (1932); C.A. Webster, *The cathedral church of St Fachtna, Ross* (Cork, 1927); *A brief account of the cathedral church of the Blessed Trinity, Waterford* (Waterford, n.d.).   11 T.M. Fallow, *The cathedral churches of Ireland* (London, 1894); J.G. Day and H.E. Patton, *The cathedrals of the Church of Ireland* (London, 1932); R.W. Jackson, *Cathedrals of the Church of Ireland* (Dublin, 1981); Peter Galloway, *The cathedrals of Ireland* (Belfast, 1992).

past history of Ireland, none of her historians have deemed it worthy of more than a brief and passing notice.' He lamented the '… meagre and inaccurate accounts …' of Christ Church contained in the various histories of Dublin and considered only Sir John Gilbert's chapter on Christ Church in his three volume *History of the city of Dublin* (1854–9) to be of any consequence. Seymour's own work was intended to supply this deficiency and its ninety pages contain a useful synopsis of the cathedral's history from its foundation until the eve of the disestablishment of the Church of Ireland. Yet as Seymour admitted, he had been unable, through illness, to consult original documents, and so his work '… cannot claim to be much more than a compilation from other works …'[12]

The restoration of the cathedral in the 1870s by the noted English architect, George Edmund Street, was the catalyst for a renewed interest in Christ Church and a welter of architectural studies ensued. These were predominantly in the form of articles in the *Irish Builder* but R.B. McVittie commemorated the re-opening of the cathedral by publishing his *Details of the restoration of Christ Church cathedral*[13] and articles by Thomas Drew, who succeeded Street as cathedral architect, were published by the Royal Society of Antiquaries of Ireland and the Royal Irish Academy.[14] Street, himself, wrote an account of his work which appeared in a handsomely bound volume in 1882[15] while the restoration also encouraged the Dublin architect, William Butler, to publish his measured drawings of Christ Church made in 1870, before Street began work on the building.[16] Street's work included a historical sketch of the cathedral by Edward Seymour and the short historical introduction to Butler's book also drew heavily on Seymour's published history, emphasising the absence of fresh historical endeavour. In 1878, John Finlayson, who had succeeded Seymour as prebendary of St Michael's, published an account of the monumental inscriptions in Christ Church[17] and in the early years of the twentieth century James Mills wrote on the chapels and crypts of Holy Trinity,[18] while the work of the Dublin antiquarian, H.F. Berry, on the Dublin trade guilds illuminated some aspects of the cathedral's associations with these confraternities.[19]

This former lack of interest in the history of Christ Church was reflected in two developments. The first was the absence of Christ Church from the series of cathedral histories published by George Bell of London between 1896 and 1910. As the diocesan cathedral of Dublin and the principal Anglican

---

12 Seymour, *Christ Church.* 13 McVittie, *Restoration.* 14 Drew, 'Ancient chapter-house'; Drew, 'Cloister garth'; Drew, 'Christchurch'. 15 Street & Seymour. 16 Butler, *Measured drawings.* 17 Finlayson, *Inscriptions.* 18 Mills, 'Notices'. 19 H.F. Berry, 'The ancient corporation of barber-surgeons, or gild of St Mary Magdalene, Dublin' in *R.S.A.I. Jn.,* xxxiii (1903), pp 217–38.

place of worship in the capital city of Ireland, Christ Church ought to have been an obvious choice for this series but instead the Irish volume was devoted to St Patrick's. Significantly, perhaps, St Patrick's already had a published history on which to draw and a distinguished scholar as dean, J.H. Bernard, later to be provost of Trinity College, to revise it for modern use.[20] Second was the revelation that not only did Christ Church not have a history but it did not even have a guide-book. According to the preface of William Butler's account of the cathedral, which was published in 1901, 'there was no guide-book to be had either in the cathedral or in the book-shops of Dublin ...' and so he had set himself the task of producing '... a popular, and at the same time technically interesting guide-book ... to meet the wishes of the ordinary tourist, as well as those of the student of history and archaeology'. The result, although more substantial than the average guide-book, was little more than a collection of paragraphs describing aspects of the fabric and fittings of the building and alluding to personalities and events in the cathedral's history. Yet this volume, largely devoid of sustained narrative or analysis was the closest approximation to a published history of Christ Church yet produced.[21]

Most of the significant investigation of Christ Church related to its archives. The forerunner was an edition in 1844 by Crosthwaite and Todd of the priory's 'Book of obits' and 'Martyrology',[22] but it was in the later years of the nineteenth century that interest in the medieval records of Christ Church grew. In 1888 the first part of a calendar of the cathedral's deeds was printed as an appendix to the report of the deputy keeper of the public records of Ireland and subsequent reports in 1891 and 1892 continued this work with an index being added in 1895.[23] The deeds had been deposited in the Public Record Office in 1872 and their ready availability together with the convenience of a printed calendar, prompted further interest in the collection. This was realised in the publication in 1891 of the mid-fourteenth century account rolls of the priory. The significance of the rolls, which had survived among the deeds, was recognised by James Mills, a member of the record office staff, who prepared them for publication and his edition also included the text of the middle English morality play 'The pride of life'.[24] The two medieval registers of the priory, the early fourteenth-century century 'Liber niger' and the sixteenth-century 'Liber albus', were calendared by H.J. Lawlor and published in 1908.[25]

Thereafter serious academic interest in Christ Church flagged. Lawlor, although he remained professor of ecclesiastical history in Trinity until 1933,

---

20 Bernard, *St Patrick's*.   21 Butler, *Christ Church*.   22 Crosthwaite & Todd, *Obits*.   23 See appendices to *P.R.I.rep.D.K. 20, 23, 24* and *27*.   24 *Account roll of the priory of the Holy Trinity, Dublin, 1337–1346 with the middle English moral play 'The pride of life'*, ed. James Mills (Dublin, 1891).   25 Lawlor, 'Liber niger'.

took no further interest in Christ Church and fostered no body of students to follow his early interests. The vacuum was filled by amateur historians from the chapter who recycled the cathedral's history in short booklets, guides and pamphlets. Architecture, antiquarianism and archives continued to be the themes which were most regularly treated as the publications of Robinson, Kennedy and Lewis-Crosby readily demonstrated.[26] The only significant exception to this was the publication by Aubrey Gwynn in 1946 of an important revision of Lawlor's analysis of the 'Liber niger'.[27]

However in the 1950s and 1960s there was a renaissance of academic interest in Irish cathedrals. Under the auspices of the Roman Catholic archdiocese of Dublin, its historical journal, *Reportorium Novum*, published articles by William Hawkes on medieval liturgical manuscripts, including those associated with Christ Church, an analysis of the medieval charters of Holy Trinity by Maurice Sheehy and articles by Geoffrey Hand on manuscripts associated with both the Dublin cathedrals and on the medieval chapter of St Patrick's.[28] Hand in particular seemed set fair to do for Irish medieval cathedral history what R.A.L. Smith had promised for English cathedral studies.[29] His research in University College, Dublin, on the administration of the Dublin cathedrals in the mid-fourteenth century provided the foundations for his articles in *Reportorium Novum* and further articles on this topic, an overview of Irish medieval cathedral chapters and a more extended examination of the chapter of Limerick cathedral followed.[30] However, just as Smith's premature death had cut short an immensely promising career, so Hand's academic shift from history to law dashed the hopes for a sustained revival in Irish cathedral history. Thereafter, apart from the work of Roger Stalley on the architectural history of Christ Church[31] and Harry Grindle's study of Irish cathedral music,[32] Christ Church received little scholarly attention until the 1990s.

---

26 J.L. Robinson, *Handbook to Christ Church cathedral, Dublin* (Dublin, 1914); H.B. Kennedy, *Christ Church cathedral, Dublin: a sketch of its history, and a description of the building* (Dublin, 1926); E.H. Lewis-Crosby, *Christ Church cathedral: its builders and restorers* (Dublin, 1940); *The ancient books of Christ Church cathedral* (Dublin, n.d. [1946]). 27 Gwynn, 'Unpublished texts', pp 281–337. 28 Hawkes, 'Liturgy in Dublin'; Maurice Sheehy, 'The registrum novum: a manuscript of Holy Trinity cathedral; the medieval charters' in *Reportorium Novum*, iii, no. 2 (1963–4), pp 249–81 and iv, no. 1 (1971), pp 101–34; Hand, 'Psalter'; Hand, 'Camb. MS'; Hand, 'Chapter of St Patrick's'. 29 R.A.L. Smith, *Collected papers* (London, 1947). I am grateful to Raymond Gillespie for alerting me to Smith's work. 30 Hand, 'Two cathedrals'; Hand, 'Rivalry'; G.J. Hand, 'Medieval cathedral chapters' in *Proceedings of the Irish Catholic Historical Committee* (1956), pp 11–13; 'The medieval chapter of St Mary's cathedral, Limerick' in J.A. Watt, J.B. Morrall, F.X. Martin (ed.), *Medieval studies presented to Aubrey Gwynn, S.J.* (Dublin, 1961), pp 74–89. 31 See Roger Stalley, *Ireland and Europe in the middle ages: selected essays on architecture and sculpture* (London, 1994). 32 W.H. Grindle, *Cathedral music* (Belfast, 1989).

The one exception to this unwillingness to pursue sustained research into the history of Christ Church was the work of William Monck Mason. The author of a history of Christ Church's rival cathedral, St Patrick's, which had been published in 1820, Mason began work on a companion volume for Christ Church but this was never printed despite the fact that engravings were prepared for it. His Christ Church history followed the St Patrick's model, which was deemed to have '... exhausted its subject ...'[33] and consisted largely of narrative which was augmented by quotations from documents in the cathedral archives. There was little extended discussion or analysis but it was a work of considerable research based on the original archives, some of which were subsequently destroyed in the fire in the Public Record Office of Ireland. Mason's history of Christ Church lay forgotten until it was purchased by Trinity College, Dublin in the 1990s[34] when Geoffrey Hand expressed an interest in editing it, an initiative that proved to be a catalyst for the present project to write a full-scale history of Christ Church.

Hand was familiar with the recent historiography of English cathedrals and it was this, in part, which had re-awakened his interest in Christ Church. Beginning with a history of York minster, which was published in 1977, there had been a considerable renaissance in the writing of the history of English cathedrals as subsequent multi-authored studies of Winchester, Chichester, Lincoln, Canterbury, and Norwich clearly showed.[35] The English cathedrals were, of course, well placed to undertake such extensive intellectual ventures successfully. Not only did they have extensive archives, and an apparently ready supply of historians who were equipped to use them, but also, in most cases, they had a substantial historiographical legacy on which to draw. St Paul's cathedral, London, for example, which as a diocesan cathedral in the English capital city might usefully be compared with Christ Church, Dublin, had a series of published histories from the seventeenth century onwards,[36] while even provincial cathedrals such as Winchester and Norwich had an impressive body of published material about aspects of their past. Christ Church, by contrast, had relatively little in the way of published history on which to draw, and, if the received wisdom were accepted, a slender archival base on which to found a new history – as everyone knew, the records of

33 *D.N.B.*, *sub nomine*.   34 T.C.D., MSS 10529–30.   35 G.E. Aylmer and R.J. Cant (ed.), *A history of York minster* (Oxford, 1977); John Crook (ed.), *Winchester cathedral: nine hundred years, 1093–1993* (Chichester, 1993); Mary Hobbs (ed.), *Chichester cathedral: an historical survey* (Chichester, 1994); Owen, *Lincoln minster*; Collinson *et al.*, *Canterbury*; Atherton *et al.*, *Norwich*.   36 William Dugdale, *The history of St Paul's cathedral in London from its foundation* (London, 1658; 2nd ed., London, 1716; 3rd ed., expanded, London, 1818); H.H. Milman, *Annals of St Paul's cathedral* (London, 1869); W.R. Matthews and W.M. Atkins (ed.), *A history of St Paul's cathedral* (London, 1957); a new history of St Paul's is in preparation under the editorship of Derek Keene.

church and state had been destroyed in the fire in the Public Record Office of Ireland in 1922. However, this perception of the cathedral's archives was mis-placed for, by Irish standards at least, the Christ Church muniments provide a remarkably coherent body of evidence for the writing of the cathedral's history.

It is true that the archives and manuscripts of Christ Church (both those which have survived in the custody of the cathedral and those which have migrated to other custodies) are by the standards of comparable English institutions unremarkable. There is no corpus of pre-Reformation liturgical books or manuscripts from the cathedral library such as survive for Durham and Canterbury; no series of registers like those of Worcester which are extant from 1301 or even those of Westminster abbey which survive from 1485; or no medieval obedientiary rolls like those of Winchester, the earliest of which survive from 1310. Yet when compared with the archives of Irish cathedrals the Christ Church collection is not merely remarkable but unique. Only two other Irish cathedrals, St Patrick's, Dublin,[37] and St Canice's, Kilkenny,[38] have substantial archives. In both instances, however, their records are essentially those of the post-Reformation church supplemented by a few pre-Reformation deeds and charters, and in the case of St Patrick's, by the 'Dignitas decani', an early sixteenth-century register containing copies of deeds and related documents from the twelfth century, and by the 'Dublin troper', a fourteenth-century liturgical manuscript with some administrative addenda.[39] On a smaller scale Waterford cathedral has a few pre-Reformation deeds, a fifteenth-century account roll, and some post-Restoration chapter acts,[40] Cork has a continuous set of chapter act books from 1624,[41] while Cloyne[42] and Kildare[43] cathedrals have fragmentary collections dating from the mid-seventeenth century. Otherwise there is little of significance which pre-dates the nineteenth century.

A glance at the wider Irish context emphasises the importance of the Christ Church collection. No significant body of records survives from the medieval period for Irish schools or universities, trade guilds or religious confraternities; the records of central government, municipal corporations and the Church have been seriously depleted; and few families have an archive which will allow them to chronicle their history in detail before the Restoration. Inadequacies in record keeping, which were commonplace in Ireland, the unsettled state of the country which militated against the accumulation of records and their safe transmission from one generation to the

37 R.C.B., C2.   38 R.C.B., C3.   39 N.B. White (ed.), *The 'Dignitas decani' of St Patrick's cathedral, Dublin* (Dublin, 1957); Dom Hesbert (ed.), *Le tropaire-prosaire de Dublin* (Rouen, 1966).   40 R.C.B., C16.   41 St Fin Barre's cathedral, Cork, B8.   42 R.C.B., C12.   43 R.C.B., C14.

next, and the destruction of the Public Record Office in Dublin by fire in 1922, all contributed to this unhappy situation. The Christ Church collection, however, is a substantial archive which chronicles in detail the activities of the dean and chapter and the development of the post-Reformation foundation, together with an important body of material, in both original and copy form, which illuminates the life of the prior and convent of the Holy Trinity before the dissolution of the religious houses. As the archives of the most important religious foundation in the most important city in Ireland the collection documents not only the life of the cathedral and its community but the interaction of that community with the wider world and especially with the corporation of Dublin, which has the only other comparable archive.

The cathedral's medieval archives and manuscripts are few in number but their very survival is in itself a matter of remark and their significance far outweighs their paucity. The fourteenth-century 'Liber niger' and the early sixteenth-century 'Liber albus' are the only extant medieval administrative records, apart from a few miscellaneous papers and memoranda, but they are supplemented by the Christ Church deeds and five fourteenth-century account rolls which survive as printed editions. The splendidly decorated fourteenth-century psalter, the thirteenth-century 'Martyrology' and the fifteenth-century 'Book of obits' reflect something of the liturgical practices of the community, while three liturgical manuscripts from the neighbouring parish church of St John the Evangelist may also have Christ Church connections. Although the medieval manuscripts do not provide a sustained and comprehensive record of life in the priory, they are sufficient to give a sense of the ways in which the administrative and liturgical life of Holy Trinity were ordered, especially when used imaginatively in conjunction with other ecclesiastical and civil archives.

The creation of registers such as the 'Liber niger' and the 'Liber albus' was in itself an indication of serious administrative activity in the priory and the content of the books gives a sense of how the community was ordered and the matters which its priors and obedientiaries considered to be important. The 'Liber niger' is largely the work of Henry la Warr, an Augustinian canon from Bristol, who became prior of Holy Trinity in the winter of 1300–1 and much of the contents reflect his career as a diplomat at the court of Edward I and his personal interest in, for example, French literature. La Warr brought the book to Dublin and it was there that he, and others, filled the blank leaves and margins with memoranda about Ireland in general, the diocese of Dublin, and Holy Trinity in particular: copies of twelfth and thirteenth century charters, a list of the founders and benefactors of Holy Trinity, and miscellaneous memoranda relating to rights, privileges and property. The register also contains two accounts of the foundation of Holy Trinity, the first quite brief and written in the early fourteenth century, and a longer version which seems to have been copied into the register in the late fourteenth or early fifteenth century. This second narrative is the source of the belief, generally accepted by historians, that Sitriuc was the founder of the cathedral and is also of value in describing Christ Church in the late fourteenth century. Its less convincing claims that the cathedral had been founded by the Danes before the coming of St Patrick and that Patrick said mass there were described by Aubrey Gwynn as 'untrustworthy', and are now subject to re-interpretation.

Similarly, the 'Liber albus', which was compiled under the direction of the sub-prior, Thomas Fich, who died in 1518, brings together copies of documents relating to possessions and privileges, a knowledge of which would have been essential for the successful administration of the priory. The earliest of these is a copy of the bull of Urban II, dated 2 July 1186, confirming the privileges of Holy Trinity and the register also contains subsequent confirmations of those privileges by, among others, King John and Pope Innocent VII. Among other important documents which are included in the 'Liber albus' are the *composicio pacis* of 1300 which regulated relations with St Patrick's cathedral; defences of fishing rights on the River Liffey, which were important sources of both food and revenue in the late fifteenth century; and the statute of Prior David Wynchester of 1493 which formally provided for the embryonic choral foundation that had been in existence since 1480.

Whilst the 'Liber niger' and 'Liber albus' are valuable resources for the history of Holy Trinity much of their novelty undoubtedly lies in their survival to the exclusion of any similar administrative codices. But perhaps the most important administrative records are the Christ Church deeds which cover the period 1174 to 1699. They have the longest chronological span of any of the cathedral's record series and are the only part of the archives which substantially cover both the medieval and the modern periods. They reflect, often graphically, not only the life of a religious community but also its interaction with the city of Dublin and beyond, and are an important bridge between the sacred and the profane worlds. The deeds were deposited in the Public Record Office in 1872[44] and were destroyed in the fire in 1922: fortunately much of the contents had been transcribed and calendared. In the middle of the eighteenth century 467 deeds, covering the period 1174 to 1684, were transcribed into three paper volumes called the 'Registrum novum'.[45] These parchment bound books contain transcripts of papal bulls, episcopal and royal charters, agreements, inquisitions, wills, acts of parliament, rentals and other documents which are mostly copied from the original deeds. However, some are taken from other sources such as the 'Liber niger', 'Liber

44 *P.R.I.rep.D.K. 5*, appendix 5, p. 82.   45 C6/3/1–3.

albus' and the 'Crede mihi'[46] and where this is the case the source is always given. The transcripts are frequently annotated with notes on the condition of the original document, both sides of papal and episcopal seals are reproduced and witness lists are never omitted. Maurice Sheehy, who examined the 'Registrum novum' in the 1960s, concluded that 'the compilers were using, for the eighteenth century, quite exacting standards of accuracy and detail'.[47] Following the transfer of the deeds to the Public Record Office the deputy keeper of the public records, Sir Samuel Ferguson, ordered the preparation of a calendar of them.[48] The entire collection was calendared, both those deeds which had appeared in the 'Registrum novum' and the remainder, and the greater part of his work was published as appendices to the reports of the deputy keeper. In an introductory note to the published index the editor, M.J. McEnery, revealed that the deeds subsequent to 1602 had also been calendared but had not been considered of sufficient importance to be printed.[49] The manuscript calendar of 499 deeds covering the period 1605 to 1699 survived the fire of 1922 and has been published as part of a new edition of the deeds in the Christ Church documents series.[50] The deeds, as found in the 'Registrum novum', the published and unpublished calendars of McEnery, and, in a few instances, elsewhere among the cathedral's muniments, number almost 2,000 items from the eve of the final quarter of the twelfth century to the dawn of the eighteenth century. They are, apart from the Dublin city assembly rolls, the most sustained record of administrative activity by any Irish institution, and more than any series in the cathedral's archives, provide an informational continuum on a wide variety of subjects: membership of the cathedral community and its interaction with the city of Dublin and beyond; land holding, estate management and hospitality; the physical condition of the building and the development of the precincts; liturgy, worship and the evolution of the choral foundation.

In addition, the collection of deeds included five account rolls covering the period 1337 to 1346. These had been calendared by McEnery but not transcribed into the 'Registrum novum'. Fortunately, however, they were printed in full in 1891[51] and so, although the original records were destroyed along with the deeds in 1922, the information which they contained has survived *in toto* as has some sense of their physical characteristics. James Mills, who edited the rolls, concluded that they comprised four distinct accounts for the years 1343 to 1346 which had been sewn together and to these he

---

46 The 'Crede mihi' is a late thirteenth century register of the diocese of Dublin. It has been printed as *'Crede mihi', the most ancient register book of the archbishops of Dublin before the Reformation*, ed. J.T. Gilbert (Dublin, 1897).   47 Sheehy, 'Registrum novum', p. 250.   48 *P.R.I.rep.D.K. 20*, pp 13–14.   49 *P.R.I.rep.D.K. 20*.   50 McEnery & Refaussé, *Deeds*.   51 Mills, *Account roll*.

added in his edition a fragment of a seneschal's account for the years 1337
to 1339. A frontispiece reproducing a portion of one of the rolls is the only
visual record of the manuscripts. The accounts, four of the seneschal of Holy
Trinity and one of the bailiff of Clonkeen, provide detailed information on
the management of the three cathedral granges of Gorman, Glasnevin and
Clonkeen and in the words of James Lydon 'preserve a mass of information on every aspect of the manorial economy of medieval Ireland'.[52] They
also detail much of the domestic life-style of the priory, for the estates were
sources not only of income for the community but also of food and drink.
An unexpected interpolation into the rolls is part of the text of 'The pride
of life', a fourteenth century morality play, which was copied by two scribes
in the first half of the fifteenth century. The scribes may have been members of the Dublin Augustinian community and the play may have been part
of a dramatic repertoire which also included the 'Visitatio sepulcri' and the
lost Christmastide plays of 1528.[53]

The medieval archives are also sufficient to give a sense of liturgical life
in the priory before the Reformation. The oldest of the liturgical manuscripts
is the 'Martyrology', a register of Christian saints and martyrs to be read in
the quire,[54] and recent scholarship suggests that it has its origins in the first
half of the thirteenth century.[55] Its calendar and martyrology have a marked
Irish dimension and the inclusion of the feasts of the translation of St Lorcán
of Dublin and St Michan, to whom a Dublin church attached to the cathedral was dedicated, suggests a Christ Church connection. Of more substantial Christ Church interest is the 'Feast of the relics' on 31 July which has
an account of the relics which were deposited in the cathedral by Dúnán, the
first bishop of Dublin, and in the time of Archbishop Gréne (Gregory). The
list differs from that in the 'Book of obits', which is the principal source for
the cathedral's relics, and the fact that it omits the *baculus Ihesu* and the
miraculous crucifix suggests that it may have been copied from a list of relics
which was compiled before these treasures were obtained by the cathedral;
that is between 1161 and 1180. The final piece of the manuscript is a copy
of the rule of St Augustine, which the regulations of the order required to
be read through once a week. However, only the first part of the rule has
been copied into the manuscript suggesting that the discipline of the community had fallen from the level which the founder of the order required. A
further indication of low standards in Holy Trinity is suggested by the many

---

52 Lydon & Fletcher, *Account roll*, p. xi. 53 For a fuller discussion of the play and its
context see A.J. Fletcher, 'The pride of life' in Lydon & Fletcher, *Account roll*, pp xxii-
xliii. 54 T.C.D., MS 576. 55 M.L. Colker, *Trinity College Library, Dublin: descriptive catalogue of the medieval and Renaissance Latin manuscripts* (2 vols, Aldershot, 1991),
ii, 1039.

errors in grammar and syntax in the 'Martyrology' and by the fact that the community had continuously recited a flawed and uncorrected text.[56]

The 'Book of obits', with which the 'Martyrology' is now bound, is a register of those for whose souls the community prayed (leading figures in the church, members of the community and benefactors) with the day of the month on which they were to be annually remembered in the priory's round of devotions. It was compiled in the later fifteenth century, although it has subsequent additions from the sixteenth century, and a succession of authorities have attributed it to Thomas Fich, the compiler of the 'Liber albus'. It is similar in general character and script to the 'Liber albus' and includes the obit of Fich in a hand which is later than the original script. It seems therefore that the book was compiled in his lifetime and probably under his guidance as part of his reorganisation of the priory archives. Many of the entries relate to members of the cathedral fraternity, through which lay people, both men and women, were admitted to participation in the religious life of the community, and so this is an important source for identifying the wider cathedral community in the late middle ages.

It was not unusual for the obits, martyrology and rule to be brought together in one volume from which they could be conveniently read daily in chapter, but when the two parts of this manuscript were brought together is not clear for the book was rebound in the 1740s by John Exshaw of Dublin for the library of Trinity College.[57] The martyrology continued to be used in the cathedral after the suppression of the religious houses as is clear from a minute in the first chapter act book[58] while entries continued to be added to the list of obits until 1558, the final one being that of Rosina Holywood, wife of Arland Usher. The volume is, therefore, not only an important reservoir of information for the history of the late medieval priory but is also a valuable source for the early years of the new foundation.

By far the most splendid of the liturgical manuscripts is the 'Christ Church' psalter.[59] It is a late fourteenth century parchment manuscript with miniatures and illuminated capitals which has been rebound, possibly in the early sixteenth century, in red leather. The psalms are preceded by a calendar and followed by creeds, litany and prayers while additions of a later date include prayers, a form of absolution, memoranda of priory business in the late fourteenth and early fifteenth centuries, and, in the hand of the seventeenth-century antiquarian, Sir James Ware, obits of nine priors beginning

---

56 Crosthwaite & Todd, *Obits*, p. lxxxvii.   57 Colker, *Descriptive catalogue*, i, 18.   58 Crosthwaite & Todd, *Obits*, p. xcii.   59 Bodl., Rawl. MS G.185. See Falconer Madan, *A summary catalogue of western manuscripts in the Bodleian Library* (Oxford, 1895); Otto Pächt, 'A Giottesque episode in English medieval art' in *Journal of the Warburg and Courtauld Institutes*, vi (1943), pp 51–70; articles by Hand and Hawkes cited in note 28.

with Robert de Lokynton in 1397 and ending with William Hassard in 1537. A colophon on folio 142 indicates that the psalter was made for Stephen of Derby, prior of Holy Trinity from 1348 until c.1382, who appears as a kneeling supplicant in one of the miniatures. The name of the artist is not mentioned in the manuscript but on stylistic grounds Otto Pächt confidently attributed it to the Master of the Egerton Genesis. It is, therefore, an English manuscript which was imported into Holy Trinity and so was part of a trade which was well established by the fourteenth century whereby English scriptoria were producing books specifically for export. As a wealthy Irish religious house but one without a significant scriptorial tradition Holy Trinity might be expected to have been a patron of this trade and may have purchased other liturgical books which have not survived or been identified. The purchase of the psalter, while generally reflecting the wealth of the community and its links with liturgical and cultural life in England, also emphasises, if not the absence of a scriptorial tradition in Holy Trinity, at least the lack of any sophisticated scriptorial practice. The manuscript is also important for the accounts and memoranda of priory business for the period 1368 to 1416 which supplement the administrative records which have already been discussed. These entries relate mostly to the priorate of James de Redenesse and may be in his own hand.[60] Perhaps, however, the principal significance of the psalter for the history of Christ Church is that it is the earliest, and the only certain, source of music in the priory, although three liturgical manuscripts (two fourteenth-century processionals and a fifteenth-century antiphonary) survive from the neighbouring church of St John the Evangelist and these may have originally been used in Holy Trinity.[61]

Clearly the collection of medieval manuscripts in Christ Church must have been much larger. Holy Trinity, as a monastic cathedral, an Augustinian foundation, and one of the largest and wealthiest corporate bodies in medieval Ireland must have had a significant collection of manuscript books. These were needed not alone for liturgical and administrative purposes but also for the education of the members of the community and one would expect there to have been gospels, psalters, graduals, antiphonaries and missals; cartularies and legal texts; books of scripture, writings of the fathers and devotional works to be read at meals at the different seasons of the year. These may have been produced locally as were the 'Martyrology', 'Book of obits' and 'Liber albus', acquired by purchase like the psalter or received as bequests. It is known, for example, that in c.1450 Thomas Westoun, rector of Newcastle-Lyons, bequeathed his breviary to the prior and convent to be

60 See Hand, 'Psalter', pp 314–19; G.J. Hand, 'The psalter of Christ Church, Dublin (Bodleian MS Rawlinson G. 185)' in *Reportorium Novum*, ii, no. 1 (1958), p. 222.   61 Fletcher, 'The pride of life' in Lydon & Fletcher, *Account roll*.

chained in the quire[62] while books of John Alleyn, dean of St Patrick's, may have come to Holy Trinity after his death,[63] and it is likely that there were many similar bequests the records of which have been lost. Little has survived, due largely, it must be supposed, to the effects of the Reformation, although the absence of any attributable Christ Church manuscripts in other collections (apart from the obits, martyrology and psalter) may suggest that the output of the cathedral scriptorium was very limited. There are no references in the account rolls to the purchase of parchment for any purpose other than business while the researches of Todd suggested that the standards of learning in the community were not high.

Whilst the medieval archives are sufficient to allow an adequate examination of the administration of the priory and to permit some sense to be obtained of liturgical life, they are seriously deficient in one respect. There are no contemporary accounts of the building of the cathedral and indeed no visual image of the building survives before the publication of an engraving in London in 1581.[64] The chronicle of Gervase of Canterbury which describes the re-building of that cathedral in the late twelfth century has no Dublin counterpart; there are no contemporary architectural drawings such as those of the west front of Strasbourg cathedral in the mid-fourteenth century; and no physical representations of the building like the thirteenth-century funerary model of Nuremburg or the early sixteenth-century architect's model of Rouen cathedral.[65] The early architectural history of Christ Church must be based not on the archives but on the evidence of the building itself and that which may be extrapolated therefrom.

The records of the post-Reformation cathedral are more abundant with, in particular, the chapter act books and the proctors' account books providing an almost complete chronological record of the administration of Christ Church from the late sixteenth century until the disestablishment of the Church of Ireland in 1871. Thereafter the records of the chapter and the cathedral board provide the framework for the interpretation of Christ Church in the late nineteenth and twentieth centuries.

The early modern period, that is from the establishment of the new foundation until the eve of the Restoration, is relatively well documented in the cathedral's archives although not continuously so. The chapter act books do not begin until 1574, some thirty-five years after the foundation of the secular chapter, while the proctors' accounts, although beginning in 1542, are sparse for the second half of the sixteenth century. For the early years of the new foundation the absence of chapter acts and the paucity of accounts

---

62 McEnery & Refaussé, *Deeds*, no. 886.   63 Crosthwaite & Todd, *Obits*, pp xxxii–xxxiv. See p. 157 below.   64 *Anc. rec. Dublin*, ii, appendix.   65 Alain Erlande-Brandenburg, *The cathedral builders of the middle ages* (London, 1995), pp 71–3, 147–52.

are serious lacunae and the imaginative use of other sources, principally the deeds and the 'Book of obits', is required to illuminate the principal issues of the time: the state of Holy Trinity on the verge of the Reformation, the conversion of the priory to a secular cathedral managed by a dean and chapter, and the administrative and liturgical accommodations which were necessary to meet the changes required by the anglican-catholicism of Henry VIII, the embryonic protestantism of Edward VI, the catholicism of Mary and the protestantism of Elizabeth. Otherwise, however, these two series provide a valuable framework, and a certain amount of the covering upon which it is possible to flesh out convincingly the history of the cathedral. The details are provided both directly and inferentially from these minutes and accounts and from two other series in the cathedral's archives, lease books and guard books, which were the products of two major re-orderings of the cathedral's archives.[66] The first of these took place in the mid-1630s when the newly appointed chapter clerk, Thomas Howell, re-organized the cathedral's records in order the better to understand and administer the estates and finances of Christ Church. To this end he copied the proctors' accounts, transcribed the leases into a large parchment book, and made an abstract of all the cathedral leases. More significantly, from the viewpoint of Christ Church historians, was the work of the eighteenth-century antiquary John Lyon, who together with three canons of Christ Church, John Owen, William Fletcher and Isaac Mann, re-ordered the deeds, leases and loose papers. The deeds were transcribed into three volumes, which became known as the 'Registrum novum'; lease books were made for the properties of the dignitaries, the vicars choral and the general 'oeconomy fund'; and the mass of loose papers was roughly sorted thematically and made up into guard books with titles such as law proceedings, rent rolls, petitions for leases, acts and orders. Together, these sources make it possible to identify the cathedral community, to determine how it administered its affairs, to form some impression of its beliefs and religious practices, and to gain a sense of how the cathedral building was ordered and how the choral tradition developed.

From the Restoration to disestablishment, and in particular from the eighteenth century onwards, the cathedral archives are as complete as anyone familiar with Irish institutions would have any reasonable right to expect. Apart from a gap between 1670 and 1686 the chapter acts run in an unbroken sequence, while the accounts are complete except for the years 1738 to 1768; Lyon's work provides ease of intellectual access to the cathedral estates; and the guard books offer an immense range of incidental information about almost every aspect of the cathedral's life. In addition, new series of records

66 Gillespie, 'Archives', pp 3–12.

begin to appear. The wider cathedral community is recorded in the registers of baptisms, marriages and burials which survive from 1717,[67] and a somewhat different community, those who were invited to preach in Christ Church on Sundays and at the great public services,[68] are listed in the series of preachers' books which begins in 1727. From the middle of the eighteenth century information about the choral foundation becomes abundant. The choir attendance books begin in 1762[69] and, more importantly, there is a large body of manuscript music for the choir and organ, which is the most extensive of its kind in Ireland.[70] The cathedral estates were surveyed by John Longfield in the early years of the nineteenth century and the resulting three volumes of maps complement Thomas Reading's important map of the liberty of Christ Church (1761) and the handful of unrelated maps and surveys which detailed aspects of the cathedral and its estates from the late seventeeth century onwards.[71]

These archives, together with the records of the diocese of Dublin, central government and the neighbouring cathedral of St Patrick, provide the sources for the articulation of the day-to-day life of Christ Church and the investigation of major themes such as the turbulent relationship between the cathedral and the archbishop of Dublin, William King, the place of Christ Church in the development of a substantial choral tradition in Dublin and, especially, the effects of the growing intervention of government in the affairs of the Church of Ireland, evidenced particularly by the Irish Church Temporalities Act of 1833 and more decisively by the disestablishment of the Church of Ireland by the Irish Church Act of 1869.

Disestablishment reduced the status of Christ Church from that of an ecclesiastical corporation with its own estates and sources of income to that of a dependent part of a voluntary Christian community. The cathedral estates were confiscated and sold by the Church Temporalities Commissioners and so the activity which had consistently contributed most to the accumulation of the cathedral's archives, the management of property, was dramatically reduced. Yet, paradoxically, it was following disestablishment that the the most significant Christ Church property, the cathedral itself, received long overdue attention. The complete restoration of the fabric between 1872 and 1878, funded by the Dublin distiller Henry Roe, and carried out under the direction of the eminent architect, George Edmund Street, resulted in the development for the first time of an architectural record of the building with drawings and sketches by Street and his successors, Sir Thomas Drew and R. Caufield Orpen, detailing the development of the building in the late nineteenth and early twentieth centuries.

---

67 Refaussé & Lennon, *Registers.*   68 C6/1/21.   69 C6/1/23.   70 C6/1/24.   71 C6/3; N.L.I., MSS 2789–90.

The records of the chapter and the board, the latter one of the adminis-trative results of disestablishment, are the principal archival sources for the history of Christ Church in the late nineteenth and twentieth centuries. As the twentieth century progressed it was the board rather than the chapter which gradually assumed the dominent role and its minutes, which are con-tinuous from 1873, are the main source for all major administrative matters, and especially finance, with the chapter concerning itself only with the reg-ulation of worship under the direction of the dean. The board minutes are supplemented by minutes and accounts of various sub-committees and by printed annual reports. Indeed as the century progressed there was a marked increase in the output of printed material from the cathedral: year books, orders of service, annual lists of morning preachers and a wide variety of ephemera relating to activity in Christ Church all of which provide detail which complement the minutes and accounts.

It is indisputably the case that there are periods of the cathedral's his-tory and aspects of its past which the muniments do not record, but nonetheless there clearly is an archive which is adequate for the needs of a respectable history. The problem, in recent years at least, has not been the lack of an adequate archive but a lack of access to it and a consequent ignorance of its potential. It is scarcely a coincidence that the only signif-icant history of Christ Church, that of Monck Mason, was written after the cathedral archives had been re-organized by John Lyon, so repeating the model of St Patrick's cathedral where Lyon had ordered the muni-ments which provided the source for Mason's history. Following Mason's work the archives remained in the cathedral library, largely unregarded but at least safe. The restoration of the building in the 1870s swept away the library but provided no appropriate alternative accommodation and the archives, without a permanent home, were inevitably at risk. Eventually they were consigned to the crypt where their inaccessibility was matched only by their physical deterioration. An examination of the collection in 1970 revealed that the manuscripts were 'sopping wet', the bindings were covered with fungus, and some had begun to crumble. A hasty rescue plan was followed by a report on the importance of the collection and expert opinion on how it might be restored,[72] all of which was ignored. The medieval manuscripts, 'Registrum novum' and the chapter act books were crammed into a poorly ventilated strong room and the remainder of the collection, much of it in a fragile condition following its incarceration in the crypt, was abandoned in unrelated piles in presses, on bookshelves and on the floor of the administrator's office. The vital precursor to the writ-ing of this history of Christ Church was the transfer of the entire cathe-

72 C6/5/8/31.

dral archive to the Representative Church Body library in the late 1980s and early 1990s. There, for the first time in its history, the collection as a whole was arranged and listed and was made available for research. The consequent emergence of a clear sense of the nature and extent of the archive has made what follows possible.

THE MEDIEVAL CATHEDRAL

II

From Hiberno-Norse to Anglo-Norman, *c.*1030–1300

Stuart Kinsella

The history of Christ Church before the arrival of the Anglo-Normans has received little more than a cursory glance, as is clear from those accounts written in the nineteenth century.[1] This lack of concern with origins has itself a long lineage. On 24 February 1326, the king's escheator, Walter de la Pulle, declared the church's origins beyond legal memory.[2] In 1383, a further investigation stated likewise, 'that it was founded and endowed by divers Irish men, whose names are unknown time out of mind, and long before the conquest of Ireland'. In *c.*1345, a weak attempt was made at identifying the founder, the unlikely Sitriuc macMurgh.[3] Not only had the founder's name become corrupted, but by the seventeenth century the foundation date too had succumbed to an inaccuracy when the ecclesiastical historian, Sir James Ware, put it at 1038.[4]

---

1 W.M. Mason, 'The history of the cathedral church of the Holy Trinity', T.C.D., MS 10529 was never published. For the MS's origins, see *Catalogue of the literary collections and original compositions of William Monck Mason, Esq., etc.* (London, 1858); Finlayson, *Inscriptions*, appendix [p. 111], *Dictionary of National Biography, sub nomine* and Douglas Hyde and D.J. O'Donoghue, *Catalogue of books and manuscripts of Sir John T. Gilbert* (Dublin, 1918); for the precentor, Edward Seymour's history, see Seymour, *Christ Church*. His collaborative work with the architect G.E. Street contained much the same material, but returned to an abbreviated style for the early period. 2 'Lands and liberties enjoyed a *principio conquesti Hibernie* were beyond the limit of legal memory', G.J. Hand, *English law in Ireland 1290–1324* (Cambridge, 1967), p. 176. 3 For inquisitions of 1326, see McEnery & Refaussé, *Deeds*, no. 220; of 1386, see Walter Harris, *The history and antiquities of the city of Dublin, from the earliest accounts, etc.* (Dublin, 1766), p. 372 and T.C.D., MS 10529; and for 1325 see Gwynn, *Irish church*, p. 53, citing an inquisition in P.R.O., chancery miscellanea, C. 47/19/1, no. 4. See also below, pp 75–94. 4 James Ware, *De praesulibus Hiberniae commentarius* (London, 1654), pp 140–1. See Gwynn, 'Origins' and Gwynn, *Irish church*, pp 64–6. For Ware, see G.V Jourdan, *Sir James Ware: historian and antiquary (1594–1666)* (Dublin, 1953).

A major obstacle in the quest for cathedral origins lies in the difficulty of definition. Twentieth-century conceptions of cathedrals are intimately associated with diocesan structures (first introduced into Ireland as part of the twelfth-century reform) and with the classic capitular system of dignitaries and canons which appeared only with the spread of Anglo-Norman power in the late twelfth and early thirteenth centuries.[5] Historians have tended to classify the Irish church before the twelfth-century reform as monastic in character and therefore have failed to consider the possibility of the existence of churches with episcopal links, literally, churches with a bishop's *cathedra*, even if that did not extend to the sort of diocesan control which later developed. More recently the importance of bishops and their churches in pre-Anglo-Norman Ireland has been increasingly recognised.[6] Such an important episcopal church may have existed in a monastic context at the settlement of 'Duiblinn' by the seventh century.[7] A number of references (some admittedly seventeenth-century) to seventh- and eighth-century bishops and abbots of Duiblinn cannot be discounted as 'plainly unhistorical'.[8] One prelate, Siadal (d. 790), was listed as abbot and bishop, which seems to represent a typical example of early Irish Christian monastic presence within the ecclesiastical enclosure, the sole occupier of which may have been St Peter's church, perhaps under the patronage of the local rulers, the Uí Fergusa. They were a minor branch of the Uí Dúnlainge dynasty and, as chief church in their túath, the bishop's area of authority probably extended to the boundaries of their kingdom.[9]

Within this symbiotic structure of church and secular polity in the Dublin area, one element failed to fit: the Viking settlement at Áth Cliath, for two reasons. First, Viking settlements in the Dublin area before the tenth century seem to have been temporary affairs.[10] Second, unlike York, where the Vikings

5 K.W. Nicholls, 'Medieval Irish cathedral chapters' in *Archivium Hibernicum*, xxxi (1973), pp 102–11. 6 For example, Richard Sharpe, 'Churches and communities in early medieval Ireland: towards a pastoral model' in John Blair and Richard Sharpe (ed.), *Pastoral care before the parish* (Leicester, 1992), pp 81–109; Colmán Etchingham, 'Bishops in the early Irish Church: a reassessment' in *Studia Hibernica*, no. 28 (1994), pp 35–62. 7 For the early evidence of bishops in the Dublin area, Howard Clarke, 'Conversion, church and cathedral: the diocese of Dublin to 1152' in James Kelly and Daire Keogh (ed.), *History of the Catholic diocese of Dublin* (Dublin, 2000), pp 23–30. 8 Clarke, 'Conversion', pp 20, 25, 27, notes 3, 42, 53–7. See also James Ware and Walter Harris, *A history of the bishops of Ireland* (Dublin, 1739), pp 303–7; Gwynn & Hadcock, *Religious houses*, p. 70 and M.V. Ronan, 'Cross-in-circle stones of St Patrick's cathedral' in *R.S.A.I. Jn.*, lxxi (1941), pp 1–8, note 12. 9 For a review of early bishops, see Etchingham, 'Bishops in the early Irish church', pp 35–62. See also Clarke, 'Conversion', pp 24, 27–9, notes 31, 59–67. 10 P.F. Wallace, 'Archaeology and the emergence of Dublin as the principal town of Ireland' in John Bradley (ed.), *Settlement and society in medieval Ireland* (Kilkenny, 1988), p. 127; H.B. Clarke, 'Proto–towns and towns in Ireland and Britain in the ninth and tenth centuries' in H.B. Clarke, Máire Ní Mhaonaigh and Raghnall Ó Floinn (ed.), *Ireland and Scandinavia in*

allied themselves with the church, in Ireland churches provided plunder and the possibility of Vikings settling at pre-existing monasteries does seem likely.[11] The first half of the tenth century was an unstable period for Dublin's Viking community with frequent changes of ruler. The accession of Amlaíb (Norse, *Óláfr*) Cúarán, king of York in 943, to the kingship of Dublin in 945 (kingships both held by his father, Sitriuc Cáech) was an important landmark in the settlement's history. Despite a lengthy sojourn in England, Amlaíb returned to Dublin in 952.[12] The period of sustained peace that followed enabled Amlaíb to establish a permanent settlement and to transform the economy from pillaging (and its by-product, slave-trading) to craftworking and commerce. By the 980s, the agglomeration of the two settlements of Áth Cliath and Duiblinn had probably occurred, producing a thriving urban economy in the Hiberno-Norse town. The axes of the conurbation were present-day Castle Street-Christchurch Place and the more steeply graded Werburgh Street-Fishamble Street and Nicholas Street-Winetavern Street, while the pattern of a defensible ridge surrounded by a confluence of waterways matches well with other Hiberno-Norse towns.[13] Of even greater significance in the longer term for Dublin were Amlaíb Cúarán's religious beliefs. His uncle Godfrid's sparing of some monasteries in 921 may already be an indication of Christian sympathies, although he sacked Kildare in 929. His father was given the sister of the Christian Anglo-Saxon king Æthelstan in marriage in 926 and Amlaíb himself was baptised in 943 under the auspices of King Edmund of England. Edmund also sponsored the confirmation of his cousin, Ragnald Godfridsson (king of York, 943–4) and it would seem likely that Amlaíb's Christianity was 'thanks to a political initiative', and although perhaps initially shallow, was certainly ingrained by the time of his death.[14]

Amlaíb's death in 980 was something of a turning point for the Dublin settlement. His son Sitriuc, who eventually succeeded him in 989, built on

the early Viking age (Dublin, 1998), pp 344–53; H.B. Clarke, 'The bloodied eagle: the vikings and the development of Dublin, 841–1014' in *The Irish Sword: the journal of the Military History Society of Ireland*, xviii (1990–2), pp 92–100; H.B. Clarke, 'The topographical development of early medieval Dublin' in Clarke, *Medieval Dublin: metropolis*, p. 67. 11 Raghnall Ó Floinn, 'The archaeology of the early Viking age in Ireland' in Clarke et al., *Ireland and Scandinavia*, p. 163; Clarke, 'Proto-towns', pp 344–53; Clarke, 'Conversion', p. 31. 12 For Dublin and York, see A.P. Smyth, *Scandinavian York and Dublin: the history and archaeology of two related Viking kingdoms* (2 vols, Dublin and New Jersey, 1975–9). See also Clarke, 'Proto-towns', pp 353–61; Clarke, 'Bloodied eagle', pp 106–7. 13 Clarke, 'Proto-towns', pp 333–4, 344–64; P.F. Wallace, 'The archaeological identity of the Hiberno-Norse town' in *R.S.A.I. Jn.*, cxxii (1992), pp 62–4. 14 Lesley Abrams, 'The conversion of the Scandinavians of Dublin' in Christopher Harper-Bill (ed.), *Anglo-Norman studies xx: proceedings of the Battle conference in Dublin 1997* (Woodbridge, 1998), pp 22–6, especially note 169; Clarke, 'Conversion', pp 33–5 and Gwynn & Hadcock, *Religious houses*, p. 130.

his father's legacy. Like his father, Sitriuc's lasting achievements occurred during a period of peace, and he is best remembered for the very Christian gesture of establishing a bishopric at Dublin and the erection of a cathedral. However, Christianity was at this time probably still very much more a matter of political allegiance than of religious conviction, as Sitriuc's blinding in 1018 of the rival king of Leinster, Bran mac Máel Morda, demonstrates.[15] Religious change was no doubt slow, presumably spaced over generations, and this would account for the absence of a cathedral in Dublin over forty years after the death of the probably Christian Amlaíb. Sitriuc's pilgrimage to Rome in 1028 when he was in his seventies confirmed his own Christianity, and his daughter is also known to have been a nun in St Finnan's convent.[16]

Possibly Sitriuc's pilgrimage to Rome in 1028 was one of personal devotion, but he may also have been aware that the re-establishment of an episcopal base in Dublin in the last years of his life would be his enduring achievement. A tradition of Irish pilgrimage to Rome ensured that he was accompanied by 'many others' (*multi alii*), one of whom may have been his prospective bishop, a young Irishman called Dúnán. His consecration is unlikely to have been by Irish bishops, given their uncanonical status in the eyes of Rome, and in the absence of any known links with York, he probably looked to Canterbury, where Archbishop Æthelnoth 'the Good' (1020–38) had previously consecrated a bishop of Denmark. Unfortunately, no evidence survives apart from the unverifiable tradition cited by Canterbury when consecrating Dúnán's successor.[17]

Recent historians have agreed on c.1030 as the date for Sitriuc's founding of a church on the present site, some time after his pilgrimage to Rome in 1028. Only two documents – the entries in the fourteenth-century 'Liber niger' and an early deed listing the cathedral's endowment – contain information as to its foundation.[18] The 'Liber niger' has two foundation narratives, the shorter being earlier, and based on an older source. The longer, and later, narrative contains the sole reference to Sitriuc as founder, stating that

> he gave to the Holy Trinity and to Donatus [Dúnán], the first bishop of Dublin, a site on which to build a church to the Holy Trinity;

---

15 Poul Holm, 'The slave trade of Dublin, ninth to twelfth centuries' in *Peritia*, v (1986), pp 332–3; Gwynn, *Irish church*, p. 62.   16 Benjamin Hudson, 'Knútr and Viking Dublin' in *Scandinavian Studies*, lxvi, no. 3 (1994), pp 323–32.   17 Abrams, 'Conversion', pp 26–8; Hudson, 'Knútr and Viking Dublin', p. 327; Clarke, 'Bloodied eagle', p. 111. See also M.T. Flanagan, *Irish society, Anglo-Norman settlers, Angevin kingship: interactions in Ireland in the late twelfth century* (Oxford, 1989), pp 7–19. For Dúnán, see Gwynn, 'First bishops'.   18 Lawlor, 'Liber niger'; Gwynn, 'Unpublished texts', McEnery & Refaussé, *Deeds*, no. 364c, and *Alen's reg.*, pp 28–30 (148b).

where the arches or vaults are now founded, with the lands as named below: Kealdulek, Recra and Portracre with their villeins and cattle and corn. And he gave also gold and silver sufficient to build a church with all its court. Then that most religious man Donatus said that he would satisfy the wish and the command of this King Sitriuc in as far as he was able.[19]

Earlier in the same narrative, references to the above arches and vaults are inaccurately associated with St Patrick and this probably relates to a later conflict over primacy between Dublin and Armagh, confusing the saint with a former bishop of Dublin, Gilla Pátraic.[20]

The dedication of the cathedral to the Holy Trinity is evident only from later sources, but given Dúnán's probable consecration by the archbishop of Canterbury, it may well have been borrowed from that cathedral. It would also have been a politically astute move to focus on the church rather than on any particular local allegiance. Holy Trinity could not have been a simpler dedication, yet it was decisively Christian and acceptable to Dúnán's fellow Irish, who presumably supported the re-establishment of the Dublin bishopric, perhaps from Clondalkin.[21] In one move, Sitriuc gave the Hiberno-Norse town a new heart, embracing its westward expansion (*c.*1010-30) by situating the cathedral at the western edge of Duiblinn's old *dún*, and unifying the Viking settlement of Áth Cliath and the older Irish Duiblinn (both roughly equidistant from the new cathedral).[22] An episcopal seat not only carried great esteem but could act as a centre for bespoke and prestige liturgy, such as Alan Fletcher describes below, accepting local patronage, and facilitating larger events such as coronations, consecrations and the burial of dignitaries.[23] Perhaps most importantly, it upgraded Dublin's status of 'unchartered town', created by his father, Amlaíb, to that of 'city', which Sitriuc must have realised.[24]

---

19 Gwynn, 'Origins', pp 45-50.   20 See David Dumville, 'St Patrick and the Scandinavians of Dublin' in David Dumville *et al.*, *Saint Patrick, A.D. 493-1993* (Woodbridge, 1993), pp 259-64 and p. 40 below.   21 Clarke, 'Conversion', pp 32-4, 41. 22 Anngret Simms, 'Medieval Dublin: a topographical analysis' in *Irish Geography*, 12 (1979), p. 33; P.F. Wallace, 'The archaeological identity of the Hiberno-Norse town' in *R.S.A.I. Jn.*, cxxii (1992), pp 40, 48, 60; Anngret Simms, 'Medieval Dublin in a European context: from proto-town to chartered town' in Clarke, *Medieval Dublin: metropolis*, pp 50-1, states that 'had the original Viking settlement at Dublin not developed in the area of the present-day castle, but rather on the site of Christ Church cathedral, the highest point inside the walled town, then the street pattern would probably have evolved in a concentric fashion around the church, which it clearly is not.'   23 See pp 129-41.   24 Clarke, 'Conversion', p. 26, note 51, citing the 'Liber angeli' in Ludwig Bieler (ed.), *The Patrician texts in the Book of Armagh* (Dublin, 1979), pp 188-9, and Colmán Etchingham, 'The implications of *paruchia*' in *Ériú*, xliv (1993), p. 149. Clarke, 'Proto-towns', p. 331

As king of Dublin, Sitriuc probably decreed the location for the cathedral, unlikely to have been concerned by pre-existing property congestion (in any case, perhaps less dense closer to the old western boundary). Indications from the 'Liber niger' that St Michael's chapel, supposedly erected with the first cathedral, was built 'out of what was left of the money and timber', suggests, along with the predominant archaeological findings of buildings in Dublin, that the early cathedral was of wood. However, the presence of a stone church in Waterford in 1100, recent evidence from Copper Alley and the crypt's own revelations of stone foundations amidst considerable boulder clay indicate that, at least in part, the early cathedral was of stone.[25] Sitriuc's endowment of 'gold and silver sufficient to build a church with all its court' is ambiguous given the phrase '*cum tota curia contulit*' which might imply a substantial household, together with the buildings in which they would operate.[26] He also established a chapel to St Nicholas on the cathedral's north side, still evident in 1541 as 'a long loft called St Nicholas's chapel situate over the cellar'.[27] Two other parish churches of St Nicholas are known to have survived: St Nicholas Within, a church just south of the cathedral precincts, and that extended under Archbishop Bicknor (1317–49) 'without' the walls of city.[28] The only early reference to St Nicholas's parish church is in a deed of 1179,[29] and it might be this church which reverted to the status of a chapel by 1541, perhaps due to a decline in popularity.[30]

The question of the existence of an episcopal residence beside the cathedral still poses difficulties. The older of the two foundation narratives in the 'Liber niger' tells that Dúnán, the first '*arch*bishop' [*sic*] made a chapel of St Michael in his palace.[31] It further states that the church of St Michael was

recognised 'the notion of cathedral and episcopal dignity' as the only justification for the oversimplification of Dublin as 'a Scandinavian city (840–1169)' stated by A.P. Smyth, *Scandinavian kings in the British Isles 850–880* (Oxford, 1977), p. 186.   25 See Stalley's suggestion that a precursor may have been Sitriuc's palace, pp 55 and 219; for St Michael's church, see Gwynn, 'Origins', p. 49.   26 The narratives are reproduced in Gwynn, 'Unpublished texts', pp 308–9.   27 McEnery & Refaussé, *Deeds*, no. 1182. When citing this deed, Butler, *Christ Church*, p. 14, is undecided as to his interpretation, which refutes a dubious suggestion that the north-eastern Lady chapel was originally dedicated to St Nicholas. The Huguenots he mentions worshipped in the Lady chapel of St Patrick's not Christ Church.   28 Bernard, *St Patrick's*, pp 15, 55 and H.A. Wheeler and M.J. Craig, *The Dublin city churches of the Church of Ireland* (Dublin, 1948), pp 31–3. Considerable overlap occurred between parishoners of St Nicholas Without and the French congregation worshipping in St Patrick's Lady chapel.   29 *Alen's reg.*, p. 3.   30 Whether as church or chapel, the continuity suggested for St Nicholas by the 1541 deed, makes it unlikely that Sitriuc was the founder of St Nicholas Within. See John Bradley, 'The topographical development of Scandinavian Dublin' in F.H.A. Aalen and Kevin Whelan (ed.), *Dublin city and county: from prehistory to present* (Dublin, 1992), p. 48, citing Gwynn, 'Unpublished texts', p. 309.   31 Bradley, 'Topographical development', p. 48.

built out of what remained of the money and timber from the rebuilding of the cathedral near the community dining hall by Archbishop Lorcán. The later narrative agrees with this, recognising Dúnán as bishop.[32] Roger Stalley shows below, however, that this building phase is Anglo-Norman, undertaken by Archbishop Cumin, (c.1184–6). Furthermore, both narratives refer to the fact that 'before there were archbishops in Ireland' (earlier narrative) or 'the city of Dublin' (later narrative), 'the site of the palace was the property of the prior and convent of Holy Trinity [in Dublin (later narrative)], and their orchard was there'. Ireland's first archbishops were created in 1111 as a result of the synod of Ráith Bressail, but Dublin had to await the synod of Kells-Mellifont of 1152. Identifying the site of the palace with an orchard owned by the prior and convent before 1152 poses two problems: first, a continuous monastic organisation was not introduced to Christ Church until after 1163 and second, both narratives agree that Dúnán erected the palace, dating it to the 1030s. To the writers of the fourteenth-century 'Liber niger' narratives, perhaps the prior and convent simply represented the cathedral as they knew it? If so, did Gréne, bishop and later archbishop of Dublin in 1152, enhance his new status by building a new palace, or perhaps expanding Dúnán's old one? Given the proximity of the present St Michael's church[33] (Dúnán's original chapel) to the western range of the cloisters where the quarters of the dean, prior and probably St Lorcán were, it is likely that the palace lay somewhere in the area beneath the road just south of the present bridge linking the cathedral with the former synod hall.[34]

It is possible to place part of the landed endowment of the church. Aubrey Gwynn identified three place names in the 'Liber niger' foundation narrative as St Doulagh's (Kealdulek), Lambay (Recra) and Portrane (Portracre), but for two reasons this is probably incorrect. First, Kealdulek is not the rural northside parish of St Doulagh's, but Gorman, the first of the cathedral's granges (Grangegorman),[35] alternatively known as 'Bealdulig' or 'Balemicamlaib'.[36] A deed, dated between 1228 and 1255, recorded in the sixteenth-century register of Archbishop Alen, refers to 'the church of Holy Trinity with all its court and graveyard, ... the grange beyond the bridge, called Kildulyc [and he notes 'Alias Cellduleg, also Gorman'], with its appur-

---

32 Gwynn, 'Origins', pp 46–9.   33 Used for the exhibition 'Dvblinia' since 1993. For the rebuilding of St Michael's church as a synod hall in the 1870s, see p. 367 below.   34 See also p. 109.   35 Otway-Ruthven, 'Church lands', p. 60. Hudson, 'Knútr and Viking Dublin', pp 333–4 perpetuates the 'St Doulough' misidentification, as does Gwynn, *Irish church*, p. 52 (although he is aware [p. 53] of the inaccuracy).   36 *Alen's reg.*, pp 3–5, 7–8, 15–16, 28–30, 80, McEnery & Refaussé, *Deeds*, nos 6, 44, 364a and c; Lawlor, 'Liber niger', no. 42 and *'Crede mihi', the most ancient book of the archbishop of Dublin before the Reformation*, ed. J.T. Gilbert (Dublin, 1897), no. i.

tenances, namely Ballymachkaeull, Machduma'.[37] The gift of Grangegorman's 878 acres by Sitriuc seems small compared to its later medieval holdings of 10,538 acres, but it would remain a core grange and that nearest to the cathedral.[38] Second, the identifications of Lambay and Portrane may be accurate, but not as part of Sitriuc's donation. The Christ Church deed relevant to this lists 'Bealdulig, Rochen, and Portracharn, granted by Cithuric, son of Absolea, earl of Dublin; Minoreni, by Macdeardan Macduba'.[39] It is probably from this deed, however, readily available in the fourteenth-century cathedral, that the entry was written into the 'Liber niger'. An earlier and more accurate version of the deed also occurs in Alen's register which lists the following donors: 'of the gift of Cithuric son of Absolea, earl of Dublin, the place where the church of Holy Trinity is actually founded and Kealdulig; Rocheir and Portrahcham, of the gift of Macdeardan mcduba, imōrē, of the gift of Donoghd son of Donald the gross, Clonchen'.[40] The transcriber of the Christ Church deed had assumed the donated property was recited first followed by the donor's name. The second entry, 'Macdeardan mcduba, imōrē', is known to be Murchad, underking of Dublin between 1054 and 1070 and son of high king 'with opposition', Diarmait mac Máel na mBó.[41] With no clear precedent, this is listed backwards and it is clear that the transcriber inaccurately assigned 'Macdeardan mcduba' as the donor's name and 'imōrē' as his non-existent property.[42]

The death of Sitriuc in 1042, probably in Wales, inaugurated a succession of weak kings of Dublin which 'must have caused discontent among young and impatient aristocrats in Dublin'.[43] It is worth noting that this rivalry was by no means limited to Irish soil, but in the areas surrounding the great 'Viking lake' of the Irish Sea, where there was an expansion of 'the Norse sphere of influence' at this time.[44] According to the life of Gruffudd

---

37 *Alen's reg.*, p. 80. Significantly, several deeds place Magduma between Grangegorman and Drumcondra, but see also, M.V Ronan, 'History of the diocese' in *Reportorium Novum*, i, no. 1 (1955), p. 38.   38 Otway-Ruthven, 'Church lands', p. 59.   39 McEnery & Refaussé, *Deeds*, no. 364c.   40 *Alen's reg.*, p. 28.   41 Clarke, 'Conversion', p. 35, note 117.   42 A third version of this deed has been published as a typeset reproduction of the Latin original in *Chartae, privilegia et immunitates, being transcripts of charters and privileges to cities, towns, abbeys and other bodies corporate 1171 to 1395* (Dublin, 1889), p. 12 [although *Alen's reg.* states f. 148b rather than f. 148d]. Otway-Ruthven, 'Church lands', p. 60, note 46 corrects the '1202' confirmation to *c*.1203–9.   43 Holm, 'Slave trade', p. 334.   44 The description of the Irish Sea as such aptly highlights its use in connecting Dublin with Galloway, Cumbria, the Isle of Man, the Wirral, Anglesey and Chester in a vast network of routeways. For a map, see James Graham-Campbell, 'The early Viking age in the Irish Sea area' in Clarke *et al.*, *Ireland and Scandinavia*, p. 105 (after Wendy Davies, *Patterns of power in early Wales* (Oxford, 1990), fig. 5). Seán Duffy, 'Ostmen, Irish and Welsh in the eleventh century' in *Peritia*, ix (1995), pp 378–396, examines the

ap Cynan (king of Gwynedd and the great-grandson of Sitriuc 'Silkbeard'), Sitriuc's son Amlaíb ruled not only the Rhinns (a peninsula of Galloway in Scotland), but Galloway itself, in addition to his base at Anglesey, and the kingdoms of Dublin and the Isle of Man.[45] Over the next seventy-five years, the Hiberno-Norse town would generally be ruled by the high king through the appointment of an under king, usually his heir apparent.[46] Only the succession of Murchad, the eldest Uí Chennselaig son and heir of Diarmait mac Máel na mBó, in 1054 brought any real stability; he was notable as the first in a series of such high king 'trainee' appointments, marking the end of the independent kingdom of Dublin and the beginning of its primacy as capital of Ireland.[47] He reigned in Dublin for sixteen years, a significantly longer period than any of his predecessors since Dúnán was appointed bishop. On the assumption that Dúnán was in his late twenties when appointed, he would have been in his late fifties at the time of Murchad's appointment. Nevertheless it is possible that this period of stability with a single leader, a fellow Irishman, may have been a productive period for both. Murchad mac Diarmata meic Máel na mBó is known also for giving the second grant of Portrane and Lambay to the cathedral,[48] and following his death in 1070 the funeral was held in the cathedral which he endowed, and probably presided over by Dúnán. It has even been suggested that Murchad may have been buried to the left of the high altar, given Dúnán's own burial on the right hand side two years later.[49]

A different dynastic duo were to mould Dublin's future for the next three decades, the Ua Briain. Diarmait mac Máel na mBó's protégé, Toirrdelbach Ua Briain, laid claim to the kingship of Ireland and, in 1075, installed his heir, Muirchertach Ua Briain, at Dublin, whose kingship until 1086 would prove most instructive for his future leadership.[50] This period was also one of change

'Viking lake' idea in great detail, and it is also used in P.F. Wallace, 'The archaeology of Viking Dublin' in H.B. Clarke and Anngret Simms (ed.), *The comparative history of urban origins in non-Roman Europe: Ireland, Wales, Denmark, Germany, Poland and Russia from the ninth to the thirteenth century* (Oxford, 1985), pp 103–146, and Wallace, 'Dublin as principal town', p. 156.   45 Seán Duffy, 'Irishmen and islesmen in the kingdoms of Dublin and Man, 1052–1171' in *Ériu*, xliii (1992), pp 95–100.   46 H.B. Clarke, 'Gaelic, Viking and Hiberno-Norse Dublin' in Art Cosgrove (ed.), *Dublin through the ages* (Dublin, 1988), pp 23–4; Seán Duffy, 'Pre-Norman Dublin: capital of Ireland?' in *History Ireland*, i, no 4 (1993), pp 13–18.   47 Clarke, 'Proto-towns', p. 332; Holm, 'Slave trade', p. 331. 48 Todd, 'Introduction' in Crosthwaite & Todd, *Obits*, pp lxvi–lxviii.   49 Clarke, 'Conversion', p. 48, note 205, citing a lecture in the cathedral crypt given by Dr Seán Duffy on 20 October 1998.   50 Anthony Candon, 'Muirchertach Ua Briain, politics and naval activity in the Irish Sea, 1075–1119' in Gearóid Mac Niocaill and P.F. Wallace (ed.), *Keimelia: studies in medieval archaeology and history in memory of Tom Delaney* (Galway, 1987), pp 399–401; Duffy, 'Irishmen', pp 101–3.

abroad. Gregory VII succeeded to the papacy in 1073 and in July, within a month or so of his consecration, he wrote urging Lanfranc, archbishop of Canterbury, to 'strive by every means open to you to ban the wicked practices which we have heard rumoured of the *Scotti* [Irish]'.[51] Gregory also wrote to 'Toirdelbach Ua Briain and the archbishops, bishops, and abbots of Ireland' in a letter probably dated to February 1074 offering assistance. Toirrdelbach undoubtedly took the pope's letter urging reform seriously, as his own and Muirchertach's careers were to demonstrate. After his consecration as bishop of Dublin in London in 1074, Gilla Pátraic would probably have acted as messenger, carrying letters to Dublin informing people of his consecration and asking for the suppression of 'the wicked marriage laws of his people', but also to Toirrdelbach to whom he addressed a 'complete agenda for a reforming council, including action against Irish marriage law'.[52]

Toirrdelbach Ua Briain was the first claimant to Ireland's kingship to control the selection of a bishop in Dublin, and it would prove to be the most significant Irish church appointment that century. Unlike his predecessor Diarmait, whose court was a centre of Anglo-Saxon resistance since the Norman invasion of England in 1066, Toirrdelbach seems to have fostered relations with William the Conqueror.[53] In this context it is significant that 'up to 1066 we can still say that English and Irish monks shared a common cultural world in which the Irish could still be teachers', in other words 'the land of saints and scholars' had experienced a remarkable continuity albeit in a somewhat attenuated form.[54] Although this faded rapidly after the Norman conquest of England, a number of communities there remained highly conservative, including the cathedral communities of Worcester, Winchester and Canterbury, and the smaller monastic communities of Winchcombe and Evesham (in the diocese of Worcester). The last Anglo-Saxon abbot of Evesham, Æthelwig (1058–78), is remembered for welcoming pilgrims from Ireland.[55]

Toirrdelbach's task in the 1070s was to install a cleric who would not only minister to the diocese of Dublin, but also begin the process of reform in Ireland. Gilla Pátraic must have seemed like the ideal candidate, an Irish protégé of Bishop Wulfstan, who no doubt shared his political sympathies for

51 Mark Philpott, 'Some interactions between the English and Irish churches' in Harper-Bill, *Anglo-Norman studies xx*, p. 190, note 16.   52 Philpott, 'Some interactions', pp 190, 193–6; Gwynn, 'First bishops', p. 10.   53 Benjamin Hudson, 'William the Conqueror and Ireland' in *I.H.S.*, xxix, no. 114 (Nov. 1994), pp 145–58.   54 Denis Bethell, 'English monks and Irish reform in the eleventh and twelfth centuries' in *Historical studies viii Dublin: papers read before the Irish conference of historians* (Dublin, 1971), p. 125.   55 Clarke, 'Conversion', p. 43, citing *Chronicon abbatiae de Evesham ad annum 1418*, ed. W.D. Macray (Rolls Series, vol. 29, London, 1863), pp 83, 91; Hudson, 'William the Conqueror and Ireland', p. 153.

the Normans, and was friendly with Aldwin, 'monk of Winchcombe, the reformer of northern monasticism'.[56] He was to be the first in a long line of similar appointments (particularly under Muirchertach) in the reforming church, and these clerics were characterised by being unrelated to the see to which they were appointed and in having experience of the church outside Ireland.[57] It is possible that it was Dúnán who sent Gilla Pátraic, whom he recognised as his successor, to Worcester to train under St Wulfstan, and Lanfranc refers to him as 'trained in monastic institutions from his youth'.[58]

Bishop Pátraic is now increasingly being appreciated for his many achievements during a decade-long episcopate. Although evidence survives only for Pátraic's successor, Gwynn has reasonably argued that it was Pátraic who managed to establish a monastic tradition at Holy Trinity for twenty years or more, two successive bishops after him being trained at Benedictine institutions in England.[59] Dublin can be seen as one of the numerous Benedictine communities founded, mostly in northern England, by a restless diaspora. Denis Bethell has termed them 'Old English', and stated that although 'intellectually these monks were highly conservative, they could scarcely be so ecclesiastically'.[60] For this reason they were ideally suited to begin a process of reform in Dublin. The aftermath of the Norman conquest of England was a period of ecclesiastical rejuvenation with monk-bishops holding positions of prominence during the rebuilding of many of the cathedrals. This 'golden age of patriarchal rule in the cathedral priories' was to be of short duration, the monks themselves taking a less prominent role as they helped to establish the pattern of the secular clergy of priests and bishops, and this model is also found in Dublin, Gréne, most likely a secular priest, succeeding the Benedictine bishops.[61] His predecessor, Pátraic, was probably also responsible for the enlargement of Christ Church cathedral to accommodate expanded needs. The 'Liber niger' records that 'In the beginning the arches or vaults were founded by the Danes before the coming of St Patrick to Ireland. In those days Christ Church had not been founded or built as it stands today.

56 Gilla Pátraic, literally 'servant of' Patrick. See Brian Ó Cuív, 'Personal names as an indicator of relations between native Irish and settlers in the Viking period' in Bradley, *Settlement and society*, p. 79; Bethell, 'English monks and Irish reform', p. 127.   57 Anthony Candon, 'Barefaced effrontery: secular and ecclesiastical politics in early twelfth centry Ireland' in *Seanchas Ard Mhacha: journal of the Armagh diocesan historical society*, xiv, no. 2 (1991), p. 8.   58 Gwynn, 'First bishops', pp 44–6.   59 Hubert Janssens de Varebeke, 'Benedictine bishops in medieval Ireland' in Etienne Rynne (ed.), *North Munster studies: essays in commemoration of the late Monsignor Michael Moloney* (Limerick, 1967), pp 242–50 and Gwynn, 'First bishops', pp 49–50.   60 Bethell, 'English monks and Irish reform', p. 127.   61 David Knowles, 'The [Norman] cathedral monasteries' in *Downside Review*, li (1933), p. 88; Bethell, 'English monks and Irish reform', p. 129.

Therefore St Patrick said mass in an arch or vault which to this day is called the arch or vault of St Patrick'. Viewing both the historical inaccuracy of this and the fact that the phrase '*sancti Patricii episcopi*' may well have been taken up, deliberately or not, as Saint rather than Bishop Pátraic, Gwynn has logically attributed the early building of the crypt to Bishop Pátraic.[62] The eastern portion of the crypt has no apparent sculptural features allowing for dating, but its plan is apsidal with three minor eastern chapels. The plan of the crypt is unique in Ireland, and given that spacious crypts of this type in England are associated with the last quarter of the eleventh century, as at Winchester (1079), Worcester (1084), Gloucester (1089), and Canterbury (1096), it would seem a reasonable assumption that Pátraic was putting into practice that which was fashionable in the Benedictine cathedral priories of England, the 'Old English' communities with which he was familiar.[63] It is unlikely that Pátraic would have demolished the Hiberno-Norse building to the west during building, and perhaps because of this constraint the apses provide deeper foundations in the east as the ground slopes away.

Toirrdelbach's appointment of his son Muirchertach to Dublin's kingship was ideal, exposing Muirchertach to international influences, and one commentator regards him as one of the few rulers who 'lifted his head above the domestic power struggle and sought to involve Ireland in the international politics of Europe'.[64] One of his earliest engagements would have been an audience with the deposed Gruffudd ap Cynan of Gwynedd *c.*1075 at which he granted assistance to him, such that he temporarily recovered power in North Wales.[65] In view of the kingdoms of Dublin and Man being joined in one form or another for almost half a century, it is unsurprising to find that in 1073, Sitriuc mac Amlaíb and two Uí Briain were killed on the Isle of Man, no doubt attempting to establish Toirrdelbach's authority there.[66] Duffy has furthermore suggested that, given Pátraic's drowning in the Irish Sea in 1084, and the fact that there is no evidence for a bishop of Man at this time, it is reasonable to suppose that he may have been carrying out his duties as bishop of the joint kingdom of Dublin and Man when he died.[67]

One task which we know Bishop Pátraic to have tackled vigorously was the organisation of a parochial system. Dublin may have been the first ter-

62 Aubrey Gwynn (ed.), *The writings of Bishop Patrick 1074–1084* (Dublin, 1955), p. 5; Gwynn, 'First bishops', pp 45–8; Gwynn, 'Unpublished texts', p. 308.   63 Francis Bond, *The cathedrals of England and Wales* (4th ed., London, 1912), pp 22–4, 136–8, 387–90, 404–6 and B.J. Ashwell, *Gloucester cathedral: a short guide to the crypt* (Gloucester, n.d. [*c.*1980]).   64 Candon, 'Muirchertach Ua Briain', p. 415.   65 Flanagan, *Irish society*, pp 62–4 and notes; Duffy, 'Ostmen', pp 394–5.   66 Candon, 'Muirchertach Ua Briain', p. 403; Duffy, 'Irishmen', p. 102.   67 Duffy, 'Irishmen', p. 107, note 68, although *Alen's reg.*, p. 301, uses the curious phrase 'bishop of only the city of Dublin'.

ritorial diocese in Ireland, but the underlying structure of parishes was not yet in place. The imposition of 'a reforming cleric into Clondalkin against the rights of Uí Rónáin' is recorded in 1076 and shows Pátraic's reforms being forced on traditional centres of Irish monasticism, as well as his establishment of parishes using the older pre-existing baile or betagh units. Accordingly, not only was there an effective Irish system of lordship (albeit without administration as centralised as it would become), which the Anglo-Normans simply fitted into 'like a hand into a glove' when they arrived, but there was also a pre-existing parochial system.[68] In 1079, 'Máel Ísu (servant of Jesus), who had been coarb, *comharba* (the founder's heir, which often continued to be hereditary) of Patrick and abbot of Armagh since 1064, came to Dublin with the chief relic of Saint Patrick, the *baculus Ihesu* or "staff of Jesus"', and was with the northern king, Máel Sechlainn, when the latter 'went into the house of Toirrdelbach, thereby acknowledging his overlordship'.[69] Gwynn suggested that Pátraic may have been present at any ceremonial recognition of lordship that occurred and, given the presence of Máel Ísu, this ceremony most likely occurred in the cathedral and might be identifiable as one of its earliest examples of prestige liturgy.[70] More importantly, Gwynn further suggested that Bishop Pátraic was 'a prime mover' in orchestrating not only reform but arranging 'a native Irish hierarchy', delayed until 1111.[71] It has been suggested that, at a reforming council held in Dublin in 1080 under the aegis of Muirchertach, presumably at Christ Church, the points raised by Lanfranc's letter were answered in the presence of the coarb of Patrick and, among others, Domnall Ua hÉnna, the chief Munster bishop, effectively bishop to Uí Briain. If so, this would highlight the importance of Dublin and its cathedral as centres of reform.[72]

Pátraic's literary and scholastic ability has received much attention as a considerable body of his work survives, exhibiting a tradition of classical and ancient Christian scholarship.[73] It seems likely that he was responsible for the production of a Dublin chronicle at Christ Church. A set of Christ

---

68 Charles Doherty, 'The Vikings in Ireland: a review' in Clarke *et al.*, *Ireland and Scandinavia*, pp 314, 324, 329, citing M.T. Flanagan, 'Henry II and the kingdom of Uí Fháeláin' in Bradley, *Settlement and society*, pp 229–39; P.J. Duffy, *Landscapes of South Ulster: a parish atlas of the diocese of Clogher* (Belfast, 1993), p. 12 and C.A. Empey, 'The Anglo-Norman settlement in the cantred of Eliogarty' in Bradley, *Settlement and society*, p. 213. Charles Doherty, 'Cluain Dolcáin: a brief note' in A.P. Smyth (ed.), *Seanchas: essays in early and medieval Irish archaeology, history and literature in honour of Francis J. Byrne* (Dublin, 2000), pp 182–8.   69 Gwynn, *Writings of Bishop Patrick*, p. 5.   70 Lawlor, 'Liber niger', pp 29, 56; *Alen's reg.*, pp 290–1; Todd, 'Introduction' in Crosthwaite & Todd, *Obits*, p. ix.   71 Gwynn, 'First bishops', p. 51.   72 Proposed by Mr Martin Holland at a conference in Maynooth in 1999. Compare also McEnery & Refaussé, *Deeds*, no. 5, and pp 49 and 62 below.   73 Gwynn, *Writings of Bishop Patrick*.

Church annals survive in the 'Liber niger', derived from those of the abbey of Winchcombe, a community which had strong links with Worcester, whence Pátraic came. Their first Irish entry is in 1087 in the early years of the episcopate of Donngus, Pátraic's successor. Four entries in the annals of St Mary's abbey (derived partially from those of Christ Church) for the years 1074, 1084, 1085 and 1095 are particular to Dublin and most likely attributable to a tradition begun by Pátraic.[74]

Pátraic 'drowned with his companions in the British [Irish] sea' on 11 October 1084. He had already sent his prospective successor, Donngus, to train at Canterbury. Donngus's consecration by Lanfranc was not for another ten months, perhaps additional preparation time, given Pátraic's sudden death, and not helped by the additional administrative responsibilities which Muirchertach had to shoulder for his ailing father. The request for his consecration seemed unanimous however, supported by Toirrdelbach Ua Briain and the bishops of Ireland, together with the clergy and people of Dublin. Gwynn pointed out that the support of 'the bishops of Ireland' was a new departure and suggested that many of the Irish bishops, probably led by Ua hÉnna, were in support of Donngus, whose importance as a symbol of ongoing reform may have been as important as his appointment to the vacant see.[75]

The period of the episcopate of Donngus (1085–95) was an unsettled one in Dublin. In 1086, not only the Ostmen, but also the men of Leinster were defending Dublin from the king of Mide. This was still the case three years later, when their leader, Donnchad mac Domnaill Remair, patronised the cathedral with a grant of the lands of Clonkeen (Kill of the Grange), its third such endowment and, according to John Bradley, an example of 'demesne lands which were in the gift of the king of Dublin, irrespective of whether he was of Irish or Norse extraction'.[76] Bishop Donngus's death in November 1095 provided Muirchertach with another opportunity to influence reform in Dublin. He appointed Donngus's nephew, the St Albans-educated Samuel. Like his father, Muirchertach seems to have consulted widely, probably by holding a diocesan synod. Samuel seems to have begun his episcopate well by expanding the bounds of the diocese beyond the limits of the city and its immediate environs, towards Fingal.[77] Bishop Samuel is perhaps best known

74 Clarke, 'Conversion', p. 43, note 167. For the annals in the 'Liber niger' see Gwynn, 'Unpublished texts', p. 314; Robin Flower, 'Manuscripts of Irish interest in the British Museum' in *Analecta Hibernica*, no. 2 (1931), pp 317–29. See also Gwynn, 'Origins', p. 51. 75 Gwynn, 'First bishops', p. 51.   76 Clarke, 'Conversion', p. 36, note 118 and John Bradley, 'The interpretation of Scandinavian settlement in Ireland' in Bradley, *Settlement and society*, p. 59.   77 A.S. MacShamhráin, 'The emergence of the metropolitan see: Dublin, 1111–1216' in Kelly & Keogh, *Catholic diocese*, pp 53–4, note 10; Candon, 'Barefaced effrontery', pp 4–5 regards as synods the gatherings at which Gilla Pátraic, Donngus, Máel Ísu and probably Samuel were present.

for his stormy relationship with Christ Church. In a letter dating probably to September 1100, Anselm, the archbishop of Canterbury, rebuked Samuel for his expulsion of the monks of Canterbury from Christ Church Dublin and for giving away 'the books, vestments and ornaments of the church ... [given by] the brothers, sons of the church of Canterbury', emphasising that they had been given to the church not the bishop. Given the appearance of annalistic material identified with Christ Church in the archives of the Cistercian abbey of St Mary's founded in 1139, it is conceivable that these derived from the same books given away by Samuel and kept locally near St Michan's, a church of his own foundation.[78]

Difficult as it is to judge Samuel, it cannot be done without reference to the two reforming synods of Cashel in 1101 and Ráith Bressail in 1111.[79] From the perspective of the emergence of cathedral and diocesan structures in Ireland, the synod of Ráith Bressail was the more important. It might have been at this synod that Dublin staked its claim for recognition as the oldest and first diocese to be refounded in the reformed canonical sense, over eighty years old, assuming Dúnán's canonical consecration.[80] The synod's decree, copied from 'the old book' of Clonenagh, since lost, survives in Geoffrey Keating's 1632 work *Foras feasa ar Éirinn*. This describes a division of the church into northern (Leath Cuinn) and southern (Leath Mogha) halves with twelve bishoprics each and two archbishoprics, Armagh and Cashel. Dublin's omission is significant, as is the extensive area of the diocese of Glendalough surrounding Dublin, stretching from Grianóg in Ratoath, County Meath, to Begerin Island in Wexford Harbour, and also from Naas, County Kildare to Lambay Island.[81] The plan seems to have been to wait until Samuel's death and amalgamate Dublin with Glendalough, where Muirchertach was promoting the Uí Lorcáin of Muiredaig (although, ironically, the reverse was to happen a century later).[82]

78 Candon, 'Barefaced effrontery', p. 20, note 62; H.J. Lawlor, 'Note on the church of St Michan, Dublin' in *R.S.A.I. Jn.*, lvi (1926), pp 15–17; H.J. Lawlor, 'The foundation of St Mary's abbey, Dublin' in *R.S.A.I. Jn.*, lvi (1926), p. 26. See also Clarke, 'Conversion', p. 41, note 157.   79 Aubrey Gwynn, 'The first synod of Cashel' in *Irish Ecclesiastical Record*, lxvi (1945), pp 81–92; 67 (1946), pp 109–22; Anthony Candon, 'Ráith Bressail: a suggested identification' in *Peritia*, iii (1984), pp 326–9; Gwynn, *Irish church*, pp 180–92.   80 See John Fleming, *Gilbert of Limerick (c.1070–1147): his writings and their origins* (Dublin, forthcoming).   81 Information from the lost book of Clonenagh is based on Geoffrey Keating, *Foras feasa ar Éirinn; The history of Ireland*, ed. David Comyn and P.S. Dinneen (4 vols, London, 1902–14), iii, 298–307. See also John MacErlean, 'Synod of Ráith Breasail: boundaries of the dioceses of Ireland' in *Archivium Hibernicum*, iii (1914), pp 1–33; Gwynn & Hadcock, *Religious houses*, p. 49; T.W. Moody, F.X. Martin and F.J. Byrne (ed.), *A new history of Ireland*, ix: *maps, genealogies, lists* (Oxford, 1984), pp 26, 101 (map 24).   82 MacShamhráin, 'Emergence', p. 53; Abrams, 'Conversion', p. 28, note 183.

The synod of Ráith Bressail was probably the last great event over which Muirchertach presided, his power declining rapidly after illness in 1114, and with it went the plan for Dublin's amalgamation with Glendalough.[83] The political situation was about to change dramatically. In 1118, Toirrdelbach Ua Conchobair, king of Connacht, expelled Domnall Gerrlámhach (another example of a Dublin king who, in laying claim to Dublin, granted the cathedral 'Balirodelf'),[84] and took Dublin and its kingship, by implication proposing himself for the high kingship. Bishop Samuel's death in 1121 would have resulted in the diocese's amalgamation with Glendalough, had the wishes of Muirchertach Ua Briain and the synod of Ráith Bressail been fulfilled. Instead, other groups wished to emphasise it as a distinct diocese: for instance, Cellach, coarb and archbishop of Armagh wanted Dublin to be part of the Irish church under his authority. Not surprisingly this generated opposition in Dublin. In 1121, in a letter to Ralph d'Escurs, archbishop of Canterbury, the burgesses and clergy of the city of Dublin proposed Gréne, or Gregory, a sub-deacon, as bishop of Dublin.[85] In this letter, they ask for Gréne's consecration, in clear defiance of Cellach, claiming that 'the bishops of Ireland are very jealous of us, and especially that bishop who lives in Armagh, because we are unwilling to submit to their ordination but wish always to be under your rule'.[86]

Following Gréne's ordination by Bishop Roger of Salisbury at his castle of Devizes, his consecration by Archbishop Ralph at Lambeth and his return to Dublin, he found that 'the gates of the city were closed against him'.[87] Cellach, archbishop of Armagh, had taken up position in Dublin, leaving a priest in his mid-twenties in charge, named Máel Máedoc Ua Morgair, or Malachy. During this time, Énna mac Donnchad meic Murchada, king of Leinster since 1117, was in effective control of Dublin and is referred to as king of both in 1122 when he formally submitted to Ua Conchobair's overlordship. It is probably some time between this date and his death in 1126 that Énna made his grant of 'Realgeallyn' to Christ Church.[88] Eventually Gréne returned to Dublin, probably, as Gwynn has suggested, when a new archbishop of Canterbury, William de Corbeil, succeeded Ralph in 1123, releasing him from from his oath of obedience. Some time between 1123 and

---

83 Duffy, 'Irishmen', p. 114; Candon, 'Muirchertach Ua Briain', p. 405. See also Clarke, 'Conversion', p. 50.   84 In Cullagh according to Dr Reeves, *Alen's reg.*, p. 4. Variously recorded as 'Baleuroolef', 'Ferannuroulb' and 'Balyorolf and Staclock with appurtenances'. See note 37 above.   85 An early indication of how Dublin's inhabitants viewed themselves, as burgesses or townsmen. See Clarke, 'Proto-towns', p. 331.   86 Duffy, 'Irishmen', pp 117–18; Duffy, 'Pre-Norman Dublin', p. 17; Gwynn, *Irish church*, p. 114; Gwynn, 'First bishops', p. 57.   87 Gwynn, *Irish church*, p. 186; Gwynn 'First bishops', pp 56–7.   88 *Alen's reg.*, p. 28; Clarke, 'Conversion', p. 36, note 120.

Cellach's death in 1129 Gréne would appear to have recognised the authority of Armagh, an annalistic obit referring to Cellach as 'the one head to
whom the Gael and the Gall, both laity and clergy, were obedient' thereby
implying Dublin's acceptance of his authority.[89]

A remarkable aspect of Gréne's episcopacy was its unsettled political context. With the possible exception of his predecessor, Dúnán, Dublin has not
since seen a longer serving bishop. The martyrology of Christ Church, in an
entry dated between 1161 and 1180, records that he was responsible for the
establishment of a shrine (perhaps his only architectural innovation) in which
to place the cathedral's collection of relics 'for greater reverence and security ... with the box [reliquary] that contained them ... and a festival with
nine lessons was appointed in their honour'. The inventory of relics and the
list of lands granted to the cathedral by patrons make it clear that there must
have been some record-keeping by the cathedral.[90] It is unlikely that the
cathedral organisation undertaking this task was Benedictine, as had been the
case under Pátraic. There is no evidence of a monastic training for Gréne,
and many authorities, the sixteenth-century scholar Archbishop Alen included,
thought the canons during Gréne's episcopate, were secular.[91]

Toirrdelbach Ua Conchobair appointed his son, Conchobar, as king of
Dublin following the death of Énna in 1126. He was overthrown by foreigners
and Leinstermen alike within the year, and his father's reponse was to raid
their respective strongholds in Leinster: Dublin and Wexford, the latter now
controlled by Diarmait 'na nGall' or Diarmait Mac Murchada (Dermot
MacMurrough).[92] Those who attacked the town met with stiff opposition
from the Ostmen, led by Torcall (Norse, *Thorkettle*)[93] which signified the
resurgence of Hiberno-Norse rule in Dublin until the arrival of the Anglo-
Normans. With this in mind, it has been suggested that Bishop Gréne was
of Norse extraction, from the Norse *Grane*,[94] which is very likely if he was
proposed by the burgesses of Dublin. It is no coincidence that the most inten-
sive period of land acquisition by the cathedral from Hiberno-Norse donors
was during Gréne's enduring episcopate, lending weight to the idea that they
may have been his fellow Ostmen. Perhaps gentle lobbying by Gréne was

89 Gwynn, *Irish church*, pp 114–15, 128; Gwynn, 'First bishops', p. 59.   90 Todd,
'Introduction' in Crosthwaite & Todd, *Obits*, pp lxvi–lxviii, suggests that the anomalous
exclusion of the crucifix was because it 'was not considered as a relic' or that it did not
originate from the foundation. He mistakenly refers to the 'west' window. See pp 15–16
above for details of the manuscript. See also Clarke, 'Conversion', p. 35, note 113.   91
Alen's reg., pp 16, 301. Lawlor, 'Note on the church of St Michan, Dublin', p. 19 also
assumed so.   92 Duffy, 'Irishmen', pp 119–20; Duffy, 'Pre-Norman Dublin', p. 17.   93
Bradley, 'Scandinavian settlement', p. 56.   94 John Ryan, 'Pre-Norman Dublin' in Clarke,
Medieval Dublin: metropolis, pp 123–4, note 101, citing Samuel Laing, *Heimskringla* (3
vols, Dutton, 1961–4), p. 84.

also responsible for Gruffudd ap Cynan, great-grandson of the founder Sitriuc, and born at the monastery in Swords, leaving 20s. in his will for the Dublin cathedral when he died in 1137.[95]

The zone controlled by the Dublin Ostmen was known as *Dyflinnarskíri*, and represented a rural hinterland which served the settlement with its agricultural produce. A survey of this area by John Bradley highlights the degree to which cathedral and 'state' were linked, and the sons of (Mac-)Torca(i)ll were highly prominent in the granting of land to Christ Church, particularly in south Dublin, known in the Anglo-Norman period as the 'lands of the sons of Torkill'.[96] Of the nineteen grants before the first mention of Richard de Clare (Strongbow), it is possible to identify only eight specifically Ostman grants to the cathedral, which might imply a greater value being placed on grants to the cathedral by the long-standing Christian Irish than by the Ostmen Dubliners themselves. Between the death of Énna mac Donnchad (1126) and the first mention of the convent (c.1163) eight grants occur, of which three are by Mac Torcaill[97] and this dominance by one family is reflected in the kings of Dublin for the period c.1133 to 1170, who were Mac Torcaill, with two successive exceptions in the 1140s: Conchobar Ua Briain of Thomond and Ottar from the Isles.[98] Not mentioned in the list of grants, but included as the first three entries in the published cathedral deeds, one Hamund Mac Torcaill also owned the lands of Kinsaley before the arrival of the Anglo-Normans.[99] Bradley's survey leaves us in no doubt that the area of south Dublin from Glencree to Bray was the 'lands of the sons of Torkill', grants to Christ Church of which include Kill of the Grange, Tully,[100] Druming, Tibradden and Taney.[101] He further suggests that Balyucharan and Tirodran granted by Mac Torcaill are probably also in the south, although four northside grants include Lambay, Portrane, Glasnevin and Drumcondra. The donors of these lands were respectively Donnchad mac Domnaill Remair, Sitriuc Mac Torcaill, mac 'Meirboillan', the Ostmen and 'Marmacruadin', not all Hiberno-Norse names by any means.[102]

---

95 D. Simon Evans, *Historia Gruffud vab Kenan* (Cardiff, 1977), p. 31.   96 Bradley, 'Scandinavian settlement', p. 56.   97 Clarke, 'Conversion', p. 36, at note 122, notes the dateable reference in the mention of the purchase, by the convent, of Glasnevin and 'Kembonnca'.   98 *Alen's reg.*, p. 28; Moody *et al.*, *A new history of Ireland:* ix, p. 209. Alen's list is mostly in chronological order, however two obvious exceptions are the grants (each of a part of Balyogan) by 'Gerrlámhach' Ua Briain, and by 'Dormlagh son of Pole' who seems to precede his father Pole mac Torcaill, Clarke, 'Conversion', pp 35–6, notes 113, 121.   99 McEnery & Refaussé, *Deeds*, nos 1–3.   100 *Alen's reg.*, p. 28, included Culaght, or Coillacht, most of which was in the Wicklow mountains, but which included some lands in the mountains of south-western Dublin, Otway-Ruthven, 'Church lands', p. 59, note 32.   101 Ronan, 'History of the diocese', p. 32.   102 Bradley, 'Scandinavian settlement', p. 59.

While Gréne might get much of the credit for eventually bringing Dublin into the Irish diocesan system, he was undoubtedly helped both by the continuing reform process in the Irish church spearheaded by Archbishop Malachy of Armagh, and a favourable political situation. In 1145 Cardinal John Paparo had been appointed by Pope Eugenius III as special papal legate to oversee what would be known as the synod of Kells-Mellifont in 1152. This would see the final integration of Ireland, including Dublin, into a national diocesan system with four metropolitan sees, the provinces of Armagh, Dublin, Cashel and Tuam, recognising the primacy of Armagh.[103] Dublin was allocated five suffragan sees: Glendalough, Ferns, Kilkenny, Leighlin and Kildare, virtually co-terminous with Diarmait Mac Murchada's kingdom of Leinster. The division of land between Dublin and Glendalough had not been considered before, given the synod of Ráith Bressail's incorporation of Dublin into the diocese of Glendalough. The arrangement initially was that the metropolitan (Dublin) was to receive one part of the diocese and 'the other to him who lived in the mountains', the latter reverting to Dublin on his death. It was 'the insolence of the Irish' to oppose this 'reversion', and both King Henry II and King John defied them, granting Glendalough to the metropolitan. The dispute was not settled until February 1216, when Pope Innocent III confirmed the union of Dublin and Glendalough.[104] The year following the synod of Kells-Mellifont its implications were examined at the council of Winchester, resulting in Pope Adrian IV's grant of Ireland to Henry II in the papal bull 'Laudabiliter'. Although viewed by later historians as a device to further Henry II's plans to invade Ireland, this was probably no more than very successful posturing by Canterbury to bolster its claims to jurisdiction over the Irish church.[105]

Such plans evolved in a particular socio-political context, and this was very much governed by the position of Diarmait Mac Murchada. In 1156, he was confirmed in his kingship by Mac Lochlainn, with the Mac Torcaill family still ruling the town under him, and was probably in a more powerful position than ever before.[106] Diarmait seems also to have been responsible for the spread of the recently introduced Augustinian canons regular in the south, mainly in Leinster, with Archbishop Malachy of Armagh pursuing a similar agenda in the north. The order has long been under-appreci-

---

103 Gwynn, *Irish church*, pp 218–33; see also Aubrey Gwynn 'The centenary of the synod of Kells [1152] in *Irish Ecclesiastical Record*, lxxvii (1952), pp 161–76, 250–64; H.J. Lawlor 'A fresh authority for the synod of Kells, 1152' in *R.I.A. Proc.*, C, xxxvi (1922), pp 16–22. 104 Otway-Ruthven, 'Church lands', p. 58, citing [McEnery & Refaussé,] *Deeds*, no. 20 and *Alen's reg.*, p. 38. See also M.V. Ronan, 'Union of the diocese of Glendaloch and Dublin' in *R.S.A.I. Jn.*, lx (1930), pp 56–72 and below p. 50.   105 MacShamhráin, 'Emergence', p. 57, citing Flanagan, *Irish society*, ch. 1 and Candon, 'Barefaced effrontery', pp 17–18. 106 Duffy, 'Irishmen', p. 128.

ated in favour of the Cistercians, whose more enduring architectural legacy caused a bias towards them as 'the great agents of change'. The canons regular were in fact far more widespread than the Cistercians, often taking over areas of traditional monasticism; however it was this flexibility, the diverse range of architectural establishments which they occupied and their seemingly lax attitude towards documentation that has made their contribution so difficult to discern.[107] The year 1162 seems to have been a high point for Diarmait when he granted land to 'his confessor, Aed Ua Cáellaide, bishop of Louth, for the use of the canons of the priory of All Hallows', the first Arrouasian house of canons regular.[108] The grant was witnessed by two (if not assenting, at least acquiescing) Mac Torcaill: Echmarcach and Aralt as well as his brother-in-law, Lorcán Ua Tuathail, recently appointed as archbishop of Dublin, in succession to Gréne who died in 1161.[109]

Diarmait's first encounter with Lorcán was when he took him hostage to ensure the loyalty of an Uí Muiredaig sub-king, Muirchertach Ua Tuathail, who ruled north Leinster for him, and whose family leader he had already killed in 1141. However, on seeing the shape of the diocese of Glendalough following the synod of Kells, which corresponded so closely to the borders of Uí Muiredaig, Diarmait married Muirchertach's daughter, and by no mere coincidence, Lorcán was appointed abbot of Glendalough the same year, at the age of twenty-five.[110] Lorcán's appointment to Dublin probably coincided with Diarmait's grant of 'Rathkyllin' to Christ Church, although this may have been a confirmation of an initial grant ('Realgeallyn') by his brother Énna whom he succeeded.[111] Lorcán had already established Augustinian canons regular at the priory of St Saviour at Glendalough during his time as abbot, and it may be that Diarmait's new priory and his own newly acquired cathedral were his next step in introducing reforming orders, the two new houses of Arrouasian canons being described as the 'third wave' in introducing the Augustinians to Ireland.[112]

---

107 See Brendan Smith's review of Gwynn, *Irish church*, in *I.H.S.*, xxix, no. 113 (May, 1994), p. 123 and Sarah Preston, 'The canons regular of the order of St Augustine in medieval Ireland: an overview', Ph.D. thesis, T.C.D., 1996, *passim*. See also Roger Stalley, *The Cistercian monasteries of Ireland* (London and New Haven, 1987). 108 M.T. Flanagan, 'St Mary's abbey, Louth, and the introduction of the Arrouasian observance into Ireland' in *Clogher Record: journal of the Clogher Historical Society*, x, no. 2 (1980), pp 223–34. See also Preston, 'The canons regular', p. 88. 109 Gwynn, 'Unpublished texts', p. 329. For further details see A.S. MacShamhráin, *Church and polity in pre-Norman Ireland: the case of Glendalough* (Maynooth, 1996), pp 154–9 and A.S. MacShamhráin, 'Prosopographica Glindelachensis: the monastic church of Glendalough and its community sixth to thirteenth centuries' in *R.S.A.I. Jn.*, cxix (1989), pp 79–97. 110 MacShamhráin, *Church and polity*, pp 154–5 and MacShamhráin, 'Emergence', p. 53. 111 Duffy, 'Irishmen', pp 127–9. See also Seán Duffy, 'Ireland's Hastings: the Anglo-Norman conquest of Dublin' in Harper-Bill, *Anglo-Norman studies xx*, p. 77. 112 Gwynn & Hadcock, *Religious*

Lorcán was consecrated by Gilla Meic Liac (Gelasius), archbishop of Armagh, in Holy Trinity, Dublin, and the changes which he introduced to the cathedral priory must have resounded throughout the province.[113] The introduction of the rule of the Augustinian canons of the abbey of Arrouaise in the diocese of Arras brought that religious discipline which Bishop Pátraic had attempted to introduce almost a century earlier and, presumably, the introduction of the monastic round once again, which is unlikely to have flourished under Gréne who lacked a monastic education. Lorcán himself, under strict self-discipline, chose to live as head of the new community at Christ Church in the monk-bishop style commonplace in the previous century in England, which his Benedictine predecessors had also tried to emulate.[114] We know that his archiepiscopal palace was within the precincts of the cathedral, and there is little reason to doubt later authorities who tell us that this was later used successively as the house of the prior and the dean.[115]

In 1166 when Muirchertach Mac Lochlainn died, the balance of power in Lorcán's metropolitan see was to change. Ruaidrí Ua Conchobair, Toirrdelbach's son (and whose brother Conchobar had been king of Dublin briefly) took Dublin and the kingship of Ireland which that gesture by now signified. Although Diarmait was to submit to Ua Conchobair, the Dubliners and many of the lords of Leinster took their opportunity to rid themselves of him, the 'Song of Dermot and the earl' putting it bluntly: 'Mac Torcaill of Dublin abandoned his lord at this moment'. The following year, at a meeting of noblemen held by Ua Conchobair, 1,000 Dublin horsemen attended led by Ragnall mac Ragnaill meic Torcaill, possibly a brother of (or perhaps even a mistake for) Ascall Mac Torcaill, king of Dublin until the arrival of the Anglo-Normans.[116] Although Diarmait returned about this time, it was not until 1169 that assistance from the Anglo-Normans arrived in Ireland in the form of fitz Stephen, de Prendergast and de Montmorency, followed shortly afterwards by Raymond le Gros and Richard de Clare, 'Strongbow'. Ua Conchobair led a united front (including the Ostmen) opposing Diarmait and his allies and in September 1170 Mac Murchada's forces spent three days in Dublin ready

houses, p. 177; Preston, 'The canons regular', p. 41.   113 *Alen's reg.*, p. 301 and Gilbert, *Chartul. St Mary's*, ii, 264–5.   114 Knowles, 'Cathedral monasteries', pp 73–96; Charles Plummer, 'Vie et miracles de S.Laurent archevêque de Dublin' in *Analecta Bollandiana*, xxxiii (1914), pp 121–86.   115 *Gir. Camb. op.*, v, 128; Walter Harris, *The history and antiquities of the city of Dublin, from the earliest accounts, etc.* (Dublin, 1766), p. 372. For evidence of the dean's quarters, see McEnery & Refaussé, *Deeds*, nos 1162, 1250, 1303, 1354, 1432; C6/1/26/5/55 and Gillespie, *Chapter act book*, pp 43, 69, 91, 143.   116 Duffy, 'Irishmen', pp 128–31 and citing G.H. Orpen (ed.), *The song of Dermot and the earl* (Oxford, 1892), pp 12–13. For Ascall mac Torcaill's name, see Giraldus Cambrensis, *Expugnatio Hibernica: the conquest of Ireland*, ed. A.B. Scott and F.X. Martin (Dublin, 1978), p. 303, note 94.

to fight. According to Giraldus Cambrensis, writing in the 1180s, many of the inhabitants of Dublin feared that the town would fall and tried to leave by sea taking with them the miraculous speaking cross from Christ Church, but the cross refused to move. Somewhat portentously, following the treacherous swapping of sides by the Ostmen, Dublin was struck by lightning, and shortly afterwards Mac Murchada and the Anglo-Normans massacred their new Ostman allies, the majority of whom (including Ascall) managed to escape to the 'isles'.[117] More significantly, after the capture of the town, an archer from the Anglo-Norman force who offered a penny to the miraculous cross at Christ Church found his penny flung back at him, allegedly because it was plundered from the archbishop's house in the precincts of the church. Such power in the Christ Church relic collection clearly impressed Giraldus, who noted 'with these and other manifestations and evidences of its power ... the cross has earned everywhere respect and veneration'.[118]

On the death of Diarmait in May 1171, Ascall returned with an army drawn 'from Man, the Hebrides, the Orkneys, and Norway', only to be defeated and beheaded'.[119] He was the last Hiberno-Norse king, and indeed, pre-Anglo-Norman leader, to grant Holy Trinity land. The cathedral deed notes 'earl [a Norse term for a non-royal chieftain][120] Hasgall's gift, the church of St Brigid and all the lands in that parish belonging anciently to Holy Trinity church'. To the south of St Bride's, one of the early churches south of the cathedral, may well have been Ascall's house which was later occupied by the earls of Ormond and known as Barons Inns.[121] Little is heard of the Mac Torcaill after this, other than Hamund Mac Torcaill whom Strongbow allowed to remain, but was eventually killed or expelled, his lands being granted to the cathedral. Henry II's arrival in Dublin in 1171 resulted in Ua Conchobair signing away the Ostmen towns of Dublin, Waterford and Wexford.[122] The same year a council of bishops at Cashel at which Henry was represented agreed to the incorporation of the Irish into the English church and the town was granted to the men of Bristol.[123]

Henry II attended the cathedral in Dublin over Christmas 1171, the year following the murder of Thomas Becket, and in turn Lorcán was present when

117 See note 44 above for the 'isles' as part of the 'Viking Lake' concept.   118 *Gir. Camb op.*, v, pp 128–30.   119 Duffy, 'Irishmen', p. 132.   120 The terms *dux* and *jarl* gave rise to duke and earl. See also Donncha Ó Corráin, 'The semantic development of the Old Norse Jarl in Old and Middle Irish' in J.E. Knirk (ed.), *Proceedings of the tenth Viking congress, Larkolen, Norway, 1985* (Oslo, 1987), pp 287–93.   121 *Alen's reg.*, p. 29; H.B. Clarke, '*Urbs et suburbium*: beyond the walls of medieval Dublin' in Conleth Manning (ed.), *Dublin and beyond the Pale: studies in honour of Patrick Healy* (Wicklow, 1998), p. 54, citing *Calendar of Ormond deeds, 1172–1350*, ed. Edmund Curtis (6 vols, Dublin, 1932–43), iii, 284, iv, 119.   122 Duffy, 'Irishmen', p. 133.   123 M.T. Flanagan, 'Henry II, the council of Cashel and the Irish bishops' in *Peritia*, x (1996), 184–211; Duffy, 'Ireland's Hastings', pp 69–85.

the treaty of Windsor was made between Henry and Ua Conchobair in 1175 following the assent of a council of bishops in Waterford to the bull Laudabiliter. Subsequent to a general council of Lateran III, Lorcán became papal legate in 1179, but did not live long in the position, dying of fever in Eu, Normandy. The deaths of Diarmait, Strongbow (1176) and Lorcán left little sign of the old régime, and at Christ Church this became apparent in several changes which occurred in the cathedral priory. The Anglo-Normans seem to have insisted on some form of reorganisation, and Gervase, the first prior listed (some time between 1172 and 1181), judging from his name, would seem to have been of Norman stock.[124] For the next century all the priors, with the exception of Columbanus (*c.*1192), bore Anglo-Norman names. The composition of the community is much less clear and probably changed more slowly. The earliest list which contains a selection of names of the community of Christ Church comes from 1300.[125] Drawn up in the context of a dispute between the prior, Adam de Balsham, and eleven canons of the house, it indicates that by this stage all the members of the community bore Anglo-Norman names. It need not be assumed that they had come from England. The names of two canons, Walter de Clontarf and Henry de Kork, suggest that recruitment among the local Anglo-Norman population had begun. Indeed from the 1170s there are other signs that the priory made some accommodations to local sensibilities. In 1173, for instance, as a result of the actions of Strongbow, it had acquired the land of Ballyboghil in County Dublin and with it one of the most prestigious relics of Ireland, the *baculus Ihesu*. This staff, by tradition given to St Patrick by Christ, acted as the symbol of authority of the pre-Anglo-Norman archbishops of Armagh and its acquisition by the priory seems to have been an attempt to merge older authority with the new Anglo-Norman institution.[126] The same may be true of the later inclusion of a number of Irish saints in the priory's martyrology.

There are two other important indications of the shifts in cathedral and priory life which took place in the century after Henry II's visit to the cathedral. From about 1200 the volume of deeds surviving from the priory increases rapidly, which suggests that some form of centralised record-keeping process had been instituted in line with those followed by similar monastic chapters in England. From the evidence of these deeds it is possible to sketch something of the organisation of the house at Christ Church. While the archbishop of Dublin was regarded as abbot of the priory, there is evidence that it insisted on a separate identity exclusive of diocesan organisation. The com-

124 I am grateful to the Revd Canon Dr Adrian Empey for this information. See also McEnery & Refaussé, *Deeds*, no. 468f, and Hand, 'Two cathedrals', pp 147–9. 125 McEnery & Refaussé, *Deeds*, no. 164. 126 M.V. Ronan, 'St Patrick's staff and Christ Church' in Clarke, *Medieval Dublin: living city*, pp 123–31.

munity elected its own prior, a right confirmed by Pope Urban III in 1186 and Pope Clement III in 1192, but to what extent the community was subject to episcopal visitation is unclear (a grey area for centuries to come). The first evidence of such a visitation is for 1300, although the priors certainly claimed exemption from archdiaconal visitation of the cathedral's prebendal churches until 1339.[127] The role and powers of the prior are impossible to reconstruct in detail, but his authority seems to have been limited by having to act with the other members of the community. Certainly in 1290–1 the prior professed himself unable to complete an important land transaction without the consent of the chapter.[128] However, outside the priory, he was regarded as an important and influential figure described by one correspondent in 1282x8 as the person 'who after the archbishop is the most worthy person in the diocese of Dublin'.[129] How the community was organised internally in the thirteenth century is uncertain, but the introduction of the Augustinian rule ensured that certain offices appeared early in the priory. A prior, sub-prior and sacrist are certainly present in the earliest surviving deeds from the 1180s, although it is 1300 before a precentor is noted.[130] The faculties granted by Gregory IX to the prior in 1234 to punish canons in the house guilty of simony or of acting while excommunicate hardly convey a very positive impression of the moral standards of the community, though without more evidence firm conclusions are impossible.[131]

The second indication of this modernisation of the community at Christ Church is found in the building activity at the cathedral priory between 1181 and 1212, the evidence for which is to be found in the quire and transepts and is discussed by Roger Stalley in chapter III. The stylistic models drawn from the west of England suggest a desire to reshape the physical appearance of the church according to contemporary English style. This Romanesque building campaign probably came to a halt early in the thirteenth century, but was revived in the 1230s with the construction of the early Gothic nave when again contemporary English architectural styles provided the models. Such activity raises questions about the financial ability of Christ Church to fund such a campaign of modernisation. The early endowment of the church has been discussed above, but it is clear from the evidence of the surviving deeds that this land bank continued to be added to in the thirteenth century by both donation and bequest.[132] In addition, the priory had a number of Dublin churches attached to it, but how much they contributed to the resources of the house

---

127 McEnery & Refaussé, *Deeds*, nos 6, 8, 164. 128 Hand, 'Two cathedrals', p. 7. 129 *Cal. doc. Ire.*, *1285–92*, p. 211. 130 McEnery & Refaussé, *Deeds*, no. 468a and f. 131 Ibid., nos 46, 104. For an example of the sort of disorder which may have been involved, McEnery & Refaussé, *Deeds*, no. 72. 132 For a list of benefactors *c.*1285, see Lawlor, 'Liber niger', pp 39–41.

is uncertain. By the time of the papal taxation of *c.*1294, two of the churches attached to the priory were too poor to pay the tax. A number of individuals remembered the priory in their wills. An early fourteenth-century valuation estimated the possessions of Christ Church at £225, although this excludes both property outside the diocese of Dublin and offerings in the church, which were calculated at £40 a year in 1300.[133] In addition, outside assistance in the form of papal indulgences to those who contributed towards the fabric of the church helped with the thirteenth-century rebuilding.[134]

The most important influences on reshaping the life of the community at Christ Church during the thirteenth century came not from internal reform but from outside pressure. The death of Archbishop Lorcán in 1180 saw the appointment of Anglo-Norman bishops to the diocese for the first time. On 21 March 1182 John Cumin, archdeacon of Bath and a favourite of Henry II, was consecrated as archbishop of Dublin and after his death in 1212 he was succeeded by Henry of London, archdeacon of Stafford, who governed the diocese until 1228. Both men were experienced royal administrators who put the skills which they had learnt at the royal court to work in the diocese of Dublin, consolidating its possessions and underpinning its liberties. Both were powerful agents for anglicisation within the diocese and their influence can be detected in the rebuilding of Christ Church and the various charters which confirmed its rights.[135]

Cumin and Henry of London were reforming bishops, concerned to align the practices of the Irish church with those of the church elsewhere in western Europe, and especially England. Cumin, for instance, summoned a provincial council at Christ Church in 1186 to legislate for perceived abuses within the Irish church and Henry presided over a similar gathering during his episcopate. In this context the monastic constitution of the diocesan cathedral at Christ Church may have been something of an embarrasment to the Anglo-Norman archbishops. In Europe as a whole, monastic cathedral chapters were already beginning to look old-fashioned by the beginning of the thirteenth century and were even giving way in England to cathedral chapters of secular clergy. Moreover, given their considerable rights to regulate their own affairs, they were less subject to episcopal influence than a secular chapter might be. Indeed it may be that the monastic chapter of Christ

133 Hand, 'Two cathedrals', pp 10–11; McEnery & Refaussé, *Deeds*, no. 513.   134 McEnery & Refaussé, *Deeds*, nos 135, 144–9, 527.   135 For assessments of these men Margaret Murphy, 'Balancing the concerns of church and state: the archbishops of Dublin, 1181–1228' in Terry Barry, Robin Frame and Katharine Simms (ed.), *Colony and frontier in medieval Ireland: essays presented to J.F. Lydon* (London, 1995), pp 41–56; Margaret Murphy, 'Archbishops and anglicisation: Dublin, 1181–1271' in Kelly & Keogh, *Catholic diocese*, pp 72–91.

Church opposed some of the reforms which Cumin attempted to introduce, most notably his attempt to merge the dioceses of Dublin and Glendalough.[136] On other issues, too, the Christ Church chapter and Cumin may not have seen eye to eye. In the 1190s, for example, the papal legate, the archbishop of Cashel, had to intervene in a dispute between the Irish prior of Christ Church, Columbanus, and the Anglo-Norman archbishop of Dublin in the course of which the Augustinians at Christ Church seem to have been expelled from the house.[137] On a more practical level monastic chapters did not provide the sort of opportunities for patronage which the newer secular chapters did and for an archbishop such as Cumin, wishing to create a reform party within the diocese, this was a considerable disadvantage.

All these factors may have been in the mind of John Cumin when in the late 1180s or early 1190s he raised the church of St Patrick to the status of a collegiate church of secular canons. On St Patrick's day 1192, Cumin and a number of other dignitaries went in procession from Christ Church to consecrate the new church to God, the Blessed Virgin Mary and St Patrick.[138] The motivation for the foundation of this college, as set out in Cumin's charter, was educational. The college was to be composed of thirteen clerks 'of approved life' who 'by their pattern of proper behaviour should be an example to others how to live and where letters are concerned should serve the education of those less cultured'. In English terms this was not an unusual endowment and Cumin does not seem to have had in mind the creation of an alternative secular chapter to rival the monastic one at Christ Church, notwithstanding the fact that his episcopal palace at St Sepulchre lay beside the new collegiate church. He did not, for example, include any provision in his charter for the government of the body of canons and no dignitaries were provided for as would have been done in the case of establishing a full chapter. However, given the difficulties of the constitution of the Christ Church chapter, Cumin may well have had in mind a gradual supplanting of the Christ Church chapter by that at St Patrick's. It was not until c.1220 that his successor, Henry of London, reconstituted the chapter of St Patrick's to include the dignitaries associated with a cathedral. Additional legislation by Henry extended the jurisdiction of the canons of St Patrick's to bring the chapter there more into line with English secular cathedrals and in particular with the chapter at Salisbury. The intention seems to have been that this new cathedral chapter would be equal, not superior, to that of Christ Church, yet in almost every way it seemed to outrank the older foundation. In terms of endowments St Patrick's was vastly more wealthy than Christ Church. According to a taxation of the diocese of

---

136 For this suggestion, MacShamhráin, 'Emergence', pp 65–70.   137 *Alen's reg.*, p. 30.
138 What follows relies heavily on the work of Geoffrey Hand, especially 'Two cathedrals', Hand, 'Chapter of St Patrick's'; Hand, 'Rivalry'.

Dublin of *c*.1294, St Patrick's was assessed at £460. 3*s*. 7*d*., while the poorer Christ Church would only have to pay £35. 18*s*. 11*d*. It may have been jealousy prompted by the rebuilding of St Patrick's following its elevation to cathedral status which prompted the Christ Church canons to begin the building of the Gothic nave in their own church, as Roger Stalley suggests.[139] Not surprisingly, such tensions crystalised around visible manifestations of rights, and none of these was more important than the election of an archbishop, normally the prerogative of the diocesan chapter under royal licence. The problem surfaced early, after the death of Henry of London in 1228. Both chapters sent representatives to London requesting royal licence to elect, but St Patrick's moved more quickly and under royal influence elected Luke, dean of St Martin's in London. While the Christ Church chapter did not dispute the choice, they objected to the St Patrick's chapter being allowed to make it alone. The matter ended up in Rome but Luke's election stood. During his episcopate Luke attempted to broker a deal between the two bodies but the resulting agreement, that the two chapters would join together for elections, was so vague that it left wide room for disagreement. Trouble flared up again in the election following the death of Fulk de Sandford in 1271, the situation not being helped by Fulk's decision to be buried in St Patrick's rather than Christ Church where his predecessors had been interred. The two chapters chose different candidates and the matter became deadlocked until 1279, when papal intervention by Nicholas III dealt with the short term problem but failed to produce a long term solution.

The death of the papally provided Archbishop William de Hotham in 1298 again produced two rivals for the see, each nominated by one of the two chapters, one candidate being Adam de Balsham, prior of Christ Church. Once again matters went to Rome and on 6 July 1300 the dean and chapter of St Patrick's were summoned before papal delegates, the archbishop, dean and archdeacon of Armagh. Within Christ Church also, things were under strain. A number of canons, including the sub-prior and the precentor, used the tensions generated by the election to accuse the unpopular prior, de Balsham, of apostasy, simony, perjury, incontinence and waste. In the midst of this mayhem the chapter of St Patrick's proposed a compromise solution, the *composicio pacis*, which promised equality of the two chapters in episcopal election. The chapter of Christ Church was unconvinced, but pressure from St Patrick's and the justiciar (crown's representative), John Wogan, forced their agreement. De Balsham was deposed by the vicar general of the diocese, who was also the dean of St Patrick's. What followed was an unedifying squabble over who should have the rights to the oblations due at the end of the year. A search of the communal chest revealed only £8 to defray

139 See p. 74.

oblations of £40 and the matter seems to have subsided. On 31 January 1301 the canons elected Henry la Warr of Bristol, who was possibly a royal diplomat, as the new prior. They were no doubt wary of promoting an existing member of the community for fear of deepening existing factions further, although recriminations would continue into the fourteenth century.[140]

The thirteenth century had not finished well for the Augustinian community at Christ Church. From being a powerful and wealthy body under Archbishop Lorcán, it had become a minor player in the politics of the diocese. It was overshadowed by the wealthier St Patrick's which seemed to have the episcopal ear, and its normal rights of episcopal election had been nullified by the squabbles with the newer body with the result that most of the late thirteenth-century bishops of the diocese were papally provided rather than locally elected. In addition, in the years 1213–1500, the chapter of St Patrick's would contribute seven archbishops of Dublin, while that at Christ Church would not produce any, an indication of the eclipse of the power of Christ Church. Moreover, the difficult relations with St Patrick's spilled over into the unedifying spectacle of the deprivation of the prior. Apart from any other reason, such a dispute, involving litigation at Rome, was ruinously expensive as the canons quickly discovered. The dispute of 1279 had cost the priory 680 marks in the appeal to Rome.[141] Such expense could not be justified in the 1290s when the demands of the crown for purveyance for the wars in Gascony and Scotland placed intolerable demands on the Irish economy and, as one commentator noted in the 'Liber niger' of Christ Church, the harvests of 1295 were extremely poor. At Christ Church the canons had particular problems since, in 1283, 'a large part of the city of Dublin and the campanile of the church of Holy Trinity' were destroyed by fire.[142] On the other hand, the fabric was sufficiently sound for the parliament of 1297 to meet at Christ Church and for the government to store its money there. Care of the fabric was an ongoing concern, and money was still being collected in 1303 for its restoration.[143] There were few spare resources to spend on feuds. Whether the cathedral at Christ Church would exist for much longer depended on some solution being found to those problems and, in particular, whether the *composicio pacis* could be made to work.

---

140 The events of 1300 can be reconstructed from a remarkable account composed within Christ Church in 1301, McEnery & Refaussé, *Deeds*, no. 164; Lawlor, 'Liber niger', pp 8–10. For la Warr, Gwynn, 'Unpublished texts', pp 298–301.   141 McEnery & Refaussé, *Deeds*, no. 111.   142 Gilbert, *Chart. St Mary's*, ii, 290, 318–19. See p. 122 below for further details.   143 Charles McNeill, 'Harris's Collectenea De rebus Hibernicis' in *Analecta Hibernica*, no. 6 (1934), p. 328.

III

The construction of the medieval cathedral, *c.*1030–1250

Roger Stalley

It is not easy to form a complete impression of the medieval architecture of Christ Church, for what remain are fragments of the middle ages, fossilised into a monument that was largely reconstituted by George Edmund Street in the late nineteenth century. While the general history of the building is clear enough, the circumstances in which the various parts were erected are frustratingly obscure. Fires, storms, a structural collapse combined with centuries of neglect, all took their toll on the medieval fabric. By the mid-nineteenth century, the cathedral presented an uninspiring appearance, a 'worn and dingy building grimed with smoke and dirt'.[1] (Plates 26, 27) Street restored dignity to the structure, but he did so at the expense of its history and archaeology. No systematic records were made as large sections of the cathedral were dismantled and re-erected between 1871 and 1878; all we have are brief descriptions of what was found.[2] One eyewitness gave a vivid impression of the excitement and the confusion:

> In excavating for the recent restorations, vaults, old walls, doorways and windows, long since covered over and forgotten, were found in all directions, and in all those old walls as well as in those taken down for rebuilding, were found voussoirs, jambstones, caps, bases, portions of columns, annulated monials and cusped tracery, used as filling stones, but which formed portions of some former buildings, now unknown.[3]

Some of this material has been preserved, but, without knowing where it came from, its value is much diminished.[4] A few years after the restoration

---

1 *Ecclesiologist*, xiii (1852), p.169. 2 The most informative account is that given in McVittie, *Restoration*. 3 McVittie, *Restoration*, pp 27n, 28n. 4 Until 1999 this material was stored at the east end of the crypt. A permanent location is yet to be established.

was complete, attention switched to the site of the old medieval cloister, where excavations were conducted by the cathedral architect Thomas Drew.

A further impediment is the lack of reliable documentation. There are no fabric rolls relating to the medieval church; nor are there any references to foundation or consecration ceremonies. Instead we have to turn to the two historical accounts contained in the 'Liber niger' for explicit references to the building of the cathedral.[5] Both were written in the fourteenth century and as a guide to what happened in earlier times they are no substitute for contemporary records. The main problem with them is knowing how to disentangle historical fact from legend and propaganda. The lack of reliable documentation, combined with massive interventions in all areas of the ancient fabric, mean that the architectural history of the cathedral will always remain somewhat elusive.

It is generally accepted that Christ Church was founded at some point between 1028 and 1036 by Sitriuc and bishop Dúnán, following the king's pilgrimage to Rome.[6] Nothing is known for certain about the design of the first church and we have to wait 150 years before we can speak with any confidence about the architecture. Although it is tempting to cast a veil over this phase of the cathedral's architectural history, the pre-Norman building deserves consideration, not least since it may have exercised an influence on the form of the later church. There is also the important question of how the cathedral came to occupy such a prominent and central position in the Hiberno-Norse town.

It is now known, thanks to the Dublin excavations of the 1960s and 1970s, that the area around the cathedral was densely populated, with tightly packed houses, well-defined property boundaries, workshops and narrow pathways. Just to the south lay a quarter which seems to have been a focus of the city's manufacturing crafts, as borne out by the discovery of dozens of trial pieces, along with the evidence of fine metalworking. There is every reason to suppose that before 1028 the site of the cathedral and its precincts was equally well populated. Thomas Drew, who excavated in the area of the cloister during the 1880s, came to the conclusion that the building was founded on a peat bog,[7] a description which sounds suspiciously like the sort of organic debris associated with the habitation levels at Wood Quay and elsewhere. Whatever the previous history of the site, the question remains as to how the cathedral managed to acquire such a strategic location. To this the 'Liber niger' gives a categorical answer, explaining that Sitriuc himself provided 'a place to build a church of the Holy Trinity, where the arches or vaults are

---

5 The texts were published in Gwynn, 'Unpublished texts', pp 308–10. The passages are translated by Gwynn, 'Origins', pp 46–8. 6 See pp 27–32 above. 7 Drew, 'Ancient chapter-house'.

now founded'.[8] What the 'Liber niger' does not explain, however, is why Sitriuc was free to release such a valuable site in the heart of the Hiberno-Norse city.

Sitriuc was a tough individual and it may be that he simply decided to undertake a piece of urban clearance, expelling the inhabitants from the site of his proposed cathedral church. Such clearances were not unknown in the early middle ages: one has only to think of Derry in 1162 when eighty houses were demolished to facilitate the reorganisation of the monastery.[9] Since Christianity was a relatively novel experience for much of the population of Dublin, wholesale clearances for the sake of the new religion may not have been all that wise.[10] It is possible, of course, that a church already existed on the site, but this is not the impression given by later records that consistently describe Dúnán as the *founder* of the church of the Holy Trinity.[11] The most likely explanation is that the site lay under the direct control of Sitriuc himself. Was it in fact the fortress of the kings of Dublin, the residence that had been ransacked and burnt by Brian Bórama after the battle of Glen Máma in 999?[12] The position at the top of the ridge would certainly have made a good strategic location for the king's headquarters. Moreover, in handing over one of his own residences to the church, Sitriuc would have been following an exalted precedent, that of Emperor Constantine himself, who presented the Lateran palace to the church following his conversion in 313. This famous donation might have been impressed on Sitriuc during his visit to Rome in 1028–9.

It has always been assumed that, like the domestic buildings in the city, the first cathedral church was made of timber,[13] though there is no evidence to support this. In fact it is far more likely that the church was constructed of stone. By the tenth century stone was in regular use for major Irish churches and several masonry cathedrals survive from this period, including those at Clonmacnois, Glendalough and Clonfert.[14] The status of a new cathe-

---

8 This comes from the longer of the two historical accounts in the 'Liber niger'. Although neither provides a reliable guide to the history of the cathedral, this is one piece of information which there is no reason to doubt, Gwynn, 'Origins', p. 46. See also Gwynn, *Irish church*, p. 52.   9 *A.F.M.*, *sub anno*.   10 The Norse population of the city does not appear to have adopted Christianity en masse before the beginning of the eleventh century, H.B. Clarke, 'The topographical development of early medieval Dublin' in Clarke, *Medieval Dublin: metropolis*, p. 63.   11 Gwynn, 'Origins', pp 48, 50; also Gwynn, *Irish church*, p. 51. See also Crosthwaite & Todd, *Obits*.   12 Gwynn, 'Origins', p. 60.   13 Gwynn, 'Origins', p. 51; repeated in Gwynn, 'First bishops', p. 38: 'Very probably it was a timber church, such as was commonly built by the Norsemen in their Scandinavian homes'.   14 For early church building in Ireland see Leask, *Irish churches*, i, 1–78; Peter Harbison, 'Early Irish churches' in H. Lowe (ed.), *Irland und Europa, Ireland and Europe*, I (Stuttgart, 1982), pp 618–29; Ann Hamlin, 'The study of early Irish churches' in Proinseas Ní

dral church in Dublin would surely have demanded that it be built of stone
rather than wood. It is important to remember that Sitriuc had seen the basil-
icas of Rome and, since the days of Bede, building in stone had been regarded
as part of the Roman way of doing things. As Aubrey Gwynn pointed out,
the connection with Rome was reinforced by the relics that Christ Church
acquired in its early years.[15]

What this first church looked like we have no means of knowing.
Although Clonmacnois and Glendalough were planned as simple rectangles,
without aisles or chancels, less than sixty feet in length,[16] it is possible that
experience abroad encouraged Sitriuc's advisers to be more ambitious. The
longer of the two historical accounts in the 'Liber niger' may be of relevance
here. It credits Dúnán with the construction of a nave with two aisles ('*cum
duobus collateralibus structuris*'),[17] an arrangement which suggests a basilican
form, rather than the simple rectangles of the early Irish churches.[18]

It is likely that Sitriuc's church survived for approximately two hundred
years before it was eventually replaced. During that time it may well have
been remodelled or extended, though there is not much evidence of this.
Amidst the hundreds of carved and moulded stones taken from the fabric in
the nineteenth century, there is none which has a Hiberno-Romanesque character. If major work had been carried out on the cathedral in the middle years
of the twelfth century, one would have expected at least some dressed
masonry to survive. Stone was a valuable commodity and material from
demolished buildings provided an obvious supply for later masons. The only
hint of pre-Anglo-Norman workmanship comes in the form of three scalloped capitals, illustrated by Street in 1882.[19] (Plate 7a) These are not sufficient to counter the impression that Sitriuc's church survived relatively
unchanged until after the Norman invasion.

The introduction of Benedictine monks, usually credited to Bishop Pátraic
(1074–84), raises the question of the domestic accommodation of the clergy.

Chatháin and Michael Richter (ed.), *Irland und Europa, Ireland and Europe*, II (Stuttgart,
1984), pp 117–26; Conleth Manning, 'Clonmacnoise cathedral – The oldest church in
Ireland?' in *Archaeology Ireland*, ix, no. 4 (Winter 1995), pp 30–3.   **15** Gwynn, 'First bishops', p. 43.   **16** Clonmacnoise measures 18.8 metres internally; the nave of Glendalough
is 14.71 metres, Manning, 'Clonmacnoise cathedral', pp 30–3.   **17** Gwynn, 'Unpublished
texts', p. 309; Gwynn, 'Origins', pp 46–8.   **18** An independent source states that Dúnán
was buried inside the church in 1074, near the high altar on the right (probably south)
side, Gwynn, 'Unpublished texts', p. 333; Gilbert, *Chart. St Mary's*, ii, p. 249.   **19** Street
& Seymour, p. 91. Until 1998 these capitals were deemed 'lost', but during the removal
of the piles of dressed masonry stored in the crypt, fragments were found by Rachel Moss.
One of the capitals surmounted an octagonal capital. Although attributed to Dúnán's church
by Street, the design of the capitals belongs to the middle years of the twelfth century.
For further discussion of the possible context of these capitals see p. 115.

Pátraic was trained as a monk at Worcester and he must have been familiar with recent developments in monastic architecture.[20] Within a few decades of his consecration, the square cloister garth surrounded by covered ambulatories was to become a norm throughout the Benedictine houses of England. Although the Benedictines at Christ Church were ejected by Bishop Samuel around 1100,[21] they may have remained long enough for new ideas to find their way to Dublin. The domestic accommodation of the clergy must have become a pressing concern again *c.*1163, when Lorcán Ua Tuathail re-established conventual life with the introduction of Arrouasian canons. Well-organised buildings were a sign of a disciplined community. If regular cloister buildings had not been erected under Bishop Pátraic and his successor in the late eleventh century, Archbishop Lorcán surely had to confront the matter in the 1160s.

The most ancient parts of the fabric at Christ Church are to be found in the quire and transepts, both erected in a late Romanesque style following the Anglo-Norman invasion. (Plates 8, 9a) The quire is much altered and rebuilt, and the remnants of the twelfth-century building are not immediately obvious. Most of the superstructure is the work of George Edmund Street. However, just to the east of the crossing, two of the original arches remain, decorated with various types of chevron ornament. The adjacent parts of the aisles also contain some original masonry, including a number of sculptured capitals. (Plate 12) The transepts are more complete, though even here there has been substantial reconstruction. Between 1871 and 1878 the north transept was dismantled almost to ground level, with the dressed masonry of the upper parts being put back in place afterwards. The arches of the triforium and clerestory, with their chevron decoration and foliate capitals, are thus largely authentic, though the plain masonry around them is not. (Plates 9a, 10b) On the exterior of both transepts virtually all the dressed stonework has been replaced, with the exception of that around the two doorways. The larger and more ornate of the portals (Plate 8) which now faces south across the ruins of the chapter house, retains a fair amount of its medieval masonry. This portal, which was moved during the renovations of 1830–3, was originally on the north side of the building.

Despite the restorations, the Romanesque transepts are still fundamentally medieval in design. There are two bays in each arm, the division into bays now underlined by nineteenth-century wall shafts. (Plates 9a, 11) At ground level, pointed arches lead into the aisles of the quire and the nave; on the south side a further arch, this time rounded in form, leads into an eastern chapel, currently dedicated to Laurence O'Toole. All the arches at this level have 'abbreviated' orders: in other words, apart from a single order

20 Gwynn, 'First bishops', pp 44–5.   21 Ibid., p. 54.

in the centre (supported on twin shafts), the underside of the arch is bare. 'Abbreviated' arches of this type were to become popular in Ireland, being used in many of the Cistercian abbeys as well as in the transepts of St Patrick's cathedral.[22] In the Laurence O'Toole chapel the inner order is decorated with roll mouldings, whereas those in the other arches are furnished with ornate forms of chevron. This contrast is further heightened by the fact that the chapel arch is round and not pointed. The interior of the chapel itself is entirely nineteenth century, though one of the tomb recesses contains fragments of earlier (fire-damaged) masonry. Between the chapel entrance and the arch to the quire aisle is a trefoil-headed recess, embellished with nail head ornament, a feature intended to hold a statue. The north transept was laid out somewhat differently from that to the south: there is no eastern chapel, its place being taken by a doorway, furnished on the outside with chevron ornament. (Plate 4)

The division between the lowest level and the triforium is marked by a string course, decorated with Greek key ornament, a rare motif in Irish Romanesque, though one that can be paralleled at Glendalough.[23] The triforium openings consist of round arches, decorated with chevron, each containing two pointed sub-arches. (Plates 9a, 10b) The inner arches rest on a single free-standing shaft (renewed by Street). The bays of the triforium represent one of the most attractive features of the cathedral: each includes five foliate capitals and amongst the subtleties it is worth noting the insertion of an extra pointed moulding between the two engaged shafts. The chevron decoration is remarkably elaborate, consisting of a syncopated pattern with floral motifs added to lozenge-shaped motifs. A mid-wall passage, which extends around both transepts, is reached from newel staircases in the south-west and north-west angles.[24] The clerestory is designed in a similar way, with mural passages and chevroned arches, but it lacks a string course to define its base: in fact the sill of the clerestory almost collides with the head of the triforium, creating a most unsatisfactory relationship. The chevron is less extravagant at this level and the openings lack the sub-arches found below.

Altogether seventy-two foliage capitals were ordered for the upper parts of the transepts, a high proportion of which still survive. (Plate 10b) A fur-

22 Stalley, *Cistercian monasteries*, p. 98. The form seems to be associated with rubble building in cases when freestone was in short supply.   23 It occurs in the hood moulding of the east window of St Mary's church. It is made of Dundry stone and almost certainly belongs to the early years of the thirteenth century. The church is described in H.G. Leask, *Glendalough, Co. Wicklow, official historical and descriptive guide* (Dublin, n.d.), pp 14–16. The string course at Christ Church was entirely replaced by Street, but original examples survive in the crypt.   24 The northern stair was built by Street, the southern one retains some of its original masonry.

ther dozen or so are now in storage in the crypt. They belong to the early stages of what is generally described as 'English stiff leaf', a technique associated with early Gothic architecture throughout Britain and Ireland. The quality of the carving underlines the point that, however cumbersome the transepts might appear, a huge amount of experienced craftsmanship was invested in the details. This impression is confirmed by the variety of the chevron decoration (at least ten different forms have been identified), making Christ Church one of the best locations in Ireland in which to study this characteristically Romanesque ornament. Chevron took time to carve, and it required masons with experience. The construction of the transepts and quire was thus an ambitious undertaking: with the chevron and the foliage picked out in colour, and the beauty of the yellow limestone not yet sullied by pollution, the architecture would have seemed quite ostentatious.

One of the problems confronting Dublin builders throughout the ages has been the lack of good freestone, the predominant local stone being a carboniferous limestone that is hard to work. For this reason Anglo-Norman builders often resorted to freestone imported from well-established quarries in England. The dressed masonry used throughout the construction of Christ Church came from quarries at Dundry, a few miles from Bristol. This is an oolitic limestone, creamy-yellow in colour, and relatively easy to carve. From the late twelfth century it was being exported to numerous sites along the coast of the Bristol Channel, as well as to Ireland.[25] The location of Christ Church beside the River Liffey made the importation of stone an attractive proposition and one that was preferable to dragging inferior supplies from the Dublin hinterland. There is a possibility that some of the blocks arrived from the quarries in England ready carved, a practice known to have been followed at some medieval sites. In some cases Dundry stone was re-used, indicating how much it was prized by the Christ Church masons. In fact there are several stones stored in the crypt which have thirteenth-century mouldings carved on opposite faces, as if the blocks were recut after a short interval, instances perhaps of the master mason over-estimating the number of pieces required. It was better to recarve a good block, rather than throw it away.[26]

One of the enigmas of the transepts is the question of whether they received a stone vault in the middle ages. In the outer angles of the south transept, there are wall shafts running from floor level to the springing of

25 The importance of Dundry stone in Irish medieval building was identified by Dudley Waterman, 'Somersetshire and other foreign building stone in medieval Ireland *c.*1175 – 1400' in *Ulster Journal of Archaeology*, 3rd ser., xxxiii (1970), pp 63–75.   26 Street failed to identify the correct origin of the freestone and used Caen stone during the restoration of 1871–8, Street & Seymour, pp 88–9, 98n.

the modern vault, and on balance it seems unlikely that the transepts would
have been left open to the roof when the nave was vaulted in stone. Street
spoke of the 'outline of groining ribs', but the evidence he described was
destroyed during the renewal of the upper walls. A photograph of the 1794
plaster vaults, taken by Millard and Robinson, provides one additional clue.
(Plate 11) On the west wall of the south transept, the eighteenth-century ribs
rested on capitals which are similar to those found in the Gothic nave, being
furnished with stiff leaf foliage and rounded abaci. While the evidence is
scarcely conclusive, it is likely that ribbed vaults were inserted over the
transepts, probably in the thirteenth century after those in the nave were
complete.

Although little remains of the superstructure of the late Romanesque
quire, the existence of the crypt confirms its original plan. (Plate 7b) Indeed,
when Street came to reconstruct the quire between 1871 and 1878 he did so
largely on the basis of what remained below.[27] The layout of the crypt is thus
crucial for an understanding of the history of the building. Its design falls
into two phases, an early section underneath the quire and transepts, and a
later section under the nave.[28] (Fig. 1) At the east end the piers are more
roughly built (there are no chamfers on the angles) and little use was made
of cut stone. While the architecture of the eastern crypt is crude in design –
'granaries of the Danes' according to one nineteenth-century commentator –
the layout coincided with the groundplan of the late Romanesque church
above. On the supposition that what looks primitive must be ancient, some
nineteenth-century writers ascribed this area of the crypt to Sitriuc's reign.
These included Thomas Drew, who confidently asserted that 'in the rude
crypt of Dublin Christchurch is found the complete and practically unaltered
church of Sitriuc'.[29]

Although it is most unlikely that Sitriuc had anything to do with the construction of the crypt, the date of the eastern limb of the cathedral remains
a matter of dispute, largely because of the confusion sown by the two historical accounts included in the 'Liber niger'. The longer version appears to
attribute the building to Strongbow and Lorcán Ua Tuathail, amongst others:

> Then after many years came Laurence, the second archbishop of
> Dublin, and Richard Earl Strongbow and the Earl Marshall and Robert
> FitzStephen and Raymond who married the sister of the Earl Marshall.

27 Street, *Report*, 1871, pp 5–11.   28 Street's opinion that the crypt is 'uniform throughout' is clearly wrong, Street, *Report*, 1868, quoted by Seymour, *Christ Church*, p. 17. In
contrast to the eastern limb, the crypt under the nave has piers made of dressed ashlar,
with decorated chamfer stops.   29 Drew, 'Christchurch', reprinted in *The Builder* (5 May
1894), p. 350.

And they built the choir of the metropolitan church (*chorum ecclesie metropolitane*), with a bell tower and two chapels.

Taken at its face value, this passage implies that building began soon after 1171, since three of the five benefactors named were either dead or had vanished from the scene by the early 1180s. Many previous writers have therefore ascribed the late Romanesque work to the time of Lorcán Ua Tuathail, but careful scrutiny of the text provides reasons for doubt. With one crucial difference, the late fourteenth-century passage repeats that found in the shorter, earlier account written soon after 1300. The one change was the addition of the name Strongbow. He was not mentioned in the earlier version and his association with the construction of the cathedral is almost certainly a myth, a story fabricated at the end of the fourteenth century to enhance the prestige of the building. Included in both versions, however, is the name of William Marshall, earl of Leinster, and this is far more significant. William became involved in Irish affairs after his marriage to Isabel de Clare in 1189. Although he paid a brief visit to Ireland in 1200, he did not spend much time in the country until after 1207, twenty-six years after the death of Lorcán Ua Tuathail.[30] Thus the four individuals associated with the quire and transepts give us a chronological span of almost half a century, from 1171 until 1219. In this context it is more appropriate to regard them as benefactors, rather than patrons of specific parts of the building.

Comparisons with English buildings point to the period 1190–1210 as the most likely time for the construction of the quire and transepts. The piers of the quire, for example, are furnished with groups of three shafts, the centre one having an ogee profile, a form widespread in the west of England from about 1190. A motif found in the outer order of the quire arches, designed like a row of ice-cream cones, is found in a number of buildings around 1200, including a doorway in the nave of St Davids cathedral.[31] The figural capitals have some of the classicising traits first seen on the portals of the Lady chapel at Glastonbury erected between 1184 and 1189.[32] (Plate 12a) Similarly the various forms of chevron used in the cathedral can be paralleled in the area of the Severn valley and Bristol Channel at much the same period, most notably at Glastonbury abbey. These connections were first noticed by Street, who provided an extensive list of features that could be matched in the English 'west country' school.[33] This led him to believe that the work at

30 G.H. Orpen, *Ireland under the Normans* (4 vols, Oxford, 1911), ii, 200–2; Sydney Painter, *William Marshall, knight-errant, baron, and regent of England* (Toronto, 1982), pp 149–54. 31 Stalley, 'Sculpture'. 32 For the Glastonbury sculpture see Malcolm Thurlby, 'The Lady chapel of Glastonbury abbey' in *The Antiquaries Journal*, clxxv (1995), pp 107–70. 33 Street & Seymour, pp 108–9. Capitals without necking rings are a well-

Christ Church was carried out between 1181 and 1212, during the episcopate of John Cumin. There is no reason to question his judgement.

Cumin is certainly a more likely candidate for inaugurating the new work than his predecessor Lorcán Ua Tuathail, whose reputation for humility and austerity scarcely seems consistent with the ornate character of the new architecture.[34] It is difficult to believe that Lorcán would have presided over a campaign directed by English masons, particularly one which utilised extensive quantities of imported stone. Assuming Cumin took the initiative in rebuilding, this could not have started until after 1184, when the new archbishop made his first appearance in Dublin. In fact plans to enlarge the cathedral may well have coincided with the provincial synod held in the cathedral in 1186.[35] As Cumin set about the work of reform in his diocese, a reconstructed cathedral church may have seemed an obvious way of announcing a new ecclesiastical order.[36]

It is important to remember that Cumin had been an official at the court of Henry II and as such he was well acquainted with major building schemes in late twelfth-century England, not least the reconstruction of the quire of Canterbury after the fire of 1174. In 1181 he was custodian of the revenues at Glastonbury,[37] and he would also have known about plans for the cathedral at Wells. Bearing this in mind, the building that went up in Dublin between 1186 and 1200 is not what one might have expected. Although the sculptural details are attractively executed, the architecture is cumbersome and inept. There are numerous geometrical irregularities in the plan: the cross-

known feature of the west country school (Harold Brakspear, 'A west country school of masons' in *Archaeologia*, xxxi (1931), p. 9), for which there are good parallels in the small doorway on the east side of the north transept at Christ Church.   34 Austerity in personal conduct did not invariably lead to austerity in architectural matters, witness St Hugh's extravagant new choir at Lincoln begun in 1192. The fact that Laurence was canonised in 1225 no doubt encouraged the author of the narrative to associate the saintly archbishop with at least part of the surviving building. It is significant that the saint's vita makes no mention of him as the builder of a new cathedral, a surprising omission if he was in fact involved in the work. The vita does however include a brief mention of St Laurence's building activities in general terms, Charles Plummer, 'Vie et miracles de S. Laurent archevêque de Dublin' in *Analecta Bollandiana*, xxxiii (1914), p. 135.   35 The synod is discussed at length in Gwynn, 'Cumin'.   36 The stylistic evidence receives some support from the longer of the two historical entries in the 'Liber niger'. Having mentioned in turn Archbishops John Cumin, Henry of London and Luke, the author explains that these three archbishops 'succeeding one another, built the chancel from the quire (*cancellam a choro*) with two collateral structures up to the place where now stands the archbishop's throne. In proof of this, Archbishop John Cumin and Luke are buried in a stone tomb on the south side of the church, but Archbishop Henry is buried on the other side, just opposite them, in a wooden tomb' (Gwynn, 'Origins', p. 47).   37 Gwynn, 'Cumin', p. 292.

ing is not an exact square, and the north and south arches of the quire are not parallel to each other.[38] (Plate 4) The steeply pointed arches that lead from the transepts into the aisles are not aligned to the triforium above and the combination of pointed and round forms is visually disturbing. (Plate 9a) As already noted, the arch of the triforium almost overlaps the base of the clerestory.[39] Comparison with Wells cathedral (begun c.1180) or the nave of St Davids cathedral, underlines the lack of architectural sophistication. Particularly noticeable is the amount of bare masonry left either side of the triforium and clerestory. In this case the stripping away of plaster during the restoration of 1871–8 and the consequent exposure of rough masonry has accentuated rather than disguised the heavy-handed appearance. (Plate 9a, 11) The fact remains that a patron of the status and experience of Cumin might have been expected to produce something better. While competent stone masons were attracted from the English west country, the cathedral seems to have lacked the guidance of an architect of proven experience or distinction.

There is a number of other peculiarities about the design of the Romanesque quire and transepts which call for comment, the first being the inclusion of an extensive crypt. (Plate 7b) During the early middle ages crypts were a common feature of the major churches of Europe, particularly those associated with relics and pilgrimage, but by the end of the twelfth century they had become obsolete almost everywhere. The presence of a crypt in Dublin is therefore of some interest. The chief question is whether it was designed to serve a structural or a liturgical function. Space in the neighbourhood of Christ Church must always have been at a premium and the brevity of the new quire may have encouraged the provision of extra space in a crypt below, perhaps as a location for some of the cathedral's shrines and relics. There is, however, no evidence that the crypt was used for liturgical purposes; there are no traces of aumbries or piscinae in the walls to indicate the presence of altars and the crypt is so rudimentary in design that the architectural setting would have been distinctly uninspiring.[40] In the fourteenth century we know it had no religious value to the priory, as portions were being leased out for secular purposes. In 1332–3 it was being used as a warehouse to store French wine, destined for the king in Scotland.[41]

---

38 The width of the quire expands slightly as it reaches the first piers east of the crossing and the start of the three-sided apse. 39 A drawing of the interior of the transept (east elevation) made between 1857 and 1872 (Plate 9b) indicates a much wider gap between triforium and clerestory, but this is contradicted both by the building as it is today and by the drawings of William Butler made shortly before the restoration. 40 If the walls and vaults were plastered and painted, the environment would of course have been enhanced, though even this would not have concealed the crude character of the architecture. 41 Tim O'Neill, *Merchants and mariners in medieval Ireland* (Dublin, 1987),

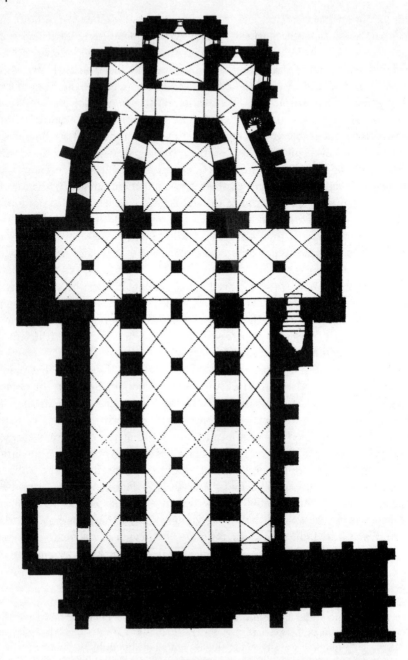

1 Christ Church cathedral: plan of the crypt (after Drew)

Moreover, the main entrance to the crypt was from outside, not from within the church.[42] Street was convinced that the crypt had no religious function, maintaining that it was built for structural reasons as a massive foundation for the church above: it has 'no artistic value', he wrote, 'its interest is wholly archaeological, and its purpose was evidently more the utilisation of foundation walls'.[43] But Street's structural explanation is not quite as compelling as it sounds, since much of the crypt was built *above* ground level, forming a substructure, rather than a normal foundation. The fact that there were external entrances to the crypt, from the cloister as well as from St John's Lane, suggests that it was intended to be used, albeit for storage or for other administrative purposes associated with the running of the priory and its estates.[44]

A second peculiarity of the late Romanesque quire is that it was very short, consisting of one straight bay before the start of the three-sided apse. (Fig. 1, Plate 4) As a consequence the stalls of the canons must have been pushed well down into the crossing, more or less as they are today.[45] This lack of space is surprising, given the desire of English cathedrals to extend the length of the quire east of the crossing. There were three straight bays at Hereford, four at Durham, Old Sarum and Norwich, and five at Chichester (by 1199). The reconstructions of Canterbury (after 1174) and Lincoln (after 1192) both involved ambitious enlargements of the east end. In this context it is odd that Christ Church embarked on a new eastern limb without any attempt to provide a spacious setting for the choir and high altar. This is all the more surprising in view of the cathedral's collection of relics, which by this time included the *baculus Ihesu*. Presumably lack of space within the old city limited the scope for eastward expansion.

A further peculiarity is the plan itself. The quire was surrounded by an ambulatory, from which three chapels opened *en échelon* at the east end, the axial chapel being slightly longer than those on either side. (Plate 6, Fig. 1) The outer walls of the ambulatory are angled inwards to correspond with the canted bays of the apse, and a spiral staircase was provided on the south side linking the crypt with the upper church.[46] If this layout was encountered in

pp 52–4. It could of course be argued that the construction of the long quire had provided more accommodation in the upper church, releasing space below. **42** The internal access was by means of a narrow spiral stair in the south quire aisle. **43** Street & Seymour, pp 86, 107. **44** It may also have been conceived as a place of burial from the start. Interment certainly took place there in the middle ages, as Sir Peter Lewis discovered when excavating in the crypt in 1565, Gillespie, *Proctor's accounts*, p. 75. **45** Street claims to have found evidence for a screen running across the nave about ten feet west of the crossing, Street & Seymour, p. 90. **46** The newel staircase was entirely rebuilt in the restoration of 1871–8. Originally it linked the crypt and quire, but Street extended it to roof level to form an external turret. A second staircase existed on the north side, but this did not descend to the crypt, Street, *Report, 1868*, p. 7; *Dublin Builder*, xiv, no

2 Winchester cathedral: plan of the late eleventh-century crypt (after Clapham).
As at Christ Church this was designed with an ambulatory and with
three parallel 'chapels' to the east.

England, one would be tempted to assign it to the 1090s rather than the
1190s. The three-sided apse, for example, was employed at the end of the
eleventh century in the churches at Tewkesbury, Gloucester and Pershore,[47]
and while there are no exact parallels for the design of the ambulatory, the
closest comparison is found in the crypt at Winchester, begun under Bishop
Walkelin in 1079.[48] (Fig. 2) Was the late Romanesque work at Christ Church
determined by an earlier building and could sections of the crypt go back to
before 1100 (perhaps begun and never completed)?[49] It is worth remembering that Bishop Pátraic (1074–84) had been a monk at Worcester, the very
area in which the parallels for the plan are to be found. The layout of the
east end would fit happily within his episcopate. Moreover, the longer history in the 'Liber niger' attributed the crypt to St Patrick; while this was
obviously absurd, it could be the result of confusion between a saint and a

296, 15 April 1872, p. 119.   **47** Roger Stalley and Malcolm Thurlby, 'The early Gothic
choir of Pershore abbey' in *Journal of the Society of Architectural Historians*, xlviii (1989),
pp 351–71.   **48** A.W. Clapham, *English Romanesque architecture II: after the Conquest*
(Oxford, 1934), p. 64. The origins of this layout can be traced to the Empire. A crypt
designed with three parallel chapels opening off an ambulatory formed part of the ninth-
century design at Corvey, Carol Heitz, *L'architecture religieuse Carolingienne: les formes et
leurs fonctions* (Paris, 1980), pp 150–1.   **49** The eastern section of the crypt is largely lacking in dressed masonry to which a date can be assigned. Some pieces of Dundry stone
are used at the entrance to the eastern chapel, and these must surely belong to the period
after 1170.

bishop with the same name. Unfortunately there is no archaeological evidence to prove the point; even if parts of the crypt do go back to the eleventh century, it is strange that Cumin's builders were prepared to retain such an archaic plan.[50]

Although the architecture of Cumin's episcopate was far from distinguished, the sculptured capitals are of high quality, and there are many parallels with carvings at Wells and Glastonbury.[51] Several capitals on the north side of the building contain figural scenes with interesting and amusing subjects.[52] (Plate 12) For example, two on the north arcade of the quire depict rustic scenes, one illustrating a shepherd with his sheep, the other a more elaborate scene with fruitpickers collecting succulent-looking fruits. The style of these lively carvings is especially close to the sculpture on the north porch at Wells cathedral (c.1205). The north transept contains one of the best known capitals, illustrating a troupe of musicians, led by a jester in an overall costume. The long flowing robes and energetic movement provide a good illustration of the classicising traits which became fashionable in English sculpture during the last two decades of the twelfth century. Also in the north transept is a double capital, each section of which has a pair of griffons with their claws implanted on human figures. With its symmetrical composition and twisting movement, this is characteristic of Romanesque art, where the struggle of man and beast was a recurring theme. Capitals in a similar idiom, though far more damaged, are to be found on the portal of the south (originally north) transept. (Plates 8, 12d) One depicts two human figures apparently attacking giant beasts, and another shows a pair of affronted birds. Further sculptures were recovered from the fabric during the restoration of 1871–8, and these include an impressive monster-head capital, carved as if swallowing the shaft below, a type with many analogies in the west country of England. None of the capitals illustrates religious themes and the combination of fantastic beasts and genre subjects is in keeping with English Romanesque fashions. What makes the Christ Church capitals especially interesting is that they were carved at the moment when Romanesque was giving way to Gothic, a change that eventually led to the disappearance of the historiated capital.

In the context of Ireland, the style and content of the Christ Church sculpture represented something totally new, a complete break with the past. The carvings were executed in relatively deep relief, a contrast to the shal-

---

50 If the crypt (and presumably the quire above) had been built under Bishop Patrick, it is difficult to understand why it had to be reconstructed a century later on exactly the same plan. 51 The sculptures are discussed at length in Stalley, 'Sculpture'. 52 Some of the capitals in the group belong to the doorway in the south transept, which was originally located on the north side of the cathedral.

low relief techniques generally employed by Hiberno-Romanesque craftsmen, and the subjects depicted were also different from the repertoire normally found in Hiberno-Romanesque. It was not long before these novel forms began to have an impact outside Dublin. The influence is especially marked in the nave of Boyle abbey, County Roscommon, giving the impression that some English or Welsh masons from Dublin had found their way to Connacht.[53] The nave at Boyle was completed in 1218 or 1220, dates which reinforce the argument that the quire and transepts of Christ Church belong to the time of Cumin, not to that of his predecessor.

The quire of the cathedral must have been finished when Cumin was buried there in 1212, but it is unclear how far work had proceeded towards the west. The thirteenth-century nave was built in an assured Gothic style, which represents a sharp break with what had gone before. (Plate 14) This next phase of construction began around 1234 and was the responsibility of a new team of masons, working under the direction of an individual of considerable talent.

The precise sequence of building is hard to unravel. We know for a number of reasons that the nave was not simply built on a piece of vacant ground to the west of the transepts. First, the late Romanesque transepts are linked to the nave aisles by pointed arches, which implies that nave aisles *already* existed (or were under construction) when the transepts were built. If the original nave was no more than a rectangular 'box', like the cathedrals at Glendalough or Clonmacnois, these arches would have served no function. The obvious conclusion is that the Gothic nave replaced an earlier nave which had aisles. Second, the Romanesque crossing could not have been finished without receiving some structural support on the western side. This could have been provided, at least temporarily, by an older building; alternatively some new work may have been carried out at the east end of the nave by the late Romanesque builders. It was common practice in the middle ages to build one or two bays of the nave in conjunction with the crossing to provide the necessary abutment. Third, some of the architectural details employed in the crypt below seem to correspond to the late Romanesque transepts rather than to the Gothic building above; the relationship is particularly obvious in the use of decorated chamfer stops. There is even a pos-

53 The features in common include triple shafts, the centre one with an ogee keel; distinctive chamfer stops, capitals without abaci etc. The chevron employed in the west window of the Cistercian abbey reproduces a type found in the cathedral and the choice of subjects used for some of the capitals is also reminiscent of Christ Church. The chevron at Boyle can be compared with that on the arch around the doorway on the east side of the north transept. The arguments are presented at greater length in Stalley, *Cistercian monasteries*, pp 87–92.

sibility that the crypt was already complete when the team of Gothic masons arrived. Finally, the plan of the crypt does not correspond with that of the nave, for, as William Butler demonstrated in 1870, the Gothic piers are not aligned with those in the crypt below. There is also the well known fact that the crypt extends only five rather than six bays to the west.[54] (Fig. 1)

It is difficult to know what to make of these observations, but taken together they suggest that the task confronting the thirteenth-century builders was not simply a question of replacing Sitriuc's nave with a modern Gothic design. Indeed the style of the crypt suggests that the old nave may have been removed soon after 1200 rather than in 1234 and there is at least the possibility that a new nave was started during the episcopate of Cumin. Although the general impression of the nave is one of supreme unity, this is not reflected in the details. The final bay at the west end, for example, is noticeably different from those further east. The mouldings of the arch are more straightforward and plain capitals take the place of the foliate types elsewhere. There is also a discrete use of billet ornament. (Fig. 3, Plate 17) The differences extend upwards throughout the whole bay. Even the vault capitals are moulded rather than foliate in form. (Plate 16a) Despite the use of billet ornament, the details tend to be more subdued than elsewhere. The workmanship has much in common with St Patrick's, which suggests that for this section of the building a band of masons was recruited from the neighbouring cathedral. As noted above, there is one further oddity about the sixth bay: the crypt does not extend underneath. Further anomalies can be detected elsewhere in the nave. The capitals on the eastern side of the fifth pier, for example, have a quite distinctive and unusual form. On the 'bell' of the capital the stems of the leaves are more numerous and the decoration is curiously extended down on to the shaft. Instead of the customary 'necking' ring, the stems terminate in a series of odd-looking blobs.[55] (Plate 16b) Other anomalies and inconsistencies were ironed out by Street during the restoration. Before 1871 less than half the piers were ornamented

---

54 The crypt under the nave was built in two stages, as can be deduced from the changes in design in the third bay from the east: (a) At this point the vaults spring from a higher point on the piers and the chamfer stops are accordingly set about one block higher. The second of the freestanding piers in the nave, which marks the point of change, has the chamfer set at two different levels on the east and west sides. (b) After the third bay the main piers are slightly wider (in a north-south direction); as a result they project further into the main body of the nave.

It is also worth noting that in the nave crypt there are no abaci or transitional features between the piers and the vault, as one normally expects in medieval architecture. In many places the relationship is decidedly uneven, with the rubble of the vault hanging forward from the face of the piers.   55 There are four major capitals which fall into this group. There is something similar on the west doors at Llandaff cathedral.

with shaft rings, but in the spirit of homogeneity Street applied them throughout.[56] (Plates 14, 27) Interestingly, the fifth pier had rings only on the eastern side, immediately below the unusual group of foliate capitals.

There is one piece of documentary evidence which may explain some of these architectural irregularities. In 1234 the prior and canons sought permission from Henry III to lengthen and widen their cathedral church, so blocking a road on the western side.[57] Most authorities have concluded that this relates to the final bay of the nave, arguing that it represents an afterthought, built when the first five bays had been finished. Assuming this bay was indeed an addition, then the rest of the nave was constructed well before 1234, perhaps in the years 1225–30. There is, however, one flaw in this argument. It presupposes that, having just completed a five bay nave, including presumably a new west facade, the canons of the cathedral changed their minds and demolished part of what they had just built – all for the sake of gaining one extra bay. Even for a cathedral with more resources than Christ Church, this would have been a profligate course of action.

It seems more likely that the 1234 request marks the start of work on the whole of the nave. A campaign lasting from c.1234 to c.1240 would not be inconsistent with the style of the building. The triforium capitals, for example, are almost identical to those used in the Lady chapel at St Patrick's, which is usually placed about 1235.[58] (Plates 16c, 16d) Moreover, the text of the 1234 document speaks of the need to lengthen and widen the cathedral, as if something more substantial than a mere bay was being contemplated. The final western bay might then have been added some years later, perhaps in the 1240s or 1250s.

The complexities of the building programme should not obscure the fact that the nave of Christ Church represents the most distinguished piece of Gothic architecture in Ireland. Although only the north elevation survives from the thirteenth century, enough remains to show the sophistication of the design. (Plate 14) It was a well-proportioned scheme, enriched by an abundance of mouldings. Each bay is defined by a shaft that runs from floor to vault, providing a vertical accent which is often missing in equivalent English designs. The bulkiness of the piers is in part concealed by a sequence of filleted shafts, alternating with a pair of thin rolls. The linear emphasis is

---

56 Freestanding piers 1 and 2 plus the eastern side of pier 5. The erratic use of shaft rings suggests that the construction of the nave had a certain piecemeal element to it. Was each bay built separately as a progressive replacement of an earlier building?   57 *Calendar of the patent rolls … 1232–47*, p. 70.   58 Michael O'Neill has recently argued for 1234 as the starting date for the whole nave, stressing the similarities that exist between the capitals of the Christ Church triforium and those in the Lady chapel at St Patrick's, Michael O'Neill, 'The architecture of St Patrick's cathedral', Ph.D. thesis, T.C.D., 1995.

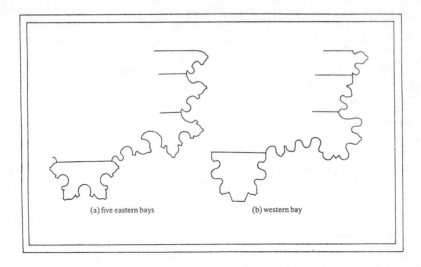

3 Christ Church cathedral: the mouldings of the main arcade of the nave:
(a) the five eastern bays; (b) the western bay.

continued in the arches above, where the soffits are furnished with mouldings of extraordinary subtlety and depth. (Fig. 3) But perhaps the most striking aspect of the design is the way in which the triforium and clerestory are
combined into a unified arrangement, with dark limestone shafts linking the
two storeys. (Plate 13) In each case there are three arches, the centre one
being finished with a trefoiled head. There were originally passageways running through the thickness of the wall at both triforium and clerestory level,
though these were blocked by Street to improve the stability of the building.[59] At the base of the triforium, a string course contributes a horizontal
element, effectively dividing the elevation into two equal parts. Apart from
the sixth bay, deeply carved foliage capitals add to the richness of the design.

The relatively low arcades, the squat piers and the profusion of soffit
mouldings recall the architecture of Wells cathedral, but this is no more than
a general impression. In fact the roots of the Christ Church design lie further north in Worcestershire. The best clues are the foliage capitals, especially those with human heads, found on the second and third piers. (Plates
15a, 15b) The examples at Christ Christ are so close to some in the village

59 The system of superimposed passages was probably determined by the earlier arrangements in the transepts. For a discussion of this feature see Virginia Jansen, 'Superposed
wall passages and the triforium elevation of St Werburg's, Chester' in *Journal of the Society
of Architectural Historians*, xxxviii (1979), pp 223–43; and Jean Bony, *French Gothic architecture of the 12th and 13th centuries* (Berkeley, 1983), pp 328–54.

church at Overbury near Tewkesbury, that they must be attributed to the same mason. (Plate 15c) There are also similarities with Worcester cathedral, where a new quire and Lady chapel were begun in 1224. The vault capitals at Christ Church, for example, are closely related to some found in the Worcester Lady chapel. Worcester also provides a parallel for one of the more peculiar details of Christ Church, the way in which the vault shaft is recessed back into the adjoining wall.[60] (Plate 14) It conveys the illusion that the huge circular pier below somehow continues upwards, being embedded in the walls of the triforium and clerestory.

The most important feature of the Christ Church design is the integration of the triforium and clerestory. (Plate 13) Between 1170 and 1185 French Gothic architects began to experiment with designs that linked the two storeys, notably in the quires of Arras cathedral, at St Remi at Rheims and at Notre Dame-en-Vaux at Chalons sur Marne and by the middle of the thirteenth century, linkage had become an important element in the French Rayonnant style.[61] In England the development is more difficult to follow.[62] The choir of Pershore abbey (begun c.1223) has a form of linkage, but in this case the triforium arches have been eliminated. A related scheme can be found in the outer bays of the transepts and Lady chapel at Worcester. A better parallel for Christ Church may have occurred in the transepts at Lichfield, but here the thirteenth-century details were obscured by a remodelling in the fourteenth century.[63] Although the picture is frustratingly incomplete, enough survives to show that the design produced by the Christ Church master was not the result of a sudden flash of genius, but represented the crystallisation of ideas which had been circulating for some time in the west of England. With its subtle recession of planes the linked triforium and clerestory at Christ Church has a balance and unity not found in contemporary English buildings. It was only with the design of the nave of York minster in 1291 that English architecture produced an equally accomplished integration of the upper storeys. The use of linkage at Christ Church, together with the continuous shafts that separate each bay, add a French tinge to what is otherwise a distinctively English piece of architecture.

---

60 Something similar is encountered in a number of English and Welsh buildings, as at Malmesbury abbey, Bindon abbey, Pershore abbey, St Davids cathedral and Llandaff cathedral. 61 Bony, *French Gothic architecture*, p. 373. 62 The linkage at Christ Church has sometimes been compared with that in the nave of St Davids cathedral and at Llanthony abbey, but in structural terms these buildings are very different, Stalley, 'Buildings', pp 71–5. 63 Warwick Rodwell, 'The development of the choir of Lichfield cathedral: Romanesque and Early English' in John Maddison (ed.), *Medieval art and architecture at Lichfield cathedral: the British Archaeological Association conference transactions for the year 1987* (1993), pp 17–35; and Malcolm Thurlby, 'The early Gothic transepts of Lichfield cathedral' in Maddison, *Medieval art*, pp 50–64.

The well-judged proportions that control the design are another impressive aspect of the Christ Church nave. The width of the bay (average 16 feet 2½ inches) was evidently used to generate some of the other dimensions. Multiplied twice it defined the level of the clerestory and multiplied three times the total height of the building (48 feet 6 inches). The floor of the triforium (24 feet 4 inches) marks the mid point of the design and stands in a ratio of 3:2 to the width of the bay.[64] The main features of the elevation were thus determined by a group of simple ratios, 1:2, 1:3, 2:3, 3:4 etc.

The nave was covered by quadripartite ribbed vaults, which, having fallen in the great collapse of 1562, were reinstated by Street.[65] (Plates 2, 3) Stone vaults exert considerable lateral force, and medieval builders spent much of their time devising ways to counter the thrusts. In France flying buttresses were usually employed, a solution that found little favour among thirteenth-century English architects. At Christ Church, as in most English buildings of the time, the master mason relied on the sheer thickness of the wall to withstand the stress, taking heart no doubt from the fact that this was not a particularly tall building. The upper walls are 4 feet 8 inches in width, which might have been substantial enough if it were not for the two passageways that run continuously through the masonry. Deprived of external buttressing, the walls rotated outwards, leading to a complete collapse of the vaults. At the top of the clerestory the main wall is 33 inches out of alignment and the whole elevation appears to have hinged outwards at a point close to the main capitals, where a change in the vertical line can still be detected.[66]

When Street replaced the masonry of the main piers in 1871–8, he claims to have been astonished by their feeble construction.[67] Loose material is said to have poured out of the core of the piers like sand, and in two cases large sections of oak about seven feet in length acted as vertical reinforcements.[68] The piers were evidently constructed with an outer ring of dressed masonry, the space in the centre being filled with rubble. Herein lies one of the principal differences between English and Irish building at the time. The scarcity

---

64 Stalley, 'Buildings', pp 71–5. In visual terms, however, it is the string course that serves as a median line and this is some 9 inches below the floor of the triforium. The unit of 16 feet 2½ inches, which seems an arbitrary starting point, may represent some local variation on the medieval perch (16 feet 6 inches).   65 The springers of the original ribs remained embedded in the upper walls after 1562, and they are visible in old photographs and prints. They served as a guide for Street's vault, though there is no way of knowing whether the medieval vault had a ridge rib like that reinstated by Street.   66 Old photographs taken before 1871 show that the bend was more gradual than it is today. As Street rebuilt the piers to the vertical, this accentuated the break in alignment at capital level.   67 The piers look stable enough in pre-1871 photographs. There is at least a suspicion that Street embellished his description in order to justify their replacement. 68 McVittie, *Restoration*, pp 48–9.

and expense of good freestone meant that both Christ Church and St Patrick's were essentially rubble buildings in which dressed masonry was used sparingly. Equivalent English buildings would have been constructed with piers of solid masonry, not with rubble cores.

Despite the uncertain chronology, we can be confident that the nave of Christ Church was erected between 1225 and 1240 during the time of Archbishop Luke. Throughout this period work was continuing on St Patrick's and it is hard to believe that the projects were unrelated. On occasions craftsmen worked at both sites, as revealed by the style of the capitals. Hardly a day could have gone by without the canons of Christ Church being made aware of the massive church rising from the ground only a few hundred yards away. With all the limitations of their site in the old city, they could not hope to compete in scale. But the decision to rebuild the nave in a rich and fashionable English style suggests that they were determined not to be outdone. There is a certain irony in the fact that, without competition from St Patrick's, Christ Church might not have commissioned such a distinguished piece of architecture.

IV

Christ Church in the later medieval Irish world, 1300–1500

James Lydon

The *composicio pacis* of 1300 seemed to have settled the differences that had arisen between Christ Church and St Patrick's, not least in the matter of electing new archbishops. When Archbishop John Leche died in 1313, the two cathedrals came together to choose a successor. They sent messengers to the king to seek a licence to proceed with the election. But they subsequently informed the Irish government 'that by hindrance of the sea and difficulties of the way' the messengers were 'prevented from coming with the king's letters testifying to his licence of choosing'. Because 'the time for choosing had almost expired', the justiciar and council granted permission for the election to go ahead. Then 'the prior for himself and his convent and the dean for himself and his chapter came before the justiciar and council here [in Dublin] and acknowledged that the said grace of election shall not act to the prejudice of the king in the future nor be used as a precedent'.[1] All seemed well and the election went ahead. But when the king's favourite, Alexander Bicknor, the treasurer of Ireland, was chosen by the canons of St Patrick's, Christ Church instead chose another powerful administrator, Walter Thornbury, the chancellor and thus senior in rank to Bicknor. More important, he had been acting as vicar-general in the absence of Leche. The dispute was solved when Thornbury decided to travel to the papal court in Avignon to press his claims. But while crossing the Irish Sea he and many others (154 according to the Dublin annalist) were drowned and subsequently the pope provided Bicknor to the see.[2]

From then on, apart from a very occasional difference, Christ Church and St Patrick's were able to go their own way. Even when they disagreed, it was

---

1 N.A.I., KB 2/5 (Justiciary Roll 7 Edward II, m. 2d), pp 7–8.   2 Aubrey Gwynn, *Anglo-Irish church life: fourteenth and fifteenth centuries* (Dublin, 1968), p. 7; J.T. Gilbert, *Chart. St Mary's*, ii, 342–3. Thornbury was carrying 'great sums received by him from divers debtors of the king in Ireland' when he drowned, so he may well have not been intent on going to Avignon (*Calendar of the fine rolls, 1307–19*, pp 188, 192).

never fundamental. In 1471 after the death of Archbishop Tregury, an election was proposed before the licence was obtained from the king. Christ
Church refused to proceed, fearing the royal reaction. But having procured
from the chapter of St Patrick's a bond of indemnity worth £100, they went
ahead and Dean Alleyn of St Patrick's was elected unanimously.[3] In 1484,
when arrangements were made to have the new archbishop consecrated as
usual in Christ Church, the dean and chapter of St Patrick's claimed the
right to have the consecration in their own cathedral. Despite an appeal to
the *composicio pacis*, the consecration went ahead in St Patrick's, leaving the
prior and convent of Christ Church to make another formal protest, repeated
subsequently at a provincial synod of the diocese of Dublin.[4]

These were minor blips, however, and in most respects the 1300 agreement was maintained. It was in Christ Church, for example, that the archbishop's cross, mitre and ring were deposited on the occasion of his death,
no matter where that happened. Even when he was away the formal handing over to Christ Church representatives still took place.[5] This was demonstrated in a spectacular way in 1449 after the death of Archbishop Richard
Talbot when the cross was deposited in Christ Church in accordance with
custom. But after the new archbishop, Michael Tregury, took office, he discovered that the cross had earlier been pledged to a Dublin tailor, Richard
White, for a loan of five marks and he ordered that it be handed over to
White by the prior.[6] When Archbishop John of St Paul in 1354 informed the
prior and canons of Christ Church of how the order of precedence was to
be regulated in future when the two chapters processed together, another
potential source of dispute was removed.[7]

On the whole, therefore, the 1300 agreement succeeded in establishing
peace between the two cathedrals and provincial synods were held in Christ
Church.[8] One sign that the new good relations were maintained was the fact
that the scholarly John Alleyn, dean of St Patrick's, bequeathed two text-
books of canon law to the canons of Christ Church when he died in 1506.[9]
Indeed it has been argued that what has been called 'the combative energies'
of the canons of St Patrick's, which before the 1300 *composicio* had been
diverted to dealing with Christ Church, were subsequently largely employed
in quarrels with the archbishop.[10] And if the canons had been successful in
retaining the precedence of their cathedral as 'the mother church',[11] so that

3 Mason, *St Patrick's*, p. 137. In the event Dean Alleyn's election was not confirmed and
John Walton was later nominated by the king and installed as archbishop.   4 Lawlor,
'Liber niger', p. 14.   5 For examples see Lawlor, 'Liber niger', pp 10–11.   6 Gilbert,
Dublin, i, 104; *Alen's reg.*, p. 156.   7 Hand, 'Camb. MS', p. 21.   8 McEnery & Refaussé,
Deeds, no. 361.   9 Gwynn, *Anglo-Irish church life*, p. 76.   10 Hand, 'Chapter of St
Patrick's', p. 248.   11 McEnery & Refaussé, *Deeds*, no. 164.

their combative energies could be employed in coping with other problems – such as that posed by the escheator, for example, in claiming royal rights over priory lands during a vacancy, or by the Dublin municipal authorities trying to prevent further acquisitions of properties – they still had to fulfil their primary duty in sustaining Christ Church as a centre of religious life.

While the canons were not monks, they were 'regular', living as a religious community under a strict rule that regulated their days and nights, even if it did not confine their activities to the priory itself. They followed the rule of St Augustine according to the custom of Arrouaise in France, from where St Lorcán Ua Tuathail had transformed the secular chapter of Christ Church after he became archbishop in 1162.[12] The community was always a small one: eleven canons in 1300, eight in 1468, and ten in 1538 when it was secularised after the Henrician reformation.[13] Arrouasian houses were always small – in England many of them had less than ten canons in the community.[14] This was one of the factors that made them popular with potential benefactors who had ambitions to establish a new community in rural areas: the endowment of land required to support a small community did not have to be extravagant. But it also meant that in Christ Church most of the canons had to accept the burden of one of the seven offices which were necessary to run the priory: prior, sub-prior, steward, cellarer, kitchener, sacristan and precentor.[15] Given the fact that the priory held extensive properties not only in Dublin but also in many parts of Ireland, and that they also had been endowed with churches, which sometimes required priestly attention, it meant that a deal of travelling outside Dublin was necessary. For example, early in the thirteenth century the church and lands at Killenaule in County Tipperary were granted to the priory on condition, according to the charter, that the canons 'build a cell on the said land, and have canons there serving God'. But for various reasons no canon was resident there, which necessitated visits by one of the community from Dublin.'[16]

This could lead to serious problems. In the mid-fourteenth century a jury found that one of the canons had gone into residence at Kilcullen, a living served by the priory, and had brought with him two of his brothers, as well as a kinswoman called Milsanda. For eight weeks he kept them there, at a cost of 10s. to the priory. Worse, his brother Nicholas was suspected of improper relations with a housemaid and, we are told, used goods valued at

12 Gilbert, *Chart. St Mary's*, ii, 266.   13 McEnery & Refaussé, *Deeds*, no. 164; Berry, *Register*, p. 172.   14 C.A. Empey, 'The sacred and the secular: the Augustinian priory of Kells in Ossory, 1193–1541' in *I.H.S.*, xxix, no. 94 (1984), p. 138.   15 For a short account of the duties of these offices see *Account roll of the priory of the Holy Trinity, Dublin, 1337–1346 with the middle English moral play 'The pride of life'*, ed. James Mills (Dublin, 1891), p. xviii.   16 Lydon & Fletcher, *Account roll*, pp 160–1.

2s. to allay suspicion. Other bits of property were sold or given away for favours (Nicholas gave the fleeces of six sheep for a supper) and through their actions the harvest was halted, at a loss of 4s. One horse, valued at 5s., died and a cart was given on loan in return for a piece of iron worth 2d. Perhaps worst of all, the canon refused to celebrate mass on the feast of the Purification; but it is indicative of the attitude of the time that what is recorded is that this led to a loss of two lb. of wax worth 16d.[17]

When Christ Church was able to find a priest to serve as chaplain to one of its churches it could prove expensive. In 1396 William Norragh, who served the church of St Sampson in Balgriffin, was brought in retirement to the priory in Dublin. There, according to the record, he was granted 'a chamber in the convent close of Holy Trinity churchyard, a pension, and an allowance of food, including both better and second quality bread, and ale, for him and his servant; with right in case of arrears or non-performance to enter and distrain the manor of Grange'.[18] No wonder that wherever possible the canons chose to service their churches themselves.

This need to travel frequently made it difficult for many of the canons, in particular those who held office, to live a full regular life as demanded by the rule. It has been suggested that even the most elementary exercise of reading a part of the rule of St Augustine each week presented difficulties, since only the first part of the text seems to have been available to the community. And even that part was so flawed textually, not least in its grammar, that it is hard to believe that the canons understood what they heard during the readings, if they listened at all.[19] But the compilation of registers like the 'Liber niger' in the early fourteenth century, or the 'Liber albus' in the early sixteenth century, shows clearly an interest in preserving important legal records such as charters. It demonstrates more than that, however, for the 'Liber niger' contains two separate narratives of the foundation of the cathedral, suggesting an interest in history on the part of some at least of the canons. Other manuscripts compiled or preserved in the priory also indicate more than just a passing interest in accounts and records, not least what is regarded as perhaps the earliest copy of an English morality play which presumably an enthusiastic canon copied on the dorse of account rolls because no other parchment was readily available.[20]

One important fact about the priory, which also helped to keep numbers down, was that no Irish were admitted, certainly from the thirteenth century onwards. Irish names do not figure among the names of the canons which

---

17 Ibid., pp 163–4.　18 McEnery & Refaussé, *Deeds*, no. 784; see also nos 265, 272, 275, 813.　19 See the comments of J.H. Todd in his introduction to Crosthwaite & Todd, *Obits*, p. lxxxvii.　20 See Alan Fletcher, 'The pride of life' in Lydon & Fletcher, *Account roll*, pp xxii–xlii.

have survived among the records. Parliament actually prohibited the admittance of Irish. The famous statute of the Kilkenny parliament of 1366 decreeing that no Irish were to be admitted to religious houses applied, of course, to Christ Church.[21] In 1380 another statute of parliament confirmed this infamous legislation.[22] Such exclusivity was common in Dublin and elsewhere in Anglo-Ireland where corporations such as trade guilds tried to maintain an English character, a fact which was condemned as against the law of charity by Richard FitzRalph, the great archbishop of Armagh, in a famous sermon in Drogheda on 28 June 1356.[23] But it did not prevent Anglo-Irish communities from enjoying the cults of Irish saints. Christ Church was no exception and many Irish saints' feast days were celebrated in the cathedral.[24]

The prior, of course, was the most important of the canons. After his election and installation he lived in the privacy of his own chamber, a set of rooms where he was able to provide lavish entertainment for distinguished visitors, including perhaps a game of chess,[25] and accommodation for the many retainers who gave public evidence of his high rank.[26] He might be asked to offer special prayer to God when great danger threatened, as happened on 11 June 1402 when the Irish were threatening the environs of Dublin. According to one source the mayor of Dublin came with the prior to pray for success against the Irish and it was 'with the help of God' that they put the Irish to flight and killed more than 400.[27]

On retirement he was allowed another chamber of his own and in some cases possibly even a pension.[28] Age, of course, could impair his ability to discharge his duties. On 25 April 1468, the archbishop of Dublin held a visitation. At a meeting in the chapter house, where eight canons were present and which lasted until noon, the record tells us that 'a serious complaint was made about the great age and infirmity of the prior'. The archbishop insisted that a coadjutor prior should be appointed, specifically to look after the estates and possessions of the house. When this was unanimously agreed by those present, what was called 'a suitable portion' of rents and debts owing

21 Berry, *Statutes*, p. 445.   22 Ibid., p. 481. Archdall, *Mon. Hib*, p. 164, on the basis of evidence no longer available, argued that legislation specifically enacted that no Irishman was to be made a canon of Christ Church.   23 Katherine Walsh, *A fourteenth-century scholar and primate: Richard FitzRalph in Oxford, Avignon and Armagh* (Oxford, 1981), pp 341–2. In 1454 the Dublin municipal assembly enacted that 'al maner of men of Iryshe blode and women' were to be expelled, repeated in 1455 and 1458, *Anc. rec. Dublin*, i, 280–1, 287, 298. In 1475 the assembly proclaimed that no one in the city was to take 'none Irisshe prentices if Irisshe blode', *Anc. rec. Dublin*, i, 352–3.   24 See Crosthwaite & Todd, *Obits*, pp xlix–li.   25 In 1451 the prior was left a chess board of ivory, with the men, and the sub-prior one of cypress, McEnery & Refaussé, *Deeds*, no. 296.   26 See Lydon & Fletcher, *Account roll*, pp x–xvi.   27 Hand, 'Psalter', pp 317–8.   28 Lydon & Fletcher, *Account roll*, p. 94.

to the priory was to be assigned to the old prior.[29] That same prior, in fact, had already engaged in activities which bordered on the criminal, though it is not sure that this was known in 1468 to either the community or the archbishop. He had leased the valuable manor of Drumsallon in County Louth to a John Begge, 'sitting in a wine tavern' in Dublin, we are told, 'without the assent of any of his brethren' and 'for so small consideration'.[30] Of course bribery had long since become part of the prior's life, not least of officials of all ranks. A blatant example occurred in 1344 when the steward recorded 2s. 8d. for 'cloth bought and given to the purveyors of the chief justiciar of Ireland that they may be more favourable to us'.[31] In that climate it is not surprising that the prior, like so many other high officials in church and state, might even use his office to promote the interests of relatives.[32]

The high rank of the prior was also manifested in the secular world by the fact that he was always summoned to the upper house whenever parliament assembled, taking his seat beside the bishops and great heads of important religious houses. So he frequently had to travel far afield from Dublin, often at great expense and considerable inconvenience. In 1346 when the prior went to attend the parliament summoned to Kilkenny his expenses on the journey came to 22s. 6d.[33]

Outside Christ Church the prior remained one of the most important figures in the Irish church. In 1447, for example, the prior was one of five who went to England on behalf of the earl of Ormond who had been accused of witchcraft.[34] Earlier, in 1326, when the famous Roger Outlaw, prior of Kilmainham, was formally accused of heresy by Richard Ledrede, bishop of Ossory, the prior of Christ Church was one of six chosen to examine and arbitrate the case. This was a particularly delicate matter, for not only was Outlaw an exceptionally important royal official (he acted as deputy justiciar in 1324, and again in 1327, 1330–1, 1335, 1336–7, and 1340–1; was chancellor from 1322–31 and later; keeper of the exchequer in 1318; deputy treasurer in 1325–6),[35] this charge of heresy was involved with the infamous Alice Kyteler witchcraft trial which touched leading Anglo-Irish families. All six found Outlaw not guilty and the annals tell us that 'for the great solemnity of his purgation, Brother Roger held a great banquet with all who wished to come'.[36] Presumably the prior joined the celebrations. He would have been well acquainted with important people in Dublin and outside and indeed elaborately entertained many such people in his chamber in Christ Church.[37]

29 Berry, *Register*, pp 172–3.   30 *Stat. Ire., 12–22 Edw. IV*, p. 47. The offence was not revealed until December 1473.   31 Lydon & Fletcher, *Account roll*, p. 94.   32 Ibid., pp 78, 92.   33 Ibid., p. 111.   34 Richardson & Sayles, *Ir. parl.*, p. 206.   35 Richardson & Sayles, *Admin. Ire.*, pp 85–7, 95, 100, 101.   36 Gilbert, *Chart. St Mary's*, ii, 368–9.   37 See Lydon, 'The text and its context' in Lydon & Fletcher, *Account roll*, p. xix.

Lavish and frequent entertainment of guests was possible because of the rich endowment of the priory in land and property, even before the English came to Ireland. It made Christ Church one of the wealthiest religious foundations in the whole of Ireland and provided an annual income well in excess of other houses. It has been estimated that in the modern county Dublin alone the land of Christ Church came to a total of 10,538 acres, most of which had been granted before the arrival of the English.[38] Even as late as 1481 the priory was given licence to accept new donations of land.[39] Since most church land in Ireland, in contrast with England, was held in frankelmoign, or occasionally in fee farm, it was free from the obligation to provide military service to the king.[40] This meant that the land was even more valuable and income not diminished. Rents in Dublin and outside, even if occasionally in arrears, were still substantial and for the most part the priory was well provided with most of the necessities of life from its own estates. Making those properties productive and a source of income could be expensive. Although labour services were required from most tenants on the estates, they were extremely limited in comparison with those enjoyed by the religious houses in England. Consequently labour had to be hired during harvest and at other times during the year and this could be very expensive.[41]

Nevertheless, Christ Church continued to enjoy a healthy income despite such charges. Leases continued to produce annual rents. When land in Balytiper was leased to John son of Walter le Wyte for twenty years, the annual rent increased yearly from 16s. to 26s. 8d., to 40s., and then to 46s. 4d. thereafter.[42] Like other tenants, the lease also specified that John owed suit of court to the prior at Clonkeen. These manorial courts, where fines were imposed and collected for the priory, provided a healthy source of revenue. In 1338, for example, the court of Balscaddan in County Dublin yielded 9s., as well as 3s. 4d. 'received of a certain fine made ... by a certain Irishman of the town of Dermotstown for having entry in 40 acres of land'; in 1344–5 the court at Clonkeen yielded 13s. 2d.

What posed the greatest threat to the financial position of the priory was the attempt of the government, in the first half of the fourteenth century, to exercise royal rights during vacancy in the office of prior. When Prior Hugh

---

38 Otway-Ruthven, 'Church lands', pp 59–61. Compare with 53,200 acres held by the archbishop and only 1,832 acres held by St Patrick's, pp 56, 61.   39 *Stat. Ire., 12–22 Edw. IV*, p. 897.   40 A.J. Otway-Ruthven, 'Knight service in Ireland' in *R.S.A.I. Jn.*, lxxxix (1959), p. 2.   41 Lydon & Fletcher, *Account roll*, pp ix–x.   42 McEnery & Refaussé, *Deeds*, no. 554. Other tenants, such as Robert Haketh at Balytiper, might have to provide 'the customary "scadbolle" of beer, equal to two gallons whenever he brews', McEnery & Refaussé, *Deeds*, no. 646, full text in Lydon & Fletcher, *Account roll*, pp 207–8.

le Jeune resigned in 1326, the escheator moved in and asserted the king's rights to income from all temporalities as escheats, until a new prior was elected and took possession of them. From then on successive escheators attempted to exercise what they claimed to be royal rights, despite the revelations of inquisitions that such rights were non-existent, mainly because the bulk of the priory's temporalities dated from endowments before the English invasion and the creation of the lordship of Ireland. Despite all the efforts of the escheators, they failed to lay their hands on any income. When the audited account of the escheator was enrolled on the pipe roll of 1337, the barons of the Dublin exchequer accepted that he accounted for 'nothing in respect of the rents and issues of the temporalities' of Christ Church which had been taken into the king's hands following the deposition of the prior, Roger Goioun, in that same year. They allowed his claim that the canons had 'levied and received to their own use the issues of the said temporalities ... having no respect to the seisin and possession of the king whereby the escheator could levy nothing'.[43] In 1347 the prior and canons appealed directly to the king in person, complaining of the continuing demands by the treasurer and barons of the Dublin exchequer for monies arising from 'the profits and issues of the temporalities of the priory during various vacancies which were taken into the king's hands by various escheators of Edward II and Edward III'. This was in spite of the fact that the king had ordered an inquisition into the facts and that he be certified of the results. Despite all, the king was never informed of what the inquisition revealed, and indeed others in 1326 and 1338, had shown that 'its granges, lands and tenements [were] given by Irishmen unknown, before the conquest, in free alms to God and the said church, and the canons serving God there'. The king, in reply to this petition, finally on 10 April 1348 ordered the Dublin exchequer 'to restore to Holy Trinity church its temporalities, and not to take them in any future vacancy of the office of prior, but to permit them to hold them as freely as previous to the time when Walter de la Pulle, escheator of Ireland, took them into the king's hands'.[44] No successful attempt was made by any escheator in future to seize temporalities during vacancies.[45]

Despite this long and sometimes bitter controversy, relations with the government and Dublin administration were generally good. Unlike St

---

43 'Cal. pipe roll 11 Edward III' in *P.R.I.rep.D.K. 45*, p. 50.   44 Philomena Connolly, 'The material in the class of chancery warrants series (C 81) in the P.R.O. London' in *Anal. Hib.*, no. 36 (1995), p. 155; *Calendar of close rolls, 1346–9*, p. 441; McEnery & Refaussé, *Deeds*, nos 220, 224, 229–31, 237. As late as 1382 yet another inquisition revealed the *same* facts, no. 253. For an excellent account of the history of this problem see Geoffrey Hand, 'The common law in Ireland in the thirteenth and fourteenth centuries: two cases involving Christ Church, Dublin' in *R.S.A.I. Jn.*, xcvii (1967), pp 105–11. For an earlier incident in 1277 see pp 98–9.   45 Lydon & Fletcher, *Account roll*, pp 156–7.

Patrick's, whose canons, it was claimed by the chapter itself in 1299, were 'for the most part the king's clerks and servants', Christ Church remained aloof from the royal administration.[46] But the priory was valuable to the administration for other reasons. As early as 1278 an issue roll of the Dublin exchequer recorded a payment of 2s. 'for making locks and keys for the chest of the treasury of Holy Trinity'.[47] Sixteen years later the records make it quite clear that this 'treasury' was in fact 'the king's treasury', situated in Christ Church, and that huge sums of money were stored there.[48] It is also clear that the exchequer itself was no longer considered a safe place in which to store the king's money and that the security of Christ Church was preferred. In 1299, 8d. was spent 'on a lock with a key for the door of the treasury at Holy Trinity' and as late as 1316 another payment of 4d. was recorded for the 'repair of a lock with a key in the treasury of Holy Trinity'.[49] But regular payments for the carriage of money back and forth to the treasury in Christ Church each term seem to have ceased in 1309.[50] By then Dublin castle and the exchequer itself had been strengthened, while the priory seemed not to offer the same level of security as in the past.

This was demonstrated in a spectacular robbery in 1311, when the culprits were caught and brought before the court of the justiciar in Dublin. The record of the proceedings tells us that they had broken open 'the coffer' of John of Exeter and stolen from it 'a book and goods to the value of 10s.'. Worse, they had stolen a precious robe, which adorned the statue of St Catherine in the cathedral, which was treated as sacrilege by the court. Perhaps most serious of all, they smashed open 'a trunk there in which money arising from oblations of divers people for the aid of the Holy Land were deposited'. It was revealed in court that it was with the connivance of one of the canons, Brother William de Clifford, that the other thief, who was also a clerk, was able to conceal himself at night in the church and so commit the robbery.[51] Later, in 1466, another thief stole a silver box weighing 33 ozs and valued at £12. 12s., which was never recovered. Fifteen years later parliament enacted that the named thief, then a fugitive, was to come to Dublin castle and remain a prisoner there until he had compensated the priory in the sum of £20. It emerged that the same box had always been kept on the high altar of the church, to hold the blessed sacrament. But it was the loss

---

46 G.J. Hand, *The church in the English lordship 1216–1307* (Dublin, 1968), p. 11. See also Richardson & Sayles, *Admin. Ire.*, p. 2. They also point out that 'common membership of a cathedral chapter doubtless fostered the esprit de corps of the king's ministers and might ease access to those in authority' (p. 3).   47 Philomena Connolly, *Irish exchequer payments 1270–1446* (Dublin, 1998), 27.   48 Connolly, *Ir. exchqr. payments*, p. 121.   49 Ibid., pp 150, 235.   50 Ibid., pp 134–5, 137, 144, 148, 150, 152, 156–8, 161, 167, 172, 174–5, 190, 209.   51 *Cal. justic. rolls Ire.,1308–11*, pp 221–2.

of a valuable piece of property, rather than the sacrilege, which seems to have been uppermost in the minds of all.[52]

It was necessary for Christ Church, as it was for all wealthy institutions and men of property, to keep well in with royal officials. In 1338, for example, a 'present' was bought for the substantial sum of 5½ marks and was sent to the treasurer. In that same year the chancellor, too, was given a gift of wine worth 5 marks. The purpose of such 'gifts' was made quite plain in 1344 when, as we have already seen, the purveyors were openly bribed 'that they may be more favourable to us', at a cost of 2s. 8d. The clerk of the chancellor was given 3s. 4d. as a 'gift of the prior, to have his counsel and help for procuring a certain writ'. And even municipal officials too, were given what the priory accounts call 'a gratuity'.[53]

One particular manifestation of the close relationship of Christ Church with the king's government in Ireland was the holding of sessions of parliament in the priory. We have seen that the prior attended the upper house, while the canons were regularly represented by proctors who joined other clerical proctors in one of the two lower houses.[54] While we cannot be sure of exactly when parliament first assembled in the priory, we do know that it was before the end of the thirteenth century. The legislation of what has been called 'the first real parliament to meet in Ireland', that of 1297, has survived uniquely in a copy preserved in the 'Liber niger' of Christ Church.[55] Not only that, it is almost certain that this 1297 parliament actually met within Christ Church.[56] By the time we reach the fifteenth century there are frequent references to sessions of parliament in the priory. The Naas parliament of May 1478 was informed of a 'false contrived trial, which was proved false before the lords in the fratry of Christ Church Dublin at the time of the parliament there held'.[57] Indeed it seems that the use of the frater was so frequent that in 1455 and 1458 it was actually referred to as 'the common house' where the commons deliberated during sessions of parliament.[58] By the time the mayor and aldermen wrote their famous letter to Cromwell in 1538, protesting against proposals to suppress the priory and confiscate its lands and property, they were able to say that it was in Christ Church that 'the Kynges Graces honorable Parliaments and Counsailles are kepyn'.[59]

---

52 *Stat. Ire., 12–22 Edw. IV*, p. 891.   53 Lydon & Fletcher, *Account roll*, pp 17, 18, 92, 94.   54 Richardson & Sayles, *Ir. parl.*, pp 125, 127, 183, 303; Richardson & Sayles, *Parl. & councils*, p. xxvii.   55 James Lydon (ed.), *Law and disorder in medieval Ireland* (Dublin, 1997), preface and pp 139–61.   56 Lydon, *Law and disorder*, p. 143. The fact that the text of the legislation, as it survives, uses the word hic ('here') twice in the preamble, most notably in recording that those summoned to attend the parliament were 'to be here (hic) on this day', seems proof enough (p. 148).   57 *Stat. Ire., 12–22 Edw. IV*, p. 607. 58 Ibid., p. 361, 525.   59 *S. P. Hen. VIII*, iii, 545.

The priory was also used for other major governmental events, when a large and grand space was required. On 17 July 1331, for example, the earl of Ulster was sworn in as head of the government in Christ Church, 'in full council' ('*in pleno consilio*') we are told.[60] This is surprising, because so many royal officials had connections with St Patrick's that it might be expected that it would be the preferred choice for what we might call great 'state occasions'. When Lionel of Clarence was in Ireland during his momentous period in office as chief governor between 1361 and 1366, he was formally and ceremoniously admitted to the fraternity of the cathedral of St Patrick's.[61] But Christ Church continued to be used for great formal public occasions. On 17 May 1333 a great assembly of notables gathered in the quire of the cathedral before the justiciar of Ireland, the treasurer, two justices, the mayor of Dublin 'and many other people, both clerical and lay'. The earl of Desmond, then held prisoner in Dublin castle on the serious charge of rebellion, was brought in, placed his right hand over the consecrated host, the chalice on the high altar, the gospel book, the holy cross, and the *baculus* of St Patrick, as well as many other famous relics. He swore to observe articles put to him, recorded by a public notary.[62]

It was there, too, that King Richard II, in an elaborate ceremony in 1395, knighted four of the great Irish lords who had earlier made submission to him, O'Neill, Mac Murrough, O'Connor and O'Brien.[63] When news of the fall of Constantinople finally reached Dublin in 1453, it was from Christ Church that the great penitential procession started out. Later, when the papal nuncio, Octavian the archbishop of Armagh, was trying to drum up support for the crusade against the Turks, it was in Christ Church that he chose to preach, granting a plenary indulgence to all who endorsed it.[64] But the most spectacular occasion of all was undoubtedly the great event which took place on 24 May 1487, when Lambert Simnel was crowned king of England and Ireland as Edward VI with a coronet borrowed from a statue of the Blessed Virgin which was held in special reverence in Dublin.[65] Those present included the archbishop of Dublin, the bishops of Kildare, Meath and Cloyne, heads of religious houses (including the prior of Christ Church), many of the leading nobility of Ireland led by Gerald Fitzgerald, the eighth

60 Richardson & Sayles, *Ir. parl.*, p. 29. 61 Hand, 'Camb. MS', p. 21. 62 Richardson & Sayles, *Parl. & councils*, p. 15. He was released from prison in June and in July his lands were restored to him, G.O. Sayles, 'The rebellious first earl of Desmond' in J.A. Watt, J.B. Morrall and F.X. Martin (ed.), *Medieval studies presented to Aubrey Gwynn* (Dublin, 1961), p. 214. 63 Edmund Curtis, *A history of medieval Ireland* (London, 1938), p. 273; Gilbert, *Dublin*, i, 105–6. 64 Mario Sughi, 'The appointment of Octavian de Palatio as archbishop of Armagh' in *I.H.S.*, xxxi, no. 112 (1998), p. 161. 65 Martin, *Crowning of a king*, pp 18–19.

earl of Kildare, and the mayor and other leading Dublin citizens.[66] The young king was then presented to the cheering crowds in a ceremonial procession through the streets around the cathedral, before a magnificent banquet was held in Dublin castle. Subsequently, after the defeat of the rebels at Stoke, the pope (at the request of Henry VII) ordered an inquiry into the part played in these events by the archbishops of Armagh and Dublin and the bishops of Kildare and Meath. Later, in 1488, when royal pardons were issued the list included the prior of Christ Church.[67] When Edgecombe, the royal ambassador, came to Dublin with the king's pardons, he compelled the bishop of Meath, who had preached the sermon at Simnel's coronation, to proclaim publicly again in Christ Church 'as well the Pope's Bull of accursing, and the Absolution for the same, as the Grace whych the Kyng had sent to hym to Pardon to every Man, that would do his Duty unto the King's Hyghness'.[68] What had seemed to be a great day in the history of the cathedral was brought to an ignominious conclusion.

An interesting example of the success of Christ Church in retaining good relations with the Dublin government is the royal warrant of 26 October 1462, which made it possible for Irish pilgrims to visit the cathedral to pray before the many famous relics which were on display there. The letter said that the king, with the assent of the acting chief governor of Ireland, 'takes into his protection all who shall come to the said church [Christ Church], as well English rebels as Irish enemies in time of war or peace for the sake of pilgrimage or presenting alms'.[69] At a time when anti-Irish feelings were rife – as we have seen, for example, the Dublin municipal assembly tried to drive all Irish men and women out of the city, and the government was otherwise engaged in protecting what it called 'the land of peace', later 'the Pale', from 'Irish enemies' – this was an extraordinary favour.

In 1450 when the Irish parliament enacted that 'lands, rents etc. granted by the king' were to be 'resumed into his hands', Christ Church was exempted from the statute. When a similar act was passed in 1460, the priory was once more exempted.[70] An even more important gesture of favour to the priory was

---

66 Michael Bennet, *Lambert Simnel and the battle of Stoke* (Gloucester, 1987), pp 5–6, 66–7. 67 *L. & P. Rich. III & Hen. VII*, i, 95–6; Mario Sughi, 'The Italian connection: the Great Earl and Archbishop Octavian' in *History Ireland*, vii, no. 2 (1999), pp 17–21. The archbishop of Armagh, in fact, vigorously opposed the coronation of Simnel (*L. & P. Rich. III & Hen. VII*, i, 383–4). 68 Donough Bryan, *The great earl of Kildare* (Dublin, 1933), pp 131–2. 69 McEnery & Refaussé, *Deeds*, no. 297. When a similar protection was later enacted in the parliament of 1491 and was confirmed by a provincial council of the archdiocese of Dublin in 1495, it was decreed that 'offenders are to be liable to the greater excommunication' and that 'if they remain obdurate for six days', then there must be an 'interdict on all places where they may be'; also confirmed in similar terms by an Armagh synod in the same year (Lawlor, 'Liber niger', pp 25–6). 70 *Statute rolls of*

the act passed at a later parliament in 1482 that the statute of mortmain was not to apply to Christ Church, which in effect meant that lands could be granted without fear of indictment.[71] As far back as 1324 the mayor and bailiffs of Dublin had complained to the king that despite the statute of mortmain religious houses, and Christ Church in particular, had 'acquired and usurped land and tenements within the city and its boundaries'.[72]

Like other religious houses, Christ Church had to contribute to the clerical subsidies granted to the king by parliaments in which the priory was represented. In the assessment for the subsidy of 1302, the priory 'with all its granges, churches and rents in the diocese of Dublin' was valued at £182. 19s. 8½d.[73] The priory regularly had to contribute its share of clerical subsidies granted in aid of the king's wars, even in Scotland, though nearly always for the wars in Ireland.[74] Indeed, that share was normally excessive. In taxes levied in Dublin, the clergy had to pay one-third and the laity two-thirds. But for the clerical subsidy, Christ Church and St Patrick's were joined together as 'the chapter', and one half of the total was levied on them.[75] Nor did the burden end there, for the prior was regularly employed as one of the assessors in levying the subsidies and then further burdened with the responsibility of collection.[76] He was even on occasion given the added responsibility of presiding over the subsequent accounting of revenues collected.[77]

Involvement in the king's wars did not end with the payment of taxation. Armies had to be fed and the priory was expected to contribute its share of food from its lands when the royal purveyors appeared with their demands. This could cause great hardship, since payment for what was seized was too often postponed, and frequently the purveyors left insufficient to feed animals on priory lands, or even to provide the seed for sowing for the year following. In 1310, when Edward II was preparing to lead yet another great army into Scotland in pursuance of what he claimed were his rights over that kingdom, the purveyors came to Gorman manor and arrested the corn there. But one of the canons, Nicholas, took some of the corn and threshed it. Charged with this offence in court, the prior argued that his men only took what was necessary to feed the animals and to provide seed. The jurors

the parliament of Ireland, reign of King Henry VI, ed. H.F. Berry (Dublin, 1910), pp 183, 175. **71** *Stat. Ire., 12–22 Edw. IV*, p. 896. See also McEnery & Refaussé, *Deeds*, no. 334. It is interesting that the reason behind this licence was the fact that 'divers of their deeds and muniments concerning their very ancient foundation are fallen to ruin and in decay' (p. 897). **72** *Anc. rec. Dublin*, i, 156. The 'laws and usages of the city' specifically ordered that citizens were not to alienate land to religious houses (p. 56). **73** *Cal doc. Ire., 1302–7*, p. 238. **74** Lydon & Fletcher, *Account roll*, pp 16–17, 157–8, Richardson & Sayles, *Parl. & councils*, pp 133, 161–2, 181; *Stat. Ire., 12–22 Edw. IV*, p. 683–5, 931. **75** Richardson & Sayles, *Parl. & councils*, p. xxxv. **76** See for example *Stat. Ire., 12–22 Edw. IV*, pp. 139, 519. **77** Richardson & Sayles, *Ire. parl.*, p 154, n. 69.

accepted this, but also returned that Nicholas had acted without licence, and on his own authority, so he was found guilty as charged. Subsequently he was released on condition that he celebrate 100 masses for the soul of the dead King Edward I.[78]

The priory had to make its own contribution in a more direct way to the defence of the *terra pacis* ('land of peace') in Ireland. In 1317, when the invading army of Robert Bruce was about to threaten the city of Dublin itself, extensive preparations were made for the defence of the metropolis and its environs from the king's enemies. The government, for example, ordered 'that all knights and other free tenants and religious of Fingal in county Dublin' should be summoned 'to make a view of arms to repel the Irish of the Leinster mountains'. The sheriff issued the summonses and among the names of fourteen who did not appear was the prior of Christ Church and he was therefore 'in grave mercy'.[79] On 21 February 1338 the account of the seneschal of the priory records that 3*d*. were spent on wine when the prior entertained the seneschal himself and Walter de Assheburne to dinner. This was before they went 'to ward', one to Kilcullen and the other to Newcastle Mackynegan in Wicklow.[80] A month later the prior himself went to the muster of troops at Clonkeen, followed four days later by the seneschal. Later still, at the end of March, the seneschal and Walter de Asshebourne 'and other men' were on their way to Clonkeen 'with horses armed for making the muster and to keep ward'. Money might have to be spent on providing armour, such as the 11*d*. 'paid for an iron head-piece for the ward'.[81] Later, when the government organised the protection of the area around Dublin, leading to the emergence of what was to become known as 'the Pale', the prior was regularly commissioned to oversee the defences.[82]

The priory's involvement in the defence of the *terra pacis* was in its own interest. Damage to property by Irish enemies and English rebels had greatly reduced income. Indeed, for many of the Dublin religious institutions it had proved impossible to find tenants for lands bordering the Leinster mountains. When the Dublin government in 1462 guaranteed the safety of all pilgrims to Christ Church, 'as well English rebels as Irish enemies', it was because of the loss of income occasioned by 'the injuries by Irish rebels to the property of Holy Trinity Church, Dublin'.[83] Even as late as 1481 the

---

78 *Hist. & mun. doc. Ire.*, pp 515–17.   79 Ibid., p. 383.   80 Lydon & Fletcher, *Account roll*, pp 9, 153–4.   81 Ibid, pp 12–13, 18. Tenants acquiring a lease might have to undertake to provide military service to the prior when required to do so, as did Robert Hakett in 1352 when he leased Tipperstone in county Dublin (p. 208).   82 See, for example, the statute of the 1455 parliament ordering that fords, bridges and river crossings were to be guarded to keep 'rebels' out, under the oversight of the prior and some others (*Stat. Ire., Hen. VI*, p. 315).   83 McEnery & Refaussé, *Deeds*, no. 297.

CHRIST CHURCH IN THE LATER MEDIEVAL IRISH WORLD 89

priory was licensed to accept land endowments.[84] Benefactions were always welcome, especially within the safer environs of Dublin. Not only was property left to the priory, sums of money were regularly bequeathed. In his will dated 30 January 1476, Peter Higley left 20s. 'to be taken out of the rent of the house in which Henry Barbor lives, in St Patrick-street'.[85]

Decline in revenues derived from land and leases made the rights enjoyed by the priory over fishing in the Liffey all the more important.[86] Over the years disputes over these rights with other religious institutions, the Dublin municipality and individuals were often protracted and sometimes bitter. It was not until July 1500 that the right of Christ Church to 'tithes of fish taken in Anilyffy' was finally accepted by St Mary's abbey after arbitration by independent assessors.[87] It was agreed that the abbey had a right to 'half the tithes of fish landed on the north side of the Fyr pole which belongs to the abbot and convent of the B.V.M. and that marks should be erected to define the Fyr pole'. This would prevent disputes in the future and in the following September two men went around and in the presence of the prior and abbot marked out the area 'with stakes and stones'.[88] One unfortunate individual, John Dyrre, a fisherman of a boat belonging to St Mary's, was formally charged by Christ Church in March 1425 with retaining tithes due for fish caught. He was found guilty by the court and sentenced to pay the tithes, two salmon or their value at 2s., as well the costs of the action, put at the huge sum of 49s. But worst of all, perhaps, 'by way of penalty for his long detention of the tithes' it was ordered that he should, 'on six days up to the feast of Pentecost, be beaten around St Michan's church [of which he was a parishioner], naked save for a loin-cloth, by the curate'.[89]

Disputes with the city authorities were more complicated. Although as early as 1180 Archbishop Lorcán Ua Tuathail of Dublin had confirmed to Christ Church not only the fishing tithes, but also a fishery as well, a later charter of King John in 1215 made a perpetual grant to the city of 'the citizens part of the water of the River Liffey together with his part of the same water, with reservations of the boats others have of ancient tenure'.[90] This inevitably led to disputes and Christ Church did not escape. In 1281 the municipality accepted the rights of Christ Church to the fishery tithes.[91] After

84 *Stat. Ire., 12–22 Edw. IV*, p. 897.   85 Berry, *Register*, pp 130–1. Frequently sums of money were left in wills 'to the works' of Christ Church, pp 28, 39, 56, 131.   86 In general see A.E. Went, 'Fisheries of the River Liffey' in Clarke, *Medieval Dublin: living city*, pp 182–91.   87 McEnery & Refaussé, *Deeds*, nos 372–3; Gilbert, *Chart. St. Mary's*, ii, 14; Lawlor, 'Liber niger', p. 26.   88 Lawlor, 'Liber niger', p. 27. For a full description of the area in which fishing tithes belonged to Christ Church see p. 25; McEnery & Refaussé, *Deeds*, no. 360.   89 Lawlor, 'Liber niger', p. 13.   90 *Anc. rec. Dublin*, i, 6; *Cal. doc. Ire., 1171–1251*, pp 89–90; *Hist. & mun. docs. Ire.*, p. 63.   91 Lawlor, 'Liber niger', pp. 12, 66.

another dispute in 1338 it was found on inquiry that the priory had 'right to tithes of fish caught in the burgage of Dublin' and that seems to have settled the matter.[92]

The Dublin city authorities were bitter about the failure, as they saw it, of religious houses within the borough to provide their fair share of what was needed for the defence of the metropolis. This was one reason why they officially resented the granting of property within the borough to such houses, though in practice there is no real evidence that individuals were in fact prevented from making grants. In fact, Christ Church does seem to have been bound by law in this matter. In July 1395, for example, when four citizens were licensed by the king to grant seven shops in Trinity Lane to the priory, it was specified that they were to be 'held in free burgage by the service of landgable', the tax levied for the defence of the city.[93]

Relations with the municipality were otherwise generally good. Of all the great religious houses in Dublin, such as All Hallows, St Thomas's, St John of Jerusalem or St Mary's abbey, Christ Church was the only one within the walls, close to the heart of municipal life. This was well expressed in 1538 by the mayor and aldermen of Dublin in a letter to Cromwell, when they pointed out that the cathedral 'standith in the middes of the said citie and chambre, in like manner as Paules Church is in London'.[94] It was close to the Tholsel, the Guildhall in Winetavern Street and other centres of the commercial as well as the municipal life of Dublin. The cistern which supplied the city with water was actually situated near the gate of Christ Church, from which a viaduct supplied the priory.[95] And the market cross, at which all sorts of important proclamations were given their first public airing to the citizens of Dublin, was only yards away.[96]

The centrality of Christ Church to civic life was manifested in an extraordinary event in 1306. Thomas Cantok, chancellor and the second most important man (after the justiciar) in the government of Ireland, was made bishop of Emly in that year. He chose to be consecrated 'with great honour' in Christ Church, the Dublin annals tell us, 'at whose consecration were the great men of all Ireland, with such a full banquet, first for the rich and afterwards for the poor, such as been unheard of in Ireland in times past'.[97] Eleven years later another event, recorded in the Dublin annals, again shows how central the cathedral was to Dublin. On 14 October 1327 seven partridges came in a line to the city and settled on the 'summit' of the brew-house of

92 Ibid., p. 58.   93 McEnery & Refaussé, *Deeds*, no. 259.   94 *S.P. Hen. VIII*, iii, 545.
95 *Anc. rec. Dublin*, i, 86–9. See also Valentine Jackson, 'The inception of the Dodder water supply' in Clarke, *Medieval Dublin: metropolis*, pp 128–41.   96 H.S. Crawford, 'The market cross of Dublin' in Clarke, *Medieval Dublin: metropolis*, pp 252–3.   97 Gilbert, *Chart. St Mary's*, ii, 333–4.

the priory. Dubliners, it was recorded, came to see and admire the spectacle. Some boys captured two of the birds alive and killed a third. The other birds then flew away to some nearby fields, which was taken as a sign of some calamity to come.[98] It was in Christ Church, too, that the archbishop, Alexander Bicknor, chose to preach a famous sermon against the sin of sloth, when he condemned the number of beggars in the city. In it, we are told, he cursed all those who refused to follow a trade, with the result that the mayor subsequently denied admission to all idlers.[99]

Christ Church had a special place in the hearts of Dubliners. Leading citizens were anxious to be buried there, making specific provision for this in their wills. In 1469, James Selyman, 'citizen of Dublin', bequeathed his 'body to be buried in the cloister of the cathedral metropolitan church of Holy Trinity', but surprisingly made no specific bequest to the priory.[100] This is remarkable as in the 'Book of obits' his death is recorded and he is described as a member of the fraternity ('*frater nostre congrationis*').[101] This meant that every year on the anniversary of his death prayers were offered for his soul by the community of the priory. Letters of fraternity would have been issued to him during his life, making him in name a participant in the religious services of the priory.[102]

Probably the most remarkable arrangement for sharing in the religious services of the priory was that made for John de Grauntsete in July 1335. He was granted, with his wife Alice, 'and all for whom they are bound as well living as dead, participation as full as the founder of our said church in all masses, matins, preces, prayers, fasts, alms, suffrages, vigils, disciplines, and in all other good deeds which by the help of God may be done, within our said church and priory as long as the world shall last'. The full arrangements are too complex to be briefly related, specifying not only the collects and other prayers to be recited at each mass while John was alive, but also the special prayers which were to be included after his death.[103] The extraordinary feature of this arrangement is that neither John nor his wife seems to have been a member of the confraternity, and while her name is entered in the 'Book of obits', his is not.[104]

Christ Church also had close relations with the municipal authorities. This is perhaps best epitomised by the fact that on 29 September 1307, at a

98 Ibid., ii, 380. 99 Ibid., ii, xiv–xv; Mason, *St Patrick's*, p. 135. 100 Berry, *Register*, p. 7. 101 Crosthwaite & Todd, *Obits*, p. 22. 102 Ibid., p. xxvii. It should be noticed that women, too, could become members of the fraternity and are recorded as *soror* (sister) in the obits. For burials see Drew, 'Ancient chapter house', p. 180. For the fraternity of St Patrick's cathedral see Hand, 'Camb. MS', p. 26. 103 Lydon & Fletcher, *Account roll*, pp 148–51; for short version see McEnery & Refaussé, *Deeds*, no. 225 and below, pp 134–5. 104 Crosthwaite & Todd, *Obits*, p. 27.

meeting of the Dublin assembly in the chapel of Blessed Mary in Christ Church, it was agreed that a meeting would be held there every year on the same date to elect a mayor of Dublin.[105] They tolerated the use of Christ Church as a safe refuge and in 1497 formally confirmed the right of sanctuary at a meeting of the assembly on 21 July: 'anyone who takes refuge there is not to be arrested within the precinct'.[106] As we have seen already, they guaranteed the safety of pilgrims, even if they were enemies of the king. Sometimes the city showed its concern for the priory in a more immediate and practical way. In 1308, when a scarcity of food threatened the priory with serious problems, made worse by a lack of means with which to buy corn, the prior decided that they would have to borrow the necessary money. He sent to the mayor of Dublin, John le Decer, plate valued at £40 as a pledge. But in a significant gesture of generosity the mayor returned the plate and with it twenty barrels of corn.[107]

The commercial community of Dublin was bound to Christ Church in a very special way. The guild of Holy Trinity, as the very name suggests, had an intimate connection with the cathedral, and more particularly with the chapel of that name. On 30 June 1451 the king confirmed the legislation of a parliament held in Drogheda, which made provision for a number of people 'to found anew a brotherhood or guild of the craft of merchants of the city of Dublin'. Both men and women were to be members, attached to the chapel in Christ Church. Elaborate regulations were laid down as to procedure and the members had a monopoly of buying and selling within the city.[108] This, in fact, seems to have been the incorporation of the old guild, rather than the creation of a new one.[109]

There was another guild, or 'fraternity', in Dublin which had Christ Church connections. This was the fraternity of St Edmund, associated with the chapel of that name which the English had established in Christ Church not long after they arrived in Ireland in the twelfth century. In 1466 a municipal ordinance recorded the names of the master and two wardens, who were responsible for what was called 'the ordinance of arrows'. This seems to have been a way of providing timber for the manufacture of arrows, presumably for the defence of the city.[110]

---

105 *Hist. & mun. doc. Ire.*, pp 227–8.   106 *Anc. rec. Dublin*, i, 383.This was confirmed by the archbishop of Dublin at a provincial council held in Christ Church on 21 September 1512 (McEnery & Refaussé, *Deeds*, no. 398). Right of sanctuary could hinder the judicial rights of the Dublin municipality, as in the 1260s when a thief was given sanctuary in Christ Church and from there was allowed to travel to Swords where sanctuary continued in the church there until he 'made his peace there' with the archbishop (*Alen's reg.*, p. 105).   107 Archdall, *Mon. Hib.*, p. 161.   108 Berry, 'Records', pp 49–51. 109 John Webb, *The guilds of Dublin* (Dublin, 1929), p. 14. Ch. 1 contains a good account of the history of this guild.   110 *Anc. rec. Dublin*, i, 325. Another ordinance on the

There is another manifestation of the Dublin context within which Christ Church functioned. In the martyrology of the cathedral many Irish saints were added to the calendar whose provenance was the diocese of Dublin – St Fintan of Howth, St Begnet of Dalkey and others. But what is more extraordinary is the huge number of other Irish saints whose feast days are inserted, eighteen in all.[111] This is a reminder that despite the inevitable anglicisation of the Irish church which occurred after the English invasion, veneration of local Irish saints returned after a time. There is no doubt that the celebration of such feast-days brought people from well outside Dublin to the cathedral. But much more important in attracting pilgrims from afar was the great collection of precious relics which was preserved in Christ Church. Some of these were exotic, to say the least: a thorn from the crown of thorns worn by Jesus; a portion of the cloth in which he was wrapped as a baby; some of the milk of the Blessed Virgin Mary (*'de lacte beate Marie virginis'*). There were many more, as well as many relics of Irish saints, including bones of St Patrick, St Brigid and St Columba. But it is interesting that in what may be called the official list of relics, primacy of place was given to the Cross (which was supposed to contain a fragment of the True Cross), followed by the staff of Jesus (*'Baculus Ihesu quem angelus beato Patricio conferebat'* – 'the staff of Jesus which an angel had conferred on blessed Patrick').[112]

The Cross was especially venerated and was frequently mentioned in wills. One citizen left 'to the Cross of Holy Trinity a silk girdle well ornamented and two rings with jewels'.[113] Agreements were regularly concluded solemnly before it, as in 1473 when a long controversy over land was finally settled, 'to which arrangement [the parties] were sworn on the Rood of Christchurch'.[114] But the staff of Jesus, too, was often employed as a solemn guarantee, as indeed it had been regularly employed in many parts of Ireland before it was removed from Armagh to Dublin after the English occupation of the ecclesiastical capital.[115] An interesting example of the importance attached to such relics by the people of Dublin is the fact that they were always willing to augment them where possible. In 1405, we are told, the citizens of Dublin raided Wales 'and there did much mischief'. But the most

same day stipulated that 'every constable in his quarter see that householders and their men have weapons according to their degree', and to punish them on holidays 'when the weather is according', for 'quoiting' instead of practising their archery (pp 325–6). **111** Crosthwaite & Todd, *Obits*, pp xlvi–xlix. **112** Ibid., p. 3. The best account of the relics is still that by Todd, pp vi–xxiii. **113** McEnery & Refaussé, *Deeds*, no. 513. **114** *Stat. Ire., 12–22 Edw. IV*, p. 155. **115** For the history of the *baculus Ihesu* see Robert Meyer, *The life and death of Saint Malachy the Irishman* (Kalamazoo, 1978), p. 137; M.V. Ronan, 'St Patrick's staff and Christ Church' in Clarke, *Medieval Dublin: living city*, pp 135–43.

significant result of the raid was that they 'brought away the shrine of St Cubius and placed it in the church of this priory'.[116]

Perhaps the greatest single manifestation of the special regard in which Christ Church was held in late medieval Ireland was the magnificent endowment of 26 July 1488 by a group of people, headed by Gerald Fitzgerald, the earl of Kildare. Two days later Christ Church agreed to an elaborate arrangement of daily masses and a special sung mass each Thursday for the benefactors, their relatives and friends.[117] The liturgy to be used was detailed, including the ringing of 'the great bell'. It is probably no coincidence that this occurred shortly after the arrival of Sir Richard Edgecombe, the royal ambassador, with terms of pardon for Kildare and others who had been involved in the Lambert Simnel affair. But the endowment, in fact, had been initiated three years earlier by John Estrete, the king's serjeant at laws and a close confidant of Kildare. He was obviously well connected with Christ Church as well, a wealthy man who had acquired much property in and around Dublin.[118] On 23 July 1485 he endowed Christ Church with land to support 'a canon to celebrate mass of the Holy Ghost for ever'. Later, on 8 October, he made provision for 'a mass in the chapel of St Laurence O'Toole, in the north aisle near the high choir'. This was to be supplemented after his death with another large endowment for a daily mass 'and every Thursday to cause the choir to sing a mass' for his soul.[119] Significantly he included his 'benefactors' in the sung Thursday mass, among them the earl of Kildare, Robert fitz Eustace (treasurer) and others who were party to the later 1488 endowment. Christ Church, at the very heart of the capital of the lordship of Ireland, continued to hold its place as what it called itself in 1300, 'the mother church'.

---

116 Archdall, *Mon. Hib.*, p. 165.   117 McEnery & Refaussé, *Deeds*, nos 1090–1.   118 Ibid., nos 1028, 1047, 1058, 1063–8, 1077, 1089. He had earlier received property in the city which he in turn granted away to two clerics, who later granted valuable property in the city to Estrete, which were then absorbed into the Kildare benefaction (nos 348, 352). 119 McEnery & Refaussé, *Deeds*, nos 348, 349.

V

The architecture of the cathedral and priory buildings, 1250–1530

Roger Stalley

By 1250, as a result of two distinct architectural campaigns, Christ Church had reached the size which it enjoys today. This did not mark the end of construction. Before the nave was finished, it must have been obvious that the short eastern limb was inadequate for the ceremonies associated with a major cathedral: there was little space around the high altar, there was no room for a feretory to display relics, and the stalls of the canons were pushed into the eastern bay of the nave, restricting the space available for the laity.[1] The cathedral of 1250 was, in liturgical terms, a most inconvenient building. It is not therefore surprising that a decision was made to extend the late Romanesque chancel to the east, forming what came to be known as the 'long quire'. In its eventual form this quire was over 100 feet long, a length which almost matched that of the nave; the cathedral thus acquired an element of symmetry, with two arms extending equally east and west of the crossing.[2] (Plate 5) The 'long quire' survived until 1872, when it was demolished to make way for Street's reinstatement of what he supposed was the original late twelfth-century chancel. Street confidently declared that 'the completely modern character' of all the features of the long quire 'made its preservation of no importance whatsoever from an antiquarian point of view'.[3] But what

1 The quire screen was placed to the west of the western arch of the crossing. Street states that he found two or three stones in situ below the floor about ten feet to the west of the crossing, Street & Seymour, p. 90. 2 Butler, *Measured drawings* gives an internal measurement of 105 feet 3 inches for the quire, whereas the plan in the C6/4, gives it as 109 feet. 3 Street, *Report, 1871*, p. 3. Street was not alone in his opinion. Many years earlier Bell had commented that the quire was 'a confused jumble of styles' and that there had been 'so many alterations in the last two centuries that there is little traces [*sic*] of the original Gothic character left' (T. Bell, *An essay on the origins and progress of Gothic architecture with reference to the ancient history and present state of the remains of such architecture in Ireland* (Dublin, 1829), p. 148).

exactly did the 'long quire' look like and was it as dull as Street maintained? Photographs taken before 1871 show it after it had been 'restored' under the direction of Matthew Price between 1830 and 1833. (Plates 22, 24b) More valuable are a series of drawings and prints made before the Price restoration, which provide a general impression of its appearance in the middle ages.[4] (Plates 23, 24a)

In order to extend the quire, it was necessary to demolish the late Romanesque apse; two twelfth-century arches immediately preceding the apse were retained, but the three arches to the east were removed. The remodelled quire was flanked by aisles, that on the south side extending almost to the east wall of the presbytery.[5] (Plate 5) The north aisle terminated well before the east end, as this area was occupied by the Lady chapel. About half way along its length, the axis of the 'long quire' shifted several degrees to the north, a change in alignment which allowed the builders to integrate the south wall of the Lady chapel with the new work.[6] From an aesthetic point of view, this was disconcerting, 'rude and unsightly' to use the words of Street.[7] As one looked east from the crossing, it was obvious that the large traceried window that filled the east wall was set at an angle.[8] Equally disturbing was the lack of regularity in the piers, lengthy sections of wall intervening between the arches that opened into the aisles. Nor were the arches north and south aligned. (Plate 22) They were not even made of the same material. While the second opening on the north side was made of stones taken from the centre arch of the former Romanesque apse,[9] the corresponding arch to the south, although Romanesque in appearance, was modelled in stucco, an arrangement presumably dating from the early nineteenth century. It was constructed with a simple two-storey elevation, without a triforium, and the crowns of the main arches appear to have come uncomfortably close to the base of the clerestory windows. One gets the impression of a building that was not designed as an integrated composition.

Drawings and prints made before 1830 show that the windows were filled with 'switchline' or intersecting tracery, a type universal in late medieval

4 Francis Grose, *The antiquities of Ireland* (London 1791–5), i, plate opposite p. 5 (the engraving was made after a drawing by Bigari dated 1780); Robert O'Callaghan Newenham, *Picturesque views of the antiquities of Ireland* (Dublin, 1826); watercolour of the cathedral from the south *c.*1800, C6/4/1; drawing by George Petrie, Royal Irish Academy collections. 5 The plan in Butler, *Measured drawings*, and the plan in C/6/4 show the south aisle stretching to the east wall of the quire, but these of course post-date the 1830–33 restoration. Pre-1830 drawings indicate that the aisle stopped one bay short of the east end of the quire, a point born out by the extended length of the final window on the south side. 6 Butler, *Measured drawings*; plan in C6/3/4. 7 Street & Seymour, p. 92. 8 Changes of alignment are of course not uncommon in medieval churches, though usually a shift in axis comes at the crossing. 9 Butler, *Christ Church*, pp 12–13.

Ireland.[10] (Plates 23a, 24a) The east window, as illustrated in a painting of c.1824, was divided into five lights, and this too was furnished with switchline tracery, apparently set under a semi-circular enclosing arch.[11] The painting suggests that the structure was in a precarious state, with timber props preventing the south aisle from collapse. The external walls were surmounted by stepped battlements, incorporating a wall-walk at the base of the roof, the wall-walk itself continuing across the east end of the quire in front of the gable.[12] Flanking the east window were square turrets containing spiral staircases.[13]

Although the enlargement of the quire did not affect the layout of the twelfth-century crypt, the alterations meant that the walls and piers of the crypt no longer coincided with the structure above. In fact solid sections of masonry in the new quire were constructed directly over voids, massive weights being supported on relatively thin panels of groin vaulting; it was a rather hazardous arrangement that somehow survived until 1872 without causing any serious problems.[14]

Documentary sources leave us in no doubt that the 'long quire', or at least a substantial portion of it, was constructed in the time of Archbishop John de St Paul (1349–62). The obits record that he built the quire '*de novo*',[15] and the 'Liber niger' explains that he 'erected the quire with the archiepiscopal throne, the great window on the eastern side of the high altar, and three other windows on the southern side between the great window and the throne'.[16] The economic difficulties of fourteenth-century Ireland, together with the trauma of the Black Death, meant that the decade between 1350 and 1360 was not a propitious time for building. In fact the form of the 'long quire', with its irregularities in planning, its simple tracery, and its re-use of old materials, appears consistent with a building campaign carried out in difficult circumstances. The history of the 'long quire' is not, however, as straightforward as hitherto assumed.

It is significant that the account of the founding of the cathedral in the 'Liber niger' lists the windows erected by the archbishop, rather than giving him credit for the building as a whole. The account mentions three windows that he built on the south side, yet we know that this part of the quire con-

---

10 Leask, *Irish churches*, iii, 117–20.   11 The drawing by Petrie in the Royal Irish Academy dated to 1821 shows the outer arch as slightly pointed.   12 This arrangement, which dates from after 1461 was common in late medieval tower houses, H.G. Leask, *Irish castles* (Dundalk, 1964), p. 86.   13 Nineteenth-century plans in Butler, *Measured drawings*, and the plan C6/3/4, show only the northern turret with a staircase, but McVittie explicitly states that there were two circular stairs beside the east window, McVittie, *Restoration*, p. 28.   14 The point was noted by Street in Street & Seymour, p. 92n.   15 Refaussé & Lennon, *Registers*, p. 70.   16 Lawlor, 'Liber niger', p. 69; Street & Seymour, 1882, p. 16.

tained at least five windows in the clerestory alone. Nor does the description refer to any north-facing windows. From this it is apparent that Archbishop John's work was limited to the eastern section of the 'long quire', where the walls of the Lady chapel prevented the insertion of windows to the north. (Plate 5) It is also worth remembering that the word '*chorum*', used in the documents, may well apply to the liturgical choir rather than to the architectural fabric. While Archbishop John certainly erected a new throne and established four new windows, he should not be given credit for the entire building.

The 'long quire' was not therefore constructed in a single campaign, a point confirmed by scrutiny of the pre-1830 drawings. (Plate 24a) The first clues can be seen in the arrangement of the windows. Those in the southern clerestory varied in both height and design: to the west came a pair of two-light windows, which were followed by a pair of three-light openings set lower in the wall. The final window to the east, was taller than all the others. Similar discrepancies in the aisle windows were noted by Bell in 1829, who added that the old stonework was 'so totally decayed, being of a soft sandy nature, that little idea can be formed of its original appearance'.[17] A further clue to the history of the building can be found in the roof over the south aisle, which was designed in two distinct sections and built at different levels. The drawings show two buttresses supporting the main walls of the quire, one of which descends behind the aisle roof. These observations indicate that the eastern half of the quire was constructed in a separate campaign and that it was originally built without an aisle, the latter being tacked on at a subsequent date. The aisleless extension included the very windows mentioned in the 'Liber niger' as being the work of Archbishop John. He was not, however, responsible for the western section of the chancel, which had already been modified many years before.

A memorandum in the 'Liber niger' records that 'in 1281, in the time of prior Adam Delamore, the new work of the presbytery was begun'.[18] Construction was probably still in progress in 1289 when a number of Irish bishops granted indulgences to those who by legacy or gift promoted the building of Holy Trinity Church.[19] Unfortunately we have no knowledge of what these operations entailed. The Romanesque apse was probably demolished at this stage, to be replaced by a chancel with at least two straight bays, but exactly how the quire terminated it is impossible to say. Nor is it clear what happened to the chapels opening off the former ambulatory. Although the amount of extra space acquired in such an operation would not have been extensive, there may have been gains in the area immediately around the high altar.

17 Bell, *Essay*, pp 147–8.   18 Lawlor, 'Liber niger', p. 66.   19 McEnery & Refaussé, *Deeds*, no. 144.

One building which has a major bearing on these developments is the Lady chapel. This was situated to the north-east of the cathedral on a site now occupied by the chapter house. (Plates 5, 21a) Regrettably, the history of the chapel is as confusing as that of the chancel. The 'Liber niger' states that it was erected *after* the 'long quire', a statement which is difficult to equate with the architectural evidence.[20] A study of the early plans suggests that the chapel already existed when Archbishop John de St Paul's workmen incorporated the south wall of the chapel into the fabric of the new quire, a decision that brought about the change of axis.[21] In this area of the cathedral there is a Gothic arch with moulded capitals, said to come from a passage which led into the chapel. Although much restored (and probably moved from its original location) the arch is of thirteenth-century character. Putting these shreds of evidence together, it is more likely that the Lady chapel was erected in the late thirteenth century, perhaps in the 1280s or 1290s following the remodelling of the quire, and that it was originally a free-standing building, located north of the main axis of the cathedral.[22]

It is now possible to summarise the sequence of events which determined the architecture of the quire. The late Romanesque quire was remodelled in the 1280s, an operation which may have been followed by the construction of the Lady chapel. The central body of the quire was then extended eastwards in an aisleless form by Archbishop John de St Paul between 1349–62. At some unknown date between 1362 and 1485 an aisle was added at the south side of the quire extension.[23]

There is one further event that throws light on this part of the cathedral. A note in the 'Liber niger' recounts that on 19 July 1461 a great storm blew in the east window and the 'falling stones broke many chests containing jewels, relics, ornaments, and vestments of the altar, and muniments, among the rest the foundation charter of Henry II ... By a miracle the staff of Jesus, though the chest in which it was kept and other relics therein were destroyed, was found uninjured lying above the stones'.[24] The fact that the chests lay

20 Gwynn, 'Origins', p. 48. 21 The 'Liber niger' adds that after the addition of the chancel 'the citizens moved by a miracle of St Laurence built the great chapel of St Mary on the north side of the *cancellum*', Gwynn, 'Origins', p. 48. The problem with this statement is that the new chancel clearly made use of the pre-existing wall of the Lady chapel. If the Lady chapel had not existed before the construction of the quire extension, windows would have been constructed to the north, and these are specifically excluded by the note in the 'Liber niger'. 22 If the Lady chapel was founded before the 'long quire' as suggested in the text, it would have been more logical to build it on the site of the future 'long quire'. Presumably this site (the location of Archbishop John of St Paul's extension) was not yet available for building. 23 This aisle existed by 1485 when it housed an altar to the Holy Ghost, a dedication changed at about that time to St Laurence O'Toole, Boydell, *Music*, p. 32. 24 Lawlor, 'Liber niger', p. 56.

close to the east window suggests that some sort of feretory existed behind the high altar. There is no reference to damage to the high altar itself, which was presumably situated well forward of the window, the space behind providing an enclosed area.[25] The following year the east window had still not been rebuilt. Edward IV agreed to take pilgrims going to Christ Church under his protection 'considering the injuries by Irish rebels to the property of Holy Trinity Church, Dublin, and the destruction of the two chief windows, comonly called Gabilles, which cannot be restored without the aid of Christians and the oblations of pilgrims'.[26] The reference to two 'Gabilles' implies that the west facade or possibly one of the transepts was also damaged in the storm. The five-light switchline window illustrated in the painting of c.1824 presumably relates to the rebuilding after 1462, so too the flanking turrets.[27] (Plate 23a) The latter recalls the turrets encountered in fifteenth-century parish churches in the Pale, notably those at Killeen and Dunsany.[28] Remains of the great east window were discovered during demolition work in 1872, as McVittie explained:

> In an old wall, about forty feet out from the end of the present presbyterium, was found the cill of a large window, the jamb of a door, and part of two circular stairs, one on either side of the large window. Many stones, supposed to have been part of this large window, were found buried beneath it. Some of them red sandstone, and different in details from any in the present building.[29]

Whether the stones pre-dated or post-dated the storm of 1461 is impossible to say, as few if any were preserved. Indeed the huge cache of worked stones which was salvaged during the restoration of 1871–8 contains almost nothing from the 'long quire' (Street's contempt for the building seems to have extended even to the masonry). The one tangible relic of the 'long quire' is an amorphous piece of buttressing, situated on the lawn to the south of the chapter house, a quietly decaying relic which perpetuates the memory of the ancient building and provides a permanent reminder of its length.[30]

---

25 An alternative explanation would be to assume that the eastern bay of the quire functioned as some sort of treasury, being sealed off from the rest of the quire. 26 McEnery & Refaussé, *Deeds*, no. 297. 27 Bell, *Essay*, p. 147, states that 'the great eastern window is circularly arched and seems to have been erected about the same period when that of the nave was rebuilt', i.e. after 1562. It seems more logical to suppose that the window dates from the reconstruction after the storm of 1461. 28 Leask, *Irish churches*, iii, 12–15. There are also parallels with the turrets at the west end of St Patrick's cathedral. 29 McVittie, *Restoration*, p. 28n. In her examination of the dressed stonework, stored until 1999 in the crypt, Rachel Moss identified a number of tracery fragments carved in red sandstone. These may well be part of the material described by McVittie. 30 The stones

The progressive enlargement of the quire of Christ Church corresponds to a pattern that can be discerned elsewhere in Ireland and Britain. During the course of the thirteenth century a number of English cathedrals built large eastern extensions in order to provide an appropriate setting for their major shrine. Thus, between 1234 and 1252, Bishop Northwold of Ely demolished the apse of his Romanesque cathedral and extended the chancel by five bays in honour of St Etheldreda.[31] Similar operations were carried out on an even more magnificent scale at Lincoln (1256–80) and at St Paul's cathedral in London (1256–1312). The impetus for these extensions ultimately came from Canterbury, where the reconstruction of the cathedral after the fire of 1174 included a splendid feretory for the shrine of Becket behind the high altar. As an important pilgrimage church, Christ Church must have been conscious of the lack of space in which to display its relics and shrines. The new extension certainly improved the situation, allowing for a more spacious sanctuary around the high altar, and perhaps a separate feretory behind. To the west, beyond the archbishop's throne, came the stalls of the canons, which were closed off from the rest of the church by a screen, located on the line of the eastern crossing piers.[32] The effect of Archbishop John's work was thus to concentrate the more sacred activities of the cathedral within the eastern limb, while at the same time releasing space for the laity in the area of the crossing. The screen was a solid structure, constructed in stone, with a doorway in the centre.[33] The door itself was provided with a lock to prevent undesirables entering the quire.[34] Above the screen were paintings of the Passion of Christ, a choice of subject that was associated with the design of quire screens throughout the medieval church.[35] A gallery or loft ran along the top of the screen, where a large crucifix or rood was displayed, accompanied most probably by the grieving figures of St John and the Virgin Mary.[36]

Previous building at Christ Church, both in the late Romanesque era and in the early Gothic period, had involved teams of workmen, at least some of whom had been trained in England. There is no evidence that this was the

mark the south-east corner of the former quire. 31 Peter Draper, 'Bishop Northwold and the Cult of St Etheldreda' in Nicola Coldstream and Peter Draper (ed.), *Medieval art and architecture at Ely cathedral* (London, 1979), pp 8–27. 32 The position of the late medieval screen under the eastern arch of the crossing is confirmed by many references in the account roll of 1564–5, Gillespie, *Proctor's accounts, passim.* 33 During the repairs undertaken in 1564 the floor of the rood loft was used for heavy building activities, which seems to rule out the possibility of a wooden screen. 34 C6/1/26/2. 35 Gillespie, *Proctor's accounts*, p. 39. 36 There are various sixteenth-century comments relating to the need to sweep the rood loft, Gillespie, *Chapter act book*, p. 25. One of the few (retrospective) references to the rood itself can be found in the proctor's accounts for 1564, Gillespie, *Proctor's accounts*, p. 37.

case with Archbishop John's extension. In terms of design it appears to have been an impoverished piece of work, (Plates 5, 24a) lacking even the geometrical tracery introduced into the quire at Tuam, begun by Archbishop William de Bermingham shortly before 1312.[37] In fact the simple 'switchline' tracery recalls the type of work encountered in early friaries, as in the chancel of the Dominican friary at Kilmallock founded in 1291.[38] It is of course possible that the pre-1461 east window was a more magnificent affair, but the absence of dressed masonry from the 'long quire' as a whole makes it difficult to evaluate the design with any confidence. The modest plan, with its aisleless chancel, can be paralleled in several Irish cathedrals, as at Cashel and Tuam, as well as in the Augustinian abbeys at Kells and Athassel. Despite his English background, Archbishop John's architectural vision did not apparently extend beyond the limits of his archbishopric. This contrasts with the approach of the prior, Stephen of Derby, who, at the very time the quire was under construction, acquired a magnificent psalter illuminated by one of the major English scriptoria.[39]

The other important addition to the cathedral during the middle ages was the crossing tower, which, though rebuilt and remodelled on a number of occasions, still survives today. (Plates 1, 21a, 24a) The history of the tower is hard to disentangle. The account of the cathedral contained in the 'Liber niger' states that a belfry (campanile) was erected by Lorcán Ua Tuathail and the Anglo-Normans soon after 1170.[40] Just over a hundred years later, in 1283, a fire, which destroyed part of the city of Dublin, also injured the campanile of the cathedral.[41] There is no mention of damage to the rest of the church and it is difficult to understand how a fire could have reached a crossing tower without causing harm elsewhere, unless of course the belfry was a free-standing structure or built to one side of the cathedral. In 1316

---

37 Leask, *Irish churches*, ii, 131–2. The quire at Tuam was built as part of an ambitious scheme to replace the old Romanesque cathedral. Only the quire was completed, though the footings of the north transept have recently been revealed, Miriam Clyne, 'Excavations at St Mary's cathedral, Tuam, Co. Galway' in *Journal of the Galway Archaeological Society*, xlv (1987–8), pp 90–103.   38 Arlene Hogan, *Kilmallock Dominican friary* (Kilmallock, 1991); Leask, *Irish churches*, iii, 117–20.   39 See pp 16–17 for details of this psalter.   40 Gwynn, 'Origins', p. 47.   41 The fire of 1283 is recorded in the annals of St Mary's Dublin: '*Combusta est civitas Dublin pro parte, et campanile ecclesie Sancte Trinitatis iii nonas Januarii*', Gilbert, *Chart. St Mary's*, pp 318–19, 290. The account was later embroidered to include the chapter house, dormitory and cloister, as in Holinshed: 'And about the same time the Citie of Dublin was defaced by fire, and the Steeple of Christ Church utterly destroyed. The Citizens before they went about to repaire their owne private buildings, agreed together to make a collection for repayring the ruines of that auntient building first begun by the Danes ...' Miller & Power, *Holinshed*, pp 198–9; compare Gilbert, *Dublin*, i, 103.

'a violent storm of rain and wind threw down the steeple', another incident which demands some explanation.[42] Crossing towers were vulnerable to collapse through differential settlement and inadequate supports, though they were not usually damaged by strong winds. Perhaps the gales destroyed a timber framed spire; or maybe the campanile took the form of a traditional Irish 'round tower', several of which are known to have fallen during storms.[43] If a crossing tower was involved in the disaster of 1316, substantial damage must have been inflicted on the fabric of the cathedral, for which there is no evidence.[44] Whatever the situation, the chapter turned their minds to the construction of a new tower, seeking a 'licence to crennelate' from Edward III in 1329.[45] Such licences were usually requested for the construction of castles or defensive towers, rather than belfries, and it suggests that something quite substantial was envisaged. The receipt of the licence in 1330 thus marks the start of building operations on the new tower.

On the eve of the Reformation, the cathedral would have been barely recognisable as the building we know today. Not only was the architectural layout quite different, but the interior was filled with altars, private chapels, statuary, paintings, shrines and secluded spaces, most of them visible only in the half light provided by burning candles. In this smoky atmosphere walls soon became grimy, which no doubt explains why the sub-prior, Richard Tristi, had the church newly whitewashed in 1430. The quire and high altar, the focus of the daily liturgy, were hidden from view behind a screen, and the altar itself was covered by some sort of tabernacle or canopy, another gift of Richard Tristi.[46] There were no chairs or seats in the nave, save perhaps

---

42 Archdall, *Mon. Hib.*, p. 163.   43 Michael Hare and Ann Hamlin, 'The study of early church architecture in Ireland: an Anglo-Saxon viewpoint, with an appendix on the documentary evidence for round towers' in L.A. Butler and R.K. Morris (ed.), *The Anglo-Saxon church: papers on history, architecture, and archaeology in honour of Dr H.M. Taylor* (London, 1986), pp 140–2.   44 In 1320 Matthew archbishop of Ardagh granted an indulgence 'to those who contributed to the reparacon of the fabric of the Church of the Holy Trinity and Holy Cross', which suggests that money was needed for the fabric fund, Lawlor, 'Liber niger', pp 20–3. Throughout the middle ages, however, the cathedral was anxious to secure funds for repairs to the cathedral so it is important not to read too much into one event. It is worth noting that the central tower of Kilkenny cathedral fell in the year 1332. In this case the reconstruction of *c.*1354 led to obvious modifications in the crossing piers, Leask, *Irish churches*, ii, 105–7.   45 15 January 1330, McEnery & Refaussé, *Deeds*, no. 223. For a discussion of licences to crennelate see Norman Pounds, *The medieval castle in England and Wales* (Cambridge, 1990), pp 102–6, 260–2. Pounds makes the point that many licences were not in fact acted upon, so the granting of a licence to Christ Church in 1329–30 does not necessarily mean that work began in that year. Out of 500 licences to crennelate listed by Charles Coulson, fifty-eight were granted to religious institutions, usually for precinct walls or defensive towers.   46 Refaussé & Lennon, *Registers*, p. 44.

a few benches for the aged and infirm. Scattered around the cathedral in various locations were eight or nine separate chapels or altars.[47]

The plan of the Romanesque church allowed for the provision of four chapels, one in the south transept and three opening off the eastern side of the ambulatory; (Fig. 1, Plate 4) the latter must have been transferred elsewhere when the quire was remodelled in the 1280s. The chapel in the south transept had vanished by 1761, and it may have even have been removed in the middle ages.[48] It was reinstated by Street in 1871–8.

One of the more ancient chapels was that dedicated to St Edmund, the Anglo-Saxon king and martyr, a favourite saint of the English crown. This was located at the west end of the south quire aisle: in 1565, for example, we hear of a discussion that took place in 'Sanct Edmondes Ille'.[49] Another early chapel was that dedicated to St Mary Alba and St Laud, sometimes described as the 'White Mary chapel'. This was situated in the vicinity of the north transept, either in the transept itself or the north quire aisle.[50] It contained an image of the Virgin Mary, presumably made of white stone or perhaps carved in wood, painted white.[51] At the east end of the south quire aisle was a chapel of the Holy Ghost, the dedication of which was changed to St Laurence O'Toole during the fifteenth century. In 1485 provision was made for a daily mass and a weekly sung mass to be performed in 'the Chapell of the Holy Goste, nowe called Seynt Laurence O Toyles Chapell, in the Southe Isle next adjoyning to the high Quere of the said church,'[52] a comment that leaves no doubt about the location. The chapel is of particular interest since this was the section of the aisle that was added to Archbishop John de St Paul's quire between 1362 and 1485.

Within the main body of the quire was the chantry chapel of Gerald Fitzgerald, eighth earl of Kildare, built in 1510, three years before his death. It contained the tomb of the earl, along with an altar dedicated to the Virgin Mary. Its appearance has been recorded in a number of illustrations, the best of which is a delicate pencil and ink drawing in the Gilbert collection.[53] (Plate

---

47 Mills, 'Notices'. 48 Early prints and engravings of the quire show a medieval (?) window in the south aisle where the walls of the south transept chapel ought to have been. The window, which is filled with switchline tracery, is consistent with other windows in the aisle, and the assumption must be that they are medieval. 49 Gillespie, *Proctor's accounts*, p. 73; Mills, 'Notices', p. 200. 50 Ibid., p. 26; repairs to the north wall of the tower mentioned the adjacent battlements of the White Mary chapel. See also Mills, 'Notices', p. 199. 51 Refaussé & Lennon, *Registers*, p. 64. 52 Boydell, *Music*, p. 32, Mills, 'Notices', p. 198. 53 A finished drawing and an unfinished pencil drawing are both bound into Gilbert's copy of Mason, *St Patrick's*. There is another drawing in Sir William Betham's *Monumenta Eblana* (Dublin Public Libraries, Gilbert MS 201, f. 25), but this is much coarser in appearance. In all the drawings only two sides are illustrated, presumably because the chapel needed only two sides, as it was located in the

19a) The chapel, which was situated in the north-east corner of the chancel, was surrounded by ornate wooden screens on its southern and western sides.[54] These were decorated with an array of Gothic tracery and decorated panelling, organised in four superimposed storeys. On the main face there were fourteen vertical panels at dado level, five of which had traceried designs, as found on tomb chests of the time. The stage above consisted of seven open arches, each subdivided into a pair of cinquefoiled sub-arches. At the base of this stage was a string course ornamented with a running vine scroll, a decoration found universally in late medieval woodwork in England, and repeated occasionally in Ireland, as on Dean Odo's doorway at Clonmacnois (c.1461).[55] The third stage included fourteen vertical panels, each surmounted by a canopy with three sub-arches. In the space below was a line of heraldic shields. Further canopy work ornamented the upper level. The background to these designs appears to lie in England, where there are obvious parallels amongst the timber screens of local parish churches.[56] In Ireland the Kildare chapel is by far the most elaborate piece of late Gothic art on record and the drawings in the Gilbert collection provide a sad and tantalising glimpse of the ornate furnishings that, throughout the country, were swept away in the aftermath of the Reformation.[57]

It was common practice in the greater churches of the middle ages for altars to be situated in front of the quire screen, on either side of the central doorway. Such altars lay immediately below the great rood, so for one of them a dedication to the cross was appropriate. This is the likely position of 'an altar before the cross', mentioned in 1353.[58]

At least three further chapels were situated in the nave. The so-called Trinity chapel, which belonged to the merchants' guild, was located in the south aisle. A special mass was held there on Trinity Sunday and a priest

---

north-east corner of the quire. Further references to the chapel can be found in Archdall, *Mon. Hib.*, p. 167; Finlayson, *Inscriptions*, p. 125; Miller & Power, *Holinshed*, pp 44, 198–9; Gilbert, *Dublin*, i, 108. Mason, contradicting his statements elsewhere, states that it was on the south side of the high altar, 'The history of the cathedral church of the Holy Trinity', T.C.D., MS 10,529, f. 79, but the very shape of the chapel shows that this cannot be correct.   54 Plans of Christ Church in the Gilbert collection mark the chapel quite clearly (number 8). The drawings are also bound into Gilbert's copy of Mason, *St Patrick's*.   55 Among dozens of examples of this motif around 1500 are the vine scrolls carved on the Beaton Panels (c.1530) in the National Museum of Scotland.   56 Francis Bond, *Screens and galleries in English churches* (Oxford, 1908). The artistic background of the Kildare chapel warrants further investigation.   57 I have not managed to establish when the Kildare chapel was destroyed. It seems to have existed in the eighteenth century and it may have been removed soon after 1743 to make way for the huge marble monument by Henry Cheere in honour of the nineteenth earl of Kildare, which is now in the south transept.   58 *Alen's reg.*, p. 208.

was hired to say masses when required for members of the guild and their families.[59] There were also burials in the chapel, but as it lay above the crypt there was very little space for interments. This no doubt explains the graves encountered in the haunches of the crypt vaults during the restoration of 1871–8.[60] The chapel was damaged by the fall of the nave vaults in 1562 and three years later its own arches and vaults were threatening collapse.[61] On the other side of the nave was a chapel in honour of St Nicholas, situated in the two western bays of the north aisle. This chapel had ceased to exist in 1541, when the cathedral leased out 'a long loft called St Nicholas' chapel situate over the cellar'.[62] A chapel dedicated to St Nicholas was one of the earliest recorded in the history of the cathedral; in the early years it was probably situated in one of the Romanesque chapels opening off the ambulatory.[63] Finally, at the east end of the nave aisle was the Barbers' chapel, mentioned in a document of 1595.[64]

Although little is known about the appearance of the various chapels, their location demonstrates that the aisles of the cathedral were not treated as continuous passageways, as they are today. Tucked away at the north-east corner of the cathedral was the Lady chapel. With a length of 66 feet, this was by far the largest and best endowed of the chapels at Christ Church, but sadly we know almost nothing about its appearance.[65] There are two eighteenth-century engravings which provide a view from the north, but it would be hard to recognise the building depicted as medieval.[66] (Plate 21a) In both prints the Lady chapel is shown as a simple box with two large round-headed windows, more classical than Gothic in appearance. The chapel was entered from the west through a thirteenth-century arch which still survives, and there was also a doorway that gave direct access to the quire.

The history of the Lady chapel is difficult to establish. According to the 'Liber niger' the chapel was constructed after the 'long quire', when the cit-

---

59 For further details see ch. viii below, especially note 45. John Gogh bequeathed a missal to the chapel in 1472, Berry, *Register*, pp 38–40.   60 McVittie, *Restoration*, p. 43. 61 Gillespie, *Proctor's accounts*, p. 43. The Trinity chapel is mentioned in 1600, Gillespie, *Chapter act book*, p. 108, and in 1667, Mills, 'Notices', p. 199.   62 McEnery & Refaussé, *Deeds*, 24, no. 1182; Mills, 'Notices', pp 199–200.   63 The altar is mentioned in the 'Liber niger', Gwynn, 'Origins', p. 47, and by *Gir. Camb. op.*, ii, 156. It is likely that a chapel (possibly that of St Nicholas) was at one time situated in the chamber opening off the fourth bay of the north aisle, evidence of which was discovered by Street in 1871–2 (Street & Seymour, p. 123).   64 Mills, 'Notices', p. 200.   65 Gilbert, *Dublin*, i, 132 gives the length of the chapel as 66 feet. The pre 1871 plan in C6/4 gives an external length of 69 feet 4 inches, whereas Reading's map of 1764 gives internal dimensions of 27 feet by 67½ feet.   66 Engravings in *The whole works of Sir James Ware concerning Ireland*, ed. Walter Harris (Dublin, 1739) and Robert Pool and John Cash, *Views of the most remarkable public buildings in the city of Dublin* (Dublin, 1760), pl. opposite p. 76.

izens of Dublin, moved by a miracle attributed to St Lorcán, 'honourably founded and built the great Lady chapel on the north side of the chancel'.[67] Written in the late fourteenth century, this account has to be taken seriously, since it deals with events that occurred only a few decades earlier. However, the evidence of the 'Liber niger' contradicts the information provided by the one remaining arch, the style of which belongs to the thirteenth century; moreover, the bend in the axis of the quire is easier to explain if one assumes that the chapel was built first. (Plate 5) The situation is further complicated by an event that took place in 1414, when John Cely, bishop of Down, consecrated an altar in honour of the Virgin Mary '*extra hostium ex parte boreali chori*'.[68] Given the location this must refer to the Lady chapel. Presumably a new and perhaps more elaborate altar had been installed. A number of benefactions to the chapel is listed in the obits during the fifteenth century: Richard Tristi, the sub-prior, for example, added decorations to the altar, and Thomas Sinothe paid for the reglazing of four windows.[69] Like the rest of the cathedral, the chapel had a battlemented roof, and it appears to have had its own bell, which was broken in 1565 and ready to fall from its frame.[70] At least part of the chapel had a tiled floor.[71] It was sometimes described as the '*magna capella*', no doubt to distinguish it from the White Mary chapel, as well as the chantry chapel of the earl of Kildare, which was also dedicated to the Virgin Mary.[72] The Lady chapel was maintained in decent condition after the Reformation, receiving a new roof in 1694.[73] It became a favourite place of burial during the eighteenth century, but in 1830 its religious status was finally extinguished, when the ancient building was ignominiously converted into a school house by the architect Matthew Price.

During the fifteenth century, the cathedral did its best to encourage pilgrims, whose oblations represented an important source of income. The two outstanding attractions of the cathedral were the speaking cross and the *baculus Ihesu*. The cross had already acquired some notoriety before the Anglo-Norman invasion and its miraculous powers were much appreciated by the local populace. When Strongbow approached Dublin in 1170, a group of citizens attempted to seize the cross as they made their escape from the city, but the cross stoically refused to budge. Following the capture of the city, Gerald of Wales explained how an archer, who had earlier raided the archbishop's house, offered a penny to the cross, and, as he turned to leave was hit in the back by the self same penny.[74] Further miracles are recounted by

---

67 Gwynn, 'Origins', p. 48.   68 Refaussé & Lennon, *Registers*, p. 52.   69 Ibid., p. 44. 70 Gillespie, *Proctor's accounts*, pp 29, 68.   71 *Dublin Penny Journal*, 3 Oct. 1835, p. 109. 72 C6/1/7/3, p. 52. It was reroofed with the aid of a gift of 40 tons of oak presented to the cathedral by the earl of Strafford from his wood at Shillelagh, Street & Seymour, p. 42.   73 See ch. xiii below, p. 268.   74 *Gir. Camb. op.*, ii, 155, v, 129–30.

Roger of Hoveden, who states that the cross was engraved ('*incisa*') with a life-like image of Christ.[75] The cross was probably of twelfth-century manufacture, but the accounts do not explain whether it was made of wood or of wood covered with precious metals. Nor is it known where it was displayed within the church.[76] The lack of information is disappointing, since a miracle-working image of Christ crucified is likely to have exerted some influence on Irish art, especially in the twelfth century.

In the later middle ages, several of the treasures of the cathedral, including the *baculus Ihesu*, were kept in a great chest, stored between the high altar and the east window of the quire. This chest was broken by falling masonry in the storm of 1461, but the *baculus* survived without damage. Like the splendid croziers preserved in the National Museum, it was no doubt embellished by bronze, silver and other precious ornaments. The staff itself, which was reputedly given to St Patrick by Christ, belonged to the church of Armagh until 1180, when it was seized by Anglo-Norman knights and presented to Christ Church.[77] In addition to these treasures, the cathedral had a host of other relics ready to impress a gullible pilgrim audience.[78] Many were no doubt provided with containers of their own, and the display of reliquaries on major feast days must have been an inspiring sight.

As well as the reliquaries, the medieval cathedral possessed a range of sculptures and other precious items, none of which survives. By 1310 it had acquired an image (as well as a relic) of St Catherine, one of the most popular of late medieval saints.[79] In 1344–5 a brother John Savage was paid 17s. for 'carving and ornamenting eighteen images for the feretory' ('*pro feretro*'), and in 1441 a silver gilt statue valued at £10 was given to the high altar by Lady Joanna Cusack of Killeen, when she was received as a sister of the confraternity of Christ Church.[80] Several benefactors provided silver and gilded chalices for the high altar, and the consecrated sacrament was reserved on the high altar in a silver box, which in 1466 was stolen by Henry Alton, 'a gentleman, late of Ardee'. The box weighed 33 ounces in pure wrought silver and the prior and convent reckoned its value at £20. Fifteen years later the cathedral was still trying to recover it.[81] These few scattered references give

---

75 *Chronica magistri Rogeri de Hovedeni*, ed. William Stubbs (4 vols, London, 1868–71), iv, 29–30.   76 In 1461 it was not apparently kept with other relics in front of the east window. The fact that it already existed in the twelfth century makes it unlikely, though not impossible, that it formed the major cross above the rood screen.   77 Gilbert, *Chart. St Mary's*, ii, p. 275, Lawlor, 'Liber niger', p. 56; Street & Seymour, p. 19.   78 Refaussé & Lennon, *Registers*, pp 39–40.   79 Archdall, *Mon. Hib.*, pp 162–3.   80 Lydon & Fletcher, *Account roll*, p. 98; Refaussé & Lennon, *Registers*, p. 48; H.M. Roe, *Medieval fonts of Meath* (Navan, 1968), p. 90.   81 *Stat. Ire., 12–22 Edw. IV*, p. 891.

us a mere hint of the illustrious objects and works of art that had been accumulated by the cathedral by the eve of the Reformation.

The introduction of the Augustinian rule at Christ Church brought with it a need to provide appropriate conventual buildings. By the thirteenth century these were laid out in customary medieval fashion around a cloister garth on the south side of the cathedral church.[82] Given the congestion in the centre of the city, it is remarkable that the priory had the space to do this. Did the cathedral already own sufficient land or was it forced to acquire new property? It is possible that the situation was assisted, at least in part, by John Cumin's decision to found a new palace for himself in the 1190s. Hitherto the archbishops lived beside the cathedral, but the founding of St Sepulchre's may have been a blessing for the canons, providing them with much needed space.[83] Nonetheless the archbishops did not surrender all their property in the neighbourhood of the cathedral, for one of the gatehouses (we do not know which) lay on land given to the priory in 1220 by Archbishop Henry of London.[84]

By 1278, if not before, the priory buildings were enclosed within a well-defined precinct, protected by stone walls and two gatehouses.[85] Unfortunately no sections of the wall survive, the last remnants being removed when the site was cleared between 1826 and 1831, though it is known that the masonry was approximately three feet in thickness.[86] While the exact boundaries of the precinct are far from clear, the general layout can be established without difficulty. (Fig. 4) Beginning to the east of the cathedral, there was a gateway opening into Fishamble Street, which by the later middle ages was fortified with a tower.[87] From this gate, the wall ran in a southerly direction, close to the line of Fishamble Street, before turning west along the

---

82 Clear evidence for the existence of the cloister does not predate the thirteenth century, but the possibility that one was laid out in the later years of the eleventh century under Bishop Patrick (1074–84) cannot be discounted. **83** A passage in the *Topographia* of Giraldus Cambrensis suggests that the archbishop's dwelling was close to the cathedral: after the capture of Dublin by the Anglo-Normans, an archer who had offered a penny to the miraculous cross in Christ Church, was hit in the back by the coin when he turned to leave. He subsequently admitted that he had plundered the archbishop's residence, *Gir. Camb. op.*, ii, 155, v, 128, 68–70. **84** McEnery & Refaussé, *Deeds*, no. 30. The gate was built 'at the entrance of the church'. **85** Ibid., nos 520, 561. **86** In 1632 a tenant sought permission to enlarge two tiny windows through a wall 3 feet thick, evidently the wall of the close, just south of the south-west gate of the old monastery, Gillespie, *Chapter act book*, p. 184. **87** McEnery & Refaussé, *Deeds*, no. 1299, Gillespie, *Chapter act book*, pp 50, 138, 212, 214. In 1634 the tower over the east gate was inhabited by Edward Carne, a tailor, who devoted his own resources to repairing the tower, Gillespie, *Chapter act book*, pp 212, 214.

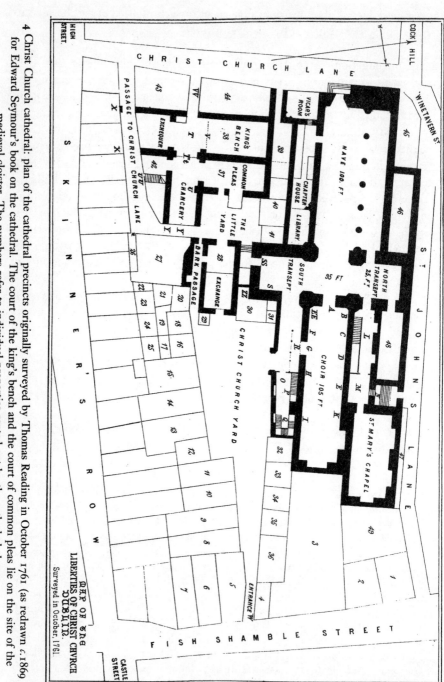

4 Christ Church cathedral: plan of the cathedral precincts originally surveyed by Thomas Reading in October 1761 (as redrawn c.1869 for Edward Seymour's book on the cathedral. The court of the king's bench and the court of common pleas lie on the site of the medieval cloister. The numbers refer to individual properties rented out by the cathedral chapter.

backs of houses in Skinners' Row (now Christchurch Place, opposite Jury's Inn). Indeed it is likely that the houses and shops erected on the north side of Skinners' Row were originally built up against the precinct wall.[88] The wall itself continued towards Christ Church Lane (not necessarily in a straight line), which it reached just to the south of the later passage beside the Four Courts. It then continued north along the east side of Christ Church Lane before reaching the cathedral. The west gate, the so-called 'great gate', was situated in this area, but its position has been the subject of some confusion. Thomas Drew, the first person to explore the layout of the conventual buildings, believed it lay at the south-west corner of the nave, 'exactly under the doorway of the present south-west porch, but some ten feet below it'.[89] Early photographs and engravings of houses in Christ Church Lane show a low arch in this position, and a narrow passage is marked in the same place in Reading's plan of 1761. (Fig. 4) Nonetheless, there are difficulties with Drew's suggestion. In 1631 both gates were protected by heavy wooden doors, with a smaller wicket gate for pedestrians, and there is no reason to suppose things were any different in the middle ages.[90] Such doors suggest important thoroughfares, suitable for bringing carts and horses into the precincts. If the gate was situated beside the cathedral, it would have led directly into the cloister, a most undesirable arrangement. Reading's map shows that by 1761 the north walk of the cloister was blocked by houses and it is hard to see how anything but a narrow passage could have led out to the street. In fact the great gate almost certainly lay at the south end of the west range, which after 1608 became one of the main approaches to the Four Courts. At the point where this passage opened into Christ Church Lane, there was a vaulted area, ten feet in width, which seems to have been the remnants of the old entrance to the priory.[91] Confirmation can be found in one of the cathedral's leases, dating from 1590. This describes a cellar, 'commonly called the vicars brewhouse', which stretched from the gatehouse to 'the Deanes Wode Celler' on the north.[92] If the gatehouse was located beside

---

88 According to Archdall, Skinners' Row existed in 1283 when shops there were set alight by a group of Scots, Archdall, *Mon. Hib.*, p. 161.   89 Drew, 'Cloister garth', p. 214.   90 In 1631 both gates were to be repaired and made new. They were to be shut at 8.00 in the evening and opened at 5.00 in the morning; the wickets were to be shut at 9.00 or 10.00, Gillespie, *Chapter act book*, p. 167. In 1564 Thomas Frenchman, a smith, was paid for mending the lock on the east gate which had perished and no longer worked, Gillespie, *Proctor's accounts*, p. 31.   91 An early nineteenth-century map in the National Library of Ireland (N.L.I., MS 21F 87) shows the corner of the south and south-west range, with a passage under the west range: diagonal lines imply it was vaulted, probably with ribbed vaults. A second map (N.L.I., MS 2790, f. 31), a copy dated 1814 of a map made by Thomas Reading, shows that at this point the passage was 24 feet long, approximately the width of west range.   92 Gillespie, *Chapter act book*, p. 69. The prop-

the church, as Drew believed, the wood cellar would have ended up in the south aisle.

The location of the gatehouse at the south-west corner of the precinct had practical advantages: stores could be brought into the priory and unloaded at the back of the kitchen, close to cellars in the south and west ranges, without causing any disruption to religious life. Anyone wishing to go through to the cloister could do so by passing through a passage under the east end of the refectory. In the context of the city, the gatehouse had a prominent location beside the cross-roads in front of the Tholsel, where the ancient market cross was situated. Such a conspicuous entry may well have encouraged the canons of Christ Church to construct a gateway with some architectural pretensions, though we have no record of its appearance.

By medieval standards, the cloister of Christ Church was small. Thomas Drew, who excavated parts of it in the 1880s, believed that it measured 84 feet in length (east to west) and 76 feet in width (north to south).[93] In the aftermath of the excavation, the area was laid out as a garden, with a square lawn in the centre representing (approximately) the site of the medieval garth. Long after the dissolution of the priory in 1539, this area was still known as the cloister, or the cloister yard.[94] Following normal monastic arrangements, the open space of the cloister was surrounded by buildings on all four sides, the northern flank being occupied by the cathedral itself. The foundations of the chapter house, which still survive to a height of several feet, enable us to determine the dimensions of the east range, which was aligned to the south transept.[95] (Fig. 1, Plate 20a) The upper floor of this range contained the dormitory, to which there are many references into the seventeenth century.

While physical remains allow us to plot the line of the east range, this is not the case with the south range, the normal location for the refectory and kitchen. But there are some clues to the position of the refectory. After 1540 it came to be known as the vicars' hall and was often used for meetings of state, with the Irish parliament assembling there on a regular basis. When the Four Courts were transferred to Christ Church in 1608, this was

erty was leased to John Bullock one of the vicars choral, who was required to close up the east door and open a new door to the west (to the street?) perhaps in effort to reduce traffic in the precincts.   93 Drew, 'Cloister garth', p. 218. My own measurements suggest a maximum north-south dimension of 59 feet 9 inches. The distance from the west wall of the transept to the nineteenth century porch (built on the west range) is 80 feet 1 inch.   94 Gillespie, *Chapter act book*, pp 168, 178. In 1631 it was described as 'the little paved church yard commonly called the cloister', Gillespie, *Chapter act book*, p. 178.   95 The west wall of the range was not precisely aligned to the transept west wall; the face of the chapter house is about 7 inches to the east of the face of the transept (west wall), underlining the fact that the transept and east range were not constructed at the same time.

one of the rooms that was taken over, being allocated to the court of chancery. (Fig. 4) It appears that the courts occupied both the south and the west ranges of the old priory, with two extra buildings – for the king's bench and common pleas – being constructed within the old cloister garth. How much of this survived the reconstruction of the Four Courts in 1695 is unclear. The evidence contained in Reading's plan of 1761 suggests that the chancery was built on the foundations of the medieval refectory.[96] The lower storey may even have survived the rebuilding of 1695. If this supposition is correct, the north-south width of the cloister would have been approximately 60 feet, rather less than Drew's assessment, making the cloister garth a rectangular, rather than a square space.[97]

When it comes to defining the west range, which contained the prior's lodgings, there is a useful archaeological clue. During his investigations, Drew claims to have found the west wall of the court of king's bench, which was erected on substantial stone foundations, over 5 feet wide. This was quite different from the walls added after 1608 as part of the Four Courts, for these were built on a cradle of oak. Drew concluded that he had discovered the east wall of the west range.[98] The west wall of the range presumably followed the line of Christ Church Lane, lining up with the west wall of the cathedral. There is however one caveat. We know that the last bay of the church was added some time after 1234, and that to build it a lane had to be blocked at the west end of the church. As the west range is aligned to this final bay of the nave, it is unlikely that it was built before 1234.

Medieval cloisters were surrounded on each side by covered walkways, and this was certainly the case at Christ Church. Given the dimensions of the cloister as a whole, this would have made for a very small cloister garth, its scale being comparable with those encountered in the Franciscan friaries of the west. The existence of covered cloister walks is proved by an entry of 1564 in the account book of Sir Peter Lewis which expresses concern that the vaults and arches of the south aisle would fall and break the roof of the adjoining cloister.[99] In Irish monasteries the cloister walks normally communicated with the central garth through a series of open arches; it is not known for certain what form these took at Christ Church, but there are fragments

---

96 The lie of the land means that the refectory could not have stood much further south than the later chancery. If the two buildings did *not* follow the same outline, it means that in 1608 the architect of the Four Courts would have been responsible for demolishing the hall where the Irish parliament had been accustomed to meet, only to replace it by a hall in virtually the same position.   97 Drew however believed that the south cloister walk was integrated into the south range, avoiding the need for a projecting walk. Although he cites no evidence, it is an interesting idea, Drew, 'Cloister garth', p. 217. 98 Drew, 'Cloister garth', p. 216.   99 Gillespie, *Proctor's accounts*, p. 43.

5 Fifteenth-century cloister arcade as reconstructed from fragments found in Cook Street (redrawn after P. Ó hÉailidhe). This cloister may have come from St Mary's abbey, but fragments of a similar cloister have been recovered from Christ Church.

in the crypt which may come from a fifteenth-century cloister arcade, the design of which has similarities with that discovered in Cook Street in 1975 and assumed to come from St Mary's Abbey.[100] (Fig. 5) We know that cloisters were erected at Christ Church in the fifteenth century, for a certain Roger Darcy, knight, left the cathedral £10 for their building.[101] It is hard to believe that the cathedral survived without cloister arcades until the fifteenth century, so we are presumably dealing with a reconstruction rather than the original scheme. Drew claimed to have found the walls on which the cloister arcades were set. His hypothetical plan, published in 1890, indicates that the cloister walks were about eight feet wide, a point which seems to be confirmed by a lease of 1631, involving a parcel of ground eight feet

100 Stalley, *Cistercian monasteries*, pp 157–9. The cloister from Cook street appears to have provided the model for those at the Cistercian abbey of Holy Cross (Tipperary), which provides a strong case for St Mary's Dublin, a Cistercian house, as their source. The fragments were re-used as rubble in a seventeenth-century wall. The cloister fragments from Christ Church, although similar in design, have somewhat different dimensions. There are at least six cloister fragments amongst the masonry in the crypt, including a section of base (a corner piece) and a piece of hood moulding with cusped ornament. I owe all this information to Rachel Moss. 101 Refaussé & Lennon, *Registers*, p. 66. Unfortunately the date of the benefaction is not known.

wide between the cloister 'pale' and the church door.[102] It is hard to envisage how the north walk of the cloister related to the walls of the cathedral, since any buttresses projecting from the south aisle would have blocked the passage.

Investigation of loose masonry in the crypt has brought to light evidence of what might have been an earlier cloister, in the form of fragmentary pieces of Romanesque scalloped capitals, which in style precede anything else associated with the cathedral. (Plate 7a) Although illustrated by Street in the 1882 volume on the cathedral, his text made no reference to their provenance.[103] The capitals belonged to freestanding columns. The scalloped form was a type widespread in England in the middle years of the twelfth century and in Dublin such capitals might well have decorated a cloister arcade with twin columns.[104]

One of the more intractable issues associated with the cloister walks is how their floor level corresponded with that of the church. Drew was adamant that the cloisters were constructed at almost the same level as the crypt, nine feet below the floor of the nave.[105] This is difficult to believe. There were two doorways opening from the south aisle of the nave, and, if the cloister walk was ten feet below, these doorways would have opened into thin air.[106] Drew made no reference to this problem, nor did he make any effort to explain how the cloisters were organised. In the absence of excavation, the only way of calculating the levels is through an examination of the entry to the chapter house, the foundations of which still remain *in situ*.[107] (Plate 20a) The threshold of the chapter house, which was presumably set at the level of the cloister, is 3 feet 8 inches below the nave floor; this is still a considerable gap, but far less than the amount postulated by Drew.[108] The

---

102 Drew, 'Ancient chapter house'; Gillespie, *Chapter act book*, pp 164, 177, 178.   103 Street & Seymour, p. 91.   104 The fragments were identified by Rachel Moss, to whom I am grateful for keeping me informed about discoveries in the crypt. She has pointed out that similar capitals were used in the cloister at Reading abbey, founded in 1121 by Henry I. At some point following Street's restoration, the capitals were smashed into small pieces, some of which were used by nineteenth-century workmen to stabilise piles of loose masonry in the crypt.   105 The crypt floor is approximately 9 feet 6 inches below the current floor of the nave.   106 Unless of course the cloister had two storeys, as at Silos in Spain for example.   107 I am fairly confident that the existing ground level, immediately outside the chapter house entrance, corresponds to the level of the medieval cloister. Nineteenth-century photographs of the excavations (Drew scrapbook, cathedral archives) show rough masonry beneath the bases, indicating that this section of wall was not visible in the original structure. Moreover, the framework for the inserted door at the entrance to the chapter house was set within a couple of inches of the same level.   108 Dr Howard Clarke has made the interesting suggestion that the level defined by the entrance to the chapter house may represent that of the pre-Romanesque cathedral and its attendant buildings.

difference is sufficiently small to have been overcome by the construction of a short flight of steps within the cloister walk.[109]

The main function of the cloister was to serve as a convenient system of circulation, allowing easy access to the various buildings of the priory, while at the same time maintaining the privacy of the community, as implied by the word cloister or *claustrum*. Judging from the meetings that took place in the priory, involving government and city officials, the cloisters had become a rather public place by the fifteenth century. They were also valued as a place of burial and by 1500 the cloister walks were probably encumbered with engraved tomb slabs and other memorials, honoring both benefactors and individual canons.[110]

The chapter house, which was an ornate and sophisticated piece of architecture, was excavated by Thomas Drew in April 1886.[111] The quality of the architecture underlines the status of the chapter house in medieval religious communities in general, a point reflected in many Irish monasteries. Doorways were frequently as lavish as those leading into the church. At Cong the Augustinians embellished the entrance to their chapter house (c.1200) with a series of chevroned arches, and the portal of the thirteenth-century chapter house at Grey Abbey, a Cistercian foundation, was equally complex.[112]

The Christ Church chapter house was rectangular in form, measuring (internally) 42 feet 10 inches by 20 feet 8 inches, dimensions which correspond to a length to width ratio of 2:1; the space was subdivided into four bays, each covered by a quadripartite ribbed vault. The interior was between 16 and 20 feet in height, to judge from ancient drawings made when the vault was still intact.[113] (Fig. 6) A stone bench, 15 inches wide, ran along the inside

---

109 The problem here is whether there would be room for such steps in a cloister walk less than eight feet wide. A further problem is access to the crypt. It is difficult to explain how the existing door into the south transept of the crypt could have been combined with the much higher door into the east bay of the south aisle of the church. Although much rebuilt, both doors have enough original masonry to suggest they belong to the years around 1200.   **110** Thus in 1469 John Selyman, a Dublin citizen, asked to be buried in the cloister, Lydon & Fletcher, *Account roll*, p. xviii.   **111** At the moment the walls of the chapter house rise to a level about 7 feet above the original floor. However most of the masonry is the result of reconstruction undertaken in 1886 and extended in the 1980s by Dublin Corporation. There is very little original masonry above the level of the bench. One course of ashlar, five and a half inches high and characterised by diagonal tooling, can be seen in the first bay and a half (from the east) on the north side and in the first bay on the south. Old photographs (Drew scrapbook, cathedral archives) show that the north-east corner was heightened with cut masonry, almost certainly under the direction of Drew. For Drew's account of the excavation see Drew, 'Ancient chapter house'.   **112** H.G. Leask, *Irish churches*, ii, 59–61; Stalley, *Cistercian monasteries*, pp 164–5.   **113** In his reconstruction of the chapter house Stuart Harrison has assumed a height of 20 feet. The only way of calculating the height of the vault is through the study of early drawings, such as those by

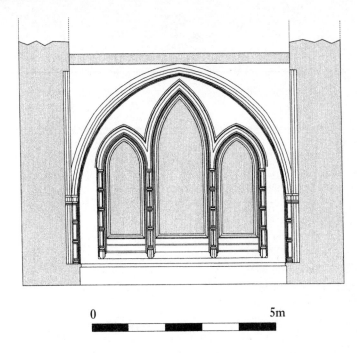

0   5m

6 Christ Church cathedral: chapter house: suggested reconstruction of the east window (Stuart Harrison). Note the relatively low level of the vault, which was necessary to ensure direct access from the dormitory to the church

face of the walls, providing ample seating for the canons.[114] It also served as a base for the responds that supported the vaults. (Plate 20a) These projected quite a distance into the building, dividing the lateral walls into clearly defined sections. The responds consisted of a substantial pier, on the front face of

Petrie and Callaghan Newenham. Both the latter depict the apex of the third transverse arch (the eastern bay of the chapter house had been removed by this stage) which can be related to the adjoining church. Petrie (probably the more reliable draughtsman) places the apex level with the springing point of the arch leading into the transept chapel. This is approximately 11 feet above the existing floor of the church (nave) which is approximately 5 feet 9 inches above the original floor of the chapter house, making a total of 16 feet 9 inches. 114 The bench consisted of a stone slab, 4 inches thick, and its top surface must have been about 18 inches above the level of the tiled floor. It ran along the north, east and south walls but not apparently across the west wall. In the south west angle a narrow strip of rough masonry, 6 inches wide at its maximum, emerges from the base of the inner wall. The floor must have been set above this masonry, which is 20 inches below the top surface of the bench. I have deducted a further two inches to represent the thickness of the tiled floor.

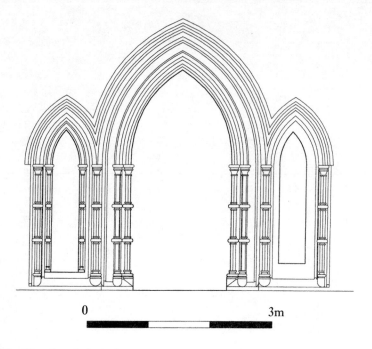

0   3m

7 Christ Church cathedral: chapter house: suggested reconstruction of the west facade
(Stuart Harrison)

which was a detached shaft, made up of short sections of stone, each held in
place by rings. As can be seen from the surviving fragments, the main body
of each respond was given an elaborate moulding, the front section of which
would have been obscured once the shafts were in place. The depth of the
respond indicates that a substantial 'formeret' or wall arch was constructed
immediately below the vaults.

The east wall was filled by a three-light window, the lower courses of
which survive. (Fig. 6) Each lancet was framed by a pointed rear arch, which
rested on detached shafts, similar to those which supported the vaults.
Detached shafts also framed the exterior of the lancets.[115] The frame of the
window was lined on the inside by a continuous moulding, extending across
the base of the window like those in the aisles of the nave (as rebuilt by
Street). The final bay of the chapter house projected beyond the east range,
giving the impression of an independent building, an impression enhanced
by buttresses on either side. That on the north side retains a nook shaft,
taking the form of a continuous keeled moulding.

115 Drew used the chapter house windows as the basis for his design for the eastern
extension of Street's chapter room (see p. 332 below).

The west facade of the chapter house was partially obscured by the cloister walk, but the central doorway and the windows alongside were delineated with considerable subtlety. The three-part composition was framed by detached shafts, portions of which survive. (Plate 20b, Fig. 7) These were made of freestone and provided with double or triple fillets, depending on their position. The doorway consisted of two orders, both supported on filleted shafts, the outer shafts being made of coursed masonry, while the inner ones were detached. It seems likely that this distinction was maintained in the arch above, with the detached shafts supporting capitals, while the coursed mouldings continued into the arch without interruption. The inside face of the door was provided with further shafts, this time detached. The most unusual feature of the whole arrangement is a broad segmental 'shaft', like a huge semi-hidden half column, which occupies the space between the inner and outer faces of the doorway. (Plate 20b) This is reminiscent of the curious treatment found in the nave of the cathedral, where, just above the capitals, there is an illusion of a half hidden pier sunk into the walls. The sophistication of the chapter house facade is revealed by the layering of the wall, which is organised so that the plane of the inner wall, containing the door and windows, is recessed some inches behind the main lines of the building.

Although it is natural to speak of a doorway, the entrance was designed to be left open, without any barrier to the outside world; even the windows alongside were probably left unglazed, at least in the original design.[116] While this might seem an uncomfortable arrangement, exposing the canons to the vagaries of the Irish climate, it was standard procedure in monastic design during the twelfth and thirteenth centuries. It is also important to remember that the west side of the chapter house received some protection from the adjoining cloister walk. At a later period – exactly when is unclear – this ascetic environment became too much for the canons. They decided to protect themselves with a solid door; crudely cut slots at the base of the jambs show where the door frames were inserted.[117] Even equipped with a door, the chapter house was not a particularly secure room and could never have been suitable for the storage of valuables.[118]

With its ribbed vault and ornate mouldings, the chapter house was an imposing chamber. According to Drew, some of the detached shafts were

116 This is suggested by the remains of the southern window where the sill and lower jambs have no trace of a glazing groove. The glass may of course have been held in wooden frames.   117 The slots are visible on both sides, approximately 7 inches wide and 4 to 5 inches deep.   118 In 1296 payments were recorded for the carriage of sacks of money to Holy Trinity and in 1299 a large lock and key were provided for the 'treasury' there. After 1316 and the Bruce invasion, the priory was deemed to be too vulnerable and no further use was made of it by the exchequer, Lydon & Fletcher, *Account roll*, p. xv.

made of dark carboniferous limestone, like those in the triforium and clerestory of the nave, a contrast of masonry that would have added to the architectural splendour.[119] The walls were apparently painted,[120] lined out perhaps with false masonry joints, as was common at the time, and the floor was covered with decorated tiles, fragments of which were recovered in the excavation of 1890–1.[121] At a relatively early stage burials took place within the room. Drew records the discovery of two decorated grave slabs, one with a floriated cross, the other with the effigy of a woman (now in the quire).[122]

A major problem that confronted monastic builders when designing a chapter house was how to combine it with the dormitory above. The vaults over the chapter house had to be kept relatively low, otherwise it was impossible to ensure direct access from the dormitory to the church, something which was *de rigueur* in monastic planning.[123] One solution, much favoured by the Cistercian order, was to divide the chapter house into six or nine vaulted bays, with the vaults supported on intermediate columns or piers. While this broke up the unity of the space, the vaults could be kept reasonably low so that they did not impinge on the sleeping quarters above. Benedictine monasteries, however, preferred chapter houses designed as a unified space, covered in a single span, making it difficult to limit the height of the vault. Many communities solved the problem by constructing a low vestibule under the actual dormitory, with the chapter house built as a separate chamber beyond the line of the east range, a solution occasionally adopted by the Cistercians, as at Mellifont.[124] If this was not practicable, efforts were made to lower the floor. The latter approach was adopted at Christ Church, where the original floor of the chapter house was some 20 inches below the level of the adjacent cloister walk.

The chief factor dictating the size of a chapter house was the size of the community. In comparison with the chapter houses of some of the English cathedrals, the example at Christ Church was modest in scale, but it was perfectly adequate for the numbers resident in the cathedral in the thirteenth century. Four canons could have been seated quite comfortably between each of the responds, so that there was adequate seating for sixteen people on each

---

119 Drew, 'Ancient chapter house', p. 40. A small fragment of this darker stone is cemented on to one of the bases on the north side.   120 A point mentioned by Arthur Champneys, *Irish ecclesiastical architecture* (London, 1910), p. 201.   121 Drew's description of the tiles is brief and ambiguous: 'There was evidence of the remains of a beautiful tesselated floor, and that a stage three feet wide, with a riser made of fine tiles three inches thick, had run along the north and south walls and across the west end', Drew, 'Ancient chapter house', p. 41.   122 Whether these were in their original positions is not entirely clear.   123 For the design of east ranges see Roy Gilyard-Beer, *Abbeys* (London, 1959), pp 25–9.   124 Stalley, *Cistercian monasteries*, pp 162–5.

side, thirty-two in all. Given the size of the Christ Church community – there were only eleven canons in 1300 – this was generous accommodation.[125] In view of the importance of the rituals that took place in the chapter house, which included public confession and the reception of new members, a dignified environment, without overcrowding, was essential. An indication of what was required for admitting novices can be gleaned from the customs of Arrouaise, as followed at Christ Church. At the appropriate time the candidate was brought into the chapter house, where he prostrated himself in the centre of the room and was interrogated by the abbot.[126] The *mandatum* or ritual washing of feet on Holy Thursday was another ceremony that required a dignified setting.[127]

In the context of Gothic architecture in Britain and Ireland, the chapter house was planned in an orthodox manner. There are numerous English examples which take a rectangular form and are vaulted in three or four bays. The thirteenth-century chapter house at Kirkham (Yorkshire), an Augustinian foundation, follows this arrangement, so too does the splendid chapter house at St Frideswide's Oxford, another Augustinian house.[128] It is more difficult to cite parallels in Ireland, since few chapter houses survive intact and they have never been studied as a group. The Augustinian priory at Newtown Trim, founded in 1202, seems to have been planned along similar lines, though it is badly ruined and has never been excavated. Judging from outlines in the soil, it was rectangular in plan, and like Christ Church it had an elaborate Gothic entrance with both engaged and detached shafts. The closest Irish parallel, however, is to be found in a Cistercian context, only a few hundred yards from Christ Church itself, in the chapter house of St Mary's Abbey, which dates from about 1200.[129] The proportions of the two buildings are almost identical.[130] As at Christ Church, the chapter house at St Mary's also has three lancets in the east wall, and it too is covered in a single span with four bays of ribbed vaulting.[131]

---

125 Lydon & Fletcher, *Account roll*, p. xix.   126 For the customary of Arrouaise as it was *c.*1230 see Ludo Milis and Jean Becquet (ed.), *Constitutiones canonicorum regularium ordinis Arroasiensis*, Corpus Christianorum continuatio medievalis, xx (Turnhout, 1970). 127 Admittedly we cannot be certain that the *mandatum* was performed by the canons in Dublin. The functions of the chapter house in the Gothic period are analysed by Sheila Bonde, Edward Boyden and Clark Maines, 'Centrality and community: liturgy and Gothic chapter room design at the Augustinian abbey of Saint-Jean-des-Vignes, Soissons' in *Gesta*, xxix (1990), pp 189–213.   128 *Kirkham priory* (London, 1980), p. 7; Nikolaus Pevsner and Priscilla Metcalf, *The cathedrals of England* (2 vols, Harmondsworth, 1985), i, 217–18. 129 Stalley, *Cistercian monasteries*, pp 130, 165.   130 The dimensions of St Mary's are 14.32 by 7.09 metres compared with 13.06 by 6.3 metres at Christ Church.   131 At St Mary's the vault ribs are supported on corbels rather than wall shafts, and, as befits its earlier date, the mouldings are less sophisticated.

While the plan of the chapter house at Christ Church was conventional, the quality of the detail was exceptional, on a par with that found in the nave of the cathedral. It must have been expensive to build and its date is a matter of great interest. Was it erected around 1225 before work on the Gothic nave began, or did it come later? There is no doubt that the design has a close relationship with the nave, for there are many technical similarities. These include the use of bases with tall round plinths,[132] the taste for triple filleted shafts, the way the detached shafts are flanked by narrow pointed rolls, the employment of buttresses with nook shafts, the use of continuous mouldings around the windows, and finally the use of multiple rings or annulets.[133] (Plates 20b, Figs 6, 7) One important detail absent from the chapter house is dog-tooth ornament, found in the final bay of the nave, but not in the nave as a whole.[134] On the basis of these analogies it would be tempting to attribute the construction of the chapter house to the same period as the nave, if it were not for one further observation. The builders of the chapter house did not use Dundry stone as found in the cathedral; instead they employed a much whiter oolitic limestone, in which the round oolites are very clear to the naked eye. This is usually described in general terms as 'Bath stone', though the location of the quarry in England has not been identified. Unfortunately the stonework is so weathered that it is difficult to assess how extensively this material was employed. As it is unlikely that the cathedral imported stone from two separate quarries at the same time, one is forced to conclude that the chapter house was erected after the completion of the nave, perhaps in the 1240s or possibly some decades later.

By the mid-thirteenth century almost eighty years had elapsed since the Augustinian rule had been adopted at Christ Church. From the start the canons would have needed a chapter house, so presumably there was an earlier building, which proved inadequate or was damaged in some way. According to Archdall, the fire which damaged the steeple of the cathedral

---

132 One detail seen on these plinths is worthy of attention. A broad fillet runs down the faces of those in the east window, as seen in the windows of the nave aisle; although reconstituted by Street, it is likely that they were based on original examples. An authentic piece survives amidst the loose stone.   133 The use of multiple rings was a feature of the aisle windows of the cathedral, one reproduced in Street's restoration. This relatively unusual technique can be paralleled in Wales, in the east windows at St Davids cathedral; in Ireland it occurs at Boyle abbey (west window *c*.1220), Graiguenamanagh (presbytery windows *c*.1210), and a doorway at St Canice's in Kilkenny (*c*.1250). The feature was first noted by Champneys, *Irish ecclesiastical architecture*, p. 140. St Patrick's cathedral, begun around 1225, provides further parallels for some of the details of the chapter house, not least the detached shaft flanked by narrow rolls.   134 Dog-tooth was also used on blind arches in one bay of the north aisle. This was dismantled by Street and not replaced, though a few stones from it are stored in the crypt.

in 1283 also destroyed the chapter house, along with the dormitory and cloisters.[135] His evidence is not corroborated by the medieval sources, which speak
only of damage to the steeple.[136] Nonetheless Drew claimed to have found
traces of fire when he excavated the chapter house and there are twelfth-century stones which bear evidence of fire damage.[137] It remains a possibility
therefore that the chapter house was rebuilt after the fire of 1283, though in
terms of style this date seems rather late.[138] The chapter house remained in
use after the Reformation, both as a meeting chamber and as a place for stor-
ing archives but by the end of the seventeenth century it had been abandoned by the clergy, who now exploited the space for commercial gain.[139] In
1699, when it was rented out to a certain Walter Motley, the room had been
divided into two separate spaces.[140] For a time in the eighteenth century it
was used as an exchange, and then, shortly after 1770, its function was transformed quite dramatically. The end walls were knocked out and the interior
levelled up with 'rubbish'. It was thus converted into an elongated archway,
allowing carriages to sweep through Christ Church yard and into the old
cloister garth beyond, making a stylish approach to the church for the more
aristocratic worshippers. This is the form in which it is illustrated in a
number of early prints, including that in Grose's *Antiquities of Ireland*
(1791–5). (Plate 23b) What remained of the old building was finally demol-

---

135 Archdall, *Mon. Hib.*, p. 161. The fire of 1283 is recorded in the annals of St Mary's
Dublin without any mention of the chapter house, dormitory and cloister.   136 See above
note 41.   137 Drew, 'Cloister garth', pp 41–2. The evidence of the fire encountered by
Drew may of course have related to post-medieval events. In the late nineteenth century
when Drew investigated the ruins, so-called archaeology amounted to little more than
'clearing out the rubbish'; evidence for an earlier chapter house may have been missed.
The fragmentary capitals of mid-twelfth date, which could come from an early cloister
arcade, bear traces of fire damage, as recorded by Rachel Moss. She has also pointed out
that there are two stones decorated with chevron ornament built into an arch in the south
aisle of the crypt that reveal traces of fire damage. Their form does not relate to anything
else in the crypt, leaving open the possibility that they come from one of the conventual buildings. Another fire damaged stone is built into the tomb recess on the north side
of Laurence O'Toole's chapel.   138 Some of the details would be consistent with a building period in the 1280s, the bases with rounded plinths, for example, and the use of
detached shafts with fillets (compare the north transept of Hereford cathedral, *c.*1270).
However the latter are also found in the west window of Llandaff cathedral which belongs
to the first half of the century, the period which seems to offer most parallels for the
Christ Church design. It is worth noting that the lower roll of the bases is furnished with
a horizontal fillet and that it overhangs the cylindrical plinth below, as in the nave of
Christ Church (especially in the triforium and clerestory) and the quire of St Patrick's
cathedral.   139 Gillespie, *Chapter act book*, pp 92–3; Gillespie, *Proctor's accounts*, pp 28
and 122 note 68; in 1699 a new chapter room was provided in the south aisle of the
church, in the space formerly occupied by the Trinity chapel.   140 C6/3/1/6.

ished between 1826 and 1831, as part of the wholesale clearances of Christ Church Yard and Skinners' Row.[141]

The chapter house was separated from the south transept by a passage, approximately 7 feet wide, which contained a staircase, leading up to the dormitory.[142] At the bottom of the stair a doorway opened into the south transept.[143] (Plate 8) The staircase thus functioned like a night stair, allow-

---

141 Already in 1794 there were proposals to demolish the chapter house 'for the purpose of enlarging the yard and making a decent and convenient approach to the cathedral', though only the section which projected beyond the east wall of the transept was dismantled at this time, C6/1/7/8, pp 14, 19. The eventual clearance was exceptionally thorough and despite strenuous efforts neither myself nor Rachel Moss has managed to identify any pieces of the chapter house vaulting amidst the stone fragments preserved in the cathedral. Perhaps it was carried away in c.1826–31 to be used as foundations or landfill elsewhere in the city. Alternatively it may have been dumped in Christ Church Yard, in which case it would have been removed in 1886, when, as Drew explains, Archbishop Lord Plunket, 'a man of directness and purpose, swept aside conventional forms, and welcomed the hungry army of unemployed into the precincts'; the resources of the Mansion House Relief Fund were 'spent in digging and removing thousands of tons of rubbish from "Christ Church Yard"', Drew, 'Ancient chapter house', p. 38.   142 Drew's comments on the staircase are contradictory. In his text (Drew, 'Ancient chapter house', pp 41–3) he speaks of stairs leading down to the crypt, whereas the plan he published in 1884 (Drew, 'Cloister garth', pp 214–18) has an inscription in this position reading 'Stairs to the dormitory'. Nowhere does Drew tell us exactly what he found.   143 Drew, 'Cloister garth', p. 216, claimed to have found traces of this doorway. It is clearly marked on Reading's map of 1761. High in the south wall of the south transept (to the west of the existing south door) are a number of stones which might have formed a relieving arch above such a doorway. Drew's description of what he found is utterly confusing; as well as referring to stairs leading to the dormitory, he also refers to 'an under flight of stairs leading to the crypt', but where this was and how it opened into the crypt is not explained (Drew, 'Ancient chapter house', p. 36, note 1). Elsewhere he mentions that 'By the side of the chapter house adjoining the transept we uncovered a flight of stone steps leading down to the crypt (which is still there)', Drew, 'Cloister garth', p. 42. Drew provided two plans of the cloister, the 1890 version showing the space between the chapter house and the south transept divided between a prison and a stairs. His 1884 plan has a continuous space with steps inscribed 'up stairs to the Dormitory'. The location of stairs is further confused by a reference of 1599 (Gillespie, *Chapter act book*, p. 105) relating to a lease on a cellar 'in the east side of the cloister ... betwixt the east pair of stayres and the north paire of stairs in the said cloyster, which cellar is commonly called the Knowd'. But where exactly were these stairs? The situation is further confused by a deed which refers to the 'Knowd' as lying between the east stairs leading to Collfabie and the north stairs leading to the steeple, the latter presumably referring to the stair in the south-west angle of the south transept, McEnery & Refaussé, *Deeds*, no. 1450. The precise location of the 'Knowde' thus remains unclear. The room was not to be used for a tavern and the dean and chapter were to maintain the vault over the said cellar. The reference to a vault makes one wonder whether this could have been that part of the crypt under the south transept.

ing the canons to descend from the dormitory to the church without going out into the cloister. The space is now occupied by the pathway which runs at a high level in front of the south transept. On the opposite side of the chapter house was the slype, a passage five feet in width, which led from the cloister through to Christ Church yard on the east. It was excavated by Drew in 1886 and its position is defined by a block of masonry which still exists just to the south of the chapter house. Beyond the slype was the dormitory undercroft, a series of vaulted chambers which extended south towards Skinners' Row. Drew exposed a piece of the east wall, where he discovered a spiral staircase.[144]

The dormitory ran the full length of the east range, extending across the chapter house, slype and undercroft. We know nothing about the appearance of the chamber in the middle ages, but it is mentioned quite frequently in sixteenth and seventeenth century documents. By this time the area had been divided into several apartments, occupied by the vicars choral. Every dormitory needed a latrine or 'reredorter', facilities which were usually located in a building that opened off the main chamber, either projecting to the east or forming an extension to the south. At Christ Church the reredorter was situated towards the south end of the dormitory and may have projected to the east in a spot that came to be known as 'Coolfabius'.[145] (Fig. 4) In 1631 we know there was a public privy at the end of the dormitory and in 1633 there were complaints that 'the great Goute under Coulfabas or Comon Privie was and continually is stopped and much annoyed by filfth cast into the same by such tennants as live over the said Coulfabas.'[146] The great 'Goute' was obviously the main drain of the priory and it was still functioning as a sewer. Thomas Drew claimed to have discovered its route, stating that he could trace its passage all the way to the Liffey.[147] His map of the cathedral precincts shows it running due north, passing directly under the ambulatory of the cathedral. As water was seeping into the crypt in the 1880s, Drew built an intercepting drain along the south side of the cathedral, diverting water into St Michael's Hill (it was during this operation that he encountered the remnants of the cloister). It is strange that the medieval builders directed the principal sewer straight under the cathedral, but, given the congestion of the precincts, they may have been faced with no alternative.[148]

---

144 Drew, 'Ancient chapter house', p. 42. 145 I have failed to discover the etymology of this word. 146 Gillespie, *Chapter act book*, pp 165, 185–6. 147 Drew, 'Ancient chapter house', p. 37. 148 There is also a substantial drain under the north aisle of the nave of the crypt (reached through a manhole). How this relates to the monastic drainage system is unresolved. In the fourteenth century there is a further reference to a water channel or 'gurgite', but its location is not known. Brother Robert of St Neots was paid 'for cleaning and making the water-channel between the door of the cellar and the gate, as in stone,

The refectory, sometimes known as the 'common house' or 'fratry' occupied the upper floor of the south range, and was built over an undercroft or basement, an arrangement found in a number of Augustinian houses, including the great abbey at Athassel.[149] At the east end a passage passed under the refectory, providing a route from the cloister to the great gate at the southwest corner of the precinct. We know nothing about the refectory itself, except that it had a fireplace. The fourteenth-century account rolls mention the purchase of fuel for the fire, along with numerous payments for wine and food. Occasionally we get a glimpse of life inside the room, as in 1397 when Maurice fitz Eustace came to the prior 'as he sat at supper in the refectory', and swore to pay the rent that he owed to the prior and community.[150] The room must have been quite spacious, for it was used for meetings of the Irish parliament on a number of occasions in the fifteenth century.[151] After 1539 the chamber was converted into the hall of the vicars choral. In practice not much changed, with the canons, now deemed vicars, climbing the stairs of the refectory each day for their meals. In 1558 a silver vessel weighing 27 ounces was given to the common table by a benefactor of the cathedral. By 1600 the common meal in the old refectory appears to have become a thing of the past, with the vicars either married or no longer living in the precincts.[152] With its main function now gone, it is not surprising that the dean and chapter were attracted by the prospect of renting the space to the judiciary. In 1608 the old refectory was converted into the court of chancery. (Fig. 4)

The priory kitchen must have been situated close to the refectory, either in the south range or in an adjoining part of the west range. In the sixteenth century the vicars' brewhouse (the buttery of the former priory) was situated in a building beside Christ Church Lane, with the dean's kitchen above.[153] This first floor kitchen was therefore situated in the west range at the point where it joined the refectory. Almost certainly this was the same kitchen that had hitherto provided food for the prior. In 1542 carpenters were paid for carrying out work in the vicars' kitchen and five years later we hear of herbs

lime and sand, with the hire of two masons, 16d.', Lydon & Fletcher, *Account roll*, p. 98. 149 Drew, 'Cloister garth', p. 217, states that 'everything points to the conclusion that the refectory was not on the ground level, but on that of the dormitories, and extended over the south cloister walk'. Further confirmation can be found in the form of maps showing property under the chancery (N.L.I., MS 21F 90; see also copy by John Longfield 1818, N.L.I., MS 2790, f. 60). There is also a reference to the 'Chancery chamber formerly the school room over the arch'. 150 Hand, 'Psalter', p. 317. 151 For example, parliament met in the refectory in 1478, *Stat. Ire., 12–22, Edw IV*, p. 607. 152 In 1603 it was reported that 'whereas their common table and manner of diet comonly called Vicars' hall, hath bene of long time discontinued, and dissolved, for that every one of them had his own family with himself', Gillespie, *Chapter act book*, p. 117. 153 Gillespie, *Chapter act book*, p. 69.

and vegetables being supplied to the hall and kitchen of the vicars choral, suggesting that the two buildings were situated alongside each other.[154] The kitchen was probably quite large: it was spacious enough in 1346 for the prior to eat there along with the prior of St Wolstan's.[155] In fact the prior was prepared to consume his meals in a variety of different rooms; as well as his own private chamber, we find him eating in the infirmary, the sacristy, and the 'chamber of the kitchen'.[156] What is not entirely clear is whether there was one kitchen serving the needs of the whole priory, or two kitchens independently serving the refectory and the prior. Certainly the prior had his own cook – in 1344 his name was John – but it seems unlikely that the cathedral had the resources to maintain two separate kitchens. There was also a bakehouse in the precincts, the oven of which had to be repaired by masons in 1344.[157] Equally important was fresh water. At Christ Church the priory received a supply direct from the municipal cistern.

The prior lived apart from the other canons, having his own apartment on the upper floor of the west range. Here he entertained in some style, to judge from the evidence of the fourteenth-century account roll. His furniture, however, was rudimentary – straw chairs, seats and stools, though the main table was more substantial: this cost 6s. 1d., a significant sum, which must have represented well over a week's work for a professional joiner.[158] At this time the prior was concerned about security, which is no surprise given the opportunities that the priory afforded to thieves or vagabonds who managed to get into the city. In 1345 a lock and key were purchased for the door of the prior's chamber at a cost of 3d.[159] It appears that the prior lived and slept in one room, though there was space for further chambers on the upper floor of the west range. In the fourteenth century a 'serving man' waited on the prior and his laundry was handled by Ymna the washerwoman.[160] After the Reformation, following the example of the medieval priors, the deans of the cathedral continued to live in the west range until about 1600. We know they used the basement as a place to store fuel, both wood and coal, and an undercroft nearby was used as a stable.[161] With the establishment of the Four Courts in 1608, the dean finally vacated a building, that for the best part of four centuries had been the home of the principal dignitary of the cathedral.[162]

---

154 Boydell, *Music*, pp 41, 43.   155 Lydon & Fletcher, *Account roll*, p. 117.   156 Ibid., pp 5, 7, 113.   157 Ibid., p. 98. It is possible that the bakehouse was another name for the kitchen.   158 Ibid., p. 97.   159 Ibid., p. 97.   160 Ibid., p. 98.   161 Gillespie, *Chapter act book*, pp 42, 143. There is a survey of the basement of the dean's house, C 6/3/5, a source to which I was directed by Edward McParland.   162 Gilbert, quoting lost memoranda rolls, states that the four courts moved to 'the house of the deans of Christ Church', Gilbert, *Dublin*, i, 133.

By the seventeenth century the various houses and chambers which clustered around the old medieval cloister were no longer used for religious purposes. A large block for the court of the king's bench and the court of common pleas was constructed in the cloister garth, filling the angle between the refectory and the west range. While the precentor and chancellor had houses in Christ Church Yard (to the east of the cloister), almost all the buildings of the old priory were rented out, along with their vaulted undercrofts and basements. The precincts were now densely populated, a labyrinth of alleys, yards, passages and vaulted basements. Almost every available corner was rented out for houses, shops, taverns or 'tippling houses'. The commercial life of the city extended right under the cathedral, and burst out through the crypt along St John's Lane, where there was a plethora of flimsy shops and outworks lining the walls of the cathedral church. Filth and garbage, along with stacks of human excrement, began to accumulate in the open spaces and there were complaints that parents were not keeping their children and servants in order. Residents had to be reminded to use the public privy and not to 'ease theire bodies in the said churchyard, cloister or other publique place'.[163] Amidst the warren of commercial and legal activity, the cathedral in its semi-ruined condition was scarcely visible, and the ancient cloisters, where children played and drunks relieved themselves, resounded to the hubbub of urban life. Two hundred years later a glimpse of this raucous era came to light when the cathedral was being restored by Street (1871–8). Tucked into a compartment in the lower walls of the north transept was a cache of clay pipes, which had been stored there, ready for sale to those who came to the precincts of the cathedral for relaxation rather than prayer.

163 Gillespie, *Chapter act book*, pp 166, 203.

VI

Liturgy in the late medieval cathedral priory

Alan J. Fletcher

Since they stood as much at an apex of secular as of spiritual life, it is easy to forget that the primary function of cathedrals in the later middle ages was the celebration of the divine office. The cathedral priory of the Holy Trinity, commonly called Christ Church, has similarly fallen a casualty to this amnesia, though partly, it must be confessed, for reasons of its own making, and this from a very early date. By 1539, it occupied so central a position in civic consciousness that it was largely in terms of its secular value that the mayor and aldermen chose to appeal to Thomas Cromwell against its dissolution.[1] To be sure, although, as will become increasingly clear, the world outside its walls would shape the liturgy conducted within, it is principally on the nature of that liturgy that this chapter will focus.

Christ Church's liturgy in the earliest days of its foundation is obscure. Our knowledge effectively begins in the late twelfth century. Very soon after Lorcán Ua Tuathail's consecration as archbishop of Dublin in 1162, he introduced the Arrouasian observance of the rule of St Augustine to the chapter of Christ Church, latterly staffed by secular canons.[2] Ua Tuathail's initiative was strengthened about three years later by the importation of Augustinian canons of the Arrouasian observance by Diarmait mac Murchada, king of Leinster.[3] From these early beginnings, and for the better part of four centuries until its signing over to the crown in 1539, Christ Church was administered by canons regular of St Augustine.[4]

The liturgical stability which this unbroken tenure must have fostered, combined with evidence of the canons' liturgical practice from both internal and external sources, permit a reasonably confident description of the liturgy of the late medieval cathedral priory. At the synod of Cashel in 1171–2 the Anglo-Roman (or Sarum) liturgy, the great exemplar and precedent for sec-

1 *S.P. Hen. VIII*, iii, p. 545.   2 *c.*1163. Gwynn & Hadcock, *Religious houses*, pp 70–1.
3 Ibid., p. 171.   4 Ibid., p. 172.

ular, as distinct from monastic, church ritual in these islands, was officially established in Ireland. A synod held at Christ Church in 1186 further determined its adoption in the churches of the Dublin province.[5] Also, the fact that the one liturgical manuscript of undisputed Christ Church provenance,[6] the 'Christ Church' psalter, commissioned for the cathedral priory by the prior, Stephen de Derby, in the late fourteenth century,[7] has a secular, rather than monastic, liturgical affiliation, would be consistent with a subscription by Christ Church to Sarum use.[8] The fact that between the years 1280 and 1299, four archbishops of Dublin are recorded in Salisbury muniments as having granted indulgences in connection with the cathedral there, circumstantially corroborates a Dublin-Salisbury link.[9] Sarum use also features in a group of three manuscripts which, though owned in the late middle ages by the nearby church of St John the Evangelist, may have arrived at that church from Christ Church. St John's stood but a few yards from the north-east end of the cathedral and from the time of Archbishop Luke of Dublin (1230–55) was served by Christ Church canons. These are the sister processional manuscripts in Dublin and in Oxford,[10] plus an antiphonary in Dublin, T.C.D., MS 79. The 'Christ Church' psalter is sumptuous, and while the other three manuscripts are less so, they nevertheless remain handsome service books, self-evidently expensive by virtue of their size and quality of manufacture.[11] The antiphonary is especially notable in this regard. Its substantial dimensions (469mm x *c.*318mm) suggest that it facilitated not one but a group of singers when in liturgical use, the sort of ensemble, in fact, that one of its historiated initials depicts, six singing clerics gathered round one large music manuscript (Plate 18a).[12] This trio of service books bears codicological witness to what other evidence suggests, that the cathedral priory was comfortably endowed, and that its liturgy should therefore not have wanted the means for being choice in execution.[13]

For convenience's sake, the pre-Reformation liturgy of Christ Church will be considered under three categories, though this should not be taken to imply that each was wholly exclusive of the other. First, there was the 'reg-

---

5 Brannon, 'Celtic rite', p. 15.   6 Bodl., Rawl. MS G 185.   7 It was produced in East Anglia however; see Hand, 'Psalter'. See also p. 143 below.   8 See p. 144 below. Sarum use was a secular use; moreover, the use of Augustinian churches was scarcely distinguishable from secular use (J.M. Harper, *The forms and orders of western liturgy from the tenth to the eighteenth century* (Oxford, 1991), p. 30).   9 Hawkes, 'Liturgy', esp. p. 34.   10 Marsh's Library, MS Z4.2.20 and Bodl., Rawl. MS liturg. d 4.   11 The processionals are most recently described in A.J. Fletcher, *Drama, performance and polity in pre-Cromwellian Ireland* (Toronto and Cork, 2000), pp 281–5. See also p. 144 below.   12 Bodl., Rawl. MS G 185, f. 81v; reproduced as a frontispiece to Boydell, *Music*.   13 For a summary description of the endowments of the medieval cathedral priory, see Lydon & Fletcher, *Account roll*, p. x.

ular' liturgy, that is, the *cursus*, a hebdomadal round of offices that formed the basic routine of canonical life. Second, 'bespoke' liturgy comprised celebrations and offices underwritten, and sometimes inaugurated, by greater or lesser benefactors and sponsoring institutions. Thirdly, there was what might be termed 'prestige' liturgy. This dignified not only high days like greater double feasts, but also occasional, prestigious proceedings like archiepiscopal consecrations and enthronements, parliaments and, in one infamous case, even a coronation.

Office books are an obvious first port of call when attempting to establish the liturgical observances of any religious congregation. Yet although Augustinian custumals in these islands are rare – only two are known to have survived – and although other evidence for their nature suggests that on points of detail they would have diverged widely,[14] the liturgical life of the Augustinian canons was, in all salient respects, the same throughout Europe.[15] The daily *cursus* of the Christ Church canons, like that of most other contemporary communities living under rule, would have been distributed over the seven familiar hours: matins and lauds (these two were reckoned as a single hour), prime, terce, sext, none, vespers or evensong, and compline. The natural day, the period between sunrise and sunset, was conceived as comprising twelve sections. Since in this part of the northern hemisphere the natural day varies considerably according to the time of year, being longest and shortest near the summer and the winter solstices respectively, the scheduling of the hours was adjustable, falling at different times throughout the year depending on the natural day's length.[16] Slotted into this flexible daily timetable were various masses: the *missa matutinalis* or morrow mass (probably what John Estrete, in a benefaction of 1485 discussed below, referred to as the 'Quere Masse'); private masses of different sorts; the mass of Our Lady; and, usually before sext, the *missa maior* or high mass.[17] And for Augustinian canons, after the morning mass followed the daily chapter, at which, as well as hearing appointed sections of the rule and the martyrology, the canons transacted administrative matters and meted out any warranted discipline.[18] The *cursus* of 'regular' liturgy took precedence; the practicalities of eating and sleeping had to fit around it.

14 J.C. Dickinson, *The origins of the Austin canons and their introduction into England* (London, 1950), pp 172–4.   15 J.W. Clark (ed.), *The observances in use at the Augustinian priory of S. Giles and S. Andrew at Barnwell, Cambridgeshire* (Cambridge, 1897), p. lxxxii. 16 See Harper, *Western liturgy*, pp 45–57.   17 A daily Lady mass was in place from at least 1335; see further below. 18 Clark, *Observances*, pp lxxxvi and xcix. For an account of how the martyrology was used in chapter at the nearby Victorine abbey of St Thomas the Martyr, see Crosthwaite & Todd, *Obits*, pp xc–xci. The obits from the book of obits and martyrology of Christ Church in T.C.D., MS 576, are reprinted from Crosthwaite's edition in Refaussé & Lennon, *Registers*.

Thus far, a liturgy has been described whose rudiments would have resembled those of the other two congregations of Augustinian canons resident in Dublin (or, indeed, of most other cathedral establishments in these islands). However, this staple was also partly customised by a 'bespoke' liturgy, the product of the cathedral priory's unique place in the life of the city. Of course, cathedral liturgies everywhere were inflected differently and distinctively in response to local factors. Many cathedrals were centres of pilgrimage, for example, owning particular relic collections that drew visitors and their offerings. Liturgy might be devised and tailored to their visits. It is appropriate to imagine that these liturgies were conducted throughout the cathedral premises of Christ Church, at the sites at which the relics were housed. Crypts were traditional places for the exhibition of relics, though whether the Christ Church crypt was ever so used is unknown. The chapel of St Nicholas, formerly at the western end of the north aisle of the nave, would have made an appropriate site for the oil of St Nicholas that Christ Church owned, just as the chapel of St Laurence O'Toole on the south side of the quire (possibly in the south transept) may have housed at least one of his numerous relics.[19] Certainly by 1461, some of the most important relics, including the *baculus Ihesu* (formerly kept in Armagh and thought to be the staff of Jesus), were housed very near the great east window.[20]

Endowments were often made on condition that the benefactors received specific liturgical recognition. The establishment of chantry and guild chapels, a form of endowment increasingly fashionable with the laity in the fourteenth and fifteenth centuries, might even entail alteration of the internal fabric of church buildings. Endowed with one or more priests who sang for the special intentions of the founders in life and for their souls after death, these chapels introduced subroutines into the *cursus*. Christ Church was no exception. The powerful eighth earl of Kildare, Gerald Fitzgerald, had his family chantry built in a high-profile position along the north wall of the quire, near the high altar, in 1510, and was buried there in 1513.[21] This was the traditional place in churches in these islands for the erection of the Easter sepulchre in which the host was deposited on Good Friday and removed at Easter matins. Thus situated, it may have been as an Easter sepulchre that the Fitzgerald chantry was conveniently made to double. Mercantile and military interests were represented at, respectively, the Holy Trinity chapel of the merchant guild, erected in the south aisle of the nave, and the chapel of

---

19 Mills, 'Notices', pp 198–200; Refaussé & Lennon, *Registers*, pp 39–40.   20 The account of the miraculous survival of the *baculus Ihesu* after the collapse of the east window in this year is published in Crosthwaite & Todd, *Obits*, pp xix–xx.   21 John Lodge, *The peerage of Ireland*, revised Mervyn Archdall (6 vols, Dublin, 1784), i, 86; see also Miller & Power, *Holinshed*, p. 44. The chapel is described p. 104 above.

the military guild of St Edmund, king and martyr, erected either in the south transept or in the western part of the south aisle of the quire.[22] These two corporate chapels will be revisited later.

The bespoke liturgy of Christ Church in the late middle ages is relatively well documented, and reads like a barometer of the cathedral priory's importance in civic and national affairs. As early as 1174, Richard FitzGilbert, second earl of Pembroke, provided a grant to maintain a light 'in the presence of the Holy Cross.'[23] Possibly the 'Holy Cross' in question was one of Christ Church's more famous relics, the miraculous crucifix.[24] One of its faculties was the power of speech, twice exercised, according to Christ Church's late medieval relic inventory.[25] By the eve of the Reformation, the cathedral priory had accumulated an impressive tally of the great and the good who courted liturgical recognition. The bespoke liturgy of Christ Church thus came to provide powerful local aristocrats with a showcase for their patronage. It was also used to blazon the civic piety and military interests of Dublin's magnates.

Clerical and lay endowments for the celebration of bespoke masses and obits mount steadily throughout the thirteenth century, and limber up to endowments of the more ostentatious sort that by the end of the middle ages were making the erection of chantry chapels possible. Henry of London, archbishop of Dublin, provided c.1220 for a perpetual commemoration of the anniversary of his death, and c.1230, Geoffrey de Tureville, subsequently bishop of Ossory, endowed a perpetual mass celebration at the 'new altar of Blessed Mary'.[26] Here we see a recent fabric installation, a new altar, becoming the site of a bespoke liturgy.[27] It was probably either in the Lady chapel north of the quire or in the White Mary chapel, possibly located in the north transept and named after an image of Sancta Maria Alba that it housed.[28] And c.1281, two members of the laity, Geoffrey Fitz Leon and his

---

22 Mills, 'Notices', pp 199 and 200 respectively.   23 'ad ministrandum lumen coram Sancta Cruce' (C6/1/6/1, p. 13).   24 See pp 46, 93 for further discussion. Or conceivably the 'Holy Cross' was a fragment of the True Cross spoken of in the martyrology; see Crosthwaite & Todd, Obits, p. 141. J.H. Todd, in his introduction to the relics in Crosthwaite & Todd, Obits, p. lxvii, takes this True Cross to be distinct from the speaking cross of Giraldus, but the basis for the distinction is not strong.   25 'bis verba sonasse legitur' ('it is read that it uttered words on two occasions'; Refaussé & Lennon, Registers, p. 39). But in the miracle of c.1170 related by Giraldus Cambrensis, it spoke only once (Gir. Camb. op., v, 128–9); possibly the 'Book of obits and martyrology' confused the miracle with another in which the cross twice threw back money offered to it by an archer who earlier that same day had pillaged the residence of the archbishop of Dublin (Gir. Camb. op., v, 129–30).   26 'ad novum Altare Beatae Mariae' (C6/1/6/1, p. 111; compare McEnery & Refaussé, Deeds, no. 30 and no. 43).   27 And compare John Cely's dedication of a new altar in 1414 noted below.   28 Mills, 'Notices', p. 199; Refaussé & Lennon, Registers, p. 64.

wife Johanna, granted an income to Christ Church on condition that they were remembered in 'the vigils, fasts, masses and prayers, as well as in all other spiritual matters' of the canons.[29] The fourteenth century accelerated the trend, and saw some particularly lavish endowments from the well-to-do, both clerical and lay, though with lay endowment becoming increasingly conspicuous. In 1327, the year before his death, Thomas Fitz John Fitzgerald, second earl of Kildare, may have inaugurated the liturgical link between the house of Kildare and Christ Church when he retained a canon to celebrate a daily mass at the altar before the 'Cross', with a special intention for the souls of the earl, of his wife, parents, friends, and of the faithful departed.[30] This may have been at the high altar, or possibly at some altar where the *crux* of Holy Trinity (the famous relic noted above?) was displayed. But the most painstakingly prescribed liturgical recognition in this century was that drafted for John de Grauntsete and his deceased wife Alice.[31] De Grauntsete was a justice of the king's bench, a valuable ally for the cathedral priory to have on its books. It seems that this time the prior and chapter took the initiative, inscribing de Grauntsete and his affinity on 9 July 1335 into the commemorative liturgy in acknowledgment of his prolonged labour on the cathedral priory's behalf. Whether this was done in response to overtures from de Grauntsete is not known, but liturgical commemoration was clearly by now a status to cherish.

The terms of de Grauntsete's commemoration are informative, and show how the granting of full liturgical honours – it is twice noted that he was to be accorded celebrations as solemn as those accorded the first founder of the cathedral priory – might impact upon the regular *cursus*. Two canons were to be appointed to celebrate daily for him, his affinity, and for the faithful departed. On his death, the same canons were to celebrate for his soul and the souls aforementioned. One canon was to celebrate daily the Lady mass, 'as is the custom'.[32] This suggests that as far as possible, the commemoration was to be accommodated within the *cursus*, an economical expedient given that this was busy enough already. The Lady mass was probably celebrated in the Lady chapel just off the north side of the quire.[33] Three collects were stipulated, one for de Grauntsete while living, the other for Alice and the souls aforementioned, and a third, for use after de Grauntsete's death. The second retained canon was to celebrate another daily mass, this time 'at the altar before the Holy Cross', and to use the same collects.[34] Both canons,

---

29 'in vigiliis, Iejuniis, Missis, & Orationibus, necnon & in omnibus aliis Spiritualibus' (C6/1/6/1, p. 249).   30 'in altari coram Cruce Sanctae Trinitatis' (C6/1/6/2, p. 479). 31 C6/1/6/2, pp 489–92 (and translated in Lydon & Fletcher, *Account roll*, pp 148–51). 32 'prout moris est' (C6/1/6/2, p. 490).   33 Mills, 'Notices', p. 198. Though conceivably the White Mary chapel was the mass venue.   34 Possibly the high altar, or perhaps one

after vesting and before the introit of each mass, were also to say either publicly or privately a Paternoster and an Ave Maria for de Grauntsete, Alice
and the aforementioned souls. In addition to this daily twin régime, de
Grauntsete's anniversary was to be celebrated in chapter and in quire whenever the dead were commemorated. Solicitous provision was made for cover
in the event of either of the two designated canons being unable to officiate.
Further, it was directed that every missal belonging to the cathedral priory
should have a prayer for de Grauntsete, Alice, and the souls aforementioned,
inscribed in it next to the *secretum* of the mass. Lest the terms of the commemoration pass out of mind, they were to be read out twice a year, in chapter, on All Souls' Day and on Quinquagesima Sunday. They were also to be
entered in the 'Book of obits'.[35] A final stipulation reveals how, as happened
on occasion, the very item donated might itself precipitate new liturgical
action. In honour of the Trinity, de Grauntsete had also given to the 'Holy
Cross' a gold ring with a precious stone, and a silver chain. (The 'Holy Cross'
may have been the well known relic mentioned above.) Ring, stone and chain
were to be suspended from it in perpetuity. The liturgical assimilation of the
offering is apparent in the fact that some rite subsequently sprang up whereby
the stone was administered to the sick who presented themselves before the
cross. It is not known whether the stone's salutary power was held to derive
from some holy association that it had contracted (it hung, after all, from a
sacred object, perhaps a very famous one) or from some peculiar virtue which,
in accordance with lapidary lore, was thought to inhere in it. Whichever the
case, de Grauntsete's gift not only commemorated him, but simultaneously
turned his donation, and by metonymic relation de Grauntsete himself, into
part of the escapement of the cathedral priory's spiritual clockwork.

Lay gifts of items of more self-evident liturgical use than gold ring and
chain – these probably began life as personal jewellery – were a favourite sort
of benefaction in the later middle ages. Indeed, many Christ Church offerings compare with ones made throughout the British Isles at this date: they
included chalices, altar linen, statues, accoutrements for statues, service books,
copes, albs and chasubles.[36] Through providing the material necessities of the

---

at which the famous Christ Church cross was displayed.   **35** However, only Alice features, on 6 June (Refaussé & Lennon, *Registers*, p. 59).   **36** For comparable sorts of
endowment in England, see Eamonn Duffy, *The stripping of the altars: traditional religion
in England 1400–1580* (New Haven and London, 1992), pp 330–1. For examples of endowments of chalices, see Refaussé & Lennon, *Registers*, pp 56 and 72 (and compare the
inscribed chalice of John Morwylle discussed below); of altar linen, pp 65 and 76; of statues, p. 68; of statue accoutrements, p. 64 and Lydon & Fletcher, *Account roll*, p. xv and
note 31; of service books, Refaussé & Lennon, *Registers*, pp 48 and 56 and Berry, *Register*,
pp 39–40; of copes, albs and chasubles, Refaussé & Lennon, *Registers*, pp 58, 75 and 86.

daily office, especially of the mass, lay people cultivated ostensible implication in sacramental action. This implication was most effectively publicised by donating items of regular liturgical use. Since the liturgy was the public and perennial site of commerce between earth and heaven, it would be here that lay folk would seek to raise enduring memorials. Thus, bespoke liturgy elevated lay liturgical participation to a more complex plane than actual physical attendance at divine offices, important though that might be. Through donating 'mass gear' (as one medieval poet described it), laity might be perpetually in attendance at the liturgy by proxy.

Furthermore they might, by proxy, touch the holy in a way they never could even if they attended in person. The gilt chalice left to Christ Church by one John Morwylle, citizen of Dublin, in 1438 is a case in point.[37] The chalice bore his name moulded on its foot, thus whenever it was elevated at mass, even if the inscription were not noticed by anyone else, it was probably noticed by the priest, not to mention by God, whose blood, after the words of consecration, Morwylle's chalice would cup. In this way, as long as his chalice lasted, Morwylle's name would have been kept in mind and the donor centred by proxy within one of the church's holiest ministrations.[38] Another telling instance in Christ Church of the late medieval lay urge to appropriate spiritual suffrage by identification – an instance going one better than the proclamation of interdependence between benefactor and liturgy such as inscribed chalices might make – was the custom of burying lay members of the confraternity of Christ Church in the habit of the Augustinian canons.[39] This comprised, essentially, a black cassock, over which was worn a white rochet or surplice, and over that again the distinctive black capa with its hood.[40] The canons would have appeared thus habited much of the time in the cathedral priory. When celebrating the hours in quire, their standard habit would have comprised cassock and surplice, quire copes also being worn for special liturgies.[41] Sometimes the fur almuce, another distinctive item

---

37 Crosthwaite & Todd, *Obits*, pp 34 and 59.   38 Ibid., p. 59.   39 The expression *canonicus ad succurrendum* or *frater noster ad succurrendum* found in the 'Book of obits' (Refaussé & Lennon, *Registers*, pp 43–6) indicates the lay practice of donning the habit on the deathbed.   40 A.J. Fletcher, 'Black, white and grey in *Hali Meiðhad* and *Ancrene Wisse*' in *Medium Ævum*, lxii (1993), p. 71. Sometimes the fur almuce, another distinctive item of canonical garb, was placed over the *capa* like a shawl (C6/1/6/2, p. 642). The accounts of the proctor John Mos in 1542 frequently mention amices, surplices, rochets, albs, and alb girdles (C6/1/26/3, f. [5]); and compare the components of the prior's habit noted in Lydon & Fletcher, *Account roll*, pp 88–9.   41 Archbishop Talbot's ordinance of 1421 stipulated that '*in matutinalibus horis, missis, vesperis & completoriis quum cum regimine chori agitur, superpelliciis secundum eorum observantiam, tegantur ad infra*' ('at matins, masses, vespers and complines, when the business of the choir is done, let them be dressed in surplices according to their observance'), C6/1/6/2, p. 642. Sacred ministers of the mass, of course, would

of canonical garb, was placed over the *capa* like a shawl. As Richard Talbot, archbishop of Dublin, decreed in 1421, the prior and convent of Christ Church were to wear 'almuces, of grey fur on the outside and of miniver on the inside, like secular canons of cathedral churches in England and Ireland use, in solemn processions.'[42] Burial in the habit, or part of it, a lay custom observed elsewhere in the British Isles and not just by benefactors of the Augustinian canons, reveals again, incidentally, how connected Christ Church was with practices outside Ireland.[43]

Alongside liturgy affirming the individual, another developed which recognized the individual as he or she existed corporately. This is not surprising since life in the late medieval city was inconceivable outside an intersecting network of corporate memberships of various sorts. The existence of a liturgy devised for the lay confraternity of Christ Church, whose members were generally recruited from the civic élite, and which may have left a palpable trace in one of the two processional manuscripts described earlier,[44] prompts the wider observation that late medieval Dublin witnessed an increase in liturgical recognition of the various corporate bodies out of which the city was constituted. In the case of Christ Church, the bodies recognized were notably mercantile and military. While any anonymous individual might contribute towards the *opus Dei* – countless pilgrim donations fell into this category and generated appreciable income[45] – it remains conspicuous that of Christ Church's less self-effacing benefactors, most belonged to the same corporate body, the Dublin civic assembly.[46] Several named benefactors were mayors and aldermen, people like Thomas Collier, entered in the martyrology as 'a brother of our congregation'.[47] During his mayoralty in 1498, Collier presided at the council meeting at which the various city guilds were assigned their pageant responsibilities for the Corpus Christi Day procession. These responsibilities were formally enrolled in the 'Chain book' of the corporation.[48] The civic élite from which the Christ Church confraternity frequently

---

have worn the traditional mass vestments.   **42** '*almusiis pellibus de Gray ad extra, & pellibus de menyner [lege menyuer] ad infra, prout canonici seculares Ecclesiarum Cathedrarum in Anglia & Hibernia utuntur, in processionibus solemnibus*', C6/1/6/2, p. 642.   **43** Christopher Daniell, *Death and burial in medieval England 1066–1550* (London and New York, 1997), pp 155–6.   **44** Dublin, Marsh's Library, MS Z4.2.20, ff 125–6v. While Mary Clark and Raymond Refaussé (ed.), *Directory of historic Dublin guilds* (Dublin, 1993), pp 37–8, may be right to say that this is a 'text of a mass for brothers and sisters of the religious guild of St John the Baptist', if the processional reflects Christ Church practice, as is probable, its mass would have served members of the confraternity of the cathedral priory.   **45** Donations to the *baculus Ihesu* were diverted to maintain the four choristers or *paraphonistae* in the 1493 benefaction of Prior David Wynchester. See note 51 below.   **46** Refaussé & Lennon, *Registers*, p. 21.   **47** '*frater nostre congregacionis*' (Refaussé & Lennon, *Registers*, p. 70).   **48** Fletcher, *Drama, performance and polity*, pp 91–6. Collier

recruited were in turn mainly merchants. Not surprisingly, then, the chantry chapel of Dublin's senior trade guild, the guild merchant, under the patronage of the Holy Trinity, came to be erected in Christ Church. Donations to this chantry would principally have come from guild members. An important endowment was made in 1451, when the guild received its charter. Four priests were retained to celebrate every day in the chapel of the Holy Trinity, Christ Church, for the health of the king and of others, and for brothers and sisters of the confraternity in life and for their souls after death.[49] The military, too, had an official permanent presence in Christ Church at their guild chapel of St Edmund, king and martyr, though less is known about it and its attendant liturgy.[50]

A final aspect of lay bespoke liturgy worth noting was endowment aimed either at enhancing the music available in the cathedral priory or at requisitioning particular musical styles. Since music was the medium of much medieval liturgy, any change to the musical establishment necessarily had liturgical repercussions. Here the most notable lay benefaction on record is that of Thomas Bennet in 1480.[51] Bennet, son and heir of John, late mayor, provided for the instruction of four choristers (*paraphonistae*) who were to assist at certain divine offices.[52] Bennet's endowment, the effective inception of the choral foundation at Christ Church, was made for all the familiar reasons: it was for the good of the souls of Bennet, his wife, father, mother and friends. As before, the required liturgical innovations, like Bennet's refurbishment of the Lady mass, celebrated in the chapel of the Blessed Virgin Mary to the north of the high altar, seem to have been accommodated within the existing liturgical round, thereby avoiding a multiplication of offices; although the benefaction might reshape the liturgy's music, the *cursus* would be left much as it had been. In 1485, another endowment with musical implications, that of John Estrete, serjeant-at-law, shows how by the late fifteenth century lay tastes in church music in Dublin had become more educated. Estrete was aware that liturgy could, in principle, be musically customised. This time, however, some multiplication of offices was necessary. In addition to establishing a daily mass of the Holy Ghost, to be celebrated at the chapel of St Laurence O'Toole by one of the canons 'after the Quere Masse … and are [before] the high Masse att the high Auter' (that is, Estrete's new mass was sandwiched into a gap in the *cursus*), Estrete also provided for a

is omitted from the list of mayors of Dublin in T.W. Moody, F.X. Martin and F.J. Byrne (ed.), *A new history of Ireland*, ix: *maps, genealogies, lists* (Oxford, 1984), p. 553.   **49** Berry, 'Records', p. 49.   **50** On the chantry of St Edmund, see Clark & Refaussé, *Dublin guilds*, p. 41.   **51** Boydell, *Music*, pp 29–31. See ch. vii for discussion of music in the cathedral priory.   **52** The establishment of the *paraphonistae* was consolidated and their duties further specified in 1493 (see Boydell, *Music*, pp 34–6).

weekly, and evidently liturgically more ambitious, Thursday mass, to be announced by a tolling bell. It was to be sung 'with playn song and sett song, yf it may be, and yf no, att the lest gode and tretable playn song.' Moreover, the rest of the convent and 'suche as kepyn the Queyr' were to assist at it.[53] Thus by the late middle ages, the *cursus* in Christ Church had acquired a heavy pendant chain of 'microliturgies', the bespeaks of the great and the good. These added to the dehistoricised and timeless *cursus* another set of liturgical routines, uniquely Dublinesque in colour.

Lastly, Christ Church was a centre of 'prestige' liturgy. This was of its nature more or less rare, a liturgy with scarcity value. It might be once-off, as in 1487, when the young pretender Lambert Simnel was crowned Edward VI in Christ Church, his crown being supplied from the head of an obliging cathedral statue;[54] or as in 1414, less showily, but with compensatory spiritual inducements to lure a congregation, when John Cely, bishop of Down, presided at the consecration of an altar to the Blessed Virgin Mary.[55] Forty days of indulgence were promised to those attending. The earliest recorded grant of indulgence for mass attendance in Christ Church was made at Perugia in 1284, when forty days were accorded to those who, being contrite and confessed, heard mass from any canon of Christ Church, or who said a Paternoster and an Ave Maria devoutly for Christ Church benefactors, and for the souls of the faithful departed.[56]

Another variety of prestige liturgy was that of the customary, but occasional, kind, like the various forms of ceremonial acclamation from 1300 onwards of the diocesan primacy of Christ Church over St Patrick's cathedral. In this year it was decided that consecrations and burials of archbishops of Dublin should henceforth take place in Christ Church.[57] Similarly, prestige liturgy would have accompanied the parliaments and great councils that Christ Church normally hosted, as well as the swearings-in of state officials.[58]

A final distinction to be entered within this category is prestige liturgy of annual occurrence. Here we encounter liturgy that could even sortie beyond the cathedral precincts and into the streets. Corpus Christi was the liturgical feast par excellence for staging prestige liturgy of this 'extramural'

---

53 Boydell, *Music*, p. 33.   54 Martin, *Crowning of a king*.   55 Refaussé & Lennon, *Registers*, p. 52. This altar may have been in the Lady chapel, or was conceivably that of the White Mary chapel.   56 McEnery & Refaussé, *Deeds*, no. 135.   57 And that Christ Church, not St Patrick's Cathedral, should have custody of the archiepiscopal cross, mitre and ring ('*Crux, Mitra & Annulus*'), C6/1/6/1, p. 375. See Hand, 'Rivalry'.   58 See note 1 above, and Richardson & Sayles, *Irish parl.*, p. 29 (the swearing-in of the earl of Ulster as lieutenant of Ireland in Christ Church in 1332). Civic officials took their oaths there too (Refaussé & Lennon, *Registers*, p. 21).

sort. Its celebration afforded, amongst other things, an opportunity to paint a festive picture over a city-wide canvas of the place that sacred power in Dublin occupied. Yet more particularly, it may have been the sacred power wielded by Christ Church that people were required to notice: for Christ Church, before any other church, was a central assembly point in the procession of the consecrated *corpus Christi* through the city streets. Thus Christ Church in this civic liturgy would have advertised yet again its place at the heart of things. The prestige liturgy of Christ Church, profoundly theatrical in spirit, could easily be dimensioned as holy pageantry in a procession already inherently dramatic, with pageant wagons on sacred and secular subjects wheeled out by the trade guilds under the supervising eye of Dublin corporation. A trace of that holy pageantry remains in a 1542 record of the carrying of the Christ Church 'fertor' ('reliquary') on Corpus Christi Day.[59]

In extant sources, however, one annual liturgy is egregious. On the reliable assumption that the two processional manuscripts owned by the church of St John the Evangelist either originated in Christ Church or at least reflect its liturgical practice, it is evident that Christ Church made impressive provision for celebrating Easter Day. The day's first liturgical observance, a prelude to a shortened office of matins, was the '*Elevatio crucis et hostie*' (the ritual of the 'Raising of the cross and host'), in which the cross and host, deposited in the Easter sepulchre on Good Friday, were ceremonially removed, the host returned to the high altar, and the cross carried through the quire in procession. A description of the ritual may make an appropriate conclusion to this chapter.

The ritual begins before dawn in a darkened church. No lights burn except the great paschal candle and the lights inside the Easter sepulchre. The clergy and the others in attendance carry unlit candles. The precentor begins, intoning the Easter anthem '*Cum rex glorie*', which is resumed by the choir. In the meanwhile, two senior priests in surplices go to the Easter sepulchre with thurifers, and a senior priest begins the antiphon '*Elevamini, porte eternales*' in a low voice. The choir responds, and the senior priest begins the antiphon again, this time a little more loudly. The choir again responds. The senior priest begins the antiphon for a third time, louder still, and the choir responds. The thurifers then cense the sepulchre and its entrance is opened. (At some point, the host is taken out of it and placed on the altar in a pyx.) The priests light their candles from the light inside the sepulchre, and from these the other lights in the church are lit. As the priests remove the cross from inside the sepulchre, a senior priest intones the antiphon, '*Domine, abstraxisti ab inferis animam meam*'. The choir responds with the psalm, '*Exaltabo te, Domine*', after each verse of which the choir repeats the antiphon

59 In the accounts of the proctor John Mos (C6/1/26/3, f. [8]).

'*Domine, abstraxisti ab inferis animam meam*', until the cross has been placed on the altar. The priests, now at the altar, intone '*Christus resurgens*', and the choir responds. The priests sing the verse '*Quesumus, auctor omnium*', the choir responds '*In hoc paschali gaudio*', and the priests sing '*Gloria tibi, Domine*'. All genuflect, and all the bells are rung. The choir sings '*Qui surrexisti a mortuis*'. The priests intone the antiphon '*Christus resurgens*', and the choir responds '*Ex mortuis*'. During this antiphon, a procession passes through the middle of the quire with two priests carrying between them the cross that they had earlier taken from the sepulchre and laid on the altar. The thurifers and candle bearers go in advance to some altar situated outside the quire and the choir follows them, the senior persons proceeding in front. When the choir have finished the antiphon and its verse, the principal priest in that place at which the procession has halted turns to the altar and sings the versicle '*Surrexit Dominus de sepulcro*'. The prayer '*Deus, qui pro nobis Filium*', follows, after which all genuflect and adore the cross, the worthier persons first of all. Then they all return without procession into the quire. Finally, all the crosses and images in the church are uncovered, and the bells are rung for matins.

The ritual makes impressive use of lights, incense, music and choreographed liturgical movement. Moreover, the matins office that the *Elevatio* prefaced went on to enact an Easter drama (the Dublin *Visitatio sepulcri*), the first play from Ireland to have survived in full.[60] *Elevatio*, matins and *Visitatio* combine in a moment of prestige liturgy, and convey strikingly the range of aesthetic resources that the pre-Reformation liturgy of Christ Church had at its disposal.[61]

---

60 See Fletcher, *Drama, performance and polity*, pp 62–77 and 281–301.   **61** It is hoped that the words and music of this Easter liturgy will be made available in a future study.

VII

Music in the medieval cathedral priory

Barra Boydell

Direct evidence for the practice of music at Christ Church cathedral during the four and a half centuries from its foundation in the early eleventh until the late fifteenth centuries is slight. The wider context of the cathedral during the medieval period, the small handful of surviving musical sources which can be linked to the medieval cathedral priory, and what is known of the practice of sacred music in Ireland during the later medieval period do however allow the broader outlines of musical practices in the cathedral to be suggested. Plainchant formed an integral part of the celebration of the daily offices and masses in medieval monasteries and cathedrals. In monasteries and cathedral priories like Christ Church the entire community formed the choir for the daily observance of the liturgy, the acquisition of a thorough familiarity with the plainchant repertoire sung throughout the church year being part of the training of a novice. In contrast with secular cathedrals like St Patrick's,[1] there is no evidence that Christ Church used singers from outside the cathedral community before the later fifteenth century.

As the previous chapter has noted, Christ Church liturgy was based on the use of Sarum in England and thus by the later twelfth century the plainchant of the Sarum rite would have been in use at Christ Church. The earlier Celtic rite, the music of which has not survived,[2] may have persisted in some Irish centres, but the situation of Christ Church as the cathedral of Dublin was quite distinct. As a Hiberno-Norse city, pre-Anglo-Norman Dublin was nominally independent from the rest of Ireland, both politically and ecclesiastically, its closest links being with the Irish Sea region. When Dúnán became the first bishop of Dublin on the foundation of Christ Church he received his authority from the archbishop of Canterbury, to whom the next four bishops of Dublin were also to swear obedience.[3] There had been

---

1 On the medieval choir at St Patrick's, see Grindle, *Cathedral music*, pp 3–4, 6–7. 2 But see Brannon, 'Celtic rite'. 3 Gwynn, 'First bishops'; the consecration of Dúnán by the archbishop of Canterbury remains uncertain.

a marked revival of church music in Anglo-Saxon England during the late tenth century when links were established with northern French monasteries, which included both monastic reform and training in the proper singing of chant, and surviving sources of the early eleventh century from Winchester and Canterbury confirm the close links between English chant and polyphony and French and Rhenish forms of the Roman liturgy.[4] Bishop Pátraic, who succeeded Dúnán in 1074, had been trained as a Benedictine monk at Worcester cathedral priory which was already noted by the ninth century for its classical tradition of Roman chant.[5] Thus it must have been the Roman liturgy which was celebrated at Christ Church in the first century and a half of its existence, not differing significantly from what would have been heard in comparable English cathedrals with the possible exception of certain specific chants sung on feast days of Irish saints.[6]

The 'Christ Church' psalter, prepared in England on the orders of Stephen de Derby (prior of Christ Church from 1348 to c.1382) is the one medieval liturgical manuscript with musical notation which can unquestionably be linked to Christ Church.[7] The music is limited to short antiphons to seventy-seven of the psalms (usually also with the reciting tones and endings) which, with their accompanying illuminations, are of inferior quality to the rest of the manuscript and may have been inserted after the psalter came to Christ Church.[8] The feature of this psalter which has attracted the most attention is the illumination which includes eight elaborate initials, two of which are of musical interest. (Plates 18a, b) On the basis of the style of illumination the psalter is thought to have been written and decorated in East Anglia. What has not previously been noted is that the eight illuminated initials reveal that the Augustinian canons at Christ Church followed secular use in their celebration of the daily office, a practice not uncommon amongst the Augustinians in contrast to other monastic orders who followed monastic use:[9] these initials serve a practical function, marking the first psalms according to secular use for matins on successive days of the week starting on Saturday (Psalms 1, 26, 38, 52, 68, 80, and 97 in the vulgate numbering), and the first psalm for Sunday vespers (Psalm 109). In monastic use these

4 Peter Lefferts, 'Medieval England, 950–1450' in James McKinnon (ed.), *Music and society: antiquity and the middle ages* (London, 1990), pp 171–2.   5 Gwynn, 'First bishops', p. 46; *New Grove*, xx, pp 523–4.   6 Hesbert identified one *Kyrie* trope in the Dublin troper (see below) which is otherwise only known from one French source and may not have been known in England: Dom Hesbert (ed.), *Le tropaire-prosaire de Dublin* (Rouen, 1966), p. 47.   7 Bodl., Rawl. MS G 185; see Otto Pächt, 'A Giottoesque episode in English medieval art' in *Journal of the Warburg and Courtauld Institutes*, vi (1943), pp 51–71; Hand, 'Psalter', pp 311–22; Hawkes, 'Liturgy'. See also pp 16–17 for further details of the Christ Church psalter.   8 Hand, 'Psalter', p. 312.   9 Harrison, *Music*, p. 48.

same psalms occupy very much less significant positions (with the exception of Psalm 109 which is likewise the first psalm for Sunday vespers).

The text of Psalm 80 (vulgate) '*Exultate Deo*' is illustrated by a miniature showing five monks in the black habits of the Augustinians making music on harp, psaltery, what might be termed a rectangular 'harp', and two straight trumpets, together with two singers. (Plate 18a) The imagery is symbolic, reflecting the words of the psalm 'Raise a song, sound the timbrel, the sweet lyre with the harp': while it does include instruments in contemporary use others, notably the rectangular 'harp', are symbolic and do not bear organological scrutiny.[10] A second miniature accompanying Psalm 97 (vulgate) '*Cantate Domino*' belongs to a widely-represented iconographical tradition in which this psalm is illustrated with a group of monks or clerics singing from music.[11] (Plate 18b) Here six monks sing from a music book placed on a lectern, four being visible full-length of whom three wear coloured copes. In view of the iconographical tradition associated with this particular psalm and of the probable English provenance of this manuscript, this illustration is not specific to Christ Church and whether the music is plainchant or polyphony cannot be determined.[12] Within the borders of the illuminated initial two grotesque rustics sing from music books in a parody of the more ordered singing of the monks.

Three liturgical manuscripts with plainchant from the church of St John the Evangelist, only yards from the cathedral and whose cure was the responsibility of the canons of Christ Church, may have originated from the cathedral. These comprise an antiphonal copied *c.*1435[13] and two processionals dating from *c.*1400 which are of particular importance as the sources for the liturgical drama known as the Dublin *Visitatio sepulcri* play.[14] These manuscripts all follow Sarum use. Although now accepted as originating from St Patrick's rather than Christ Church, the 'Dublin troper'[15] dating from *c.*1360 with later additions is nevertheless of particular interest for the light it casts on Dublin cathedral music during the later fourteenth century.[16] The major

10 Like this rectangular 'harp', fantastic instruments on Irish high crosses may derive from late antique David imagery; see Ann Buckley, 'Music-related imagery on early Christian insular sculpture: identification, context, function' in *Imago musicae*, viii (1991), pp 165ff. 11 Christopher Page, 'An English motet of the 14th century in performance: two contemporary images' in *Early Music*, xxv (1997), pp 7–34. 12 Some *Cantate Domino* miniatures do clearly show the singers performing polyphonic music; see Page, 'English motet'. 13 T.C.D., MS. 79 (formerly MS. B.I.4); see also Hawkes, 'Liturgy', pp 44–6; Brannon, 'Celtic rite'. 14 Marsh's Lib., MS. Z4.2.20; Bodl., Rawl. MS liturg. d 4; transcribed in Máire Egan-Buffet and A.J. Fletcher, 'The Dublin *Visitatio sepulcri* play' in *R.I.A. Proc.*, xc, C (1990), pp 159–241; see also Hawkes, 'Liturgy', pp 40–4. For a discussion of the links with Christ Church for the *Visitatio sepulcri* manuscripts, Lydon & Fletcher, *Account roll*, p. xxxii. 15 C.U.L., Add. MS 710. 16 Facsimile in Hesbert, *Tropaire-prosaire*; see also Hawkes, 'Liturgy ', pp 35–8; Hand, 'Camb. MS.', pp 17–23.

part of this manuscript, the troper itself (ff.32r–131v), contains plainchant for the ordinary of the mass, frequently embellished with interpolated tropes, along with sequences for various feasts including two in honour of St Patrick, and Marian sequences which are likely to have been sung at the votive mass of the Virgin. While one of the two sequences in honour of St Patrick ('*Laetabundus decantet*', f.101v–102r) uses the same melody as a popular Christmas sequence probably of French origin ('*Laetabundus exsultet*', f.41v), the second ('*Laeta lux est*', f.50v) could have been composed in Dublin.[17] Also likely to have been composed in Dublin are thirteen of the Marian sequences for which this is the only known source and a further eight for which this is the earliest recorded source.[18] However, none of the tropes can be shown to be Irish.[19] This manuscript is best known for the three-voice *Angelus ad Virginem* inserted in a later hand. This religious song, of English or French thirteenth-century origin, enjoyed wide popularity in the late middle ages and is referred to by Chaucer in 'The miller's tale'.[20] A setting for three voices, it is unique to the Dublin manuscript and may be a locally-notated version of the improvised polyphonic tradition of descanting.[21]

Although plainchant was sung on a daily basis, and chantries within the cathedral such as that of four priests granted to the Guild of the Holy Trinity in 1451 could have had a musical dimension,[22] it is unclear to what extent polyphonic music was sung at Christ Church. In view of contemporary links with southern England, it is very possible that polyphony similar to that in the eleventh-century Winchester troper (the earliest surviving practical source of liturgical polyphony in western Europe)[23] was sung in the pre-Norman cathedral. Within the context of his introduction of the Augustinian canons *c.*1163, a thirteenth-century life of Lorcán Ua Tuathail mentions the emphasis he placed on music as part of the overall presentation of religion to the people, alongside 'proper priests' and church decoration. Apparently referring to the introduction of distinct new musical practices, possibly the introduction of polyphony sung by experienced singers, it also states that he made 'regular singers [stand] around the altar that they might praise the holy name of the Lord; and he introduced order to the celebrations, and made sweet measures [modes] into their sounds'.[24] Significantly, a strong tradition of

17 Hesbert, *Tropaire-prosaire*, pp 20 (n. 6), 21, 58, 60, 79f. 18 Ibid., pp 21, 63–5, selected transcriptions and commentary, pp 86–96. 19 Ibid., p. 57. 20 E.J. Dobson and F.L. Harrison, *Medieval English songs* (London, 1979), pp 176–83, 266–8, 303–5; John Stevens, 'Angelus ad Virginem: the history of a medieval song' in *Medieval studies for J.A.W. Bennett* (Oxford, 1981), pp 297–328; Iain Fenlon, *Cambridge music manuscripts, 900–1700* (Cambridge, 1982), pp 79–81; Hesbert, *Tropaire-prosaire*, pp 105–10, 186–7, 192–3. 21 Dobson & Harrison, *Medieval English songs*, p. 178. 22 Berry, 'Records', p. 49. 23 Corpus Christi College, Cambridge, MS 473. 24 '*Fecitque regulares cantores circa altare,*

polyphonic music is associated with at least some Augustinian houses in Britain[25] and the existence of a precentor at Christ Church in 1300[26] suggests a concern with musical practices which may have gone beyond the regular cycle of plainchant. The evidence from England suggests that by the thirteenth and fourteenth centuries polyphony had become a normal part of the musical celebration of the office and mass, especially on major feast days, and that the practice of improvised descant was particularly widespread.[27] There is no reason to suppose that Christ Church cathedral was an exception to this practice but, apart from *Angelus ad Virginem* and the assumed parallels with English cathedrals for which polyphonic repertories are known, the evidence of the few other known sources of medieval Irish sacred polyphony provide the only glimpses of what may have been sung.[28]

Two short examples of polyphony surviving from later twelfth and thirteenth century Ireland show that early polyphony in Ireland was closely linked with and not behind practices elsewhere in western Europe. A psalter written in the middle or second half of the twelfth century includes a short passage set for three voices using a *Benedicamus* melody of the Sarum rite as the lowest voice.[29] This is early in the European context for three-part music. A late twelfth/early thirteenth-century gradual which may have originated in the Benedictine monastery at Downpatrick (later to become a cathedral) includes a short piece of two-part polyphony, the verse '*Dicant nunc*' from the processional Easter antiphon '*Christus resurgens*'. This is unique in providing the only musical concordance for a polyphonic piece from before the later twelfth century, the same music occurring in a manuscript from Chartres dating from *c.*1100.[30] This gradual also demonstrates links with Winchester, whose importance as a centre of polyphony in the twelfth century has already been noted. A fragment of a four-voice motet of English origin dating from before 1325, '*Rota versatilis*', the complete music and text for which has been

vt laudarent nomen Domini, et dedit in celebrationibus decus, et in sono eorum dulces fecit modos'; copy *c.*1400 of lost mid-thirteenth century original, Charles Plummer (ed.), 'Vie et miracles de S. Laurent, archvêque de Dublin', in *Analecta Bollandiana*, xxxiii (1914), pp 137–8.   25 Mary Berry, 'Augustinian canons' in *New Grove*, i, p. 697.   26 McEnery & Refaussé, *Deeds*, no. 164.   27 Harrison, *Music*, ch. 3.   28 F.L. Harrison, 'Polyphony in medieval Ireland' in Martin Ruhnke (ed.), *Festschrift Bruno Stäblein zum siebzigsten Geburtstag* (Kassel, 1967), pp 74–8.   29 B.L., Add. MS 36,929; illustrated in Françoise Henry and G.L. Marsh-Micheli, 'A century of Irish illumination (1070–1170)', in *R.I.A. Proc.*, lxii, C (1964), plate xlii; transcribed in Harrison, 'Polyphony', p. 78.   30 Bodl., Rawl. MS C 892, f. 67v–68r; Marion Gushee, 'The polyphonic music of the medieval monastery, cathedral and university' in McKinnon, *Music and society*, p. 151, transcribed in Harrison, 'Polyphony', p. 78, reproduced in J.F. Rankin, *Down cathedral* (Belfast, 1997), p. 61; see also E.W.B. Nicholson, *Early Bodleian music* (London, 1913), iii, pp lxxxivf, pls LXI–LXIV, who suggested Waterford as the provenance.

reconstructed from four fragments including this one, was bound into a four-teenth-century missal of the Augustinian canons proper of the church of St Thomas the Martyr, Dublin.[31] The link with Dublin Augustinian canons, while not those of Holy Trinity, makes this source of particular interest. The only other polyphonic music known from a sacred context in medieval Ireland, some fragments of mensural notation inscribed probably in the later fifteenth century on pieces of slate found at Smarmore, County Louth,[32] suggest that more sophisticated polyphony may have been sung not only in larger cathedrals and monasteries but also in smaller, more isolated communities.

These examples of polyphony and possible parallels with English cathedrals provide little more than circumstantial evidence that polyphonic music was sung in the cathedral. Holy Trinity was a small community, but polyphony of this period was normally sung with only one or two voices to a part. It has been suggested that a low level of literacy prevailed amongst the canons during the later fourteenth and fifteenth centuries,[33] which in turn might suggest that the ability to read the complex musical notation required for composed poly-phonic music may not always have been present amongst this small community. However, the unusually high level of sophistication of the late fourteenth-century *Visitatio sepulcri* play associated with Christ Church suggests that the argument in favour of a low level of literacy amongst the canons at this period may not be valid.[34] Even were composed polyphonic music not widely sung at Christ Church, improvised polyphony must surely have been heard more frequently. Improvisatory musical practices, however, seldom leave their mark in the records and, unless sources of polyphonic music from the later medieval period which can firmly be linked to Christ Church come to light, the question of how often, how elaborate, or how well composed polyphony was sung within the cathedral during the middle ages must remain unanswered.

The presence of the play 'The pride of life' in the fourteenth century account roll of the priory of the Holy Trinity draws attention to the involvement of the Augustinian canons in the performance of drama.[35] Apart from a stage direction for the character of Nuncius to sing (doubtless a secular and not a liturgical song) when he says 'I must sing wherever I go',[36] there are no indications of music in 'The pride of life'. However, the music and text

31 B.L., Add. MS 24,198; Margaret Bent, 'Rota versatilis: towards a reconstruction', in Ian Bent (ed.), *Source materials and the interpretation of music: a memorial volume to Thurston Dart* (London, 1981), pp 65–98, incl. transcription; facsimile in F.L. Harrison and R. Wibberly (ed.), *Manuscripts of fourteenth-century English polyphony* (London, 1981), pp 3–8. 32 National Museum of Ireland, accession nos 1961: 12, 24, 34, 41; transcribed and illustrated in Harrison, 'Polyphony'; see also A.J. Bliss, 'The inscribed slates at Smarmore' in *R.I.A. Proc.*, lxiv, C (1965), pp 33–60. 33 Lydon & Fletcher, *Account roll*, p. xx. 34 Egan-Buffet & Fletcher, '*Visitatio sepulcri*', p. 165. 35 Lydon & Fletcher, *Account roll*, pp xxii–xlii, 126–42. 36 Ibid., p. 136.

for an Easter play, the *Visitatio sepulcri*, survives in the two processionals dating from *c.*1400 from the church of St John the Evangelist,[37] and the priory of Holy Trinity continued to be actively involved in the performance of liturgical drama right up to the eve of the Reformation. The music of the *Visitatio sepulcri* includes the liturgical hymn '*Te Deum laudamus*' and the sequence '*Victime paschali laudes*', as well as phrases linked both textually and musically to earlier continental Easter plays, but it also includes music and text which is unique.[38]

From the tenth century primitive organs were used in some monasteries and cathedrals, most famously at Winchester which may have had links with Christ Church a century later. By the early fifteenth century organs were becoming more widespread and a cathedral of the relative importance of Christ Church may have had one or more instruments. Unsupported claims that there was an organ at Christ Church in 1358 and that a new organ was built there in 1470 remain unconfirmed,[39] although at St Patrick's cathedral 'a pair of organs' had been bequeathed for use in the Lady chapel in 1471.[40] While musical activity in the cathedral priory during the medieval period would have been overwhelmingly within the broad context of the liturgy, the prior, both as a member of the upper house of the Irish parliament and as head of the leading religious house in Dublin, frequently had occasion to entertain important visitors and benefactors. On these occasions musical entertainment might be called for, as in 1338 when he entertained the visiting justices and payment was made to the justices' trumpeters in the refectory and also to 'a certain little harper'.[41] A further extra-liturgical allusion to music occurs on one of the twelfth-century capitals in the cathedral on which is carved a number of figures including musicians or minstrels.[42]

During the fifteenth century it was increasingly the practice for cathedrals and larger monastic institutions to elaborate the celebration of the liturgy, in particular of the Lady mass, by the singing of polyphony and the addition of boys' voices. This development typically took place first in the secular cathedrals, and so too in Dublin it is first noted at St Patrick's cathedral in 1431, but it was to be some time before it was adopted at Christ Church. When it did take place in 1480 it marked perhaps the most significant development in the musical life of the cathedral up to that time and formed the foundation for the cathedral's subsequent choral tradition.

37 See note 14.   38 Egan-Buffet & Fletcher, '*Visitatio sepulcri*', pp 182f.   39 W.H. Grattan Flood, 'Irish organ-builders from the eighth to the close of the eighteenth century' in *R.S.A.I. Jn.*, xl (1910), pp 229–34; 'The organs of Christ Church cathedral, Dublin' [n.d.] newspaper article C6/6/4/2/8, source unknown.   40 Berry, *Register*, p. 26.   41 Lydon & Fletcher, *Account roll*, p. 19.   42 Stalley, 'Sculpture', fig. 40.

THE EARLY MODERN CATHEDRAL

VIII

The coming of reform, 1500–58

Raymond Gillespie

Between 1500 and 1558 the assumptions on which the political and religious life of Ireland rested were transformed. Politically the Dublin administration, headed by an Englishman after 1534, began a campaign to extend its authority outside the Anglo-Irish Pale. The replacement in 1541 of the traditional style of the rulers of Ireland as 'dominus Hiberniae' with the new 'rex Hiberniae' was not merely cosmetic. The influx of New English administrators who oversaw the consequent changes had a long term impact. Administrative changes were accompanied by religious change, on the tacit assumption that the ruler's religion should be the religion of his subjects also. The nature of that religion was an open question. It remained unresolved in 1558 whether it was to be the anglican-catholicism of Henry VIII, the more radical Protestant world of Edward VI or the catholicism of Mary. This religious debate impacted directly on the community which worked and worshipped around Christ Church.

Insofar as the history of an undying monastic corporation such as that of the early sixteenth century Augustinian priory of Holy Trinity or Christ Church can have clear cut turning points, the resignation of William Hassard as prior of the house in 1537 was, in retrospect at least, pivotal. Hassard had been prior for seventeen years, having been elected by the chapter to succeed Richard Skerret in 1520.[1] Most of his life was spent in the priory, witnessing a deed as early as 1493.[2] The route by which Hassard became prior was a traditional one, from canon to sub-prior on the death of Thomas Fich in January 1518, and prior two years later.

The office of prior to which Hassard succeeded was an influential one.[3] Within the community he presided over chapter meetings and allocated tasks,

---

[1] The 'Book of obits' dates Skerret's death to 13 March 1519. The election was delayed as Hassard was still sub-prior in February 1520 but was prior by July 1521 (Refaussé & Lennon, *Registers*, p. 63; McEnery & Refaussé, *Deeds*, nos 408, 409). [2] McEnery & Refaussé, *Deeds*, no. 357. [3] Technically the abbot of the community was the archbishop

although the extent to which the house was an autocracy or a communal enterprise is masked by its legal form. The prior also acted as a bridge between the monastic cathedral and the wider worlds of church and state. Christ Church had a twofold function of monastic house and cathedral, although much of the diocesan administration was based at St Patrick's. Hassard was both prior and dean of the cathedral church and hence an important diocesan figure. In the absence of the archbishop the prior of Christ Church, sometimes assisted by the dean of St Patrick's, acted as keeper of the spiritualities of the see, symbolised by his custody of the archiepiscopal cross.[4] These functions were not honorific. During the vacancy after the death of Archbishop William Rokeby in 1521 Hassard confirmed the election of the prior of All Hallows and the new abbot of St Thomas's as well as suspending an interdict imposed by the bishop of Ossory on the earl of Ormond.[5]

The friendships which the prior made in this ecclesiastical world are revealed in the entries in the cathedral's 'Book of obits'. Peter Mann, the prior of Holmpatrick, and Walter Hancock, prior of All Saints, were both remembered in the cathedral's masses as were some persons unconnected with monastic houses such as John Allyne, dean of St Patrick's.[6] These contacts were not restricted to Dublin as members of other Augustinian houses, such as Cartmel in Cumbria and Llanthony in Monmouthshire, were also included as was a Benedictine monk from St Werburgh's in Chester, which had Dublin contacts.[7]

The prior's contacts were not solely religious. He was responsible for the defence of the house's temporal rights. For this reason gaps between priors were usually short. The prior petitioned parliament or the corporation of Dublin and was the named party in legal actions involving the canons.[8] He was also a member of the upper house in parliament. Through these contacts the prior was well known in élite Irish society. Prior Skerret, for example, was friendly with the earl of Ormond. Such links may account for the inclusion in the obits of Thomas Plunket of Dunsoghly, chief justice of common pleas, and Richard Delahide, chief baron of the exchequer, in 1514 and 1539.[9] Such contacts imposed obligations on the prior, including that of hospitality, and he was excused from living the common life with the rest of the convent, having instead a house at the west end of the church.[10]

of Dublin, *Alen's reg.*, p. 286.   4 Lawlor, 'Liber niger', p. 11; *Cal. Carew MSS, 1515–74*, p. 60.   5 B.L., Add. Charters 7043, 7044; *Irish mon. deeds*, pp 137–9.   6 Refaussé & Lennon, *Registers*, pp 40, 53, 75.   7 Ibid., pp 77, 81.   8 *Anc. rec. Dublin*, i, 383; McEnery & Refaussé, *Deeds*, nos 378, 405, 401, 429.   9 Edmund Curtis (ed.), *Calendar of Ormond deeds* (6 vols, Irish Manuscripts Commission, Dublin, 1932–43), iv, pp 28, 316; Refaussé & Lennon, *Registers*, pp 41, 59.   10 For the location of the house B.L., Add MS 4813, f. 7.

Given these responsibilities priors could not give their undivided attention to the day-to-day management of the convent. A sub-prior acted in their absence. There were four sub-priors in the early sixteenth century. Thomas Fich, who died in 1518, was succeeded by Hassard who after his appointment as prior had three sub-priors in succession: Richard Walsh, William Loghan and Richard Ball. Lack of evidence makes it difficult to measure the effectiveness of these men but one, Thomas Fich, stands out since he reorganised the priory muniments in the early sixteenth century.[11] There were few other officials in the house apart from the precentor and sacrist who were responsible for the organisation of worship in the church. A canon must have acted as cellarer to ensure food supplies and part of a cellarer's account survives for 1541.[12] No treasurer is mentioned among the priory's officers which may suggest decentralisation among the other officials.

The community over which Hassard presided fluctuated between eleven and twelve canons, slightly higher than the ten which was the late fifteenth-century average for the house.[13] In Irish terms this was a large establishment. Only the Cistercian houses of St Mary's in Dublin and Mellifont could muster larger communities with sixteen and fourteen members respectively at the dissolution of the religious houses in the late 1530s. On average only four 'conventual persons' from each dissolved house received pensions.[14] By comparison with Augustinian houses elsewhere Christ Church was a small community. Carlisle, which was both a cathedral and an Augustinian priory on the edge of English authority, had a community of fourteen canons and five novices in 1521 and St Andrews, a similar institution in Scotland, had thirty canons in 1555. The stability of the Christ Church community over time suggests that some target, possibly determined by available resources, was being aimed at. Of the twenty-eight English Augustinian houses in the 1530s whose wealth lay in the same range as that of Christ Church (£100–£150) the mean size of the community was ten, about equal to Christ Church.[15]

A profile of the Christ Church community can be constructed using the biographies of the thirty-five canons associated with the house between 1500

11 For further details, Gillespie, 'Archives', pp 8–9.   12 McEnery & Refaussé, *Deeds*, no. 431.   13 Ibid., nos 1158, 1154, 1131, 1121, 1109, 357, 353, 1046, 346; *Irish mon. deeds*, p. 242; Newport B. White (ed.), *Registrum diocesis Dublinensis* (Irish Manuscripts Commission, Dublin, 1959), p. 33; 'Dillon papers' in *Anal. Hib.*, no. 20 (1958), p. 27.   14 Calculated from the pensions paid in *Fiants Ire., Hen. VIII*.   15 D.M. Robinson, *The geography of Augustinian settlement in medieval England* (2 vols, Oxford, 1980), appendices 14, 20; I.B. Cowan, and D.E. Easson, *Medieval religious houses: Scotland* (2nd ed., London, 1976), p. 96; Mark Dilworth, 'Canons regular and the Reformation' in A.A. MacDonald, Michael Lynch and I.B. Cowan (eds), *The Renaissance in Scotland* (Leiden, 1994), pp 172, 177.

and 1540. With one exception their surnames suggest they were of English
or Anglo-Irish origin, which defined the cathedral as a centre of Anglo-Irish
civility. The only native Irishman, Nicholas Owgan, appears in a list of canons
at the reorganisation of the priory.[16] It may be that he came to Christ Church
when his own community was dissolved, since some Irish Augustinian houses,
such as Great Connell in Kildare, had a number of native Irish canons.[17]
Two of the canons at the dissolution in 1540 were English. Robert Castle,
sometimes known as Paynswick (probably after his birthplace in Gloucestershire), a canon of the Augustinian house of Llanthony in Gloucestershire,
was in Ireland to manage the priory's estates at Duleek. William Owen came
to the Dublin house after the dissolution of the Augustinian house at
Haghmon in Shropshire in 1539.[18] Surname evidence suggests that most
Christ Church canons were drawn from prominent Dublin families such as
Ball, Kerdiff, Loghan and Stanihurst. Prior Richard Skerret may have been
from Dublin or from the main branch of the family in Galway.[19] Some were
certainly from outside the city. Thomas Lewet, who died in 1528, was from
Clonmel and N. Loghan, first listed as a canon in 1478, was ordained at New-
town Trim in County Meath.[20]

   Most Christ Church canons came from well-established families with
backgrounds in the law, land, trade or the church. John Highly, for instance,
was the son of a modest Dublin merchant, Peter Highly.[21] More specula-
tively William Loghan and Laurence Hancock may be related to John Loghan
and Nicholas Hancock, both merchants and former mayors of Dublin who
died in 1529 and 1547 respectively, and John Kerdiff to Sir John Kerdiff,
chief justice of common pleas.[22] The decision to enter the Augustinian priory
was clearly a complex one. Some Dublin families who provided canons had
well-established links with the house. The surnames of many of the sixteenth-
century canons, such as Hassard, Cantrell, Fich, Lambkyn, Heyne and
Loghan, appear in the cathedral's 'Book of obits' before the sixteenth century.[23] At least some of these families saw the church as a career path for
their children. Prior Richard Skerret, who died in 1518, was almost certainly
a brother of Robert Skerret, prebendary of Tipper, Mulhuddart and Castle-

---

16 McEnery & Refaussé, *Deeds*, no. 432.   17 For example M.C. Griffith, *Calendar of inquisitions formerly in the office of chief remembrancer of the exchequer: County Dublin* (Irish
Manuscripts Commission, Dublin, 1991), p. 44.   18 For Castle see below; Owen signed the
deed of surrender at Haghmon in 1539 (*Eighth report of the deputy keeper of the public records
[of England]* (London, 1847), p. 22) and by early 1540 was in Christ Church (McEnery &
Refaussé, *Deeds*, no. 432).   19 Hardiman, *Galway*, p. 19.   20 McEnery & Refaussé, *Deeds*,
nos 1147, 972, 313.   21 Berry, *Register*, p. 131.   22 Refaussé & Lennon, *Registers*, pp 46,
74.   23 Ibid., pp 46, 56, 69 (Cantrell); 40, 41, 45, 46, 63, 71 (Hassard); 53, 54, 63, 77
(Heyne); 47, 51 (Lambkyn); 45, 46, 54, 60, 65 (Loghan); 42, 49, 52, 55, 61 (Fich).

knock in St Patrick's, who died in 1519 and left 40s. to Christ Church. Thomas Fich, who died in 1518, was probably a brother of Geoffrey Fich, dean of St Patrick's, who also endowed the priory at his death and Nicholas Kerdiff, chancellor of St Patrick's from 1502 until 1522, may have been related to John Kerdiff of Christ Church.[24] For others the route to Christ Church was more indirect. Richard Walsh, the sub-prior who died in 1521, had been ordained before entering the community. Walsh had served as a chaplain in St Werburgh's and, presumably unable to find a benefice, entered the community.[25] Prior Hassard may have followed a similar path since a William Hassard was a chaplain in Ardee in 1483.[26]

The careers of the thirty-five individuals who served in the community between 1500 and 1540 fall into two categories, those who spent their entire lives in one community and those who were more peripatetic. Witness lists of deeds and the entries in the 'Book of obits' record the core of the community who spent their entire ministry in Christ Church from their profession in their late teens or early twenties until their death. John Hassard, for instance, first appears as a member of the convent as witness to a deed of 1479 and thereafter witnessed deeds regularly until his death as 'sacerdos et canonicus', recorded in the obits under 1516. John Kendyll's career ran from 1493 until 1529. Richard Walsh, already ordained when he entered the priory, first featured in 1502 and died as sub prior in 1521.[27]

The lives of these members of the priory were built around prayer and study as prescribed by the Augustinian rule which was flexibly executed. Central to this was the *opus Dei*, the recital of the monastic office and the mass. The offices consisted of the night prayer of matins, followed by prime, terce, sext, nones, vespers and compline at sunset. The morning, or Mary mass was celebrated after the office of prime and high mass after terce. Other masses might be included according to the liturgical season. In 1493, for instance, a daily mass of St Mary is mentioned along with the mass of Jesus on Fridays during Lent.[28] The flexibility of the Augustinian rule meant that the entire community would not participate in every event since pastoral or administrative concerns prevented such commitment. The rather late evidence of the purchase of a total of 2,200 mass breads in the proctor's account of 1542 suggests that, allowing for two masses a day, probably no more than

24 Lawlor, *Fasti*, pp 96, 168, 137, 43, 63; Refaussé & Lennon, *Registers*, pp 48, 63, 42, 52–3.   25 McEnery & Refaussé, *Deeds*, no. 380.   26 Ibid., no. 335.   27 For Hassard, McEnery & Refaussé, *Deeds*, nos 1020, 353, 1042, 346, 357, 1080, 1082, 1112, 1109, *Irish mon. deeds*, p. 242, Refaussé & Lennon, *Registers*, p. 41; for Walsh, McEnery & Refaussé, *Deeds*, nos 380, 1112, 1131, *Irish mon. deeds*, p. 242, Refaussé & Lennon, *Registers*, p. 50; for Kendyll, McEnery & Refaussé, *Deeds*, nos 357, 1109, Refaussé & Lennon, *Registers*, p. 72.   28 McEnery & Refaussé, *Deeds*, nos 357; Lawlor, 'Liber niger', p. 17.

three of the community of twelve would be present and communicating at each mass.[29]

Private masses were said to fulfil the terms of chantry endowments. These could be said in the side chapels such as the Mary chapel. The Holy Ghost chapel on the south side of the quire was a chantry for the mass of the Holy Ghost. Only one family chantry existed, that built by Gerald Fitzgerald, eighth earl of Kildare, by 1512 in the north aisle of the quire.[30] The precentor, who in 1539 was Walter White, managed the liturgical round aided by a sub-precentor or sacrist, a post held by John Mos in 1539. He cared for the church and its contents. From 1493 a choirmaster was employed to train the choir.[31]

Ecclesiastical needs were met in a number of ways. Perishable goods such as oil and bread and wine for communion were purchased from city suppliers.[32] More enduring was the accumulated plate and vestments. The fourteenth-century psalter, for example, was probably still in use in the church until at least the 1540s.[33] From time to time cloth was purchased to make surplices and embroiderers paid to decorate them. The priory also acquired material by bequest. In 1525 Christopher Ussher, a former mayor of Dublin, bequeathed a set of red velvet vestments to the priory. John Savage, another mayor, who died in 1499, also bequeathed vestments and both men were remembered for this in masses.[34]

Outside the daily liturgical round it is difficult to be precise as to how the community spent its time. There was a daily chapter meeting before terce at which a chapter of the rule and extracts from the gospels were read and convent business transacted. To judge from the surviving deeds the cathedral business was transacted only once a year.[35] At least some of the canons' time was spent in pastoral work and in study. The community's small size exempted it from the Augustinian requirement to maintain a student at Oxford. However two early sixteenth-century Dubliners, Walter White and Thomas Fich, had studied at Oxford.[36] Collections of theological texts, such

---

29 C6/1/26/3, no. 2.   30 Miller & Power, *Holinshed*, p. 44; *The annals of Ireland by Friar John Clyn and Tady Dowling*, ed. Richard Butler (Dublin, 1849), p. 33.   31 McEnery & Refaussé, *Deeds*, no. 431; Lawlor, 'Liber niger', p. 17.   32 C6/1/26/3, no. 2.   33 Hand, 'Psalter'.   34 Refaussé & Lennon, *Registers*, pp 43, 86; C6/1/26/3, no. 2; for this issue generally Margaret Murphy, 'The high cost of dying: an analysis of *pro anima* bequests in medieval Dublin' in W.J. Shiels and Diana Wood (ed.), *The church and wealth: studies in church history*, xxiv (Oxford, 1987), pp 111–22.   35 Much of the material in the 'Book of obits', including the rule, the gospel passages and the martyrology seems to have been for use in the chapter.   36 *Chapters of the Augustinian canons*, ed. H.E. Slater (London, 1922), pp xxxvi–xxxvii, 125; A.B. Emden, *A biographical dictionary of the university of Oxford to 1500* (3 vols, Oxford, 1952), ii, 735; A.B. Emden, *A biographical register of the university of Oxford, 1501–1540* (Oxford, 1974), p. 624.

as those in the 'Liber niger' which was used into the sixteenth century, were available but how frequently they were consulted is unknown. The community was keen to acquire new works and bequests were made to them. The books of John Alleyn, the dean of St Patrick's, including works on canon law, were appropriated by the priory despite the dean's wish that they be sold for the poor.[37]

An alternative career path followed by a minority of the canons at Christ Church was a more peripatetic one. These individuals witnessed only one or two deeds suggesting they spent only a short period in the house. Thomas English, for example, witnessed only one deed, in 1518, and Thomas Heuet and Patrick Monsell appear only in 1522.[38] Some of these men may have been passing through on their way to other houses or to benefices or may have been attached to the cathedral temporarily for some reason. Henry Levet, who witnessed one deed in 1505, was an Augustinian who was appointed a papal judge delegate in Dublin in 1503.[39] The mobility of some clergy highlights the fact that the Augustinian canons were not an enclosed order and that they involved themselves in the wider community. John Hassard was a curate in a city church, Thomas Water served as Mary priest in the nearby St Werburgh's from 1510 until 1513 and Richard Heyne may be the absentee rector of the same name in the parish of Loughbracken in County Dublin in 1526.[40] Such external contacts may have served to defuse the tensions which must have built up in an all-male community, but the lack of visitation evidence makes it impossible to make judgements about the spiritual or moral life of the community.

These interchanges between the Augustinian house and the wider world indicate that the cathedral had functions wider than those of a monastic church. At a national level it was the meeting place of the Irish parliament, which sat in the frater (refectory) of the priory. So used was the lord deputy to attending parliament at Christ Church that he stored his parliamentary robes there.[41] At a regional level it acted as a spiritual centre for the Pale and the home of two of the most famous relics of early sixteenth-century Ireland, the *baculus Ihesu* and the miraculous speaking crucifix, as well as a collection of other relics.[42] This made it an important pilgrimage centre. The business

---

37 The circumstances of Alleyn's bequest are dealt with in Crosthwaite & Todd, *Obits*, pp xxvii–xxxiii, 5, 52.   38 McEnery & Refaussé, *Deeds*, no. 1131, 'Dillon papers', p. 27.   39 McEnery & Refaussé, *Deeds*, no. 383; *Cal. papal letters, xvii, pt 1 (Alexander VI, 1495–1503)*, ed. A.P. Fuller (Dublin, 1994), no. 989.   40 J.G. Smyly, 'Old deeds in the library of Trinity College, Dublin' in *Hermathena*, lxxxii (1948), p. 118; J.L. Robinson, 'Churchwardens' accounts, 1484–1600, St Werburgh's, Dublin' in *R.S.A.I. Jn.*, xliv (1914), pp 134, 142; Griffith, *Inquisitions*, p. 18.   41 *Stat. Ire., 12–22 Edw. IV*, p. 607; *L. & P., Hen. VIII*, xv, 486.   42 Refaussé & Lennon, *Registers*, pp 40–1 for an early sixteenth-century list.

pilgrims brought to the city was valued since in 1497 both parliament and corporation promised them immunity.[43] The majority of the pilgrims were probably drawn from the Dublin hinterland. One pilgrim came from Glenmalure in Wicklow in 1504, while some came from the southern part of Armagh diocese. In 1495 the prior thought it worth asking only the provincial councils of Armagh and Dublin to legislate against those molesting pilgrims travelling to the cathedral. Holy Cross provided an alternative attraction for the south and west of the country and Christ Church was not included in a series of penitential pilgrimages to be made by Heneas MacNichaill in 1518 from the Irish part of the Armagh diocese.[44]

At a more localised level there were strong links between the citizens of Dublin and the cathedral. The number of town's people who attended mass in the cathedral was probably fairly small, most devotion being focused on parish churches. However, there were other ways in which the Dublin laity could associate themselves with the cathedral church. At an institutional level the most powerful guild in the city, the Trinity or merchants' guild, had its chapel in the south aisle of the nave. In life, the chapel provided a religious focus for the guild members who maintained the chapel and gathered there on Trinity Sunday to attend mass before their annual celebrations. After death, members of the guild and their families could be buried in the chapel and avail of the masses said by the priest hired for that purpose.[45]

On an individual level there were opportunities to benefit from the intercessions of the monastic clergy by becoming a member of the cathedral congregation or confraternity. Most Dublin parish churches and St Patrick's had such groups.[46] The 'Book of obits', which noted the date of death of the confraternity members on which they would be remembered at mass, records some sixty-three members of the confraternity who died after 1500, thirty-eight men and twenty-five women. Most were from the city and its immediate hinterland, Chapelizod, Dundrum, Castleknock and Malahide. Surname evidence suggests they were mainly from Anglo-Irish backgrounds.[47] Most were from the upper social levels including, in 1550, a goldsmith. Some had been mayors which suggests they were members of the Trinity guild, and hence merchants. Members might ask to be buried in Christ Church and, in return, leave bequests in their wills.[48]

---

43 *Anc. rec. Dublin*, i, 383, full text in Crosthwaite & Todd, *Obits*, pp xxv–xxvi.   44 Lawlor, 'Liber niger', p. 28; McEnery & Refaussé, *Deeds*, nos 361, 362; Aubrey Gwynn, *The medieval province of Armagh* (Dundalk, 1946), pp 268–9.   45 B.L., Eg. MS 1756, ff 12, 12v, 13v; for another copy of the guild material Dublin City Libraries, Gilbert MS 78, ff 36, 38, 48.   46 Hand, 'Camb. MS', pp 26–8.   47 Refaussé & Lennon, *Registers*, pp 40, 41, 45, 61, 64.   48 For example James Selyman (Berry, *Register*, p. 7, Refaussé & Lennon, *Registers*, p. 55) or Robert Norreys (McEnery & Refaussé, *Deeds*, nos 309–11, Refaussé & Lennon, *Registers*, p. 83).

The cathedral played a part in the lives of the wider community also. As an urban property owner with eighty-five properties the cathedral played an important part in the urban land market. Its urban rental was twice that of any other monastic house in the city.[49] Of the twenty-nine individuals recorded in the 'Book of obits' who were not clergy or members of the confraternity nine were priory tenants. In a more public way the nave of the church, separated from the quire by the rood screen, formed a public space for all manner of transactions. In 1527 the citizens gathered there to be interrogated about their actions in crowning the pretender Lambert Simnel. Public notaries also operated in the nave taking depositions from clients in legal actions in the church courts. Examinations and depositions were often sworn on the *baculus Ihesu* or the 'Rood of Christ Church' as a way of invoking divine sanction against perjury.[50] As was observed in the 1540s, Christ Church was to Dublin what St Paul's was to London: a centre for civic religion.

The maintenance of the cathedral church for sacred and secular activities and provision for the canons required finance. The bulk of this income came from land, in contrast with St Patrick's which drew its wealth from church livings. The origin of most of this landed endowment lay in piecemeal medieval grants although property was still being acquired into the sixteenth century. In 1511, for instance, John Bourke left the priory two houses in the city parish of St Nicholas Within 'for prayers for his and his parents' souls forever' and in 1534 Richard Freeman gave his property to the church. By the 1540s the priory's endowment amounted to some 10,538 acres in county Dublin together with urban property and the income of churches both in Dublin and elsewhere.[51]

In terms of management the priory's property fell into two main types. First there were the large manors of Grangegorman, Clonkeen and Balscadden, which were operated as demesne by officials appointed by the priory. The sergeant of Grangegorman, for example, features in a deed of 1508. In all cases manorial courts operated in the early sixteenth century.[52] These were the most profitable of the priory's property producing between two thirds and a half of the house's income in the 1540s.[53] Secondly there

49 This is derived from the rental of £45 for 1542 in C6/1/26/3, no. 2; the next closest was St Mary's at £23. The urban rentals of other houses are in N.B. White (ed.), *Extents of Irish monastic possessions, 1540–41* (Irish Manuscripts Commission, Dublin, 1943). **50** B.L., Sloan MS 1449, f. 152v; Curtis, *Ormond deeds*, iv, 365–6, 23, 27–8; *Stat. Ire., 12–22 Edw. IV*, p. 155; Crosthwaite & Todd, *Obits*, p. xv; H.F. Twiss, 'Some ancient deeds of the parishes of St Catherine and St James, Dublin' in *R.I.A. Proc.*, xxxv, C (1919), pp 290–1. **51** Lawlor, 'Liber niger', p. 36; McEnery & Refaussé, *Deeds*, nos 390, 423–5; Otway-Ruthven, 'Church lands', pp 58–61; *Alen's reg.*, pp 255–7. **52** *Alen's reg.*, p. 258, McEnery & Refaussé, *Deeds*, nos 387, 1114, 1134. **53** C6/1/27.

was the directly managed urban property. The deeds of this property indicate a fairly active management policy in the early sixteenth century. Leases made between 1500 and 1540 were short. Only four were made for lives the remainder being for less than fifty-nine years. Thirty-one years was the most common term, somewhat longer than the twenty-one years normal on the estates of the earls of Kildare and Ormond. Clauses for the repair of property were usual as were provisions for re-entry clauses for the non-payment of rent. In some cases leases were used as part of a property development strategy. A number of leases contain clauses for building and in the case of the commercial property on the north side of the church outstalls were to be built or repaired.[54]

It is more difficult to describe the relations between priory as landlord and the tenants. On only one occasion, in 1551, did the dean and chapter prosecute a tenant in court for failing to repair buildings. More subtle pressures were probably brought to bear.[55] There are indications in the surviving deeds that relations between the priory and its tenants were flexible and accommodations reached. In 1532, for instance, a Dublin merchant was promised first refusal on the purchase of the property he leased. Promises were also made about leases on property adjoining existing leaseholds.[56] Extensions to leases were negotiable at a suitably increased rent.[57] Rents might also be staggered to suit tenants as in the case of one tenant who took a lease for thirty-seven years in 1528, paying 6s. 8d. for the first seven years and 8s. thereafter.[58]

In addition to this landed property there were other rights which also produced income. The tithe of fish from the Liffey, which provided both income and food for the priory, was jealously guarded against encroachment.[59] There was also income from the oblations within the cathedral which might be significant. In 1542 ringing of bells for monthly and yearly minds brought in £1. 12s. 2d., funerals 15s. and other small offerings £26. 6s. 8d. The proceeds from the offerings at the *baculus Ihesu* was enough to support the maintenance of the singing boys.[60] The priory also had fourteen parish churches and a number of chapels within the diocese of Dublin. Four churches outside the diocese came under its care but it is unlikely that these produced much income.[61] Of the Dublin diocesan churches Stillorgan was united to Clonkeen in 1551 because of its poverty while another, Balscadden, was

---

54 McEnery & Refaussé, *Deeds*, nos 1158, 1168, 1174, 1115, 1112.   55 N.A.I., RC6/1, p. 28.   56 McEnery & Refaussé, *Deeds*, nos 1155, 1144.   57 Ibid., nos 1143, 1140, 1155. 58 Ibid., nos 1151, 1156.   59 Lawlor, 'Liber niger', pp 27, 32.   60 C6/1/26/3, no. 2; Lawlor 'Liber niger', p. 17; McEnery & Refaussé, *Deeds*, no. 357.   61 *Alen's reg.*, pp 255–7 and the low level of proxies on p. 277 also suggests poverty; N.B. White (ed.), 'The reportorium viride of John Alen' in *Anal. Hib.*, no. 10 (1941), pp 180–217.

valued at less than the diocesan average in the 1540s.[62] Outside the diocese the parish of Philipstown in County Louth was among the poorest in the diocese of Armagh as measured by its procurations.[63] Only one of the livings, that of Balgriffin, had an endowed vicarage, the others being served by chaplains. In the case of Kilcullen in Kildare there was a number of chaplains including William Rothe, an Augustinian canon of Cartmel.[64] Another source of income was linked to the cathedral church's governmental connections. One example is the 6s. 8d. paid annually to the prior and canons for singing 'hymns and anthems' in the law courts at the end of the Michaelmas and Hilary terms. In the late fifteenth century Henry VII had granted the priory a subvention of £20 per annum because of its impoverished state, the subvention being charged on the fee farm of Dublin.[65]

Despite this apparent wealth Christ Church was not a particularly rich house. The valuation of Pale monasteries in 1536 estimated its income at £100 per annum although in 1544 this was raised to £160.[66] In monastic terms this was about a third of the income of the larger Dublin monasteries such as the Cistercian house of St Mary's or St Thomas's and it was on a par with the relatively modest establishment at All Hallows. Carlisle, by contrast, had an income of £597. 14s. 7d. in 1540 split between temporalities of £252. 2s. 7d. and spiritualities of £345. 12s. 0d. The mean for English Augustinian houses was £201.[67] In parochial terms Christ Church was not particularly well off. If the annual income were divided among ten canons it would provide an average income of £16 a year whereas the average benefice in Dublin diocese in the 1530s netted £22. 6s. 8d. although the most frequently occurring value of benefices was under £5.[68]

The Augustinian community at Christ Church presided over by William Hassard was neither rich nor poor by Irish standards, neither a powerhouse of spirituality nor a centre of immorality. It was, rather, a group of men who sought their salvation in a community which was shaped by the needs and pressures of everyday life. They were part of the world of late medieval Dublin but separated from it by the legal status of the priory in which they lived and by the style of life which they adopted. Events after 1537 would subject them to even more of those worldly pressures.

62 McEnery & Refaussé, Deeds, no. 444.　63 L.P. Murray, 'A calendar of the register of Primate George Dowdall' in Louth Archaeological Journal, vii (1929–32), pp 88–9.　64 McEnery & Refaussé, Deeds, no. 376.　65 Ibid., no. 394, Lawlor, 'Liber niger', pp 16–17; N.A.I., Ferguson MS iv, f. 213.　66 L. & P., Hen. VIII, xi, 564; S. P., Henry VIII, iii, 489.　67 Robinson, Geography of Augustinian settlement, i, 128, appendix 14; Henry Summerson, Medieval Carlisle (2 vols, Kendal, 1993), ii, 598.　68 Steven Ellis, 'Economic problems of the church: why the Reformation failed in Ireland' in Journal of Ecclesiastical History, xli (1991), p. 250.

Why William Hassard resigned as prior of the Augustinian canons of Christ Church in 1537 is unclear. His action was certainly unusual. Only one other prior in the recent history of the convent had resigned, William Lynton, who resigned in 1475, seven years after being described as being of 'great age and infirmity'. Hassard was certainly a considerable age, having been a member of the house for forty-four years at the time of his resignation. He may also have been ill as he died on 7 January 1538. For such a man the pressures generated in the late 1530s were considerable. The passage in England of an act for the suppression of the lesser monastic houses in the spring of 1536 set the agenda for change in Ireland. In May 1536 a bill for the suppression of eight Irish monastic houses was introduced into the Irish parliament and a commission issued for their dissolution. Another three were added in November.[69] Two others, St Wolstan's and Grane, had already been closed by agreement with their community. Even if the prospect of dissolution was not sufficient to worry Hassard there were other ominous signs. In England Wolsey had begun reform of the Augustinians, closing over twenty houses. In Ireland reform also meant closure, seven of the thirteen dissolved houses were Augustinian.[70] In addition the Irish property of the Augustinian house at Llanthony in Gloucestershire had been seized under the act of absentees in 1536. The Augustinian bishop of Kildare, Walter Wellesley, was concerned enough by May 1536 to write to Thomas Howard, duke of Norfolk, seeking reassurances about the future of the Augustinian house at Great Connell. In Mullingar the Augustinian canons took practical action by alienating as much monastic property as possible at the best price. If Hassard believed Christ Church might be safe because of its size and location proposals made in autumn 1536 to dissolve St Thomas's in Dublin and the Knights Hospitallers at Kilmainham suggested otherwise. One crumb of comfort in this situation was that the commission issued in May 1536 to effect the dissolution of the religious houses seemed to be a dead letter. However it was reactivated in the spring of 1537. Any hope of popular resistance was quashed in the summer of 1537 when the citizens of Dublin proposed that the Augustinian house of All Hallows be granted to the corporation. A resolution seemed imminent of the long standing problem of having two cathedrals in Dublin by dissolving the monastic Christ Church. This was hardly a situation the elderly Hassard wanted to deal with.

Another development may have unsettled Hassard. The archbishopric, vacant (and therefore under Hassard's control) since the murder of John Alen

---

69 For the history of the dissolution, Brendan Bradshaw, *The dissolution of the Irish monasteries under Henry VIII* (Cambridge, 1974).   70 J.C. Dickinson, 'Early suppression of English houses of Augustinian canons' in Veronica Ruffer and A.J. Taylor (ed.), *Medieval studies presented to Rose Graham* (Oxford, 1938), pp 66–75.

in July 1534, was filled in January 1536 by the English Augustinian friar, George Browne. Browne was consecrated at Lambeth on 19 March and arrived in Dublin in July. It seems likely that the relationship between the new archbishop and the prior was uneasy. Browne supported the Henrician reform which gained ground in Dublin with the enactment of the supreme headship in May 1536. Browne's first sermon in Christ Church in early December brought enthusiastic comments from some reformist members of the congregation, one commenting that he had 'set forth the word of God so sincerely that both unlearned and learned give him high praise and those that favour the word of God are very glad of him and pray for him to continue'.[71] Browne was not an easy man to deal with. Early in 1537 he began to make accusations of fraud involving episcopal land against government officials. Indeed Brown may have pressurised Hassard to resign for Dean Fich of St Patrick's was certainly encouraged to follow this course.[72] Such manifest changes in the traditional order both in organisation and personnel may well have convinced Hassard he should resign. Browne meanwhile was anxious to introduce a more reform-minded prior.

Precedent suggested that the natural successor to Hassard should be the sub-prior, Richard Ball. However the community chose the younger Oxford educated Walter White who signed himself 'prior electus' in April 1537.[73] In theory the chapter elected the prior but in practice no election could take place without the archbishop's approval. As abbot he had to agree to the nomination before its confirmation.[74] Browne considered Ball and White too closely linked with the old order. A new candidate emerged, Robert Castle, a canon of the Augustinian house of Llanthony who had come to Ireland before 1534 as proctor of their lands at Duleek.[75] Castle won favour as a member of a community that had accepted the royal supremacy, although he was in Ireland in 1534 when the other canons of Llanthony had signed the deed of acceptance. After the confiscation of the Irish property of Llanthony in 1536 he became redundant. He was given a share in the £15 paid to the two proctors of Duleek and permitted to hold a benefice.[76] The priorate of Christ Church seemed, from Browne's point of view, to be both economically and administratively advantageous. Castle, on the other hand, seems to have been less enthusiastic about the appointment which he held until his

---

71 *L. & P., Hen. VIII*, xi, 509, printed in M.V. Ronan, *The Reformation in Dublin* (London, 1926), pp 44–5.   72 Murray, 'Tudor diocese', pp 52–4, 116–18.   73 *Cal. Carew MSS, 1515–74*, p. 161 where the document is misdated to 1540.   74 *Alen's reg.*, p. 290. 75 N.A.I., Ferguson MSS iv, f. 24; White, *Extents*, p. 314.   76 *Seventh report of the deputy keeper of the public records [of England]* (London, 1846), p. 290; Victoria County History, *A history of the county of Gloucester* (11 vols, London, 1907–76), ii, 90; *L. & P., Hen. VIII*, xii, pt 2, 465; D.S. Chambers, *Faculty office registers, 1534–49* (Oxford, 1966), p. 65.

death in 1543. He seems to have wished to leave Ireland and in 1542 he professed himself willing to take a benefice worth £50 a year in England to escape from the cathedral.[77]

If the members of the Christ Church community hoped that stability would return after the appointment of the new prior that hope was short-lived. Royal commissioners arrived in Ireland in autumn 1537 with authority to suppress further monastic houses. A sharp letter from the king to Archbishop Browne in July demanding more rapid reform ensured that life in Christ Church would remain unsettled. Towards the end of 1537 policy in England was moving towards the suppression of the major monastic houses. The dissolution of All Hallows in autumn 1538 suggested that this would be true for Ireland also. Even before this there were signs that traditional life in the priory was under threat. In late 1537 Archbishop Browne ordered the erasure of the name of 'the bishop of Rome' from all liturgical books and in the case of St John's parish, which was under the control of Christ Church, this was done.[78]

References to relics in the liturgical books of St John's parish were also removed which may prefigure the campaign against images in 1539. In February 1539 a commission was issued for the destruction of shrines. The precious metals and jewels were to be sent to the Irish exchequer. Christ Church yielded £35. 15s. 6d. worth of valuables, the second highest amount after the £40 from Our Lady's shrine in Trim, which marked it off as one of the most important pilgrimage sites in the Pale area. What happened to the relics themselves is more problematical. Of the fate of most of the relics noted at the beginning of the 'Book of obits', including the miraculous speaking crucifix, nothing is known. The *baculus Ihesu*, however, was described as being burnt in 1538 in both the annals of Loch Cé and Connacht. While Browne had no liking for relics and would have liked to have seen them removed from the cathedral, he explicitly denied destroying them.[79] There are later references to suggest that the *baculus*, or a very good imitation of it, survived in lay hands in the late sixteenth century and in 1686 the Catholic synod of the diocese of Meath ordered that anyone who used the veil of St Brigid, the gospels of Colmcille or the *baculus Ihesu* without ecclesiastical permission would be subject to sanctions.[80] It seems likely that the *baculus* was not destroyed but, like the miraculous statue of Mary at Trim, was taken into lay hands where it remained until the late seventeenth century.

---

77 *L. & P., Hen. VIII*, xvii, 382.   78 Hawkes, 'Liturgy', p. 45; *S.P. Hen. VIII*, ii, 540. 79 Charles McNeill, 'Accounts of the sums raised by the sales of chattels of some suppressed Irish monasteries' in *R.S.A.I. Jn.*, lii (1922), p. 14; *S.P. Hen. VIII*, iii, 35.   80 H.F. Hore, 'Irish bardism in 1561' in *Ulster Journal of Archaeology*, 1st ser., vi (1858), p. 167; P.F. Moran (ed.), *Spicilegium Ossoriense* (3 vols, Dublin, 1874–84), iii, 118.

From the summer of 1538 the campaign for the total suppression of monastic houses in England gained momentum and in May 1539 a commission was issued for the dissolution of the remaining religious houses in Ireland. By December 1539 the commissioners, who had been working their way southwards from Dundalk, began to deal with Dublin. In the case of the cathedral they met popular resistance for the first time. Christ Church had a civic importance. One measure of popular support is that in the 1530s Dubliners continued to be added to the list of cathedral obits at the same rate as earlier in the century. The mayor and corporation complained to the English architect of the dissolution, Thomas Cromwell, that the dissolution of Christ Church would be 'a great comfort and encouraging of our sovereign lord the king's Irish enemies'. Moreover they were supported by the lord deputy and council who argued that Christ Church had a civic role, since 'it stands in the high place as St Paul's does in London', but it also had a national function, being used for 'parliaments, councils and the common resort and in term time for definitions of matters by judges and learned men'.[81]

The commissioners were forced to yield. A compromise already tried in England was reached. The monastic house was converted into a secular cathedral, on the grounds that this returned it to its original constitution. By 12 December 1539 the commissioners had produced a scheme for the reorganisation of the priory, creating dignitaries and vicars choral with property allocated for their support.[82] The commissioners had acted beyond their authority and in January 1540 the prior and convent petitioned the king for letters patent to transform them into a dean and chapter and so styled themselves in deeds from this date onwards.[83] There was some doubt as to the sufficiency of letters patent and a bill to confirm the change was drafted for the Irish parliament of 1541 as part of the more general legislation to confirm royal title to dissolved monastic houses.[84] However, this was not utilised when the use of letters patent to create secular cathedrals in England allayed fears about their sufficiency. On 10 May 1541 Henry VIII granted letters patent which confirmed the arrangements set out by the commissioners in December 1539. There was one significant difference. In the original scheme the crown would appoint only the dean, all other dignitaries being elected by the chapter. In the patent all dignitaries became royal appointments.[85]

81 *S.P. Henry VIII*, ii, 545 (for the dating of this Bradshaw, *Dissolution*, p. 118, n.2); iii, 130–1.   82 McEnery & Refaussé, *Deeds*, no. 431; for the same technique elsewhere in Ireland, *Cal. pat. rolls, Ire., Hen. VIII–Eliz.*, p. 84.   83 McEnery & Refaussé, *Deeds*, no. 432; this is the letter referred to in the lord deputy's letter of 19 January 1538 misdated as January 1539/40 in *S.P. Hen. VIII*, ii, 544.   84 D.B. Quinn, 'Bills and statutes of the Irish parliaments of Henry VII and Henry VIII' in *Anal. Hib.*, no. 10 (1941), p. 158.   85 For the text C6/2/32/3 and translated in C6/2/32/4–5. For the comparison of the schemes, N.L.I., MS 98, f. 39v.

This was not, as the newly constituted dean and chapter would have hoped, the end of the matter. Dublin now had two secular cathedrals. Some officials viewed this as excessive. The lord deputy therefore withheld the patent from the cathedral chapter and in August 1542 proposed that Christ Church should be converted into a parish church and an administrative centre. This threw doubt on the chapter's legality and few deeds were made by them in 1542 and 1543. The matter was raised again in June 1543 when the king seemed enthusiastic about the proposal and asked for further investigations. As with the commissioners in 1539 the council met with opposition, the corporation arguing that without Christ Church the city would be 'totally defaced and disparaged'. The scheme was eventually dropped in January 1544 when it was discovered that the annual income of the cathedral was only £160. 6s. 8d.[86] Attention turned instead to the wealthier St Patrick's and in 1546 instructions were given by the king to St Leger to accept the surrender of that cathedral.[87]

By 1544 the future of Christ Church as a new secular cathedral seemed secure. There were, of course, changes. The relics had been removed. The role of pilgrimage centre disappeared and the monastic office was no longer said. The canons were now secular clergy, dispensed from their monastic vows. A cathedral chapter in which the dean was *primus inter pares* replaced the absolute rule of the prior. The creation of this chapter had implications for the management of cathedral assets. Whereas the priory lands and livings had been run for the benefit of the house they were now allocated between the various dignitaries and vicars of the cathedral. Much of the urban property was set aside for the maintenance of the church fabric and worship.[88] This had two immediate effects. First, the old system of property management began to break down. In some cases the chapter resorted to leases to individuals of large amounts of property as a way of managing their assets.[89] Second, it was realised that property could belong to an individual rather than the community. Some former canons, released from their vow of poverty, exploited this fact. By 1547 Christopher Rathe, a former canon who became the chancellor's vicar at the reorganisation, held land in Lusk as well as the tithes and oblations of the parish of Corristown and a house near the cathedral.[90] Others were slower to become property owners. John Curragh received a lease of land in Oxmantown in 1548 but the lease was endorsed 'lessee might not take this lease, being a member of the chapter'. Walter White received a lease of tenements near the cathedral but did not enforce it while the current occupants were alive.[91]

86 *S.P. Hen. VIII*, iii, 414–16, 468, 484, 489–90. 87 Mason, *St Patrick's*, p. 450. 88 For the allocation McEnery & Refaussé, *Deeds*, no. 431. 89 McEnery & Refaussé, *Deeds*, nos 1186, 1195. 90 Ibid., nos 1207, 1215, Griffith, *Inquisitions*, pp 117, 118. 91 Ibid.,

Despite all these signs of change there were even more powerful forces working for continuity. All the former canons were given a place in the new order. Prior Castle became dean. Richard Ball, the former sub-prior, Walter Whyte, formerly precentor, and John Mos, the sub-precentor, became precentor, chancellor and treasurer respectively. The other canons were created vicars choral. Most radically the vicars choral were made members of the chapter although they were not in the strict sense prebendaries. The model may well have been the arrangements in St Patrick's where the senior vicar choral, the dean's vicar, had a seat in the chapter but not a vote.[92] In a British Isles context, however, this was very unusual. It caused some initial confusion and from 1540 to 1542 leases were made in the name of the dean and chapter but from 1543 they were made by the dean and chapter with the consent of the vicars choral. Thus in effect the chapter of the priory became the chapter of the secular cathedral. In lifestyle too there was continuity. Initially property in the precinct was not leased and the new vicars choral continued to keep a common hall as the canons had done.[93] Only one member of the new chapter seems to have moved out, William Owen, the Shropshire canon who had only recently arrived at Christ Church, leased a house in Skinners' Row.[94]

In liturgy too there was considerable continuity between the old priory and the secular cathedral with the mass remaining at the centre of the life of the community. The 1541 charter had been explicit on the function of the new institution. It was 'to serve almighty God and perpetually pray for our [the king's] good estate while we live and for our soul when we shall quit this life and for the souls of our ancestors'.[95] There was debate over the form of that prayer. Archbishop Browne introduced the 'form of the beads' in 1538 which attempted to provide guidelines for prayer which exhorted 'confidence and trust in our saviour Jesus Christ' and not in prayers to the dead, confession or the power of the pope. The result was a debate with Bishop Staples of Meath which was partly carried on from the pulpit of Christ Church.[96] The effect of Browne's scheme was negligible and names continued to be added to the obits list. According to the settlement of December 1539 it was one of the functions of the dignitaries to 'celebrate second mass daily and the mass of the Blessed Virgin Mary and high mass on the festivals proper to the same' and in 1546 the choir was to sing the lady mass and anthem daily and the Jesus mass on Friday. Mass continued to be said in the quire which was closed to the laity, indicated by the replacement key for the door of the quire bought in 1542. The appearance of the celebrant remained the

nos 1219, 1221.   **92** Mason, *St Patrick's*, p. 89.   **93** McEnery & Refaussé, *Deeds*, no. 1207.   **94** Ibid., no. 1202.   **95** C6/2/32/3; Henry was included in the obits, Refaussé & Lennon, *Registers*, p. 43.   **96** *S. P. Hen. VIII*, ii, 564.

same. The proctor's accounts of 1542 mention albs, amices, maniples, girdles and rochets.[97] While the mass remained central to the life of the cathedral it was supplemented by the seasonal round of other feasts which were celebrated. The proctor's accounts of 1542, for example, record expenditures at Corpus Christi, Candlemas, St Mark's day, St George's day, Trinity Sunday and rogation week as well as breakfast for the 'singers of the passion'. A visitor to the cathedral in 1544 would certainly still have recognised the world of the priory a decade earlier.

The priory had managed to salvage much of its prestige and practices as a secular cathedral under the conservative reform of Henry VIII. At his death in January 1547 its future seemed secure. The dissolution of St Patrick's effected in the dying days of the old king's reign was executed under Edward VI, thus ensuring that Christ Church would be the only cathedral for the diocese of Dublin. The cathedral benefited from that dissolution since all the plate, jewels and ornaments were to be transferred to Christ Church.[98] Commensurate with its new status the choir of Christ Church was to be enlarged with an annual exchequer grant of ten marks each for six priests and four marks for two child choristers.[99] The stipend for one of the clergy was assigned to Christopher Rathe who was already a vicar choral of the cathedral. Two others recruited under this scheme, Richard Betagh and John Claregenet, had been vicars choral of St Patrick's.[100]

Despite the promising start to the history of the Edwardian cathedral the movement for a more radical reformation which grew in that reign presented problems to the conservative institution. Further reform was signalled by Browne in the autumn of 1547 but it was not until November 1548 that political circumstances allowed him to issue his 'book of reformation'.[101] The 'book' probably followed the decrees issued in England in 1547 and 1548 for the removal of images, sacramentals, relics, pilgrimages, prohibitions on veneration of the saints and alterations to the canon of the mass. By late 1549 the mass itself was under attack. In the following year the first Edwardian prayer book was being enthusiastically promoted by the Dublin administration although Browne claimed that in 1551 mass was celebrated at Christ Church by the authority of the lord deputy, Anthony St Leger.[102] In reality the eucharistic liturgy was little changed in the first prayer book and wafers

---

97 McEnery & Refaussé, *Deeds*, no. 431; C6/1/26/3, no. 2. 98 Mason, *St Patrick's*, pp 152, 163. 99 McEnery & Refaussé, *Deeds*, nos 439–40; the enlargement was confirmed by Mary, McEnery & Refaussé, *Deeds*, no. 448, Mason, *St Patrick's*, p. 153. 100 *Cal. pat. rolls Ire., Hen. VIII–Eliz.*, p. 143. 101 For the general context, Brendan Bradshaw, 'The Edwardian reformation in Ireland' in *Archivium Hibernicum*, xxxiv (1976–7), pp 83–99. 102 P.R.O., S.P. 61/3/45.

and the traditional liturgical vestments continued in use until 1553. More ominous was the 1552 revision of the prayer book which was much more explicitly Protestant in its formularies.

The reaction to these developments shown by the community at Christ Church was limited. Only one man seems to have had difficulty with the changes, William Walsh who had come to the cathedral after the dissolution of St Patrick's as one of the six new vicars choral. Walsh may have been a Cistercian at St Mary's abbey but his career between 1539 and 1547 is not known. By 1557 he was in Spain and was about to return to Ireland with a grant of £10 from Philip II and a promise that he should be prior of Mellifont. It seems likely that he had left the cathedral over the Edwardian prayer book.[103] That Walsh was alone indicates that the Edwardian reforms had a restricted impact on the cathedral.

The man largely responsible for the stability of the cathedral over this period of change was the dean, Thomas Lockwood, who had become dean on Castle's death in 1543. Lockwood was a conservative churchman. He had been part of the pre-Reformation church as archdeacon of Nobber in 1538, archdeacon of Kells in 1541 and in 1542 became prebendary of Yago in St Patrick's.[104] His theological position was indicated at the ordination of John Bale as bishop of Ossory at Christ Church in February 1553. Bale, an English radical reformer, insisted on ordination according to the second Edwardian prayer book. This was agreed to after some hesitation by Browne and Lord Chancellor Cusack. As the ordaining bishops were about to impose hands according to the rite

> Thomas Lockwood (Blockhead he might well be called) the dean of the cathedral church there desired the lord chancellor very instantly that he would in no wise permit that observation to be done after the book of consecrating bishops which was last set forth in England by act of parliament alleging that it would be both an occasion of tumult and also that it was not yet consented to by act of their parliament in Ireland. For why he much feared the new changed order of the communion therein to hinder his kitchen and belly.[105]

While Bale's judgement was characteristically harsh it does reflect Lockwood's dislike of the new liturgy.

---

103 *Fiants Ire., Hen. VIII*, no. 94; *Cal. pat. rolls Ire., Hen. VIII–Eliz.*, p.143; *Cal. S.P. Ire., 1509–73*, p. 140 refers to 'Sir James Walsh sometime chantor of Christ Church' but this seems to be a mistake for William.   104 N.A.I., R.C. 9/8, pp 184, 223, 237, 300; Griffith, *Inquisitions*, p. 87; Lawlor, *Fasti*, p. 185.   105 John Happé and John King (ed.), *The vocacyon of John Bale* (New York, 1990), p. 52.

Lockwood's genius in preventing innovation lay in his political acumen. He could adapt to changing circumstances as in 1557 when he was appointed to a commission to recover chalices and church plate despite the fact that in the 1530s he had been one of the instruments of disposing of monastic chattels.[106] At times his activities may have sailed close to the wind to judge from a number of pardons granted to him in 1542, 1550, and 1552.[107] Lockwood clearly recognised the political role of the dean of Christ Church. He was a member of a number of local commissions to hear disputes and for gaol delivery. He served as a justice of the peace for County Dublin and was a privy councillor from 1544 to his death.[108] Politically he was well connected. His elevation to the prebend of Yago in 1542 was certainly due to his political connections since Yago was in the hands of the crown, attainted from the earl of Kildare after the rebellion of 1534. In particular he was associated with a conservative reforming faction within the Irish government. He was executor of the will of Sir William Brabazon, the Irish vice-treasurer, and it may be through Lockwood's influence that Brabazon appears in the cathedral 'Book of obits'.[109] Brabazon and Lockwood were part of a wider circle including the lord deputy, Anthony St Leger. He supported the Henrician Reformation, was rather less enthusiastic about Edward's innovations but to Marian restorers seemed to be a secret Protestant. Evidently he was a conservative reformer, a description which might characterise Lockwood also.[110] Lockwood's views were probably reinforced by the growing conservatism of Archbishop Browne in the 1550s who, it was claimed, in the summer of 1554 'made a Catholic sermon in Christ Church at Dublin'.[111]

Despite Lockwood's dislike of innovation there were changes in the role and functions that Christ Church performed under Edward. The bonds which had linked priory and city, the guild chapels and the confraternity, began to dissolve and were reshaped. The entries in the obits for the 1540s and 1550s are largely of those who were not members of the confraternity. Between 1500 and 1540 only sixteen of the seventy-two individuals (or 22 per cent) who were recorded in the 'Book of obits' were not members of the confraternity but between 1540 and 1560 that had risen to 65 per cent of the twenty new entries. Many of these were civic officials, such as former mayors or officials of the Irish government, indicating a conscious attempt to define a role for the cathedral in the wider world and to cultivate groups of supporters.

106 *Cal. pat. rolls Ire., Hen. VIII–Eliz.*, p. 369.   107 Ibid., pp 161, 202, 275.   108 Ibid., pp 112, 354, 369, 189, 227, 346, 350, 355, 434; *Cal. Carew MSS*, 1515–74, pp 226, 189, 279; *L. & P., Hen. VIII*, xix, pt 1, 526.   109 N.A.I., R.C. 6/1, pp 67–8; *Cal. pat. rolls Ire., Hen. VIII–Eliz.*, p. 434; Refaussé & Lennon, *Registers*, p. 62.   110 Ciaran Brady, *The chief governors* (Cambridge, 1994), p. 69.   111 Murray, 'Tudor diocese', pp 153–5; Bodl., Rawl. B479, f. 94v.

Moreover the state began to look upon the cathedral as a centre for ceremonial and from 1548 the cathedral became the normal venue for swearing-
in chief governors of Ireland.[112]

The conservative influence of Lockwood on the Christ Church community
during the attempted introduction of radical change under Edward VI made
the transition to catholicism under his sister Mary all the easier. Mary succeeded her brother in July 1553 and on 22 August, according to a Dublin
chronicle, 'the mass began again and the communions put down'.[113] The rev-
olution was not as dramatic as it might seem. According to a chapter act of
1555 or 1556 the liturgical round at the cathedral consisted of a rood mass,
a second mass and a Jesus mass in Lent, a pattern very similar to the priory's
schemes of 1495 and 1540. The internal layout of the cathedral also seems
to have required little adjustment to meet the new circumstances. The rood
loft and screen were still in place in 1565. The arch above the rood still had
a painting of the story of the Passion which had probably belonged to the
priory. Some items which had fallen into lay hands may have been restored
to the church.[114] Other elements may have been new such as the symbols of
the Passion, later removed, which were unusual decoration in Irish churches
before the mid-sixteenth century.[115] Certainly by 1556 the cathedral was fully
equipped for traditional Catholic worship. An account of the swearing-in of
the earl of Sussex as lord deputy in that year mentions the use of censers,
holy water sprinklers and processional crosses as well as copes for the cathedral clergy. 'Calaber amices', traditional wear for Augustinian canons, were
specified in orders of 1557.[116]

What distinguished the innovations made by Mary from what had gone
before was the speed with which they were made. The changes under Henry
VIII were, in many respects, superficial or gradual. The conservatism of
Lockwood ensured that little of the radical Edwardian reformation penetrated
Christ Church. What was more threatening to the Christ Church chapter
was Mary's decision to restore St Patrick's in 1555, again raising the spectre
of a surplus cathedral in Dublin. Lockwood was personally distressed with
this news since during the suppression he had styled himself dean of St
Patrick's. He considered he had some right to the position at the restoration
but became only prebendary of Rathmichael.[117] Mary clearly felt uncertain

---

112 B.L., Sloan MS 1449, ff 162, 162v, 164v, 165, 165v, 167.   113 B.L., Add. MS 4822,
f. 113.   114 Gillespie, *Proctor's accounts*, pp 35, 37–40; Gillespie, *Chapter act book*, pp
23–4.   115 Raymond Gillespie, 'Irish funeral monuments and social change, 1500–1700'
in Raymond Gillespie and Brian Kennedy (ed.), *Ireland: art into history* (Dublin, 1994),
pp 161, 164.   116 *Cal. Carew MSS, 1515–74*, pp 258, 278–9.   117 Lawlor, *Fasti*, pp
44–5, 144.

about the Christ Church chapter and when the new Catholic bishop, Hugh Curwen, appeared in the diocese after his consecration in September 1555, he carried a letter from the queen to the chapter spelling out their duty to obey him.[118]

Some of the canons found it impossible to make the adjustment to the new order and others were probably deprived because they had married. Richard Ball, who had been a canon of the priory since at least 1511 and precentor at the reorganisation in 1540 was replaced in 1553 by one of the vicars choral, Christopher Rathe, although the chapter leased him a house near the cathedral.[119] Walter Whyte, precentor of the priory and chancellor since 1540 was deprived in May 1553, he too being granted a house by the chapter. He was replaced by another vicar choral, John Herman.[120] John Mos, the treasurer and former sacrist of the priory, remained in place but died in 1556 and was replaced by a third vicar choral, John Kerdiff. As a result of these changes new people appeared in the chapter. Christopher More, a vicar choral in St Patrick's until 1547 and then chaplain at St George's chapel which was supported by the city, became a new vicar choral.[121] Mary may also have tried to enlarge the chapter to bring it more into line with that of a secular cathedral. The witness list to the orders of 1557 records in addition to the normal quota of dignitaries and vicars two other prebendaries, Thomas More and Robert Lyde or Hyde, although no prebends are assigned to them.[122]

It was not only cathedral worship and administration that were affected by the Marian changes. The restatement of the traditional doctrine of the efficacy of masses for the dead gave new life to the guild chapel of Holy Trinity. In 1566 the Trinity guild accounts record the hiring of a priest for the chapel and the guild also contributed to the cathedral. In 1557 a sustained programme of refurbishment of the chapel was begun with almost £9 being spent in that year. In the following year £2. 15s. was disbursed on 'hangings and deckings of Trinity chapel and to the priest that kept the mass in the said chapel and other necessary affairs'.[123] The guild, at least, was convinced that the Marian reforms were there to stay.

118 Printed in Ronan, *The Reformation in Dublin*, pp 432–3; Mant, *Ch. of Ire.*, i, 238. 119 *Irish mon. deeds*, p. 242, McEnery & Refaussé, *Deeds*, nos 431, 1318; *Cal. pat. rolls Ire., Hen. VIII–Eliz.*, p. 326.   120 McEnery & Refaussé, *Deeds*, nos 431, 1221, 1250, 1259; *Cal. pat. rolls Ire., Hen. VIII–Eliz.*, p. 325.   121 McEnery & Refaussé, *Deeds*, no. 1246; Lawlor, *Fasti*, p. 213; Dublin City Archives, M.R. /35, f. 86.   122 Gillespie, *Chapter act book*, p. 24; McEnery & Refaussé, *Deeds*, nos 1246, 1250; More may have been a former chantry priest of the St Anne guild, H.F. Berry, 'History of the religious gild of St Anne' in *R.I.A. Proc.*, xxv, C (1904), p. 41. Hyde or Lyde was probably a former Cistercian from St Mary's abbey, *Fiants Ire. Hen. VIII*, no. 94.   123 Dublin City Archives, M.R./35, ff 135, 140, 141, 146, 153.

In a paradoxical way the restoration of catholicism under Queen Mary marked the end of the old order at Christ Church. By 1558 it was clear that even given the queen's personal enthusiasm for religious orders, the old conventual life would not be restored and Christ Church would remain a secular chapter. How long it would survive was a problem posed by the re-establishment of St Patrick's which raised the difficulty of two cathedrals in a relatively poor city. By the mid-1550s the personnel of Christ Church were changing rapidly. Half of the chapter of 1540 were either dead or had been deprived and the new arrivals had no experience of the monastic ethos. The change in attitudes is revealed in the abandonment of the old systems of land management and by the acquisition of lands by members of the secular chapter. Moreover there were signs that the Marian catholicism was rather different to that traditionally practised. The cathedral made no attempt to acquire new relics as objects of devotion. Instead, the symbols of the Passion, which focused attention on the suffering Christ of the mass, were set up. The changing imagery of devotion was one reflection of changing priorities among the cathedral personnel, which in turn reflected the transformation of the religious, social and cultural significance of the cathedral in sixteenth-century Dublin.

IX

The shaping of reform, 1558–1625

Raymond Gillespie

It was not clear to contemporaries in the immediate aftermath of the death of the Catholic Queen Mary in November 1558 what changes would be made in the Irish church. Nearly ten months elapsed before the newly re-appointed lord deputy, Thomas Radcliffe, earl of Sussex, arrived in Ireland with instructions for religious reform. The 1560 parliament clarified the position, at least in the short term, with the passage of the acts of supremacy and uniformity.[1] However, given the experience of religious volatility over the previous twenty years, it was not certain that the reforms of Elizabeth would be any more enduring than those of her father or her siblings. After more than a decade it became apparent that the reforms of 1560 could cohere into a workable ecclesiastical order. Between the accession of Elizabeth in 1558 and that of Charles I in 1625 the Church of Ireland community shaped its identity as a minority, rather introverted, community now facing a resurgent Tridentine catholicism. In that process it formulated relationships with its sister church in England and catholicism. The community at Christ Church was a prime mover in these developments.

The pace of religious change at Christ Church after the accession of Elizabeth I was slow. By Easter 1559 the mass was still being celebrated. The Trinity guild required its members to attend mass at its chapel in Christ Church on the octave of Easter and to offer 1d. each day on pain of a fine of a pound of wax for lights in the chapel.[2] By the end of the summer the return of the lord deputy, the earl of Sussex, signalled changes. When he attended Christ Church in August Nicholas Dardis, one of the stipendiaries, sang the litany in English, probably in the context of mass, which was the practice in England over the previous months.[3] The pace of change quickened with the

---

1 Henry Jefferies, 'The Irish parliament of 1560: the Anglican reforms authorised' in *I.H.S.*, xxvi, no. 102 (1988), pp 128–41.   2 B.L., Eg. MS 1765, f. 18; Dublin City Libraries, Gilbert MS 78, f. 56.   3 T.C.D., MS 591, f. 20; B.L., Add. MS 4813, f. 65.

summoning of a parliament to meet at Christ Church from 12 January until 1 February 1560 and by its dissolution acts of uniformity and supremacy were in place which authorised the use of the Book of Common Prayer from the summer of 1560.[4]

By May 1560 the cathedral was being renovated to meet its new role. The walls were 'new painted' and it was decided 'instead of pictures and popish fancies to place passages or texts of scripture on the walls'.[5] However significant traces of the older world remained. By 1564 the rood screen was still in place, although the rood had gone, and the 'painted board that was in the arch over the rood where the story of the Passion was presented' survived until it was taken down as part of rebuilding works. Stained glass also remained and one window with a picture of St Laurence was repaired in 1564.[6] If features such as the rood screen survived, their functions disappeared. The new liturgy made no distinction between nave and quire and most worship from the mid-sixteenth century was conducted in the quire. The precentor, Peter Lewis, noted in January 1565, 'diverse gentlemen in the quire at service'.[7] The nave continued to be used for services and a range of other quasi-religious functions. It was there that Richard Dixon, the bishop of Cork, was required to sit in 1570 in public penance for bigamy and in 1578 James Bedlow of Dublin had to stand barefoot before the pulpit for denying the royal supremacy.[8] Both nave and quire were opened up in a dramatic way after 1560.

The change in the internal organisation of the cathedral church in the early 1560s was paralleled by a shift in personnel. The Elizabethan legislation required the subscription to the oath of supremacy. At Christ Church a significant number failed to do so. Three of the four dignitaries were deprived for non-subscription. Only the compliant Dean Lockwood, who had survived all shifts in religious emphasis from the 1540s, obliged. The case of the other members of the chapter is less clear. John Lyde or Hyde, who had been appointed under Mary, failed to take the oath and was deprived while Christopher More, also a Marian appointment, did subscribe.[9] The other seven vicars who signed Marian chapter acts all feature in the Elizabethan chapter act books or as witnesses to deeds suggesting that they subscribed.

The same seems true of practice at St Patrick's after Sussex's return, B.L., Add. MS 4791, p. 11. William Haugaard, 'The English litany from Henry to Elizabeth' in *Anglican Theological Review*, li (1969), pp 191–9.   **4** For the parliament at Christ Church, Bodl., Rawl. B 484, f. 34v; T.C.D., MS 591, ff 19v, 20.   **5** N.B. White (ed.), 'The annals of Dudley Loftus' in *Anal. Hib.*, no. 10 (1941), p. 235.   **6** Gillespie, *Proctor's accounts*, pp 39, 48.   **7** Ibid., p. 49.   **8** Richard Caulfield, *A lecture on the history of the bishops of Cork and cathedral of St Fin Barre* (Cork, 1864), p. 18; T.C.D., MS 772, f. 18v; C6/1/7/1, f. 19.   **9** *Fiants Ire. Eliz.*, nos 226, 227.

The fate of those who failed to take the oath is not clear. Most remained in the city. The former chancellor John Herman was there in 1569 when he was described as a 'chaplain' and the former precentor Christopher Rathe died in Dublin in 1564. The conservative corporation of Dublin appointed John Kerdiff, the Marian treasurer of the cathedral, to be custos of the former leper house of St Stephen.[10]

These deprivations mark a significant break in the history of Christ Church since for the first time none of the chapter had experience of the Augustinian house of the early sixteenth century. The chapter could now establish a new identity. It was less constrained than its English counterparts for no statutes had been made to govern its actions nor were there any Injunctions to guide church business such as had been issued in England in 1559.[11] This lack of direction, together with the problem of two cathedrals in one city, clearly exercised the late sixteenth-century administration. In 1565, for instance, it was proposed to grant a new constitution to Christ Church and dissolve St Patrick's and again in 1584 Sir John Perrot attempted a dissolution of St Patrick's and a re-endowment of Christ Church 'whereby Christ may devour St Patrick' but nothing was done in either instance.[12]

In this context the cathedral began to carve out its role. By the 1570s there is evidence that the community of Christ Church had settled down to an orderly existence. The surviving deeds from 1539 to 1570 suggest that the chapter met rather irregularly, between once and five times a year, but by the early 1580s, when the entries in the chapter act book become frequent, three or four meetings a year, usually once a quarter, took place. Records of meetings were formalised by the keeping of a chapter act book, beginning in October 1574. There was some administrative confusion after the death of Dean Lockwood in 1565. John Garvey was appointed but without the necessary letters patent. This was only resolved in 1574.[13] An attempt to regularise cathedral life is suggested by the drawing up of orders for the management of the body in October 1574, 1575 and 1576. In part these were

---

10 N.L.I., GO MS 209, p. 17; Gillespie, *Proctor's accounts*, pp 28, 109; *Anc. rec. Dublin*, ii, 42.   11 Lehmberg, *Reformation*, pp 91–4, 142–5.   12 P.R.O., SP63/13/51; Charles McNeill (ed.), 'The Perrot papers' in *Anal. Hib.*, no. 12 (1943), pp 8–9; *Cal. S. P. Ire., 1574–85*, p. 524. The fate of St Patrick's is dealt with in Murray, 'Tudor diocese', pp 329–70. For government inability to grapple with this problem in an English context, James Saunders, 'The limitations of statutes: Elizabethan schemes to reform new foundation cathedral statutes' in *Journal of Ecclesiastical History*, xlviii (1997), pp 445–67.   13 *Cal. S. P. Ire., 1574–85*, p. 20 where Archbishop Loftus described Garvey as 'dean elect' in April 1574. The irregular manner of Garvey's appointment gave rise to problems later, *Cal. S. P. Ire., 1633–47*, pp 223–4. For his subsequent career, Brian McCabe, 'An Elizabethan prelate: John Garvey' in *Breifne*, vii (1987–8), pp 594–604.

drawn from contemporary experience but older precedents were sought and some of the regulations for the Marian cathedral were copied into the beginning of the first chapter act book.[14] It is clear that the monastic ethos which provided rules for ordering business in an informal way was now dead.

Many of the functions which Christ Church fulfilled in the late sixteenth century were those of a diocesan cathedral. The liturgical round of morning and evening prayer continued, the eucharist was celebrated, the poor were cared for and there was a grammar school attached to the church.[15] Morning and evening prayer formed the basis of this worship and in the winter of 1564–5 candles were regularly bought to light the quire for evening prayer.[16] More importance was attached to morning prayer. In the 1575 orders regulating cathedral life, fines were imposed on clergy absent from morning prayer while none were payable for missing evening prayer.[17] Such worship was supplemented more infrequently by celebration of the eucharist. It is only in the 1590s that the proctor's accounts are detailed enough to chart this activity. By that stage accounts for the purchase of bread and wine suggest a monthly communion, normally on the first Sunday of the month.[18] In comparison with Dublin parish churches this was a frequent celebration. The St Werburgh's churchwardens' accounts for the 1580s and early 1590s indicate that the eucharist was celebrated at Easter and possibly also at Whitsun.[19] The communion service was rather different from the mass which it superseded. It was no longer seen as a linking of earth and heaven and hence it had no benefit for the dead. One effect of this was the ending of the cathedral fraternity and no entries were made in the 'Book of obits' after June 1558. The communion was now a gathering of the faithful. The intention that this would be an inclusive rite is suggested by the taking of an offering for the poor before the prayer for the whole estate of the church. Such alms replaced the endowment of a chantry or the saying of masses. By 1565 a poor box was securely placed in the quire as well as a box for offerings beside the quire door. When Lord Deputy Fitzwilliam attended communion at the cathedral in the 1570s and again in the 1590s he made an offering to the poor of between 10s. and £1.[20]

Christ Church fulfilled another role not normal in cathedral churches. To a greater extent than ever before it became the church of the Dublin castle administration. It was the place of worship of the lord deputy when he was in Dublin and on ceremonial days it was the venue for celebration. On St

---

14 Gillespie, *Chapter act book*, pp 23–8. 15 For the school, Gillespie, *Chapter act book*, p. 27. 16 Gillespie, *Proctor's accounts*, pp 30, 31. 17 Gillespie, *Chapter act book*, p. 26. 18 C6/1/26/3, nos 4, 6, 8, 9. 19 R.C.B., P326/27/2/15, 17, 18, 19, 20. 20 Gillespie, *Proctor's accounts*, p. 97; Northampton Record Office, Northampton, Fitzwilliam of Milton MSS, Irish, nos 34, 37, 41, 42, 46, 55.

George's day 1578, for instance, the lord deputy, Sir Henry Sidney, rode to the cathedral in his red mantle and order of the garter with the mace and sword being borne in state. The quire was hung with blue broadcloth for the occasion.[21] It was not only state religious ceremonial that the cathedral became associated with. It became a centre for a wide range of public ceremonial. Lords deputy were usually sworn in there, apart from the late 1560s and early 1570s when the church was undergoing repairs. It was where knights were created and by 1567 the arms of the knights of the garter were displayed on one side of the quire.[22] More publicly the bells of Christ Church were rung on state occasions and in 1570 the lord deputy decreed that the rebellious earl of Thomond should submit himself not only in Dublin castle but also publicly 'in the high church of Dublin called Christ Church' as Feagh O'Byrne was also required to do in 1578.[23] The precincts of Christ Church were also an important public space where the government conducted business. Continuing the medieval tradition the parliaments of 1560 and 1569–71 were held there and the privy council usually met there.[24]

If fostering closer links between church and state was a feature of life at Christ Church in the 1560s and 1570s the maintenance of older, civic links was also a priority. Despite the shift towards protestantism this did not alienate the cathedral from its civic connections. Such contacts were enhanced through institutions such as the Trinity guild chapel in the cathedral and in the 1570s the barber surgeons seem to have established their chapel there also.[25] Moreover, when the increasingly fragile fabric of the cathedral needed repair it was to the city and its inhabitants that the cathedral chapter looked. After the collapse of the vault of the church in April 1562, discussed by Roger Stalley below, the funding to prop up the structure was provided by the lord deputy, the earl of Sussex, and funds were sought from the crown.[26] The bulk of the cost of repair was borne by individual subscriptions. Over the

---

21 T.C.D., MS 772, f. 18.   22 B.L., Eg. MS 2642, ff 281–1v; T.C.D., MS 772, f. 18. For lords deputy being sworn in *Cal. S. P. Ire., 1508–73*, p. 394; *Cal. Carew MSS, 1575–88*, p. 312; James Perrot, *The chronicle of Ireland*, ed. Herbert Wood (Dublin, 1933), p. 183. For knighthoods *Cal. Carew MSS, 1603–25*, pp 384–5; *Cal. Carew MSS, 1589–1600*, pp 235, 238, 240.   23 'Henry Sidney's memoir of his government of Ireland' in *Ulster Journal of Archaeology*, 1st ser., v (1851), p. 308; *Cal. Carew MSS, 1575–88*, p. 141.   24 Jon Crawford, *Anglicising the government of Ireland* (Dublin, 1993), pp 32, 52. For examples of privy council business transacted at Christ Church, P.R.O., SP63/17/57, 58; Gillespie, *Proctor's accounts*, p. 28.   25 T.C.D., MS 1447/6, ff 37v, 39v, 44; C6/1/26/3, no. 7.   26 For the details of this, Gillespie, *Proctor's accounts*, pp 13–14; P.R.O., SP63/7/45. Lord Deputy Sidney also paid for the repair of Strongbow's tomb in 1570 possibly because it was an important civic marker for payment of debts; B.L., Add. MS 4183, f. 88v; Bodl., Rawl. MS B 484, f. 33. For a full treatment of the collapse see ch. xi.

next forty years many of those who appeared on the list of subscribers, or their families, were to become identified with recusancy in the city. Margaret Ball, who contributed grain, was imprisoned for recusancy in 1580 and Christopher Fagan, who gave 1,000 slates, was a committed Catholic by 1600. One of the sons of another contributor, the wife of James Bath of Drumcondra, became a Jesuit.[27] Clearly in the 1560s an affection existed between the city population and the cathedral which transcended nascent denominational boundaries. At an institutional level also the corporation of Dublin contributed to Christ Church. In 1580 a benevolence was granted to the church by the corporation. In 1582 the rent from the dissolved house of St Mary's was also given to the cathedral and a further grant was made in 1584. When the steeple of the church cracked in 1588 the corporation provided labour of one man from each house in the city towards its repair.[28]

The reformed cathedral was able to straddle a number of worlds. The accounts of the precentor, Peter Lewis, suggest that some of the rituals of a more traditional religion were maintained at the cathedral in the 1560s. Month's minds continued to be rung and traditional saints' days were observed. St Catherine's day, according to Lewis's accounts for 1563, was 'kept holy day from work all that day'. Although St Catherine was included in the revised Church of England calendar of 1561 the feast was not a red-letter day. However, St Catherine had been one of the saints associated with pre-reform Christ Church and a relic of her had been in the cathedral. The feasts of St Thomas Becket and the Assumption of the Blessed Virgin were observed without any authority. Observance of Becket's feast had been forbidden by Henry VIII but a relic of the saint had also been among the cathedral's collection suggesting an established cult.[29] Again good relations between the urban world and the cathedral are suggested by the fact that the Jesuit, Edmund Campion, was allowed access to the cathedral records in 1570 when he was compiling his history of Ireland, probably due to the mediation of the Dubliner Richard Stanihurst.[30] While there is no doubt that Christ Church was a Protestant church in the late sixteenth century there were enough points of contact with the past to ensure that it could command allegiances from the population of a diocese in which confessional boundaries had not yet hardened.

The death of Dean John Garvey in 1595 marked a significant break in the life of the Christ Church community. The political and religious problems

27 Gillespie, *Proctor's accounts*, pp 22–3; Colm Lennon, *The lords of Dublin in the age of reformation* (Dublin, 1989), pp 89, 156–7, 213. 28 *Anc. rec. Dublin*, ii, 146, 168, 187, 211, 221; Dublin City Archives, MR/35, p. 365; MR/17, f. 19. 29 Gillespie, *Proctor's accounts*, pp 39, 47, 101; Refaussé & Lennon, *Registers*, p. 39. 30 Edward Campion, *Two bokes of the historie of Ireland*, ed. A.F. Vossen (Assen, 1968), pp 86, 104, 108, 115, 116.

confronting his successors were rather different from those with which he grappled. Most immediately the cathedral entered an economic crisis in the late 1590s. According to the proctor's accounts for the 1580s and 1590s cathedral income slightly exceeded expenditure but not sufficiently so to deal with a crisis. The problem of rent arrears, running at 10 per cent of rental income, was not addressed.[31] The fabric of the church gave cause for concern. In 1562 the vault had collapsed causing extensive damage which was repaired in 1564–5 and further work was carried out in the early 1580s. Despite this Archbishop Loftus of Dublin could claim in 1584 that Christ Church was 'altogether ruinous and decayed'.[32] The cracking of the steeple in 1588 and the explosion of gunpowder on Wood Quay in 1597 further damaged the fabric badly.[33]

Increased cathedral income from its rented property was called for to meet the cost of repairs but that proved difficult to achieve. In the late sixteenth century the chapter concentrated on maintaining a steady income from its property by continuing the pre-Reformation tradition of making leases for modest periods, although there was some lengthening in the term of leases. Before 1540 the most common lease was for thirty-one years. From 1540 to 1560 forty-one years was the norm although fifty-one and sixty-one year leases were not unknown. However, four-fifths of leases made in this period were for terms less than fifty-one years. Relatively few fee farm grants were made, the only significant one being the alienation of the manor of Grangegorman to Francis Agard in 1560. This was not done voluntarily. Agard had been a speculator in dissolved monastic property and as that market dried up in the late 1550s he turned his attention elsewhere. Using his position as secretary to Sir Henry Sidney, a former lord justice, Agard acquired a queen's letter requiring the chapter to make the grant and thus no appeal was possible.[34] In comparison to Carlisle, a former Augustinian cathedral on the edge of English authority, and cathedrals in Wales, Christ Church was not significantly out of line. The Henrician statutes for the English cathedrals of the new foundation had limited leases to sixty years for urban property and twenty-one years for rural property (measures extended to all ecclesiastical property in 1570) and Carlisle in the main adhered to those rules. In the large Welsh diocese of St Davids during the 1560s, however, roughly half all the leases made were for periods of forty or more years which is closer to the Christ Church pattern.[35]

From the 1560s, however, the Christ Church leasing policy changed. Problems with the cathedral fabric left the chapter in much greater need of

---

31 C6/1/26/3, nos 4–8.   32 P.R.O., SP63/110/33.   33 C6/1/26/3, no. 4; C6/1/26/1, ff 19, 23.   34 C6/1/26/1, ff 6–13v. Agard was buried in the cathedral and a monument to him exists in the south transept, Refaussé & Lennon, *Registers*, p. 120.   35 Lehmberg, *Reformation*, pp 172–4; National Library of Wales, Aberystwyth, SD/Ch/B/1.

ready cash and this weakened their bargaining power with prospective tenants. In the 1560s the chapter began to take entry fines for the first time, sometimes in money but also in material for the repair of the church and this practice re-emerged in the 1580s.[36] Sixty-one year leases became the norm in the 1560s and remained so for the remainder of the sixteenth century. The length of individual leases does not, however, tell the whole story. Throughout the late sixteenth century the practice developed of granting reversionary leases of property before the original lease had expired. A few of these had been made in the 1540s but in the 1560s nine, three times the number made in the 1540s, were granted as the demand for money for repair of the church grew. Attempts were made to reduce this number in the 1570s and 1580s but problems with the fabric meant that the number of reversionary leases granted in the 1590s grew to sixteen. In a few cases such grants were an attempt to give security to a tenant who had invested capital in buildings on his property. In most cases it was forced on the chapter by the need to mortgage future rent increases to the present need for funds in the form of entry fines.[37] The practical effect of this may be seen in the case of one house in the parish of St Nicholas which was originally leased in 1548 for sixty-one years but in 1571 a reversionary lease was made for a further sixty-one years which meant that the lease would not expire until 1670.[38] Another lease of 1548 granted one of the cellars under the church from 1558 for sixty-one years but before this could expire another reversionary grant was made in 1598 for sixty-one years in consideration of £4 for repairing the church.[39] A further reversionary lease of 1541 for forty-one years, which was due to expire in 1596, had another reversion made in 1562 in consideration of stone provided for repair of the cathedral.[40] In at least some cases a number of these leases were acquired by one individual who could then petition the chapter for a long lease of the property.[41] It is clear that the chapter realised this would present problems in the future. They were aware of the rising land market and in contrast to cathedral chapters in England, they raised rents when possible. The rent of one property in Glasnevin was doubled between 1584 and 1619.[42] Rents were also increased when making reversionary leases but in the absence of evidence on sixteenth-century Irish rent movements it is impossible to judge how realistic those increases were.

Not surprisingly there was considerable demand for leases of Christ Church property not only from the Dublin mercantile community, who were

36 McEnery & Refaussé, *Deeds*, nos 1284, 1286, 1318, 1326, 1342, 1364, 1368, 1372. 37 For reversions as a result of improvements, McEnery & Refaussé, *Deeds*, nos 1317 and partly 1392. 38 McEnery & Refaussé, *Deeds*, nos 1216, 1321. 39 Ibid., nos 1222, 1408. This was assigned in 1651 for five times the annual rental. 40 Ibid., nos 1182, 1284. 41 C6/1/17/1, p. 236 for example. 42 C6/1/17/2, pp 3, 5.

the traditional lessees of the lands, but from within the cathedral community itself, especially the vicars choral. Indeed in 1594 John Bullock, one of the vicars choral and later verger, was ordered to stop requesting leases from the chapter.[43] In the early seventeenth century when the future interests had become so great as to preclude further grants, a secondary market (the profits of which did not accrue to the chapter) developed in the assignments of leases which were used to allow investors realise their gains in a buoyant land market. Thus a lease of 1592 of the great farms of Glasnevin for 119 years was sold in 1650 for £215 or fifty-seven times the annual rent and a 1594 lease of Draycott's farm, to commence in 1624, traded at £50 (or fifteen times the annual rent) in 1650.[44] In the city a reversionary lease made in 1590 for £3. 4s. changed hands for £143 in 1629 and in 1660, with a limited life span, it could still command £50.[45]

By the beginning of the seventeenth century the only solution to the economic difficulties of the church lay in a thorough reorganisation of its landholding. Other problems needed reform including the lack of statutes for the church and the rather irregular composition of the chapter in which the vicars choral were members. The simplest solution to these problems was thought to be a new charter. In 1602 Dean Wheeler was given leave to be absent in England for six months to expedite this. While the queen approved the charter she died before the document could be sealed, the new patent being made in July 1604.[46] This made the churches of St Michael, St Michan and St John prebendal rather than simply the livings of the dignitaries' vicars, confirmed the property of the cathedral and made provisions for the issuing of statutes.[47] However the new charter in itself was not sufficient to deal with the problem of long leases. As early as February 1603 the English privy council had instructed the Irish lord deputy and council that the queen was considering the seizure of the property of those Christ Church tenants who had fee farm grants but was prepared to allow them to compound for their lands.[48] Elizabeth's death ended this initiative but the king's letter of 1603 for the new charter provided for a commission to examine alienation of cathedral land. By 1605 the commission was established and by June 1606 it had identified a number of properties that had been alienated.[49] Some property was recovered under this commission including the lands of Grangegorman, Loughlinstown and the property granted to Walter Harrold in 1592. In return

43 Gillespie, *Chapter act book*, p. 87; for Bullock's leases, McEnery & Refaussé, *Deeds*, nos 1360, 1400, 1403, 1423.   44 C6/1/17/2, pp 4, 4a, 5. These properties with a combined rental of £16. 10s. in the 1590s were released at £40 in 1660, p. 67.   45 C6/1/17/4, p. 226.   46 *Fiants Ire. Eliz.*, no. 6705; C6/1/26/1, ff 46–6v; *Cal. S. P. Ire., 1603–6*, p. 99.   47 C6/2/32/1.   48 C6/1/6/3, p. 1228; *Cal. S. P. Ire., 1574–84*, p. 278 where it is misdated to 1580.   49 C6/1/6/3, pp 1231, 1256–60, 1259–67.

for Wheeler's efforts this property was assigned to the deanery and re-set on shorter leases.[50] Some of the disputed properties, such as that held by Lord Fitzwilliam at Simmonscourt, remained in contention with the cathedral into the 1640s.[51] Other solutions would have to be found for the cathedral's financial difficulties.

The death of Garvey marks another turning point in the history of the cathedral. John Garvey was the last Irish-born man to serve as dean before 1660. He was also the last Irish-born member of the late sixteenth century chapter and those appointed after him were from a rather different ecclesiastical tradition. After the 1580s a shift occurred in the nature of the career pathways of the church's clergy. Traditionally a route had developed from vicar choral to a canon's stall and even to a dignitary's place. The ascent of William Dermot illustrates the process. Dermot was the native Irish nephew of a Franciscan hermit who, although he had been in Dublin in the 1540s, first appears at Christ Church as a vicar in 1557. By 1561 he had become prebendary of St Michan's and by 1563 he was chancellor, an office he held until his death.[52] Most of these men were not university graduates although some might be sent there after their appointment to Christ Church while others, such as Dermot, seem to have acquired a working knowledge of practical subjects such as canon law.[53]

By the 1580s new forces were at work in the recruitment of the chapter. In St Patrick's the dean was elected by the chapter and the other canonries appointed by the archbishop but in Christ Church the dignitaries were royal appointments. This made posts at Christ Church attractive and accessible to New Englishmen, particularly those with access to patronage such as royal chaplains or the chaplains of Irish lords deputy. John Garvey's successor, Jonas Wheeler, was a chaplain to Queen Elizabeth and his successor in 1618, Ralph Barlow, was chaplain to Lord Deputy Chichester.[54] The attraction of these posts is easy to understand. According to the taxation of the church in 1616 the deanery was the third richest in Ireland after those of St Patrick's and Waterford, worth about £200 a year in the early seventeenth

50 Gillespie, *Chapter act book*, pp 84, 126, C6/1/17/2, p. 55; C6/1/26/1, ff 37-46v.   51 For legal action over the Simmonscourt property, N.A.I., RC6/1, p. 303; Chancery pleadings, K2 and for legal action over a lease of 1547 at Stagob, Chancery pleadings, K233. 52 Dublin City Archives, EXPL/1283a, 1285; McEnery & Refaussé, *Deeds*, nos 1287, 1291, 1274, 1288; Gillespie, *Chapter act book*, p. 24; *Cal. pat. rolls Ire., Hen. VIII-Eliz.*, p. 477; he received a grant of English liberty in 1570, McEnery & Refaussé, *Deeds*, no. 1566.   53 *Fiants Ire. Eliz.*, nos 2438, 416, 794; for Dermot's knowledge of canon law *Fiants Ire. Eliz.*, nos. 2379, 3014, 3244. He was probably part of an older apprenticeship tradition of training canonists, Murray, 'Tudor diocese', pp 64-87, 97-100.   54 J.B. Leslie, *Ossory clergy and parishes* (Enniskillen, 1933), p. 16; John Lodge, *Desiderata curiosa Hiberniae* (2 vols, Dublin, 1772), i, 206.

century (although Archbishop Loftus had claimed it yielded only £50 in 1584).[55] The precentorship, held by three former chaplains to the lords deputy from 1587 to 1634, was second in wealth only to that of St Patrick's. The treasurership and chancellorship were inferior only to those of St Patrick's and Ferns.[56] It is difficult to estimate the resulting wealth of the holder of a Christ Church post. At one end of the scale is the claim by the chancellor, John Harding, in 1641 that he had lost £2,463 as a result of the rebellion of that year although this included church livings, lands in Armagh and debts due to him rather than the direct income of his chancellorship.[57] At the lower end of the ecclesiastical hierarchy, the 1599 will of Laurence Bryan, who held the living of St Michael's since 1586, suggests more modest prosperity. While the living was valued at £7 a year in 1615 Bryan had managed to accumulate nine houses, some in the city, and a farm at Esker in county Dublin, much of which was held on lease from the cathedral.[58]

It was clear by the 1590s that Christ Church was also a road to further preferment. Every dean after John Garvey to 1649 became a bishop and three of the seven precentors acquired bishoprics. Moreover, it was increasingly rare for any member of the chapter to hold only his Christ Church post. In 1580 the only pluralist was John Garvey, who was also archbishop of Armagh. By 1600 half the chapter held another post and by 1613, when two members of the chapter were deprived for non-residence, all were pluralists.[59]

The emergence of Christ Church as a source of financially lucrative posts, and the importance of patronage through the royal household as a way to those posts, had a significant effect on the composition of the chapter. Personnel from England, where possibilities for clerical advancement were growing slimmer, looked to Ireland. These men were, in the main, university graduates. Of the twenty-six appointments to the chapter between 1585 and 1625 twenty-one can be identified as graduates. Of these fourteen came from Cambridge, four from Trinity College, Dublin (these mainly in the 1620s) and three from Oxford. This preponderance of Cambridge graduates shaped the theological outlook of the chapter. Late sixteenth-century Cambridge was well known as a centre of moderately puritan, godly clergy and the colleges

---

55 P.R.O., SP63/110/33; for estimates, R.D. Edwards, 'The letter book of Sir Arthur Chichester' in *Anal. Hib.*, no. 8 (1938), p. 91; *Cal. S. P. Ire., 1603–6*, p. 169; *Cal. S. P. Ire., 1625–32*, p. 428. The deanery property was set at £227 in 1633, McEnery & Refaussé, *Deeds*, no. 1512. 56 Bodl., Rawl. A 419. It was claimed that the deanery of Christ Church was over-taxed, *Cal. S. P. Ire., 1615–25*, p. 130. The three precentors who held chaplaincies were Robert Richardson (*Cal. Carew MSS, 1589–1600*, p. 228), Robert Grave and Thomas Ram (J.B. Leslie, *Ferns clergy and parishes* (Dublin, 1936), p. 7). 57 T.C.D., MS 809, f. 305. 58 N.L.I., GO MS 290, pp 19–20; B.L., Add. MS 19836, f. 6v; McEnery & Refaussé, *Deeds*, no. 1349; Gillespie, *Chapter act book*, p. 68. 59 Gillespie, *Chapter act book*, p. 135.

which were the centres of this activity, Christ's, St John's, Trinity and
Emmanuel, were the homes of 40 per cent of the appointments to the chapter.[60] This does not mean that the chapter of Christ Church became a centre
of puritan dissent with strong views on matters such as the unacceptability of
vestments. In 1613, however, Archbishop Abbot of Canterbury complained
that the dignitaries and prebendaries in the Dublin cathedrals did not attend
worship wearing their surplices and academic hoods.[61] Rather than become
involved in divisive issues the chapter's concern was to promote Christ Church
as a centre of godly preaching and true reformation. This concern seems clear
from a list of books borrowed from the cathedral library about 1607.[62] These
books are concerned in the main with the refutation of catholicism and the
promotion of a spirituality based on the works of English godly authors such
as William Perkins and Hugh Broughton. A strong Calvinist streak in the theological outlook of the chapter is suggested by the presence of works by
Theodore Beza and Francis de Jon, professor of theology at Leiden.

Preaching was central to the task of promoting a godly reformation and
lectures became increasingly important in the cathedral from the 1590s.
Indeed when Precentor Ram became bishop of Ferns in 1605 he took, rather
unusually, as his episcopal seal the image of a preacher in the pulpit.[63] By
1603 the lord deputy could claim that there was as much preaching in Dublin
as in any English city with a lecture every week at Christ Church. Even the
Protestant polemicist Barnaby Rich could comment favourably in 1610 that
'I dare be bold to avow it that there is never a pulpit within the city of
London (Paul's cross only excepted) that is better supplied than the pulpit
at Christ Church in Dublin' where there were many 'grave preachers'.[64]
Supplying a pulpit was a costly undertaking and Archbishop Loftus claimed
in 1585 that Christ Church 'neither hath nor is able to maintain one
preacher'. Initially government help was available and later an indirect subvention through Trinity College assisted.[65] Providing preachers from a chapter of seven was a difficult task and outsiders were frequently invited to
preach. Humphrey Fenn, the puritan controversialist who was also a fellow
of Trinity College, Dublin, frequently preached in the cathedral in 1596 and

---

60 These calculations are based on Leslie, 'Fasti'. For Cambridge, Patrick Collinson, *The
Elizabethan puritan movement* (London, 1967), pp 125–8.   61 T.C.D., MUN/P/1/72.
How long this lasted is unclear. By 1622 Edward Hill, prebendary of St John's wore a
surplice in his church (R.C.B., P328/5/1, p. 42) and in the 1630s Irish bishops preaching in Christ Church wore rochets whereas in other churches they preached without episcopal dress, Laud, *Works*, vii, 291–2.   62 Gillespie, 'Borrowing'.   63 T.C.D., MS 6404,
f. 57.   64 *Cal. Carew MSS, 1601–3*, p. 432; Barnaby Rich, *A new description of Ireland*
(London, 1610), p. 55.   65 P.R.O., SP63/115/27; *Cal. S. P. Ire., 1611–14*, p. 116. Lord
Deputy Fitzwilliam may personally have supported a lectureship in Christ Church in
1594, Northampton Record Office, Northampton, Fitzwilliam of Milton, Irish, no. 46.

1597 for instance.[66] Preaching was shared with the much larger chapter of St Patrick's. A preaching list from 1622 suggests that in the course of a year the dean would preach quarterly at morning prayer and three times a year at evening prayer. Other members of the chapter preached at least once a year at morning and evening prayer although some might preach twice.[67] The weekly lectures, held at the cathedral as a supplement to sermons, were handled somewhat differently. Students from the newly established Trinity College, Dublin lectured in combination. In 1600, for instance, John Richardson, the future bishop of Ardagh, delivered an expository lecture on Isaiah on Fridays while on Sunday mornings Henry Welsh, later prebendary of Donaghmore in St Patrick's, gave a theological lecture. Sunday afternoons were reserved for James Ussher, the future archbishop of Armagh, who delivered an address on controversy in which, according to his biographer Nicholas Bernard, 'he did so perspicuously ever concluding with matter of exhortation that it was much for the confirmation and edification of Protestants which elder sort of person living in my time I have heard often acknowledge'.[68] Apart from a break in 1603 these lectures continued into the 1630s.

How successful this programme of godly reform was in the 1590s and early 1600s is difficult to measure. At least part of its momentum was provided by government backing and the belief that converts to protestantism could still be made.[69] However, one result was that relations with the city became less cordial than before. As early as 1596 the corporation moved one of its stations, formerly kept at Christ Church, to the more religiously conservative church of St Audoen's.[70] After the pro-Catholic revolt of the Munster towns in 1603 the situation deteriorated more dramatically. Within the central government decisions were made that more effective measures should be taken against a resurgent catholicism. In Dublin the problem of recusancy came to a head in late 1603 with the failure of the mayor-elect for 1604, Robert Skelton, to take the oath of supremacy. In November 1603 mandates were issued to some of the most prominent Catholic citizens to go to their parish church or 'to give your personal attendance upon our mayor of our city of Dublin ... at such time as he shall upon the same day repair to the cathedral church commonly called Christ Church ... to hear divine service and sermon and then and there to present and show yourself before the said deputy general and council and there continue during such service and sermon'.[71] Only

---

66 *Cal. Carew MSS, 1589–1600*, pp 244, 248, 245, 253–4.   67 *Ordo habit et fact Dominica prima in Adventu ann dom 1622*, Society of Antiquaries, London, Proclamations, Ireland, no. 18. For other lists from which a similar pattern emerges T.C.D., MS 575, f. 95; MUN/P/1/400; Chetham Library, Manchester, MS A 677, pp 613–7.   68 Bernard, *Ussher*, pp 34–5.   69 For example the lectures in the cathedral were funded by the government in 1602, *Cal. S.P. Ire., 1611–15*, p. 116.   70 *Anc. rec. Dublin*, ii, 298.   71 *Cal. S.P. Ire., 1603–6*,

the mayor and seven aldermen attended. Six others were fined £100 and two others £50. Among these were two tenants of the cathedral and the son and nephew of two others.[72] In the following eight months others, including a number of Christ Church tenants, were summoned on mandates but refused to attend church and were fined.[73] None of the leases of these men was renewed. When the mandates controversy came to an end in 1607, after the intervention of the London government, considerable damage had been done to relations between the cathedral and the Catholics of the city.

What the chapter thought of the policy of conversion by compulsion is not clear but it seems likely that at least some disapproved. The precentor Thomas Ram, for instance, was probably unhappy. He claimed at the metropolitan visitation of his diocese of Ferns in 1622 that 'I never (till of late) proceeded to the excommunication of any for any matter of religion but contented myself only to confer with divers of each diocese [Ferns and Leighlin] both poor and rich and that in the most familiar and kind manner that I could, confuting their assertions by the touchstone of all truth, the holy scriptures'.[74] Similarly the prebendary of St Michan's, Meredith Hanmer, while a noted controversialist, had befriended the Jesuit Henry Fitzsimon while in prison suggesting some mutual respect.[75] Whatever the chapter as a whole may have thought, the heavy-handed intervention of one section of the Dublin administration had breached irretrievably the relationship between cathedral and city.

The cathedral's survival of the economic crises of the 1590s and the political upheavals of the first decade of the seventeenth century posed further problems. The reforming zeal which characterised the 1590s waned. By the 1615 regal visitation the chapter had lost most of the enthusiasm which it had displayed in the 1590s. By 1615 the dean and precentor were both recorded as absentees and the chancellor, Nicholas Robinson, was described as 'aged'. The treasurer, Christopher Hewetson, had held his post for twenty years and, although described as resident, was also vicar of Swords. The younger prebendaries held out more hope for the future. Edward Hill in St John's was 'a very sufficient man and a preacher' and John Egerton of St Michael's was 'a good preacher'.[76] However, there is little doubt that the chapter was atrophying. Between 1605 and 1615 it met on average just over

---

pp 346–7.   72 Ibid., p. 349. The tenants of the cathedral were John Eliot and Edmund Malone (Gillespie, *Chapter act book*, pp 92, 123). William Shelton was a nephew of John Shelton and Walter Seagrave a son of Christopher (Gillespie, *Chapter act book*, pp 104, 51). 73 Lennon, *Lords of Dublin*, p. 178.   74 *Second annual report of the commission ... respecting the public records of Ireland (1812)* (Dublin, 1815) p. 264.   75 Henry Fitzsimon, *Words of comfort to persecuted Catholics*, ed. Edmund Hogan (Dublin, 1881), p. 60.   76 B.L., Add. MS 19836, ff 6–6v.

twice a year in comparison to the average of over five meetings a year in the 1590s. After the death of the chapter clerk Christopher Bysse in 1614 it was not thought worth replacing him. Hence the chapter had no administrative focus until a new appointment was made in the 1630s. As a result the chapter met fitfully, if at all, in the early years of the 1620s.[77]

The early seventeenth century also saw a reorientation of the cathedral's relationships with both the city and the state. The souring of relations between the government and the city in the mandates controversy and the rise of recusant catholicism meant that Christ Church was no longer a centre for civic religion but rather a sign of the rifts within the city. The mayor still attended Christ Church on Sunday and an agreement of 1607 with the corporation meant that some members of the Trinity guild accompanied him. As a result the mayor's seat in the church was refurbished in 1608 and new cushions were supplied.[78] However, tensions still remained. The Protestant polemicist Barnaby Rich wrote of the corporation in the 1610s: 'I know not any of them that is a papist that on Sunday morning will first hear mass then after that they will bring the mayor to Christ Church and having put him into his pew they convey themselves to a tavern till the sermon be done that they bring the mayor back again to his home'.[79] How widespread this problem was it not clear but those who surveyed the state of Ireland in 1622 commented that of the twenty-four aldermen in Dublin only two went to church.[80]

Tensions between cathedral and city manifested themselves in a number of ways during the early seventeenth century but the most obvious one was over the existence of a liberty, excluded from the jurisdiction of the city, at Christ Church. The origin of the liberty lay in the exemption of the medieval religious house from civic control, a privilege inherited by the Protestant cathedral. Those who lived and worked there were exempt from the need to be freemen of the city and members of guilds. They were also exempt from taxes.[81] Until the 1580s this was not a significant problem since the liberty had few residents but in 1581 the first lease of property within the former cloisters was made and by 1635 some fifteen properties had been let.[82] The social world of the liberty comes into clearer focus in 1631 when the dean and chapter made regulations for the management of the liberty which were signed by all the householders.[83] Of the forty-one signatories the occupations of fourteen can be determined from other sources. Half described themselves

77 Calculated from Gillespie, *Chapter act book*.   78 *Anc. rec. Dublin*, ii, 483; iii, 72; Dublin City Archives, MR/35, pp 642, 740.   79 C.L. Falkiner, 'Barnaby Rich's "Remembrances of the state of Ireland"' in *R.I.A. Proc.*, xxvi, C (1906–7), pp 138–9.   80 B.L., Add MS 12496, f. 33.   81 For St Patrick's claim to be free from taxation, Mason, *St Patrick's*, pp 183–4.   82 Gillespie, *Chapter act book*, pp 38–9; C6/1/26/3, no. 24.   83 Gillespie, *Chapter act book*, p. 168.

as merchants, some operating shops in Christ Church Yard, three were shoe-makers, two cutlers and there was also a goldsmith and a tailor. Some of these were wealthy people. Merchants, such as Thomas Bird or Edward Carney, claimed considerable losses as a result of the outbreak of rebellion ten years later and another, Arthur Champion, had amassed enough money to purchase himself an estate in Fermanagh.[84] Not all were as powerful as this and the illiteracy of about a quarter of the residents of the liberty may suggest a poorer substratum but the liberty represented a considerable con-centration of wealth outside corporation control.

The existence of such liberties, and the consequent tension with the cor-poration, were not unusual in English cathedral towns but the situation in Dublin was more strained. The religious differences between corporation and cathedral sharpened tensions and the fact that the corporation's rights were themselves under attack by central government in the first two decades of the seventeenth century made them even more sensitive to the existence of lib-erties. As early as 1580 the corporation had tried to link the provision of funds for the rebuilding of the cathedral to limitations on the development of the liberty.[85] The issue became pressing in the early seventeenth century as the liberty began to expand. In 1609 the Holy Trinity guild seized goods of traders in the liberties of both Christ Church and St Patrick's and prosecutions were initiated.[86] By 1613 a second guild, that of the tailors, became involved in a dispute with Christ Church over its liberty and this gave rise to a trial in king's bench.[87] Both guilds appealed to the corporation for support and received it.[88] The matter appeared before the Irish privy council in 1617 but within a few years its ruling was in dispute.[89] Throughout the 1620s and 1630s the jurisdictional dispute continued, widening briefly in 1625 to the issue of the cathedral's holding of manorial courts in the county of the city of Dublin, with seemingly no prospect of a resolution.[90] Such problems did not sever relations between the city and cathedral. Dean Wheeler, for example, was made free of the city in 1607 and held city leases. The bell-ringers of Christ Church also continued to undertake civic functions such as the ringing of bells in the morning and evening to alert the citizens to passing time, although dis-putes over payment for this service became more frequent.[91] Such tensions

---

84 T.C.D., MS 810, ff 116, 122; N.L.I., MS GO 298, pp 31, 33; Gillespie, 'Champion', pp 53–6. The goldsmith was also clearly a substantial figure as he could allow one cus-tomer's debts to top £28 in 1637, B.L., Add. MS 46921, f. 184. For the operation of shops, McEnery & Refaussé, *Deeds*, nos 1510, 1526, 1527, 1541. 85 *Anc. rec. Dublin*, ii, 146. 86 *Hastings MSS*, iv, 4; B.L., Eg. MS 1765, ff 28–9, 35; N.A.I., Chancery pleadings, E55; C6/1/26/4, no. 1. 87 C6/1/6/3, pp 1269, 1270–1; C6/1/26/3, no. 9. 88 *Anc. rec. Dublin*, ii, 12, 30, 36–7, 54, 122–3, 167. 89 *Alen's reg.*, pp 303–4. 90 C6/1/26/14 no 2; C6/1/6/3, pp 1307–8; C6/1/26/13, nos 1–2, 4, 44; *Anc. rec. Dublin*, iii, 189. 91 *Anc. rec. Dublin*, ii, 474, 476; iii, 133–4, 186, 231.

meant that the city was less well disposed to the cathedral than in the sixteenth century, especially in funding repairs to the church. The cathedral
would have to look for other supporters in the seventeenth century.

The most obvious body to which the cathedral could turn for support in
a volatile world was the state. Links between cathedral and government were
already established. The state contributed to the maintenance of the church
with a £60 grant each year dating back to Edward VI's reign.[92] Money was
also paid to the choir who sang anthems and said prayers in the exchequer at
the end of the law terms.[93] Individual lords deputy might offer support as in
1608 when Lord Deputy Chichester gave the cathedral part of the find of
Catholic vestments at Armagh, 'chiefly one rich cope of cloth of gold he gave
to Christ Church in Dublin for to make a cushion and pulpit cloth for the
pulpit which is used for that very purpose there at this day'.[94] Other deputies
had been well disposed towards sextons and choristers and made payments
to them although for such benevolence they might also hope to exercise rights
of patronage in appointments to the choir and other offices.[95] The cathedral
continued as a centre of state ceremonial. In 1622, for instance, when Lord
Deputy Falkland was sworn-in the letters patent were handed over across the
communion table at Christ Church.[96] Indeed by the 1630s so important was
the swearing-in at Christ Church that when Lord Deputy Wentworth refused
to go there 'the common voice ... [was] said to murmur that their ancient
customs are by him slighted'.[97] The linkage between state and church is clearly
seen in the burials recorded in the funeral certificates registered in the office
of arms. Of the fifty-two individuals recorded as being buried in the cathedral between 1595 and 1616 twenty-nine were either minor government officials or related to officials. Only two burials were of civic figures.[98]

In return for acting as the state church Christ Church looked increasingly
to the government for financial support for maintenance of the building.
However, the early seventeenth-century Irish finances were perilous and the
government tried to move the burden elsewhere. In 1601, for instance, they
hoped that levies on army pay might fund the restoration of the church but

92 *Cal. S. P. Ire., 1611–14*, p. 116; *Cal. Carew MSS, 1601–3*, pp 418, 504; *Cal. Carew
MSS, 1603–24*, p. 185. There was a threat to this during the 1622 enquiry into Irish
finances but it was allowed (Exeter College, Oxford, MS 96, f. 9; Gillespie, *Chapter act
book*, pp 146–7, 152).   93 For example N.A.I., Ferguson MS xi, 179, 225, 249, 262, 280,
285.   94 C.L. Falkiner (ed.), 'William Farmer's chronicle of Ireland from 1594 to 1613'
in *English Historical Review*, xxii (1907), p. 539.   95 For example, *De L'Isle and Dudley
MSS* (3 vols, H.M.C., London, 1925–36), i, 412, 417; Bodl., Add. MS C 39, f. 13v;
Northampton Record Office, Northampton, Fitzwilliam of Milton MSS, Irish, nos 30,
32 37, 38, 40. For lords deputy exercising patronage, Bodl., Rawl. C 439, ff 3, 4; Gillespie,
Chapter act book, pp 84, 146.   96 T.C.D., MS 6404, f. 11v; *Cal. S. P. Ire., 1615–25*, p.
346.   97 B.L., Add. MS 29587, f. 19v.   98 N.L.I., GO MSS 64–6.

this failed and the exchequer was charged with the levy.[99] When the matter surfaced again in 1611, as preparations were being made for the summoning of a parliament in Ireland, the state tried to evade the problem. Legislation was proposed for the re-edifying of cathedrals but exempted those in sufficient repair to be useable and declared that the dean and chapter should pay for the necessary work at Christ Church.[100] Other sources of funding had to be found and Sir James Ware recorded that the archbishop of Dublin, Thomas Jones, contributed significantly to repairing the church.[101] However such personal largesse could not continue and in the parliament of 1615 a committee of the house of commons was established to consider how funds might be raised for work to the church.[102] Donations of £107 were raised but even basic work required expenditure of £125.[103] The state was approached again and attempted to deal with the problem by establishing a lottery to raise £500 for work on the cathedral. The patent to operate the lottery was granted to a soldier, Henry Southey, who entered bonds for the £500 in chancery.[104] The scheme was not a success and generated complaints that others were not allowed to operate lotteries in the same way. There was also grumbling about the immorality of lotteries in 'begetting idleness in the resorters to the same, pilfering in servants and great detriment [to] many wages'.[105] The required finance was not raised and one man, Humphrey Farnham, who had advanced money to allow the works to proceed in expectation of recouping it later, found himself out of pocket.[106] However, sufficient funds were raised to ensure that the cathedral fabric was now sound and the lawyer Luke Gernon in his 1620 description of Dublin observed of the city's two cathedrals 'St Patrick's is the more vast and ancient, the other is in better repair'.[107] The episode had revealed that the cathedral's new patron was less generous than the city had been.

The second institution to which Christ Church looked for support, this time theological, was the newly founded Trinity College, Dublin. Created in 1592, mainly as a centre for the education of future Church of Ireland clergy, a link between the cathedral and college was natural. The students in the new college were said to resort 'to solemn service in the cathedrals' in 1616 and for the convenience of its students Trinity maintained a seat 'in the eye of the state' in the cathedral. Students were expected to attend the church and to give an account to their tutor of the sermons they heard there.[108] As

---

99 *Acts privy council, 1601–4*, pp 128–9. This may be the reason Wheeler carried bills of exchange from England in 1602, C6/1/26/1, f. 46; P.R.O., AO1/288/1084, m.10r. 100 *Cal. Carew MSS, 1603–24*, p. 154. 101 Ware, *Works*, i, 355. 102 *Commons' jn. Ire.*, i, 48. 103 C6/1/26/6, no. 38; C6/1/26/12, no. 1. 104 *Cal. S. P. Ire., 1615–25*, pp 279–80; B.L., Add. MS 19839, f. 32v. 105 B.L., Harl. MS 3292, f. 2v. 106 C6/1/26/2, no. 13; Marsh's Lib., MS Z3.2.6, nos 48–50. 107 C.L. Falkiner (ed.), *Illustrations of Irish history* (London, 1904), p. 351. 108 T.C.D., MUN/P/1/88, 99; *The particular book*

students entered the ministry their future careers might bring them close to the cathedral. Edward Hill, the prebendary of St John's from 1613 to 1630, was a graduate of Trinity College as was one of his successors, Dudley Boswell. Both John Bradley, the chancellor from 1627 to 1635, and John Egerton, prebendary of St Michael's from 1612 to 1625, were Trinity alumni, Bradley having been a senior fellow in the college before coming to the cathedral. Student links were not, of course, the only ones between college and cathedral. Dean Wheeler, for instance, was a tenant of the college and also sent his son there. By 1610 some of the manuscripts which the cathedral had no further use for, including the 'Book of obits', were in the college library.[109] Close links were clearly developing between the two institutions.

One of the most significant ways in which Trinity College influenced the life of the cathedral in the early seventeenth century was through the preachers and lecturers it provided for the Christ Church pulpit. Whatever about its administrative torpor the cathedral had a considerable reputation as a centre for godly preaching. In 1624 the puritan chaplain of the earl of Cork, Stephen Jerome, compared it to St Paul's Cross or Spittalfields in London or York and Lincoln for the quality of its sermons and lectures, echoing the earlier comments of Barnaby Rich.[110] In 1611 the government had provided £40 to the provost of Trinity College to supply a lecturer for Christ Church, the post rotating among the senior fellows. Attempts were made to attract well-known godly preachers to fill the post. In 1612 James Ussher, then professor of theological controversies in Trinity, tried to lure a Colchester preacher, Mr Eyre, to Dublin with the promise of the lectureship in Christ Church and in 1621 it was hoped that Ussher's scholarly friend Samuel Ward of Ipswich would accept a Trinity professorship and Christ Church lectureship.[111] The financial problems of the government led to the funding being withdrawn in 1618 but the College continued to provide preachers for the Friday lecture from its own fellows, including William Bedell, the future bishop of Kilmore.[112]

It is difficult to measure the long-term influence of the college on the theological ideas of the Christ Church clergy. None of the cathedral clergy committed their views or sermons to print and no library lists survive for cathedral personnel. It is highly probable that the existing godly ethos of the cathedral in the 1590s was reinforced and deepened by the influence of the

---

of Trinity College, Dublin, ed. J.P. Mahaffy (London, 1909), ff 32v, 34v, 50v, 63, 73v, 86v. **109** T.C.D., MUN/D/67b-c; Mahaffy, Particular book, ff 26, 32, 35, 37v, 47v, 51v, 56v, 61, 74v, 79v; Gillespie, 'Archives', p. 4. **110** Stephen Jerome, Ireland's jubilee or joyes io paean (Dublin, 1624), p. 169. See p. 185 above. **111** J.W. Stubbs, The history of the university of Dublin (Dublin, 1889), p. 27; Ussher, Works, xvi, 315, 318; Mahaffy, Particular book, ff 193v. **112** Cal. S. P. Ire., 1615–25, pp 189, 201. That the funding was actually withdrawn is suggested by a petition in the 1620s to have it restored, Ussher, Works, xv, 391. The lectures seem to have petered out in the 1630s but were revived, C6/1/7/2,

college. Trinity's early seventeenth-century preoccupation with theological controversy together with the ideas of election and damnation underpinned by the philosophical works of Peter Ramus, widely used in the college, undoubtedly shaped, and was shaped by, the cathedral clergy. It is possible to reconstruct a little of their mental world from the books they borrowed from James Ussher, bibliophile, Trinity professor and later archbishop of Armagh. According to two borrowing lists kept by Ussher before 1625 Christopher Hewetson, the treasurer of Christ Church, borrowed Ussher's manuscript catechism by the English Presbyterian Thomas Cartwright, a 'book of secular priests against Jesuits' and a scriptural commentary by the godly English preacher Hugh Broughton. The prebendary of St John's, Edward Hill, also borrowed works by Cartwright and Broughton. Edward Donelan, prebendary of St Michael's, lent Ussher the more mainstream, if uninspired, *Survey of Christ's suffering and descent into hell* by Thomas Bilson, bishop of Winchester. Dean Barlow clearly had a taste for controversial works since he borrowed from Ussher the strongly puritan work *An answer to a sermon preached ... by George Downham*. Catholic controversial works such as that by William Fulke and the Jesuit Robert Parsons's *Defence of the censures* were in the hands of Nicholas Robinson, the chancellor, and Thomas Baugh, successively prebendary of St Michan's and St Michael's, respectively.[113] Christ Church was a community absorbed in godly Calvinist thought and concerned more with the elect than the perceived reprobate.

By the middle of the 1620s it was clear that the cathedral community of Christ Church had retrenched behind the walls of the close. The civic role, prominent a century earlier, had now all but collapsed. Moreover, any attempt to reach out to the Catholic community of the city had been abandoned. The 1615 visitation admitted that the three prebendal churches of the cathedral were staffed by good or sufficient preachers and the visitation of 1630 confirmed that the fabric was in good repair and furnished with all the required ornaments. Yet despite these resources the parish of St Michan had 320 recusants in 1617–18, St Michael's 190 and sixty-eight in St John's parish. By 1630 most of the inhabitants of St Michan's were described as recusants and 'most part' of St Michael's fell into that category. Only in St John's was there a majority of Protestants.[114] In addition to this within 150 yards of the cathedral a Jesuit house had established itself

---

f. 15v. For preachers, Mahaffy, *Particular book*, f. 171v, *Tanner letters*, ed. Charles McNeill (Irish Manuscripts Commission, Dublin, 1943), p. 85; Nicholas Bernard, *Certain discourses* (London, 1659), p. 350.   113 T.C.D., MS 790, ff 49, 169v; Bodl., Rawl. D 1290, ff 1–2v. 114 M.V. Ronan (ed.), 'Royal visitation of Dublin, 1615' in *Archivium Hibernicum*, viii (1941), pp 11–12; M.V. Ronan (ed.), 'Archbishop Bulkeley's visitation of Dublin, 1630' in *Archivium Hibernicum*, viii (1941), pp 75–8; John Meagher, 'Presentment of recusants in Dublin, 1617–18' in *Reportorium Novum*, ii, no. 2 (1959–60), pp 272–3.

in Back Lane, where the dean's orchard lay, and it was fully equipped for mission with the latest in European ecclesiastical fittings.[115]

Those who lived around Christ Church were not unaware of these developments and could not continue to ignore them indefinitely. There were already rumblings of discontent from some Protestants. Henry Leslie preaching in the cathedral on 30 October 1625, a day of humiliation occasioned by the outbreak of plague in England, saw this as a warning for Ireland of the dangers of failing to establish a godly society and in particular the sin of tolerating catholicism.[116] The message was not a new one. George Andrews, dean of Limerick, preaching in Christ Church before the lord deputy the previous year had spelt out a similar message.[117] Even earlier the young James Ussher preaching before the government in the cathedral in 1601 predicted that Ireland would pay for the sin of tolerating catholicism forty years later as the application of his text required.[118]

Apart from pulpit orators others began to show unease about the way the world of Christ Church was organised in the late 1620s. When Ralph Barlow, the dean of the cathedral, was being considered for the archbishopric of Tuam in 1628 he applied, as his predecessors who had been elevated had done, to hold his deanery *in commendam* with the bishopric. The response which he received was rather different from the usual approval. Both the king and William Laud, the newly appointed bishop of London, objected, claiming that to hold two senior posts together would be detrimental to the church. It was only after a great deal of special pleading that the bishopric could not 'support the dignity of such a calling' that the holding of the two posts was allowed but London officials were unhappy about the situation in Christ Church.[119] It is clear that the style of reform that had evolved in the late sixteenth and early seventeenth centuries was not sufficient to meet the demands now being placed upon it. How the church was to be modernised was a problem which would preoccupy the cathedral for the next forty years.

---

115 Brereton, *Travels*, pp 141–2.   116 Henry Leslie, *A warning for Israel in a sermon preached at Christ Church in Dublin, the 30 of October 1625* (Dublin, 1625), pp 4, 10.   117 George Andrews, *A quarterion of sermons preached in Ireland* (Dublin, 1625), sermon 1. 118 Bernard, Ussher, pp 39–40; the text was Ezekiel 4.6, 'Thou shalt bear the iniquity of the house of Judah forty days: I have appointed thee each day for a year'. The reference was later understood to relate to the outbreak of the rebellion in 1641.   119 B.L., Sloan MS 3827, f. 151; Laud, *Works*, vi, 258; B.L., Add. MS 18824, no. 50.

X

The crisis of reform, 1625–60

Raymond Gillespie

By the middle of the 1620s it was clear that protestantism, albeit in a rather introverted and lack-lustre form, had established itself in many parts of Ireland. The form that protestantism would eventually take was less clear. A number of possibilities was emerging. One option was that the episcopal Calvinism of the early seventeenth century would undergo a reinvigoration. Another was that a sacramentally based style of worship, which brought communities together around a corporate ritual, such as was becoming the norm in England, would emerge. A third possibility was that the godly worship of English dissent might be adopted in Ireland. Between 1625 and 1660 all these forms were part of the expression of protestantism at Christ Church cathedral. A revival in the traditional worship of the Church of Ireland in the late 1620s blended into a Laudian experiment which saw the eucharist as the main channel of sacramental grace. The collapse of that paradigm in the 1640s gave way to a style of worship dictated by the ideas of Independency in the 1650s before the restoration in 1660 of a Church of Ireland rather different to its early seventeenth-century counterpart.

Signs of revival in the activities of the Christ Church community can be detected from April 1627. The momentum for change was a fear of a Catholic revival. War between England and Spain in late 1625 saw Ireland, the favoured invasion route for England, ill-prepared. The inability of the Irish exchequer to fund adequate defence forced Charles I to offer his Catholic Old English subjects twenty-six concessions or 'graces' in return for a subvention towards the Irish army. Fears of a *de facto* toleration of catholicism began to grow in Dublin. This was condemned in a private meeting of the Irish bishops in November 1626 attended by both Dean Wheeler and Precentor Ram of Christ Church in their episcopal capacities. On 22 April 1627 a clarion call was issued from the pulpit of the cathedral by George Downham, bishop of Derry, who declared toleration of catholicism sinful and a dishonouring of God. According to one witness 'all the Protestants in the church cried Amen, Amen' but a more sober contemporary observed that it was 'an excellent and learned sermon'.[1] The message was hammered home on successive Sundays before being taken by the bishops to the lord deputy himself.

Concern for the propagation of protestantism in the face of a potential Catholic revival was already on the mind of Lancelot Bulkeley, the archbishop of Dublin, and the cathedral chapter. In his visitation of the cathedral in early April 1627 the archbishop laid down new orders which were to be obeyed in the church.[2] The chapter itself underwent a reinvigoration, meeting five times in 1627 alone, or almost double the annual average for the previous ten years. These were not isolated incidents. Over the next three years as fears of Catholic plots waxed and waned there were calls for reform. Stephen Jerome, a chaplain to one of the lords justice, the earl of Cork, preaching in Christ Church in 1631 attacked those who rejected the godly as 'papist, hypocrite, idolater, blasphemer, drunkard, atheist, profane person, murderer [and] devil incarnate'.[3]

Despite these intermittent pressures for revival the chapter found it difficult to develop a long term reform strategy. The reasons are not difficult to discover. The two most senior individuals in the chapter, the dean and precentor, were pluralists and most of the others were elderly. In January 1630 however Edward Hill, prebendary of St John's for almost twenty years, died having 'foretold his own death a day or two before. He was suspected to have used magic.'[4] In April the chapter chose as his replacement John Atherton, an English cleric from Somerset who had come to Ireland two years earlier in somewhat dubious circumstances.[5] The reasons for his selection are unclear but probably owed much to his patron, Adam Loftus, the lord chancellor and lord justice, to whom Atherton was chaplain.[6]

In many ways Atherton was an inspired choice. He had a reputation, acquired at Oxford, as a canon lawyer which made him familiar with the workings of a cathedral chapter despite his lack of capitular experience. Moreover the preoccupation of senior figures in the chapter with their own affairs meant that they left him to devote his considerable energy to the running of the cathedral. In July 1630 he was appointed sub-dean and in 1632

---

1 Bodl., Carte MS 1, ff 85–6; Bernard, *Ussher*, pp 62–4; Robert Ware, *The second part of foxes and firebrands* (Dublin, 1682), p. 70; T.C.D., MS 6404, ff 43v, 66.   2 Gillespie, *Chapter act book*, pp 148–9.   3 S[tephen] J[erome], *The souls sentinel ringing an alarm against impiety and impenitence* (Dublin, 1631), sig A3.   4 T.C.D., MS 6404, f. 108v.   5 For Atherton, Aidan Clarke, 'The Atherton file' in *Decies*, no. 11 (May 1979), pp 35–54.   6 Atherton is described as 'a new chaplain of his lordships' in February 1630, B.L., Sloane MS 3827, f. 173; *The life and death of John Atherton* (London, 1641), sig A2v, and he continued until at least 1635, *Hastings MSS*, iv, 62.

was given an open power of attorney by the dean.[7] Atherton's impact on the church was dramatic. A new chapter clerk was appointed in May 1630, the chapter in the 1620s having managed without a clerk. The number of chapter meetings soared from three or four a year to nine by 1630 and eleven in 1634. Discipline among the vicars choral was increased and more offences were recorded in the chapter act book than before. By the middle of the 1630s there were signs of a new reformation within the precincts of Christ Church. Atherton's reforms ensured that when the new lord deputy, Thomas Wentworth, earl of Strafford, was appointed in July 1633 with an agenda of aligning the English and Irish churches in doctrine and practice, the chapter of Christ Church was already moving in that direction. The arrival of John Bramhall, sub-dean of Ripon since 1624 and a member of the chapter at York, as treasurer in September 1633 simply speeded up the process.[8]

While the reforms of the 1630s can be seen as part of a process already under way at Christ Church there was one significant innovation in worship. On 21 June 1633 the Irish auditor-general, Sir James Ware, recorded in his diary 'the communion table at Christ Church was set up after the manner of an altar, north and south, and upon the Sunday following viz. 23 June the epistle and gospel and ten commandments were read there by Mr Atherton, prebend of St John's'.[9] The effect for the congregation which met in the quire was to reorientate worship away from the pulpit and reading desk where the word of God was proclaimed towards the Eucharist celebrated at the altar. The increasing importance of the eucharist as the main channel of sacramental grace can be seen in two ways. First, the physical setting of the altar was dramatically improved. Previously the communion table stood in the middle of the quire but in its new fixed position it was raised up and paved around with steps provided for access, innovations also executed in Atherton's prebendal parish of St John in 1635–6. It was also railed off from the worshippers and painted as were the ten commandments which adorned the wall behind it.[10] New communion silver was also acquired. Four 'great flagons' were bought in 1636–7 but more was also purchased. Among the Christ Church silver sold to St Canice's, Kilkenny in 1683 were two London-made chalices of 1635 and a basin made in Dublin in 1638 which were presumably acquired in the 1630s.[11] Secondly, attendance at the communion service was

7 Gillespie, *Chapter act book*, pp 180–1.   8 J.T. Fowler, *Memorials of the church of SS Peter and Wilfred, Ripon* (3 vols, Durham, 1882–5), ii, 287, 279–83.   9 T.C.D., MS 6404, f. 116v; for the works, C6/1/26/3, no. 23.   10 C6/1/23/1, no 27; R.C.B., P328/5/1, p. 139.   11 Graves & Prim, *St Canice's*, p. 52. Waterford cathedral tried to reclaim some of its silver in 1637, James Graves, 'The ancient fabric, plate and furniture of the cathedral of Christ Church Waterford' in *R.S.A.I. Jn.*, ii (1852–3), pp 76–7. The cathedral at Cork ornamented its altars as the result of a bequest in 1638, St Fin Barre's cathedral,

increasingly seen as important. The orders for the vicars choral instituted in January 1634 required that every vicar attend the communion service on pain of a fine of 40s. for the first offence, £4 for the second and expulsion for the third. This represents a significant increase on the fine of 2s. 6d. stipulated for the same offence in the 1627 orders.[12] The communion service became a gathering of all the community rather than simply an elect. The covenant theology which had underpinned George Downham's 1627 sermon in the cathedral was being replaced with the Arminian view that God's grace was available to all people. That view was being articulated in the writings of the new treasurer of Christ Church, Edward Parry, and during the trial of Archbishop Laud in 1640 it was alleged that William Chappel, then provost of Trinity College, Dublin, held similar views and he 'did maintain ... in Christ Church Arminianism'.[13]

The refurbishment of the altar indicates the increasing attention paid to the importance of orderly worship in a beautiful setting. The setting of Christ Church left something to be desired. Within the cathedral the traveller William Brereton described the quire in 1635 as 'but plain and ordinarily kept, the body of the church a more stately building'.[14] This was a matter that required attention and in 1638 a major refurbishment of the quire was undertaken with extensive repairs, re-glazing and re-plastering, the walls being coloured with russet and ochre.[15] The importance of music in the liturgy was also expanded, as Barra Boydell demonstrates below. While the chapter were certainly involved in these changes they were also being approved at a higher level with the plans being forwarded to Laud by Wentworth.[16] Outside the church there were also problems. The development of shops in the liberties during the early seventeenth century together with the older practice of letting commercial space in the vaults did not make for a tranquil setting. John Bramhall, the newly appointed treasurer, reported to Archbishop Laud in August 1633 that

> the vaults from one end of the minster to the other are made into tippling houses for beer, wine and tobacco, demised all to popish recusants and by them and others so much frequented in time of divine service that although there is no danger of blowing up the assembly above their heads yet there is of poisoning them with the fumes.[17]

Cork, B8/1, p. 43. **12** Gillespie, *Chapter act book*, pp 148, 205. There was a similar tightening up of the rules governing the vicars choral in Cork, St Fin Barre's cathedral, Cork B8/1, pp 34, 36–8. **13** Edward Parry, *David restored*, ed. John Parry (Oxford, 1660) esp. pp 7, 10–11; Laud, *Works*, iv, 299. **14** Brereton, *Travels*, p. 138. **15** C6/1/23/1, no. 27. **16** *The earl of Strafford's letters and despatches*, ed. William Knowler (2 vols, London, 1799), ii, 157, 169. **17** *The works of ... John Bramhall*, ed. A.W. Hadden (5 vols, Oxford,

In response to such complaints the lord deputy and council issued orders for the management of the cathedral in November. By December Wentworth claimed these were being implemented and Archbishop Laud regarded them as a model for developments elsewhere.[18] Christ Church, as the church used by the government of Ireland, was to be the flagship for a religious experiment that could not be allowed to fail.

To make a reality of this experiment in worship and to ensure its continuity at least two things were required, appropriate personnel and finance. Changes were made in the composition of the chapter at Christ Church on a scale not witnessed since the 1560s. The government had been concerned about the puritan character of the Christ Church chapter for some time and William Bedell claimed that before his appointment as bishop of Kilmore in 1629 he had been refused the deanery of Christ Church because of his theological views.[19] Between 1632 and 1635 all the members of the chapter, with one exception, were replaced. Thomas Ram, the precentor, and Christopher Hewetson, the treasurer, had died, the others resigned. How much pressure was applied is not known but in 1634 Dean Barlow, who was also archbishop of Tuam, felt obliged to resign the deanery he had striven to retain in 1628, so it could be conferred on someone 'whose abilities and conversation may be answerable to the eminency of the place'.[20] The motivation behind these changes is suggested by the fact that of the seven members of the chapter in 1635 four had been brought directly from England. Most of the newcomers had been chaplains in Wentworth's household and hence conversant with new styles of Laudian churchmanship. One other member, John Atherton, had arrived only a few years earlier after spending time in the diocese of Bath and Wells where many of the new Laudian reforms had first been tried out.[21]

To judge from the career paths of those appointed in the mid-1630s Christ Church was used as a way of introducing promising English talent into the Church of Ireland. The chapter produced four bishops before 1640. John Bramhall became bishop of Derry, Atherton was elevated to Waterford and Lismore and Tilson and Chappel became bishops of Elphin and Cork respectively. Tilson's successor as dean, James Margetson, was also intended for greater things since Henry Bridgeman, the Restoration dean of Chester,

1842–5), i, lxxix.   18 *Cal. S. P. Ire., 1633–47*, pp 17, 31–2; Gillespie, *Chapter act book*, pp 202–4; Laud, *Works*, vii, 61; T.C.D., MS 6404, f. 117v; Knowler, *Letters and despatches*, i, 173.   19 Shuckburgh, *Bedell*, p. 53.   20 Laud, *Works*, vi, 398; *Cal. S. P. Ire., 1633–47*, p. 86. Bramhall had originally been considered for the deanery but was appointed bishop of Derry instead, Knowler, *Letters and despatches*, i, 329. For Tilson who was appointed, Knowler, *Letters and despatches*, ii, 361.   21 Margaret Steig, *Laud's laboratory: the diocese of Bath and Wells in the early seventeenth century* (London, 1982), pp 325, 344.

later claimed that Wentworth had promised him the deanery of Christ Church in succession to Margetson.[22]

Measuring the effect these men had on the life of the cathedral is difficult but it is possible to quantify one aspect of their impact. In the later 1630s the number of occasions on which the chapter met rose significantly. Between 1635 and 1640 the number of chapter meetings rose to an average of ten a year from six in the early 1630s and in 1640 alone thirteen meetings were held. Average attendance also improved from five canons in the early 1630s to six between 1635 and 1640. In some cases the improvement was dramatic. Dean Barlow was one of the poorest attenders at chapter meetings, managing less than half in the early 1630s, but his successors managed sixty out of sixty-two after 1635. Precentor Ram, whose attendance record was worse than the dean's, was succeeded by men who missed only five out of sixty-two meetings.[23] While it is impossible to make any judgement on the spirituality of those who guided the cathedral through the late 1630s they were certainly enthusiastic administrators.

The second requirement for the success of the Laudian religious experiment was money. The cost of the refurbishment of the cathedral alone was considerable and was frequently commented on by Archbishop Laud in 1637 and 1638.[24] In 1630–1 the cathedral expended £139 on the maintenance account but by 1638–9 this had risen to £344.[25] Some of the initial shortfall between income and expenditure may have been personally funded by Lord Deputy Wentworth but if the experiment was to endure the problem of the low level of income from the cathedral endowment had to be tackled.[26] A government attempt to assign lands to the church in the abortive plantation of Connacht in lieu of exchequer payments was unsuccessful.[27] However, where new leases of existing cathedral property could be made in the 1630s rents were dramatically increased. Property let in Lucan in 1635 saw the rent treble from the previous letting in 1578 and the dean's property at Prior's Land, first leased in 1572 at £2 a year was re-leased at £8 in 1639. In other, mainly urban, cases rent was not increased but new leases had building covenants.[28] Another way of maximising the revenue from Christ Church lands was to manage the existing property more efficiently. This approach

22 Bodl., Carte MS 34, f. 559.   23 Calculated from Gillespie, *Chapter act book* and C6/1/7/2. At St Fin Barre's in Cork the number of meetings barely increased at all in the 1630s, St Fin Barre's cathedral, Cork, B8/1.   24 Laud, *Works*, vi, 502, 522; vii, pp 368, 383, 425, 447–8, 465.   25 C6/1/23/1, nos 17, 21.   26 A loan to the cathedral from Wentworth of £150 in 1635 was repaid in 1639, Cheshire Record Office, Chester, DLT/B43, p. 2.   27 Sheffield City Library, Wentworth Wodehouse MSS, Strafford letter book 20, no. 129.   28 C6/1/17/2, pp 89–91; C6/1/17/4, pp 382, 383, 401–2. For the breaking of the Prior's Land lease, C6/1/26/2, no. 8.

was two-fold. In the early 1630s Atherton had begun a campaign to collect arrears of rent and by the middle of the 1630s most of these had been cleared. Growing demand for property in the cathedral liberty in the 1630s was used to maximise income. As property in this area became more sought after so small pieces of land that had been hitherto ignored attracted attention and a number of leases of such property was made in the late 1630s.

By the 1630s, however, much of the cathedral property was entangled in a skein of sixteenth-century reversionary leases, many of which would not expire until the 1660s. Thus few new leases could be made to take advantage of the increasing demand, and hence higher rents, for property around Dublin. The only realistic approach to this problem was to attempt to break some of the older leases. This was not a simple process. Attempts had been made in the early 1630s by John Atherton to recover long standing arrears and some alienations. In 1632, for example, the dean and chapter attempted to extract the tithes of Grangegorman from John Agard through a suit in chancery. In the following year proceedings were taken against John King over the tithes of fishing in the Liffey.[29]

The national process of recovering alienated church lands spear-headed by Bishop Bramhall began late in the diocese of Dublin. It was March 1637 before Dean Tilson ordered an examination of the title to cathedral property held on long leases.[30] In the following year action was begun against Simon Luttrell over the lands of Stagob which he held under a lease of 1547.[31] By late 1639 the process was gathering momentum and the bishop of Derry, John Bramhall, was appointed to summon the tenants of cathedral land held on long leases to produce the evidence for their title.[32] To consolidate potential gains from this process legislation was introduced into the parliament of 1640 to confirm the cathedral's land titles. This foundered on a dispute over the lands of Simmonscourt claimed by Lord Merrion. There was an attempt to resurrect the bill in 1643 but legislative underpinning of the cathedral's property titles proved abortive.[33]

While considerable strides had been made in the 1630s towards establishing both English personnel and styles of worship in Christ Church the fragility of the new order was demonstrated after the removal of Lord Deputy Wentworth from Ireland in late 1640 and the execution of Archbishop Laud in May 1641. The full import of these events was felt in Ireland during the

29 C6/1/6/3, pp 1294–9, N.A.I., RC6/2, pp 104, 98; Gillespie, *Chapter act book*, pp 178–9, 189–90.   30 E.P. Shirley (ed.), *Papers relating to the Church of Ireland, 1631–9* (London, [1874]), pp 48, 51; C6/1/26/23, no. 6.   31 C6/1/26/15.   32 B.L., Harl. MS 2102, ff 51–4; C6/1/26/13, nos 8, 9; C6/1/26/2, nos 20 23, 29, 33; C6/1/7/2, pp 48–9.   33 *Commons' jn. Ire.*, i, 304; *Lords' jn. Ire.*, i, 130–1; C6/5/8; C6/1/6/3, pp 1337–8, 1339–40, 1341–9.

trial and execution of Wentworth's supporter the chancellor of Christ Church and bishop of Waterford and Lismore, John Atherton, in the wake of Wentworth's fall.[34] Four days after the execution on 6 December the Irish lord deputy, Christopher Wandesford, died and was buried at Christ Church. His daughter recalled that 'such was the love that God had given to the worthy person that the Irish did set up their lamentable hone, as they call it, for him in the church which was never known before for any Englishman done'.[35] The conjuncture of the two events must have raised doubts in the minds of the Christ Church community as to whether the lament was for all the old order.

If the progress of the Laudian experiment in worship and church government ground to a halt by the beginning of 1641 it came to a dramatic end in October of that year when news broke of a rising of native Irish in Ulster and the discovery of a plot to seize Dublin castle. The immediate reaction of the Christ Church community was panic, fuelled by rumour and uncertainty. Pamphlets published in London in the closing months of 1641 played on local fears by retelling fabricated stories, probably based on rumour, of how the rebels had stacked gunpowder under the cathedral which they intended to detonate when the lords justice were at church.[36] Such stories played on traditional fears of the gunpowder plot of 1605, the celebration of which had long been part of the political calendar by the 1640s. Other rumours about the fate of the church came from Protestants fleeing to Dublin in advance of the rebels. Anne Capper of Finglas, for instance, reported that in early December 1641 she had heard rebels 'affirm that by Christmas next following mass should be said in Christ Church Dublin' and Robert Maxwell, rector of Tynan, said that he at been told by a friar at Drogheda 'I hope ... to say mass in Christ Church Dublin within eight weeks'.[37] More worrying was the report from Wicklow which claimed that rebels had said 'that some of them would have St Patrick's Church and some Christ Church wherein they said all the English treasure was, which treasure they would have

---

34 Clarke, 'The Atherton file'.   35 *The autobiography of Mrs Alice Thornton*, ed. Charles Jackson (Durham, 1875), pp 25, 39.   36 *A gunpowder plot for blowing up the chiefest church in Dublin when the lords and others were at sermon on Sunday October 31 1641* (London, 1641), sig A2v; *A copy of a letter concerning the traitorous conspiracy of rebellious papists in Ireland* (London, 1641), p. 4.   37 T.C.D., MS 809, ff 6, 261; MS 810, f. 22v. This became a trope frequently repeated in the pamphlet literature, *A continuation of the Irish rebel proceedings with our victories over them* (London, 1642), p. 6; Nicholas Bernard, *The whole proceedings of the siege of Drogheda* (London, 1642), pp 34, 81; *A false and scandalous remonstrance of the inhumane and bloody rebels of Ireland* (London, 1644), p. 74; *A full and impartial account of the secret consults, negotiations, strategems and intrigues of the Romish party in Ireland from 1660 to the present time* (London, 1690), p. 15.

amongst them'.[38] As the war dragged on into December the chapter moved its records to Dublin castle for safe keeping.[39] Some members of the chapter became concerned for their safety and left the city. By the beginning of 1642 only the chancellor, and the prebendaries of St Michan's and St John's remained. The precentor, Richard Washington, had fled at the news of the outbreak of the rising as had William Carville, chaplain to the marquis of Ormond and prebendary of St Michael's. Carville was deposed from his living in February 1642 for non-residence.[40] The dean, James Margetson, may also have left the country as he was absent from chapter meetings after January 1642 for almost eighteen months. Some vicars choral also felt unsafe and one of them, Thomas Lowe, went to London where he found a place in St Paul's for his talents.[41]

When those who remained near the cathedral came to terms with the initial shock of the rising they were faced with the problem of how to deal with their changed situation. Many were immediately affected by the war. One former resident of the cathedral liberty, Arthur Champion, was murdered by the insurgents in the first days of the rising. Two others, the merchants Thomas Bird and Edward Carney, later claimed considerable financial loss as a result of the war. The chancellor, John Harding, estimated his losses at almost £2,500 and the chapter clerk, Thomas Howell, lost a more modest £230.[42] There were more immediate inconveniences. Troops were billeted on the liberty from late 1641 and by 1644 there were almost 141 men stationed there.[43] In addition to these local inconveniences the whole city was overcrowded with refugees from other parts of the country who not only had to be fed but also were potential carriers of disease. Henry Jones, the bishop of Meath, claimed in his 1679 sermon at the funeral of James Margetson that the dean had fed and clothed such refugees until he could no longer afford to do so 'the course of his revenues here being every way stripped'.[44] Such charitable acts could not hope even to contain the situation which rapidly worsened and mortality rose. The registers of the prebendal parish of St John, which lay immediately north of the cathedral, reveal that the number of burials in 1642 was almost four times that of the previous year. Of the 416 interred in 1642 a quarter were described as 'poor

38 T.C.D., MS 811, f. 135v.   39 C6/1/7/2, f. 50.   40 Washington died in London in 1651, Armagh Public Library, Robert Ware's MS history of the city of Dublin, 1678, p. 267; Bodl., Carte MS 164, ff 319–20; C6/1/7/2 ff 50–4; Bodl., Carte MS 3, f. 596. 41 C6/1/7/2, f. 53v, 58.   42 Gillespie, 'Champion', pp 58–9; T.C.D., MS 809, f. 305; MS 810, ff 116, 122.   43 Anc. rec. Dublin, iii, 398; Calendar of the manuscripts of the marquess of Ormond (old series, 2 vols, H.M.C., London, 1895–9), i, 148, 158, 179.   44 Henry Jones, A sermon at the funeral of James Margetson, late archbishop of Armagh ... preached at Christ Church, Dublin, August 30, 1672 (London, 1672), pp 27–8, 37–8.

English who having fled to the city for refuge died in the parish of St John and a further thirty-nine were described as 'poor soldiers', presumably quartered on the parish.[45]

It is hardly surprising that the reactions of some of the cathedral community to the rising would be extreme. Hugh Cressy, who had been prebend of St John's before becoming dean of Leighlin in 1638, saw the events of the 1640s as God's judgement for the sacrilege and schism which he thought the Reformation had brought about and he responded by converting to catholicism and became a Benedictine monk at Douai in 1646.[46] A rather different response was that of the sub-dean, John Harding, who invited a series of hard-line clergy to preach violently anti-Irish sermons in the cathedral. Edward Dunsterville, preaching at the funeral of Sir Simon Harcourt in March 1642 described the Irish as ravening wolves. In May 1642 Faithful Teate, temporarily in charge of Trinity College, claimed in a Christ Church sermon that the war in Ireland was 'against our anti-Christian and bloody adversaries' and that revenge had to be sought. Teate was removed from his college position and was forced to flee to England.[47] Harding also arranged for the Christ Church sermon of Stephen Jerome in late 1642. Jerome saw the rebellion as a consequence of Charles I's marriage to the Catholic Henrietta Maria and spoke of kings who endangered their kingdoms by marrying the daughter of Jezebel. For Jerome both English cavaliers and Irish rebels were birds of the same feather. William Bulkeley, archdeacon of Dublin, later tried to depict Jerome as an isolated, unbalanced figure but it is clear that he had powerful sympathisers.[48] Harding's own views are evident from his Dublin publication of a sermon by a Tewkesbury preacher, John Geree, entitled *Ireland's advocate* to which he wrote a preface. This characterised the war as 'a quarrel this day in Ireland between the limbs of Antichrist and the Lord Jesus in his truth and members'. Reprinted at London in 1643, as negotiations for a cessation were beginning in Ireland, it attracted highly unfavourable comment, was judged treasonable and burnt by the common hangman. Harding was arrested, tried by an ecclesiastical court in Dublin, stripped of the chancellorship of Christ Church and his Trinity College, Dublin doctorate of divinity and degraded from the priesthood. He was handed over to the state for trial but was exchanged for royalist prisoners at Chester. Harding eventually became a Baptist preacher in

45 *The registers of St John the Evangelist*, ed. James Mills (Dublin, 1906), pp 56–9, 64. 46 Hugh de Cressy, *Exomologesis* (Paris, 1674), esp. pp 8–12, 16–21.   47 *Cal. S. P. Ire., 1633–47*, p. 383; Edward Dunsterville, *A sermon at the funeral of … Sir Simon Harcourt* (London, 1642), pp 7, 8; Faithful Teate, *A soldier's commission, charge and reward* (London, 1658), pp 14, 16, 23.   48 Bodl., Carte MS 4, ff 40, 44, 50, 54–64; *Lords' jn. Ire.*, i, pp 189, 190, 191, 192, 194.

Cork much to the disgust of the governor of Drogheda, Arthur Aston, who referred to him in 1649 as 'the apostate Harding'.[49]

Most of the Christ Church chapter in the 1640s were more compliant, having been carefully selected. By 1643 the dean, the treasurer and the prebendary of St John's were all that remained of the 1641 chapter. The new prebend of St Michael's, Henry Hall, and the new chancellor, John Creighton, were both domestic chaplains of the marquis of Ormond, the lord lieutenant. Edward Parry, the treasurer was later described by his son as a man much obliged to Ormond 'for many noble favours'.[50] As the Dublin government, financially bankrupt and short of military supplies, moved to negotiate a cessation with the forces of the confederation of Kilkenny, which was eventually concluded in September 1643, it took no chances of opposition from within the establishment.

The cessation of 1643 allowed cathedral life to return to something approaching normal. Chapter meetings became more frequent and attendances improved dramatically. With the exception of two meetings at the end of 1644 all the canons were present from 1643 to 1645. Cathedral records were recovered from the castle and the chapter clerk, Thomas Howell, began to survey the state of the church's property.[51] By 1645 the chapter were confident enough to proceed against the Trinity guild to repair their chapel in the nave of the cathedral.[52] This comforting interest in the minutiae of everyday life could not disguise the fact that the world of the mid-1640s was, for the cathedral, insecure. The chapter were uncomfortably aware that one of the issues in the negotiations for peace then taking place was the ownership of church buildings. Only the two Dublin cathedrals and that of Cork were left in Protestant hands by 1643. Kilkenny, Limerick and Cloyne had been appropriated by Catholics and Kildare, Armagh and Ross were severely damaged in the war.[53] There were ominous signs that Catholics were casting their eyes in the direction of Christ Church. From at least the early 1640s the papacy had appointed a dean of the cathedral, first William Berrey and after his death in 1644 Patrick Cahill, the parish priest of St Michael's.[54] There

49 John Geree, *Ireland's advocate* (London, 1643); Bodl., Carte MS 7, f. 516; Carte MS 10, f. 710; Carte MS 12, f. 513; Carte MS 15, ff 99, 609; T.C.D., MS 6404, f. 136v ; *Calendar of the manuscripts of the marquess of Ormond* (new series, 8 vols, H.M.C., London, 1902–20), i, 92. By 1663 Harding was back near Dublin, Bodl., Carte MS 33, f. 254. His son became a Presbyterian minister at Bandon, Presbyterian Historical Society, Belfast, Diary of John Cooke, 29 Oct. 1701. 50 Bodl., Carte MS 14, ff 285, 387; Parry, *David restored*, sig A2v; C6/1/7/2, f. 56v. 51 C6/1/26/13 no. 5; C6/1/17/10. 52 B.L., Eg. MS, 1765, f. 29v; Dublin City Libraries, Gilbert MS 76, f. 117; C6/1/7/2, f. 62. 53 Graves & Prim, *St Canice's*, pp 40–2; Bodl., Carte MS 155, ff 136v–7; Maurice Lenihan, *Limerick: its history and antiquities* (Dublin, 1886), pp 588–9; T.C.D., MS 812, f. 203; MS 839, f. 43. 54 Nicholas Donnelly (ed.), 'The "Per Obitum" volumes in the Vatican

were rumours that this might be made more than a titular appointment. One story circulating in London in 1641 told of how a mob had barged into a Dublin cathedral and had mass celebrated there.[55] None of these fears was allayed by the correspondence to Dean Margetson from his predecessor Henry Tilson, now bishop of Elphin, about his treatment at the hands of the confederates in the mid-1640s.[56]

If the world after the cessation of 1643 seemed religiously unstable economic life was more unsettled and the problem of financing the Christ Church establishment soon posed itself. While economic activity around Dublin certainly increased after the cessation it did not regain its pre-war level. Some new leases of property were made by the chapter but return on them was small. When the 'crook chamber' in the liberty was leased to a Dublin merchant in 1644 the chapter were obliged to accept a rent two-thirds of that set in 1599.[57] Signs of economic difficulty were everywhere to be found. The organist's salary was reduced in November 1642 and the inability to collect rents during the war meant that by November 1643 the vicars choral were distraining rents from their tenants and vacant vicars choral places left unfilled. By 1644 the sexton added his voice to the complaints pointing out that he had not been paid for two years and when John Brookbank was appointed precentor in 1646 he was unable to sue out his patent 'for want of means'.[58] More frightening was that up to the end of 1645, although less frequently than before, bodies were still being found near the cathedral on the streets of St John's parish and had to be buried at parochial expense.[59]

The clearest evidence of the cathedral's economic difficulties in the early 1640s is provided by the history of the community that lived in the liberty. Of the forty-one individuals who were resident in the liberty in 1631 only two remained at the beginning of 1648 and the number resident in 1648 was almost half of its 1631 level.[60] At least one resident, Simon Esmond, had died before the war began but most population dislocation resulted from war.[61] Up

archivio' in *Archivium Hibernicum*, i (1912), p. 34; Brendan Jennings, 'Ecclesiastical appointments in Ireland, August 1643–December 1649' in *Collectanea Hibernica*, no. 2 (1959), p. 25.   55 Edward and Peter Razzell (ed.), *The English civil war: a contemporary account* (5 vols, London, 1996), ii, 57–8. The story is without foundation; its origin seems to be an event in Derry, Michael Perceval Maxwell, *The outbreak of the Irish rebellion of 1641* (Dublin, 1994), p. 131.   56 Bodl., Carte MS 15, ff 428, 510, 543, 545–6, 578, 652.   57 McEnery & Refaussé, *Deeds*, nos 1450, 1550.   58 C6/1/7/2, ff 54v, 56; Bodl., Carte MS 164, f. 77. For Brookbank's losses in the rising, T.C.D., MS 812, ff 186–7.   59 R.C.B., P328/5/1, pp 243, 252.   60 Gillespie, *Chapter act book*, p. 168; Dublin City Archives, MR/5, p. 9. The throughput of individuals was greater than this suggests since some lived in the liberty between these two dates but appear on neither list, such as William Brigham, T.C.D., MS 810, f. 278.   61 For Esmond, Mills, *Registers of St John the Evangelist*, p. 26.

to one third of the inhabitants of the liberty may have joined the government army.[62] Others found life in the liberty intolerable and moved elsewhere. At least four of those who lived there in the 1630s can be identified with a fair degree of certainty in the registers of other Dublin parishes after 1648. Others within the cathedral felt that life in its precincts was becoming too difficult or dangerous by the end of 1646. John West, who had been appointed in March 1646 to deliver the weekly lecture at Christ Church, left for England in November with his wife, child and baggage.[63] Some resolution of the economic and other problems of the cathedral was urgently needed.

The position of the city of Dublin improved dramatically in the middle of 1647. When the king was captured by parliament at the end of the first civil war in England the Irish lord lieutenant, the marquis of Ormond, was left without clear instructions. In July 1647 he withdrew to England to consult with the king. He had little alternative but to surrender the city to the recently landed parliamentary army under the command of Michael Jones. The parliamentary blockade on the city was lifted and trade restored. Within the liberty of the cathedral there was an influx of new residents listed on the cess lists of 1648. Some of these were already Dublin residents who wished to take advantage of the economic upturn in late 1647. Simon Smallwood lived in the parish of St John in the 1630s and Ridgely Hatfield had moved into the liberty in 1643.[64] Eighteen others were recent arrivals. One, William Benson, was a soldier while another, John Preston, came from Lancashire on seeing the possibility of profit in Dublin.[65] Of the eleven whose occupations can be established, usually because they later became freemen of the city, one described himself as a gentleman, three as merchants, three as tailors and three defined themselves as a cloth-drawer, shoemaker and smith respectively. These were not poor refugees. Christ Church yard contributed the highest cess payment per head for the army in 1648 followed closely by the parish of St Audoen, an average resident of the liberty paying 14s. The new occupants of the liberty were substantial figures who would play a part in any upturn of the cathedral's fortunes.

If the events of mid-1647 augured well for those who lived around the cathedral they were much less auspicious for the cathedral establishment itself. On 19 June the parliamentary commissioners struck at the very rationale for the existence of a cathedral by proposing the abolition of the Book of Common Prayer. The Dublin clergy expected this since in May they had

---

62 This estimate is too high since it is based on a comparison of names on the 1631 list with the army muster rolls in H.M.C., *Ormond MSS*, o.s., so it is uncertain whether the individuals are the same.   63 Bodl., Carte MS 16, f. 672; Carte MS 164, f. 343.   64 Mills, *Registers of St John the Evangelist*, p. 33; T.C.D., MS 810, f. 275.   65 N.L.I., GO MS 87, p. 111. Benson is described as a lieutenant in the cess book.

petitioned the Irish house of lords asking for their protection should this occur. Not surprisingly the clergy reacted negatively but the prohibition became effective on 24 June 1647. In early July the Dublin clergy rather futilely objected claiming that the Protestants of the city were 'much grieved' for the loss of the liturgy.[66] Without the rationale of liturgical worship the cathedral began to disintegrate. No chapter minutes were kept after the meeting of 14 June 1647 although the chapter may have met in some attenuated form since leases made by them survive for 1648 and 1649.[67]

The disintegration of Christ Church as a cathedral can be measured by the departure of its establishment. Between May and June 1647 the evidence of signatures on the petitions to the parliamentary commissioners and attendance lists in the chapter act book show all the chapter, with the exception of John Parker, prebendary of St Michan's who had left in April, as being present in Dublin. By September 1647 John Brookbank, the prebendary of St Michael's, with five others (probably including John Creighton, the chancellor), had fled to England.[68] By the end of 1647 Dean Margetson was in Manchester where he was imprisoned before being exchanged for other prisoners. In June 1650 he was in London, wanted by the parliamentary commissioners because he had 'carried away all the plate, records and evidences of the said church [Christ Church] to the great prejudice and danger of the public'.[69] By November 1649 when the archbishop of Dublin, Lancelot Bulkeley, preached a farewell sermon to his clergy in St Patrick's, Dudley Boswell, the prebendary of St John's, was the only member of the Christ Church chapter present. He was briefly imprisoned for being present when the Book of Common Prayer was used. He died on 27 July 1650.[70] The treasurer, Edward Parry, was also in the city although not at Bulkeley's sermon and two days after Boswell's death he succumbed to the plague ravaging Dublin. Of the chapter which witnessed the prohibition of the Book of Common Prayer in 1647 only one member, the chancellor, John Creighton, would be restored to his position in the 1660s.[71]

As the cathedral organisation slowly disintegrated between 1647 and 1649 contemporaries may not have fully understood the enormity of the changes which were taking place. Some did. When the sexton, William Wood,

---

66 Bodl., Carte MS 20, f. 551; Carte MS 21 ff 165–6, 241v–2, 284–5; Carte MS 65, ff 384–5.   67 C6/1/7/2, f. 72v; McEnery & Refaussé, *Deeds*, nos 1559–68. The chapter at Cork met until November 1646 and then once in August 1649 to elect a new bishop. St Patrick's chapter met till March 1650.   68 Bodl., Carte MS 21, f. 441. Creighton later claimed to have left about this time, C6/1/7/2, f. 99v.   69 Jones, *A sermon*, p. 28, Royal Society of Antiquaries of Ireland, Dublin, Richard Langrishe's notes for an introduction to the Christ Church chapter act books, in vol 2, pt 2.   70 Ware, *Works*, i, 356.   71 For details of Creighton's reinstatement, see p. 256 below.

received a lease of a property in Ship Street from the chapter in April 1649
he quickly sold it on to Nicholas Fitzgerald taking a quick profit possibly
influenced by the formal abolition of deans and chapters by the English parliament on 30 April 1649.[72] Others assumed that the events of 1647-9 were
a temporary difficulty. The chapter itself seems to have begun a building
programme in August 1648, to judge from the evidence of leases, which suggests confidence in the future.[73] Others saw a situation on which they could
capitalise. The Trinity guild, for instance, in 1648 demanded the return of
rights in the Trinity chapel which they claimed the dean and chapter withheld from them and in 1649 appointed John Parry, minister of St Audoen's,
as their chaplain and continued to appoint preachers in 1651 and 1652.[74] Such
victories were pyrrhic ones.

By the end of 1649 Christ Church had ceased to be in any sense a cathedral
church. Its property was seized by the parliamentary commissioners. In future
the income from the Christ Church lands would be brought to the treasury
for the Dublin precinct and used to relieve poor soldiers, widows, orphans
and later to pay the salaries of godly ministers.[75] Those who had earlier served
the cathedral became redundant. The sexton, William Wood, died shortly
afterwards but the chapter clerk, the stipendiaries, lay vicars choral and the
choristers became unemployed. Some, such as the organist Randolph Jewett,
went to England while others took up posts in the city. John Tadpole, one
of the vicars choral, was parish clerk of St John's throughout the 1650s.[76]
For ex-employees of Christ Church the 1650s were difficult years. While the
problem of the cathedral establishment was resolved by its dissolution the
building posed more of a problem. Unlike many Irish cathedrals and some
English ones, such as Carlisle, Christ Church was largely undamaged as a
result of the war. It could not simply be abandoned since it had a symbolic
role as the church of the Irish administration and a centre where civic ritual
was enacted. On a more mundane level it performed important civic functions such as the regulation of urban life by the ringing of its bells. Thus
Christ Church could not be without a verger to ring the 6 a.m and the 9
p.m. bell. After the death of William Wood, John Hatten was appointed to
fulfil this role.[77]

Given these considerations it is hardly surprising that throughout the 1650s
Christ Church continued to be used as a church and in particular the church
of the new Irish administration. A near contemporary life of one Independent
minister who came to Dublin in the 1650s, Samuel Winter, described how

72 McEnery & Refaussé, Deeds, no. 1566.   73 Ibid., nos 1562-5.   74 B.L., Eg. MS 1765,
ff 39v-40, 41v, 42; Dublin City Libraries, Gilbert MS 78, ff 119-20, 124, 126.   75 B.L.,
Eg. MS 1761, ff 18v-19.   76 See pp 266-7.   77 Anc. rec. Dublin, iii, 512.

'in the city of Dublin (where they [the commissioners for Ireland] continued the greatest part of their time) he preached sometimes twice every Lord's day in Christ Church before the commissioners, the lord mayor, the aldermen of that city, many gentlemen and others resorting to his ministry'.[78] In the early 1650s the dominant religious grouping within the administration were Independents. Hence it was those ideas that were most often heard from the pulpit in Christ Church. It could also be used as a venue to confute others. In 1656 Winter used a series of Christ Church sermons, possibly up to seven, preached before Lord Deputy Fleetwood and the parliamentary commissioners to confute what he regarded as the heretical ideas of believer's baptism.[79] On more formal occasions the government resorted to Christ Church to repent or give thanks for God's punishment or blessing. Henry Jones, the former bishop of Clogher, was appointed to preach in Christ Church on 8 August 1656, a day of thanksgiving for the parliamentary victories at Dungan's Hill and Rathmines in 1647 and 1649 respectively. Two months later Samuel Winter preached on 23 October 'being the commemoration of the Lord's signal deliverance by his timely discovery of [the] bloody design' in 1641 and on 5 November Henry Wooten occupied the Christ Church pulpit to give thanks both for the victory of the Commonwealth navy over the Spanish and also for the anniversary of the discovery of the gunpowder plot in 1605.[80]

The adoption of Christ Church by the Irish administration as its church solved the problem of the maintenance of the fabric. During the 1650s most Irish churches were maintained by levies on corporations or by their congregations.[81] Since Christ Church had no parochial responsibilities it had no source of funding. Such money as was required was provided by the commissioners for Ireland. In November 1654 the commissioners general of revenue were instructed to consider how 'the public meeting place at Christ Church Dublin' was to be maintained and further consideration was given to the matter in 1655. Between January 1656 and October 1659 almost £204 was expended on maintenance.[82] While this fell short of the expenditure by the chapter in the early seventeenth century it ensured against disrepair and made it possible for it to be used again at the Restoration.

A more difficult problem for the Irish government was the role which Christ Church should play in the Cromwellian propagation of the gospel. A

---

78 *The life and death of the eminently learned, pious and painful minister of the gospel Dr Samuel Winter* (London, 1671), p. 9.   79 Samuel Winter, *The sum of diverse sermons preached in Dublin* (Dublin, 1656).   80 N.A.I., MS M2817, p. 42.   81 T.C. Barnard, *Cromwellian Ireland* (Oxford, 1975), pp 168–71.   82 N.A.I., MS M2817, pp 11, 18, 13, 109. Waterford, by contrast fell into decay, Graves, 'Ancient fabric', pp 78–82, and St Patrick's had to be extensively repaired by subscription in 1661, Chetham's Library, Manchester, MS A 677, pp 342–3.

congregation needed to be settled there and in August 1651 one was established under the care of John Rogers, one of the first godly ministers to be
settled in Ireland. He commanded a government salary of £200 a year.[83]
Rogers, from the heartland of English puritanism in Essex, attracted a following at Christ Church which was different from anything which the church
had previously seen. Rogers's conception of a church was of 'a fellowship
called out of the world and united to Christ as members to the head all one
with another'. The rules governing this voluntary association were set down
in a church covenant which all members of the congregation were bound to
accept. The covenant drafted for the church which met at Christ Church contained twelve clauses binding the members into 'one body with one mind in
all sweetness of spirit and saint like love to each other'. Members were to
avoid divisions, to watch over each other (reproving each other when necessary) and to contribute spiritually and financially to the well-being of the
church.[84]

Membership of this company of gathered saints was not automatic. Those
who wished to join had to provide evidence of their conversion in the form
of a spiritual autobiography before selection as members. In the case of Christ
Church, Rogers preserved some forty-five autobiographies from his congregation of which twenty were women and twenty-five men. From these spiritual testimonies a profile of his congregation can be constructed.[85] Almost all
were recent arrivals in the city. Two women, Elizabeth Chambers and Mary
Turrant, described their experiences in Ireland in the early stages of the rising
before fleeing to England to return in the late 1640s. The others came between
1647 and 1650 since they described their conversion experiences as being in
England. Nine of the men had come to Dublin as soldiers, including John
Hewson the governor of Dublin, and four of the women were wives of soldiers. One man, Henry Johnson, described himself as a merchant and another,
Ralph Swinfield, had spent time in New England before coming to Dublin.

This was not a local church which anyone might attend. There were, for
instance no native Irish names among the members nor did those who lived
in Christ Church Yard worship there. They had little in common with most
of those who had worshipped in Christ Church in the early 1640s. When the
former chapter clerk, Thomas Howell, met a future member of Rogers's congregation, Humphrey Mills, in 1648 they came to blows over Howell's assertion that the parliamentary force were 'fools and traitors and all who took
their part' were the same.[86] What held Rogers's congregation together was
their conversion experience. Despite Rogers's preservation of the congrega-

---

83 St John Seymour, *The puritans in Ireland* (Oxford, 1921), pp 21–4; B.L., Eg. MS 1762,
f. 6v; John Rogers, *Ohel or Beth Shemesh* (London, 1655), p. 350.   84 Rogers, *Ohel*, pp
352, 459–61.   85 Ibid., pp 386–419.   86 Gillespie, *Thomas Howell*, pp 11–12.

tional testimonies it is difficult to reconstruct those experiences since the surviving texts were edited to make then conform to an ideal model.[87] The
descriptions usually take a standard form: a sense of sin, often awakened by
the preaching of a godly minister, a period of searching and finally a conversion often by spectacular divine intervention such as a blinding light or a
dream. This emphasis on experience rather than doctrine as a touchstone of
regeneration attempted to draw together individuals of different theological
views within one godly assembly. Some, such as John Hewson, were convinced Independents but others in the congregation held to the idea of
believer's baptism. Certainly in 1652 the Baptist meeting in Waterford condemned Rogers for creating a congregation in which some were 'joined in
fellowship with such as so fundamentally differ in judgement and practice,
to wit such as agree not with you about the true state of the visible church
nor the fundamental ordinance thereof [baptism]'.[88] In the early years of the
Cromwellian administration in Ireland such distinctions might be buried but
by 1652 they were becoming sharper. As a result John Rogers's experience
at Christ Church was not a happy one. It was, he later recalled, 'a time of
troubles and afflictions, distractions and disturbances' which originated in
the theological diversity of the church. By March 1652 he had returned to
England with a certificate from the commissioners for Ireland that he had
been 'painful and industrious' in the work of the ministry at Christ Church.[89]

Rogers's departure and the scattering of his followers raised the problem
of how Christ Church would be supplied with preachers. The difficulty was
resolved in December 1652 by establishing a rota of Dublin ministers to
occupy the pulpit as they agreed among themselves. The first five preachers
included the Baptist Thomas Patient and four Independents, among whom
were Samuel Winter and John Murcot.[90] This solution was possible because
of the recent influx of godly ministers into Dublin. As Winter's biographer
noted 'after some other ministers coming forth from England the commissioners used to request one or other of them to preach in the morning reserv-
ing Mr Winter for the afternoon at which time was the greatest auditory'.[91]
By 1655 the four preachers at Christ Church included Winter and Patient
and also Thomas Harrison, chaplain to the newly-appointed commissioner
for Ireland, and later lord deputy, Henry Cromwell. By 1656 Harrison and
Winter had monopolised all the preaching in the church, squeezing out more
radical figures such as Patient.[92]

This shift in the Christ Church preachers was symptomatic of a more

87 Nigel Smith, *Perfection proclaimed* (Oxford, 1989), pp 33–43. 88 Rogers, *Ohel*, p. 302.
89 Ibid., pp 48–9, 54; B.L., Eg. MS 1762, f. 30. 90 B.L., Eg. MS 1762, ff 54v–5. 91
The life and death ... of Samuel Winter, p. 9. 92 Seymour, *Puritans*, pp 33, 34, 213;
N.A.I., MS M2817, pp 29, 91.

fundamental change in religious policy within Ireland. In the late 1650s Henry Cromwell came increasingly to rely on moderate Presbyterians and compliant former Church of Ireland members to govern Ireland to the exclusion of the former radicals.[93] Some former members of Rogers's congregation at Christ Church opposed such a move and Col Hewson vehemently opposed Harrison's appointment in Dublin.[94] Tightening of attitudes is also clear in the treatment of radical sects who appeared at Christ Church. When in 1656 and 1659 Quakers interrupted the preachers they were quickly removed and in one case imprisoned.[95] This conservative shift in attitudes is also apparent from the composition of the Christ Church congregation. From the lists of those who were buried in the church in the late 1650s and a few names of seat holders it seems that none of Rogers's congregation now attended the church and the new congregation were drawn from Dublin's social élite.[96] In other ways too there are signs of social conservatism. In 1655, for example, it was ordered that the seating in the pews of Christ Church was to be allocated by the council, presumably in order to reflect social order.[97] The spiritual equality of experience evident in Rogers's congregation was being replaced by a well-defined social hierarchy.

Those who met in Christ Church in the late 1650s met primarily for the preaching of God's word. The themes of these sermons were probably those of standard godly expositions. One set of sermons on prayer by Thomas Harrison were later published as *Topica sacra* in 1658. This offered practical advice about wrestling with God in prayer and was reprinted as a minor spiritual classic into the nineteenth century. Other sermons had a more political theme. In the 1680s Robert Ware alleged that one of the Christ Church preachers, Enoch Gray, delivered a sermon which claimed that 'hell was paved with king's crowns and bishop's mitres'.[98] Whatever the themes the style of preaching was powerful. One listener to Thomas Harrison's sermon on the death of Oliver Cromwell preached in Christ Church noted he preached from notes 'in a full and fluent manner, extracting tears from the eyes and sighs from the hearts of his hearers' and John Murcot's preaching in the church was 'with the highest evidence and power upon the hearts and spirits of those that heard it'.[99] Moreover this was preaching that was intended

93 T.C. Barnard, 'Planters and policies in Cromwellian Ireland' in *Past and Present*, no. 61 (1973), pp 31–69. **94** B.L., Lansd. MS 821, f. 222. **95** Abraham Fuller and Thomas Holms, *A compendious view of some extraordinary sufferings of the people called Quakers* (Dublin, 1731), pp 106–7; Richard Greaves, *God's other children* (Stanford, 1997), p. 65. **96** N.A.I., MS M2817, p. 28; Finlayson, *Inscriptions*, pp 74–6. **97** N.A.I., M2817, p. 26. **98** Robert Ware, *The hunting of the Romish fox* (Dublin, 1683), p 232; Seymour, *Puritans*, p. 213; N.A.I., MS M2817, p. 60. **99** Thomas Harrison, *Threni Hybernici* (London, 1659), sig A3v; John Murcot, *Saving faith and pride of life inconsistent* (London, 1652), sig A3.

to be taken seriously. In 1653 and again in 1655 the mayor of Dublin was ordered to ensure that 'vain and idle people' would not come to Christ Church and wander around nave or aisles to distract either ministers or people during prayer or the sermon.[100] When the hearers left the church they were meant to take the message with them. Thomas Harrison urged his hearers in Christ Church to meditate on what they had heard advising 'every one of you that would do any good on it to pick out something from every sermon they hear to be repeated upon their knees in secret'.[101]

Such preaching had to be supplemented by other ways of advancing the religious knowledge of the Christ Church congregation. In July 1655 the Irish council appointed a weekly lecture to be held in the church on Monday morning at ten o'clock which was to be given by the Dublin ministers in rotation.[102] In April 1656 the importance of catechising was recognised when the Independent Samuel Mather, of the New England puritan family, was appointed to catechise children at Christ Church on Sunday afternoons. He was succeeded by Nathaniel Brewster, the minister of St Audoen's.[103] All this imposed heavy demands on the Dublin clergy and in 1655 readers were introduced to read the psalm or to pray at a salary of £30 a year. Many of these were preachers on trial and many soon moved off to their own churches. The first appointee, Thomas Bridsall, became preacher at Newcastle, County Dublin, in 1657 and was succeeded at Christ Church by Josiah Smith who in turn became the minister of the congregation at Ballymote in County Sligo in 1659. His Christ Church place was taken by John Goldbourne, a former Church of Ireland minister and fellow of Trinity College, Dublin who was schoolmaster at St Patrick's school through the 1650s.[104]

The task of propagating God's word, whether read or preached, which these men undertook, was seen as a converting ordinance intended to awaken a sense of sin and repentance. As such it was open to all. The communion service, on the other hand, was for those already admitted to the fellowship of the church and who were regarded as worthy communicants. Infrequent as the service was it provided a powerful bonding force for worshippers. In the 1680s a rather hostile witness, Robert Ware, described a communion service conducted by Samuel Winter at Christ Church. The communion rails surrounding the altar of the 1630s had been taken down and the bread and wine were administered to those present sitting 'for which purposes several tables (upon those days) were placed together in length from the choir up to altar in Christ Church Dublin. This his fraternity were also, for further dis-

100 N.A.I., MS M2817, pp 23, 84.   101 Thomas Harrison, *Topica sacra* (London, 1658), p. 172.   102 N.A.I., MS M2817, p. 25.   103 Ibid., pp 41, 42.   104 Seymour, *Puritans*, pp 207, 221, 121, 215; N.A.I., MS M2817, pp 28, 61, 65, 127; Barnard, *Cromwellian Ireland*, p. 195.   105 Ware, *Hunting of the Romish fox*, p. 228; for the communion rails

tinction's sake, to call one another brother or sister'.[105] The normal social distinctions observed in the allocation of seats for preaching were dissolved and a new set of bonds, those of the spiritual equality of the godly community, were created around the sacrament. Thus in the 1650s word and sacrament held together the community based on Christ Church but in a rather different way from that which the reformers of the 1630s envisaged.

Following the death of Oliver Cromwell in September 1658 the Cromwellian experiment in government and religion came under increasing strain. In May 1659 the 'Rump' of the Long Parliament had reassembled in England and Oliver's son Richard resigned from the protectorate. Henry Cromwell was recalled from Ireland and with him went his chaplain Thomas Harrison. This necessitated a rearrangement of the preaching scheme in Christ Church in September 1659.[106] The old régime was given a final push in December 1659 in a conservative military coup which seized Dublin castle. New commissioners were appointed for Ireland in January 1660 and a convention was summoned for February to decide the future of the country. From the Christ Church perspective the most pressing question was the form of ecclesiastical settlement that would emerge. Resentment towards the religious radicals in Dublin was already evident. In February 1660 one of the assistant preachers at Christ Church, Enoch Gray, was prevented from preaching and threatened by porters and watermen with being stoned or thrown into the river.[107] Earlier in December 1659 the congregation of the church ordered a red pulpit cushion with crimson silk lining and a gold fringe, suggesting a move from godly austerity.[108] The possibility of some form of religious toleration was suggested by the invitation to the Presbyterian Samuel Cox to preach in Christ Church before the convention in March 1660.[109] In reality more powerful pressures were at work. Probably in late May Charles Coote, one of the commissioners for the government of Ireland, wrote

> I have with great difficulty prevailed upon Mr Bury [one of the Presbyterian inclined commissioners] for the adding of four ministers at Christ Church by means whereof I do undertake the common prayer book will be sufficiently used there but what the consequences will be I know not, but I am sure if it had not been done gradually by such

being replaced in 1663, C6/1/26/3, no. 30. Similarly John Murcot in his Christ Church sermon referred to his congregation as 'brethren', Murcot, *Saving faith*. **106** N.A.I., MS M2817, p. 60. **107** *A sober vindication of Lt General Ludlow* (London, 1660), pp 2–3. **108** C6/1/26/6, no. 15. **109** Sem Cox, *Two sermons preached at Christ Church … before the honourable general convention* (Dublin, 1660). **110** Bodl., Carte MS 31, f. 3.

way as this it would have had great disturbances.[110]
In the event Coote need have had no fears for the reception of the prayer
book since the drive for the revival of episcopacy proved unstoppable. When
Henry Jones was invited to preach in Christ Church on 24 May to celebrate
the proclamation of Charles II in Dublin ten days earlier he was styled bishop
of Clogher.[111]

The process of returning Christ Church to its cathedral status was swift.
Robert Mossom was appointed the new dean of the cathedral (James
Margetson now being archbishop of Dublin) on 25 September 1660 and most
of the remainder of the chapter were appointed by February 1661.[112] The
new chapter had already held its first meeting on 2 November 1660. To judge
from the proctor's accounts they inherited a building that had been little
damaged during the interregnum. The theological position of the congregations of the 1650s had obliged them to remove the altar rails and the font.
These were restored and a new organ installed.[113] There was also some
remodelling of the seating in late 1660. More pressing was the need to recover
the documents and the ornaments of the church which had been scattered
in the 1650s. Some documents, such as the chapter act book, seem to have
been kept by the chapter clerk, Thomas Howell, who had been in Dublin
throughout the 1650s. The whereabouts of others were known to Margetson.[114] John Platt, the verger, was ordered to receive the ornaments of the
church that had been preserved in lay hands during the 1650s. Mrs Hatten,
the wife of Platt's predecessor as verger, returned two pewter flagons, various candlesticks and the 'standing eagle' lectern which she had and Mr
Williams restored various cushions together with chairs and footstools.[115]
Finally in December the floor of the chapter room was broken in an attempt
to find the chapter seal which had been hidden there in the late 1640s but
either it was not found or was too damaged to use and a new seal based on
the older design was engraved.

By 23 April 1661, the day appointed for Charles II's coronation in
London, Christ Church cathedral was a working entity again. According to
the *Mercurius Publicus* of 2 May 1661 the day was celebrated in Dublin by a
state procession of the lords justice from Dublin castle with 'all sorts of music
played before them' until 'they passed to Christ Church where after divine
service and anthem the lord primate made a most excellent sermon'. On their

---

111 Henry Jones, *A sermon preached at Christ Church before the general convention of Ireland,
May 24 1660* (London, 1660). The process has been traced in J.I. McGuire, 'The Dublin
convention, the Protestant community and the emergence of an ecclesiastical settlement
in 1660' in Art Cosgrove and J.I. McGuire (ed.), *Parliament and community* (Belfast, 1993),
pp 121–47. 112 Bodl., Carte MS 41, f. 76. 113 C6/1/26/3, no. 30. 114 C6/1/26/6,
no. 16. 115 Ibid., no. 5; C6/1/7/2, ff 78v, 84v, 90, 94v.

return from the church 'the conduit did run plentifully with wine and the ordnance several times discharged in very good order'.[116] A month later in a more sober mood John Parker, the former prebendary of St Michan's and now bishop of Elphin, mounted the pulpit of Christ Church to commemorate the first anniversary of the Restoration in a sermon. He concluded

> The children that are yet unborn and the generations which are yet to come shall bless God for this day, the day which was restoration of our king, of our church, of our religion, of our laws, of our liberties, of all that we call venerable, good, honourable or sacred.[117]

For the listening chapter of the newly restored cathedral it might have seemed that the old order had indeed returned but experience was to show that the developments of the later seventeenth century were about innovation rather than a return to a golden age.

116 *Mercurius Publicus*, no. 17, 2 May 1661; the same story appears in *The kingdom's intelligencer*, no. 18, 6 May 1661. Both are transcribed in B.L., Add. MS 6308, f. 30. For another account, *Hastings MSS*, ii, 363.   117 John Parker, *A sermon preached at Christ Church before both houses of parliament, May 29 1661* (Dublin, 1661), p. 48.

XI

The 1562 collapse of the nave and its aftermath

Roger Stalley

Just over twenty years after the Augustinian priory had been dissolved, the end of the middle ages at Christ Church was marked in physical terms by a cataclysmic event. On 3 April 1562 the precinct was shaken by a noise that must have sounded like an explosion or a rumble of thunder. It came from the cathedral itself, where the high vaults of the nave had come crashing to the ground, a catastrophe still evident in the fabric today. In a classic illustration of ribbed vault mechanics, the thrust of the thirteenth-century vaults forced apart the upper walls of the nave, in the case of the north elevation pushing it some two feet out of vertical alignment.[1] (Plates 2, 14) While the north elevation survived intact, the consequences were far more devastating on the opposite side, for here the falling vaults demolished the clerestory and much of the arcade below. The tomb of Strongbow was a victim of the disaster, the original monument being smashed by the falling masonry. The great collapse is recorded in a contemporary inscription, part of which remains in the south aisle. The words are brief but telling: 'THIS WAL FEL DOWN IN AN 1562 THE BILDING OF THIS WAL WAS IN AN 1562'.[2] The collapse left almost half the cathedral in ruins. When the dust eventually settled – and there must have been a great deal of dust – it would have been immediately obvious to the dean and chapter that the nave, piled high with débris, would not be used again for many years. Sections of the slated roof, which lay above the stone vault, had also fallen, leaving the body of the church open to the

---

1 It must be noted that there is no absolute proof that stone vaults were erected over the thirteenth-century nave, though the presence of stone springers shows that they were envisaged. For the purposes of this study it is assumed that a stone vault was erected and that this is what fell in 1562.   2 The inscription was originally longer. It starts with the words: THE RIGHT HONORABL THE LO OF SUSSEX LEUTNT … but the full text is now lost. Further fragments, which mention the name of Dean Lockwood, have recently (1999) been recovered among the loose masonry in the crypt (Butler, *Christ Church*, p. 8).

elements.[3] The story of Christ Church over the next three hundred years is a tale of continual repairs, partial restorations, regular calamities and almost permanent anxiety about the possibility of further disasters.

The cause of the 1562 collapse has been attributed to the lack of secure foundations, a view popularised by Sir Thomas Drew in the late nineteenth century: 'The church all stands over a peat bog', he wrote. 'After heavy rains the bog slipped on the sloping hill-side. The groined roof fell in, thrusting out the north side of the triforium 2 ft, and ruining the south side'.[4] Drew's interpretation is straightforward but not very plausible. In his role as cathedral architect, he may have encountered a dark peaty subsoil within the precincts of the cathedral, material which would now be recognised as the residue of habitation levels rather than bog. There is in fact no evidence that Christ Church was built on a bog, or that the original foundations were inadequate. Archaeological soundings in the crypt in April 1999 demonstrated that early habitation levels, if they existed, were cleared away by the medieval builders, who excavated down to boulder clay. The walls were then inserted into foundation trenches.[5] Moreover there is no trace of the type of settlement within the crypt which might have led to the destabilisation of the walls above. In fact a glance at the remaining north elevation of the nave shows that the wall began to bend quite sharply above the level of the main piers. (Plate 2, 14) The problems clearly lay higher up the building.

Several of those who witnessed the reconstruction of the cathedral in the 1870s under the direction of George Edmund Street were appalled by the poor quality of the thirteenth-century masonry. Thus McVittie recounted that 'the northern wall was built of rubble masonry of a very indifferent kind, being in many parts quite hollow'.[6] Even the main piers, which appeared to be constructed of freestone, were built with a rubble core. One spectator claimed that when these piers were dismantled 'the hearting of rubbish gushed out as sand'.[7] Christ Church was essentially a rubble building, where the walls were vulnerable to mortar decay, a factor which almost certainly contributed to the collapse.[8] The building was not as solid as it looked.

---

3 It is not possible to assess the full extent of the disaster. Parts of the south aisle, where the Trinity chapel was situated, were still partially intact in 1564, and Street gives the impression that the outer wall of the aisle survived until 1871, Street & Seymour, p. 68. It is difficult to accept McVittie's assertion that the collapse broke the floor, allowing masonry to plunge through the groin vaults of the crypt (McVittie, *Restoration*, p. 6).   4 Drew, 'Christchurch'. Similar views were expressed by T. Bell, *Origins. An essay on the origins and progress of Gothic architecture with reference to the ancient history and present state of the remains of such architecture in Ireland* (Dublin, 1829), pp 146–7 and by Butler, *Christ Church*, p. 29.   5 Linzi Simpson, 'Archaeological assessment in the crypts of Christchurch cathedral, Dublin' (22 April 1999), p. 8.   6 McVittie, *Restoration*, pp 59–60.   7 Street & Seymour, p. 112.   8 Problems with mortar are discussed briefly by Robert Mark,

Photographs taken before the 1871–8 restoration suggest that the lean of the piers on the north side was more acute than is the case today. (Plate 27) The two western piers are known to have had a double deflection, leaning both to the north and to the west.[9] The buttressing undertaken in the eighteenth century makes it clear, that, even after the collapse of 1562, the north wall continued to rotate outwards. (Plates 21a, 25a) How much of this was the result of bad design? The upper walls of the cathedral were required to withstand the lateral forces of a stone ribbed vault, without any additional support from flying buttresses. In England, where the use of flying buttresses was viewed with some suspicion, this was a standard way of designing a great church. In some cases, as at Salisbury and Wells, 'flying' buttresses were hidden within the roofs of the aisles, an expedient not adopted at Christ Church.[10] Moreover, although the upper walls of the cathedral are almost five feet thick, the solidity of the masonry was compromised by the insertion of passages at both triforium and clerestory level. (Plate 13) The clerestory passage was a common feature of major English buildings, so this in itself should not have caused problems, especially as Christ Church was a low building by English standards.[11] But combined with rubble masonry and the gradual decay of mortar, the structural limitations of the design may have become significant. Even so, it is difficult to believe that the collapse on 3 April 1562 happened without warning. There must have been some sign of the spreading of the vault and the likelihood of impending collapse; it seems that the newly constituted chapter failed to act, or at least failed to act with sufficient alacrity.

The disaster at Christ Church was far from unique, for the history of medieval architecture is studded with records of similar calamities: one occurred in 1186 at Lincoln, when the fall of the vaults effectively cut the cathedral in two – 'scissa est' to use the words of a contemporary chronicler.[12] Far better known is the collapse of the high vaults in the choir of the French cathedral at Beauvais in 1284, the cause of which has been the subject of much analysis.[13] More relevant to Christ Church is the collapse which took place at St Patrick's cathedral in 1544, when the vaults at the west end of

---

Experiments in Gothic structure (Cambridge, Mass., 1982), pp 18–19. The nature and behaviour of the mortars used at Christ Church deserve more investigation.   **9** McVittie, *Restoration*, p. 49.   **10** Bracing arches of this type were inserted under the aisle roof by Street.   **11** The height to the top of the vaults is approximately 48 feet 6 inches, whereas Salisbury and Wells attain heights of over 70 feet.   **12** Otto Lehmann-Brockhaus, *Lateinische Schriftquellen zur Kunst in England, Wales, Schottland vom Jahre 901 bis zum Jahre 1307* (Munich, 1956), ii, 25.   **13** Mark, *Experiments in Gothic structure*, pp 58–77; Stephen Murray, *Beauvais cathedral, architecture of transcendence* (Princeton, 1989), ch. 6. For early vault collapses see Roger Stalley, *Early medieval architecture* (Oxford, 1999), ch 6.

the nave disintegrated. Although funerary monuments were destroyed, this disaster was not as severe as that at Christ Church, the main walls of the building escaping without serious damage.[14]

The most immediate task confronting the authorities at Christ Church in April 1562 was to seal off those parts of the cathedral that were still useable. A temporary screen or window was quickly erected under the eastern crossing arch, allowing the quire to remain in use while repairs were undertaken in the nave. Nonetheless the conduct of services, particularly on feast days, was badly affected, and government officials transferred their allegiance to St Patrick's. These included the lord deputy, who attended St Patrick's on Sundays and feast days 'until the south wall of the nave of Christ Church was rebuilt and a new roof made'.[15] With the quire enclosed, the next task must have been to clear away as much of the débris as possible. Some roof timbers were sold to local merchants, but according to Street, ' a great portion of the rubbish was left where it lay', being levelled, and then 'paved over', an expedient which presumably saved both time and labour.[16] On 25 May, less than two months after the collapse, masons began to repair the church, the principal task being to reconstruct the south elevation of the nave. This was a major operation, carried out with remarkable speed. The stonework was completed in a little over two years and by the autumn of 1564 preparations were being made for the construction of a new roof.

The restored south elevation was not a distinguished piece of architecture. (Plates 3, 26) No attempt was made to reinstate the thirteenth-century arcade, and the three eastern bays were replaced by a solid wall, entirely separating the nave from the aisle.[17] Two arches were constructed in bays four and five, but these were considerably lower than their thirteenth-century predecessors. The arches themselves were furnished with simple chamfered mouldings and they rested on an octagonal pier and octagonal responds. The latter were furnished with an exaggerated moulding half way up, echoing, in a crude way, the shaft rings on the medieval piers opposite. The sixth and final bay was enclosed by solid masonry. In later years the blank walls were used to display a variety of tombs and monuments. The reconstructed elevation was divided by string courses into three horizontal sections, the proportions of which bore no relationship to the medieval work. At triforium level a series of nine pointed arches, devoid of ornament, opened into what seems to have been a mid-wall passage and the clerestory above was designed

14 W.M. Mason states that 'the great stone arch which covered the west aisle fell in and destroyed many monuments', Mason, St Patrick's, p. 8.   15 Ibid., p. 165.   16 Street & Seymour, p.125.   17 This wall was built over the arches of the crypt, and it was probably at this time that the openings in the crypt between the main nave and the south aisle were first blocked off.

in an equally curious manner, with a variety of different-sized windows, spaced at irregular intervals. In front of the windows was a passageway, emulating that found in the thirteenth-century building; near the east end was a broad double window, the rear arch of which rested on a free-standing octagonal pier.[18] The sixteenth-century masons made no attempt to reinstate the ancient dressed stonework, which was exploited merely as a useful source of rubble. Not all the thirteenth-century work, however, was lost in the collapse. The eastern respond, with parts of the triforium and clerestory, survived, along with sections of the first two piers. All were encased in sixteenth-century masonry. Street was able to salvage some stones from the eastern arch, which he re-used in his restoration.[19] The west facade of the cathedral, along with the four-light window with switch-line tracery, also dates from after the 1562 collapse. (Plate 25a) As for the former south aisle, this was converted into a semi-enclosed space, which continued in use as the Trinity chapel until 1699, in which year it was converted into a library and chapter room.[20]

The impoverished character of the reconstruction underlines the urgency of the situation that confronted the chapter in 1562. Speed rather than quality was uppermost in the minds of the clergy. The later years of the sixteenth century are not associated with enterprising church building in either Britain or Ireland, and the work at Christ Church reflects the rather limited ambi-

---

18 One of the clerestory windows was composed of twin lancets on the outer face and these were set within a rectangular frame, clearly illustrated in the *Dublin Penny Journal* of 1835. This sixteenth-century technique was employed at Lislaughtin friary (Kerry) and it also occurs in Scotland at Biggar (Clydesdale) (Roger Stalley, 'Ireland and Scotland in the later middle ages', in J. Higgitt (ed.), *Medieval art and architecture in the diocese of St Andrew's: the British Archaeological Association transactions for the year 1986* (London, 1994), p. 111, pl. XIX).   19 Street & Seymour, p. 121. The pre-1871 plan in the R.C.B. shows the two thirteenth-century piers outlined within the southern wall of the nave, as if they still existed embedded in the masonry. The illustration in the *Dublin Penny Journal* of 1835 depicts the thirteenth-century vault respond and vault springer in the south-east angle of the nave. The latter are also marked on the elevation by Butler, *Measured drawings*. Seymour reports that in 1868 Street removed some of the plaster on the sixteenth-century wall to establish how much of the thirteenth-century arcade survived, but he discovered that only the eastern arch remained, 'and that in a very shattered and damaged condition', Seymour, *Christ Church*, p. 42.   20 Shown on the map of Thomas Reading, 1761. The history of the south aisle is difficult to disentangle. Sections of it survived until 1564, when arches in the vicinity of the Trinity chapel were dismantled, Gillespie, *Proctor's accounts*, pp 41–3. It appears that it was repaired or reconstructed after the main south (clerestory) wall of the nave. Butler marks a series of two-light windows on his plan (Butler, *Measured drawings*), whereas the *Dublin Penny Journal* for 1835 clearly shows a large window with elaborate switch-line tracery. For the conversion to a chapter room see C6/1/7/3, f. 108.

tions of the period. In Dublin there may have been added reasons for working fast. Although the crossing tower had survived the fall of the vaults, there
were fears that it too might soon disintegrate. There were times in the 1560s
when the proctor, the official in charge of the fabric, found himself fighting
to save the building on several fronts.

The immense difficulties which faced the cathedral are brought sharply
into focus in the account book of Sir Peter Lewis, who served as proctor for
the year beginning in November 1564. This is one of the most informative
documents in the whole of Irish architectural history, a remarkably detailed
list of expenditure, down to the last pickaxe and wheelbarrow. As well as
financial details, there are descriptions of specific operations, as for example
the strengthening of a pier in the crypt, or the manner in which stone was
extracted from local quarries. During his year of office Lewis was responsible for works in almost every part of the cathedral.

One of the principal tasks was the construction of a new roof over the
nave. Any thought of reinstating a stone vault was obviously out of the question, and the main need was to erect a timber roof with its outer covering of
slates. In October masons were at work on the upper walls and a great crane
was set up on the north side in preparation for lifting heavy timbers. By early
November scaffolds were being erected, with hurdles of wickerwork laid out
between timber poles and spars. By 17 November the building was ready to
receive six roof couples (i.e. six main rafters), which were lifted into position under the direction of John Brenaghe, the chief carpenter, over the next
two days. Following a break for winter, work resumed in earnest in February,
continuing until 13 April 1565. During this period the main frame of the
roof was completed, and the accounts give detailed specifications of some of
the timber components, like the six 'schrudes', ten inches square and twenty
two feet long, which were sold at a discount to Christ Church by a local merchant. Timber from the old roof was also re-used. Tady, the 'helier' or slater,
had begun preparing laths for the roof in late December, and there are many
payments to him for 'hewing', sorting and pinning slates. From January the
slaters were absent for about five months, but on 10 May Tady and his men
were back, laying laths on the roof itself. There were occasional problems,
as in late May, when eight great 'spikes' were needed by John Brenaghe to
nail some spars or rafters that had warped. Work seems to have progressed
from east to west, with the process of lath-laying reaching the west end by
19 June. Meanwhile slates were lifted to the upper reaches of the cathedral,
some of them being stored temporarily above the vault of the south transept.[21]

---

21 Gillespie, *Proctor's accounts*, p. 94 where the reference is to the 'south vault' . While
this might refer to the vault over the south aisle, it is difficult to believe that this could
have survived the collapse of the south (clerestory) wall in 1562.

Welsh slates were employed and on 2 June a certain Patrick Terell of Clontarf was paid to go to Beaumaris 'to bryng a lode of sklats for Chrystis churche'. Most slates, however, were purchased from local merchants like Nicholas Fitzsimons, who appears to have operated as a builders' supplier. Throughout the accounts there are many payments for the purchase of roofing materials, such as laths from Wexford, slates and slate pins, the latter bought in vast quantities at a cost of 7d. per thousand. In October the installation of gutters and battlements marked the completion of the roof, which had taken just under a year to build. The last entry in the account book, on 22 October, gives a flavour of these activities: 'Workyng apone the tabllment stonys for the gutters of the southe syde of the churche, the battalling a longe with gutters and rydders all a longe neyer hande to the stepulle. iiij massons, j boy'.[22]

An ancient wooden frame still survives above the nineteenth-century vault of the nave, and there is every likelihood that this corresponds to the roof built in 1564–5 by John Brenaghe and his assistants.[23] It consists of a series of trusses, two per bay, which are reinforced by an additional tie and a collar. Arched braces link the central tie beam to the lower edges of the rafters. The collar and tie have sockets at their midpoint, implying that the roof was designed to take some form of king post. The one concession to architectural embellishment in what is otherwise a fairly rudimentary piece of carpentry were wall posts terminating in decorated corbels, the latter just visible in the woodcut in the *Dublin Penny Journal* of 1835. (Plate 3) The most reliable impression of the roof as it existed before the Street restoration is conveyed by a nineteenth-century watercolour in St Patrick's deanery, even though it shows only a small section of the structure.

Over the course of four centuries the roof has been modified by a number of additions and reinforcements. Early additions included the diagonal braces that now link the central tie and the collar.[24] More substantial changes occurred during the Street restoration. At this stage the king post was reinforced by a pair of vertical planks, bolted either side of the existing timbers, and the lowest tie beam was removed since it interupted the line of the proposed new vaults. Once the old tie was cut out, a replacement was inserted a short distance above. During this operation the wall posts, complete with their decorated terminals, were sawn off; the latter now hang from the frame of the roof as crude, abbreviated stumps. The nineteenth-century additions are fairly easy to detect, since they are held in place by iron bolts, a contrast

---

22 Gillespie, *Proctor's accounts*, p. 117.   23 There appears to be no accurate survey of this roof. Dendrochronological investigation would confirm whether or not it belongs to the late sixteenth century.   24 The roof was examined on 5 July 1999 and the author is glad to acknowledge the help he received on this occasion from Rachel Moss and Stuart Kinsella.

to the wooden dowels used before. As one of the oldest surviving examples in the country, the roof of the Christ Church nave deserves to be better known.

Throughout the reconstruction of the cathedral in the 1560s, the body of the nave was used as a builders' yard. Carts loaded with mortar and other materials were dragged into the church, the masons prepared stone there and this was where Tady the 'helier' cut and sorted his slates. The space was of course open to the sky, but some protection from the elements was provided in the north aisle, where the roof (though not the vault) survived the collapse.

As work proceeded on the nave roof, Lewis became increasingly troubled by the condition of the crossing tower. He began by reinforcing the eastern crossing arch, work carried out under the direction of Henris, the chief mason. A timber support was erected within the arch, a space described in the accounts as 'the great wyndo in the rode loff'.[25] The top of the rood screen was used as a base for this operation and wooden stairs were made to facilitate access to the scaffolds, allowing labourers to carry up stone and mortar to the masons. When the arch was repaired, the timber supports were left in place, perhaps to serve as additional reinforcement to the tower. The timbers were covered by wooden boards, including some painted with scenes from the Passion, which had to be cut and nailed in place. The quire was thus separated from the rest of the church by a wall of timber, filling the space above the rood screen.

By early December, Lewis had turned his attention to the arch leading into the north quire aisle. The masonry in this area was badly distorted, and, as Lewis himself explained, the 'wall was rent very sore and I was in great dout of hit'.[26] He came to an agreement with Henris the mason to block up the arch, leaving a smaller opening as a doorway. (Plate 9b) The intention was obviously to provide a solid wedge or buttress running north from the north-east crossing pier, which implies that this pier was rotating outwards.[27]

At the start of the new year preparations were being made for the reconstruction of the north-east pier itself, along with the north crossing arch. Thus on 4 January three masons were 'working apone whytt stonys for the neyw worke for the coynes to seat in the arche'.[28] The process of quarrying

---

25 Gillespie, *Proctor's accounts*, p. 37.   26 Ibid., p. 41. Exactly where the breach lay is not made clear.   27 Gillespie, *Proctor's accounts*, pp 41, 43. In 1562 the merchant Thomas Fitzsimon had given the cathedral a consignment of white Flanders stone for the repairs of the pillars (McEnery & Refaussé, *Deeds*, no. 1284). Some of this material was evidently used in the blocking of the north quire aisle. On 13 December there were payments for timber boards used for the centering of the door within the blocking wall.   28 Gillespie, *Proctor's accounts*, p. 48.

and cutting stone for the pier and arch took several months and on 25 April Lewis himself went to the quarry at Milltown to choose stone 'for owre neywe pyller'. By this time it was apparent that reconstruction of the north-east pier alone was not going to be sufficient, and that the corresponding pier underneath in the crypt was in need of reinforcement. Thus began one of the most dramatic episodes in the architectural annals of the cathedral.

On 14 May a boat-load of stone from Clontarf was shifted into a section of the crypt leased out to Patrick Gough. For the next week this area was the scene of intense activity. Six masons assisted by labourers worked by candlelight, the candles themselves costing 12*d.* per day. Having excavated the area around the pier, the space was filled with a carefully laid mixture of oak timbers and well-cut stone – 'great brod blacke stonys of Clontarffe and of Doddyr Wattyr'.[29] Over the next few days the pier was gradually built up, the masons using extensive quantities of lime, as noted in the accounts.[30] It is still possible to see the extra buttresses inserted by Lewis and his team, one of the few pieces of Irish architecture that can be dated, not just to a year, but to an exact week.

Once work in the crypt was complete, operations switched to the north-east crossing pier. Lewis solemnly notes that six masons began 'apone the neywe work, the base of the pyller in the northe syed, und[er] the stepulle, to stay hit that was sore rassyd'.[31] The intention was to buttress the existing piers and to construct a new supporting arch underneath the old one, a difficult task which took almost six months. During June and July large quantities of masonry were gathered from the quarries, with the actual task of laying the stones beginning on 30 July. During August and September seven masons were employed, four of them laying and three of them dressing stone. 'Great long stones', one of which was eight feet in length, were employed to bind the new work with the old.[32] By the middle of August work had reached the base of the arch and two days were spent on the preparation of wooden centering. It took a further four days to erect the inner order, the keystone being fixed on 23 August. On this day the masons worked until nine o'clock in the evening, not daring to leave until they had inserted their 'clossnge stone' (i.e. keystone). For this they were rewarded by Lewis with five pence worth of good ale.[33] Work subsequently followed on the outer order, described in the accounts as the 'upper arch' or the 'wings',[34] but progress was hampered by a lack of suitable stone, which forced the masons back to the quarries. Unfortunately, all trace of the arch, the building of which is described so vividly in the account book, was obliterated in subsequent reconstructions of the tower.[35]

---

29 Ibid., p. 75. During the operation Lewis describes how he found two skulls ('ii dede skolles of menys heds') between two pillars of the crypt.   30 Ibid., p. 77.   31 Ibid., p. 78.   32 Ibid., pp 96, 101.   33 Ibid., p. 103.   34 Ibid., p. 104.   35 It is unlikely that the

During his year as proctor, Lewis also supervised repairs to the quire. The rafters immediately adjacent to the tower were replaced in October, and the roof above was re-slated immediately afterwards. Tady was engaged for seven weeks on this task, working by candlelight well into the evening.[36] The following September the roof of the quire was 'sore shaken with storms' and Tady spent a further ten days on repairs.[37]

The various tasks undertaken in 1564–5 were all supervised by the proctor himself, and one gets the impression of someone who took an active part in directing operations, both at the cathedral and in the quarries. Sir Peter Lewis was not however a professional builder. He was a cleric who came to Ireland probably as a chaplain to Sir Anthony St Leger in the 1530s, becoming precentor at the cathedral in 1561. He had already been involved in works at the castles of Carlingford and Greencastle, so he was reasonably experienced when he took on the office of proctor at Christ Church.[38] The accounts give the impression of an energetic administrator, well-informed on building matters, a man capable of getting things done efficiently. Most of the tasks accomplished during the year were basic structural operations and there is no suggestion that the proctor himself had any special skills in architectural design.

Lewis supervised a substantial workforce. In August 1565, for example, nineteen men were at work, a team which included seven masons and four slaters. During the course of the year the number of masons employed at the cathedral rose from five to seven, the chief mason being Henris, who was paid at a higher rate, receiving 10d. per day. Henris fell sick on 27 March 1565 and he was subsequently absent from work for a month. The other masons were paid at variable rates, Ferdoghe for example receiving 8d., and Brene 7d. None was apparently a specialist, each man taking his turn in the quarries, as well as dressing and laying stone. The masons, who had their own workshop at the cathedral, known as the 'manger',[39] could not have worked without the services of a smith, and a certain Thomas Frenchman was paid on a regular basis 'steeling' crowbars, picks, punches and chisels. The hardness of the local stone was frustrating and Lewis complained of the adverse effects it was having on the masons' tools, 'the stone beying so hard that hit ettys the stelle wery sore'.[40]

work of Lewis survived the reconstruction of the tower in the early seventeenth century. Illustrations of the crossing before 1871 show simple chamfered piers supporting a single broad arch, also chamfered: this does not accord with the double order described in the account roll.   36 Gillespie, *Proctor's accounts*, pp 28–9.   37 Ibid., p. 108. The storm also damaged the roof of the Lady chapel.   38 Ibid., pp 11–13.   39 The workshop was probably situated in the nave. It was cleaned out by the carpenters on 26 February 1564, Gillespie, *Proctor's accounts*, p. 58.   40 Ibid., p. 102. When the masons were working in the quarry at Clontarf, a local smith, described as 'Smythe of Clontarff', was employed instead of Thomas.

The carpenters at Christ Church were led by John Brenaghe, who was assisted by Thomas Leynam and John Keting. As well as constructing the roof frames, they erected scaffolds and hoists, and carried out sundry repairs to such equipment as wheelbarrows and cranes. The slating of the roof was the responsibility of Tady, the 'helier' or slater, who was aided by two or three assistants. The various groups of skilled workmen were supported by a band of labourers, each paid 7d. per day. They were hired when needed, their numbers fluctuating between six and twelve. To them fell the task of loading masonry at the quarries, shifting material into the cathedral, and carrying stones, slates and mortar up the scaffold. Most of the workers, both skilled and unskilled, were paid by the day, with food being provided as an extra. In fact some of the most intriguing details in the accounts concern food and drink: on one occasion the workers rejected Lewis's home-brewed ale as too sour, forcing him to go out and buy alternative supplies.[41] Although most of the labour force was paid by the day, there were times when the skilled workmen were paid by 'task', in other words for particular operations. Thus Henris the mason agreed to block the arch of the north quire aisle for a specific price, and Tady was given a set sum of 40s. for slating on 23 May 1565.[42] When work was successfully completed, special rewards were due: thus on 19 December 1564 the masons and slaters were given two quarts of Gascon wine for their efforts, and when the pier in the crypt was successfully buttressed, the proctor was so relieved he bestowed upon the children at dinner time a terstin or tester (equivalent to five and a quarter pennies).[43]

The proctor's relief was understandable, for he faced a continuous series of crises and mishaps. As well as his fears about the stability of the tower, high winds and storms during the winter affected progress on the roof. There was an ever-present fear of theft, which meant that materials had to be safely locked away. It was considered too dangerous to leave small pieces of stone outside the cathedral; on one occasion iron bars were stolen from the chapter house windows.[44] Building has always been a dangerous undertaking and there were plenty of minor accidents at Christ Church: a tub full of mortar fell off the scaffold; the slaters managed to break a window in the quire as they lowered a ladder down from the battlements by rope; carts and wheelbarrows suffered regular breakages. In June 1565 one of the carpenters cut down an ash tree in the proctor's orchard to make new barrows for the quarry, 'for all the barrows was borcken in the cory with great stonys'. Three months later on 15 September a cart overloaded with stone from Milltown disintegrated in front of St Patrick's cathedral.[45] The most serious incidents, however, occurred at the quarries themselves. Along the Dodder valley, at

41 Ibid., p. 98.   42 Ibid., p. 78.   43 Ibid., pp 45, 103, 75.   44 Ibid., pp 66, 106, 116.
45 Ibid., pp 86, 109.

Milltown and Clonskeagh, stone was cut from the bed of the river, an operation which involved the construction of dams to divert the water, but in
June 1565 heavy rain in the Wicklow mountains raised the level of the river
and swept away the dams. The dangers of quarrying were further underlined
four months later, when a bank of earth fell on one of the masons. He was
dragged out by his legs, bleeding at the nose and mouth, but, Lewis notes,
with some nonchalance, 'we sawyed his leffe with great a doo'.[46]

The shortage of good freestone has always presented difficulties to builders
in Dublin, and things were no different in the sixteenth century. During the
year 1564–5 stone was obtained from at least five different sources. (Fig. 8)
A small consignment was obtained from the ruins of St Mary's abbey, the
Cistercian house which had been dissolved twenty-five years earlier.[47] 'White
Flanders stone', which was highly valued by the masons, was used for some
sections of the north crossing arch and the north quire aisle. But most of the
stone employed was obtained from quarries in the immediate locality of the
city, from Finglas, Clontarf and Milltown. None of the quarries was organised on a professional basis, and in each case masons from Christ Church
were sent to cut the stone themselves. Several different sites were exploited
along the Dodder valley, some of them identified by the proctor. On 6 June,
for example, he notes that he found a good quarry in the middle of the river,
where he then made a dam. Water must have seeped into the area, since large
bowls were needed as ladles to keep the quarry dry.[48] Once the stone was
extracted from the river bed, it had to be cut into manageable pieces and
loaded on to carts for the journey to Christ Church. The carts cost 3s. 6d.
per day to hire, a considerable expense. This cost could be avoided when
Clontarf stone was used, since the latter could be loaded straight into boats
and floated up the river Liffey to Wood Quay, just below the cathedral. The
boats were loaded at low tide and floated off at high water. But quarrying at
Clontarf was difficult. As the beds were located on the shoreline, they were
flooded at high tide, and, as at Milltown, bowls and scoups were needed to
keep the works dry.[49] Moreover, the stone was so tough that it broke the
points of picks and crowbars, forcing Lewis to return to the quarries in the
Dodder valley. In both quarries the stone in question was the dark-coloured
carboniferous limestone, often described as Dublin 'calp', a notoriously hard
stone to cut.[50] Expeditions were also made to Finglas, 'to seke for good and
thycke stonys' for the arch under the steeple.[51] Despite sporadic quarrying

46 Ibid., pp 87, 115.   47 Ibid., p. 28.   48 Ibid., p. 83.   49 Ibid., pp 50–2. The beds
sloped down under the water level, and Lewis complained that, as they followed the beds
underground, the 'watter cam wery myche apone us'.   50 Thanks to Dr Ian Sanders and
Professor George Sevastopoulos of the geology department T.C.D.   51 Gillespie, *Proctor's
accounts*, pp 83, 98.

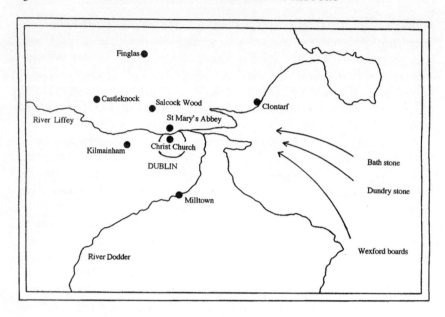

8 Map of Dublin and its hinterland, showing the source of building materials supplied to Christ Church, both in the middle ages and in the sixteenth century.

here and at Clontarf, the bulk of the stone used at Christ Church came from the river Dodder.

Much of the timber used in the reconstruction was obtained from Wexford. A dozen timbers, eighteen feet long, were bought from 'a man of Weyxford' in August 1565, and Wexford 'boards' were used on a regular basis for water channels and gutters. Wattle for scaffolding was obtained from local sources, much of it from Kilmainham, and a payment was made to the 'woodkeeper' at Kilmainham for his goodwill.[52] Timber was also obtained from Castleknock, in the form of 'five great trees', as well as from Salcock Wood (between Grangegorman and Cabra).[53] The brisk trade in local timber underlines the extent to which the hinterland of Dublin was still extensively forested. (Fig. 8)

Other materials supplied to the works included tallow and pack thread. Tallow was smeared on to crane ropes to prevent the fibres rotting, and pack thread was used in laying out arches and centering to ensure they were correctly aligned. More predictable were the supplies of nails, which included seven inch long 'spike' nails, costing 16d. per hundred.[54] Lime, obtained from Castleknock, was supplied by two merchants, Seggyrson and Bounell. As for equipment, this included a wide variety of tools, as well as ladders, pulleys,

52 Ibid., p. 36.   53 Ibid., pp 65, 31, 103, 122 n. 72.   54 Ibid., pp 31, 42, 72.

cranes, buckets, along with sieves and rakes, the latter used for refining sand. Although the account roll is limited to a single year and concerns the restoration of the cathedral rather than its initial construction, it nevertheless provides a remarkably vivid impression of all the activities required for the construction of a great ecclesiastical monument.

After the sudden illumination provided by the account roll, the architectural history of the cathedral vanishes into semi-obscurity for the next two hundred years. There are glimpses of further crises and emergency repairs, but it is difficult to form a clear picture of what took place. A new pavement was laid in the nave by 1570, albeit at a higher level than before, and the lord deputy, Sir Henry Sidney, paid for the reinstatement of Strongbow's tomb.[55] Sidney, was not, however, prepared to waste money on new sculpture and an existing effigy, dating from about 1330, was merely substituted for the broken one. (Plate 19b) The historical subterfuge is revealed by the arms displayed on the shield, which are those of FitzOsbert, not those of the earl of Pembroke.[56] There is in fact no certainty that the replacement even came from Christ Church.

Repairs to the roofs of the cathedral continued during the 1570s, by which time the condition of the tower again began to cause alarm.[57] Continual efforts were made to secure additional funds for repairs and maintenance: between 1577 and 1592 a series of benefactions and fines was directed towards the 'reparacon of the decaied steple'.[58] It appears that the efforts of Sir Peter Lewis had been in vain, and that the cathedral was now faced with rebuilding not just the crossing tower, but other parts of the fabric as well. In 1584 Archbishop Loftus stated that Christ Church was 'altogether ruinous and decayed'.[59] The previous year the chapter had arranged for the names of donors, along with the size of their gifts, to be recorded in a special book, the donations being intended for 'the re-edification of the cathedral, the fabric whereof was reduced to a state of utter decay, insomuch that a great part of

55 Sidney's role is made plain in a sixteenth-century inscription in the south wall, printed in full in Butler, *Christ Church*, p. 25. According to a note by Sir James Ware the replacement tomb was brought from Drogheda by Peter Lewis and he adds (rather puzzlingly) that it was the stone in memory of the earl of Drogheda who was beheaded in Drogheda (1464), Bodl., Rawl. MS B 484, f 33 (I owe this reference to Ray Gillespie). Seymour, *Christ Church*, p. 43 has the same report.   56 John Hunt, *Irish medieval figure sculpture 1200–1600* (2 vols., Dublin and London, 1974), i, 136; Butler, *Christ Church*, p. 25.   57 McEnery and Refaussé, *Deeds*, nos 1326 and 1338 mention slates. One lease is dated 1572, the other to 1574, and in both cases 4000 slates are mentioned. This is puzzling since the major task of re-roofing was over by 1565. It is possible that the slates, or the money for their purchase, were provided in the 1560s on the understanding that leases would be granted or renewed in the future.   58 Gillespie, *Chapter act book*, p. 41 *et passim*; see also pp 180–1 above.   59 P.R.O., SP63/110/33.

it was obliged to be razed to its foundations'.[60] The phrasing is significant, for it seems that the chapter was considering a comprehensive reconstruction of the cathedral, a point borne out by the terms of other benefactions. In 1585 the lord deputy, Sir John Perrot, granted 100 beeves 'towards rebuilding the walls of Christ Church' and in the same year a grant was received from the corporation of Dublin 'towards the building of Christ Church'.[61] On 22 September 1588 the situation became even more desperate. During a sermon by the archbishop, an ominous crack was heard coming from the direction of the tower, a sound which brought a rapid end to the archbishop's discourse.[62] Sections of the tower were apparently dismantled soon afterwards, though we know nothing about the details of what happened. The tower had been reconstructed by 1619, since Archbishop Thomas Jones, who died in that year, placed three weathercocks on the top.[63] Jones himself is usually given credit for financing the rebuilding.

Although the tower was subsequently remodelled by Street, the basic fabric belongs to the reconstruction carried out about 1600. (Plates 1, 24) On both the east and north sides, the walls of the tower retain the marks of two earlier roofs, showing the tower's lengthy history before the restoration of 1871–8.[64] The doorways are constructed with two large 'voussoirs', a technique universal in Irish tower houses of the later middle ages. (Plate 21b) One such door, giving access to the ringers' chamber, has arch stones decorated with punched dressings and drafted margins, embellishments consistent with a date at the beginning of the seventeenth century.

Given the financial circumstances of the cathedral about 1600, it is not surprising that the tower was built to a relatively austere design. The stark masonry was relieved only by shallow corner turrets and simple battlements, the latter less elaborate than those later added by Street. (Plate 24) A string course was located just above the level of the adjacent roofs, and, although this was remade in 1871–8, it follows the original line. The belfry, which now has large openings designed by Street, had two-light windows with simple curvilinear tracery. The most striking feature of the old tower was the presence of large clock faces, square in shape, that occupied the space immediately above the belfry windows. These were changed to a circular form in 1845, before being removed altogether twenty-five years later. Most of the external masonry up to the level of the battlements is ancient; so too the newel stair in the south-west turret, where only the topmost section was

60 Gilbert, *Dublin*, i, 114. 61 Street & Seymour, pp 29–30; H.F. Berry, 'Minute book of the corporation of Dublin known as the "Friday book", 1567–1611' in *R.I.A. Proc.*, xxx, C (1913), p. 486. I owe the latter reference to Edward McParland. 62 Street & Seymour, p. 31. 63 Ibid., p. 35, Gilbert, *Dublin*, i, 116. 64 These roof creasings are visible from within the roof spaces of the quire and north transept.

rebuilt in the nineteenth century.[65] The present slated roof, designed by Street, is far steeper than that depicted in the old engravings. There are two storeys within the tower, the ringers' chamber above the crossing vault, and the bell chamber proper. Access to the ringers' chamber is curiously awkward and ill-planned: after climbing the spiral stairs in the south-west corner of the transept, one has to go outside and proceed along the transept wallwalk to the external doorway at the base of the tower. From this point an internal staircase gives access to the ringers' chamber and the upper levels of the tower. Inside the cathedral, the tower was supported on roughly constructed arches, approximately ten feet lower than the those inserted during the restoration of 1871–8. Street took a poor view of the seventeenth-century crossing arches, which accentuated the divisions between the various parts of the church.

As well as the major work of the crossing tower, repairs were carried out in other parts of the cathedral. In 1593, for example, the roof of the chancel was replaced under the direction of the carpenter, Richard Enos, the chapter specifying that each side must be furnished with three courses of purlins.[66] But no sooner had one problem been solved than another appeared. In 1597 the cathedral was damaged by an explosion of gunpowder at Wood Quay, a blast which probably blew out some of the window glass. The accident was later cited as an argument to extract funds from the crown.[67]

Despite the many repairs carried out since 1562, reports continued to speak of the 'ruinous' condition of Christ Church. The cathedral was further disappointed by the failure of a lottery, which had been established in 1620 with the idea of producing a £500 bonus for the fabric fund.[68] In 1627 eighteen and a half years of unpaid rent was demanded from the Four Courts, the cash being needed urgently for 'necessary reparacons'.[69] So great was the decay of the fabric at this time that the lord deputy and members of the council refused to worship in Christ Church during rough and stormy weather.[70] As for the nave, it was a forlorn and uninspiring place, the north

---

65 The stair is entered from the outside of the tower from the western wall walk of the south transept, which in turn was reached by the stair turret in the south-west angle of the transept. It is possible that the medieval crossing tower was reached by the interior passage along the late Romanesque clerestory to the base of a newel stair inside the southwest crossing pier.   66 Gillespie, *Chapter act book*, p. 85.   67 C6/1/26/3, no. 4; C6/1/26/1, ff 19, 23. A letter of James I speaks of the great dilapidations into which the church had fallen 'by reason of a mischance in firing powder of the late queen's provision some years past', Street & Seymour, p. 31. Since the reign of Edward VI, the state had contributed £60 each year towards the maintenance of the cathedral, see p. 190 above. 68 See p. 191 above.   69 Gillespie, *Chapter act book*, pp 144–5, 151–3.   70 In its anxiety to raise money, the chapter may have been guilty of exaggeration, for three years later a visitation stated that the fabric was in good repair.

aisle windows blocked by shops and outworks along St John's Lane, and the south aisle cut off by the ponderous masonry of 1562–4. This part of the cathedral was not used for services, as Sir William Brereton recounted in 1635: 'the chancel is only made use of, not the body of the church, wherein are very great strong pillars, though very short; the chancel is but plain, and ordinarily kept; the body of the church is a more stately building'.[71] Brereton clearly appreciated the quality of what was left of the early Gothic design.

The stone vaults over the transepts were apparently dismantled at some point after 1565. Both transepts are covered by pendant roofs of seventeenth-century character, and, as they are designed to be seen from below, they must have been erected after the removal of the vaults.[72] The pendants in the south transept still survive, but those in the north transept were sawn off when a stone vault was reinstated in 1871–8. The roofs were designed with simplified hammer beams, a fact which adds considerably to their historical interest; in the south transept the hammer beams are supported by attractive double curved braces.[73] (Plate 10a)

The arrival of Wentworth as lord deputy and the reform of the chapter in the 1630s brought a more energetic approach to the affairs of the cathedral.[74] Amongst the proposed reforms was a reorganisation of the rented spaces in the crypt, which had long been used as 'tippling rooms for beer, wine and tobacco'. These prosaic activities were condemned in a famous letter of 1633 by the treasurer, John Bramhall, the contents of which were repeated by Wentworth in correspondence with Laud.[75] Commerce however won out over morality and some forty years later identical criticisms were voiced by the earl of Ormond.[76] There is some evidence that Wentworth and his advisors revived the idea of replacing the cathedral church with a new building. In a letter to Laud of 1638 Wentworth commented: 'For the building of Christ Church, now that his Majesty and your Lordship approve of the way, I trust to show you I neither sleep nor forget it' and the following year the archbishop laments that, due to economic conditions in Ireland, 'it' cannot begin this year.[77] Had Laud and Wentworth survived in power, the medieval fabric of Christ Church might have been swept away.

71 Brereton, *Travels*, p. 138. 72 A small drawing dated 1827 in the R.C.B. describes the south transept principal as being of seventeenth-century date, and, given the age of the timbers and the use of wooden dowels, this seems very likely. The north transept was in a poor state by the early nineteenth century with the north wall overhanging St John's lane by up to two and a half feet. Once this outward rotation started, the vaults would have been in jeopardy, C6/1/8/11, ff 140–2. 73 The couples of the north transept roof still retain their assembly marks in the form of horizontal strokes. 74 See p. 197 above. 75 Gillespie, *Chapter act book*, pp 202–3; Gilbert, *Dublin*, i, 119. 76 Gilbert, *Dublin*, i, 124. 77 Ibid., i, 121.

1 The cathedral from the south-east, showing the choir as rebuilt by
George Edmund Street in 1871–8

2 The interior of the cathedral looking east towards the chancel screen.
Comparison with the illustration in the *Dublin Penny Journal* (shown opposite)
reveals the extent of the reconstruction undertaken in 1871–8
(photograph by Brendan Dempsey).

3 The interior of the nave in 1835 as illustrated in the *Dublin Penny Journal*, with the Byfield organ of 1752 visible above the chancel screen. The contrast between the two sides of the building is very apparent, a result of the hasty rebuilding of the south side of the building after the collapse of the vaults in 1562.

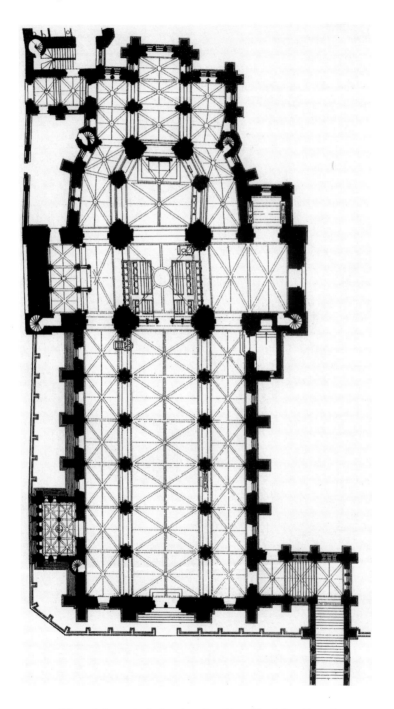

4 Plan of the cathedral as it existed in 1882 (after Street).

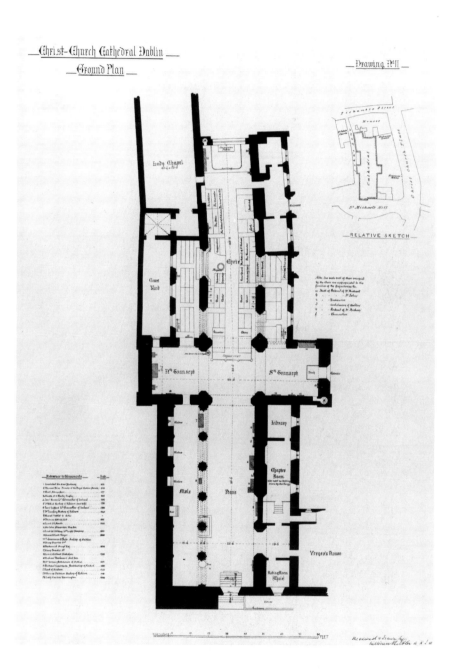

5 Plan of the cathedral drawn by William Butler in 1870–1, shortly before the start of Street's restoration.

6 Interior of the quire. The triforium and clerestory are entirely the work of Street, but a few sections of the lower arches, identified by dark masonry, were recovered from the old building.

7 **(a)** (left) Three Romanesque capitals recovered from the walls in 1871–8, which appear to pre-date the existing cathedral. They were smashed in pieces soon after this drawing was made (after Street).

(b) (below) The east end of the crypt as drawn by H.W. Brewer, the artist who prepared most of the engraved drawings for Street & Seymour's commemorative volume of 1882.

8 The exterior of the south transept, with the ruins of the chapter house in the foreground. The Romanesque doorway in the facade of the transept was moved to this position in 1831.

9 (a) (above) The interior of the south transept, showing the upper levels of the east wall. While the vault and much of the masonry was renewed in 1871–8, the arches of the triforium and clerestory belong to the period around 1200.
(b) (below) Section through the transepts depicting the east elevation. The presence of the Telford organ indicates that the drawing was made between 1857 and 1871 (compare plate 3).

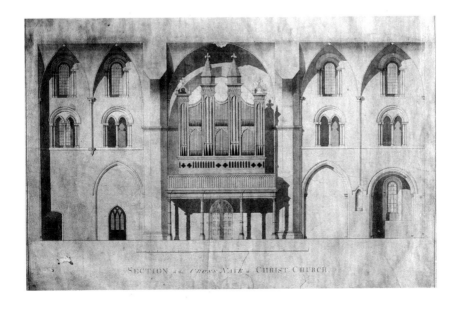

SECTION of CROSS AISLE CHRIST CHURCH

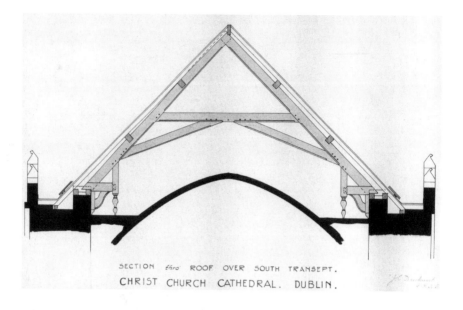

SECTION *thro* ROOF OVER SOUTH TRANSEPT.

CHRIST CHURCH CATHEDRAL. DUBLIN.

10 (a) (above) Roof over south transept as drawn by J. Dewhurst in the 1920s. The decorated pendants and double curved braces were designed to be seen from below, indicating that the roof was erected long before the plaster vault of 1794.
   (b) (below) The interior of the south transept, showing a detail of the east triforium, finished with early 'stiff leaf' capitals and chevron ornament.

11 The interior of the south transept, west wall, as photographed by Millard and
Robinson before 1871. The plaster vault was erected by Edward Parke in 1794
(photograph courtesy of National Library of Ireland).

12 Romanesque capitals from the transepts and choir carved about 1200:
(a) a troupe of 'entertainers' playing musical instruments; a jester is visible to the
right (north transept). (b) a paired capital showing griffons enveloping human
busts; this capital was discovered during the restoration of 1871–8, having been
obscured by masonry since 1564 (north transept). (c) a group of fruitpickers, one
of whom holds an oval basket filled with giant raspberries or blackberries (choir,
north side). (d) affronted beasts, one being ridden by a man with flaming hair
(south transept doorway). (e) foliate capital with berries (north transept).
(f) foliate capital with nailhead ornament, one of many sculptured capitals taken
from the fabric in 1871–8.

13 A view of the north elevation of the nave showing the unified design of the thirteenth-century triforium and clerestory, linked together by continuous shafts.

14 The interior of the nave showing the thirteenth-century north elevation which survived the collapse of the vaults in 1562.

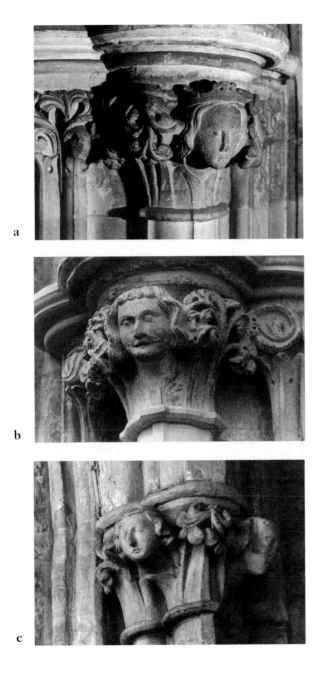

a

b

c

15 (a & b) sculptured capitals with protruding heads belonging to the piers of the thirteenth-century nave. (c) capital in similar style, perhaps carved by the same craftsman, at Overbury (Worcestershire).

a

b

c

d

16 Capitals from the nave: **(a)** moulded capitals from the west face of the fifth pier; such capitals were introduced in the final bay of the nave. **(b)** foliate capitals from the east face of the fifth pier; the curious 'blobs' on the necking are unique in Irish architecture. **(c)** capital from the triforium of the nave (east bay); the design is comparable with work produced for the Lady chapel of St Patrick's cathedral. **(d)** capital from St Patrick's cathedral (choir triforium, west bay; photograph by Edwin Rae); the foliage has obvious similarities with that found on the Christ Church capital illustrated in (b).

17 The interior of the nave, showing the westernmost bay. This final bay was an addition to the nave as first built, a point revealed by a number of minor changes in the design.

18 The Christ Church psalter (Oxford, Bodleian Library Ms. Rawl. G. 185). The illuminations in the psalter are remarkable for the painter's interest in foreshortening and three-dimensional modelling, qualities which reflect some knowledge of Trecento painting in Italy. (a) (above) Initial E to Psalm 80 (*Exultate Deo*), 68v. (b) (below) Initial C to Psalm 97 (*Cantate Domino*), 81v.

19 (a) (above) The Kildare chantry chapel established by 1512. The chapel, evidently constructed of wood, was removed from the cathedral before 1830 (Dublin City Libraries).

(b) (below) The 'tomb of Strongbow'; the original tomb was destroyed in the collapse of 1562, and this early fourteenth-century effigy was introduced as a substitute soon afterwards.

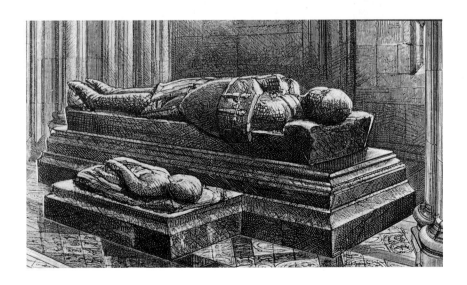

20 The thirteenth-century chapter house. **(a)** (right) the responds which supported the vault; the projecting rings were designed to hold detached shafts (probably in a contrasting dark stone). **(b)** (below) the doorway, with its cluster of moulded shafts; below the curious semi-cylindrical pier embedded in the jambs is a crude rebate cut to install a wooden door.

The North Prospect of the Cathedral Church of the Holy Trinity in Dublin

21 (a) (above) The cathedral from the north as engraved in 1739 for *The Whole Works of Sir James Ware Concerning Ireland*, edited by W. Harris. This provides a rare view of the old Lady chapel, visible at the extreme left. (b) (left) The entrance to the tower; this doorway, which belongs to the years around 1600, is reached from the wall-walk above the south transept.

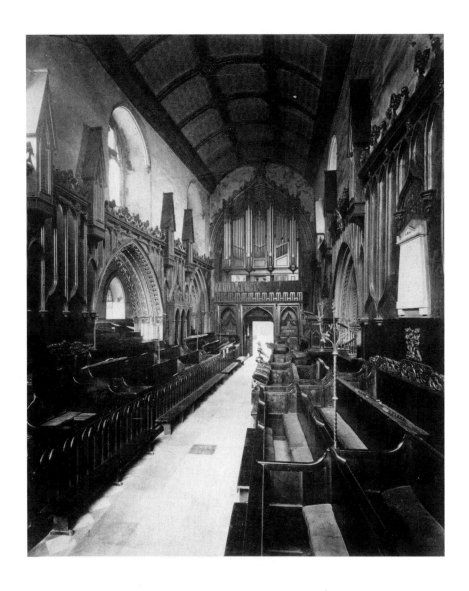

22 The interior of the long quire looking west, as photographed by Millard and Robinson shortly before 1871. The view into the nave is blocked by the Telford organ. The furniture and fittings belong to the restoration of Matthew Price 1830–3 (photograph courtesy of National Library of Ireland).

23 (a) (above) The exterior of the long quire in 1824, before the restoration of
Matthew Price. The wooden props suggest the south aisle was in a dilapidated
state at this time. (b) (below) The cathedral from the south-east as engraved for
Grose's *Antiquities of Ireland* (1791–5). Although the end walls of the ancient
chapter house had been removed, the building was still substantially intact.

24 (a) (above) The cathedral from the south, as shown in a lithograph in R. O'Callaghan Newenham's *Picturesque Views of the Antiquities of Ireland*, 1826. This illustrates the quire and transept before the restoration by Matthew Price in 1830–3. **(b)** (below) The cathedral from the south as photographed by Millard and Robinson shortly before 1871. Comparison with the illustration above reveals the extent of the changes introduced by Matthew Price.

25 (a) (above) The exterior of the cathedral from the west as seen in a drawing by George Petrie, engraved in R. Cromwell's *Excursions through Ireland*, 1820.
(b) (below) A similar view today, which reveals the extent of Street's reconstruction.

26 The interior of the nave looking west (south side) as photographed by Millard and Robinson shortly before 1871. The section of the nave, erected in 1562–4, was demolished in Street's restoration (photograph courtesy of National Library of Ireland).

27 The interior of the nave looking west (north side) as photographed by Millard and Robinson shortly before 1871. Slight inconsistencies in the design of the medieval piers were removed during the restoration by Street (photograph courtesy of National Library of Ireland).

28 Furnishings ancient and modern: **(a)** (above, left) an evangelist, detail from the pulpit, designed by Street and installed in 1878. **(b)** (above, right) detail of the brass gates at the entrance to the chancel; the handle and lock were executed with meticulous care by 'Mr Potter of London'. **(c)** (left) the ancient lectern, thought to date from the later middle ages, though much restored in more recent times.

29 Portrait of Henry Roe, as published in the commemorative volume of 1882.

30 (a) (above) The nave during the course of the restoration of 1871–8 as photographed by Millard and Robinson (National Library of Ireland). The north aisle has been entirely removed and the main arches of the north elevation are shown propped up with timber baulks. (b) (bottom, left) one page from the book of mouldings prepared during the restoration of 1871–8; this drawing shows the mouldings of the mullion and arch of the west window. (c) (bottom, right) a thirteenth-century capital, one of several removed from the fabric in 1871–8; the vertical slit was cut by the nineteenth-century masons; by inserting a piece of stiff card or paper, the profile could be recorded with greater ease.

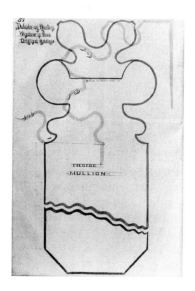

31 Photograph of George Edmund Street *c.*1869 (courtesy of Paul Joyce).

32 Street's original design for the synod hall, as proposed in his second report (1871). The location of the site on the old claustral buildings would have blocked views of the cathedral from the south

But thanks to the addition of various props and buttresses, Christ Church managed to survive without serious mishap for another two hundred years. Alterations involved matters of taste and liturgy, rather than structural changes, with most attention focussed on the quire. In 1679, Charles II contributed £100 towards the repair and adornment of the quire, though we do not know what this entailed.[78] In 1725 the floor of the quire was paved with black and white flags, following contemporary fashion, and by this time the whole interior was white-washed on a regular basis.[79] In the same year the west window was reglazed, almost certainly with clear glass. White walls and plain glass, along with black and white paving, gave a distinctively Georgian flavour to the ancient architecture. By the end of the century, the first hints of the Gothic revival began to appear. In 1794 neo-gothic plaster vaults were constructed over the transepts and crossing, work carried out under the direction of the cathedral architect Edward Parke.[80] (Plate 11) Although demolished during the Street restoration, their appearance has been recorded in a number of photographs and drawings.[81] These indicate that each transept was covered by two bays of ribbed vaulting, the ribs being moulded in medieval fashion. Photographs also reveal the extent to which the walls were encrusted with accumulated layers of plaster and whitewash.

Edward Parke rebuilt the vaults in plaster in full realisation that the walls of the transept would not support anything heavier. The upper sections of the north transept overhung St John's Lane by over two feet, and in 1829 Parke gave a sombre report on the future of the building, arguing that money spent on repairs would be wasted.[82] The only solution was to reconstruct the greater part of the cathedral, a view which echoed that of Wentworth two centuries earlier. Although the north clerestory of the nave no longer supported a stone vault, the walls still appeared to be rotating outwards. To counter the problem a huge buttress had been added at the north-west angle at some point before 1739, and when various sheds and outworks were removed from the outer face of the north aisle in 1753, the masonry was found to be so badly decayed that it was necessary to encase the entire facade with a huge block of battered masonry.[83] (Plates 21a, 25a) Despite these mea-

---

78 Ibid., i, 124. The quire had been replastered and whitened in 1668, C6/1/8/2, f. 389.
79 In 1707 the chapter came to an agreement with Edward Johnson to plaster the ceiling and whitewash the church for a period of twenty-one years, at a rate of £9 per year. This agreement did not apparently last its full term, for in 1726 the church was in need of whitewashing, three years having elapsed since this was last done, C6/1/8/4, f. 18; C6/1/8/5, ff 3, 10.   80 C6/1/8/8, f. 19.   81 The vaults are also illustrated in a nineteenth-century watercolour of the interior and in a drawing by the Reverend Narcissus Batt, 'Sketches of Irish antiquities', volume 8 (Ulster Museum).   82 C6/1/8/10, f. 51; C6/1/8/11, f. 139. See p. 354 below.   83 The buttress, but not the encasing wall, is shown on the engraving of 1739 used to illustrate Ware, *Works*, i, opposite p. 299; Street

sures, the fabric remained in a precarious condition. When Archbishop Smyth offered £1,000 for the erection of a spire in 1769, the offer was declined in view of the fragile condition of the crossing tower.[84] The proposal was obviously inspired by St Patrick's, where a spire had been added to Minot's tower twenty years earlier.

The fall of the nave vaults in 1562 inaugurated a despiriting period in the architectural history of the cathedral. For over three hundred years the chapter struggled to maintain the fabric, and there were times when even the congregation felt their lives were in danger when they entered the building. From the late sixteenth century the need for fundamental reconstruction was obvious, but it was not until the fortune of Henry Roe was placed at the disposal of the cathedral that this became a reality.

& Seymour, p. 49.   84 Gilbert, *Dublin*, i, 127; Street & Seymour, p. 49.

XII

The establishment of the
choral tradition, 1480–1647

Barra Boydell

The Henrician Reformation was to change profoundly the structure and establishment of Christ Church cathedral, but from the musical point of view arguably the most significant shifts from earlier practices had taken place in the late fifteenth century. In 1480 Thomas Bennet, son of a former lord mayor, made a grant to maintain four singing-boys to serve in the choir and Lady chapel.[1] A feature of late medieval worship was the growing devotion to the Virgin Mary reflected in the establishment of Lady chapels often with boy choristers who sang in the votive masses and antiphons. In most instances in England where Lady chapel choirs with boys were established an almonary school already existed, so that boys were already to hand and provided for.[2] Bennet's endowment suggests that this was not the case at Christ Church, so that everything – provision for the boys' sustenance as well as their musical training and the organisation of the music – needed to be created. The result is one of the most extensively documented examples of the establishment of a Lady chapel choir in the English or Irish contexts. The four boys are described as '*paraphonistae*', a term only otherwise recorded at the chapel of St Anthony's Hospital, London, in the 1460s.[3] This possibly reflects the characteristic desire of monastic houses to avoid using the term '*chorista*' which was often used for full-time professional choirboys of the secular collegiate churches and cathedrals like St Patrick's. At Christ Church the boys were to be trained in music, to sing plainsong and polyphonic music ('set song or pricksong and other more learned musical chants') daily both in the high quire and at the Lady mass in the Lady chapel, and the practice of singing more

---

1 Boydell, *Music*, pp 29–31; Refaussé & Lennon, *Registers*, p. 68.   2 Roger Bowers, 'The almonary schools of the English monasteries, *c.*1265–1540' in Benjamin Thompson (ed.), *Monasteries in medieval Britain* (Harlaxton Medieval Studies vi, Stamford, forthcoming). 3 Information from Roger Bowers; it may be significant that St Anthony's Hospital, which was in the process of being secularised, had formerly been in Augustinian hands.

complex polyphony in the cathedral was to be developed. Since this musical training presupposes the existence of a music teacher or director, the foundation of the cathedral choir school which was to survive until 1972 can effectively be dated to 1480, even though it would be found necessary to put such arrangements on a more formal footing thirteen years later.

In 1485 a grant by John Estrete included provision for the choir to sing every Thursday in the chapel of St Laurence O'Toole a mass with plainsong and polyphony ('sett song') using music ('by note') or, if this was not possible, at least 'good and treatable plainsong'.[4] This suggests that the anticipated mastery of polyphony had not yet been achieved, and in 1493 prior David Wynchester established a stipend for a music master to teach the four boys and provide for their food, clothing and accommodation financed by offerings to the '*baculus Ihesu*', as well as by rents from certain specified church properties and other donations.[5] The boys must have had a master since 1480 who was paid in some informal manner, this 1493 charter putting existing arrangements on a sound and regular basis. The master's duties included teaching the boys plainchant, polyphony and descant (polyphony improvised over plainchant) for the daily mass of the Blessed Virgin and for the mass and antiphon of Jesus on Fridays in Lent, as well as at other services as might be determined. The master and the boys were to be provided with food and drink, as well as a room for sleeping and for teaching. Bennet's grant of 1480 and Estrete's of 1485 have a further significance within the context of Christ Church's close links with the citizenry of Dublin as reflected in the 'Book of obits' in which a majority of those commemorated comprise 'a roll-call of civic and gentry families who were prominent in the Dublin area particularly in the later fifteenth and earlier sixteenth centuries'.[6] When a choir of boy choristers had been instituted at St Patrick's in 1431 the initiative had come from the archbishop of Dublin. At Christ Church in the 1480s it came from a leading citizen concerned to elaborate the cathedral's liturgy through the provision of boys' voices.[7]

The choir was most probably augmented, as in most cathedrals and larger collegiate churches, by lay clerks trained in the singing of polyphonic music.[8] Clerks, sometimes married, are occasionally mentioned in leases and in the 'Book of obits', but the meaning of 'clerk' (or '*clericus*') here is ambiguous.[9]

---

4 Boydell, *Music*, pp 32–3.   5 Ibid., pp 34–7.   6 Refaussé & Lennon, *Registers*, p. 21.   7 Further on music at Christ Church as a reflection of the cathedral's links with both the city and, after the Reformation, with the government, see Boydell, 'Cathedral music, city and state'.   8 In 1519 in a set of statutes written for Augustinian canons (as at Christ Church) Cardinal Wolsey forbade the singing of polyphony by the canons. Laymen, seculars and boys were, however, permitted to sing with polyphony and organ at the Lady mass, the Jesus mass, and on other occasions when music might be sung outside the conventual choir. Harrison, *Music*, pp 191–2.   9 C6/1/3, f. 46; Refaussé & Lennon, *Registers*,

However, three choral clerks were included at the new foundation in 1539, implying that these positions were already in existence. The fact that the vicars choral at the new foundation were constituted from the existing canons shows that at least some must have been proficient in the singing of polyphony, but in the absence of surviving music or other records the musical repertoire remains a matter of conjecture. The number of choirboys at Christ Church was small compared not only with the six at St Patrick's but also with the larger numbers common in many cathedrals in England and reflects a smaller overall size of choir.[10] It seems unlikely that this small choir would have even approached the standards represented by some of the more elaborate sacred music surviving from England at this period,[11] but up-to-date polyphonic music of a more modest style, including works composed by the master of the choristers of the time, would undoubtedly have been sung. Composed polyphony was not however necessarily sung when the boys were present.[12] Undoubtedly the most elaborate occasion at which the newly-established choir participated would have been the coronation of the pretender Lambert Simnel on 24 May 1487 when the full panoply of regal magnificence, including music, must surely have been employed.[13] Like the provision of choristers, organs were increasingly used to enhance the liturgy in the later fifteenth and early sixteenth centuries by which period they had become normal in cathedrals.[14] Although there is no confirmed evidence for organs at Christ Church before 1539, it is very probable that they were used.[15] The late medieval tradition of liturgical drama continued up to the eve of the Reformation: in 1528 Prior Hassard, together with the priors of St John of Jerusalem and of All Hallows, 'caused two plays to be acted [at Hoggen Green to the east of the city] the one representing the Passion of our Saviour and the other the several deaths which the apostles suffered',[16] and payments were made in 1541 and 1542 for 'singing the Passion' and 'playing the Resurrection'.[17]

Under the arrangements for the new foundation of Christ Church set out in 1539[18] the eight canons of the former priory who were not dignitaries were transformed into vicars choral along the model of St Patrick's, a secular cathe-

pp 49, 50, 67.   10 For numbers of choristers in cathedrals at the reformation, Lehmberg, *Reformation*, p. 199.   11 Most notably the Eton choirbook compiled 1490–1502, edited by Frank Harrison in *Musica Britannica*, x–xii (London, 1956–61).   12 Roger Bowers, 'The musicians of the Lady chapel of Winchester cathedral priory, 1402–1539' in *Journal of Ecclesiastical History*, xlv (1994), p. 223; on the practice of improvising over a plainchant, S.B. Meech, 'Three musical treatises in English in a fifteenth-century manuscript' in *Speculum*, x (1935), pp 242–58.   13 Martin, *Crowning of a king*.   14 Lehmberg, *Reformation*, pp 214–15.   15 See also p. 148 above.   16 Walter Harris, *History and antiquities of the city of Dublin* (Dublin, 1766), p.144.   17 Boydell, *Music*, p. 41.   18 Ibid., pp 37–41.

dral, rather than minor canons as was usual in cathedrals of the new foundation. Like minor canons, however, all the vicars were in holy orders, although
this requirement was later to lapse; unusually, the vicars choral were all made
members of the chapter. The eight vicars were divided into four principal vicars:
dean's vicar, succentor's or precentor's vicar (later more often called chanter's
vicar), chancellor's vicar, and treasurer's vicar; and four 'vicars minor'. As well
as the four boys there were three choral clerks, very possibly former lay clerks:
the organist and master of the boys, the sacrist who also assisted the singers at
masses, and a third who assisted the celebrant at mass. The clerks or additional
singing men, normally two in number up to the Restoration, came to be known
as stipendiaries in the late sixteenth century, a term which would continue in
use until disestablishment.[19] Although it was nominally the succentor's duty to
teach the boys singing, in practice this was delegated to the organist and master
of the boys who was to be sufficiently trained in plainchant, polyphony and
singing descant in order to instruct the boys. The chancellor's vicar was responsible for the correction of any mistakes in the Latin texts of the choirbooks,
payments in 1542 for 'paper for songs' and to John Kerdiff, the first succentor, for rebinding music books being the earliest references to choirbooks.[20]

The choral duties following the new foundation, modelled on those of St
Patrick's, represent substantially a continuation of those outlined between
1480 and 1493.[21] High mass and Lady mass were celebrated daily including
polyphonic singing with choirboys and organ, the boys playing instruments
in the Lady mass 'during the time of their child's voice', and a Marian
anthem or antiphon was performed daily with organ. This suggests that
(unspecified) instruments joined with the voices in polyphonic music and
that unbroken boys' voices were not now used in the music for the Lady
mass, a practice which would mark a change from the late fifteenth century.[22]
The rood mass was also celebrated daily except Friday by one of the minor
vicars 'with lowered voice', probably chanting. Jesus mass was celebrated
with organ and polyphony ('solemn singing') 'according to the practice of St
Patrick's' early on Friday morning in lieu of first mass, and the Holy Ghost
mass celebrated on Thursdays with 'singing and choristers and other ministers as is the practice', also suggesting polyphony. Plainchant masses for the
state of the king were celebrated thrice weekly at the high altar, and masses
at the altar of the Holy Ghost for the cathedral's benefactors on Mondays,

19 Ibid., p. 56.   20 Ibid., pp 41–2.   21 Ibid., p. 42.   22 Instrumental teaching for choirboys, at this period most probably keyboard instruments, is documented in English cathedrals, Ian Payne, *The provision and practice of sacred music at Cambridge colleges and selected
cathedrals c.1547–c.1646* (New York and London, 1993), pp 134f, and Jane Flynn, 'The
education of choristers in England during the sixteenth century' in John Morehen (ed.),
English choral practice, 1400–1650 (Cambridge, 1995), p. 189.

Wednesdays and Saturdays appear also to have been with plainchant. The organist played whenever mass was celebrated with polyphonic singing, as well as at matins on the eight principal feasts and major doubles, when polyphony was apparently also sung. When Robert Heyward was appointed organist and master of the boys in 1546, in addition to defining many of the above duties, he was to instruct the choristers in polyphony and 'discant to four minims' (that is, improvisation over a plainchant melody) and to procure 'suitable songs' at the expense of the cathedral.[23]

Following the dissolution of St Patrick's in 1547 the choir at Christ Church was enlarged by six priests and two boys funded out of the exchequer, at least two of the new priests, Richard Betagh and John Claregenet, being former vicars choral at St Patrick's.[24] In recognition, the choir sang each term at the court of exchequer, a custom which continued until disestablishment.[25] The enlarged choir was confirmed in 1555 when St Patrick's was restored as a cathedral and Christ Church subsequently retained items including musical instruments and organs which it had received from St Patrick's, but the number of boys on the foundation would return to four by 1604.[26]

The daily office had ceased to be celebrated after the new foundation but many of the former liturgical practices continued. Even following the first use of the English liturgy in 1551 there is nothing to suggest that at Christ Church the survival of the choir was threatened during the Edwardian reformation when Dean Lockwood exerted a restraining influence on the demands of more Protestant reformers. The new prayer book was at best vague as to the role of music and the evidence from English cathedrals shows an adapting of older musical practices to new circumstances rather than any profound change.[27] The daily office and the Roman liturgy were restored under Queen Mary: in orders dating from c.1557 the attendance of the dignitaries, prebendaries and minor vicars at the various masses was defined. Apart from the prebendaries and a senior dignitary singing high mass and other daily masses and the dignitaries singing mass on all principal double and major double feasts, it is only for the daily Lady mass sung by five minor vicars and for which 'for the more honour of God's divine service ... certain of basses and countertenors' were to be appointed that there is clear reference to polyphonic music.[28] The choirboys' duties are not mentioned.

On 30 August 1559 in the early months of the reign of Queen Elizabeth I the litany was sung in English at Christ Church when the lord deputy, the

23 Boydell, *Music*, p. 42.   24 Above, p. 168.   25 Boydell, *Music*, p. 43; *Cal. pat rolls Ire., Hen. VIII–Eliz.*, p. 143; see also Bumpus, 'Composers', pp 83–4.   26 McEnery & Refaussé, *Deeds*, no. 448; Boydell, *Music*, pp 45–6, 85.   27 Payne, *Provision and practice*, p. 23.   28 Boydell, *Music*, pp 44–5.

earl of Sussex, took his oath.[29] Music at the cathedral entered a new phase with the definitive establishment of the Anglican rite and became more secularised as the former monastic traditions were discarded. There is no information on the musical repertoire at this period, but the fact that payments for candles 'for the choir at service' which were regularly bought for evensong through the winter of 1564–5 cease after early February 1565[30] suggests that polyphonic music (which would have been sung from music books which would need to be lit) was not sung during Lent. In the 1560s, like the canons of the pre-Reformation priory, all vicars were clerics living within the precincts under the watchful eye of the dean and chapter and dining together in their common hall.[31] In common with most English cathedrals, as the century progressed and the links with the monastic past faded, this practice declined and had fallen into disuse by 1604 as the choirmen increasingly married and lived with their families.[32] In 1638 the six priests or vicars were described as having families, and five of them as having chambers near Christ Church.[33] This more outward-looking view is reflected in the developing links between the city and state and the cathedral as a centre of Protestant reform. As a permanent, professional body of musicians the cathedral choir was on occasion called on to provide music outside the precincts, for example for the lord deputy, Sir Henry Sidney, between 1568 and 1570 and for the lord mayor on station days in the 1590s.[34] Reciprocally, the lord deputy's musicians accompanied the cathedral choir on important occasions such as Christmas eve and the celebration of the queen's accession (17 November) in the 1590s.[35] The vicars' income came from property defined in the 1539 arrangements and subsequently added to,[36] but they also took out leases on property in the city which they sub-rented as an additional source of income.[37] Rents were paid not only in money but also, in the sixteenth century, in the form of food or even of a tablecloth for the vicars' hall.[38] Robert Heyward's income as organist and master of the choristers in 1546 included malt, a livery coat, firewood, a room in the precincts and daily board at the vicars' table, in addition to a yearly stipend.[39]

Discipline amongst the vicars was, in the sixteenth century as later, a recurring problem. In the later 1550s fines for absence from mass were specified, vicars were forbidden to sleep outside the precincts without good cause, and more general concerns included their behaviour at mealtimes and avoid-

29 T.C.D., MS 591, f. 20; B.L., Add. MS 4813, f. 65.   30 Gillespie, *Proctor's accounts*, p. 54.   31 Boydell, *Music*, pp 51, 52–4, 79–80.   32 Ibid., pp 58–9; compare Lehmberg, *Reformation*, pp 194–5.   33 Boydell, *Music*, p. 72.   34 Ibid., pp 84–5.   35 Ibid., pp 80–1. 36 Ibid., pp 37, 43; C6/1/3, ff 80v–82v.   37 The deeds and chapter acts make frequent mention of property leases to individual vicars choral.   38 Boydell, *Music*, pp 42–3.   39 Ibid., p. 42.

ance of arguments and disputes.[40] The earliest recorded chapter meetings in the 1570s were largely concerned with establishing guidelines for the running of the cathedral and these included rules of conduct affecting the vicars and other members of the cathedral. Apart from attendance, matters of concern between 1574 and 1579 included violent behaviour, the wearing of arms within the precincts or city, and staying out after nine o'clock or allowing any strange women 'or of ill fame' into the vicars' chambers at 'undue' times, while tensions between Irish and English vicars are evident in the reference to disputes arising out of any 'difference between nations'.[41] The redefining and imposing of penalties for non-attendance at services in the cathedral and questions of behaviour and personal appearance were to occupy the dean and chapter's attentions on many subsequent occasions. The cathedral grammar school must have been attended not only by the foundation choirboys but also by other boys, some only beginning their musical training, others doubtless supplementing the choir at certain services, but these additional boys are rarely mentioned.[42] In addition to music, their curriculum included reading, writing and grammar,[43] and choristers would continue to be lodged, fed and clothed by the cathedral until the nineteenth century, their gowns in the sixteenth and early seventeenth centuries being made of coloured broadcloth with canvas collars and faced with fur.[44] Barbers were employed to shave the vicars, dean and chapter and to cut the choristers' hair.[45]

Since earliest times the tower of Christ Church had housed one or more bells regarded as significant in the life of the cathedral and the city.[46] An entry in the 'Book of obits' for 1424 records the death of John Kyrcham 'maker of our bells' and is the first known reference to the casting of bells in Ireland.[47] Kyrcham was a member of the Christ Church community and his three bells continued in use (a sexton would ring the angelus bell at 4.00 a.m. and the curfew bell at night[48]) until they were found to be cracked in 1597 and were re-cast in 1610.[49] Payments for repairs and maintenance had at times to be made: in 1564 Thomas Frenche, a smith, was paid for making buckles for the tongue of the great bell and of the second bell; a saddler,

40 Ibid., pp 44–5, Gillespie, *Chapter act book*, p. 24.   41 Boydell, *Music*, pp 51–4.   42 In 1575 the school master William Weyrand was allowed to miss morning prayer 'for that he must apply the youths in the grammar school', Boydell, *Music*, p. 52.   43 Boydell, *Music*, p. 44; compare Flynn, 'Education of choristers', pp 180–99.   44 Boydell, *Music*, pp 44, 79–81; Gillespie, *Proctor's accounts*, p. 79.   45 Boydell, *Music*, pp 41, 84; McEnery & Refaussé, *Deeds*, no. 1292; Gillespie, *Proctor's accounts*, p. 83.   46 Sections in the music chapters relating to the cathedral's bells have been supplied by Leslie Taylor, honorary ringing master of the cathedral society of ringers.   47 Refaussé & Lennon, *Registers*, p. 66.   48 J.L. Robinson, 'Dublin cathedral bells, 1670' in *R.S.A.I. Jn.*, xlii (1912), pp 155–62.   49 A.M. Frazer, 'Old bells of Dublin' in *Dublin Historical Record*, vi (1943–4), pp 50–62.

Gylles, was paid for leather parts, and Mathew Hamlyn for grease for the bells for Christmas.[50] On Good Friday 1565 nails and well-seasoned Wexford wood were required to mend the wheel of the Mary bell which was ready to fall from its stock.[51] Hamlyn, who was awarded twenty shillings a year for ringing the bell for morning prayer in 1576, [52] was referred to as Mary clerk, the term 'clerk of St Mary's' also occurring later. In 1593 Thomas Bradie was to be paid an amount at the discretion of the proctor to knoll the bell at five and six o'clock in the morning and at six and nine o'clock at night,[53] showing the dual use for and expectations of the bells: to ring both for the services of the church and for the city at large as signallers of time. A century later John Dunton would describe the bells going to the tune of a psalm and a clock face on four sides of the tower, indicating mechanical chiming.[54] Resonances of earlier practices are apparent in 1565 when the mayor of Dublin, Richard Fyan, gave a gift of half a beef to the cathedral to ring the knell for the soul of Christopher Rathe, the Catholic precentor of the cathedral under Mary I.[55]

In 1604 a new constitution for the vicars choral was drawn up under James I which would prevail until disestablishment.[56] The three prebendaries were no longer to be vicars choral whose number was now established at six, but in practice the position of sixth vicar was often left unfilled and the choir suffered from a shortage of members during the unsettled years after 1641.[57] It became the practice for the three prebendaries to be assisted by vicars choral who had to be in holy orders so that they could discharge these duties and in 1634, only two of the five vicars then being priests, the other three were required to take minor orders.[58] The unusual arrangement whereby many choirmen belonged to both Christ Church and St Patrick's cathedrals, often being appointed as a vicar choral in both cathedrals, may first have arisen following the re-opening of St Patrick's as a cathedral in 1555, some of its former choirmen having been appointed to Christ Church when St Patrick's was dissolved in 1547. Certainly from the 1620s a majority of the vicars choral of Christ Church are known to have belonged to both cathedrals, a situation which resulted in the vicars enjoying substantially increased incomes.[59] An augmentation of the choir proposed in 1638 within the context of Laudian reforms and the use of the incomes belonging to the guild of St Anne resulted in some additional appointments being made, but

---

50 Gillespie, *Proctor's accounts*, pp 45, 46.   51 Ibid., p. 68.   52 Gillespie, *Chapter act book*, p. 28.   53 Ibid., p. 86.   54 Dunton, *Teague land*, p. 380.   55 Gillespie, *Proctor's accounts*, p. 109.   56 Boydell, *Music*, p. 85.   57 Ibid., pp 60, 78.   58 Ibid., pp 68–9.   59 See Cotton, *Fasti*, ii, 84–9, 202–12; the paucity of records from St Patrick's before 1639 prevents a more accurate comparison of choir members, although Cotton does also note some common vicars choral in 1546.

these were short-lived and there were still six vicars choral following the Restoration.[60] Neither was a planned increase from four to six choirboys in 1638 realised. In addition to the vicars choral there were normally two stipendiaries, often appointed in the expectation of promotion to a vicar's place, but a vicar usually held his post for life unless he voluntarily resigned or was dismissed for absence or other misdemeanour. The shortage of basses in the choir was a recurring problem. Around Christmas 1613 'Mr Hoskins our bass' was in England and anthems had to be adapted or singers hired from St Patrick's.[61] There are references to 'the bass' in 1617 and 1626–7, while the excess of tenors and the scarcity of basses and countertenors was commented on in 1638.[62] Significantly, Thomas Bateson's anthem 'Holy, Lord God Almighty' composed c.1612 has only a single bass part, although scored for seven voices.[63] Vacancies in the choir were filled or applied for with reference to the appropriate voice,[64] but sometimes a place was sought by petition sponsored by the lord deputy in which cases the dean and chapter might feel bound to oblige even if there was technically no vacancy, as happened in 1592, and on other occasions special circumstances such as poverty might be pleaded.[65] Choirboys might also be appointed following a petition, usually by the boy's father or a close relative, or a plea on compassionate grounds supported by the organist.[66] A position as a choirboy brought with it free education, clothing and upkeep and must have been much sought after by parents. Choirboys with good voices may not always have been easy to find and in 1596–7 the mother of one choirboy was paid for her son to continue in the choir when she was considering removing him.[67] The terms of Thomas Bateson's contract as organist and master of the boys in 1609 only mentions his teaching them to sing,[68] but a set of *In nomines* (an important genre of viol consort music) belonging to the cathedral in the early seventeenth century suggests that the choirboys were taught the viol as part of their musical education and organ would certainly also have been taught.[69]

60 Boydell, *Music*, pp 96–7.   61 Ibid., p. 82; C6/1/26/3/10, f.3v; Hoskins was described in the account book of St Anne's guild as the 'great bass' (Royal Irish Academy, MS 12.D.1, f.29v).   62 Gillespie, *Chapter act book*, p. 139; C6/1/26/3/13, f. 4r; Boydell, *Music*, p. 73.   63 B.L., Add. MSS 17,792–6; New York Public Library, Drexel MSS 4180–5; transcribed in Boydell, *Music*, pp 187–93, recorded on *Sing (CD)*; on the origins of these MSS, *New Grove*, xvii, 716.   64 Boydell, *Music*, pp 69–70, 85–6.   65 Ibid., pp 55–6, 78.   66 Ibid., p. 59; C6/1/7/2, ff 39, 58v; Boydell, *Music*, p. 78.   67 Boydell, *Music*, p. 81; this choirboy may be the Anthony Wilkes who was organist of St Patrick's c.1606 (Grindle, *Cathedral music*, p. 224) and a stipendiary at Christ Church between 1625 and 1627 (C/6/26/1/3/11, f. 3r; Gillespie, *Chapter act book*, p. 149); on the difficulties in finding talented boys, Lehmberg, *Reformation*, p. 203.   68 Boydell, *Music*, p. 62.   69 T.C.D., MS 571, f. 140v, see also Gillespie, 'Borrowing'.

The role of music within the cathedral-state links which had been developing since the Reformation were further emphasised in 1638 within the context of government attempts to control the recusant guild of St Anne, developments in which the cathedral choir played an important role.[70] Both in order to bring the activities of the guild under closer church and state control and as a means of raising funds to pay for the elaboration of the cathedral and its services under the Arminian influence, a commission under the direct control of Lord Deputy Wentworth proposed that St Anne's guild would now use Christ Church rather than St Audoen's church for its services and that its revenues would be used in part to enlarge the cathedral choir and to increase the salaries of its members.[71] Since at least 1606 two choirboys and six men from either Christ Church or St Patrick's choirs, as well as the organist of Christ Church, had received regular salaries from St Anne's guild for singing in St Audoen's church.[72] Now, in 1638, the revenues of St Anne's were to be used to increase the number of vicars at Christ Church to ten, at least four of whom were to be priests, and two boys were to be added to bring their number to six. Furthermore, reflecting the Arminian desire for the elaboration of cathedral services, two cornetts and two sackbuts were to be provided for to accompany the choir, this enlarged choir attending on the two anniversaries of the guild which would continue to be celebrated in St Audoen's. Although some appointments were made under the terms of this certificate it appears that the planned expansion never came fully into effect.[73]

Lax practices within the church were addressed as part of Archbishop Bulkeley's reforms in the 1620s. A set of orders for the choir drawn up in 1627 following his visitation emphasised punctuality and the wearing of gowns and surplices as appropriate, the latter on Sundays and holy days.[74] The organist was to serve in the choir when not needed at the organ, and all vicars and stipendiaries were to take communion whenever it was served in the cathedral. New regulations in 1634 instigated under John Atherton further increased choir discipline: choir members were required to sit together, not

---

70 On St Anne's guild, Colm Lennon, 'The chantries in the Irish reformation: the case of St Anne's guild, Dublin, 1550–1630', in R.V. Comerford, Mary Cullen, J.R. Hill, Colm Lennon (ed.), *Religion, conflict and coexistence in Ireland: essays presented to Mgr Patrick J. Corish* (Dublin, 1990), pp 6–25; on the role of the choir in cathedral-state relations, Boydell, 'Cathedral music, city and state'.   71 Boydell, *Music*, pp 71–3, 86–8.   72 Account book of St Anne's guild, Royal Irish Academy, MS 12.D.1.   73 C6/1/7/2, ff 33, 33v, 38; in the proctors' accounts that survive for the years after 1638 the names of only five vicars and continuing references to only four boys still occur (C6/1/26/3/27–28); however, the St Anne's guild accounts continue to list payments to singers (and to sackbut players at Christmas 1639) up to May 1652 (Royal Irish Academy, MS 12.D.1, ff 72r–92r).   74 Boydell, *Music*, p. 64.

to talk during services, each 'respectively [to] perform his due part' when singing anthems, and to sing the doxology at the end of every psalm.[75] In 1639 the vicars were told not to laugh or jeer at any of their fellow singers following complaints that divine service was not performed in a 'due formal and becoming manner and decency'.[76]

The organists and masters of the choristers are not known between Robert Heyward in the 1540s and Walter Kennedy, a vicar since 1586 and referred to as organist in 1594.[77] Following Kennedy's resignation in November 1595 George Goshan, a former choirman who had since left Dublin, returned as organist until February 1596 when John Farmer arrived from England.[78] Farmer became a vicar choral in 1596 but was threatened with dismissal in 1597 for returning to England without licence.[79] It is not known when he ceased to be organist but he was apparently living in London in 1599 when his *First set of English madrigals* was published and there is no record of him at Christ Church after 1597.[80] Farmer's setting of the Lord's Prayer, his only sacred work to have remained in the repertory, dates from before his Dublin years.[81] Richard Myles, a vicar choral, was paid in January 1600 for training and selecting the choirboys,[82] but four months later John Fido, a trouble-some character who was briefly organist or vicar choral at Worcester, Lincoln and Hereford (on three occasions) in the 1590s and later at King's College, Cambridge, Wells, and again at Hereford and Worcester, was appointed to train the choristers for the choir.[83] It is likely that Myles and Fido (neither of whom are heard of again at Christ Church) also acted as organists.[84]

Thomas Bateson, formerly organist of Chester cathedral and best known for his two books of madrigals (London, 1604 and 1618), was installed as a vicar choral on 24 March 1609 and formally as organist and choirmaster on 5 April.[85] He had already been engaged on 9 March as organist at St Audoen's church, a position held throughout the first half of the seventeenth century by the organist of Christ Church.[86] Bateson was appointed for life, remaining at Christ Church until his death in 1630.[87] As well as playing the

75 Ibid., pp 66–9.   76 Ibid., pp 74–5.   77 Cotton, *Fasti*, ii, 82; Boydell, *Music*, p. 85; for succession list of organists to 1800, Boydell, *Music*, pp 250–1; compare Shaw, *Organists*, pp 407–16.   78 Boydell, *Music*, pp 26, 80–1.   79 Ibid., p. 57.   80 *New Grove*, vi, 402; E.H. Fellowes claimed that Farmer returned to Dublin where he remained until the spring of 1599 (*The English madrigal composers* (Oxford, 1921), p. 241).   81 Published in Thomas East, *The whole booke of psalms* (London, 1592).   82 Boydell, *Music*, pp 57–8.   83 Boydell, *Music*, p. 58; on Fido, Watkins Shaw, *The organists and organs of Hereford cathedral* (Hereford, 1976), pp 10–12; Payne, *Provision and practice*, pp 76–7.   84 Although he does not appear in the records after 1600, Grindle lists Myles as organist from 1600 to 1608 (*Cathedral music*, p. 222).   85 Boydell, *Music*, pp 60–3.   86 Royal Irish Academy, MS 12. D. 1, f. 23v; see also Boydell, 'Cathedral music, city and state'.   87 Boydell, *Music*, pp 65, 86.

organ, for which he was allowed a deputy, he taught and was granted full authority over the choirboys and also sang in the choir. His stipend as vicar choral was supplemented by £8 13s. 4d. (English) annually and he was provided with a house within the precincts. In 1612 Bateson was granted the first music degree awarded by Trinity College, Dublin,[88] and in 1616 he was instrumental in providing a new organ for the cathedral. The copying of Bateson's contract into the chapter acts, the only occasion this was ever done for an organist in the cathedral's history, reflects the importance placed by the dean and chapter on the appointment of such a relatively prominent English musician, an appointment which falls within the context of the increasing numbers of Englishmen brought to Christ Church as part of Protestant Reformation policy.[89]

Randall (Randolph) Jewett, who took over as organist directly after Bateson's death in March 1630, was, like Bateson, formerly at Chester.[90] He may possibly have been related to John Jewett from Fethard, County Wexford, a countertenor in the choir of Christ Church from 1620 to 1640.[91] Within months of taking up his appointment Jewett was disciplined for disobedience and admonished daily to teach the choristers singing.[92] The following year his salary was increased to £15 annually on condition of good service (it was further increased to £20 in 1634) and Richard Galvan, a choir member, was paid as an assistant organist.[93] Jewett was the first person to combine the posts of organist at both Christ Church and St Patrick's cathedrals as was later to become common.[94] He was appointed a vicar choral in June 1638 but by July Benjamin Rogers was acting as organist, being formally appointed in 1639.[95] Jewett remained as master of the boys until December 1639 (and possibly up to 1643 when he was organist at Chester cathedral).[96] By January 1645 he was back in Dublin as a vicar (and apparently organist) at St Patrick's and in July 1646 he successfully petitioned for a vicar choral's place at Christ Church.[97] Whether or not he acted as organist during this final year before cathedral services were suppressed in 1647 is not clear: the position of organist at St Audoen's church (usually held by the organist of Christ Church) was granted in July 1645 to John Hawkshaw 'in the absence of Randall Jewett', but

88 Brian Boydell, 'Thomas Bateson and the earliest degree in music awarded by the university of Dublin' in *Hermathena*, cxlvi (1989), pp 53–60.   89 On Bateson's appointment see further Boydell, 'Cathedral music, city and state'.   90 Boydell, *Music*, p. 82; *New Grove*, ix, 613.   91 See Boydell, *Music*, pp 85–6; the death of a chorister named James Jewett, possibly a son of either Randall or John Jewett, is noted in 1636, C6/1/7/2, f. 16.   92 Boydell, *Music*, p. 65.   93 Ibid., pp 61, 69.   94 Grindle, *Cathedral music*, p. 224.   95 Boydell, *Music*, pp 69, 70–1, 74–5; C6/1/7/2, 19 June 1638. Shaw, *Organists*, p. 409 incorrectly states that Randall Jewett was in deacon's orders by 1638, this reference being to John, not Randall (see Boydell, *Music*, p. 71).   96 Boydell, *Music*, p. 75.   97 Shaw, *Organists*, p. 417; Boydell, *Music*, p. 78.

reverted again to Jewett in July 1648.[98] Benjamin Rogers's tenure as organist was short-lived, for in 1641 he was a lay clerk at Windsor,[99] his departure possibly prompted by the rebellion of that year and the cathedral's worsening financial conditions which led the following year to the organist's salary being halved.[100] The organ at Christ Church in the late sixteenth century was small enough to be moved into the quire on special occasions and in 1612 Henry Alyngton was paid for mending 'the organs'.[101] Four years later Bateson was contracted to build a new instrument costing £35.[102] It was reported in 1635 that damage was being caused to the organ by people sitting or standing too close to it, but there is no information about where it was located.[103]

The assistance of the lord deputy's musicians at services in the 1590s has already been noted and musicians were employed on the occasion of a visitation between 1615 and 1617.[104] The use of instruments on a regular basis is suggested by the dissatisfaction expressed by William Bedell (later bishop of Kilmore and Ardagh) between 1627 and 1629 with 'the pompous service at Christ's church in Dublin, which was attended and celebrated with all manner of instrumental music, as organs, sackbuts, cornetts, viols, etc'.[105] The object of Bedell's complaints is corroborated by a payment in 1629–30 'to them that played on the cornetts',[106] but his puritanical views did not prevail. During the 1630s Christ Church became the flagship for Laudian reform in Ireland and this is directly reflected in the provision for instrumentalists to adorn the music.[107] Seats for a violinist and a sackbut player were provided between 1636 and 1638, two sackbuts and two cornetts were paid in March 1638 for their 'service and attendance', and later in the same year it was suggested that two sackbuts and two cornetts should play every Sunday in Christ Church.[108] This growing use of instruments from the late sixteenth century reflects contemporary practice at many English cathedrals, although the specific use of a violin in 1636 is exceptional before the Restoration.[109] While they may also have played voluntaries and other purely instrumental music, the musicians playing 'in the choir and helping our vicars' in 1594–5 shows that they did accompany the voices as well.[110]

The increasing evidence for the purchase and copying of new music at this period also reflects developments at English cathedrals.[111] Paper was

98 Royal Irish Academy, MS 12.D.1, f. 74r; Jewett was organist and master of the choristers at Winchester cathedral from 1666 until his death in 1675 (New Grove, ix, p. 613). 99 New Grove, xvi, 102. 100 Boydell, Music, p. 77. 101 Ibid., pp 80–1. 102 Ibid., pp 63, 82. 103 Ibid., p. 70. 104 Ibid., p. 82; on the use of instruments in English cathedrals, Payne, Provision and practice, pp 147–55. 105 Shuckburgh, Bedell, pp 153–4. 106 Boydell, Music, p. 83. 107 See further Boydell, 'Cathedral music, city and state'. 108 Boydell, Music, pp 70, 71, 83, 84; on Laudianism and cathedral music, Payne, Provision and practice, pp 80–92. 109 Payne, Provision and practice, pp 148–9; Boydell, Music, p. 83. 110 Boydell, Music, p. 80. 111 Payne, Provision and practice, pp 73–8.

bought, music copied and choir books bound between 1594 and 1598 and in 1613,[112] and a year later two service books bought and three services copied.[113] Existing music was repaired or bound in 1625–6 and 1634–5, service books, unspecified anthems and a 'service book for the organist' bought on various occasions during the 1630s, and in 1632–3 boxes were provided in the choir 'for each vicar to put his books in'.[114] None of the above payments mentions composers or specific titles and no music manuscripts of this period survive from Christ Church. The close links between Christ Church and English cathedrals suggest a common repertoire represented by composers like Gibbons, Weelkes or Tomkins which survives in hand-copied choirbooks from English cathedrals, no collections of printed Anglican liturgical music (as distinct from psalm settings) appearing between 1565 (Day's *Certaine notes*) and 1641 (Barnard's *The first book of selected church musick*). Organists and some of the vicars choral undoubtedly would have composed anthems or services for Christ Church, but few pieces of music associated with the cathedral during this period can be identified. Bateson's full anthem 'Holy, Lord God Almighty' is believed to have been composed for the occasion of his being conferred with a Mus.B. degree from Trinity College Dublin in 1612, the text being chosen to honour both Trinity College and Christ Church (dedicated to the Holy Trinity). It survives in two sources (one incomplete), both copied by John Merro of Gloucester in the 1620s.[115] A book entitled *Anthems to be sung ... in the cathedrall church of the Holy and Undivided Trinity in Dublin* published in 1662 contains texts (but no music) of fifty-one verse anthems, nearly all by composers prominent in the earlier seventeenth century, and many of these anthems must have been in the cathedral's repertoire at that time. Four anthems are included by Randall Jewett and two by Benjamin Rogers. It is possible that some of these date from their Christ Church years.[116]

Choral services at some English cathedrals were already ceasing from late 1642[117] but in Dublin cathedral services would continue for some years, although financial difficulties affecting the choir had been growing. As early as 1639 the choir had petitioned for payment 'in respect of the uncertainty of the state of the church', in 1641 choir payments were in arrears, and in November 1643 the vicars choral and prebendaries complained that they had not received any rents 'for a long time'.[118] Complaints by the chapter in

---

112 Boydell, *Music*, pp 80–1; the payment in Nov. 1613 for '11 ruled paper books for church songs' was to Andrew Auden, an otherwise unrecorded Dublin stationer.   113 Boydell, *Music*, p. 82.   114 Ibid., pp 75, 82–4.   115 See note 63.   116 T.C.D., shelf mark r. f. 53; for a fuller discussion of the contents, Boydell, *Music*, pp 174, 176.   117 Collinson *et al.*, *Canterbury*, p. 450; Owen, *Lincoln*, p. 75; Payne, *Provision and practice*, pp 170–1.   118 Boydell, *Music*, pp 74, 77; C6/1/26/3/28, f. 4v.

February 1645 that service in the choir was 'slenderly performed for want of number, and fit and able men' must have reflected the climate of the times as much as the age and ability of the choirmen.[119] There is however no mention of any direct threat to the cathedral music and in July 1646 the chapter could still look forward to the continuing existence of the choir, promising the next vacancy as a vicar choral to John Heydock, the oldest stipendiary.[120] Stipendiaries were appointed as late as 14 June 1647 at the final recorded chapter meeting before cathedral services ceased,[121] some of the choirmen continuing thereafter to sing at St Patrick's cathedral for a further three years before all cathedral services ceased in Dublin.

119 Boydell, *Music*, p. 78.   120 Ibid., p. 78.   121 C6/1/7/2, f. 71v; Boydell, *Music*, p. 79.

THE MODERN CATHEDRAL

XIII

Restoration and reorganisation, 1660–1830

Kenneth Milne

Although there were many similarities between the structures of church and state in the 1630s and the 1660s, so many changes had taken place in personnel, property and policy in the course of the interregnum that there could be no return to the *status quo* that had obtained at the end of Charles I's reign. The cathedral building had continued in use as a place of worship, however changed in form that worship had been. Furthermore, it had been attended by a prestigious congregation, whose physical safety and comfort would not have been neglected. The task facing the restored dean and chapter, so far as the fabric was concerned, had mainly to do with the re-ordering of the interior of the church for a return to Anglican worship.

What was restored bore the hallmarks of Wentworth's Laudian experiment,[1] and Ormond, the viceroy, who exerted himself energetically in the interests of the established church, was 'a man of exemplary piety' who 'found in the daily offices a source of strength in his difficult post'.[2] His duchess contributed to the cost of adorning the building with a rich crimson pulpit cloth and canopy and donated two silver flagons.[3] The Caroline tradition of eucharistic doctrine was evident in the Book of Common Prayer of 1662, and the embellishment of communion table and sanctuary showed clearly that Christ Church intended the sacrament to be celebrated in a setting of some splendour. Candlesticks (presumably, contrary to post-disestablishment practice, intended to hold lighted candles) were part of the magnificent 'royal plate' presented by William III, a suitably secure iron chest being provided for it in 1710.[4] By 1663, there were carved communion rails and pulpit cloths with scarlet fringes.[5] In 1668 black and white tiles were laid inside the altar

---

1 See ch. X above. 2 F.R. Bolton, *Caroline tradition*, pp 51, 187. 3 C6/1/4, p. 2.
4 C6/1/7/4, 30 Sept. 1710. A detailed description of the royal plate by M.S.D. Westropp is appended to Lawlor, 'Chapel of Dublin castle'. 5 C6/1/26/3; C6/1/4, f. 2.

rails and fifty-six ounces of gold and purple silk were purchased for the altar cloth and communion table.[6] A description of work on the sanctuary in 1725 referred to the 'altar of the communion table in the choir of the church' being enlarged, with new rails and new gilding, the floor of the choir to be new-flagged with black and white squares, and a piece of crimson velvet with gold lace being inserted 'for the middle panel over the communion table'.[7] In 1734 a reward was offered for the capture of a thief who made off with the silk lace surround of the communion table carpet, presumably that newly provided in 1725.[8] A sum of £10 14s. was expended in the year 1679–80 on carving the king's arms and shields.[9]

In a sense, the chapter as it was reconstituted in 1661 had undergone a greater transformation than that experienced by the building. John Creighton, the chancellor, was the sole survivor of pre-Commonwealth years. He returned from exile to find that, his death being assumed, the chancellorship had been given to the Revd James Vaughan. Creighton petitioned the lords justices for reinstatement, and they found in his favour. Vaughan was asked to make way, which he did, and was shortly afterwards appointed warden of Galway.[10] The six new appointments had much in common with their pre-decessors. Three members of the chapter, the dean, the treasurer and the prebendary of St Michael's, were Englishmen who came to Ireland in 1660, presumably for ecclesiastical preferment. All three seem to have got it. Mossom, the dean, became bishop of Derry in 1666, and William Fuller, the treasurer, was not only simultaneously dean of St Patrick's, but became bishop of Limerick in 1664. However, William Reresby, from Yorkshire, prebendary of St Michael's, was back in England within a year as a prebendary of Lincoln. The other four members of the chapter had all been in Ireland before 1660. William Lightburne had been the Cromwellian minister at St Audoen's and Thomas Bladen (son of William Bladen, the king's printer in Ireland in the 1640s), prebendary of St John's. Of the chapter members at the Restoration, five were graduates of Trinity College, Dublin, as at least were four pre-interregnum. By 1681, of the eight members of the chapter of Christ Church, five (possibly six) were Trinity graduates, though at least two of these were not Irish-born.

How the Restoration chapter was selected is not entirely clear, though it has always been recognised that chaplaincy to the lord lieutenant was a sure path to advancement in the Church of Ireland, if not necessarily as far as the bench. Only one out of four of those who served the first duke of Ormond as chaplains during his terms as viceroy attained episcopal rank.[11]

6 C6/1/4, f. 173.   7 C6/1/7/5, 5 Apr. 1725.   8 C6/1/7/5, 12 Feb. 1734.   9 C6/1/4, p. 40.   10 C6/1/7/2, f. 100; Leslie, 'Fasti'; Hardiman, *Galway*, p. 247.   11 F.E. Ball, 'Some notes on the households of the dukes of Ormond' in *R.I.A. Proc.*, xxxviii, C (1928–9),

It is, however, noteworthy that cathedral dignities frequently came their way. Three chaplains were successive deans of Christ Church: John Parry (1666–77), William Moreton (1677–88) and Welbore Ellis (1693–1705), Parry having been treasurer for a few months in 1660. Precentorships went to Henry Hall (1647–60), Thomas Hinde (1679–80) and Peter Drelincourt (1681–1722), and chancellorships to Benjamin Phipps (1670–82) and Nathaniel Wilson (1682–3). Likewise, we find erstwhile chaplains among the prebendaries. Henry Hall began his association with the cathedral as prebendary of St Michael's. Daniel Witter held that stall from 1662 to 1665. John Parker (from 1643 to 1660) and Daniel Neyland (from 1661 to 1668) were successively prebendaries of St Michan's, while the egregious Thomas Bladen was prebendary of St John's from 1660 to 1695.

Robert Mossom was the first of the post-interregnum deans of Christ Church. The chapter acts record his installation by the archdeacon and most of the chapter on 2 February 1661, who

> having the organ playing, and the singers of the church going before them singing holy hymns, brought the said Dr Mossom into the choir of the said church, and before divine service and sermon instituted him, and after in like manner brought him again into the chapter house, where, after taking the oaths required in that behalf, he was placed in a chair and obtained a voice in the chapter as was usual.[12]

A native of Lincolnshire, and a Cambridge graduate, Mossom was in favour in political circles in England, having an outstanding record both as a royalist and churchman during the interregnum. He had been a particularly strong advocate of the rights of clergy who had suffered economically and otherwise at that time, having, as he said, 'tasted the bitterest of sufferings', though able to maintain his family in some 'plentiful subsistence'.[13] It is not surprising that, while expressing his willingness to work in Ireland, he had let it be known that this would involve him in great expense. Believing that his income in Dublin would be uncertain, he also obtained the precentorship of St Patrick's. The endowments of the established church had suffered considerably as a result of the political upheavals of the 1640s and 1650s, and when the crown restored to the church various revenues lost previously by confiscation, it was Mossom who brought to Ireland the royal letters of glad

---

pp 1–20.   12 C6/1/7/2, f. 85. Special emphasis was placed on the first four of the 1634 canons, prescribing the use of the *Book of Common Prayer* and no other, and declaring that those who denied the necessity of episcopal consecration were worthy of excommunication. 13 *D.N.B.* sub 'Mossom, Robert'; *An apology in the behalf of the sequestered clergy presented to the high court of parliament, 1660* (London, 1760), p. 12 (margin).

tidings that enabled the various dignitaries concerned to collect their newly-released incomes.[14] In 1666 Mossom received preferment to the see of Derry, Bramhall, the primate, indicating to the archbishop of Dublin that he would like the consecration to be held in Christ Church, and the chapter agreeing.[15] John Parry succeeded Mossom, and when Parry was appointed bishop of Ossory in 1672 he retained the deanery of Christ Church, by no means the first or last time that Christ Church was to have an episcopal dean.

William Moreton, who came to the cathedral in 1677, presided over the chapter for the rest of the century. When he was made bishop of Kildare in 1682, he obtained a licence to continue to hold the deanery *in commendam* 'by reason of the poverty of the see',[16] a link that continued until it was broken in 1846 under the provisions of the Church Temporalities Act of 1833. The diocese of Kildare seems not to have had a residence for its bishop, and so Moreton continued to live in the dean's mansion near the cathedral, as did his successors for generations to come. The other dignitaries, all crown appointments,[17] seem to have performed their duties adequately, but the same could not be said of at least one of the prebendaries, Dr Thomas Bladen. A veritable vicar of Bray, Bladen served as a Commonwealth minister until 1660,[18] and was to survive several serious accusations of negligence as prebendary of St John's, including a petition by the churchwardens to the dean and chapter in 1669, in which he was accused of behaving 'negligently, carelessly, uncomfortably, unconscionably and uncharitably'.[19] The complaints against Bladen throw some light on what parishioners in the prebendal parishes expected of their clergy, for the two churchwardens, George Kennedy and Thomas Morton, beg to be given 'a faithful minister'. They list sixteen causes of complaint, such as refusing to answer sick calls (in the case of one urgent call Bladen 'flew into a passion', allegedly saying that 'he would not be made a pack-horse'). This was not the only time that another minister had to be sent for. Worse still, it was reputed that he had refused to baptise a sick child, while on other occasions charging for baptisms. He had, allegedly, not administered holy communion since Easter (this was January) and, in the summer of 1668 had absented himself for two months without appointing a deputy. In fact, the chapter had authorised a period of absence, but he had overstayed it, and had had to be recalled.[20] There was much else besides, including alleged abuse of the consistorial court to obtain dues. Bladen survived, only to be arraigned in 1691 for his allegedly simon-ical behaviour 'in the late calamitous time of the late King James II', when

14 *Hastings MSS*, iv, 100.   15 C6/1/7/2, f. 143v.   16 Cotton, *Fasti*.   17 For exam-ple, Dr James Vaughan presents his letters patent of appointment to the chancellorship and John Parry his to the treasurership, C6/1/7/ 2, ff 86v–7.   18 J.B. Leslie, *Succession list of the clergy of Ardfert* (Dublin, 1940), p. 17.   19 C6/1/7/2, f. 172.   20 Ibid., f. 161v.

his ambitions extended to episcopal office in England. Using every legal device open to him he held his prebend until his death.[21]

In addition to the dignitaries and those associated with the music (the organist, organ-blower, stipendiaries, vicars choral, and the singing-boys and their master), various other functionaries played their part in the life of the institution. There were the 'readers', for instance. The prebendaries were paid £20 a year to read services in the cathedral and were expected to attend also on Sundays and holydays. They employed as 'readers' clergy who would say the daily offices for them, and in particular the morning prayers at six o'clock. When the income of the prebendaries from their property fell in 1689, the cathedral undertook to pay the readers out of the 'oeconomy', the cathedral's corporate income.[22] Another participant in the liturgical sequence was the cathedral verger, sometimes referred to as the dean's verger and sometimes as sexton. He was provided with a new gown in 1703[23] and his verge was repaired in 1708.[24] His duties were not entirely ceremonial. He could, for instance, find himself discharging such unenviable tasks as boarding up the rooms of an absconding cathedral tenant,[25] or taking custody of an offender,[26] or collecting (by distraint) arrears of cess due on the beadle's salary.[27] The beadle, or constable, had duties related to law and order in the precincts. The chapter's business was serviced by the chapter clerk,[28] who, among other things, attended to the formalities when vicars choral and stipendiaries were admitted, receiving a fee for his pains.[29]

These elaborate cathedral structures existed primarily for the maintenance of the daily round of public worship and the liturgical marking of major occasions in public life. The cathedral, understandably, made much of its status as chapel royal, a distinction formalised in 1672 by letter of Charles II to the lord lieutenant in which the king referred to Christ Church as 'that our said cathedral church and royal chapel', many of whose 'great and ancient privileges, immunities and jurisdictions, granted and confirmed by many of our royal predecessors' had, through the disorders of recent years 'been lost or embezzled'.[30] Its legal standing as such was questioned from time to time,[31] and considerable doubts about the legal basis of the cathedral's traditional claims were expressed

---

21 C6/1/7/3, f. 78 (19 Oct. 1691; 5 Dec. 1695). The chapter minutes record the fact that his widow, daughter of Lord Blayney, claimed (and obtained) the income due to him up to the previous Michaelmas. Bladen inherited his powers of survival from his father William, the king's printer in Ireland and editor of the first Irish newspaper, who retained his office under Cromwell (Robert Munter, *The history of the Irish newspaper 1685–1760* (Cambridge, 1967), pp 6–7).   22 C6/1/7/3, 31 Oct. 1689.   23 Ibid., 1 Feb. 1703.   24 C6/1/7/4, 7 Aug. 1708.   25 C6/1/7/2, f. 108.   26 Ibid., f. 119.   27 Ibid., f. 124.   28 Gillespie, *Thomas Howell*.   29 C6/1/7/2, p. 246.   30 Letter dated 14 June 1672, copy in P.R.O., SP 63/331/89.   31 See p. 282 below.

by H.J. Lawlor in 1923.[32] However, the dean and chapter (who seem to have relied on precedent, and may have been unaware of the survival of the letter of 1672) were satisfied that the chapter acts clearly showed 'that the said cathedral is recognised as his majesty's chapel royal in Ireland both before and after the building of the present chapel in Dublin castle',[33] and such benefactions as that of Charles II in or about 1668 'towards the adorning of the seat of the right honourable his majesty's lieutenant and privy council of this kingdom and of the seat of the chief governor's lady' signify a special place for Christ Church in national life.[34] Public perception was clear on the matter. John Dunton, the London bookseller who travelled Ireland in the late 1690s, attended morning service at Christ Church and commented 'Hither the government come to church as the king's chapel royal. They sit over the great door of the quire and the ascent to it from the aisle is by two large stair-cases'.[35]

By 1760, when George III succeeded to the throne, there were no fewer than twenty days of commemoration in Ireland, celebrated with varying degrees of pomp, though by no means all of them were observed by the cathedral. 30 January, however, was an occasion of some ceremony, when throughout the 1720s and 1730s the lords justices processed to Christ Church to hear a sermon commemorating 'the barbarous and bloody murder of that pious martyr King Charles I'.[36] 23 October was a particularly auspicious date, marking as it did the discovery of the plot to seize Dublin castle in 1641. Leaders of state and city attended Christ Church, the duke of Rutland being the last viceroy to attend the cathedral for this occasion in 1784, the political climate changing thereafter, at least at government level.[37] In the 1780s, St Patrick's day received official recognition.[38] The weekly round of daily and weekly services continued, with its own high festivals, crowned by Easter, and we have a description of the celebration of Holy Communion at Christ Church on Easter Sunday 1675:

> The most reverend the lord archbishop of Dublin [Michael Boyle], chancellor of Ireland, having performed the communion office with

---

32 Lawlor, 'Chapel of Dublin castle', pp 34, 66–7.   33 C6/1/6/4/3/7. There was more to the argument than a question of dignity. The matter of the provenance of the royal plate was at issue. William Butler wrote (1901) that on Christ Church ceasing to be the Chapel Royal in 1814, when Francis Johnston's building was opened, the plate was transferred there (Butler, *Christ Church*, pp 40–1). But Lawlor, in the absence of any record of this transfer, conjectured that the plate had always been in the castle, coming to Christ Church in 1922 for the first time.   34 C6/1/4/, f. 1.   35 Dunton, *Teague land*, p. 380.   36 James Kelly, '"The glorious and immortal memory": commemoration and Protestant identity in Ireland 1660–1800' in *R.I.A. Proc.*, xciv, C (1994), pp 42–52. Commemoration', pp 25–52. 37 Jacqueline Hill, *From patriots to unionists: Dublin civic politics and Irish Protestant patriotism, 1660–1840* (Oxford, 1997), p. 242n.   38 Kelly, 'Commemoration', p. 48.

singular decency and good order, he himself reverently took the sacred communion and gave it to the ministers of the altar, then to the lord lieutenant, to the peers and royal council, and to a numerous concourse: all received it with singular devotion; having for associates in giving it the most reverend the archbishop of Armagh, primate of all Ireland, the right reverend the bishop of Meath, the chief of the bishops of Ireland; after the metropolitans and three dignitaries of the Church, there were doctors in divinity to administer the cup, each one making a godly brief exhortation to the receiver for a due receiving of it, the lord archbishop having read at the communion table a grave and pious homily, exhorting to a right preparation for receiving the venerable sacament, as is usually done in all churches upon such an occasion.[39]

It was not exceptional for the lord lieutenant to be there. He attended on Sundays and holy days throughout the year, the offices of morning prayer and evening prayer being sung each Sunday, with the addition of a celebration of holy communion (as required by the canons of the Irish church) monthly. Edward Wetenhall, the precentor for 1675–8, claimed that the 'ancient custom of sermons on Sundays and holy days continued in cathedral and collegiate churches' and this is borne out by the Christ Church preachers' books.[40]

   In 1733 the dean and chapter agreed to a rota whereby the dignitaries and prebendaries took turns at preaching on Sundays, commencing with the dean on Advent Sunday.[41] A comparison of the rota with the preachers' books makes it clear, not only that the members of the chapter often preached by proxy, but that several of them appear never to have preached at all. The deans were honourable exceptions, being regular preachers. The compilation of the rota implies that by 1733 the cathedral had abandoned any hope of maintaining the ancient practice whereby the dignitaries of St Patrick's had taken their turn of preaching at Christ Church, an obligation from which they were seeking to extract themselves at least as early as 1701, when the dean of Christ Church complained that they were not doing their duty.[42] In 1708 Christ Church recorded its 'disappointment' in the matter and asked the chapter of St Patrick's to impose sanctions on those of its members who neither took their turn nor 'supported their turn' with the necessary engagement of a substitute.[43] In 1714, St Patrick's asked for reasons why the agreement should be kept, and the best answer that Christ Church could come

39 Bolton, *Caroline tradition*, pp 167–8.   40 Wetenhall, *Of gifts and offices*, p. 783; C6/1/21/1–16, for the years 1727–1943.   41 C6/1/7/5, 15 Dec. 1733.   42 C6/1/7/3, 13 Jan. 1702.   43 C6/1/7/4, 28 Dec. 1708.

up with was that it was very ancient. Dean Welbore Ellis is reputed to have blamed Jonathan Swift for bringing the custom to an end.[44]

Three services were held each weekday, beginning with the six o'clock prayers in St Mary's chapel, morning and evening prayer being sung later in the day. By early nineteenth century, the early morning prayers were said at 8.00 a.m. in winter and 6.00 a.m. in summer. Sometimes they were said by a vicar choral, who received an additional emolument for so doing. Thus the Revd John Jones, a vicar choral from 1728 to 1738 was paid £15 per annum (increased to £20 some months later) for performing the service in place of the Revd Ralph Sedgwick, whose name does not appear among those of either vicars choral or other clergy.[45] In 1698 the six o'clock prayers were said by the Revd Walter Atkins (or Atkin), a minor canon of St Patrick's.[46] A leaflet of 1719, listing the services in Dublin cathedrals and churches gives those at Christ Church as 6 and 10 a.m. and 4 p.m., with holy communion being administered on the first Sunday of the month.[47]

There were those among the dignitaries who cared greatly that things should always be done decently and in order, and not only on major occasions. Edward Wetenhall, precentor, whose exhaustive treatment of preaching, singing and praying has already been referred to, was conscious of the ever present risk of liturgy being treated as entertainment, his dissertation being 'designed to make people more sober, and regular and serious in public worship'. Not that cathedral worship was to everyone's taste, then as now, and there survives an extraordinarily unflattering description of divine worship at Christ Church, published early in the eighteenth century, purporting to be that of two northerners (or Scots), ship-hands sailing from Portaferry, and cast adrift in Dublin one Sunday morning.[48] They were distracted from their search for a more acceptable form of worship by the sight of the lord mayor going to Christ Church. They followed him in, but were far from edified. They noted the 'two great stairways', the 'brass bird' and the 'table railed round with two books on it and two brass candlesticks with candles.' They noted a functionary with keys, admitting people to their seats. Nor were they seduced by the 'whistle pipe', noting that when the clergy approached the end of the church where the table was 'they bowed as they

44 Irwin Ehrenpreis, *Swift: the man, his works, and the age* (3 vols, London, 1962–83), iii, 73.   45 C6/1/7/5, 15 May, 17 Aug. 1730.   46 C6/1/7/3, 24 Mar. 1698; Leslie, 'Biographical evidence', R.C.B., MS 61/4/1, pp 42–3.   47 *An address to absenters from the public worship of God: with an answer to their pleas* (3rd ed., London and Dublin, 1719). 48 *The northcountryman's description of Christ Church in a letter to a friend* (n.d. [1720]). Could it be, as the catalogue for the Gilbert collection speculates, that this was a piece of Swiftian malice? Though ordained deacon and priest at Christ Church, Swift's attitude was hostile, both for personal and official reasons. See Ehrenpreis, *Swift*, ii, 100–2.

went'. But most of all they were conscious of a great deal of coming and
going on the part of both clergy and congregation.

Maintenance of the building was an ongoing (and sometimes neglected)
obligation on the dean and chapter, and the funding of it was, or ought to
have been, a first charge on the income of the cathedral oeconomy. While
rents and fines from the living constituted the oeconomy's major source of
money, the dead also brought in revenue, for burial within the cathedral was
something to be desired by Dublin's civic and political élite, and the associated fees, such as those laid down in 1661,[49] posed no deterrent. The clergy
who conducted the burials were entitled to dues, as were the organists who
played and the choristers who sang. Payment was exacted for opening the
grave, the nearer the sanctuary the more expensive, and there was also a
charge for 'palls, pulpit-cloths and other mournings'. All such fees were
regarded, in part, as an entitlement of office, but were also seen as a contribution to the maintenance of the building.

Jealous though they were of their own personal interests and of their
trusteeship, the dean and chapter had certain funds at their disposal for charitable purposes also. For instance, in January 1699,[50] they entered into an
agreement with the churchwardens of St John's for the distribution of bread
to the poor, and asked one of their number, the prebendary of that parish,
to ensure that this was done. Some cathedral employment was regarded as
an entitlement to charity, and emoluments seem from time to time to have
been supplemented by gratuities. In 1730, payments of £6 each were made
to three men and 40s. to a woman, Jane Corbet, who was also awarded £3
per annum to buy mops and keep the quire clean.[51] She was a verger's widow,
and in the promotions consequent on her husband's death, she was made
organ-blower,[52] and got paid for washing the boy choristers' surplices,[53] none
of which seems to have rendered her ineligible for charity payments that
appear mostly to have been paid in December.[54] Regular small payments were
made over a number of years to the Revd Isaac Leake, 'a disordered clergy-
man'.[55] Harsh winters bore heavily on the poor, and that of 1739–40 was, to
quote the chapter minutes, 'calamitous'. The very considerable sum of £40
was allocated by the chapter for relief: £20 for the poor of the precincts and
liberties, and £20 for general distribution to the poor of the city [56] during 'a
long extraordinary cold season', as Swift recorded.[57] The cathedral acknowl-

49 C6/1/7/2, f. 95. For a full treatment of burial practices at Christ Church see Refaussé
& Lennon, *Registers*.   50 C6/1/7/3, 19 Jan. 1699.   51 C6/1/7/5, 7 Dec. 1730.   52
Ibid., 18 Nov. 1731.   53 Ibid., 4 Dec. 1732.   54 Ibid., 6 Dec. 1731, 4 Dec. 1732, 3 Dec.
1733. For a detailed account of the cathedral's 'servants', their personalities, duties and
conditions of work, see Gillespie, *Thomas Howell*.   55 C6/1/7/5, 26 Apr. 1731, 10 June
1734, 5 Dec. 1737.   56 Ibid., 23 Jan. 1740.   57 St Patrick's and many parishes also

edged a particular responsibility for boy choristers whose family circumstances deteriorated, and when one boy's father died, not only did the chapter seek for a master to whom he might be apprenticed, but also undertook to pay the apprenticeship fee.[58] It was enlightened self-interest to look after the welfare of the boys, and to make membership of the choir attractive to families, many of which must have valued the association with the cathedral, not only for reasons of prestige but also for the economic benefits that it brought.

Edward Wetenhall's account of how things were ordered at Christ Church in the 1670s, says that the 'children' were brought up 'in the art of music and in some other parts of good literature, as we find them capable.' Music, grammar, 'humane learning' and religion comprised the curriculum.[59] Sir James Ware described Thomas Seele, provost of Trinity and dean of St Patrick's from 1666 to 1675, as being 'the son of an officer of Christ Church ... from whence he derived little more than his education, until he was better provided for in the college'.[60] But the fact that there would appear usually to have been only two teachers for the boys (the master of the choristers and one other) was not, given the handful of scholars, exceptional for the time. Our modern concept of classroom management was unknown, and a form of group tutoring was the norm. Furthermore, at least from the 1760s, the boys were taken in by Trinity College *gratis*, some in due course returning to the cathedral as vicars or stipendiaries.

The maintenance of the cathedral establishment and its liturgical life depended on the provision of adequate financial support, and given the uncertainties at the time of the Restoration, it is not to be wondered at that the newly-appointed dean, Robert Mossom, together with several other deans-designate, before embarking for Ireland in September 1660, petitioned the government to the effect that, while they were ready to travel to take up their assignments, they had to give thought to 'the need for support and subsistence during the coming winter', and sought assurances (such as the bishops had obtained) that the income from their several offices would be forthcoming.[61] Mossom's immediate anxieties were allayed, but it took time for claims of one kind or another to be settled. For example, the tithe entitlements of the vicars choral and choirmen of both the Dublin cathedrals were confirmed only in 1671.[62] However, the established church fared better than most other property-holders under the Restoration land settlement, for, with the restoration of the monarchy came also the restoration, for the most part, of eccle-

---

responded charitably to the crisis (Ehrenpreis, *Swift*, iii, 899–900).   **58** C6/1/7/5, 18 June 1739.   **59** Wetenhall, *Of gifts and offices*, pp 532, 543. For more detail of the boy choristers' conditions, see ch. xiv.   **60** James Ware, 'History and antiquities of Dublin collected by his son, 1678', 2 vols, transcript in the Gilbert collection, i., 346.   **61** *Cal. S. P. Ire., 1663–5*, p. 466.   **62** *Calendar of treasury books, 1669–72*, pt 2, p. 846.

siastical property to its former owners.[63] 'His majesty's gracious declaration' of 1660 vested in the king, through the Irish parliament, all land confiscated since 23 October 1641 as a 'consequence of the rebellion', with general exception of the land held on that date by the church and Trinity College.[64] The process of restitution was to some extent delayed by the clear indication from the crown that justice was to be tempered with mercy when dealing with leases entered into during the interregnum. The records of Christ Church tell of several instances when tenants who gained possession of property during that period were allowed to remain,[65] and when disputes arose the dean and chapter were known to act as mediators, as in the case of two claimants to a house in High Street, one of whom had actually built it, while the other obtained a twelve year lease under 'the late dissolved government'.[66]

A comparison of the surviving rent rolls of 1639 and 1664 helps us to assess the impact of the Cromwellian period on Christ Church's real estate. Much of it lay in the twenty or so neighbouring streets and lanes, with outlying possessions in the counties of Dublin, Meath, Kildare and Louth. Examination of the rent rolls suggests that in 1639 rents could have been expected to bring in about £400 per annum, most of which seems to have been collected. The figure for 1664 was £430, £366 being collected (of which about one tenth was arrears).[67] There is a list of rents not received after the Restoration, but also a list of rents improved.[68] Dean Parry (1666–77) drew up 'a rent roll of the deanery ... as I found the rents thereof when I was admitted dean'.[69] Certain rents related to property 'within the mansion house [deanery] or precincts of Christ Church', much of this income being regarded as the dean's own. Furthermore, a rent roll of the dean and bishop of Kildare 'as delivered by Dr Moreton the late dean' (1677–1705), amply illustrates how important the Christ Church income was to the bishop of Kildare: the dean took in four times as many rents as did the bishop (though not of four times the value).[70]

Owning property was one thing, managing it quite another, and corporations such as cathedrals were notorious until modern times for the poor administration of their estates. There were several reasons why this should have been so. Just as municipal corporations tended to grant to their members long leases of borough estates on favourable terms, so did ecclesiastical corporations. Likewise, bonds might be forged with influential, even powerful, friends, through mutually advantageous leases. Cathedral servants might,

63 14 & 15 Car. II, c. 2, s. 103.   64 L.J. Arnold, 'The Irish court of claims of 1663' in *I.H.S.*, xxiv, no. 96 (1985), p. 417; 14 & 15 Car. II, c. 2 lists the provisions for the respective religious and civic institutions.   65 C6/1/7/2, ff 90–90v.   66 Ibid., f. 90.   67 C6/1/26/4/1; C6/1/26/4/3; C6/1/3/1.   68 C6/1/26/3/6; C6/1/26/3/11.   69 C6/5/8/1(b).   70 C6/5/8/4(a).

in the same way, have their emoluments enhanced, and charity be dispensed, either to the dependents of former chapter members, or, indeed, to men and women who, though having no legal claims on the cathedral, were deemed to be deserving of its charity.

It is easy to find examples in all such categories. Charles Cobbe was bishop of Kildare (and therefore dean of Christ Church) from 1732 to 1743. In the latter year he became archbishop of Dublin, and six years later, in 1749, leased property from the dean and chapter for twenty-one years at £37 3s. 6d. per annum.[71] The archbishop's accounts also throw light on another aspect of property management: the imposition of fines when leases were renewed. Often these fines were substantial, and it is intriguing to read in the archbishop's papers that between 1743 and 1750 fines received by the see of Dublin totalled £7,087 11s.[72] The archbishop of Tuam held land in Oxmantown from the cathedral, as did a prominent layman, Lord Chief Justice Domville, while the earl of Meath, lord of the neighbouring liberty of Thomas Court and Donore, was a tenant.[73] Likewise Alderman Drury in the 1660s, though his rank did not shield him from being summoned for arrears of rent.[74] George Grierson, the king's printer, held land at Swords from the chancellor, and his lease was renewed for twenty-one years in March 1737, at the existing rent of £6 per annum, with no mention of a fine.[75]

The cathedral's most prestigious tenant, though by no means either its most remunerative nor least troublesome, was the crown. The Four Courts and their ancillary services sat in the precincts of Christ Church. While undoubtedly it was to the cathedral's advantage to have such instruments of state in its vicinity, arrears of rent from that quarter were by no means unknown,[76] and disputes arising from the leases could be vexatious and protracted, in particular when the dean and chapter allegedly suffered crown encroachments on other parts of their estate. Not, indeed, that the revenue from this particular property was especially great, amounting to £12 6s. per annum in 1639, which remained virtually unchanged until 1717.[77]

Some property attached to dignitaries and prebendaries from which, either individually or corporately, they drew revenue. Lands belonging to the dean and chapter were leased to, amongst others, the registrar and chapter clerk.[78] Of a somewhat different species was the leasing in 1667 to John Tadpole

---

71 Newbridge House, County Dublin, Archbishop Cobbe's account book, 31 May 1749.
72 Charles Agar, archbishop 1801–9, had longed for Dublin with its two palaces and demesnes, temporalities of £6,000 per annum and 'fines now worth £5,000' (P.R.O.N.I., Normanton papers, T. 3719/C/12/54).   73 C6/1/7/2, f. 292.   74 Ibid., f. 131v.   75 C6/1/7/5, 3 Dec. 1733, 21 Mar. 1738.   76 For examples, C6/1/7/2, f. 159v, and C6/1/26/14, no. 51.   77 C6/1/26/14, no. 57; C6/1/26/4/3, f. 103; Bodl., Rawl. MS B 493.   78 C6/1/7/2, f. 354; C6/1/7/3, p. 150.

(senior), a vicar choral, of a lease of all the profits from butchers' stalls in St John's Lane on market days, in return for his keeping the area cleaned and paved.[79] Property could be assigned in recognition of services rendered, as happened in the case of Robert Douglas, who in 1661 petitioned for (and obtained) some concessions relating to his lease due to 'his procuring several books, writings, et cetera' belonging to Christ Church which were seized during the time of 'the late usurping government'.[80] Mossom, the first post-Restoration dean, was credited with having been a good steward of Christ Church property.[81] He died, bishop of Derry, in 1679, but his widow long survived him and in 1695 negotiated the renewal (for a £500 fine) of the lease of a property belonging to Christ Church, originally leased to her husband.[82]

So much for the property belonging to the 'cathedral oeconomy'. There was also a considerable amount of property which belonged to individual dignitaries and others. As was to be expected, the dean's revenues were the greatest, including not only income from bricks and mortar, but from tithes and fishing rights on the Liffey (which he farmed out).[83] His total income from all sources was put at £200 per annum in the mid-1770s.[84] The other dignitaries similarly had income from property and tithes. The prebendaries of St Michael's, St Michan's and St John's either had designated houses, or accommodation in lieu thereof, and some other property as well.[85]

The dean and chapter were not the only property-holding body. There was a minor corporation, 'the prebendaries and vicars choral of Christ Church', and there was another corporately-held fund, that of the vicars choral and stipendiaries of Christ Church and St Patrick's, known as 'the augmentation estate' which possessed additional grants of rents and tithes made by Charles II on recognition of the role played by the two Dublin cathedrals as pillars of Anglo-Protestant rule in Restoration Ireland. Like other ecclesiastical property, the assets of these two bodies (which included tithes) had been confirmed to them at the Restoration. The property of the prebendaries and vicars choral was managed by a steward, whose duties included distributing their dues to the members half-yearly, less any penalties they might have incurred.[86] The actual setting of leases appears to have been carried out by the dean and chapter, but always, it was carefully noted, with the consent of the members of the corporation concerned.[87] Dean Mossom's care of the estates of the cathedral

79 C6/1/7/2, f. 154. For an account of the place of the Tadpoles, senior and junior, see Barra Boydell, *Music in Christ Church cathedral from the late fifteenth century to 1647* (Dublin, 1997). 80 C6/1/7/2, f. 94v. 81 Ibid., f. 143v. 82 C6/1/7/3, 23 and 29 Apr. 1695; C6/1/17/5, nos. 499 and 600 (which puts the fine at £500, whereas the sum recorded under 23 April 1695 is £400). 83 C6/1/7/2, f. 89v. 84 Mant, *Ch. of Ire.*, ii, 659. 85 For example, C6/1/7/2, f. 108; C6/1/7/2 f. 354; C6/1/7/5, 15 Apr. 1737, 5 Feb. 1739. 86 C6/1/7/2, ff 110–110v. 87 For example, Ibid., ff 92–92v.

oeconomy extended also to that of the prebendaries and vicars choral, whose rent-roll he 'perfected'.[88] The income from rents for the half year to Michaelmas 1712 totalled £136 11s. 6d., and after the steward had had his cut, and various incidentals had been paid, the beneficiaries received £1 15s. each.[89] It was, indeed, important to have an accurate rent roll and equally important to gather in the rents. Arrears of rent constantly figure in the records as a matter of major concern. Historians of English cathedrals suggest that income from rents picked up when deans and chapters appointed professionals to see to the matter, and that this was, in the main, a late eighteenth-century practice.[90] But much earlier than that, in 1662, Christ Church appointed an agent, John Hetherington, to deal with a worrying accumulation of arrears 'and several usurping claims'. He was empowered by special letter of attorney and paid £20 per annum for his work.[91] The problem did not go away, and four years later, in 1666, was still causing concern.[92] In 1667 the dean reported that great difficulties were being experienced in collecting rents, with consequent problems in keeping the building in repair, and he accepted the chapter's request that he should take on the office of proctor himself.[93]

The dean and chapter were concerned to maintain the value of their property and to protect it from 'intrusions'. In 1661 they ordered Henry Ward to pull down a shed that blocked a passage through the close,[94] and the following year, W. Colley, a trunk-maker, was in trouble for infringing the liberties and franchises by additions to his new dwelling-house in Skinners' Row.[95] In 1737, the dean and chapter gave orders that certain building work in the precincts was to stop as it was obstructing light to the chapter house.[96] Critics such as Archbishop King alleged that the chapter neglected the cathedral as the result of pursuing the legal battle with him described below,[97] yet, despite the performance of deans and chapters under whom the state of the building was often described as 'ruinous', we must take due note that they were not entirely neglectful. In 1663, John Mills was directed to begin repairs on the cathedral where he certified it to be 'ruinous'.[98] Work on the roof of St Mary's chapel began in 1694, Henry Kinch being paid £40 fortnightly for 'framing and raising the roof'.[99] Two years later, Trinity chapel was converted into a chapter house, a consequence of having leased the original chapter house to the lord mayor and corporation in 1695.[100]

The years between the Restoration and the Williamite wars saw the resumption of normal cathedral life, insofar as Anglican order was reinstated and

88 Ibid., f. 144.   89 C6/1/18/1.   90 Collinson et al., Canterbury, pp 245–6; Atherton et al., Norwich, p. 93.   91 C6/1/7/2, f. 105.   92 Ibid., f. 146v.   93 Ibid., f. 152.   94 Ibid., f. 93v.   95 Ibid., f. 109.   96 C6/1/7/5, 15 Apr. 1737.   97 See p. 281 ff below.   98 C6/1/7/2, f. 115.   99 C6/1/7/3, 21 Apr. 1694.   100 Ibid., 19 Feb. 1695; 2 Dec. 1696.

administration followed much the same lines as had been the case heretofore. But this was to be a period of turbulence where the cathedral's external relationships were concerned, and Christ Church found itself embroiled with such formidable adversaries as the crown, the city and the archbishop. As they rejoiced at the Restoration, little did the dean and chapter envisage that in a mere thirty years' time another major disruption would be visited on the cathedral. Not, this time, by a regicide power such as Cromwell's, but by the very crown itself, in the person of the Catholic monarch, James II.

During James's short but (from the Protestant point of view) devastating reign, Irish Catholics looked for a restoration of a different kind, returning to them their lands and position in public life, and to their church its proper status in the kingdom. William King was dean of St Patrick's for the troubled years from 1689 to 1691, during which he experienced two spells of confinement in Dublin castle for his strongly expressed Protestant and Williamite views. According to King the Catholic Sir Thomas Hackett, James's appointee as lord mayor of Dublin, extended the power of that office 'where the mayor's power was never owned'. He sent his warrant and committed the officers of Christ Church, Dublin, to the stocks, because he fancied they did not make the bells ring merrily enough for the birth of the Prince of Wales.[101]

The cathedral bells had also rung out, possibly more enthusiastically, three years previously when the accession to the throne of the then heirless James II had been greeted with suitable ceremony at Christ Church on 6 February 1685.[102] The lord lieutenant had processed to the cathedral accompanied by troops of grenadiers and horse, the streets lined on both sides with soldiers. Then followed trumpeters, pursuivants, the bishops of the Church of Ireland (two by two), privy councillors and many others. A banquet followed at Dublin castle, where, after the second course, his majesty's style was proclaimed, and there was ringing of bells and fireworks. There was to be yet more bell-ringing, on Palm Sunday, 24 March 1689, when a much chastened James II arrived in Dublin in order to retrieve his kingdoms. The display of loyalty that greeted the king in Dublin that Palm Sunday was genuine. The Catholic population, whose interests he and his chief governor Tyrconnell had sedulously advanced, had much to thank him for, and the Church of Ireland continued, if tentatively, to give its allegiance. The members of the established church might resent the king's policies whereby he sought to remove restraints on Catholics, and might even protest at the catholicisation of the legal, civic and military professions. But, though bishoprics remained unfilled (their perquisites going, in part, to pay stipends to the Catholic bish-

101 William King, *The state of the Protestants of Ireland under the late King James's government* (Dublin, 1730), p. 104.   102 Bodl., Rawl. MS A 482, f. 3.

ops) the Church of Ireland had, thus far, suffered little damage other than to its prestige.

James was, indeed, cautious in advancing the Catholic cause. He took account of advice that restoring the Catholic religious and clergy to their livings and churches 'may be inconsistent at present with the promotion of your majesty's affairs in England'.[103] Furthermore, he was no less conscious of his royal prerogatives in the church than his predecessors had been, and let his considerable displeasure be known in 1687 when several benefices belonging to Christ Church were filled without his nomination or knowledge. He made clear his expectation that no such promotions would again happen in his kingdom without his or his ministers' recommendations.[104] Nor does he seem to have been pleased at what he considered to be the undue haste shown in the taking over of churches from the Church of Ireland. In the early years of his reign, two places of worship had changed to Catholic use: the chapel of Dublin castle, where the viceroy sometimes worshipped, and the very recently consecrated chapel of the Royal Hospital, Kilmainham. The viceroy's brother, Archbishop Talbot (who held the see of Dublin by papal provision from 1669 to his death in 1680) had, allegedly, told Tyrconnell's secretary in 1672 that he hoped to have high mass at Christ Church at Christmas.[105] The diary kept by an anonymous Protestant, in an entry under 7 January 1688, records that it was 'reported ... that Christ Church was to be given to the papists'.[106]

Count d'Avaux, the French diplomat who accompanied James on his Irish expedition reported to Louis XIV that when 'he took the liberty of informing the king [James] that the Roman Catholic authorities and the Catholics of the town had taken possession of one of the principal churches '*qui est une sainte chapelle*' [Christ Church?]', James had thought ill of it, because he was resolved to have the first mass said in that church, so he intended to have it closed and re-opened on his arrival in Dublin.[107] D'Avaux advised James that, being faced with a *fait accompli* he had better leave things as they were, the alternative being to return the church to the Protestants. According to the diarist, James told Bishop Dopping of Meath that had he been in town, Christ Church would not have been taken, but since it had been, he could not

---

103 'The reduction of Ireland, 1689–91', Royal Irish Academy, MS 24 6 vi, f. 1, 'Proposals to King James for taking away the penal law [*sic*] and restoring the Romish clergy, etc. to all their livings in Ireland: July 1690'.   104 Bodl., Rawl. MS 139b, f. 99.   105 *A full and impartial account of all the secret consultations, negotiations, strategems, and intrigues of the Romish party in Ireland, from 1660 to the present year 1689* (London, 1690), pp 15–16. 106 'A diary of events in Ireland from 1685 to 1690' in *Calendar of the MSS of the marquess of Ormond, K.P., preserved at Kilkenny castle* (H.M.C., London, 1920), n.s., viii, p. 347.   107 *Négociations de M. Le Comte D'Avaux en Irlande 1689–90*, ed. James Hogan (Irish Manuscripts Commission, Dublin, 1934), p. 550.

restore it without 'disobliging the Irish, whose interest was all he had to trust to'.[108]

The year 1689 had seen a degree of panic among Dublin Protestants, tempered with a prudent acquiescence, though by July of that year they were gaining in confidence as news of the relief of Derry and of Williamite successes in the north filtered through. Even before that, D'Avaux was telling Louis that measures had to be taken to disarm the Dublin Protestants,[109] having already told James that he estimated that there were 6,000 armed Protestants in Dublin, who had promised their support to William. It was against this background that many churches were searched for arms. Cathedral records tell that on Monday 25 February, Christ Church was 'seized for to receive arms', but restored the Saturday following. On Wednesday 7 August, it was searched and seized, though 'on Sunday 25 August the keys were again restored'.[110] On Monday 26 August, from his place of imprisonment in nearby Dublin castle, William King recorded that ' at 8 in the morning I heard the chimes of Christ Church, from whence I concluded that the church was restored, which I found to be true, but much out of order.'[111] Writing some years later, King gave details of another incident involving Christ Church

> ... and because there chanced to be a sword and case of pistols found on 6 September 1689 in some outward by-place in Christ Church, Dublin, one Wolfe, the sub-verger, was committed to Newgate, indicted and found guilty, and had [the] good luck to escape [with] his life, the chief justice declaring it was treason, though Wolfe was only indicted for a misdemeanour.

The anonymous diary quoted above, describes exhaustive searches for arms, and how 'only the sexton and ringer of Christ Church had hid a saddle and two cases of pistols ... for one of his neighbours, for which they were put in Newgate, and the church shut up'.[112] The chapter act book records that 'on Saturday late at night being the 26 October 1689 the keys of Christ [sic] were taken from the sexton and mass held therein the next day after'.[113] This tallies with King's journal entry of 27 October that 'Christ Church was seized and mass said in it. They went to it in great state, a regiment or more being drawn out and lining the streets'.[114]

---

108 'Diary of events', p. 373.   109 D'Avaux to Louis, 26 June 1689; D'Avaux to James, 4 June 1689, in *Négociations*, pp 218, 262.   110 Scribbled notes in different hands in the chapter act book, C6/1/7/3, ff 12–13.   111 H.J. Lawlor (ed.), 'Diary of William King, D.D., archbishop of Dublin, during his imprisonment in Dublin castle' in *R.S.A.I. Jn.*, xxxiii (1903), p. 264.   112 'Diary of events', p. 369.   113 C6/1/7/3, 25 Feb. 1689; 7 Aug. 1689.   114 'Diary of William King', p. 399.

It would appear, therefore, that following several incidents earlier in 1689, such as searches for arms and temporary closures, Christ Church finally oberved Roman Catholic liturgical order (however the king may have felt about it) on Sunday 27 October 1689. It seems that James did not attend for some time (perhaps he was in Kilkenny, where he spent much of the winter of 1689/90).[115] However, to quote the anonymous diary once more, 'Notwithstanding the report of the king's displeasure for taking Christ Church, and that he said he would never come hither, yet this day [17 November 1689] he went to mass there, attended very meanly, much worse than the deputy [viceroy] used to do'.[116]

William Moreton, bishop of Kildare and dean of Christ Church, and many of his fellow clergy, made good their escape from Dublin shortly after James II's arrival. Moreton therefore, like his archbishop, Francis Marsh, featured in the list of those included in an act of attainder passed by James II's Irish parliament that met from 7 May to 18 July 1689. The king exercised his prerogative and appointed the Revd Alexius Stafford dean (but not bishop of Kildare, there already being an occupant of that see by papal provision). Our knowledge of affairs at Christ Church under Alexius Stafford is fragmentary, consisting mainly of 'some papers of Stafford, pretended dean of this church and his chapter in 1689',[117] and we know disappointingly little about Stafford himself.[118] But from what we do know, he came from a long-established County Wexford family of Old English extraction that had a record of military service to the crown. Like many aspirants to the priesthood from south Leinster, he was trained at St Patrick's College, Lisbon, one of the smaller Irish colleges, founded in 1593 and sending home between two and five secular priests each year.[119] He was ordained priest on 10 August 1675 in the church of Our Lady dos Socorres by the suffragan bishop of Lisbon,[120] and while we know nothing of any ministry in his home diocese of Ferns (if indeed he ever returned to it) he was signatory to a wedding ceremony in September 1682 in one of London's Catholic chapels, describing himself as 'Alexius Stafford, Catholic missioner in England'.[121]

But his gifts were not confined to those of the priesthood and he was a man of many parts. He was appointed a master in chancery by James and

115 J.G. Simms, *Jacobite Ireland* (London, 1969), p. 133.　116 'Diary of events', p. 373. 117 C6/1/26/6/32.　118 Two 'literary remains' survive: a manuscript dissertation of his 'Compendium logica Conunbriensis' inscribed with details of his authorship (Marsh's Library, Z4.5.3) and a volume 'ex libris Alexii Stafford, Dublin MDCLXV' (T.C.D., G. e. 25).　119 T.W. Moody, F.X. Martin, F.J. Byrne (ed.), *A new history of Ireland:* iii, *early modern Ireland 1534–1691* (Oxford, 1976), pp 616, 624; Hugh Fenning, O.P., 'Irishmen ordained in Lisbon 1660–1739' in *Collectanea Hibernica*, nos 34 and 35 (1992–3), p. 75.　120 Fenning, 'Irishmen ordained'.　121 *Registers of the Catholic chapels royal and of the Portugese Embassy Chapel, 1662–1829*, i, *marriages* (Catholic Record Society, London, 1941), p. 28.

also sat in the parliament of 1689 for the borough of Bannow, County Wexford. Charles O'Kelly, who also sat in that parliament, described him as '... the celebrated Doctor Alexius Stafford, doctor of the civil and canon laws, dean of Christ Church, master in chancery, member of parliament, and preacher to the King's Inns' who was chaplain [to King James Royal Regiment] of Irish Foot Guards.[122]

It was the last of these roles that cost him his life at the battle of Aughrim, as with crucifix in hand, Stafford passed through the line of battle and pressed into the foremost ranks, loudly calling on his fellow-soldiers to secure the blessings of religion and property by steadiness and attention to discipline.[123] To men like Stafford, the Williamite wars in Ireland were a crusade, and another account of Aughrim, ' written by an intelligent Jacobite who was evidently in close touch with the affairs of the time',[124] describes him as 'an undaunted zealot and a pious churchman, who fell in front of the royal regiment as he was encouraging them in the final charge.'[125]

Stafford's death, the fact that James appears not to have appointed a successor to him and, above all, Dean Moreton's return following the Williamite victory, render academic any debate as to Stafford's legitimacy as dean of Christ Church. Suffice it to say that, as with all conflicts, the winner defined the truth, and so, when the ancien régime was restored, all references were to the 'pretended' Dean Stafford. Nonetheless, whatever the legality of Stafford's status, cathedral business continued to be transacted, and a dean and chapter were in place. There are minutes of a chapter meeting held on 22 January 1690, though an attendance of only three dignitaries is recorded: Mr (sic) Dean, Mr Chancellor and Mr Treasurer. Listed elsewhere on a loose sheet among the papers relating to Stafford's period are the names of several clergy: Revd Fr Maguire, Revd Fr Leary, Revd Fr Stafford and others. At least one chapter member, John Glendie, appears to have held on to his prebend of St Michael's, as did Bladen, the great survivor of both the Cromwellian and Jacobite periods, who remained at St John's.[126] According to William King, Dean Glendie (he was also dean of Cashel) suffered some public humiliation for it.[127]

We know something of the sermons that were preached when Stafford was in office, even if only from hostile sources. Archbishop King records how 'one Mr Moore preached before the king in Christ Church in the beginning of the year 1690. His sermon gave great offence; he told his majesty

122 Charles O'Kelly, *Macaria excidium, or the destruction of Cyprus*, ed. J.C. O'Callaghan (Dublin, 1850), p. 453.   123 O'Kelly, *Macaria*, p. 453.   124 J.G. Simms, 'Introduction' to J.T. Gilbert, *A Jacobite narrative of the war in Ireland: 1688–1691* (Dublin, 1892; reprinted Shannon, 1971), p. v.   125 Gilbert, *Jacobite narrative*, p. 148.   126 See p. 258 above.   127 King, *State of the Protestants*, p. 247.

CHRIST CHURCH CATHEDRAL: A HISTORY

that he did not do justice to the Church and churchmen'. James 'highly resented this, and the preacher was banished, or voluntarily withdrew from court ...'.[128] More to the king's taste were the homilies of Fr Hall,[129] who predicted that under the new dispensation Ireland would once again be the *insula sanctorum*. Preaching before the king on one occasion he took for his text 'and the time of this ignorance God winked at; but now commanded all men everywhere to repent'.[130]

Among the members of the congregation at the cathedral were those who were eager to convey the gist of what was being said to King in his imprisonment. Others did as much for Nathaniel Foy, shortly to be bishop of Waterford, who was apprised of the sentiments expressed in several sermons preached by a doctor of the Sorbonne, and systematically refuted them.[131] But, of course, liturgically, what occasioned the greatest satisfaction to the court, and dismay to the Williamite citizens of Dublin, was that these sermons took place in the context of mass celebrated according to the Roman rite, remarkable mementoes of which, the tabernacle and candlesticks, have survived.

Most of the very scant manuscript material from these few years in the cathedral archives takes the form of correspondence with Stafford.[132] These letters usually relate to matters of property and the collection of rents. A certain Edmund Burke sought reimbursement for 'service done for the reverend fathers the dean and chapter of Christ Church', clearly in the collection of rents in Dublin and elsewhere. There would appear to have been little disruption of tenancies, the only complaint recorded (when Moreton had been reinstated) taking the form of a petition from some tenants for abatement of rents, on account, among other things, of 'rents extorted from them by the late pretending Dean Stafford and his brethren'.[133] An undated letter to Stafford from Joseph Byrne, of Queen's County, refers to a property holding of his in Skinners' Row. Whatever the nature of the boon he sought, he had been advised by Stafford that the property in question was held from the vicars choral and had nothing to do with the dean. Seemingly the integrity of the vicars chorals' endowment was observed by the new régime, to the chagrin of Byrne who vowed that 'I would rather pay you one pound than any Protestant in Ireland a penny.'[134]

The period of Roman Catholic presence at Christ Church was very brief, little more than seven months. While there were alarms and excursions from time to time prior to the actual takeover, and much uncertainty, the life of the cathedral continued. For most of James II's reign, the clergy and laity who served Christ Church had been resigned to enduring a relatively short

---

128 Ibid., p. 18.   129 Simms, *Jacobite Ireland*, p. 134.   130 King, *State of the Protestants*, p. 246. The text cited is Acts xvii, 30 (Douay version).   131 Phillips, *Ch. of Ire.*, iii, 167. 132 C6/1/26/6/32.   133 C6/1/7/3, 13 Nov. 1690.   134 C6/1/26/6/32.

Catholic interlude. He was fifty-two years of age when he succeeded his brother Charles II, and until the birth of his heir in June 1688 it was anticipated that on his death the Protestant succession would resume. It was to King James that the chapter had protested at the treatment meted out to Wolfe, though with what degree of confidence of redress we cannot tell.[135] And it is noteworthy that there is a payment to that same devoted servant Wolfe in the proctor's accounts 'for helping to bury the plate' so that it would not fall into Jacobite hands, complemented by later disbursements to him 'for taking up the plate', to a carman 'for bringing it home', and to a woman for 'scouring' it.[136] It must have given the same Wolfe great satisfaction to ring the bells for three days in celebration of William's victory.[137]

Things quickly returned to their normal pattern after the Boyne. There was, of course, the sensitive matter of juring (that is, giving oaths of allegiance to William and Mary as rightful monarchs) and non-juring. But the Irish clergy, understandably, had less tender consciences in this matter than had their English brethren. Among the chapter only John Fitzgerald, archdeacon of Dublin, resigned and moved to London as early as February 1690, being unwilling to swear fealty to William and Mary.[138] Another who swam against the tide was Charles Leslie, who challenged William King's account of the Jacobite period, claiming that King could not name a single church taken over either by James's order or connivance, other than Christ Church, 'for his own use, which was always reputed as the king's chapel'.[139]

The cathedral's quarrels with the Dublin municipal authorities had to do with its secular rather than its ecclesiastical prerogatives, but were nonetheless bitter for that, and were more enduring. A royal commission on the state of the Irish municipal corporations that reported in 1835–6 identifed four manorial jurisdictions in Dublin. These were the earl of Meath's liberty of Thomas Court and Donore, the archbishop of Dublin's liberty of St Sepulchre's, the dean of St Patrick's liberty (which was an enclave within the archbishop's) and, lastly, the manor of Glasnevin or Grangegorman and the liberty of Christ Church, where the dean and chapter had jurisdiction. The commissioners explained that the liberties had their origin in crown grants: the manor of Glasnevin or Grangegorman exercising authority confirmed by James I's charter of 1603 to the dean and chapter.[140] The dean and chapter, when their privileges were queried, cited a much older source, Pope

---

135 Above p. 271.   136 C6/1/26/16/10, no. 10.   137 Ibid., no. 10.   138 Leslie, 'Fasti'. 139 Charles Leslie, *An answer to a book entitled The state of the Protestants in Ireland under the late King James's government* (London, 1692), p. 2.   140 *Municipal corporations (Ireland), appendix to the first report of the commissioners (report on the city of Dublin, [part II])*, [26], H.C. 1836, xxiv, p. 289.

Urban III, who, in 1186, by his apostolical authority ('as he calls it') granted them many privileges.[141] The nineteenth-century commissioners put it very clearly '[the liberties] are all remnants of the feudal polity in which they originated, the object of which was to make a powerful individual or ecclesiastical corporation responsible for the good order of that particular district which was their private property'.[142]

Whereas the archbishop's liberty of St Sepulchre and the earl of Meath's liberty of Thomas Court and Donore not only exercised legal jurisdiction but also performed many quasi-municipal functions, such as the provision of a water-supply and public lighting, this was not the case in the liberty of Christ Church, nor did parliament make provision for them to do so, as it did with St Sepulchre's and Thomas Court and Donore. It is worth noting, however, that while not possessing a market jury for regulating and adjudicating on market transactions as the earl of Meath's liberty did, a certain market jurisdiction did exist in the cathedral's manor of Grangegorman. Seizures of bread and butter were carried out there in 1767 and 1776 'by the grand jury of the liberty of Grangegorman.'[143]

The dean and chapter had certain jurisdictions in their manors, and they regarded their regulatory duties in the precincts as analogous to those of the earl of Meath in his liberty. But while exercising autonomy in some spheres, for most practical purposes Christ Church was heavily dependent where public services were concerned on its larger neighbour, the city corporation. In 1698, for example, while the seneschal (the liberty's legal officer) 'in acknowledgment of the privileges of this church' authorised the city treasurer to cut off the water supply to certain consumers in the liberty for non-payment of water-rent,[144] the city was the supplier.

The liberty of the dean and chapter of Christ Church, with its perimeter wall and gate (with a dwelling over it)[145] was small, a warren of alleyways, entries and buildings of mongrel ancestry, uncertain age, and only too certain dilapidation. Dean Mossom admitted its tininess to Ormond, the lord lieutenant, conceding that while the houses in the precinct were few, yet 'by virtue of immunity of the same, of considerable value and of benefit to the church's revenue which by breach of their privileges will be diminished'.[146] An enumeration of 1695–6 gave the number of houses in Christ Church Yard (part of the precincts) as seven, with twenty-three hearths, and the number of dwellings in the liberty as thirty-two, with fifty-five hearths.[147] The infor-

---

141 C6/1/26/14, no. 18, p. 1.   142 *Mun. corp. Ire. Rep., Dublin II*, p. 307. For further discussion of the liberties, see ch. ix.   143 *Freeman's Journal*, 26 May 1767, 14 April 1767, 16 July 1776.   144 C6/1/7/3, 2 Sept. 1698.   145 C6/1/7/5, 10 Oct. 1730.   146 C6/1/26/13, no. 16.   147 'An enumeration of houses, hearths and people in Dublin, 1695–6 by John South, a commissioner of revenue in Ireland' in *Anc. rec. Dublin*, vi, 577.

mation provided by mid-eighteenth century mortality bills similarly testifies to a very small community: the number of weekly baptisms and births in the liberty of Christ Church being usually 'none', occasionally 'one', rising to an exceptional three births in 1754, as compared with thirty-four births in St Patrick's liberty, and fifty-three deaths there.[148] The population of Dublin city in 1778 is estimated to have been about 154,000.[149]

Who actually resided in the close? There were, of course, the dean's mansion house and the houses of the dignitaries, most of which were sub-let. The use of the term 'ancient' mansion house suggests that it had fallen out of use as a residence for the dean. This may, in part, account for an ambitious building programme embarked upon in 1731 to provide houses for the dean, the chanter (precentor) and the chancellor in Fishers' Alley, off Fishamble Street, on land belonging to the cathedral. The treasurer was to receive an equivalent allowance, until he, too, could be provided with a residence. Furthermore, houses were to be built for the prebendaries of St Michael's and St Michan's in their respective parishes. The parishioners of St John's already provided their incumbent with a house, so he was to receive an allowance instead.[150] The designs for the dignitaries' houses were drawn up by the surveyor-general, Edward Lovett Pearce, who was given responsibility for seeing the work through.[151] Complications ensued. Mrs Sarah Medcalf petitioned the dean and chapter to complain that the construction of the houses was damaging her property.[152] There is a reference in 1662 to the vicars' rooms 'in the old [priory] dormitory'.[153] It was, with their formal consent, leased out. However, many years later, in 1738, the 'vicars' lodging' which they had long since vacated,[154] in what was called 'the close', having been viewed by the proctor and prebendaries, was judged to be in a ruinous condition,[155] and, later still, in 1740, the vicars were directed either to repair the building or, 'for the safety of the people', pull it down.[156] There were shops and stalls in the precincts, the former conventual buildings having been secularised in this manner. The tower over the east gate of the close was leased out.[157] There had been a ban on ale-houses in the precincts, but (the chapter records of 1661 concede) 'through the licentiousness of the times, "tippling houses" have come into existence, the Lord's Day is profaned, and the neighbours inconvenienced'. From November, the law would be invoked against offenders,[158] though in fact several proprietors were licenced to trade in alcohol. But Patrick Tallant's lease for 'a room or study' used as a with-

148 Dublin bills of mortality, 1752–6 (Dublin City Libraries, Gilbert collection).   149 Hill, *From patriots to unionists*, p. 197.   150 C6/1/7/5, 4 June 1731.   151 Ibid., f. 58, 12 Aug. 1731.   152 Ibid., f. 70, 26 Apr. 1732.   153 C6/1/7/2, f. 112.   154 See p. 242. 155 C6/1/7/5, 30 Apr. 1739.   156 Ibid., f. 164, 29 Mar. 1740.   157 C6/1/7/2, f. 93. 158 Ibid., f. 98v.

drawing-room for the court of common pleas, seems eminently respectable.[159] Christ Church Yard was a popular address with the makers of musical instruments: John Carroll, George Ward, Thomas Molyneaux and Thomas Dunne, violin makers, and such music publishers as William Neale and James Hoey.[160] Edward Davis, barber, was granted a house over the small shop 'newly erected' at the south-east end of the old chapter-house.[161]

Cheek by jowl with these premises were the buildings occupied by state institutions, most prominent among them, the Four Courts. Some of these official buildings were, in fact, leased from the cathedral, the offices of the chief remembrancer, for instance.[162] The law courts were a much-valued presence, to judge from a petition to the common council of the city in 1684, when there was talk of moving them to another site.[163] This would ruin many of those citizens 'whose livelihood depends on the concourse of people who attend the said courts'. The courts and the cathedral seem to have interpenetrated one another to some extent, the dean and chapter being served by the attorney-general with a writ of intrusion in 1717.[164] Amidst this agglomeration of dwelling-places, lawyers' chambers, tippling-houses, tradesmen's shops and hucksters' stalls, stood the cathedral of the Holy Trinity.

The exempt jurisdiction attaching to the dean and chapter's liberty, formalised by Charles II,[165] was something with which even the government had to reckon. While the viceroy felt unable to exempt the cathedral precincts from having troops quartered in it, he agreed to submit for the dean's approval details of the seven soldiers and one sergeant to be billeted there, the names of those on whom they were to be quartered to be announced by the verger in church.[166] In 1679, the dean was again required to provide 'quarter and victuals' for as many privates of a company of foot-guards as could be accommodated in the inns, ale-houses and victualling houses of the liberty.[167]

Taxation could also cause friction. In 1667, the commissioners of the newly-instituted hearth tax required a return of the number of hearths in the liberty, and addressed their demand to 'the verger or proper officer serving within the liberty of Christ Church'.[168] The verger was uncooperative.[169] When, in 1672,[170] the lord lieutenant levied £1,200 on the city for its defence, and the lord mayor asked that £18 be raised in the liberty of Christ Church,

---

159 Ibid., f. 102.   160 See Barra Boydell, 'Prickers and printers: the purchase and copying of music at Christ Church cathedral, Dublin, in the 17th and 18th centuries' in *Long Room*, xliii (1998), pp 20–8; 'The development of the Dublin music print trade to 1800' in *Long Room*, xli (1996), pp 25–33.   161 C6/1/7/2, f. 106.   162 C6/1/7/4, f. 135.   163 *Anc. rec. Dublin*, v, 346.   164 C6/1/7/4, f. 99.   165 See p. 259 above.   166 C6/1/26/13/16.   167 C6/1/26/13/32.   168 C6/5/8/1c.   169 C6/1/26/13/23.   170 C6/1/26/13/25–6.

the dean and chapter objected that, while prepared to pay their share, the matter was being handled in such a way as to constitute an infringement of their liberties. They were soothed when, by order of the privy council, they themselves were authorised to carry out the assessment. The liberty of Christ Church was called upon to make by far the smallest contribution to the levy for the city work-house in 1730: £4 3s. 9d., a mere 0.3 per cent of the total assessment on the parishes.[171]

Where law and order were concerned, there was no doubt that the dean and chapter, and the seneschal and beadle (or constable), exercised an undoubted jurisdiction, and many examples survive of how they discharged their duties. One of the earliest tells how in 1663 the dean and chapter committed into the custody of the verger one of the 'inhabitants within the franchises of the said church', on foot of a complaint by one of the city sheriffs that the offender had displayed 'opprobrious words and ill-carriage' towards him.[172] The seneschal of the manor or liberty was a lawyer, appointed by the dean and chapter, and the office continued well into the nineteenth century, though the 1835 commissioners condemned the fact that there was no proper court-house, and that he heard his cases for the several manors mostly in public-houses.[173] Sir Thomas Drew, the cathedral's architect in the late nineteenth century, told the historian G.T. Stokes that he had been present when the vice-chancellor of Dublin University deputised for the seneschal in the court of the dean's liberty.[174] From time to time, the inhabitants of the precinct were summoned to meet the dean and chapter as a grand jury for discussion of liberty matters touching, for example, local tax (the cess),[175] the beadle's stipend being a major call on the proceeds,[176] and we shall see how Dean Moreton invoked the jury's aid in a dispute with the archbishop.[177] Relations between cathedral and city were close, at least formally, and the city fathers' devotion to the established church was not in question. The population of Dublin was predominantly Protestant, the one third of the population who were Catholic living mainly outside the walls,[178] and a surprising element of continuity of civic personnel, for example among the aldermen, persisted from pre-Cromwellian times. The lord mayor, council and board of aldermen regularly attended Christ Church, and when, in 1679, it was reported that the seats of the councillors and their wives were somewhat out of repair, the corporation directed that £50 be raised by the masters and war-

171 R.V. Dudley, 'Dublin parishes 1660–1729: the Church of Ireland parishes and their role in civic administration of the city', Ph.D. thesis, 2 vols, T.C.D., 1995, i, 14.   172 C6/1/7/2, f. 119.   173 Mun. corp. Ire. rep., Dublin II, p. 304 and Select committee appointed to inquire into the operation of the small debt jurisdiction of manor courts in Ireland, H.C. 1837, xv, p. 91.   174 Stokes, Worthies, p. 219.   175 C6/1/7/2, f. 101.   176 For example C6/1/7/2, f. 109.   177 See p. 283 below.   178 Dudley, 'Dublin parishes', i, 47.

dens of the city guilds (which elected the council members).[179] In 1681, the city agreed to contribute towards the 'beautifying' of Christ Church.[180] But contiguous jurisdictions, such as those of the liberty and municipality, were bound to come into conflict from time to time and on occasion the cathedral felt constrained to assert its prerogatives and there could be strained relations with the city of Dublin, a municipality that trebled in population between the mid-seventeenth and mid-eighteenth centuries, growing from about 40,000 in 1660 to 180,000 by the year 1800.[181]

Towards the end of the seventeenth century, a major confrontation arose. The dean and chapter's case[182] was that on 10 July 1684 an officer of the liberty, Parsons by name, was on his way, staff in hand, to answer a summons by the sheriff and bailiff of the county, with whose jurisdiction the cathedral had no quarrel, attending the quarter sessions there and lodging its prisoners in Kilmainham gaol. Parsons met, accidentally or otherwise, the lord mayor and city sheriffs and being asked where he was going, told them that his destination was the quarter sessions at Kilmainham. He was taken into custody by the city marshall, and 'hurried back to the Tholsel'. However, when the lord mayor disappeared into an inner room, Parsons made his escape, back to the cathedral precincts a short distance away. A city sheriff and forty constables followed in hot pursuit into the liberty, whereupon a 'rabble of people with swords, clubs and other weapons, broke into Parson's house to fetch him out'. Hearing of the fracas, and fearing worse trouble, the dean, Moreton, ordered that the gates be shut. Nonetheless, the inhabitants of the liberty were 'barbarously beaten, wounded and dragged away by the hair of their heads', to be gaoled by the lord mayor. After a few hours, the dean had bailed them out, but the lord mayor indicted several of them.

Protracted legal proceedings followed, the lord mayor and corporation insisting that the precincts were always part of the liberties of the city, and claiming that this was demonstrated by the fact that the corporation was preceded into the cathedral by the city sword, on occasions when the lord lieutenant was not present. Furthermore, the city claimed, there were precedents for the lord mayor's action in the present dispute. The seneschal and inhabitants had customarily attended city quarter sessions, felons had been convicted there for crimes committed in the liberty, and, on occasion, nuisances in the liberty had been removed and the perpetrators punished by the city. The dean and chapter rejected everything, including the city's claim that the inhabitants of the liberty had been the sole rioters. As for bearing the sword in the cathedral: that was simply to encourage the lord mayor to attend! The

---

179 Anc. rec. Dublin, v, 179.   180 Ibid., v, 214.   181 Hill, From patriots to unionists, p. 19.   182 The source for the account that follows is C6/1/26/14, which contains not only statements of the dean and chapter's position, but also the city's response.

cry of the dean and chapter was 'We seek none of the city's liberties, but endeavour to preserve our own'. The lord lieutenant and the Irish privy council were drawn into the dispute and ordered a cooling-off period. Soon hostilities were resumed, and while rarely attaining the degree of animosity engendered by the above incident, jurisdictional disputes were to occur from time to time for as long as the liberty remained as a legal entity.

The proctor's accounts for 1673–4[183] record under the heading of 'extraordinary disbursements' a payment of £3 12s. 6d. for a treat at the archbishop's visitation of the cathedral in May, and in 1686 the dean, William Moreton, invited the archbishop, Francis Marsh, to a 'treat' on a similar occasion.[184] But such felicitous relations between the cathedral and its archbishop were not to endure, for when William King, who had moved from the deanery of St Patrick's to the bishopric of Derry in 1691, was translated to Dublin in 1703, and the letters patent appointing him to Dublin were inspected by the dean and chapter of Christ Church, they saw in them signs of trouble ahead, and objected to several clauses impinging, as they believed, on their prerogatives.[185] The letters patent were dated 11 March 1703. On 19 May, the dean, having been admonished by the new archbishop to summon the chapter with a view to his enthronement, did indeed convene it, but for the purpose of consulting with the members as to the archbishop's right so to admonish him. Their response was in the negative.[186] Furthermore, according to a minute of 14 April, the dean and chapter entered a caveat against the passing of the letters patent which, they claimed, contained 'an unusual clause'. A pamphlet of the time identifies the offending clause as insisting on the archbishop's right of enthronement in either Christ Church or St Patrick's. According to the Christ Church version of events, the archbishop thereupon resolved never to attend the cathedral until he had been enthroned there, and kept his vow.[187] Stokes attributes the animosity between Moreton, the English tory from Christ Church, Oxford, and King, the Irish whig, with a Trinity College, Dublin background, to their political incompatibility.[188] This cannot have helped matters, especially at a time of acute political feeling. Again, King had been dean of St Patrick's, and there may well have been sensitivities on that score, especially since Narcissus Marsh (successor to Francis, but no relation), on his translation from Dublin to Armagh in 1703 had appointed King to be 'administrator of the spiritualities of the diocese of Dublin'.[189] Nor should it be forgotten that Moreton (bishop of Kildare as

183 C6/1/15/1; C6/1/26/14, no. 15, p. 8.   184 C6/1/7/3, 30 Mar. 1687.   185 Ibid., 14 Apr. 1703.   186 Ibid., 19 May, 5 July 1703.   187 *A short state of the case of the dean and chapter of Christ Church Dublin* ([Dublin, 1704]), pp 1–2.   188 Stokes, *Worthies*, p. 212.   189 C6/1/7/3, 23 Feb. 1703.

well as dean) had archiepiscopal ambitions himself, having been mentioned in high quarters as a serious candidate for the see of Dublin when it fell vacant in 1693 on Francis Marsh's death, though at least some of the lords justices regarded Moreton as a firebrand, and not untainted by jacobitism.[190]

The potential for friction also existed in the cathedral's claims to be a royal peculiar. Narcissus Marsh, King's predecessor, had informed a correspondent that the dean and chapter claimed that because Christ Church was where 'the state goes to church', it must be a chapel royal, and therefore exempt from episcopal visitation.[191] And there are references, admittedly in what can only be described as cathedral propaganda, to his majesty's royal cathedral.[192] To King, Christ Church was 'a nest of corruption'. Matters first reached crisis pitch in 1703 when the newly appointed Archbishop King summoned the prebendaries of Christ Church to attend his visitation, to be held at St Patrick's and St Audoen's. According to the chapter acts, the prebendaries were ordered by the chapter not to go,[193] and, therefore, given their oath of canonical obedience to the dean (itself, in the view of the archbishop, an innovation), they could not answer the summons.[194]

There was much to-ing and fro-ing between legal tribunals, both in Ireland and England. Then, in April 1704, a citation from the archbishop was affixed to the chapter house door calling on the dean and chapter to appear before his grace on 24 April.[195] This, they recalled, was the day of the year when, traditionally, they solemnly received the archbishop at the cathedral. It was, they asserted, 'the ancient custom for the archbishop to come before prayers to the west door of the church, and thence to be sung into the choir'.[196] Having considered the citation, the chapter authorised the dean to take any action that he considered essential to the preservation of the cathedral's prerogatives. King sent word that he could not come for prayers (his vow not to worship there, presumably, inhibiting him) but, *after* prayers, on 24 April, he appeared at the west door, was met by the dean and chapter, and conducted to the chapter house. Once there, he was on the point of holding his visitation when the dean 'desired him' to retract his citation, which 'contained several things destructive to the privileges and constitution of this church'.[197] His grace declined to do so, and the dean 'dissolved the chapter', and the members withdrew, leaving the archbishop alone with his entourage. The dean deemed the occasion to be a chapter meeting, while the archbishop construed it as a visitation, for he then adjourned what he deemed to be his visitation until 29 April, and a further citation was affixed to the chapter house door.

---

190 *Calendar of state papers, domestic*, 1693, pp 400, 405.   191 Mant, *Ch. of Ire.*, ii, 169.
192 *A continuation of the case of the dean and chapter of Christ Church Dublin* ([Dublin, 1704]), pp 1–2.   193 C6/1/7/3, 5 July 1703.   194 *A short state*, p. 2.   195 C6/1/7/3, f. 150.   196 *A short state*, p. 3.   197 Ibid., p. 3.

On 29 April, the archbishop duly returned to the cathedral, 'without his robes', according to the cathedral's account of the proceedings. He made his way to the quire as prayers ended, and (Moreton being, diplomatically, elsewhere) took possession of the dean's stall. He declared that he was holding his visitation, pronounced the dean 'refractory' and the prebendaries 'contumacious', and, considerably upping the ante, called on them to show cause why they should not be excommunicated. He next called on the vicars choral to appear. They declined, pleading their oath to the dean. Three weeks later, on 23 May, the archbishop again appeared at Christ Church, this time in his robes, took possession of the dean's stall, declared that he was continuing his visitation, ordered the sexton to break open the door of the throne and had his vicar-general enthrone him.

Relations continued to deteriorate, culminating in a further visit by the archbishop, when, once again from the dean's stall, he declared Moreton suspended, announcing that when his visitation resumed he would pronounce the dean's excommunication.[198] Clearly, however, a high churchman like Moreton could scarcely feel comfortable in such a situation. The cathedral put the most favourable construction possible on the affair, depicting the dean as anxious to prevent schism, and conscious that the censures of the church ought not to be disregarded. The dean sent messengers to the archbishop with an appeal. They were denied an audience. Whereupon, the dean decided that he would not be excommunicate until the queen's pleasure in the matter were known. 23 August was the day appointed by the archbishop for his resumed visitation, and, the six o'clock prayers having ended, the dean ordered that the cathedral doors be locked, and the old chapter house ('now disused'), where the archbishop was likely to hold his 'pretended visitation', shut up. At ten o'clock the archbishop arrived in Christ Church Yard, was unable to gain admission to the church, and the vicar-general 'pretended' to adjourn the visitation to St Patrick's: his grace all the while 'sitting in his coach'.[199] Doubtless, by this time the curiosity of the inhabitants had been aroused, and, especially since it was a market day, a crowd was gathering. The dean assembled the jury of the precincts 'who', a pamphlet explains, 'are bound to hinder all routs, riots, and other invasions of their privileges'. The jury advised him to shut the gates of the liberties. In a heartfelt expression of weariness, in yet another pamphlet, Moreton said 'It is a very unhappy thing to be dean in any place where the archbishop of Dublin has been, or is concerned'.[200]

This was but one of several disputes between cathedral and archbishop. Another, in 1708,[201] related to the archiepiscopal suspension of the prebendary

198 Ibid., p. 3.   199 Ibid., pp 2–3.   200 *Fifth continuation of the case of the dean and chapter of Christ Church Dublin* ([Dublin, c.1704]), p. 21.   201 C6/1/7/4, 13 Jan. 1708.

of St John's for not appearing at a visitation. By this time, Moreton had been translated to Meath which then lay in the province of Armagh, and the archbishop of Armagh, Narcissus Marsh, had advised the lord lieutenant, Ormond, that to move Moreton to Meath (should it become available) could well be in the best interests of the Church, the archbishop of Dublin having made it clear that he would gladly make up the quarrel with Moreton's successor.[202] But such was not to be the case, doubtless to the satisfaction of Moreton who, in thanking Ormond for his promotion, spoke of Christ Church as having many 'royalties', and appearing from its charter to be '... a peculiar of the crown's own making'. Ominously, he expressed the hope that his successor would 'take up the gauntlet that I lay down',[203] and far from earlier events being merely a test of strength between Moreton and King, the pace of confrontation accelerated, if anything, under Welbore Ellis, Moreton's successor. Archbishop King claimed that Moreton 'is gone out with a stink having left the oeconomy sunk with this suit and delapidated the deanery by renewing the lease at his going off on vile terms'. He offered an olive branch to the new dean saying that far from 'desiring or expecting that you should part with any of its [the cathedral's] privileges, it being my resolution as well as intention to preserve the rights of all the clergy inviolable.'[204] In fact, Welbore Ellis kept up the good fight over all the issues, for instance in 1708, in relation to the archiepiscopal suspension of the prebendary of St John's referred to above,[205] and in 1715, when dean and chapter refused to institute the archdeacon, on the grounds that the oath of canonical obedience to the dean had not been taken. But eventually, matters having reached the house of lords in London, Archbishop King was vindicated, and could write in November 1724 'I visited Christ Church the 27th of last month, and was received there with submission, on which the contempt was purged'.[206] Not to have pursued the matter would, in his view, have constituted 'a great blow to episcopal power'. Soon he was claiming to have found the dean and chapter amenable to one of his major complaints against them, the failure to provide for cures. On 21 January 1730, King's successor, John Hoadly, having taken oaths before the dean and chapter of St Patrick's, was met at the door of Christ Church by its dean and chapter, who conducted him to his throne. 'He presented his letters patent and then the dean took his grace by the right hand and brought him into the throne.' Prayers were then said, and the archbishop was 'sung out of the said choir'.[207]

202 Primate Marsh to Ormond, 21 July 1705, 'Diary of events', p. 167.   203 Moreton to Ormond, 28 Aug. 1705, 'Diary of events', p. 179.   204 King to Ellis, 22 Aug. and 30 Oct. 1705, T.C.D., King correspondence, MSS 750/3/217, nos 228–9.   205 C6/1/7/4, 13 Jan. 1708.   206 C.S. King, *A great archbishop of Dublin, William King* (London, 1908), p. 246.   207 C6/1/7/5, 21 Jan. 1730.

There is nothing in the hundred or so years from the 1730s to the 1830s to compare with the shocks that the established church of Ireland sustained in the century that preceded and followed those dates. There were, of course, manifold changes, both to the cathedral building, to its environs, and to what went on in them. The Act of Union (1800), Catholic emancipation (1829) and municipal reform (1840) undermined the cathedral's claims to peculiar national and civic status,[208] as did the designation of what had previously been regarded as the viceroy's chapel in Dublin castle as a chapel royal (1814), a development that elicited surprisingly little recorded comment from the dean and chapter at the time. The daily and weekly liturgical round continued, but while the arrangements for their maintenance were efficient in theory, at least one dean, Charles Lindsay, found them honoured in the breach as well as the observance, as we shall see. Irregular attendance at services by chapter members was nothing new, if we read between the lines of such eighteenth-century chapter acts as made provision for stipendiaries to be available 'to assist the prebendaries in reading prayers',[209] and that each of the two readers on Sundays should be provided with a sermon, in case the member of chapter on duty failed to appear.[210] A new rota of Sunday preachers and weekday attendance was agreed in 1808, the existing one having proved 'inconvenient'. All chapter members were to take their turn, with the exception of the archdeacon of Dublin, though his presence was to be desired whenever he could attend.[211]

Besides the large group of those whose sphere was the liturgical and musical life of Christ Church, there continued to be numerous others whose services were vital to the ordered life of the institution, no less hierarchical in status, and equally likely to benefit from family connections (with the difference that benefits could be enjoyed in both the male and female lines). James Hewitt, for instance, seems to have been the eighteenth-century equivalent of Thomas Howell of an earlier age.[212] He was verger in 1767,[213] and his wife Esther was appointed sextoness in 1779.[214] In 1802, there is a reference to James Hewitt, sexton, his wife Jane, both of whom had care and tuition of the boy choristers,[215] and Mr James Hewitt, senior, verger (who received a £20 gratuity for the 'extraordinary trouble and attention' he had paid to collecting rents).[216] What must surely have been a signal boon was granted James Hewitt, junior, in 1808 when the cathedral defrayed the cost of a tablet he erected in one of the aisles to the memory of his father and sister.[217] He himself became verger, and died in 1810.[218] In 1833, Jane Hewitt

---

208 Aspects of this change can be traced in Refaussé & Lennon, *Registers*, pp 32–3.   209 C6/1/7/6, f. 61v.   210 C6/1/7/7, p. 112.   211 C6/1/7/8, pp 448–52.   212 Gillespie, *Thomas Howell*.   213 C6/1/7/6, f. 116.   214 C6/1/7/7, p. 127.   215 C6/1/7/8, p. 204.   216 Ibid., p. 206.   217 Ibid., pp 452–3.   218 C6/1/7/9, p. 56.

had custody of 'the inside door of the south aisle and front seats between the pillars', attended peeresses 'and other ladies of distinction', and kept the entrance to the robing-room clean, all for £20 per annum.[219] When she retired later that year, at her own request, she was awarded a pension of £10 per annum.[220] The verger was clearly the most important of the cathedral servants. From time to time, the office was combined with that of sexton: the 'verger and sexton' was superannuated in 1749,[221] and Thomas Jones was elected verger and sexton in 1763, the beadle being appointed to succeed him.[222]

A detailed schedule of 'officers and servants' was drawn up by the dean and chapter to coincide with the re-opening of the cathedral after major renovation in 1833. The verger was 'general superintendant', paid £80 per annum, while the sexton (whose wife also had duties) received £36 and £5 respectively. Next came the aforementioned Jane Hewitt (£20 per annum), which was the sum also received by the beadle and constable. The beadle's duties were largely indoor, including tolling the bell, while the constable lit stoves, acted as scavenger and kept the yard, 'flower-ground' and graves.[223] As well as receiving pensions and superannuation, the servants received Christmas bonuses to augment their incomes. Somewhat different was the gratuity paid to the verger 'at the audit', on his good behaviour, mentioned in 1767, and increased from £10 to £20 in 1807.[224] Presumably the dean and chapter considered their servants to be adequately rewarded when they erected notices requesting the public to observe the rule that gratuities to the attendants were forbidden.[225]

Perhaps the most common feature running through the chapter act books for these years is the elaborate formula whereby members sought the sanction of their peers to absent themselves from the cathedral and appoint a proxy to attend meetings in their place. Pluralism and non-residence were endemic in the established church of Ireland in the eighteenth and early nineteenth centuries, and to our way of thinking clergy who held several, often widely separated, dignities and cures and were by definition incapable of residing in some of them or of personally discharging their duties in them all, constituted a flagrant abuse. We need look no further than the chapter of Christ Church for a prime example: Henry Cotton, theologian and bibliographer, who was installed treasurer in 1832,[226] had come to Ireland ten years previously as domestic chaplain to his father-in-law, Richard Lawrence, archbishop of Cashel. In addition to his stall at Christ Church, Cotton held the offices of archdeacon of Cashel and dean of Lismore (from which he drew

219 C6/1/7/11, p. 250.   220 Ibid., p. 250.   221 C6/1/7/6, f. 27v.   222 Ibid., f. 88v.
223 C6/1/7/11, pp 250–1.   224 C6/1/7/6, f. 63v; C6/1/7/8, p. 421.   225 C6/1/7/11, p. 251.   226 Ibid., pp 240–1.

no emoluments, and where he died). More often than not, he was represented by his proxy at chapter meetings. But the ecclesiastical system that permitted such a ministry sustained scholars like Cotton, enabling him to visit diocesan libraries and chapter houses throughout Ireland as he researched his monumental six-volume *Fasti ecclesiae Hibernicae*. Charles Lindsay, son of the dean, was not only his father's archdeacon as bishop of Kildare, where he had a parish, but was also perpetual curate of Monkstown, in the diocese of Dublin. In 1816, his father explained to Archbishop Brodrick of Cashel (who was coadjutor to the ailing archbishop of Dublin and something of a disciplinarian) that his son seldom missed a Sunday at Monkstown, and that when he did it was to visit his rectory in Kildare, where there was neither a glebe house, not the prospect of one.[227] The dean emphasised that Charles discharged all his obligations conscientiously, and he claimed that it was the importance that he, the dean, attached to a scrupulous attention to duty, that lay at the root of a long-running and tempestuous dispute with most of his chapter. Dean Lindsay considered his main adversary in the chapter to be Richard Graves, 'an essentially eighteenth-century divine',[228] fellow of Trinity and, by 1814, professor of divinity, a man immersed in academic life and college politics. Undoubtedly, he took very much into account the financial implications before embarking on any changes in his responsibilities, yet while deeming the prebend of St Michael's, to which the dean and chapter appointed him in 1801 as 'too trifling a preferment to be sought for its own sake', he admitted that it held out prospects, and also gave him opportunities for pastoral work. Although he had a curate, he himself visited and instructed the children. The 'prospect' presumably included the rectory of St Mary's, which fell vacant in 1808. His succession to St Mary's was complicated by the fact that Graves had, apparently, promised his support to another, less senior, candidate, who, according to Graves's biographer, was totally unacceptable to the other dignitaries, and the affair led to 'most unseemly divisions in the chapter'. In the event, Graves was not to be presented to St Mary's until 1823.[229] By then he was also dean of Ardagh, having refused that office as being less lucrative than a college fellowship, until he had been assured of 'an arrangement being proposed by which he could resign his fellowship for the divinity chair'.

We can detect from the earliest days of Lindsay's deanship an attention to discipline. Within weeks of his installation we find rules for the procedure at chapter meetings being recorded, and a detailed valuation of cathedral

227 N.L.I., Brodrick MSS, 8863/2, Lindsay to Brodrick, 1 July 1816.   228 R.B. McDowell and D.A. Webb, *Trinity College, Dublin, 1592–1952* (Cambridge, 1991), p. 136. 229 *The whole works of Richard Graves, D.D ... with a memoir of his life and writings*, ed. R.H. Graves (4 vols, London and Oxford, 1840), i, lxiii.

property instituted.[230] No scholar himself, he may consequently have had little patience with Graves's priorities. The fact that the matter at issue between them was the latter's alleged neglect of his duties is not immediately clear from the chapter acts, but Lindsay made it abundantly clear in his correspondence with Archbishop Brodrick, who had little relish for involvement. The dispute was a protracted one, and bitter divisions among chapter members surfaced during debates about appointments to prebendal stalls in 1809.[231] Lindsay wrote (in a memorial lodged with Archbishop Brodrick on 30 April 1810) that normally the archiepiscopal visitation could be met by the dean, on behalf of himself and the chapter saying, 'all things are well with us'. But that was not possible now, 'our condition is disordered and stands in need of graver counsel than our own', the dean declaring that he was at odds with all but the most recent members of his chapter.[232]

Lindsay's account of events, however ex parte, does tally with the more formal entries in the chapter minutes. There was much squabbling over precedent, much flourishing of parchments and much recrimination. On one occasion the dean quit the chair, only to discover that the meeting continued, decisions being made and recorded in his absence, the joint registrars having been, in Lindsay's words, 'intimidated' into doing so.[233] His use (abuse, allegedly) of the chapter seal was raised, and much debate ensued as to whether or not the treasurer had called the dean's behaviour 'infamous'. And, while this 'long paper war', as he described it, between dean and chapter apparently ended with the chapter submitting 'in words' to his jurisdiction, they continued their policy of 'reducing me to a cypher'. He addressed the lord lieutenant, looking for something to be done, even asking that the prince regent (this being one of George III's periods of incapacity) be informed of the matter.

Lindsay claimed that since his advent to Christ Church in 1804 he had striven to correct abuses there. He had gone to divine service only to find none of the chapter present, no inferior ministers either, and had been compelled to conduct the entire service himself. For eight years they had refused to listen to his complaints about the persistent absence of the precentor,[234] and even when his objections were recorded in the books, 'they would not attend to it'. Dr Graves's object had been 'to make a total sinecure of his prebendal stall'.

---

230 C6/1/7/8, pp 287, 306–7.   231 Ibid., p. 488 et seq.; C6/1/7/10, f. 526 et seq.   232 N.L.I., Brodrick MSS, 8863/2.   233 The sources drawn upon for the following account of Lindsay's dispute with the chapter comprise the chapter acts (despite certain entries being obliterated as part of the feud), copy of Lindsay's address to the lord lieutenant and correspondence with Archbishop Brodrick (N.L.I., Brodrick MSS 8858, 8863/1 and 2).   234 N.L.I., Brodrick MSS 8863/1, Lindsay to Brodrick, 20 April 1814.

> Let [him] deny his constant complaints and murmurings in the chapter against what he calls the severity of his prebendal attendances. Why does he not resign what he cannot overtake? and why, I ask him, is a congregation to be disturbed by the entrance of Dr Graves (perhaps being the preacher) into his stall after morning service on Sunday at the beginning of the communion service?

To all of which Archbishop Brodrick, following his visitation in 1814, responded with soothing words to the effect that he would use every means in his power to restore peace and friendship.[235]

While peace (but scarcely friendship) may gradually have come about, Lindsay's troubled relationships were not at an end, and he was to face a more formidable adversary, Archbishop William Magee, described by R.B. McDowell as 'the [Prince] Rupert of the episcopal bench'.[236] Magee evinced Lindsay's zeal for much-needed discipline, for Archbishop Cleaver, his predecessor, had been mentally ill for most of his archiepiscopate and the diocese and province were described as being 'utterly void of pastoral care'.[237] The dispute between Lindsay and Magee arose over interpretations of the archbishop's right of visitation, a long-standing source of friction.[238] A 'protestation' of the dean and chapter (united in defiance) asserted that, while a formal, annual visitation of the cathedral was traditional, Christ Church was exempt from the archbishop's jurisdiction, only the lord chancellor and keeper of the great seal having that prerogative. They referred to a visitation convened by the archbishop on 17 June 1824 at St Patrick's as 'a certain pretended business' and to 'the pretended adjournment thereof' to 8 July. The sub-dean was authorised to attend the 'pretended adjournment' to present his grace with the protestation, and with an objection to the act of contumacy against the dean and chapter declared by the archbishop at the original 'pretended' visitation on 17 June.

The archbishop was conciliatory, an exchange of documents was agreed upon, and in August the dean and archbishop had 'a long conversation'. The lord chancellor heard (and dismissed with costs against them) the dean and chapter's case, the archbishop having produced papers that undermined their position. They surrendered, and agreed to attend a further adjournment of the visitation (on 26 August) 'to purge ourselves of our contempt, and submit to his grace's ordinary visitation.' Honour was saved to some extent by the fact that at the heart of the dispute lay the case of John Smith, a stipendi-

---

235 Ibid., Cashel to Kildare, 23 April 1814. The attendance lists in the chapter act books show that for several years the precentor never appeared, even at visitations.   236 R.B. McDowell, *Public opinion and government policy in Ireland, 1801–46* (London, 1952), p. 22.   237 C6/1/7/9, f. 113.   238 C6/1/7/10, pp 252–62, 270, 272, 280.

ary chorister dismissed in 1823 who had appealed to the archbishop to hold a visitation to hear his appeal. Smith appeared before the dean and chapter of Christ Church, apologised, was restored, and received retrospective payment.[239] Magee's biographer wrote that the archbishop's candour, consideration and kindness were such that none of his clergy murmured at the strictures of his exercise of jurisdiction.[240] He showed these qualities in his dealings with Christ Church, and Lindsay, who, it has to be remembered, was bishop of Kildare, and so one of Dublin's suffragans, survived all these vicissitudes. He was still dean in 1840, when Archbishop Whately conducted a visitation, and *omnia bene* was entered in the chapter act book.[241]

The cataclysmic political events of late eighteenth-century Ireland seem largely to have passed the cathedral by, though undoubtedly they undermined the context to which it had been accustomed. The bishop of Cloyne preached in defence of the constitution in February 1787, a time of political uncertainty, and it was resolved that the chapter's expression of thanks to him should be published.[242] But the only reference we have to the rebellion of 1798 concerns the delay experienced by the dignitaries of Armagh cathedral in proceeding with a memorial to Archbishop Robinson, to which Christ Church contributed £50.[243] The dean and chapter may well have been unaware that at least one resident of Christ Church Lane, Rourke, a watchmaker, was a member of the Dublin Society of United Irishmen.[244] In 1803 (though before Emmet's abortive rising) an address to the king spoke of the 'desperate designs of traitors'.[245] The designs of those politicians who united the two kingdoms and the two established churches by the Act of Union of 1800, though they must have exercised the minds of the dean and chapter as individuals, pass without corporate comment, despite the enormous implications both constitutional and economic for the cathedral, yet in the early years of the nineteenth century, the dignitaries were still ruminating on the results of the transfer of the Four Courts across the river in 1796! Even municipal reform as effected by a statute of 1840,[246] changing (ever so slowly) the character of Dublin corporation from conservative Protestant to nationalist Catholic, and the sweeping away in 1859 of the jurisdiction of manorial courts,[247] which had been so tenaciously defended in past years, seem scarcely to have caused a ripple, perhaps because there were even more pressing matters calling for attention in consequence of the Church Temporalities Act that had hit both church and cathedral in 1833 as will be described in a later chapter.[248]

239 Ibid., p. 306.   240 A.H. Kenney, *The works of the Most Reverend William Magee, D.D., lord archbishop of Dublin ... with a memoir of his life* (2 vols, London, 1842), i, lv.   241 C6/1/7/12, p. 92.   242 C6/1/7/7, pp 208–9.   243 C6/1/7/8, pp 187–9.   244 R.B. McDowell, *Proceedings of the Dublin Society of United Irishmen* (Dublin, 1998), p. 139.   245 C6/1/7/8, p. 246.   246 3 & 4 Vict., c. 108.   247 22 Vict., c. 14.   248 See pp 315 et seq. below.

The moving of the Four Courts had been an unwelcome change, much argued against when in prospect, and the impact on the area around the cathedral was alleged to be have been disastrous as predicted.[249] Consequent on the removal of the Custom House to the east (which happened in 1791) and of the Four Courts to the west, 'property in the central parts of the city has diminished very much in value'.[250] Only the corn market remained 'to preserve the value of the contiguous property', a situation that has to be seen against the background of the economic depression that Dublin experienced in the aftermath of the Union.

By 1805, the chapter act book was recording that 'houses in Christ Church Lane and Chapter Court have evidently lessened considerably in their value ... and are now in a very neglected state and if not properly attended to and repaired will soon fall into ruin'. Furthermore, 'they are mostly inhabited by persons of an inferior class who do not appear either inclined or capable of keeping their premises in repair'.[251] Not, indeed, that the crown had been an ideal tenant, the Four Courts having been 'delivered up in so dilapidated a state' that other tenants would have been sued for damages.[252] Some temporary use was made of the premises, for instance as a verger's house, as late as 1810,[253] but demolition was the chosen path after 1800 (except for those parts used for the education of the choirboys) and the resulting materials were sold off.[254] In fact the area around the two cathedrals, where demolition and a consequent population shift took place on a large scale, was exceptional in Dublin, as also were developments in the George's Street area, where again Christ Church was a significant property-owner.[255]

That the dean and other dignitaries lived elsewhere cannot have helped to preserve the amenities of the neighbourhood. George Stone (1743–5) declined to live in the dean's house in Fishamble Street, and received £60 per annum in lieu thereof.[256] Likewise his successor, Thomas Fletcher (1745–61), soon moved out of the deanery for health reasons.[257] Any thought of the dean returning to the house had been abandoned by 1759, when the deanery, with its yard, garden, stables, coach-house and lodge, were leased for forty years (though admittedly with a conditional clause whereby the lease could be ended on twelve or, in certain circumstances, six month, notice).[258] Six years later, the same tenant (Johnson, an apothecary) had also taken out leases on the adjoining houses in Fishamble Street 'formerly allotted' to precentor and chancellor.[259] By 1794, the treasurer and the prebendaries of St

249 See p. 278 above.   250 C6/1/7/8, p. 191.   251 Ibid., p. 357.   252 Ibid., pp 235–8.
253 C6/1/7/9, p. 68.   254 C6/1/7/8, p. 152.   255 Mary Daly, 'Late nineteenth and early twentieth century Dublin' in David Harkness and Mary O'Dowd (ed.), The town in Ireland (Belfast, 1981), p. 242.   256 C6/1/7/6, f. 9.   257 Ibid., f. 25v.   258 Ibid., f. 69.   259 Ibid., f. 104v.

Michael's and St Michan's had moved out – the prebendaries in order to facilitate the laying out of 'a more convenient approach to the cathedral'. All received compensation and allowances.[260]

The dignitaries were sensitive to any suggestion that they were governed by self-interest in their choice of abode, especially when, in the early years of the nineteenth century they were seeking government support for the development of the area around the cathedral, and, indeed, of the building itself. They petitioned parliament in 1806 about the decayed state of the area west of the castle and south of the river, with its many narrow and inconvenient passages, asserting that only the legislature could ameliorate the situation.[261] The houses built in the early eighteenth century by the dean and chapter on a piece of ground in Fishamble Street belonged to the cathedral oeconomy.[262] Now they lay derelict, but the dignitaries expressed their intention, when funds permitted, 'to clear away the present extensive ruins of the precincts and to resume their habitation when rebuilt in the manner prescribed by the several charters.' This never happened.[263]

All was not change and decay. Though St Michan's parish had already been divided,[264] by 1791 the numbers attending the divided parish and St Mary's were so large as to necessitate the creation of a further new parish by annexing part of St Michan's to St Mary's and creating St Thomas's. The dean and chapter contributed financially to the development.[265] In 1791, following consultation with the clergy of St Mary's, St Thomas's and St Michan's, the cathedral would not agree to the Lying-in Hospital (the Rotunda) making a parish church of its chapel.[266] The dean and chapter had a share in the patronage of the new St George's.[267] The established church was not alone in building and improving city churches, especially in the years following the granting of Catholic emancipation. In 1852, the superior of the Franciscan chapel of Adam and Eve was written to, pointing out that work on building there was intruding on Christ Church property, and asking 'what arrangement they are disposed to make'.[268] On a wider stage, cathedral lands were being leased for quite different purposes. The Royal Canal Company had an interest in land in Meath and Dublin, and the Grand Canal Company wanted ground for its Naas extension.[269] When it was proposed in 1816 that the railway carrying stones from the quarry at Dalkey for the new harbour wall under construction at 'Dunleary' should pass through cathedral land, the

---

260 C6/1/7/8, ff 15–17.   261 Ibid., pp 366–8.   262 See p. 000 above.   263 In the early 1990s the former St Werburgh's School in St Werburgh Street was largely restructured and is now the Christ Church deanery.   264 By 9 Will. III, c. 16 (1697).   265 C6/1/7/6, ff 40v, 83v. John Jebb, the cathedral treasurer, was elected first rector of the new parish. 266 C6/1/7/7, pp 298–300.   267 Ibid., pp 346–7.   268 C6/1/7/12, pp 298–9.   269 C6/1/7/7, p. 310; C6/1/7/8, p. 154.

dean and chapter raised no objection,[270] and they leased land in perpetuity for the construction of the Dublin and Kingstown Railway that opened in 1834.[271]

Eighteen hundred and six was a year when the proctor's statement of accounts was encouraging: a balance of £10,251, of which £2,152 was in debentures resulting from the sale of property to the Wide Streets Commissioners.[272] Between 1810 and 1814 the dean and chapter claimed to have spent £2,735 on the cathedral from the sale of part of the oeconomy estate,[273] and (partly, no doubt, because of the cost of providing for the boy choristers[274]) had borrowed £500 from St Patrick's.[275] The financial situation seems rapidly to have deteriorated. In view of 'the distressful state of the finances of this church' a range of economies was adopted: fees to readers were reduced, and savings made on lighting and heating. The dean undertook to continue to donate his house-money to the oeconomy.[276] Evening service was discontinued. The clerical vicars choral lost the fees they had received for assisting the prebendaries in reading prayers, being deemed to be in receipt of sufficient remuneration. By 1817, funds were in better shape.[277] In 1819, while assets in the proctor's hands stood at £11,571, this was almost entirely in debentures or government securities,[278] and once again, in 1820, revenue was insufficient for expenditure. It is easy to understand, therefore, why the dean and chapter were turning to government for help, if to little avail. While the cathedral might proclaim its financial embarrassment,[279] parliament also was experiencing a degree of embarrassment caused by growing public perception of the established church of Ireland as an over-endowed and maladministered adjunct of the state. Dean and chapter might (and did) say that only the state could rescue them from the predicament of having insufficient resources for the tasks in hand, and that there was little that they could do to break out of the vicious financial circle in which they found themselves. But when the state did eventually intervene, it was to require the re-distribution of resources within the Church of Ireland, and Christ Church was to prove a loser rather than a beneficiary.

In 1769 the niceties of the cathedral's rights as set out in the 'Liber albus' were consulted by the corporation where the riding of the franchises was concerned,[280] and well into the nineteenth century there were occasions when the seneschal summoned the jury of the manor to settle appropriate matters.[281] Likewise, the dean and chapter continued to appoint a constable to police their jurisdiction, and stood on their dignity from time to time. The dean, in

---

270 C6/1/7/9, p. 325.   271 C6/1/7/11, p. 269.   272 C6/1/7/8, p. 410.   273 C6/1/7/9, pp 276–82.   274 See p. 345 below.   275 C6/1/7/9, p. 277.   276 See p. 291 above.   277 C6/1/7/9, f. 358.   278 C6/1/7/10, p. 64.   279 Ibid., p. 108.   280 C6/1/7/6, f. 124; C6/1/7/8, pp 258–60.   281 C6/1/7/8, p. 479.

1816, drew the attention of the lord mayor to the fact that the city regalia had
been carried 'out of and beyond the lord mayor's jurisdiction', and the lord
mayor was duly contrite,[282] though years previously he had been obliged to
leave the city mace in the cathedral on ceremonial occasions 'for want of any
sort of officer to carry it', the mace-bearer having his hands full.[283] In 1817,
when it was revealed that there were 175 indigent residents of the precinct,
and a committee for the relief of the city poor made a donation to assist them,
it was returned to the donors, with the message that the dean and chapter
themselves would 'make provision for the poor within their precincts out of
their own funds', and proceeded to allocate £50 for the purpose.[284]

But such gestures of independence were not always possible, and there
had to be sharing of amenities with the city. While there was some street
lighting in the liberty, seven lamps in all (presumably provided and maintained by the cathedral),[285] the provision of the other public utilities posed
problems. The city corporation had a paving board from mid-eighteenth century[286] and there seems to have been an arrangement whereby the sweepings
of the precincts were taken to the corporation carts for removal.[287] Cooperation
with the government-nominated paving board (which itself had moments of
conflict with the municipal authorities) may have been less damaging to the
cathedral's *amour propre*, and not only did the chapter seek the paving board's
services to gravel and maintain the footpaths on the east side of the precinct,
but also authorised and paid for flagging and curbing on the west side, the
actual work being carried out under the paving board's auspices.[288]

A recurrent and more substantial occasion of dispute related to the perennial problem of infringements of the liberty's manorial jurisdiction. Such
petty judicial prerogatives were to be swept away mid-nineteenth century,
but while they lasted the dean, chapter and seneschal clung to their privileges. The infringement of the cathedral's franchises by a city under-sheriff,
who without the seneschal's warrant, executed a writ on a resident of Christ
Church Yard, caused the cathedral to assert

> ... that although Christ Church be in the inside of the city of Dublin,
> yet it is not any part of the city of Dublin, but an exempt jurisdiction
> where neither sheriffs of the city or county can execute a writ with-
> out the proper officer of the precincts,

and the city made amends.[289] In that same year, 1803, the seneschal sought
support from the archives for inhabitants who refused jury service in city

---

282 C6/1/7/9, pp 336–7.   283 *Anc. rec. Dublin*, viii, 485.   284 C6/1/7/9, f. 352.   285
C6/1/7/8, p. 4.   286 13 & 14 Geo. III, c. 22.   287 C6/1/7/7, p. 326.   288 C6/1/7/11,
pp 90, 91.   289 C6/1/7/8, p. 266.

courts.[290] A later seneschal, Henry Cole, was compensated by the dean and chapter for costs he sustained in defending a case (subsequently abandoned) charging him with false imprisonment for debt. The county gaol accepted debtors sent by his court, the superior courts respected his right to do so, and he claimed to have maintained the rights of his court even as far away as Blackrock and Kingstown![291] While the Irish Municipal Reform Act of 1840[292] transformed the basis on which Irish local government operated so far as the towns and cities were concerned, the manorial courts retained their functions until 1859, when they were abolished.[293]

The Wide Streets Commission was a statutory body whose activities impinged on both city and cathedral. Established in 1758,[294] the commissioners are credited with shaping the city of Dublin as we know it today. The city's role in urban planning was largely reduced to that of a client, from time to time submitting memorials to the commissioners, and seeking to have attention given to various necessary works. The environs of Dublin castle were central to the commissioners' work, and those of Christ Church scarcely less so. We first see evidence of their activities when, in 1778, the dean and chapter declined to renew leases in George's Lane and Dame Street because of plans to open a street from the lower north gate of the castle to College Green.[295] Similarly, in 1785, the dean and chapter informed a tenant of the impossibility of renewing a lease pending the commissioners' decision on 'opening a commodious passage to the church',[296] a development which the corporation offered to support.[297]

The cathedral could see some advantages in prospect, not least a financial one. While suffering from the post-Union property slump, at least it could anticipate a ready (if compulsory) purchaser.[298] However, the commissioners' funds were limited, and sales did not always raise as much as the dean and chapter would have liked. They were particularly disappointed at the commissioners' price for the Dean's Orchard in 1812.[299] Nonetheless, the proceeds from the sale of property in High Street and Christ Church Lane in 1814 amounted to £2,735, which was invested in 3½ per cent government stock.[300] In 1804 the dean and chapter resolved to set up a committee to consult with the various parties having an interest in developments in the environs of the two cathedrals. It comprised, in addition to their own representatives, representatives of the lord mayor and corporation, the archbishop,

290 Ibid., pp 258–9.   291 C6/1/7/11, pp 159–60.   292 3 & 4 Vict., c. 108.   293 22 Vict., c. 14.   294 31 Geo. II, c. 19.   295 C6/1/7/7, p. 105.   296 Ibid., p. 184.   297 Anc. rec. Dublin, xv, 516.   298 Another official source of revenue was the purchasing of land in 1805 for the erection of martello towers numbers 6 and 7 in south County Dublin (C6/1/7/8, f. 337).   299 C6/1/7/9, p. 203.   300 The legislation (31 Geo. II, c. 19) governed the manner in which income from sales to the commissioners was to be handled.

the dean and chapter of St Patrick's 'and such noblemen and gentlemen as may be concerned' to promote the view that the opening of the streets in the vicinity of Christ Church would greatly benefit the public. Copies of the resolution were given to chapter members for distribution.[301]

There was communication between chapter and commissioners on a regular basis, including occasions when Thomas Sherrard, the commissioners' secretary, waited on the dean and chapter at the cathedral.[302] For instance, the cathedral made an urgent request in 1815 that rubble in Christ Church Lane be removed as it made the passage of carriages to the great door highly dangerous. The commissioners went one better, and had the area levelled and shingled.[303] Presumably it was with some relief that the dean and chapter referred complaints about the main sewer from the residents of Christ Church Yard to the commissioners.[304] Despite constant lobbying it was not until 1817 that major decisions were made for the area surrounding the cathedral, based on plans drawn up by Sherrard. To facilitate the carrying out of these proposals, the cathedral sold property to the value of £5,948, consisting mainly of old shops, the gate-house, the old court of chancery, 'Mr Bates's toy shop', the Cheshire Cheese in Skinners' Row and the Bull's Head in Fishamble Street.[305] Of the sum raised, by far the greatest share went to the oeconomy, the rest being divided between several dignitaries, and, as the law dictated,[306] invested in government debentures, the oeconomy and the individuals concerned benefitting from the interest that accrued.

George IV's visit to Ireland from 12 August to 3 September 1821 provided an incentive to expedite development of the area. By July the commissioners had cleared much of the ground around Christ Church, which, according to the dean and chapter 'after no long time ... must be rebuilt or fall into utter ruin',[307] and offered 'if encouraged' to provide a plan for the area that would leave ample room 'for the site of a new cathedral church and chapel royal'. The residents of Skinners' Row, Castle Street and Fishamble Street urged the commissioners to do something about dangerous walls that remained, and 'the daily nuisance and indecencies' on waste ground, and the constant dust.[308] Some débris from demolished buildings survived until at

---

301 C6/1/7/8, p. 310.   302 For example, Dublin City Archives, Minutes of the Wide Streets Commissioners, vol. 29, ff 241–2 and vol. 32, f. 284.   303 Dublin City Archives, Wide Streets Commissioners, vol. 27, ff 140–1.   304 C6/1/7/7, ff 114–16.   305 Niall McCullagh, *A vision of the city: Dublin and the Wide Streets Commissioners* (Dublin, 1991), pp 9–10; C6/1/7/9, pp 381–4.   306 7 Geo. III, c. 7, s. 1 prescribed a procedure whereby the proceeds from the sale of property pertaining to individual dignitaries was paid to a trustee or trustees appointed by the said dignitaries, and approved by the dean and chapter. This procedure was adhered to (C6/1/7/6, ff 120–1).   307 C6/1/7/10, pp 144–5. 308 Ibid., p. 147.

least 1826, when the cathedral raised the matter yet again with the commissioners, emphasising the improvement to the city that would ensue (particularly if it were found practicable to erect residences for the dean and dignitaries).[309] By 1828, having failed, it seems, to elicit any response to their proposals for a re-built cathedral, the dean and chapter were attempting at least to prevent the commissioners from leasing ground contiguous to the cathedral as being 'detrimental to the object of the rebuilding of this cathedral church'. But the most that Christ Church obtained from the commissioners towards achieving its hopes for a new, greatly enhanced, building was an agreement to commute ground belonging to the commissioners in Skinners' Row for cathedral property in Ship Street.[310] In 1831 the commissioners presented the dean and chapter with their proposals for Skinners' Row, and these met with approval.[311]

The early decades of the nineteenth century were a time of considerable and well-founded anxiety and disappointment on the part of the cathedral authorities, as it became clear how limited was their capacity to influence decision-making by such bodies as the Wide Streets Commissioners. References, such as that quoted above to the cathedral's role as chapel royal, betray a nostalgia that would be of little avail in the face of the realities soon to be brought to bear on the temporalities of the Church of Ireland by a government at Westminster that was bent on reform.

---

309 C6/1/7/11, p. 12.   310 Ibid., pp 106, 109–20.   311 Ibid., p. 217. The surviving south-side of Skinners' Row was in compliance with the wishes of the residents renamed Christchurch Place, in 1833 (C6/1/8/11, p. 235).

XIV

The flourishing of music, 1660–1800

Barra Boydell

The Restoration in 1660 marked not only a return to choral services but also a new era in cathedral music as cathedrals sought to emulate the elaborate music of the Chapel Royal at St James's, and the *Book of Common Prayer* of 1662 gave for the first time formal recognition to the singing of anthems. Charles II underpinned the role of the Dublin cathedrals as pillars of Anglo-Protestant rule by increasing the incomes of the cathedral choirs in 1665 so that they could better maintain their 'great and solemn service'. He granted the proceeds of forfeited lands known as the augmentation estate, the half paid to Christ Church being divided equally among the six vicars choral and the stipendiaries, more or less doubling the value of these positions.[1] Furthermore, it became usual to offer singers positions in both cathedral choirs, the exceptional level of income thus enjoyed meaning that Dublin could attract cathedral musicians of the highest quality. Effectively the one choir now served both cathedrals. The nine vicars choral nominated at St Patrick's in October 1660 were all included amongst the six vicars choral and now eight stipendiaries appointed at Christ Church in September 1661, these fourteen constituting the twelve vicars and two stipendiaries listed at St Patrick's the following January. The four boys apprenticed at Christ Church in December 1662 were also in St Patrick's choir.[2] While the number of vicars choral remained six by statute, the stipendiaries soon settled (with some variation, dropping as low as two in 1689–90) at six, at which number they would remain until disestablishment.

During the break in cathedral services before 1660 choirmen had sought their living as best they could, in what Edward Wetenhall, precentor between

---

1 C6/1/27/3/1, pp 169–71; Seymour, *Christ Church*, p. 73; salaries to stipendiaries recorded in the proctors' accounts, £15 each per annum from the 1660s up to the nineteenth century, represent only part of their income. See also ch. xiii. 2 St Patrick's chapter acts, R.C.B., C2/1/3/2, ff 256, 279 [3, 26]; Boydell, *Music*, pp 96–7, 156–7; in addition the choir of St Patrick's also had four 'petty canons'.

1675 and 1678, described as 'mean, miserable and illiberal ways' and regarded as the cause of weaknesses he perceived in cathedral music.[3] After 1660 the collection of rents due to the vicars choral and the assigning of leases occupied both John Hawkshaw, a former vicar choral and now organist,[4] and Richard Hosier as dean's vicar and vicars' steward.[5] The choir stalls needed to be rebuilt, a temporary organ used pending the building of a new instrument in 1664–5, and the musical repertoire re-established and renewed.[6] Although Hawkshaw and Hosier were the first vicars to be appointed, in February 1661,[7] and the full choir was not formally installed until October, the new choir participated in the ceremony held in St Patrick's on 27 January 1661 at which twelve bishops were consecrated and at the installations of the dean and other dignitaries in Christ Church in February and March 1661.[8]

Twice-weekly rehearsals were introduced in 1661 and new rules for the choir were drawn up in 1662.[9] Strict regulations governing attendance included morning and evening service daily and choirmen were to take communion on solemn feasts and at least once quarterly. There is a new emphasis on musical standards, each choirman being required to be able to sight-read 'ordinary anthems'. Appropriate behaviour, dress and appearance at services were required and due reverence expected towards senior members of the cathedral. Any choirman striking another, swearing, being drunk or an 'incontinent liver' faced expulsion, and none was to keep an alehouse or tavern. These rules followed complaints about the behaviour of choirmen including one who had received a black eye in a tavern brawl.[10] At the same time the oath sworn by vicars choral on their admission emphasised obedience, daily attendance at services and specified that they had not committed simony in seeking their position.[11] By the late eighteenth century rules relating to the appropriate singing of responses and the antiphonal chanting of psalms, both sides joining in the doxology, were reflecting changes in the practice of psalm chanting.[12] Half the choir now attended weekday services as had been the practice since mid-century[13] and, echoing views expressed

---

3 Wetenhall, *Of gifts and offices*, pp 538–9, see Boydell, *Music*, p. 163.   4 Cotton stated that Hawkshaw was appointed organist in 1646, but his source is not known (*Fasti*, ii, p. 84); Hawkshaw was however organist of St Audoen's church, a position normally held by the organist of Christ Church, between 1645 and 1648 (accounts of St Anne's guild, Royal Irish Academy, MS 12.D.1, f. 74).   5 Boydell, *Music*, p. 156; C6/1/7/2, ff 91v, 92, 94; C6/1/26/5, f. 29v; C6/1/26/12/2, f. 2r; C6/1/26/12/3.   6 Boydell, *Music*, pp 132, 133, 134.   7 Ibid., p. 96.   8 Mason, *St Patrick's*, pp 192–3; C6/1/7/2, ff 85, 87, 89.   9 Boydell, *Music*, pp 97–100.   10 Ibid., p. 97; C6/1/7/2, f. 106v.   11 Boydell, *Music*, p. 158.   12 Rules for the choir (1789), Boydell, *Music*, pp 125–6; compare Nicholas Temperley, 'Music in church' in H. Diack Johnstone and Roger Fisk (ed.), *The Blackwell history of music in Britain*: iv, *the eighteenth century* (Oxford, 1990), p. 361.   13 C6/1/23/1.

by Wetenhall a century earlier, the selection of music was to be approved by the dean and chapter. Weekly rehearsals, at which attendance was a frequent problem, were only held on Saturdays from 1703,[14] but despite problems with individual choir members[15] the standard of the choir was praised in the mid-eighteenth century. Mrs Delaney commented in 1731 on the 'good voices and a very sweet organ' and Handel expressed satisfaction at the singers in his oratorio concerts who were largely members of the cathedral choirs.[16]

Morning and evening services on weekdays and Sundays formed the bulk of the choir's duties (by the 1760s evening service was not usually attended by the choir),[17] but more elaborate services were held on occasions of both church and state ceremonial. Reflecting practices at the Chapel Royal in London, during the deanery of William Moreton from 1677 instrumentalists were increasingly used to accompany the choir at important services.[18] On these occasions symphony anthems with instrumental accompaniment (such as those by Humfrey, Blow, Cooke and others in the Hosier MS from Christ Church, c.1670s)[19] would have been played, but after 1685 the use of musicians declined.[20] State days such as the monarch's birthday were often marked by additional payments to the vicars, and at the centenary celebration of Trinity College in 1695 the choir sang in Purcell's ode 'Great Parent, Hail!', an event which took place in the college rather than the cathedral.[21] During the eighteenth century the cathedral was the venue for public celebrations including state visits by the lord lieutenant, the celebration of English military victories and peace celebrations such as the treaties of Utrecht (1713) and Aix-la-Chapelle (1749), and state anniversaries. On these occasions *Te Deums* and celebratory anthems were performed, often composed by cathedral musicians or by the master of the state music.[22]

The increasingly public role of the cathedral is reflected in the growing opportunities for choirmen to sing outside the cathedral, which however were repeatedly opposed by the dean and chapter. In 1663 a stipendiary had been

---

14 Boydell, *Music*, p. 106. 15 Compare Dean Swift's comments on choirmen, Grindle, *Cathedral music*, pp 39–40. 16 Lady Llanover (ed.), *Autobiography and correspondence of Mary Granville, Mrs Delaney* (5 vols, London, 1861–2), i, 294–5; Donald Burrows, 'Handel's Dublin performances' in Patrick Devine and Harry White (ed.), *Irish musical studies*, iv (Dublin, 1996), p. 56. 17 Boydell, *Music*, pp 158, 169–70; no choir attendance records survive between 1664 and 1762. 18 Ibid., pp 136, 137, 138, 139; compare Wetenhall, *Of gifts and offices*, pp 533–4. 19 Durham cathedral, dean and chapter library, MS B 1 (see further below). 20 Musicians are next mentioned on the queen's birthday in 1703, Boydell, *Music*, p. 143. 21 Boydell, *Music*, pp 136, 137, 138, 139; Helga Robinson-Hammerstein, 'With great solemnity: celebrating the first centenary of the foundation of Trinity College, Dublin, 9 January 1694' in *Long Room*, xxxvii (1992), pp 27–38. 22 Boydell, *Music*, p. 109; Brian Boydell, *A Dublin musical calendar 1700–1760* (Dublin, 1988), pp 35, 126, 170, 253.

disciplined for singing in the theatre and this problem was to become common in the eighteenth century.[23] Following their participation in some of Handel's concerts in 1741 choir members were forbidden to sing at any concert without special leave of the chapter (an injunction repeated with reference to the boys in 1771),[24] but the cathedral choirs did constitute a body of trained singers who could usefully be called on for appropriate occasions. The choirboys sang in the annual birthday ode in honour of the monarch at Dublin castle[25] and participation in charitable performances was permitted. It was in this light that members of the combined cathedral choirs sang both as soloists and chorus in the first performance of Handel's 'Messiah' in Fishamble Street on 13 April 1742.[26] When the Lying-In Hospital (the Rotunda) sought permission in 1772 for some of the choir to perform in charity oratorios in a theatre during Passion week permission was only granted with assurances that the choir would be physically separated from any stage players.[27] Boy trebles were popular at the Rotunda charity concerts in the 1760s and 1770s, while cathedral choirmen and organists also played at or conducted these concerts.[28] In April 1788 the cathedral itself hosted charitable concerts when three Handel commemoration concerts were held in aid of decayed musicians, the Meath Hospital and the Lying-In Hospital, and permission was readily given for choir members to sing at charity sermons.[29] Within their own private circles, however, the choirmen sang glees and catches, often of a ribald nature quite foreign to their professional duties, the Hibernian Catch Club (still in existence) having been founded, reputedly in c.1680, by the vicars choral of the two cathedrals.[30] It was for convivial men's clubs such as this that Richard Woodward, choirman and later organist, composed his catches.[31]

The choirboys maintain a shadowy existence being only rarely mentioned in the records. A proposed increase to six choirboys in 1664 was not apparently realised,[32] but their total number did increase from six to eight in 1761,

23 Boydell, *Music*, p. 100.   24 Ibid., pp 112, 113, 118; for Dean Swift's less prosaic injunction against the choirmen of St Patrick's in 1741, Boydell, *Musical calendar*, p. 76.   25 T.J. Walshe, *Opera in Dublin, 1705–1797* (Dublin, 1973), p. 26.   26 Burrows, 'Handel's Dublin performances', pp 67, 70.   27 Boydell, *Music*, p. 119; the performance in question was of 'Messiah' on 16 April (Brian Boydell, *Rotunda music in eighteenth century Dublin* (Dublin, 1992), p. 93); compare Boydell, *Music*, pp 121–2 and Boydell, *Rotunda music*, pp 109, 226.   28 For William Brett and Robert Tuke (choirboys), Samuel Murphy as organist in 1771 and Langrish Doyle as conductor in 1790, Boydell, *Rotunda music*, pp 68, 94–5, 215, 221.   29 Boydell, *Rotunda music*, p. 168; 24 Feb. 1786 (St Ann's church), 1 Dec. 1800 (St Mary's and the Rotunda chapel); C6/1/7/7–8.   30 Boydell, *Musical calendar*, p. 267; Bumpus however stated that the Hibernian Catch Club was founded 'in the middle of the last [i.e. eighteenth] century' (Bumpus, *Stevenson*, p. 11).   31 *Songs, canons and catches*, op.1 (London, 1761).   32 Boydell, *Music*, p. 101, but 'the

St Patrick's contributing a quarter of the cost.[33] Most of the boys at this period sang in both cathedral choirs and in 1777 it was agreed to apprentice them simultaneously to both cathedrals.[34] From 1660 the boys were apprenticed for seven years, swearing an oath to behave themselves, to avoid 'taverns, unlawful houses, gambling, and immoral practices' and, although they were probably only about eight when apprenticed, not to get married without permission.[35] Punishments could be severe, including being committed to the cathedral's prison or even being discharged with cancellation of apprenticeship.[36] On completing their apprenticeship or when their voices broke the boys were paid a gratuity and apprenticed to a trade (unless they remained in the choir as adults).[37] The cathedral might retain the services of former choirboys, in one instance even encouraging further musical education through the provision of a spinet.[38] Organ tuition meant that boys could deputise for the organist on occasion, and in the later seventeenth century the boys were also taught lute and violin, with theorbo for continuo.[39] A harpsichord bought in 1702 and a spinet five years later reflect changes in continuo practice and by 1781 the cathedral owned two fortepianos.[40]

After 1660 as the positions of organist and master of the choirboys increasingly became, like the choir, common to both cathedrals the duties of each post were separated, a practice which had begun in 1638 when Randall Jewett remained master of the boys after Benjamin Rogers became organist.[41] Subsequently there was only to be one twenty-year period from 1776 when Richard Woodward (junior), Samuel Murphy and Langrish Doyle successively combined the two posts. Until 1800 the master of the boys was responsible for their food, accommodation and clothing, and for their musical education, a 'writing master' looking after their general education.[42] From the Restoration to the mid-eighteenth century the master of the boys was always a priest and usually either dean's vicar or chanter's (precentor's) vicar, but thereafter the post was typically given to lay choir members (not necessarily

---

four chorister boys' are mentioned in 1666; compare Boydell, *Music*, p. 133.   33 Ibid., pp 116, 118.   34 Ibid., p. 122; on choirboys as members of both choirs compare boys listed in St Patrick's chapter acts and mentioned at Christ Church in the chapter acts; in the absence of lists of boys at Christ Church before the mid-nineteenth century it is difficult to determine their full complement at any one time.   35 Boydell, *Music*, pp 100, 107, 156–7.   36 Ibid., pp 101, 136, 146; C6/1/7/7, p.120.   37 Gratuity first mentioned in 1676–7, Boydell, *Music*, p. 136.   38 Boydell, *Music*, p. 117.   39 Ibid., pp 135, 136, 137, 169; on the identity of the theorbo, Linda Sayce, 'Continuo lutes in 17th and 18th century England' in *Early Music*, xxiii (1995), pp 666–84.   40 Boydell, *Music*, pp 106, 143, 144, 151, 152; the pianos were repaired by Ferdinand Weber (who most probably made them) and subsequently by his widow.   41 See page 248.   42 Boydell, *Music*, pp 135, 138; C6/1/7/4, 24 Nov. 1713; for Wetenhall's views on the education of choirboys in the 1670s, Boydell, *Music*, pp 163–4.

vicars choral) who were prominent musicians. Richard Hosier was the first master of the boys following the Restoration, a position he also held at St Patrick's.[43] The treble solos in Hosier's anthems[44] and an anthem in the Hosier MS dated 1669 by Walter Hitchcock (then a choirboy at St Patrick's and probably also Christ Church)[45] reflect his activities as music teacher to the boys.[46] In contrast Nicholas Sanderson, Hosier's successor after his death in 1677, was admonished in 1691 for, amongst other faults, teaching the boys to sing not 'according to art but by rote'.[47] William Lamb, a stipendiary and a prominent countertenor,[48] was master of the boys from 1746 to 1758 and the first to be neither a vicar choral nor ordained. His successor, Revd Samuel Murphy, took his Mus.D. from Trinity College Dublin in 1768 and has the unusual distinction of having twice been master of the boys, from 1758 until he resigned in 1768 and from 1777 following the early death of Richard Woodward (junior) until his own death in 1780. During the latter period Murphy also succeeded Woodward as cathedral organist, which post he had held at St Patrick's since 1769.[49] The combining of the posts of organist and master of the boys under Woodward, Murphy and Doyle (1780–97) coincides with a period when music flourished at Christ Church and vocal standards were high. Subsequent appointments however were less successful: Doyle's successor John Clarke(-Whitfield), a respected if conservative composer, returned to England and resigned within a year, reputedly because of the outbreak of rebellion in 1798.[50] John Spray, an outstanding tenor singer, was appointed master in December 1798. His quarrelsome disposition may have contributed to his resignation two years later, despite his remaining a prominent vicar choral until his death in 1827: in 1800 he was involved in a dispute with Revd Charles Osborne (now master of the boys) over a choirboy's solo singing.[51] On Osborne's appointment responsibility for the boys' housing and care was delegated, initially to the verger James Hewitt.[52]

From 1670 the cathedral bells increase in number once every century until the twentieth century. The augmentation beyond three bells from 1670 brought a different sound and a different dynamic into play, the ringers

43 R.C.B., C2/1/3/3, p. 80; for full listing of masters of the boys up to 1800, Boydell, *Music*, pp 252–3.   44 For example Boydell, *Music*, pp 195–205.   45 R.C.B., C2/1/3/2, ff 327v [74v], 376.   46 The 'Hosier MS', Durham, MS B 1, pp 124–31; see further Boydell, *Music*, pp 176–9.   47 Boydell, *Music*, p. 102.   48 Boydell, *Musical calendar*, p. 282; Burrows, 'Handel's Dublin Performances', pp 63, 70.   49 Boydell, *Music*, pp 116, 118, 122, 123; Grindle, *Cathedral music*, p. 224.   50 Boydell, *Music*, pp 128, 129; C6/1/7/8, pp 108–10; Seymour, *Christ Church*, p. 76; Clarke-Whitfield later became professor of music at Cambridge, *New Grove*, iv, 449.   51 Boydell, *Music*, pp 128, 130, 131–2; see also Bumpus, *Stevenson*, pp 14–15; John Matthews, chantor's vicar, had looked after the boys between Michaelmas 1797 and 1798, Boydell, *Music*, p. 153.   52 Boydell, *Music*, pp 130–1.

thenceforth existing as a body of practitioners and friends, ringing for state days and celebrations and for divine service on Sundays, while the sextons and vergers continued for some time to have the duties of daily tolling. In response to a petition to the chapter in 1670 the Society of Ringers was granted right of access to practise at their pleasure, the verger being directed to keep the bells in good order.[53] The bells in question were made by the Purdue brothers, Roger and William, of Bristol and Salisbury, with Irish partners William and Tobias Covey. They were cast in Dublin using the three old bells and additional metal from artillery parts from the king's storehouse. The motivator of this improvement was Dean John Parry who, as well as acquiring the artillery parts, gained the assistance of the city authorities to raise funds in return for which the lord mayor and council asked that the dean and chapter ensure that the great bell of Christ Church be rung at four in the morning and nine at night 'as formerly hath been accustomed' and without charge on the mayor, sheriffs, commons, citizens or their successors.[54] This arose from the fact that after the Reformation the citizens had arranged that payment for the continuation of the four o'clock and nine o'clock bells be made from the city funds. The city accounts between 1618 and 1658 reveal constant requests from successive sextons of Christ Church and sometimes from their widows for payment of arrears (the curfew bell continued to be rung by the sexton until the early nineteenth century, but the morning bell was soon given up by common consent).[55] The city officials collected £276 as a contribution to the cost of the new bells.[56] Six bells, all with full wheels, were sufficient requirement for the formation of a society of ringers and the beginning of the growth of change-ringing, a new art developing in England since 1650. The one society (Phil Crofts, Mr Dodson and the Society of Ringers are listed in the reply to the petition) could begin ringing in Christ Church in July 1670 and in St Patrick's in September when eight bells by the same makers were in place, all part of a great scheme of bell acquisition for the ornamentation of Dublin begun and carried through by Dean Parry who was also precentor of St Patrick's.[57] The sharing of one band of ringers for the two cathedrals continued until the late nineteenth century.

Tobias Covey had to recast the tenor in 1687.[58] In 1697 the ringers were paid ten shillings for ringing on a day of thanksgiving for peace and the following year Ellinor Byrne of Fishamble Street received ten shillings for meat and drink for the ringers on a state day.[59] Clearly, ringing for state days was lucrative and enjoyable, but it could also prove to be hazardous due to the

53 Murphy & Taylor, *Bells*, p. 14.   54 *Anc. rec. Dublin*, iv, 446–7.   55 J.L. Robinson, 'Dublin cathedral bells, 1670' in *R.S.A.I. Jn.*, xlii (1912), pp 155–62.   56 C6/1/4.   57 Robinson, 'Bells', p. 159.   58 C6/1/7/3, f. [3r].   59 C6/1/26/16/13: 1697, p. 9, 1698, f. [2v]; C6/1/7/3, 24 Mar. 1698.

importance of bells as an instrument of public rejoicing: in 1688 when Dublin was in the hands of Catholic supporters of James II and opponents of his Protestant challenger, William of Orange, the lord mayor alleged that the bells of Christ Church did not ring merrily enough for the birth of the Prince of Wales, the Catholic heir to the throne, and sent his men to place officers of Christ Church in the stocks. Affronted, they claimed first that the mayor had no jurisdiction, second that nobody apart from the mayor noticed a lack of merriness, and third that if they did not ring merrily enough 'it was the ringers' fault, not theirs'. Thus protesting, they were dragged off.[60] This confirms that it was the ringers with their new-fangled art who were in charge of the bells, and clearly the mayor was ignorant of the fact. But what can the mayor have meant by merry ringing? Did he mean fast ringing? With limited notes, merriness is hard to regulate except by speed. Even now, and more especially in the old days of heavy wooden headstocks and slow-turning bells on plain bearings, fast ringing might have been beyond the power of ringers, or simply not their habit. This raises the question of how exactly bells are rung in the manner practiced at Christ Church since 1670. The full wheel is crucial to the art, and at each time the note sounds the bell is near its highest point travelling through 360 degrees. The bells are not static but swinging and swooping, and the control which a ringer must exert is a result of expertise gained through experience so that the sequences rung are correct and the sounding out of each note is separate from all the others. We cannot tell what precisely the ringers were ringing in 1670 – whether called-changes or methods – since no record survives. As for the instrument on which they performed their art, in 1733 it was found that the tenor was cracked (this was a re-casting by Covey in 1687 of the Purdue tenor), while in 1716 the second bell had also been recast.[61] The four Purdue bells, with the substitutes, were replaced in 1738 by a splendid eight made by Abraham Rudhall of Gloucester, of which five remain, the others having in their turn been re-cast in the nineteenth century, two by Murphy of Dublin and the other by Taylor of Loughborough.[62]

After the temporary use from 1661 of an organ belonging to John Hawkshaw which was small enough to be carried 'from church to church',[63] a new organ was built by George Harris in 1665 to which Lancelot Pease added a choir (or 'chair') organ in 1667 at a cost of £80 pounds, thus completing the provision of a full 'double' organ for the cathedral.[64] Pease settled in Dublin, becoming both a stipendiary at Christ Church and vicar choral at St Patrick's.[65] Thirty years later a new organ was needed. An agreement was

---

60 King, *State of the Protestants*. See also p. 269.   61 Murphy & Taylor, *Bells*, pp 17–19. 62 Ibid., pp 19–20.   63 Boydell, *Music*, p. 132.   64 Ibid., pp 133, 134, 159–61.   65 C6/1/7/2, f. 150; Cotton, *Fasti*, ii, 205; Pease had built organs for King's College,

sealed with the English organ builder Bernard Smith in November 1694, a deposit of £50 having been paid to Richard Battell, sub-dean of the Chapel Royal.[66] However, Smith failed to fulfil the agreement and in May 1697 Renatus Harris (who was currently building an organ at Limerick cathedral and had just completed one for St Patrick's) was engaged at a cost of £1,200 to install the organ he had built for a direct competition between himself and Smith at the Temple, London (from which Smith had emerged triumphant).[67] Dublin city council contributed £50 towards the cost, with lesser contributions from others including the bishop of Kilmore, Edward Wetenhall (the former precentor).[68] The decision to engage John Baptist Cuvillie in 1698 both as organ tuner and to add to Harris's instrument ensured the services of the leading organ builder in Ireland of the early eighteenth century. Cuvillie's additions in 1699 which would make it suitable 'for all manner of voluntaries, French or Italian grounds whatsoever' included a tremulant 'which no organ in England can show the like, for they have not found out to make a Tramblan [sic] stop'.[69] When the Harris-Cuvillie organ needed to be replaced in 1750, despite the presence in Dublin of a number of organ builders the dean and chapter approached John Byfield of London (who had formerly acted briefly as organ tuner after Cuvillie's death in 1728). Byfield's new instrument was installed in 1752 at a cost of £800,[70] Byfield taking the old organ back to England where it survives today in Wolverhampton, though rebuilt.[71] With subsequent repairs and additions, Byfield's organ remained in use until 1856. By 1766 or earlier Ferdinand Weber was looking after the organ,[72] followed after 1784 by William Castles Hollister until his own death in 1802.[73] In 1791 the organ was moved to the quire screen which had formerly been occupied by the lord lieutenant's seat.[74] Prior to this, at least since the Harris organ of

Cambridge and Canterbury cathedral before coming to Ireland. 66 Boydell, *Music*, pp 103, 140. 67 Ibid., p. 104; agreement dated 26 May 1697, McEnery & Refaussé, *Deeds*, no. 1932; see also Boydell, *Music*, pp 141–2. 68 Boydell, *Music*, pp 142, 143. 69 Ibid., pp 104, 105, 167–9; on Cuvillie, Barra Boydell, 'John Baptiste Cuvillie, Ferdinand Weber, and the organ of Trinity College chapel, Dublin' in *The Organ*, lxxii (1992), pp 15–26; Barra Boydell, 'St Michan's church, Dublin: the installation of the organ in 1725 and the duties of the organist' in *British Institute of Organ Studies Journal*, xix (1995), pp 74–96; Denise Neary, 'Music in late seventeenth and eighteenth century Dublin churches', M.A. thesis, St Patrick's College, Maynooth, 1995. 70 Boydell, *Music*, pp 111, 115; Boydell, *Musical calendar*, pp 166, 168, 170; for the specification of Byfield's organ, Boydell, *Music*, p. 265. 71 Brian Boydell, 'Organs associated with Handel's visit to Dublin' in *British Institute of Organ Studies Journal*, xix (1995), pp 59–60; for Robert Stewart's opinion of the Harris organ in Wolverhampton, Vignoles, *Memoir*, pp 130–1. 72 Boydell, *Music*, p. 147; the accounts are missing between 1738 and 1766. 73 Ibid., p. 124; C6/1/7/8, p. 209. 74 C6/1/7/7, pp 310–11; Boydell, *Music*, pp 126–7.

1697 if not earlier, the organ had occupied a gallery towards the north-east end of the quire with a curved projection in front used by solo anthem singers who would ascend to the organ loft for their solos.[75]

John Hawkshaw was organist from the Restoration until his death in late 1688 or early 1689.[76] Like Randall Jewett before the Commonwealth he was also organist at St Patrick's, this pattern becoming common (but not invariable) until disestablishment.[77] For a period of nearly ten years after Hawkshaw's death various people acted as organist but none for very long. Thomas Godfrey, organist at St Patrick's since 1686, held the post for a few months from January 1689, followed by Thomas Finell, a stipendiary and also organ tuner in succession to Lancelot Pease, until Christmas 1690 when Thomas Morgan was appointed. Within little more than a month Morgan had gone to England 'to attain the perfection of an organist' and Finell resumed the post.[78] In November 1691 the position was offered to Peter Isaac, organist and master of the choristers at Salisbury cathedral and formerly a stipendiary at Christ Church and vicar choral at St Patrick's. Isaac was appointed on 31 March 1692 (he also became organist at St Patrick's) but he died only two years later while visiting England.[79] Again Thomas Finell took over until the arrival of Daniel Roseingrave from Salisbury (where he had succeeded Isaac) in November 1698.[80] In the late sixteenth and early seventeenth centuries most or all of the organists appear to have been appointed from England.[81] The change after 1660 to local appointments shows a growth in confidence and musical standards at Christ Church, while Isaac and Roseingrave, the only organists to be appointed from England, both had links with Dublin.[82] Their appointment may have been part of a conscious

---

75 In 1710 the organ was situated next to 'the seat in the gallery wherein the lady mayoress sits', as it was before 1791 (Boydell, *Music*, p. 109); in the 1680s Dineley merely refers to the 'organ gallery' without stating where it was sited (F. Elrington Ball, 'Extracts from the journal of Thomas Dineley, or Dingley, Esquire, giving some account of his visit to Ireland in the reign of Charles II' in *R.S.A.I. Jn.*, xliii (1913), pp 275–309); John Jebb, *A few observations respecting Christ Church cathedral and its precinct* (Dublin, 1855), pp 10–11.   76 For a listing of organists before 1800, Boydell, *Music*, pp 250–1.   77 Grindle, *Cathedral music*, p. 224; Shaw, *Organists* (Oxford, 1991), pp 410, 418–19.   78 Boydell, *Music*, pp 102–3.   79 Ibid., p. 103; C6/1/7/3, 23 Apr. 1688; Lawlor, *Fasti*, p. 222; Shaw, *Organists*, p. 419.   80 Roseingrave was also granted a stipendiary's income but without the attendant duties, Boydell, *Music*, pp 103, 104, 105, 106; Grindle incorrectly states that Robert Hodge is named as organist in 1697 (*Cathedral music*, p. 223).   81 On the possible political reasons behind the appointment of English organists, see Barra Boydell, 'Cathedral music, city and state'.   82 On Roseingrave's possible Dublin antecedents (although the name is also found in early seventeenth-century England), Boydell, *Music*, p. 263, n. 123.

policy to introduce musicians with broader experience but Irish connections at a time when both the cathedrals and Dublin cultural life were being re-established following the Williamite war. All succeeding organists of Christ Church until the early twentieth century were Irish (until Charles Kitson was appointed from England in 1913), many having been trained as choristers in the cathedral.

Daniel Roseingrave's appointment coincided with the completion of Renatus Harris's new organ. His son Ralph succeeded him in 1727 until his own death in 1747, the two Roseingraves being organists of both cathedrals for nearly half a century as well as being important composers of cathedral music. George Walsh became organist on Ralph Roseingrave's death and was succeeded in 1765 by Richard Woodward (junior), undoubtedly one of the most gifted musicians to serve Christ Church cathedral during the eighteenth century.[83] His father Richard (senior) had joined the choir from England in 1751, Richard (junior) becoming a choirboy.[84] In 1771 he took his Mus.D. at Trinity College, Dublin, in the same year publishing his *Cathedral music*, the earliest publication of cathedral music by an Irish composer.[85] He died at the age of thirty-three in November 1777, a year after his father had resigned the post of master of the boys in his favour. Samuel Murphy was elected both organist, a position he already held at St Patrick's and Trinity College (where members of the choirs of both cathedrals sang on Sundays since the 1760s), and master of the boys for a second time.[86] Langrish Doyle, who succeeded to both positions in 1780, had been a choirboy at both cathedrals and a stipendiary of Christ Church before becoming organist at Armagh in 1776.[87] Like Murphy he was also organist in Trinity College.

The Restoration musical repertoire at the two Dublin cathedrals can be traced from two sources: a printed volume of *Anthems to be sung at the celebration of divine service in the cathedral church of the Holy and Undivided Trinity in Dublin* (1662)[88] and an early Restoration music manuscript from Dublin, the Hosier MS.[89] *Anthems to be sung* contains the texts of fifty-one verse anthems of the later sixteenth and early seventeenth centuries by composers including Gibbons, Byrd, Nathaniel Giles and Bull.[90] Composers associated

83 Boydell, *Music*, pp 114, 117; further on Woodward, Eithne Donnelly, 'Richard Woodward: a study of his life and music', M.A. thesis, N.U.I. Maynooth, 1998.   84 Boydell, *Music*, pp 115, 116; C6/1/7/6, f. 70.   85 *Cathedral music consisting of one compleat service, seven anthems, several chants and Veni Creator Spiritus* (London, 1771).   86 Boydell, *Music*, p. 122; on music at Trinity College chapel, Lesley Whiteside, *The chapel of Trinity College, Dublin* (Dublin, 1998).   87 Boydell, *Music*, pp 123–4; Grindle, *Cathedral music*, p. 50.   88 T.C.D., shelf mark r. f. 53.   89 Durham cathedral, dean and chapter library, MS B 1; see also Brian Crosby, 'An early Restoration liturgical music manuscript' in *Music and Letters*, lv (1974), pp 458–64, and Boydell, *Music*, pp 176–9.   90 On the use of such volumes, Wetenhall, *Of gifts and offices*, p. 487, in Boydell, *Music*, p. 161.

with Christ Church include Randolph Jewett (four anthems) and Benjamin Rogers (two) and at least some of these anthems may have been composed locally. Only two anthems unquestionably post-date the Restoration: Richard Hosier's 'Now that the Lord hath readvanc'd the crown' (Consecration anthem) and John (or Thomas) Holmes's 'O God that art the well spring',[91] the music for both of which is in the Hosier MS. In contrast, the music in the Hosier MS which dates from the 1660s and 1670s is very much more up to date. This is the earliest known collection of post-Reformation church music from Ireland and the unique source for a number of anthems by Dublin composers. There are six anthems by Richard Hosier, the main copyist of the manuscript, and one each by John Blett, a stipendiary between 1661 and late 1665/early 1666 and vicar at St Patrick's,[92] and Walter Hitchcock, who remained a choirman at St Patrick's and Christ Church at least until 1690–1.[93] There are also two anthems by Benjamin Rogers, one of which ('I beheld and lo', which is unattributed in the manuscript) may date from his Dublin years. The anthems by Hosier, Blett and Hitchcock are all verse anthems with short four-part choruses, predominantly chordal in style and including final 'Hallelujahs' in four of Hosier's anthems.[94] Each anthem opens with a brief organ introduction and the verses, most often declamatory in style, usually alternate sections for each soloist although there are occasional duets. The harmonic language is limited and at times rough-hewn. Many contemporary churchmen were concerned at secular influences on sacred music as evident in much of this repertoire. Edward Wetenhall was a strong advocate of the role of music in worship and made practical suggestions to improve cathedral music and choirs while being critical of anthems and services which 'savour more of curiosity of music, than design of devotion'.[95] Dean Moreton enquired in 1679 if the anthems sung at Christ Church were 'fit to excite and employ Christian devotion' and performed 'with due art and decency'.[96]

The choral repertoire needed to be re-established and developed in the years after the Restoration and there was considerable activity in the purchase and copying of music.[97] Cathedral music continued to circulate mainly

91 Attributed to John Holmes in *Anthems to be sung* ... and to Thomas in the Hosier MS. 92 Boydell, *Music*, pp 97, 134; Lawlor, *Fasti*, p. 214.   93 R.C.B., C2/1/3/3, 8 Jan. 1672; Boydell, *Music*, pp 136, 140.   94 Hosier's 'Now that the Lord' (Consecration anthem), 'Thou O God art praised in Sion' and Blett's 'Ad te Domine: Thou art O God' in Boydell, *Music*, pp 195–211; Hosier's 'Now that the Lord' and Rogers's 'I beheld and lo' recorded on *Sing (CD)*.   95 Boydell, *Music*, p. 162.   96 Ibid., p. 165.   97 Ibid., pp 132, 133, 134, 135, 136, 137, 138, 139, 140; Dublin stationers and printers named in these payments include Samuel Dancer, Nathaniel Thomson, John North, Mary Crooke, and William Winter; see also Barra Boydell, 'Prickers and printers: the purchase and copying of music at Christ Church cathedral, Dublin, in the 17th and 18th centuries' in *Long Room*, xliii (1998), pp 20–8.

in hand-copied manuscripts well into the eighteenth century and there is no evidence for music printing in Dublin before 1685,[98] so payments for 'printed anthems', 'music books', 'anthem books' and 'service books' would have included word books like the 1662 volume of *Anthems to be sung*. Choir members also copied and wrote music for which ruled music paper was bought from London.[99] Nicholas Sanderson, master of the choirboys, was asked in 1692 to prepare a new set of 'service anthem books' which he copied over the next two years. He was also appointed to look after the music books and be responsible for copying new music, this marking the beginning of the practice of paying someone (usually the chanter's vicar) as keeper of the choirbooks.[100] None of the music copied at or acquired by Christ Church (or St Patrick's) is known to survive from between the Hosier MS and the collection of later eighteenth and early nineteenth-century part-, score-, and organ-books from Christ Church.[101] The repertoire sung during this intervening period can be assumed, as later, to have been comparable with that of English cathedrals.[102] Two anthems written by Bartholomew Isaacs, a vicar at Christ Church from 1684 to 1687, may date from his Dublin years although copied in England,[103] but two creeds and four services composed for Christ Church by Daniel Roseingrave[104] are amongst works which are lost (the anthems and a service which do survive by Daniel Roseingrave are thought to pre-date his Dublin years,[105] although some of the music attributed to Ralph Roseingrave in the surviving Christ Church choir-books could be by Daniel). Christ Church choirmen who were paid for composing anthems in the early eighteenth century are George Rogers in 1704, John Harris five years later, and both John Church and Ralph Roseingrave in 1735–6.[106]

A wordbook entitled *A collection of anthems, as the same are now performed in the cathedral church of the Holy and Undivided Trinity*, Dublin published in 1745 provides a view of the repertoire in the mid-eighteenth century.[107] Most of the 186 anthems are verse anthems and contemporary or recent composers predominate, Maurice Greene with forty-eight anthems being by far the most popular followed by Croft and Boyce. The later seventeenth cen-

98 Barra Boydell, 'The development of the Dublin music print trade to 1800' in *Long Room*, xli (1996), pp 25–33.   99 Boydell, *Music*, pp 132, 133, 137, 138, 140; on the production of music paper, Robert Thompson, 'Manuscript music in Purcell's London' in *Early Music*, xxiii (1995), pp 605–18.   100 Boydell, *Music*, pp 103, 140.   101 C6/1/24/1–5.   102 When Robert Hodge returned from a visit to England in 1697 he brought music for St Patrick's cathedral including verse anthems by Blow, Purcell and Tucker, and services by Aldrich, Blow, Child and Purcell (Grindle, *Cathedral music*, pp 32–3).   103 Spink, *Cathedral music*, p. 226.   104 Boydell, *Music*, pp 106, 142.   105 Spink, *Cathedral music*, p. 228.   106 Boydell, *Music*, pp 107, 144, 147.   107 B.L., shelf mark 3438.i.3.

tury is less well represented, Blow and Purcell having thirteen anthems each, Aldrich and Humfrey seven each, while the sixteenth and early seventeenth centuries are only represented by two anthems each by Farrant and Gibbons and one each by Byrd, Hooper and Tallis. A subscription for 'a book of anthems' in 1724 was most probably for William Croft's *Musica sacra: or select anthems in score* published in that year, and in 1742 the cathedral subscribed to Maurice Greene's *Forty select anthems*, copies of which survive in the cathedral library.[108] Subsequent purchases of printed music include Boyce's *Cathedral music* (3 vols, 1760–75), John Alcock's *Six and twenty select anthems in score* (1771), James Nares' *Twenty anthems in score* (1778), *Thomas Ebdon's Sacred music ...* (*c.*1789), John Stafford Smith's *Anthems, composed for the choir-service of the Church of England* (*c.*1793), and William Hayes's *Cathedral music in score ...* (1795). James Kent's *Twelve anthems* (1773) was bought in 1797 but no copies survive in the cathedral.[109] In most cases the subscription lists show that Christ Church bought as many or more copies than any other subscribers including major English cathedrals. The only Christ Church cathedral composer who published church music at this period was Richard Woodward whose '*Veni Creator Spiritus*' was composed for the consecration of the bishop of Cloyne on 31 May 1767 and whose *Cathedral music* (1771) was purchased between 1772 and 1774.[110]

By the end of the eighteenth century Christ Church cathedral had built up a substantial library of the contemporary printed cathedral repertoire. Much of the music however continued to exist in hand-written part-books and scores. Twelve choir-books were copied in the mid-1720s of which eight were bound, and some of Greene's anthems were copied in 1735 (Greene did not publish any anthems before 1743).[111] On being appointed chanter's vicar in 1743 John Church was asked to 'examine and collect the scores of such good music as are to be met with in the old choir-books' and to examine and report on music recently copied by John Mason, one of the vicars choral.[112] This may mark the beginnings of the surviving series of scorebooks, two of which are dated 1746. In the 1760s and 1770s various choir members copied music[113] but the most prominent copyist was John Mathews who was paid regularly for music copying and related expenses over a twenty year period until his death in 1799 and who was the major scribe of the surviving score- and part-books.[114] Composers represented by the greatest num-

108 Boydell, *Music*, pp 113, 146. 109 Ibid., pp 115, 125, 127, 148, 149, 150, 152, 153. 110 *Veni Creator Spiritus, op. 1* (Dublin, 1767); revised in *Cathedral music op.3* (London, 1771); modern edition, Boydell, *Music*, pp 229–33; see also Boydell, *Music*, p. 149; Woodward's 'Sing o ye heavens' recorded on *Sing (CD)*. 111 Boydell, *Music*, p. 146. 112 Ibid., p. 113. 113 Ibid., pp 117, 121, 147, 148, 150, 151. 114 Ibid., pp 123, 127, 129, 150, 151, 152, 153, 154; Eamonn O'Keeffe, 'The score-books of Christ Church cathe-

bers of anthems in the score-books are Boyce followed by Greene and Handel (choruses from oratorios included). Local composers of the later eighteenth or early nineteenth century are also prominent: John Stevenson is the fourth most-represented composer with nineteen anthems (in all eight services and twenty-six anthems by Stevenson survive in the combined manuscript collections of the two Dublin cathedrals), followed by Shenton with seventeen, equal to Kent. A choirboy at Christ Church from 1773 and stipendiary from 1781, Stevenson became a vicar choral in 1800 (a position he had held at St Patrick's from 1783), received an honorary doctorate of music from the University of Dublin in 1791 and was knighted in 1803, the first musician so to be honoured.[115] Best remembered today for his accompaniments to Moore's *Irish melodies*, Stevenson was highly regarded in his day and a noted bass singer. He was to remain one of the most popular composers in the Dublin cathedral repertoires well into the nineteenth century.[116] Robert Shenton was dean's vicar from 1758 to his death in 1798. To dismiss him as a composer whose 'output was as considerable as his lack of inspiration' is perhaps a little harsh;[117] while in a largely conservative Handelian idiom, verse anthems such as 'The beauty of Israel' and full anthems like 'O God my heart is ready' are not without merit, even if at times lapsing into a repetitive and somewhat uninspired style.[118] The most popular composers of services in the score- and part- books are Aldrich, King and Stevenson (five each), and Child, Dupuis and Shenton (four each).

A number of Christ Church musicians in addition to Shenton and Stevenson are represented in the score- and part-books. Some of the twenty-two anthems, both verse and full, attributed to Ralph Roseingrave certainly merit revival.[119] To the five anthems and one service by Richard Woodward which also appeared in his *Cathedral music* can be added five services by Edward Higgens, vicar choral from 1765 to 1769,[120] one anthem by Samuel Murphy (of exceptional length and probably written as his doctoral exer-

---

dral Dublin: a catalogue' in *Fontes artis musicae*, xliv (1997), p. 43.   115 C6/1/7/7, pp 48, 140, 136–7.   116 See also pp 382–3 below; for a fuller discussion of Stevenson, Bumpus, 'Composers'; Stevenson's 'By the waters of Babylon' and 'I looked and behold' recorded on *Sing (CD)*.   117 Grindle, *Cathedral music*, p. 178.   118 'The beauty of Israel' in Boydell, *Music*, pp 218–28, recorded on *Sing (CD)*; see also Carol Cunningham, 'Selected eighteenth century anthems by composers at Christ Church cathedral Dublin', M.A. thesis, N.U.I. Maynooth, 1997; Andrea Moran 'Three eighteenth century anthems from Christ Church cathedral, Dublin', M.A. thesis, University College Dublin, 1994. 119 C6/1/24/1/17, 23–4; C6/1/24/3/11–16, 55, 56, 58–60; 'I will cry unto God' in Boydell, *Music*, pp 212–17; see also Cunningham, 'Selected eighteenth-century anthems', Andrea Moran 'Three eighteenth-century anthems'; there are also two services by Roseingrave; Roseingrave's 'Bow down thine ear' and 'I will cry' recorded on *Sing (CD)*. 120 C6/1/24/1/20; C6/1/24/3.

cise),[121] and one service by George Walshe (described by John Bumpus in 1900 as 'really fine and scholarly' and still in regular use at Christ Church at the end of the nineteenth century).[122] Other works only attributed by surname may have been written by [Thomas] Godfrey (organist in 1689),[123] [Peter or Bartholomew] Isaac,[124] and [John] Marsh (a chorister in 1746–7 and apprentice to the organist the following year).[125] There are also five anthems and a service by either Timothy or Charles Thomas Carter, the former a chorister and choirman from before 1730 to his death in 1772, the latter a choirboy in the 1760s but not subsequently associated with the cathedral.[126] While Roseingrave, Woodward and Stevenson are certainly the finest of this group, the music of these Christ Church composers does vary considerably in quality.[127]

The lack of wider recognition afforded to a composer like Woodward, despite his unquestioned ability and his publication of a collection of cathedral music in London in 1771, reflects the problem of cathedral musicians in Dublin composing for a religious and social minority in their own country but largely ignored by the cathedral tradition in England. The situation was exacerbated by the lack of a vibrant, outward-looking tradition in English cathedral music at the time. A general decline of standards has been noted in eighteenth-century cathedral music arising out of a combination of the declining real incomes of choir members leading to disinterest and disaffection, and the prevalent stagnation of cathedral practice.[128] In marked contrast to most English cathedrals, however, music thrived at Christ Church during the later eighteenth and early nineteenth centuries. This is seen not only in the presence of some of the cathedral's most active composers during the century between Ralph Roseingrave's appointment as organist in 1727 and the death of John Stevenson in 1833, but also in the amount of purchasing and copying of music that took place especially in the later eighteenth century, and in the often demanding solo writing in anthems by Shenton, Woodward and Stevenson which reflects musical standards which were certainly not depressed.[129] The reasons for this can be attributed to a combina-

---

121 C6/1/24/1/22; see Cunningham, 'Selected eighteenth-century anthems', pp 50–7. 122 C6/1/24/1/15, 21; C6/1/24/3/7–16, 55–6; C6/1/24/8; Bumpus, 'Composers', p. 93. 123 Two anthems and one chorus (incomplete), C6/1/24/3/1–7; C6/1/24/4/1, 3–4, 7. 124 One anthem ('Let God arise'), incomplete and also attributed to Purcell, C6/1/24/4/1, 3, 6. 125 One anthem (incomplete), C6/1/24/3/21, 25. 126 C6/1/24/1/12, 14, 16, 22, 24; Grindle, *Cathedral music*, p. 180, but the identity of the various members of the Carter family active as musicians and composers in Dublin is not as clear-cut as Grindle implies. 127 For a more detailed discussion, Grindle, *Cathedral music*, ch. 9. 128 See Temperley, 'Music in church', pp 358–9. 129 Boydell, *Music*, p. 95; Cunningham, 'Selected eighteenth-century anthems'; see also Grindle, *Cathedral music*, p. 189.

tion of Dublin's flourishing musical life in the eighteenth century and the financial position of the choir members. Not only was the income of a vicar or stipendiary/petty canon at either Dublin cathedral high by English standards thanks to Charles II's grant of 1665,[130] but most choirmen enjoyed positions at both cathedrals and thus received double incomes but without commensurate duties since during the later eighteenth century (and up to the restoration of St Patrick's in 1865) weekday services were not held at St Patrick's.[131] The Dublin cathedrals could thus attract first-class singers and musicians from England and Ireland. Furthermore, the benevolence of the chapter towards its choir members and dependants suggests that money was not generally a problem and there is little evidence of the loss of morale amongst choirmen common at English cathedrals. Despite the chapter's misgivings, many organists and choir members, both adults and boys, were contributing to the active public musical life of Dublin in the later eighteenth century, thereby enhancing both their incomes and their musical careers.[132] Christ Church enjoyed a vibrant and confident musical life at a time when Anglican cathedral music has more usually been perceived as having been 'never at so low an ebb'.[133]

130 For income figures for the nineteenth century, see pp 339–40 below.   131 Grindle, *Cathedral music*, pp 45–6.   132 Organists and choir members of both cathedrals are frequently cited in Boydell, *Rotunda music*.   133 Preface to John Alcock, *Collection of six and twenty select anthems* (1771), cited after Bernarr Rainbow, *The choral revival in the Anglican church* (London, 1970), p. 244.

XV

The stripping of the assets, 1830–1960

Kenneth Milne

John Henry Newman said that he regarded 14 July 1833 as the day on which the Oxford Movement began,[1] for it was on that day that John Keble preached his historic assize sermon attacking the Irish Church Temporalities Bill, then before parliament, and which, a few days later, would pass into law.[2] Central to the act's purpose was the reduction of two Irish archbishoprics to bishoprics, and the amalgamation of several other dioceses. The intention of these changes was to divert funds from certain sees to purposes that, in the opinion of the government, might be more profitably employed by the church. Where Keble, Newman and the other Tractarians were concerned, the secular power was interfering with the affairs of the spiritual, and they perceived in this the thin end of a wedge that would eventually see the established churches of Ireland and England becoming mere departments of state. The full title of the statute of 1833 that is commonly called the Church Temporalities Act is 'An act to alter and amend the laws relating to the temporalities of the Church in Ireland'. It received its first reading in the house of commons on 23 April 1833 (after an abortive start some weeks earlier). The clauses of most specific interest to Christ Church did not appear in the first version,[3] but were added at the committee stage in the house of lords, appearing in the statute as clauses xlix and l, whereby, on the voidance of the see of Kildare, it was to be united with the dioceses of Dublin and Glendalough, and the dean of St Patrick's was to assume the deanery of Christ Church also.[4]

In the stream of parliamentary papers that provided government with the evidence it needed for the institution of reforms in the church were the reports of his majesty's commissioners on ecclesiastical revenue and patronage in Ireland.[5] These reports made it clear that the revenues of the bishop of Kildare

---

1 J.H. Newman, *Apologia pro vita sua* (London, 1959), p. 122.   2 3 & 4 Will. IV, c. 37.
3 H.C. 1833 (59), i, 339.   4 H.C. 1833 (431), i, 499.   5 *First report* (H.C. 1833, xxi); *Second report* (H.C. 1834, xxiii); *Summary of the digest of the inquiry into the archiepiscopal revenues*

largely arose from his connection with Christ Church, and that out of Bishop Charles Lindsay's gross revenue of £6,507 practically everything came from rents or renewal fines from his property as dean. Furthermore, his position as dean gave him a voice in the election of the three prebendaries, six vicars choral and six stipendiaries, as well as in the appointment to the benefices of St Mary's, St Paul's and St Thomas's. Added to all this was a voice in alternate appointments to the parish of Barronstown in the diocese of Armagh. However, the temporalities of the deanery of Christ Church were deemed to be those of the bishop of Kildare, and, therefore (as was the case with the revenues of suppressed bishoprics), passed to the newly formed ecclesiastical commissioners. The church had strenuously argued against suggestions that these funds might be at the disposal of government for a variety of non-ecclesiastical purposes, and had won that argument. But this victory was of little or no value to Christ Church whose deanery was, when the holder of the office vacated it, to be rendered virtually penniless.

The archbishop of Dublin, Richard Whately, was not enchanted with the prospect of assuming (as the act prescribed) the metropolitical responsibilities of the suppressed archbishopric of Cashel, nor of the see of Kildare – though the former did not come his way for a further five years, nor the latter for thirteen, when vacancies occurred. In correspondence, Whately described the addition of Kildare to his responsibilities as 'the last straw'.[6] But the chief secretary, Edward Stanley (one of the chief architects of the Church Temporalities Act), considered it reasonable to add Kildare's fifty benefices to Dublin and Glendalough's 114.[7] While Whately did not receive the temporalities either of Cashel or Kildare, an amendment to the bill in the house of lords gave him the patronage of those benefices that were solely in the gift of the dean of Christ Church.[8] For some years, while Lindsay of Kildare still lived, Whately persisted in his opposition to the proposal. He wrote to the lord lieutenant in 1842,[9] proposing a union of Kildare and Leighlin (which would have necessitated detaching that see from its new partners, Ossory and Ferns) and the archbishop also made an abortive attempt in 1847 to have the law changed by introducing a bill that would have allowed for the restoration of the bishopric of Kildare.[10] The proposed legislation proceeded as far as a second reading in the house of lords, Whately admitting that he would derive great benefit from being relieved of the see of Kildare

(H.C. 1833 [243], xxvii).   6 D.H. Akenson, *A Protestant in purgatory: Richard Whately, archbishop of Dublin* (Hamden, Connecticut, 1981) p. 85, Oriel College, Oxford, Whately MSS, letter book, no. 280.   7 *Hansard 3*, 1833, col. 943.   8 H.C. 1833 (594), i, 587.   9 Richard Whately, *Charge to the clergy of the dioceses of Dublin and Kildare delivered at the visitations of those dioceses respectively in July 1847* (Dublin, 1847), p. 37 ff.   10 Church Temporalities Acts Amendment (Ireland) Bill, 1847.

and its re-constitution in its own right. He referred to some exploratory talks with the fellows of Trinity College, whereby the provostship would be annexed to Kildare to provide an income. The fate of Christ Church was not mentioned. The bill attracted little support and, on the advice of the bishop of Salisbury, Whately withdrew it.[11] Further legislation (4 & 5 Will. IV, c. 90) made it obligatory on the dean and chapter to seek sanction from the ecclesiastical commissioners before proceeding to fill vacant prebends or other dignities. These restrictions were observed when, for example, the precentorship was filled in 1835,[12] and again when the prebendary of St Michael's was filled in 1844.[13]

The Church Temporalities Act also provided that, on the separation of the see of Kildare from the deanery of Christ Church the dean of St Patrick's was to be dean of Christ Church 'for ever'. This was to happen automatically, 'without election or other ceremony', to quote the statute. Charles Lindsay, bishop of Kildare, died in office on 8 August 1846, aged eighty-seven years. The chapter acts for 3 September 1846[14] record as follows

> The Honourable and Very Reverend Henry Pakenham, dean of St Patrick's has by the death of the late lord bishop of Kildare and the operation of the Church Temporalities Act, 3 & 4 Will. IV, c. 37, section l, become dean of the deaneries of St Patrick's and Christ Church without any oath or ceremony whatsoever and has this day taken his seat at the chapter of this cathedral accordingly.

In an undated copy or draft letter, Pakenham wrote to the registrar of Christ Church

> Delicacy of feeling has always hitherto prevented my making any enquiry into what have become my new duties. I speak, therefore, under correction. But if I am borne out by the constitution of the cathedral ... I would nominate the same individual as my sub-dean who exercised that power under the late dean. I believe it to be the Revd Mr Chichester.[15]

Pakenham received from Henry Cotton, treasurer of Christ Church, an assurance, dated 14 August 1846, that the chapter 'will be glad to receive you among us as our head', trusting that the new dean will 'firmly preserve the

---

11 *Lords jn.*, lxxix, 1847, p. 336 ff; *Hansard 3*, xciii, 753–5.   12 C6/1/7/12, p. 36.   13 Ibid., pp 145–6.   14 Ibid., p. 243.   15 Pakenham to dean and chapter of Christ Church, copy or draft, n.d., Tullynally castle, Pakenham papers, Y/12. Seen by kind permission at P.R.O.N.I. (temporary reference T. D. 5777).

rights and privileges of Christ Church'.[16] Pakenham may have felt rather as Whately did about assuming these additional responsibilities. Certainly, a correspondent, W.G. Monsell, wrote

> I cannot congratulate you on the new position [in] which the law of the land has just placed you. I shall rather condole with you, on your own account, and on account of the injury it inflicts on our church by removing from Christ Church its own individual head, and by heaping on you a vast increase of work. The new arrangement cannot work out.[17]

It did, however, last for over thirty years, and Pakenham has been credited with being assiduous in discharging his obligations to Christ Church, which the record of his chapter attendances bears out. For instance, between September 1846 and September 1847 the chapter of Christ Church met on eleven occasions, and 'Mr Dean' headed the list of those present on all but three of them. (His successor at both cathedrals, John West, has been charged with evincing less dedication to Christ Church than Pakenham had,[18] yet he regularly chaired chapter meetings there.) Pakenham died in December 1863, the same month in which Richard Chenevix Trench was appointed to succeed Whately as archbishop and the new archbishop's first impression of Christ Church must have contrasted starkly with memories of his previous milieu, Westminster abbey. His consecration was arranged for 1 January 1864, and he came to Dublin several days earlier to attend Pakenham's funeral at St Patrick's. He visited Christ Church, and found it shrouded in mourning drapes, which he asked to have removed in time for the service of consecration.[19] But quite apart from the signs of mourning, the cathedral itself must have been a far from cheering sight, to judge from what we know to have been its structural condition. Major developments affecting the building were already in train, and more were to come, culminating in the major restoration by G.E. Street in the 1870s described in chapter xvii. By then, however,

16 Cotton to Pakenham, 14 August 1846, Pakenham papers.   17 Monsell to Pakenham, 11 August 1846, Pakenham papers.   18 See, for example, H.A. Boyd, 'The cathedral system in the Church of Ireland since the disestablishment', B.Litt. thesis, 1950, T.C.D., copy in R.C.B., describing West as 'an avowed partisan of St Patrick's', who took little interest in his sacred charge on Dublin's hill', pp 179–80. An appreciation of West published in the *Irish Ecclesiastical Gazette* at the time of his death (11 July 1890) refers to his parochial ministry at St Peter's, his term as archdeacon of Dublin and his years at St Patrick's, but never mentions Christ Church, where he was dean for eight years. In the cathedral *Year book* for 1933 (p. 16) Dean Kennedy refers to West's 'undisguised partiality for St Patrick's and neglect of Christ Church'.   19 J. Bromley, *The man of ten talents: a portrait of Richard Chenevix Trench, 1807–86* (London, 1959), p. 159.

equally radical changes had overcome the cathedral's constitution in the shape of the Irish Church Act of 1869, whereby the Church of Ireland was disestablished, ceased to be the state Church and was largely disendowed. The stripping of the assets of Christ Church, begun by the Church Temporalities Act, was to be largely completed by the Irish Church Act.[20] The period of time immediately following disendowment and disestablishment posed challenges for those who directed the fortunes of Christ Church no less awesome than those faced by their seventeenth-century forebears. In some ways, the nineteenth-century challenges were more fundamental. The dean and chapter of 1660 and 1690 had to reconstitute cathedral life according to tradition. But disendowment and disestablishment effectively swept away the status quo for all time. The very constitution of the cathedral was radically changed and the economic structures that underpinned it were dramatically weakened. When the accelerating deterioration of the building is taken into account, as well as the major difficulties and controversies that a comprehensive restoration brought in its train, then the magnitude of the task facing the dignitaries of the 1870s and 1880s is apparent.

Under disestablishment, the dean and chapter ceased to be a corporate body for legal purposes, though continuing as an ecclesiastical entity.[21] But as with all individuals who lost property entitlements under the Irish Church Act, there were complex arrangements for compensation. These led, as might be expected, to a great deal of correspondence between the dean and chapter and the commissioners for church temporalities about financial matters.[22] The life interest of individual dignitaries and others was protected under the Irish Church Act, and they were awarded annuities. The prebendaries successfully claimed that they had rights of succession to the parishes that were in the cathedral's gift, and were compensated accordingly when that patronage was abolished,[23] it being said in the house of commons, when the bill was in debate, that 'they [the prebendaries] invariably exercised these rights of patronage in their own favour'.[24] Likewise the stipendiaries (after a struggle) had their claims of succession to vicar choralships admitted.[25] Some indi-

---

20 The deep resentment in Church of Ireland circles against W.E. Gladstone, the prime mover behind the statute, seems to have dissipated by 1880. Cruising with friends on the Irish Sea in August of that year, his diary records: 'Reached Dublin in time to land suddenly & go to Christ Church. The congregation all agog. Out of doors an enthusiastic extempore reception.' (*The Gladstone diaries*, ed. H.C.G. Matthew (13 vols, Oxford, 1968–94), ix, 573). The cathedral preachers' book records the visit (C6/1/21/14, 29 Aug. 1880).   21 Irish Church Act, 1869, clause 13.   22 I am indebted to Mr Tom Quinlan of N.A.I. for this information. The records of the Irish church temporalities commissioners in N.A.I. are as yet unavailable for public consultation.   23 W.L. Bernard, *Decisions under the Irish Church Act, 1869* (3rd ed., Dublin, 1873), p. 145.   24 *Hansard 3*, cxcvi, col. 766.   25 Bernard, *Decisions*, p. 46.

vidual cases were raised when the bill was going through the commons. Cavendish Bentinck, M.P. for Whitehaven, urged the claims of those musicians who had held 'high office' in English cathedrals, and moved to Armagh or Dublin for better incomes, and he cited the case of 'Dr Stewart of Christ Church' as an example, who would never have come to Ireland but for the conditions then attaching to the post.[26] However, when Seymour, proctor-to-be, claimed indemnity for the loss of prospective emoluments, he was refused on the grounds that the proctorship was seen as an agency for receiving rents, not as an office within the meaning of the act.[27]

The first of January 1871 was the date on which the whole property of the Church of Ireland was vested in the commissioners, and there was a flurry of renewal of leases by the chapter in the preceding months, entailing long leases and substantial fines.[28] On 31 December 1870, the day before disestablishment came into force, the dean and chapter, enjoying their last day as a legal corporation, resolved to donate to Trinity College the jacobean tabernacle and candlesticks and the medieval 'Liber niger' and 'Liber albus'. On that very day, Archdeacon Lee conveyed the books to the library in Trinity. Soon, however they were back at Christ Church, for legal opinion had decreed that they were held in trust by the new Representative Church Body, and could not be given away.[29] Another key date was 30 June 1871, by which, under the provisions of the act, the newly established Representative Church Body had to claim church buildings which, like other assets of the church, had since 1 January 1871 been vested in the new commissioners of church temporalities. Duly, the Representative Church Body reported in 1871[30] that it had sent claims to the commissioners for the cathedrals of St Patrick's and Christ Church in the diocese of Dublin, both being required, as the commissioners themselves confirmed, 'for religious purposes'.[31] In the case of Christ Church, the verger's house was included, but virtually all other corporate assets, found by the 1868 royal commission of inquiry to consist solely of the proceeds of the oeconomy, remained with the commissioners.

Within weeks of the passing of the Irish Church Act, the provincial synods of Armagh and Dublin (which were entirely clerical bodies) met to make arrangements for convening a church convention of clergy and laity. By February 1870, the convention was in session, and addressing the major tasks of providing the newly-disestablished church with a constitution and a representative trustee body. The state of limbo in which the Irish cathedrals

26 *Hansard 3*, cxcvi, col. 754.   27 C6/1/7/13, p. 299; Boyd, 'Cathedral system', p. 149. 28 For example, chapter meetings of 2 December and 31 December 1870 (C6/1/7/13, pp 295–6, 310).   29 C6/1/7/13, pp 309–10, and Boyd, 'Cathedral system', p. 162.   30 *Journal of the general synod*, 1871, p. 9.   31 N.A.I., Irish Church Temporalities Commission MSS, 'Lists of churches applied for by the Representative Church Body'.

found themselves in 1870, while the General Convention and its successor, the general synod, debated what should be done with them, came to an end in 1872 when several statutes were passed determining their future status. There were, indeed, members of the general synod who saw no future for cathedrals at all,[32] in which sentiment they were scarcely more radical than royal commissioners who, reporting in 1868, declared that Christ Church could best fulfil its vocation as a parish church.[33] On the other hand, the proposals originally put to the general synod in 1872 envisaged that Christ Church, not St Patrick's, should be a national cathedral, and the number of canons was put at twelve to allow for a representative from each united diocese. It was only as the proposed legislation passed through the general synod that the role of 'a national cathedral' passed to St Patrick's, because, so it was claimed, of the views of Mr Henry Roe. In 1862, Henry Roe, with his brother George, had inherited George Roe and company of Thomas Street, Dublin's major distillery, covering seventeen acres. Roe was a man of considerable wealth and influence, who wished to make a significant contribution to the disestablished church in thanksgiving for many mercies received and unforeseen prosperity (as he put it in a letter to the archbishop).[34] So munificent was his contribution, over many years, but particularly in the restoration of Christ Church by George Edmund Street, and the building of the synod hall, that the family fortune was much diminished thereby.[35]

The statute that emerged from the general synod in 1872[36] gave Christ Church the constitution that in broad outline governs it today, though the detail has greatly changed. The deaneries of the two cathedrals were separated, the archbishop becoming dean of Christ Church (a role to which he was no stranger, having headed the chapter at Westminster). On 27 June, Dean West resigned and the archbishop was installed as dean of Christ Church. This was the last occasion on which the cathedral was open for some considerable period of time. In that month, the chapter considered a letter from Street, seeking the closure of the quire, 'in order that we may proceed to take it down', and an act of the chapter 'resolved that during the restoration of the cathedral the celebration of divine service be suspended ...'[37] The archbishop appears not to have treated the office of dean as a sinecure. For,

32 See debates in the *Daily Express* for April 1872.   33 *Report of her majesty's commissioners of the revenues and condition of the established church (Ireland)* [4082], H.C., 1867–8, xxiv, p. ix. For a previous occasion on which this was mooted, see ch. viii, note 86.   34 Quoted in the cathedral *Year book 1933*, p. 16. For a note on the *Year books*, see n. 120 below.   35 *Truths about whiskey*, published by J. Jameson and Son, William Jameson and Company, John Power and George Roe and Company (Dublin, 1878), pp 6–7; E.B. McGuire, *Irish whiskey* (Dublin, 1973), pp 248, 339; F.G. Hall, *The Bank of Ireland 1783–1946* (Dublin, 1949), p. 504.   36 Chapter 4 of 1872.   37 C6/1/7/13, p. 328.

while the chapter meeting at which he was installed was the one at which it was decided to close the cathedral to allow for major restoration work, and chapter meetings became infrequent, many of those held during the difficult period of the restoration were held at the archbishop's palace on St Stephen's Green, and were chaired by 'His Grace, the Dean'. Years later, when Archbishop Trench retired, the chapter expressed its warm appreciation of his commitment to the cathedral, particularly because since disestablishment he 'was surrounded by great trials and difficulties in his work'.

The general synod statute that made the archbishop dean and ordinary of Christ Church also reconstituted the chapter. The benefices formerly appropriated to the three prebends were separated from them, the prebendaries being given the option of resigning either from the parish or their prebendal stall. The prebendaries of St Michael's, St Michan's and St John's were to be residentiary canons, required to be 'skilled in chanting' and 'bound to such residence as the dean and chapter determine'. Together with the dean, precentor, chancellor, treasurer, archdeacon of Dublin and archdeacon of Glendalough, and twelve canons (six from Dublin and six from Glendalough) they comprised the chapter. From among them, the archbishop would chose a sub-dean, who, like the precentor and the three residentiary canons, was 'bound to residence', in order that there might be at least one residentiary canon and one other member of the chapter 'at every divine office'. These arrangements were soon to be modified in the light of experience. A joint meeting of the chapter and the newly-created cathedral board in 1873[38] considered and approved draft legislation (enacted in 1874)[39] whereby eight, rather than six of the twelve canons were to be from Dublin, the Glendalough representation being reduced to four. All twelve must hold cures in their respective dioceses and be resident there, and the acceptance of any external position would constitute resignation from the canonry. Furthermore, members of the chapter would in future sit in the diocesan synod of Dublin and Glendalough as members of their respective dioceses. Among further amendments to the constitution of Christ Church that soon followed were the removal of the 'residentiary' obligation from the prebendaries of St Michael's, St Michan's and St John's, simply conferring those titles on the three senior canons, and under the Roe endowment[40] the appointment of three residentiary 'minor' canons, 'skilled in chanting', who would not be members of the chapter. Provision was also made for the archbishop at some future date to appoint a dean, should he see fit.[41]

The working out of the provisions of the Irish Church Act of 1869 were to cause many problems for Christ Church, not least in that differences arose

38 C6/1/13/1, pp 42–3.   39 Chapter 1 of 1874.   40 See p. 324 below.   41 Chapter 2 of 1879.

between the chapter and those bound to it by annuities, and in particular the choirmen who had become 'annuitants' and who engaged the chapter in a long and litigatious dispute as to what might be expected of them as the cathedral's liturgical life changed.[42] Even less edifying was a wrangle with one of the cathedral's most devoted dignitaries, Edward Seymour, the precentor, who over several years sustained a lengthy argument with his colleagues as to what his duties entailed, specifically resisting their requirement of his presence at Sunday evensong. Throughout 1880 the argument continued, a board resolution of December of that year (proposed by Henry Roe, Seymour's cousin) calling on 'His Grace the Dean' to consider how best 'the present disunion' might be ended.[43] Yet three years later, when Seymour resigned, another board resolution (again proposed by Roe) paid tribute to Seymour, crediting him with the original concept of the Street restoration, and with influencing 'his kinsman' Mr Henry Roe 'to undertake this great work'.[44] These great constitutional and economic changes were accompanied by vast problems with the fabric of the building, to be examined in detail in chapter xvii, but mention must be made here of the manner in which Roe's munificence and Street's talents came to associate Christ Church with the concept of a specially-built synod hall. The diocesan synod of Dublin, which had in mind the provision of suitable accommodation for the meetings of the general synod, appointed a 'Christ Church cathedral and synod-house committee' in November 1870.[45] Having considered whether or not the nave and transepts of the cathedral would do, since that was 'where the synods of the Church of Ireland have been formerly held', the committee, whose membership included the dean of Christ Church and St Patrick's (Dean West) and such luminaries as the duke of Leinster, concluded that the cathedral was not the appropriate location for the meetings of the general synod 'as it is proposed to be restored', but that the adjoining St John's Church would make a suitable temporary meeting place.[46] Then came Roe's offer to erect the synod hall in addition to what he was doing for the cathedral. As he put it: 'It is my earnest desire that this cathedral (when restored) may prove useful to the Church of Ireland at large by being connected, as in past ages, with her synodical government ...' The offer was brought to the general synod, proposed by the archbishop of Dublin, and seconded by the marquess of Kildare. It was accepted.[47] Street prepared plans, proposing that St Michael's would be a more appropriate nucleus for the new hall than St John's. Neither of them, in Street's opinion, was architecturally worthy of conservation, but

42 See p. 375 below.   43 C6/1/13/1, pp 246–7.   44 C6/1/13/1, pp 335–7. See also p. 382 below when Seymour's contribution to the life of Christ Church is considered in more detail.   45 *Journal of the general synod, 1871*, pp 151 ff.   46 Ibid., p. 152.   47 Ibid., pp 156–8.

building on the St John's site would greatly damage the view of the newly-restored cathedral.[48]

Roe's generosity was not at an end. The cathedral plate was giving cause for concern, and there had been discussion as to how it might be repaired. By a happy chance, the subject came up as Street and Roe, *en route* from Kingstown to Holyhead, conversed on the mailboat.[49] Roe offered to provide the restored cathedral with new chalices, 'more in keeping with the character of the cathedral and more convenient', on condition that none of the existing plate was disposed of. Needless to say, this offer also was accepted. Nor did his benefactions end there. He purchased for the cathedral several houses (shortly to be demolished) that had been part of the cathedral's pre-disestablishment estate,[50] and paid for the new episcopal throne[51] and in 1881 for a boardroom table (designed by Drew, by then the cathedral architect).[52] When that same year, the lord mayor's offer to defray the cost of restoring the corporation seat was accepted,[53] Roe had the ancient 'state or royal seat' reconstructed. In this new pew the royal arms of the Stuarts, which it was surmised had been mutilated in Cromwellian times, were incorporated.[54] In addition to all this generosity towards enhancing the fabric and furnishing of Christ Church, Henry Roe gave evidence that it was a place of worship, not an architectural showpiece, that he wished to preserve, by entering into a financial agreement with the Representative Church Body in 1873 to secure the liturgical and musical tradition of the cathedral.[55]

The Roe endowment was a recognition by Henry Roe that the sum paid by the commissioners of church temporalities to the Representative Church Body to pay the annuities of those pre-disestablishment vicars choral and choirmen who had commuted would, year by year, be reduced as annuities were paid and annuitants died. To arrest the reduction of this capital sum, Roe donated £20,000 on condition that the Representative Church Body agreed that £20,000 of the commutation capital held by them was added to Roe's donation to make a sum of £40,000. The interest on this was to be used to maintain choral worship at the cathedral: morning and evening prayer daily, and holy communion on Sundays, Christmas Day and Ascension Day. Additionally, in 1878 Roe engaged to give Christ Church a further £500 per

---

48 *Christ Church cathedral, Dublin, and the synod hall for the Church of Ireland: observations on the proposed restoration of the cathedral and suggestions as to the site for the new synod hall* (Dublin, 1871), p. 4 (reprinted from the *Irish Builder*). The synod hall opened on 6 April 1875, three years before the cathedral was ready for worship (*Year book 1933*, p. 18). **49** *Year book 1933*, p. 18. William III's 'royal plate' was of course, now at the Chapel Royal in Dublin Castle (see p. 260 note 33 above). **50** C6/1/13/1, pp 76–7. **51** C6/1/7/14, p. 17. **52** C6/1/13/1, p. 288. **53** Ibid., pp 294–5. **54** C6/1/7/14, pp 23–4. **55** Copy is to be found between pp 8–17 of C6/1/13/1.

year during his lifetime. One half of the sum was to be put towards the salary of the sub-dean, a key figure (especially since the assumption of decanal powers by the archbishop) who almost invariably chaired the board meetings, and the other moiety to help further the cathedral music.[56]

A board sub-committee, reporting in 1885, pointed out that since the inception of the scheme under the Roe endowment, circumstances had made aspects of it inappropriate. The cost of maintaining the music had increased, but only three clergy were in receipt of salaries (not five as originally envisaged), and no residences were provided. The number of annuitant clergy bound to the cathedral had diminished to one. Following consultation with the archbishop and Henry Roe, an obligation to support ten choirmen was substituted, but the stipulation regarding daily choral services remained.[57] A constitutional innovation under the 1872 act of general synod was the creation of a registered vestry, open to every male member of the Church of Ireland who was an accustomed member of the congregation for at least a year and had made a minimum financial contribution to cathedral funds. The most important duty of the vestrymen was to elect, triennially, the cathedral board, itself an innovation, charged under the statute with management of the cathedral finances and the employment of lay staff. All appointments that were not in the gift of the archbishop, dean, or chapter fell to the board.

There was substantial chapter representation on the board and, during the period when the archbishop was dean, the sub-dean usually chaired the board, while the dean chaired the chapter. In the initial years the business transacted by chapter and board was often scarcely distinguishable but gradually their ways parted as their respective duties became more clearly defined, and it is increasingly to board rather than chapter transactions that the historian must look to see how the cathedral was developing. The first board, elected by the Easter vestry of 1873 comprised, in addition to the cathedral dignitaries, a strong representation of business and professional life, including, not surprisingly, Henry Roe, the cathedral's supreme benefactor.

As the re-opening date approached much thought had to be given to arranging, not only for worshippers, but also for the considerable number of visitors who wished to inspect the glistening new edifice, a number of them doubtless attracted by the unwelcome publicity that Street's work drew from some evangelical circles. For, while the cathedral re-opened to the delight of many, there was dismay on the part of others who saw in Street's remarkable transformation of the old building clear signs of an incipient Catholic revival within the Church of Ireland in the very year (1878) that new restrictions were imposed on 'ritualistic' practices through the canons ecclesiastical in the revised *Book of Common Prayer*. The leading critic was a member

56 C6/1/13/1, p. 104.   57 Ibid., pp 406–8, 416.

of the cathedral chapter, Canon William Marrable, a pronounced evangelical who regarded ritual of all kinds as detrimental to the preaching of the gospel.[58] Several months before the re-opening, he raised objections to aspects of the restored building and its ornaments, as a result of which a member of the board, Dr George Battersby Q.C., paid a visit and declared all to be perfectly legal.[59] Far from satisfied, Marrable entered a formal protest at the board meeting of 28 March 1878[60] deeming the proposal to re-open the cathedral in May 'premature', because of the need to remove 'certain structures with devices therein'. He particularly objected to the depiction of the crucifixion in the east window, which would cause those whose custom it was to 'bow eastwards' thereby to infringe the second commandment. The screen offended him, not only because it was surmounted by a cross, but also because it separated clergy and congregation, thereby preventing members of the congregation from satisfying themselves that the relevant rubric was obeyed during the prayer of consecration. Altogether, the arrangements gave the communion table the appearance of a 'Romish altar'. Marrable's terms were mild by comparison with those employed by *The Rock*, a strongly evangelical periodical that deemed the restored cathedral 'in all its arrangements an unimpeachable reproduction of a Romish mass house'.[61] Marrable took his case to the Dublin newspapers, and offended some other members of the chapter by so doing, and by referring to 'distinct acts of idolatry' being practised in the cathedral, such as bowing before a representation of the crucifixion. His colleagues complained that he had not specified that such acts of devotion were practised by members of the congregation, and not by the clergy, and he expressed his regret for this.[62] The *Irish Ecclesiastical Gazette*, a journal that took a liberal stance on such issues (and had defended Canon Richard Travers Smith of St Bartholomew's against similar attacks from Marrable[63]), noted that his criticisms had little support in the diocese, as was evident from debate at the diocesan synod.[64] The *Gazette* further reported that a motion condemning the east window and the screen, proposed in the general synod, was lost by 146 votes to 86, after a debate lacking in acrimony.[65] Differences of opinion of another kind arose over the manner in which Street had consigned most of the cathedral monuments to the crypt. Thomas Drew, the cathedral architect, had reported in 1881 that many of them were falling to pieces,[66] and throughout 1883 and 1884 the Lindsay family urged that the bishop's monument should be returned to the nave.[67]

58 Leslie, 'Fasti', p. 103. 59 C6/1/13/1, p. 103. 60 C6/1/7/13, pp 372–4. 61 *Irish Ecclesiastical Gazette*, 1 June 1879. 62 C6/1/7/13, pp 431–2. 63 Kenneth Milne, *St Bartholomew's: a history of the Dublin parish* (Dublin, 1963), p. 23. 64 *Irish Ecclesiastical Gazette*, 1 Dec. 1879, supplement, p. 8. 65 *Irish Ecclesiastical Gazette*, 1 May 1879. 66 C6/1/13/1, p. 262. 67 C6/1/7/14, pp 72–3, 84–5.

While deprecating the fact that the monument had sustained injury, the chapter maintained that memorials were better exhibited in the newly drained and gaslit crypt. They eventually conceded that Lindsay's monument could be re-sited 'in the monk's porch', and also met a request from Roe that the Abbott and Stevenson memorials should be withdrawn from the crypt and placed in the transepts.[68]

Street's somewhat drastic treatment of the cathedral monuments, the occasion of much furious press correspondence at the time,[69] continued to make ripples. Even Strongbow's 'tomb' had not been immune, and in 1890 Drew was given permission 'to collect again the fragmentary memorials connected with Strongbow which were separated from the tomb and stuck in divers places by an ignorant clerk of works'.[70] Thomas Prior was one of Ireland's most influential economics writers of the early eighteenth century and the founding of the (Royal) Dublin Society owed much to him.[71] His monument in the cathedral was executed by Van Nost the younger in 1756 and Bishop Berkeley wrote the inscription.[72] At the request and expense of the Royal Dublin Society it was moved in 1890 from 'a dark corner in the crypt' to the south-west porch.[73] Restoration of Cheere's memorial to the nineteenth earl of Kildare, in the south transept, was paid for by the duke of Leinster at much the same time.[74] In 1910, the Auchmuty, Abbott and Fletcher monuments were removed from the crypt to the west end of the nave.[75] In 1897, the corona, formerly hung in the quire, was moved to the synod hall.[76] The old eagle lectern was repaired in 1910. Drew considered that it was one of four cast from the same mould in about 1520, the other three being in England. The lions supporting the stem had been lost in the course of time, and they were now replaced by facsimiles of those on the identical lectern at Coventry.[77]

New memorials were added: that to Archbishop Trench being unveiled on 20 January 1888,[78] and Archbishop Plunket's brass in 1899.[79] The latter depicted the archbishop wearing a scarf with crosses 'such as were never worn by his grace', according to a critic. The manufacturer of the brass was asked for an explanation and the offending crosses were erased. Protestant

---

68 For the location of the monk's porch, see p. 371.   69 See p. 372 note 93.   70 C6/1/7/14, p. 184. Recent professional sorting of stones relegated to the crypt under Street's auspices throws light on what Drew was referring to.   71 Terence de Vere White, *The story of the Royal Dublin Society* (Tralee, [1955]), pp 10, 60.   72 Homan Potterton, *Irish church monuments, 1570–1880* (Belfast, 1975), pp 30, 86.   73 C6/1/7/14, p. 183. Also correspondence with Royal Dublin Society affixed to p. 183.   74 *Annual report 1890*, p. 9; Potterton, *Irish church monuments*, p. 40.   75 C6/1/13/2, p. 166; *Annual report 1910*, p. 11.   76 C6/1/13/2, pp 15, 19.   77 *Annual report 1910*, pp 7–8; *Year book 1958*, p. 17.   78 C6/1/7/14, p. 155   79 Ibid., p. 229.

susceptibilities may well have been behind a threatened (but, in the end, not proposed) chapter resolution alluding to the marble figure of Christ 'extending his arms to bless' donated to the cathedral in 1947 and placed in the chapter room.[80] There seem to have been no difficulties in 1930, when a metal cage was fixed to the wall to enclose the casket reputedly containing the heart of Archbishop Lorcán Ua Tuathail, but it was agreed to take no action 'at least for the present' on a suggestion that the casket be opened.[81] A report by a sub-committee of the board, dated May 1938, recorded the need for repair to the tabernacle and candlesticks dating from James II's reign, cautioning that due account must be taken of the 'susceptibilities' of Catholic visitors when these articles were being arranged.[82] Estimates were sought for the restoration of the tabernacle, though work was postponed indefinitely.[83]

Duties of sexton, beadle and robe-keeper had to be re-defined from time to time, the beadle, on duty from 7.30 a.m. to 7 p.m. (when he closed the church) being responsible for tolling the bell for weekday services.[84] There was a gate-keeper, for whom a wooden shelter was provided.[85] In 1886, influenced by the response of some English cathedrals to the 1881 Open Spaces Act, Dublin corporation agreed with Christ Church to lay out the grounds as a public garden, and to maintain them. It was not, however, intended to be a play-ground.[86] Arrangements for visitors were highly organised. Shortly after the re-opening, admission to the cathedral was by sixpenny tickets, issued from 12 noon to 4 p.m. daily at the south-west porch, the sexton (who issued them) receiving commission on sales.[87] The assistant sexton, who also received commission, conducted visitors through the cathedral and crypt. Gratuities were prohibited, and when, in deference to criticism of the sale of tickets, the board replaced them with voluntary contributions, the verger and assistant verger had their salaries adjusted in compensation.[88] It was not long, however, before it was noted that many visitors made no contribution.[89] The board attached importance to attracting visitors, and thereby revenue, and some years later decided to circulate photographs of the cathedral to the principal hotels and clubs so that 'strangers arriving in town might then be induced to visit the cathedral'. The precentor agreed to get estimates of the cost of providing a drawing of the building with service times. Special fund-raising sermons were planned, one of which was to be held 'when summer visitors frequent Dublin',[90] and in 1879 forms were printed advising the public that 'after the temporary support given to the cathedral by the provisions of the Irish Church Act which preserve the particular services of cer-

80 C6/1/7/15, 4 Dec. 1948. 81 C6/1/13/2, pp 327, 351. 82 C6/1/2/13/2, pp 380–2. 83 C6/1/7/15, 27 May 1938. Postponed, in fact, until 1997! 84 C6/1/13/1, pp 108–9. 85 Ibid., p. 174. 86 C6/1/7/14, pp 111–2. 87 C6/1/7/13, pp 397–9. 88 Ibid., p. 419. 89 C6/1/7/14, p. 17. 90 C6/1/13/1, p. 205.

tain of the annuitant clergy and others' income 'does not even approach the requisite expenditure'. The document credits Henry Roe with virtually single-handedly providing the cathedral with a fixed income of £788, though expenditure is £1,850.[91] There were, of course, church collections, but these were not sufficient to make up the deficit, amounting to £620 2s. 9d. in 1878 (about one quarter of which went to charities) and £411 17s. in 1879 (£48 3s. 9d. going to charity).[92]

Changes were still taking place in the environs of Christ Church, the most important being the cutting of a new thoroughfare, Lord Edward Street, between Cork Hill and Christchurch Place in 1886. The matter had first been considered by the dean and chapter in 1876, and representatives had been appointed to watch over the cathedral's interests in the matter.[93] When Drew submitted the corporation plans for the new street to the board, they met with approval, and a satisfactory meeting of board and corporation representatives at the City Hall followed in 1882.[94]

What the Church Temporalities Act had begun in stripping Christ Church of its assets the Irish Church Act largely completed, and financial circumstances were not such as to encourage proposals for giving the cathedral a dean of its own. Archbishop Trench wished to divest himself of the office, and in 1883 let it be known that he had in mind to appoint Dr H.H. Dickenson, who among other positions held the chaplaincy of the Chapel Royal.[95] However, the plan fell through because the cathedral was not in a position to assure the archbishop that it could compensate Dickinson for the loss of his existing emoluments. In 1885, it was decided to set aside £100 per annum for an endowment fund for the deanery, and some further encouragement came later that year when substantial sums arising from a bequest were distributed by the Representative Church Body to a number of cathedrals towards their deans' salaries. Christ Church, having no dean within the meaning of the endowment, was at first excluded, but the Representative Church Body relented, and agreed to allocate £2,000 towards the deanery of Christ Church, the annual interest to be added to the capital, but the aggregate sum to be allocated elsewhere should there be no dean within five years.[96] This must have served to concentrate minds on the matter, and consideration began to be given to the implications for the cathedral of having a dean to itself, the archbishop making it clear that he would retain the position of ordinary of his diocesan cathedral.[97] In June 1887 Archbishop Plunket

---

91 C6/1/7/13, pp 420–1.   92 C6/1/13/1, p. 192. Printed statements of accounts of the years 1881, 1882 and 1883 are to be found in the chapter act book.   93 C6/1/7/14, pp 22–3.   94 C6/1/13/1, pp 286, 299–301. A wit suggested that the thoroughfare be named Street Street or Roe Row, C.T. McCready, *Dublin street names* (Dublin, 1893), p. 34.   95 C6/1/13/1, pp 361–3.   96 Ibid., pp 402, 411.   97 C6/1/7/14, pp 105 ff.

informed the chapter that he intended to resign as dean, and would appoint one of the canons, William Conyngham Greene, to the vacancy,[98] following an exchange of letters between cathedral and archbishop, the board having guaranteed a salary of £400.[99] With Greene's installation on 21 October 1887, the chapter was headed by a dean who held no other ecclesiastical cure for the first time in three centuries (if we except the Jacobite period).[100]

W.C. Greene led the cathedral into the twentieth century. He held office until 1908, being followed by James Hornidge Walsh (1908–18), Harry Vere White (1918–21), Herbert Brownlow Kennedy (1921–38), Ernest Henry Cornwall Lewis-Crosby (1938–61) and Norman David Emerson (1962–66). All were Trinity graduates and incumbents of Dublin parishes who had served as dignitaries on the chapter. As deans, they all faced the perennial problems of maintaining the liturgical life of the cathedral, keeping the building in repair (the Caen stone used in Street's restoration proved far from serviceable) and perhaps most intractable of all, balancing the books. They also had to meet the pressures posed by a sensitive period of transition in the cathedral's relations with state, city and diocese.

The other dignitaries, like the rest of the canons, being parish clergymen, could give little time to ministering at Christ Church beyond the several weeks' 'residence' that was expected of them. So it fell to the dean, assisted by several minor or residentiary canons, to conduct the liturgical life of the cathedral. A custom whereby the latter were styled 'canon' was discontinued in 1896, as it was deemed to 'efface' the distinction between the chapter and those appointed by it. Henceforth they were to be clerical vicars.[101] The headmaster of the grammar school was generally a clerical vicar, the others for the most part holding part-time appointments. Cathedral business was increasingly discharged by the board, rather than the chapter, which met less frequently and came to confine itself to formal and liturgical matters. The board drew on the expertise of some of Dublin's leading professional and business figures, and membership was opened to women by statute of the general synod in 1920.[102] As a consequence, the names of five women were added to the vestry roll in 1921, though over the years very few were elected to places on the board. One such was Lilian Duncan (Lil Nic Donnchadha), who served throughout the 1950s and 1960s. She was a distinguished graduate in Celtic studies who played a leading role in the Irish revival movement, in particular through Cumann Gaelach na hEaglaise (the Irish Guild of the Church), which began to hold its monthly services in Irish at Christ Church in 1962.[103]

Board and chapter were never free for long from anxiety about finance. In the immediate post-disestablishment period the cathedral was, in a sense,

98 Ibid., pp 141–2.   99 Ibid., p. 141.   100 Ibid., pp 143–4.   101 Ibid., pp 211, 233–4.
102 Chapter 8 of 1920.   103 See Risteárd Giltrap, *An Ghaeilge in Eaglais na hÉireann*

living off its past, comprised of endowments of one kind or another. These were made up of capital sums to meet the above-mentioned payment of clerical and choir annuitants, the Roe endowment and an endowment attaching to the dean's stipend. As was explained in the *Annual report* for the year 1909, such money was tied to specific purposes, and all other expenditure was defrayed from a general fund that depended on donations and church collections. Giving to this fund was not, the board complained, 'the assistance which the cathedral might reasonably expect from the wealthier members of the church in the diocese of Dublin and Glendalough.'[104] A symptom of the state of cathedral finances was the dispensing with the services of two supernumery choirmen in 1905.[105]

In 1910, the board wrote to the chapter noting that in recent years there had been a marked decrease in the size of congregations, and a consequent fall in collections.[106] It attributed the decline in large measure to a departure from 'the older school of cathedral music' and asked for its return. Dean and chapter undertook to endeavour to meet the board's wishes, and were as good as their word.[107] Archbishop Bernard wrote to the chapter in 1918, commenting on the 'beautiful Sunday services', but adding that they were 'intolerably long'. Very soon, the morning anthem was dropped, as was the evening sermon.[108] In 1916, the vicars choral applied for a pay rise 'to meet the unprecedented rise in the cost of living during the past two years', claiming that the purchasing power of the sovereign was only 45 per cent of its previous value. The chapter refused the application, referring to the cathedral's heavy overdraft (though they shortly relented).[109] The cathedral's cost of living had also risen, by 100 per cent in the case of fuel.[110] From time to time, the general fund was in credit, but seldom for long, and a credit balance in 1950 had by 1957 been transformed into a steadily increasing debt.[111] By 1960 it amounted to £503, and when the honorary treasurer, L.E. Dawson, was retiring the following year, he described the job as 'even more frustrating and unrewarding than that of a parochial treasurer, with expenditure ever on the increase, and very little more money coming in, or likely to be'.[112] Despite these vicissitudes, the cathedral maintained its giving to charitable causes at home and abroad, though the level of giving waned with the cathedral's circumstances.[113] Dean Lewis-Crosby, in particular, never

---

(Dublin, 1990), *passim*.   **104** C6/1/13/1, between pp 498–9.   **105** C6/1/13/2, p. 93. **106** *Annual reports* show a steady decrease from £369 in 1905 to £197 in 1910. Whatever changes may have been made to the music (see p. 383) income from offertories continued to fall.   **107** C6/1/7/14, p. 349.   **108** Ibid., pp 421–4.   **109** C6/1/13/2, pp 222–9. **110** *Annual report 1916*, p. 5.   **111** C6/1/13/3, p. 64.   **112** *Annual report 1960*, p. 4; Dawson to chapter clerk, 7 Dec. 1961, loose letter between 6 Apr. 1961 and 19 Oct. 1961 (C6/1/7/15).   **113** These are listed annually in the preachers' books, C6/1/21/14–16.

allowed the cathedral to forget its social obligations. Group discussions were held to address 'some of the social sores that mar our city's life', and he envisaged a 'new Ireland' free from want and idleness.[114]

A new source of revenue, with considerable potential, was beginning to be tapped. While the building had for long attracted visitors, particularly in the wake of Street's restoration, the number was showing appreciable growth. It was noted, for instance, in the annual report for 1928,[115] and must have received a boost in 1957 when the national carrier, C.I.E. agreed to include Christ Church on some of its city tours.[116] The impact of a growing tourist industry on the economy of the city – and the cathedral – was beginning to make a mark.

Though the chapter and board never completely gave up their ambition to provide the dean with an official residence, financial constraints always frustrated their hopes. In the year of Walsh's appointment, 1908, there were thoughts of acquiring Pearce's old deanery building in Fishamble Street,[117] whose future use by the united schools of St Werburgh's, St John's and St Audoen's was in question,[118] and in 1911–12 the chapter considered the matter further.[119] Nothing happened, though in 1911, 'pending provision of a residence', the dean was granted an allowance of £80 per year towards the cost of his house. But the allowance lapsed, and in 1952, when the matter came up again, the board stated that it was not in a position to provide either a deanery or a house allowance. There had, however, been one significant addition to the cathedral's property. In 1891, chapter and board accepted plans put forward by Sir Thomas Drew, the honorary architect, for changes to 'the east end of the grammar school' (as he put it), facing the newly-opened Lord Edward Street approach. The development included a room for the gentlemen of the choir and a library, and took longer than anticipated to complete owing to difficulties in procuring limestone, and the need to excavate to a depth of fifteen feet.[120] According to an article in the cathedral *Year book* for 1923–4,[121] the triple east window of the extension is a replication of the east window of the medieval chapter house.

The Caen stone that Street had employed so lavishly was a continual source of anxiety. As early as 1890 Drew was warning the board (of which

---

114 *Year book 1942–3*.   115 *Annual report 1928*, p. 4.   116 C6/1/13/3, p. 65.   117 See p. 277 above.   118 C6/1/13/2, pp 146, 178–9.   119 Ibid., pp 178–9.   120 C6/1/13/1, p. 520; C6/1/7/14, pp 184–5; *Annual report 1892*, p. 9. Drew's extension caused anxiety in 1949 when the keystone in the library arch was found to have shifted (C6/1/13/2, 24 June 1949) and again in the 1990s, when considerable work had to be done to stabilise the building.   121 See p. 16. The *Year book*, or *Calendar, Year book and blotter*, appeared annually from 1922 to 1959 inclusive, resuming publication in 1963. From 1938 until 1956 it was unpaginated.

he was a member) that the sandstone was starting to decay and that costly renewal would soon have to be faced.[122] A special fund was started for 'replacing Caen stone in the outer walls of the cathedral' with stone of a more durable nature, and three years later there was a further appeal for £1,500 for the same purpose.[123] In 1908 Drew reported on the dangerous condition of the stone-work overhanging St John's Lane. A hoarding was immediately erected, and the offending parapet removed.[124] Later that year, the standing committee of the general synod was informed of the pressing need for restoration work on the St Michael's Hill bridge.[125] In 1943, under Dean Lewis-Crosby's leadership, Christ Church embarked on a five-year plan to raise £5,000 for restoration work, and having spent £4,000 by 1946, had to put a stay on the work because of lack of funds.[126] Keeping up with the times, such as replacing gas by electricity in 1908 and experimenting with sound amplification in 1958, also involved expenditure.[127]

The members of the twentieth-century chapter and board were preoccupied with much the same kind of business that had engaged the attention of their predecessors. But the context within which they operated, national and ecclesiastical, was undergoing profound change. From 1916 to 1922 central Dublin was to be the scene of street warfare, and was soon to be the capital of a virtually independent Irish Free State. The part, if any, that Christ Church would in future play in national life had to be re-defined. Similarly, while the cathedral's relationship with the dioceses of Dublin and Glendalough had already been re-defined by post-disestablishment statutes of the general synod, the implications, financial and otherwise, of the new dispensation called for imagination and energy. The matter of the royal plate has already been referred to. There was correspondence as early as 1914 between dean and chapter and the Revd C.W.O. Mease, dean of the Chapel Royal, seeking an assurance that he would do all in his power to have the plate returned to Christ Church should the Chapel Royal cease to be used for Church of Ireland worship.[128] Mease referred the matter up, and in his reply stated his opinion that the enquiry was premature.[129] The cathedral did not allow matters to rest there, and by 1922, when the political die was cast, corresponded with Mr James MacMahon, the under-secretary, who made it clear that several options were open to the lord lieutenant, which included sending the plate to London. Another option was to put it in the vaults of the Bank of Ireland for safe keeping.[130] In the event, Christ Church got possession of it,

122 *Annual report 1889*, p. 12.   123 C6/1/13/2, p. 101; *Annual report 1909*, p. 7.   124 C6/1/13/2, pp 139–40.   125 Ibid., p. 143.   126 Ibid., 24 Sept. 1943, *Annual report 1946*, pp 4–5.   127 C6/1/13/2, pp 137, 171; C6/1/13/3, p. 73.   128 C6/1/7/14, pp 386–7. 129 Ibid., pp 386–7.   130 Ibid., pp 441, 443.

Mr MacMahon declaring that it would be safer in the cathedral strong room than in the bank![131]

Throughout these years of intensifying challenge to British rule in Ireland, the cathedral maintained its tradition of loyalty to the crown. Memorial services for Queen Victoria were held in 1901,[132] and when the king and queen visited Ireland in 1903 the dean and chapter presented an address of welcome at Dublin castle,[133] though the royal couple, an invitation being suggested, were unable to attend Christ Church on the Sunday of their visit.[134] Similarly in 1911, a letter from St James's palace regretted that Christ Church would not be on the itinerary of a royal visit in July.[135] But the next communication from the crown, acknowledging a resolution of sympathy from the cathedral on the occasion of the death of George V, was conveyed, as protocol dictated, through the Department of External Affairs of the Irish Free State.[136] There is little evidence in the cathedral records of the prevailing turbulence created by world war and civic disturbance in the early decades of the century, much as they impinged on the lives of those who served and worshipped there. The board had to cancel a meeting scheduled for 28 April 1916, because 'owing to the outbreak of the Rebellion it could not be held'.[137] No services were held on Sunday 30 April 'owing to Insurrection'.[138] Damage was caused to the roofs, windows and stonework by the 'troubles' of 1922.[139] An offer to the cathedral of a tricolour used in 1916 was declined, and it went instead to the National Museum.[140] Much more acceptable was the flag of 'H.M.S. Dublin', a survivor of the battle of Jutland (1916). A committee of Dublin citizens, together with members of the business community, had raised funds to provide the ship with a brass band and other amenities, and the ship's company, in return, presented the Dublin Chamber of Commerce with their battle-scarred ensign. The chamber gave it to the cathedral, and it was committed to the crypt.[141] The thanksgiving service held in June 1918 'for the overthrow of the enemy' was attended by the lord lieutenant, and attended by the largest congregation since the opening ceremony in 1878,[142] and in 1919 permission was granted to the Boys' Brigade to erect a memorial to 300 past members who had lost their lives in the war.[143] Memorial services were held in November 1918 for boys from the diocese, and in March 1919 for those from the Dublin intermediate schools.[144] A mere twenty-two years later, daily prayers were being said for 192 men on active service in

131 C6/1/13/2, p. 277.   132 *Annual report 1901*, p. 7.   133 *Annual report 1903*, p. 8.
134 C6/1/7/14, pp 269–70.   135 Ibid., pp 361–2.   136 Department of External Affairs to Dean Kennedy, 27 Feb. 1936, looseleaf letter in C6/1/7/15 between entries for 24 Jan. 1936 and 24 Apr. 1936.   137 C6/1/13/2, p. 217.   138 C6/1/21/16.   139 *Annual report 1925*, p. 7.   140 C6/1/7/15, 17 June 1958.   141 C6/1/13/2, p. 430; *Year book 1942–3*.   142 *Annual report 1918*, p. 5.   143 C6/1/7/14, p. 425.   144 C6/1/21/16.

World War II,[145] all of whom survived the hostilities.[146] Despite the uncertainties created by that war, restoration work continued,[147] while the necessary precautions against air raid damage were taken.[148] The dean wrote in the *Year book* for 1941

> Our government has been trying to hold to a position of neutrality. As citizens we must respect that attitude. But let us remember that in its spiritual warfare against evil, and its call to help those who suffer, the church can never be neutral.

In 1938 Dr Douglas Hyde, the distinguished Celtic scholar and language revivalist, who was a son of the rectory, was inaugurated as Ireland's first president under the 1937 constitution. Board and chapter sent him their congratulations.[149] But a much more signal sign of the cathedral's wish to identify with the new state came in 1940, with the introduction of the annual Citizenship Service to seek 'the blessing of Almighty God on the people of Dublin and those who are responsible for the life of its peoples'.[150] It has been regularly held since, attended by government, municipal, academic and industrial representatives, together with members of the diplomatic corps, their presence in the cathedral conveying something of the international, national and civic world outside its doors. In the early years, most of those who participated were members of the Church of Ireland, or at least Protestants of one tradition or another, but with the great relaxation in interchurch relations that followed Vatican II, the character of representation has changed, President de Valera being the first Roman Catholic president to attend in person in 1967. It had been customary until 1924 (when the city administration was temporarily vested in commissioners) for Protestant lord mayors and members of the corporation to attend Christ Church at Christmas and Easter, robed and occupying the civic pew. The custom was resumed for a time when the corporation was restored in 1930.[151] The corporation had long contributed to the upkeep of the cathedral grounds, in return for the citizens being given access to them,[152] though the board was not always successful in its attempts to have the municipal contribution increased.[153]

---

145 *Annual report 1944*, pp 5–6.   146 *Annual report 1945*, pp 4–5. Their names are listed in *Annual report 1946*, pp 10–11.   147 *Annual report 1945*, p. 6.   148 C6/1/13/2, p. 473. The dean and chapter wrote in sympathy with their equivalents at St Paul's and Coventry when their cathedrals suffered air attacks (C6/1/13/2, pp 434, 437).   149 C6/1/7/15, 29 Apr. 1938; C6/1/13/2, p. 381.   150 *Our church review* (Dublin and Glendalough diocesan magazine), Nov. 1940.   151 H.B. Kennedy, *Official guide to the cathedral church of the Holy Trinity commonly called Christ Church* (Dublin, 1931), p. 27.   152 See p. 328 above.   153 For example, C6/1/13/2, 28 Mar. 1945; C6/1/13/3, p. 16.

Whatever reservations the cathedral may have harboured in the matter, the annual report of 1893 admitted that there was no misconduct in the precincts, despite them now being 'frequented by numbers of children under no control, and by some of the lowest class of street idlers'.[154] Minutes of a chapter meeting of September 1955 record that 'the dean referred to the proposal to erect civic buildings north of the cathedral, and stressed the point that such buildings might obscure a vista of the cathedral, and might conflict architecturally with the cathedral buildings'.[155] He further reported that a meeting with the corporation had taken place, that the corporation had shown courtesy and concern for the cathedral's position 'in our city', and that a reduction of twenty feet in the height of the proposed buildings was being considered.[156] The development of the site that eventually took place falls outside the scope of this chapter; suffice it to say here that the dean and chapter of the time were somewhat sanguine in their expectations of the modifications proposed by the corporation in the 1950s. But if there were occasions of disappointment, there was also the encouragement that the cathedral drew from a growing appreciation of its place in the city on the part of the wider Dublin community, as seen in the liberal response from business firms to an appeal for funds to restore the fabric of the building in 1980.[157]

Yet main onus for safeguarding Christ Church had to rest with the Church of Ireland people of Dublin. This had been put to them in no uncertain terms in 1918, when it was explained that while endowments carried much of the cost of maintaining cathedral life, they were not intended to relieve the parishes of their duty.[158] In 1922, when finances were in an especially bad way, the archbishop chaired a meeting of incumbents in the chapter room, and they agreed to ask their parishes for a minimum annual contribution of £1 to Christ Church. There were about 100 parishes in Dublin and Glendalough,[159] and of the minority of parishes that responded, several soon dropped out, and others reduced their donation. Clearly, other avenues of approach to the parishes had to be explored, and so came about 'the Friends of Christ Church', formed in 1929 (only two years after the first such body in connection with an ancient cathedral was formed at Canterbury).[160] Dean Kennedy declared that the motivation behind this initiative was financial, and that it was linked to the launching of a special appeal to those church people throughout the diocese who were not on the vestry register. The inten-

---

154 *Annual report 1893*, p. 10.   155 C6/1/7/15, 29 Sept. 1955.   156 Ibid., 30 Nov. 1955.
157 *Annual report 1946*, pp 4–5.   158 *Annual report 1918*, p. 5.   159 C6/1/13/2, p. 270.
160 *Year book 1930*, p. 13; Keith Robbins, 'The twentieth century, 1898–1994' in Collinson *et al.*, *Canterbury*, p. 314.

tion, soon accomplished, was that the 'Friends' would provide the cathedral with an auxiliary source of income for specific projects, but more than that, would provide a bond with the parishes, and thus constitute a major step in the transition of Christ Church from its pre-disestablishment character as a rather self-contained, largely self-perpetuating corporation, whose personnel were dependent for their emoluments on property and other endowments, scarcely responsible to the diocese at all, into a mother church serving the diocese, and calling on it for support in return. The 'Friends'' initial donations to the cathedral were modest in scale, but by 1950 included such substantial projects as paying for the repair of the north wall of the chapter-house.[161] Two years later, they defrayed the cost of installing electric storage heaters.[162] In 1958 the 'Friends' paid for the restoration of two monuments in the crypt.[163] A ladies committee was formed in 1946,[164] and a junior branch was inaugurated in 1950.[165] In 1946, the Friends of Belfast cathedral paid a visit to Dublin, the first of many visits by other cathedral 'Friends' to be recorded,[166] and in 1955 the 'Friends of Christ Church' initiated what has become an increasingly ambitious item on their yearly programme by taking an outing – the first one being to Tara and Trim.[167]

The cathedral recognised that goodwill must be reciprocal, and when the nine-hundredth anniversary service of 1938 was being planned, the parish clergy were invited to apply for reserved seats. That was the year of Dean Lewis-Crosby's installation, and at his second chapter meeting, he appealed for co-operation in making Christ Church the 'mother church of the diocese', and it was agreed that the cathedral should be represented in the pages of the diocesan monthly review.[168] The following year, it was suggested to the parochial clergy that they send representatives to the cathedral on those days when their parish was remembered in prayer,[169] and agreement was reached with the Mothers' Union for the refurnishing of the chapel of St Laurence O'Toole for their use.[170] Whether by consulting with diocesan youth organisations about setting up a chapel for them,[171] or by bringing large crowds to learn more about Christ Church through the annual St Stephen's Day lectures, Lewis-Crosby reached out to diocese and city, and sought to bring diocese and city into the cathedral. He was prepared to go to the parishes to plead the cathedral's cause,[172] while urging the members of the chapter to raise money from their parishioners for the cathedral organ fund.[173] But money was not the only nexus. An annual 'quiet day' for the clergy had

161 C6/1/13/2, 26 May 1950.   162 C6/1/13/3, p. 14.   163 *Year book 1958*, p. 13. 164 C6/1/13/2, 29 Mar. 1946.   165 Ibid., 28 Apr. 1950, C6/1/13/3, p. 3.   166 C6/1/13/2, 31 May 1946.   167 C6/1/13/3, p. 46.   168 C6/1/7/15, 15 Dec. 1938. 169 Ibid., 9 Mar. 1939.   170 C6/1/13/2, p. 418.   171 C6/1/7/15, 3 Apr. 1951.   172 Ibid., 17 Sept. 1943.   173 Ibid., 2 Feb. 1943.

been a long-standing diocesan engagement.[174] There was a cycle of prayer for the parishes, and the incumbents were encouraged to pray for Christ Church as it prayed for them during the week when their particular parish was remembered there.

Dean Lewis-Crosby died in office in his ninety-seventh year on 18 May 1961. His successor, Norman David Emerson, a distinguished historian, chairman of the Irish Committee for Historical Sciences, contributor to Alison Phillips' *History of the Church of Ireland* and member of the Royal Irish Academy, was installed in January 1962. He brought to the office not only his erudition, but also his long experience of the centre city parish of St Mary's and its people. Preaching at Christ Church on the occasion of the death of Seán O'Casey, who, like one of the leading interpreters of O'Casey's work, Sara Allgood, had been baptised in St Mary's, the dean spoke of the playwright as one who had 'immortalised the hopes and fears, the loves and hates of the plain people of this city'.[175] Dean Emerson died in office, on 12 January 1966, after a comparatively short tenure of under four years. The fact that more than fifteen months were to pass before the archbishop appointed a successor was a sign that he, like others in the diocese, believed that some serious thinking had to be done about the future of Christ Church.

---

174 *Year book 1923–4*, p. 6.   175 *Year book 1965*, pp 12–13.

XVI

Music in the nineteenth–century cathedral, 1800–70

Barra Boydell

The musical establishment at Christ Church was to flourish in the early nineteenth century despite the decline in the cathedral's status and revenues following the Act of Union and the removal to other parts of the city of the Four Courts, sessions, Royal Exchange, corn market and custom house, all previously near the cathedral. Christ Church appears largely to have avoided the 'perfunctory and listless fashion' in which music was performed at most English cathedrals in the early nineteenth century,[1] Monck Mason claiming in 1820 that 'there is not ... a cathedral in Great Britain wherein the choral service is better performed than in those of St Patrick's and Christ Church'.[2] Public interest in the elaborate solo anthems of John Stevenson and others, performed in a manner more theatrical than sacred, encouraged the continuation of the healthy musical tradition which had existed in the later eighteenth century. When the high church revival began to take effect, existing musical practices were reformed but there was not the need at Christ Church as in so many cathedrals to rebuild a lapsed musical tradition.

The vicars choral and stipendiaries continued to enjoy exceptional salaries for the period, a situation which, in a plea for the proper funding of cathedral music in order to ensure high standards, Canon Seymour later acknowledged to be 'a bright exception to the general rule'.[3] A lay clerk at an English cathedral in the mid-nineteenth century might expect between £40 and £80 a year (Durham was an exception at nearly £115),[4] but in 1835 the stipendiaries at Christ Church each received £114 12s. 2¼d. and the vicars choral £196 18s. 5¼d., to either of which incomes might be added £156 6s. 6¾d. as

---

1 William Gatens, *Victorian cathedral music in theory and practice* (Cambridge, 1986), p. 6. 2 Mason, *St Patrick's*, cited in Bumpus, 'Composers', p. 81. 3 Edward Seymour, *The cathedral system* (Dublin, 1870), p. 22. 4 Philip Barrett, *Barchester: English cathedral life in the nineteenth century* (London, 1993), p. 188.

a vicar at St Patrick's. As a vicar at both cathedrals and vicars' steward Robert Jager earned an exceptional £468 11s. 8d.[5] The Dublin cathedrals could thus attract the finest Irish and English singers. An advertisement in 1858 elicited twenty-six applications, all with one exception from England, many from leading cathedrals.[6] The vicars nonetheless guarded their rights with vigilance. At the end of the eighteenth century some of the revenues of the choir had been appropriated by the dignitaries of the two cathedrals, John Spray being largely responsible for rescuing these revenues which included a total of £238 12s. 9d. reclaimed in 1808 and owing to the vicars since 1794.[7] In 1855 the vicars were to challenge the decision to transfer the rights and revenues of dean's and precentor's vicars to the prebendaries of St Michael's and St Michan's respectively.[8]

Most choirmen continued to belong to both choirs until after disestablishment[9] but since the later eighteenth century, weekday services were sung only at Christ Church. Evensong, usually with three or four singing men present (but not infrequently only the reader and organist with, presumably, some boys), was rare on Saturdays, and often held only three times a week or even suspended for periods of many months.[10] In 1843 John Jebb, a central figure in the high church revival of choral practices in the mid-nineteenth century, regretted the poor attendance by choirmen at morning weekday services in a choir so richly endowed.[11] A visitor in the early 1860s wrote of the 'dreary service' performed by one singing man and five small boys, and Robert Stewart later recalled the weekday services at that time as being 'starved, sometimes trebles only were present, and rarely more than one man for each of the other parts, and that only on Thursdays and Fridays when the dean ... used to attend.'[12] If weekdays made only light demands on the choir, Sundays were different. Some choir members sang at Trinity College (and after 1814 also at the Chapel Royal in Dublin castle), leaving the service after the anthem, with the full choir singing at Christ Church in the morning and at St Patrick's in the afternoon. Sunday evening services had been discontinued at Christ Church in 1814 and were not resumed until St

---

5 Returns to ecclesiastical commissioners, after Grindle, *Cathedral music*, pp 61–2. 6 Pakenham papers, P.R.O.N.I., T.D. 5777, Y/12/5. 7 C6/1/7/8, p. 484; C6/1/15/2, 1808–9; Bumpus, 'Composers', pp 81, 117. 8 Letter from vicars choral to the dean and chapter, 6 June 1855, Pakenham papers, P.R.O.N.I., T.D. 5777, Y/12/3; C6/1/7/13, p. 2. 9 Choirboys at St Patrick's continue to be named most years in the visitation lists but at Christ Church they are only named in passing references in the chapter acts or in the proctors' accounts after 1833–4 in connection with accommodation costs. The earliest Christ Church school attendance book dates from 1863–5 (C6/1/23/8). 10 C6/1/22/1; C6/1/23/5–7. 11 John Jebb, *The choral service of the united church of England and Ireland* (London, 1843), p. 121. 12 William Glover, cited after Bumpus, 'Composers', p. 148; Vignoles, *Memoir*, p. 189.

Patrick's was closed for renovation in 1862,[13] but when St Patrick's re-opened in 1865 its dean and chapter understandably wanted to reinstate the Sunday afternoon service popularly referred to as 'Paddy's opera' due to the crowds attracted by the performances of solo anthems.[14] Initially Christ Church only granted permission for the three surviving Robinson brothers, outstanding singers of their day, and three other choirmen to attend while still maintaining their own Sunday afternoon service, but some months later they relented, moving evensong to 7.00 p.m. with the attendance of the full choir being required.[15] With three full services on Sundays (plus Trinity College and the Chapel Royal in the mornings for some) the vicars choral and stipendiaries unsuccessfully sought in 1869 to be released from the Sunday evening service in Christ Church.[16]

Around 1840 the deans of the two cathedrals apparently agreed not to promote any choirman to one cathedral who already held a post at the other, a decision which is reported to have had a deleterious effect on the choirs since singers of high quality were no longer attracted from England and which was consequently revoked.[17] There is no reference to this decision in the chapter acts of either cathedral (nor by Seymour in 1869).[18] However, Joseph Robinson did resign as a stipendiary at Christ Church when he was elected a full vicar at St Patrick's in 1843, and the few new singers appointed to each choir during this period were not members of the other cathedral choir before 1865 when Samuel Dobbin, a vicar choral at Christ Church, was appointed to the same position at St Patrick's.[19] Despite occasional difficulties, the effective sharing of the choir between the two Dublin cathedrals could have benefits when a threat to the choir at the one cathedral was countered by its essential role at the other: when St Patrick's was closed for rebuilding in 1862–5 and Christ Church in the 1870s the continuation of services in the other cathedral provided continuity for the choirmen, while the threat to the existence of St Patrick's choir may have contributed to the dropping of a proposal in 1868 to suppress the choir of Christ Church and reduce the cathedral to the status of a parish church.[20]

The dean and chapter talked of the 'increasing excellence of the choir' in 1810[21] and Monck Mason's praise a decade later has been noted. Standards must have begun subsequently to lapse since steps were taken in 1840–1 to

13 C6/1/7/9, p. 279; C6/1/23/6–7; C6/1/22/1; see also C6/1/7/13, pp 129, 202. Bumpus states incorrectly that 'at Christ Church, from 1807 to 1825 ... there was evening service on Sunday at 7' ('Composers', p. 146).   14 C.V. Stanford, *Pages from an unwritten diary* (London, 1914), p. 37.   15 C6/1/7/13, pp 200, 203, 208.   16 Ibid., p. 278. 17 *Dublin University Magazine*, xxxvii (1851), p. 500; Bumpus, *Stevenson*, p. 26.   18 Seymour, *Christ Church*.   19 C6/1/7/12, p. 162; Lawlor, *Fasti*, p. 243.   20 Seymour, *Christ Church*, pp 74f. See p. 321 above.   21 C6/1/7/9, p. 78.

improve matters with increased fines for absence unless choir members arranged for another 'of like quality of voice' to attend on their behalf, and the problem of ageing or infirm choir members was addressed by appointing substitutes paid out of the vicar's or stipendiary's salary. A year later the chapter could record regular and satisfactory attendance at services over the previous year.[22] In 1843 Jebb reported that the cathedral's music was recovering from the 'most secular taste' which formerly prevailed and he wrote that 'nothing can surpass [the vicar chorals'] musical skill, great pains having been taken in the selection of qualified singers'.[23] In his desire to reform cathedral music and services along high church lines, Jebb was an outspoken critic of the secular, 'operatic' style of music represented by the solo anthems of composers like Stevenson, which he described as 'an abominable perversion of sacred things'.[24] However, the evidence both of contemporary commentators and of the repertoire revealed by extant service lists from the 1840s and later suggests that music at Christ Church before the choral revival of the mid-nineteenth century took full effect was anything but 'incompetent and careless', as the situation prevailing in most English cathedrals at the time has been described.[25] The regret expressed by an anonymous writer in 1851 that 'the true cathedral style (that is the choral) has made way for the exhibition of solo singing in some half-dozen anthems repeated Sunday after Sunday' is not borne out by these service lists.[26]

Following his appointment in 1864 Dean West (who was also dean of St Patrick's) introduced changes aimed at improving the quality and efficiency of the music which reflected the choral revival developing in the wake of the Tractarian and high church movements in England.[27] The attendance of a countertenor, tenor and bass was required at matins, at which all twelve choirboys now sang, these services also being held during the boys' school holidays. Evensong was now held daily except Saturdays although the boys did not usually attend.[28] Revised choir regulations the following year were designed to promote 'greater reverence and efficiency in the performance of divine service'. Attendance and punctuality were emphasised, music for processional anthems was to be easy to carry (a reminder that heavy, bound part-books were often used), music should be selected with regard for the

22 C6/1/7/12, pp 92, 103, 104f., 112, 123. 23 Jebb, *Choral service*, pp 104, 392. 24 John Jebb, *Three lectures on the cathedral service* (2nd ed., Leeds and London, 1845), pp 115–16. 25 Bernarr Rainbow, *The choral revival in the Anglican church, 1839–1872* (London, 1970), p. 257. 26 *Dublin University Magazine*, xxxvii (1851), p. 500; 'Christ Church cathedral: course of services and anthems ... [1850 to 1851]' (cathedral archives). 27 See especially Gatens, *Victorian cathedral music*. See p. 317 for the arrangement under the Church Temporalities Act whereby the dean of St Patrick's held the deanery of Christ Church. 28 C6/1/7/13, pp 195, 223; C6/1/23/9.

available strengths of the choir, be requested in good time and not changed without urgent cause, should be adequately rehearsed at least by the choristers, and placed in order on the desks before the service (a practice first noted in 1848 and formally instituted in 1850).[29] Arrangements for singing verse anthems were not to be changed during the service and the organist was to give the starting note for anthems and chants clearly.[30] By 1869 Seymour commented that the choir could 'fairly challenge the history of the past to show a more efficient or effective body ... or one whose tone could bear comparison'.[31]

In the early part of the century the two most prominent choir members were John Spray, who had come to Dublin from England in 1795 and was described on his memorial in St Patrick's as 'the first tenor singer in the empire', and Sir John Stevenson who in 1814 was appointed organist of the new Chapel Royal at Dublin castle. Stevenson's anthems, which contain many elaborate tenor and bass solos written for Spray and himself, were strongly influenced by Haydn, leading to criticism later in the century when Haydn's style was considered too secular for church music. Jebb commented in 1843 that 'with all his faults, however, [he] is far superior to many trashy and flimsy contemporaries, who have in England obtained a much wider fame'.[32] Permission continued to be given for the choir to sing at sacred or charity occasions, including the opening of a new church in Westmeath in 1802 and a visit to Belfast in October 1813 to sing in concerts organised by Edward Bunting to benefit the poor house, including the first Belfast performance of 'Messiah'.[33] Nevertheless, participation at a concert in the theatre in 1822 'for the relief of the peasantry in the distressed parts of Ireland' was only allowed because it was to be 'unmingled with any theatrical performance' and the musicians were performing *gratis*.[34] The unauthorised appearance of choir members at public concerts, however, remained strictly forbidden. In 1823 John Spray and John Smith (subsequently professor of music at Trinity College from 1845 to 1865) challenged their being punished for singing at a public oratorio performance in St Patrick's for which they were paid, the dispute eventually going to court.[35]

The earliest attendance lists for boys survive from the 1860s. By the 1830s (and possibly earlier) the choirboys of Christ Church and St Patrick's were

29 C6/1/15/4, 1848–9; C6/1/7/12, p. 275.   30 C6/1/7/13, pp 230–1.   31 Seymour, *Christ Church*, pp 71, 83.   32 Jebb, *Choral service*, p. 392; see also p. 312 above.   33 C6/1/7/8, p. 231 (the church is not identified in the chapter acts, but may have been a chapel of ease on the estate of Richard Malone, Baron Sunderlin, at Ballynahown, Co. Westmeath); C6/1/7/9, p. 208; *Belfast Newsletter*, 15 Oct. 1813.   34 C6/1/7/10, p. 167. 35 Ibid., pp 224–33, 275f., 286; John Erck, *An account of the ecclesiastical establishment subsisting in Ireland, as also an ecclesiastical register ...* (Dublin, 1830), pp 293f.

no longer combined but attached exclusively to one cathedral. The core of foundation choirboys apprenticed to Christ Church was increased from four to six in 1832 and the non-foundation choirboys, who attended the choir and the school on the same basis, to six in 1847 'for the more certain supply of well-qualified choristers'.[36] The full complement now stood at twelve, with some further boys in the school (between five and seven in the mid-1860s) who might become choirboys in later years.[37] Whereas the master of the boys had formerly always been a musician, from the early nineteenth century the writing (or 'classical') master assumed overall responsibility for the boys' education. Though typically a former choirboy, the music master was not necessarily a member of the choir. The last master to combine overall responsibility with teaching music was Charles G. Osborne. Following complaints about his education of the boys in March 1806 Francis Robinson, father of four brothers (Francis James, William, John, and Joseph) who would be members of both cathedral choirs and dominate Dublin musical life through much of the nineteenth century, took over as writing master until 1820.[38] Robert Tuke succeeded Osborne as music master in 1807, followed two years later by John Elliott who resigned in 1814. William Hamerton subsequently held the position until 1830.[39] Care of the boys, previously held by the late verger, James Hewitt, was assumed by John Elliott one year after his appointment.[40] This arrangement must have been considered financially advantageous since Francis Robinson subsequently offered to care for them at a price which he doubtless felt was profitable (although in 1817 he had to be compensated for losses incurred).[41] Richard Beatty succeeded William Hamerton as music master in 1830, remaining until 1873 by which time he was in his seventies.[42] The chapter acknowledged in 1850 that the high standards achieved by the choir owed much to his care and attention in training the boys.[43] A committee appointed to examine ways of making economies in the running of the cathedral recommended in 1852 that the duties of music master and organist be combined and that the office of writing master be abolished on the next vacancy, but no action was taken.[44] Charles Osborne junior, writing master from 1821, has been confused with his namesake (probably his father)

36 C6/1/7/11, pp 248f.; C6/1/7/12, p. 255.   37 C6/1/7/9, p. 36; C6/1/23/8; C6/1/25/1/1.   38 C6/1/7/8, pp 373, 381; C6/1/15/2–3; on the Robinsons, Caitriona Doran, 'The Robinsons, a nineteenth-century Dublin family of musicians, and their contribution towards the musical life in Dublin', M.A. thesis, N.U.I. Maynooth, 1998.   39 C6/1/7/8, p. 419; C6/1/7/9, pp 39, 41, 258, 279; C6/1/7/11, p. 188; Tuke should not be confused with his namesake (possibly his father), a former choirboy and stipendiary who had died in 1797 (see p. 301 note 28).   40 C6/1/15/2, 1809–10.   41 C6/1/7/9, pp 285, 362.   42 C6/1/7/11, pp 129, 188; C6/1/13/1, p. 22; Beatty concluded his apprenticeship as a choirboy in 1814–15, C6/1/15/3.   43 C6/1/7/12, p. 279.   44 Ibid., p. 296.

who had been master of the boys earlier in the century.[45] He was accused in 1832 by one parent of beating his son, an accusation which was not upheld by the chapter although the parents withdrew the boy from the choir.[46] Further complaints however in the following year led to Osborne's resignation.[47] Thereafter the post of writing master was held by a succession of senior clergy, two of whom had musical interests: both John Crosthwaite, precentor's vicar and schoolmaster from 1834 to 1837, and his successor John Finlayson (master until 1852) were minor composers of church music and in 1852 Finlayson published a volume of anthem texts sung in Christ Church.[48]

While the incomes of the choirmen remained high, the cathedral's declining revenues in the early years of the century demanded that economies be made and the costs of looking after and educating the choirboys was one aspect which came under scrutiny. In 1801 the dean and chapter of St Patrick's were invited to discuss 'an arrangement for the support of the school of their common choir'[49] but by 1814 Christ Church claimed to be carrying a disproportionate share of the cost of the school. Increases in the contributions from Trinity College and St Patrick's were sought, St Patrick's agreeing to support one of the Christ Church boys provided its own boys could assist at the services in Christ Church. A proposal that boys should no longer board within the precincts but live with their parents who would be paid an allowance was rejected by the parents. A compromise was reached, newly-appointed boys now living at home but existing choirboys being boarded out with people appointed by the chapter but living beyond the precincts.[50] By 1819 however this was proving inconvenient and all boys were accommodated within the dean's lodgings or by the verger or the schoolmaster. In 1832 it was finally decided to dispense with boarding and the payment of an accommodation allowance to parents was successfully reintroduced.[51] St Mary's chapel (the medieval Lady chapel) was now rebuilt for use both by the dean and as school rooms for the boys. Regular hours were appointed for the choir school which was divided into two classes to allow both the music master and the schoolmaster to teach at the same time.[52] The boys' musical education and training occupied the first part of the morning before

45 C6/1/15/3, 1820–1; Grindle, Cathedral music, pp 68–9.   46 C6/1/7/11, pp 237f., 248.   47 Ibid., pp 372, 373.   48 For two anthems by Crosthwaite, C6/1/24/1/33; Finlayson composed The general confession, responses and litany. Set to music … (London and Dublin, n.d.); see also A collection of anthems as sung in the cathedral of the Holy Trinity … (Dublin, 1852); Bumpus, 'Composers', pp 133, 134; Jebb, Choral service, p. 453.   49 C6/1/7/8, p. 158.   50 C6/1/7/9, pp 257, 265–6, 271–4, 278–9.   51 C6/1/7/10, pp 96, 101; C6/1/7/11, pp 191, 248; C6/1/15/3, 1827–8. In 1819 there was some opposition to the new plan and two boys were re-bound according to the old indentures, C6/1/7/10, p. 105.   52 C6/1/7/11, pp 233, 238.

matins. School hours were from 12.00 noon to 3.00 p.m. daily (these times were brought forward by half an hour in 1852 when the morning service was changed from 11.00 a.m. to 10.00 a.m.)[53] and the curriculum, similar to that of any contemporary grammar school, included reading, writing and grammar, mathematics, geography, history, Greek, Latin, and religion.[54] Pianos were bought on a number of occasions for the boys, as was a harpsichord as late as 1816–17, their keyboard training including Cramer's studies and Corfe's *Principles of harmony and thorough-bass explained*.[55] In 1814 the organist was asked to look after a senior chorister who could play the organ, the boys continuing as before to learn the organ and occasionally to act as deputies.[56] William Telford was asked in 1845 to quote for a two-manual organ for the use of the boys, but no payment for such an instrument appears in the accounts.[57] Prizes were instituted in 1867 for the two best choirboys at sight-reading and playing a fugue.[58] Concern to maintain the standards of the school led in 1845 to an examination of how both teachers were managing their duties and the drawing up of new regulations for the school.[59] An examination of the musical abilities of the choirboys in 1852 resulted in a satisfactory report on all the boys both vocally and instrumentally, but in the same year the presentation of silver medals to those who had satisfactorily completed their term of service, introduced by Dean Pakenham in 1846, was discontinued, although certificates were later introduced.[60] In the 1840s book prizes as rewards for good conduct were sometimes given.[61] An offer by Trinity College in 1864 of free education to choirboys in recognition of their contribution to its own chapel services was welcomed by the chapter as a means of attracting boys of 'a superior class' to enter the choir.[62]

The Byfield organ of 1752 was described in 1810 as 'imperfect and ruinous' and insufficient for the present-day needs.[63] Frederick Hollister was replaced as organ tuner by William Hull who carried out some repairs.[64] When Henry Leaman embarked on further repairs and additions in 1817 which included increasing the range of the instrument he uncovered such poor quality work by Hull that further work was called for, the dean paying the additional cost.[65]

---

53 Ibid., p. 274; C6/1/7/12, pp 300f.   54 See orders for schoolbooks between 1820 and 1845, C/6/1/21/1.   55 C6/1/15/2, 1804–5; C6/1/15/3, 1816–17, 1820–1, 1829–30; C6/1/15/4, 1864–5; C6/1/7/8, pp 226, 346; C6/1/7/10, p. 143; C6/1/7/12, p. 137; C6/1/7/13, pp 174, 184; C6/1/12/1, 15 May 1817, 6 Mar. 1818, 5 Sept. 1819.   56 C6/1/7/9, p. 273; C6/1/7/12, p. 354; C6/1/7/13, pp 272, 278.   57 C6/1/7/12, p. 225. 58 C6/1/7/13, pp 36, 90, 99, 253.   59 C6/1/7/12, pp 216, 217, 225.   60 Ibid., pp 244, 292, 294, 299; C6/1/7/13, p. 87.   61 C6/1/21/1, 3 Aug. 1841, 9 July 1843, 18 Nov. 1846.   62 C6/1/7/13, pp 175–6.   63 C6/1/7/9, pp 72, 76f.   64 Ibid., p. 141; C6/1/15/2, 1809–10, 1810–11.   65 C6/1/7/9, pp 342f., 344f., 348f., 373f.; see also C6/1/15/3, 1815–17.

The alterations to the long quire in 1831–3 included replacing the existing organ loft and making changes to the back of the organ case to improve visibility within the cathedral.[66] In 1832 William Telford, appointed organ and piano tuner in 1833, repaired the organ and added open and stopped diapasons to the great organ and double open diapason and principal to the pedals.[67] The organist Robert Prescott Stewart later recalled the modified Byfield organ as having been a 'very feeble instrument ... without one single redeeming feature', although he did at the time approve Telford's substitution in 1844 of a new swell organ of twelve stops and wider compass.[68]

The decision to build an entirely new organ by Telford was reached in 1856, Revd William Chichester O'Neill, prebendary of St Michael's, contributing significantly towards the cost.[69] It was the first organ in Ireland in which pneumatic action was extensively used and was ready at the end of

---

66 C6/1/7/11, pp 217, 227; Jebb, *Choral service*, pp 197, 202. See p. 224 below.   67 C6/1/7/11, p. 250; 6/1/7/12, pp 24f.; C6/1/15/3, 1832–3, 1833–4; the full specification of the organ as improved by Telford was given in the chapter acts for 11 April 1836: Three benches of keys from GG to F in alt.

Great ('to Bass C'): great open diapason, great stopped diapason, open diapason, stopped diapason, principal, flute, twelfth, fifteenth, sesquialtra, cornet, trumpet, double open diapason.

Choir ('GG to F in alt'): stopped diapason, dulciana, flute, principal, bassoon, open diapason to middle C.

Swell ('fiddle G to F in alt'): open diapason, dulciana, stopped diapason, principal, flute, hautboy, trumpet.

Pedals ('one and a half octaves'): double open diapason, great unison diapason, principal.

'The organ contains 1593 pipes the longest of which (the Double GG open diapason pedals) is twenty feet long by two feet ten inches, diagonal, diameter, the shortest ¾ of an inch long. The wind is supplied by two horizontal bellows; the largest is ten feet long by five feet wide loaded with 4½ cwt. of metal.'   68 Letter from R.P. Stewart to Dr Marks, 4 July 1853, Pakenham papers, P.R.O.N.I, T.D. 5777, Y/11/6; Vignoles, *Memoir*, p. 131; C6/1/7/12, p. 190.   69 C6/1/7/13, pp 26f. Telford's proposed specification was as follows:

Great ('CC to G. 56 notes'): double open diapason, great open diapason, second open diapason, flute harmonique, stopped diapason, principal, gomohorn [*sic*, gemshorn?], twelfth, fifteenth, sesquialtra of 4 and 5 ranks, trumpet, clarion.

Choir ('CC to G. 56 notes'): bourdon (stopped), small open diapason, stopped diapason, viol de gambo tenor C, principal, flute (open) tenor C, fifteenth, cor anglaise.

Swell ('CC to G. 56 notes'): bourdon (stopped), open diapason, dulciana tenor C, stopped diapason, flute harmonique (octave), principal, fifteenth, flageolet, mixture of 3 ranks, contra fagotto, trumpet or cornopean, oboe, clarion, vox humana (tenor C). Tremolo in the swell organ.

Pedal ('CCC to F. 30 notes'): double open diapason, double stopped diapason, open diapason.

1857. Increasing practice by the choirboys on the new organ meant that the organ blower had to be engaged daily instead of twice a week and requests came from former choirboys who wished to play it, but permission was not given to church organists who already had an instrument to play on. Stewart was extremely critical of Telford's instrument, describing it as 'notoriously defective in the bass', coarse, uneven and not as was proposed.[70] Repairs were made and in 1870 agreement was reached for Telford to add four further stops (a clarionet in the choir, a contra fagotto in the swell, and a violone and a trombone in the pedal organ) which would complete the instrument. The organ screen was also to be removed and the organ resited in the north transept.[71] However, before this work was completed Telford advised the removal of the organ to St Bride's church for safe keeping during Street's rebuilding of the cathedral and the outstanding improvements to the instrument were not completed until 1878.[72] Seymour wrote in 1869 that Telford's organ had not received justice both because of its being incomplete and because of its location: originally planned for the north transept, it was put on the quire screen 'with the tower-arch separating the instrument in two, and thus destroying its balance of tone by shutting out the pedal organ into the nave of the church and thus depriving the instrument of bass'.[73] A photograph of the long quire c.1870 shows the organ effectively separating the choir and nave. (Plate 22) The former Byfield organ was sold to St Nicholas's church in Cork and following the closure of St Nicholas's in 1998 the case, reduced in size and all that remains of the original instrument, was donated to Christ Church.

Langrish Doyle, organist since 1780, recommended in 1805 that his nephew William Warren (a former choirboy) should be appointed his assistant and in 1814 Warren succeeded Doyle although since 1812 both had received the full salary of £60.[74] The organist's salary was increased in 1814 to £80, at which level it remained (allowing for a change in 1825 when the Irish and English currencies were combined) until it rose to £100 in 1845 and £125 in 1865.[75] Francis Robinson became assistant organist in 1814, officially resigning when he was elected a stipendiary in 1829 although contin-

Coupling actions: great manuals to pedals, swell manuals to pedals, swell to great. Unison, swell to great. Octave above, swell to great. Octave below, swell to choir manuals

Movements: Pneumatic action in great manuals acting in couples, 4 composition pedals in the great organ, 3 composition pedals in swell organ.   70 C6/1/7/13, pp 59–61. 71 Ibid., pp 68ff, 302, 307, 309f.; C6/1/15/4, 1857 to 1860; the 'clarionet' stop was first proposed in 1866 (C6/1/7/13, p. 237).   72 C6/1/7/13, p. 328; see also p. 380.   73 Seymour, *Christ Church*, pp 86f.   74 C6/1/7/8, p. 347; C6/1/7/9, p. 187; C6/1/15/3, 1812–13.   75 C6/1/15/3, 1814–15; C6/1/7/9, p. 273; C6/1/7/12, p. 225; C6/1/15/4, 1865–6.

uing to act as deputy for which he was paid until September 1833.[76] With some difficulty the dean persuaded a reluctant Dr Warren to retire in 1833 on full salary because of his age.[77] Francis Robinson's brother John, a stipendiary as well as organist at St Patrick's from 1830, now acted as organist but on his stipendiary's fee without additional pay. Following Warren's death in 1841 Robinson acted as organist on Sundays and sang on weekdays, with Matthias Crowley as assistant organist playing on weekday mornings. A suitable chorister was allowed to play on weekday afternoons and occasionally on Sundays.[78] Robert Prescott Stewart, who succeeded as assistant organist in April 1843, became cathedral organist the following year on the death of John Robinson, a position he was to hold for fifty years.[79] Stewart was also organist at Trinity College chapel during the same fifty-year period and at St Patrick's between 1852 and 1861, conductor of the University Choral Society from 1846 and later of the Dublin Philharmonic Society, professor of music at Trinity College, Dublin from 1862 and a professor of theory at the Royal Irish Academy of Music from 1872. However, with weekday services played by the deputy organist or by choirboys, the training of the choirboys in the hands of Richard Beatty, and choir rehearsals 'more often than not confined to a haphazard ten minutes at the piano while the surplices were being put on',[80] the Sunday services were his only regular duty in the cathedral. Stewart was highly regarded in his day as a musician, organist, and composer. His anthems and services are representative of an age when artistry was at times outweighed by religiosity and academicism.[81]

Christ Church was unusual in the earlier nineteenth century in that the members of the church processed at every service into the choir with the organ playing, a practice more usually reserved elsewhere for greater festivals and days of ceremony.[82] The canticles were always sung to services on Sundays, Wednesdays and Fridays, being chanted on other days with a full anthem sung. The playing of a voluntary after the morning psalms on Sundays (except when communion was held) had gone out of use by the 1840s, but a voluntary was played while the preacher ascended the pulpit for the sermon, after which the anthem was sung.[83] While criticising the singing of a lengthy verse anthem at this point, Jebb was thankful that the former practice of the verse singers of the anthem going up to sing from the organ loft had gone out of use because it interrupted the service and only left the

76 C6/1/7/10, p. 299; C6/15/3, 1833–4.   77 C6/1/7/11, pp 263, 277, 285; C6/1/15/3, 1841–2.   78 C6/1/7/12, pp 118f.   79 Ibid., pp 52, 186.   80 Stanford, *Pages*, p. 42.   81 For differing views of his achievements as a composer, Bumpus, 'Composers', pp 140f, and Grindle, *Cathedral music*, pp 199f. Stewart's 'Thou, O God' is recorded on *Sing (CD)*. 82 Jebb, *Choral service*, pp 229, 232.   83 Ibid., pp 487, 494; John Jebb, *A few observations respecting Christ Church cathedral and its precinct* (Dublin, 1855), p. 14.

weaker choir members to sing the responses.[84] The prayers and latter part of the litany were chanted by the dean's vicar with harmonised responses peculiar to Dublin being sung up until 1826 or 1827 when the unison responses of Winchester were adopted, although the harmonised responses continued in use at St Patrick's. By the 1840s Tallis's or the Winchester responses (often harmonised) were most frequently sung on Sundays, without the organ, having replaced Stevenson's setting.[85]

A volume of anthem texts published in 1821 provides a view of the available repertoire at the time.[86] Most of the 261 anthems are verse, while the composers are overwhelmingly of the eighteenth century with Greene (twenty-five anthems), Boyce (twenty-four) and Croft (twenty-one) remaining the most popular. John Stevenson is next with twenty anthems, while the other local composers are Robert Shenton and Richard Woodward (nine and five anthems respectively), with John Spray, John Smith and Samuel Murphy represented by one each. Apart from Purcell (seven anthems) and Blow (five), earlier composers are barely represented. The earliest regular music lists from 1846 and 1849–50 suggest the beginnings of an interest in earlier composers: apart from Tallis's responses, services by Gibbons and Tallis and anthems by Batten, Gibbons and Farrant (and to a lesser extent Tye, Byrd and others) were sung on a number of occasions. The most frequently heard composers of anthems were almost all of the eighteenth century, headed in 1849–50 by Blow (the one seventeenth-century exception) followed by Roseingrave, Hayes, Ebdon, Greene and Croft, in that order.[87] The noting down of the anthems and other music initiated in April 1846 marks a response to the proposal first made in 1839 by John Peace and repeated four years later by John Jebb that the practice in cathedrals of publishing such lists beforehand would avoid the 'indecency of the boys roving about with messages' during the services,[88] a practice which at Christ Church (not specifically by the boys) had already called for comment by the dean and chapter in 1789.[89] Apart from John Stevenson whose music straddles the late eighteenth and early nineteenth centuries, nineteenth-century Christ

---

84 Jebb, *Choral service*, pp 373f.   85 Ibid., pp 261, 355, 446; 'Christ Church cathedral: course of services and anthems … 26 April 1846 [to] 24 Oct. 1846', and successive volumes (cathedral archives).   86 Revd Morgan Jellett, *A collection of anthems sung in his majesty's chapels royal, and in the cathedral churches of England and Ireland …* (Dublin, 1821); the spine bears the title *Anthems as used at Christ Church and St Patrick's cathedrals, Dublin*. I am grateful to Stuart Kinsella for making available his copy which bears the inscription 'John S. Bumpus. From Sir Robert Stewart at Christ Church cathedral, Dublin. Sunday August 16 1891'.   87 'Christ Church cathedral: course of services and anthems … 7 Jan. 1849 [to] 6 Jan. 1850' (cathedral archives).   88 John Peace, *Apology for cathedral service* (London, 1839), p. 60, cited after Rainbow, *Choral revival*, pp 250–1; John Jebb, *Choral service*, p.375.   89 Boydell, *Music*, p. 126.

Church composers represented in the cathedral's score-books are William Warren (one service), John Smith (one service), and John Crosthwaite (two anthems, one based on Haydn), with some service settings by Stewart bound into an eighteenth-century volume at a later stage.[90] There is also an anthem by Richard Gaudry (1800–24), organist at St Ann's church, Dublin, while David Weyman's *Melodia sacra* (first published Dublin, 1812) containing arrangements of the psalms for between one and four voices was widely used throughout Ireland before the first Irish church hymnal appeared in 1864.[91]

The cathedral bells continued to be rung by the one band of ringers for the two cathedrals until the 1870s when a disagreement with the St Patrick's authorities led to the complete withdrawal of the Society of Ringers from St Patrick's and its adherence to Christ Church alone.[92] The re-casting of two bells by Murphy of Dublin in 1844 and 1845 was the subject of praise from Dean Lindsay who wrote: 'The dean and chapter ... were not aware when they employed you, at different times, to recast two of their church bells, and to adapt them to the tones of eight in the diatonic scale that such an attempt had ever before been made in Ireland. I am happy to say that in both cases you have thoroughly succeeded'.[93] It has been the experience at Christ Church that hybridisation of the peal as it was modified and expanded (so that three makers are now represented) is a musical success, and that the sweeping away of the old, which was sometimes urged by founders,[94] would have been both a pity and a waste. Murphy's re-casting work in the 1840s was not the end of his contribution to Christ Church's bells: in 1878 he would be commissioned to add further bells for an enlarged peal installed as part of the restoration of the cathedral.

While records relating to the bell-ringers are slight before the twentieth century, an account in the belfry records of an expedition to Liverpool to inspect bells made by Murphy for a Roman Catholic church displays sentiments of national and local pride and even, so early, of ecumenical friendliness:

> Sometime around the year 1867 or 1868, Thomas Murphy ... received an order to cast a set of bells for St Saviour's R[oman] C[atholic] church, Salisbury Street, Liverpool. The bells were duly cast and delivered, Murphy employing an English bell hanger, one Thistlewood by name, to hang them. He, being displeased at not having the found-

90 C6/1/24/1/12. Grindle comments that Smith's music 'rarely rises above mediocrity', *Cathedral music*, p. 196.   91 Grindle, *Cathedral music*, p. 66.   92 Murphy & Taylor, *Bells*, pp 24–5.   93 Letter from Dean Charles Lindsay to Murphy of James's Street, bell-founder, 20 Dec. 1845, in Murphy & Taylor, *Bells*, p. 25.   94 Murphy & Taylor, *Bells*, p. 28.

ing as well, determined the opening peal should be a failure, [in] which he undoubtedly succeeded, casting the blame on the Irishman's work. Murphy, to ensure a fair trial, and subsequent payment of his account, induced the [Dublin] Company of Cathedral Ringers to cross to Liverpool and see what they could make of the bells; the Ringers' Company deputed Messrs. E. Curtis and R. Curtis, Robert Yeates and Chas. McGlinn to go and do their best ... they proceeded to the tower to find it in the possession of a local band of ringers (who had evidently been squared by Thistlewood) and doing their best or worst to show that the bells could not be rung (two great hulking fellows tugging for all they were worth at the little 16 cwt tenor). Strange to relate the Dublin men found great difficulty in ringing the bells themselves and, paying a visit to the bell chamber, lo!, the cat was out of the bag. The spaces between the gudgeons and brasses was [sic] found to be packed not with grease but with cotton waste. The waste was soon removed and the bells were merrily ringing, their full and sweet tone being wafted over the surrounding neighbourhood, in a succession of rhythmic sounds, due to the able conductor of the Dublin Company. Was ever such a narrow-minded piece of villainy recorded before![95]

The mid-nineteenth century had witnessed significant challenges to both the cathedral and its music, the very existence of the cathedral and its choir even being brought into question in 1868. Following the reopening of the reconstructed cathedral in 1878 the aftermath of disestablishment would present even greater challenges for the choir which would have profound effects as the twentieth century progressed.

---

95 The Murphy bells for St Francis Xavier church, Everton, Liverpool, were installed in 1870 and replaced in 1920 by Taylor of Loughborough, *The Ringing World*, no. 4577, 15 Jan. 1999.

XVII

George Edmund Street and the restoration of the cathedral, 1868–78

Roger Stalley

The re-opening of the cathedral in 1878, which brought to an end seven years of building and reconstruction, was a joyous and momentous occasion. Over fifteen hundred people, including four hundred clergy and scores of other dignitaries, were packed into the church for the special service held on the morning of 1 May. The sermon was preached by the archbishop, Richard Chevenix Trench, who proudly described what had been achieved: 'In place of a ruin, or what was verging to a ruin, we have this place of perfect workmanship which you see, so costly and so complete, and in every detail displaying a master's hand'.[1] Listening to his words were two individuals of special relevance: one was Henry Roe, the whiskey distiller whose wealth and generosity had made the restoration possible; the other was George Edmund Street, the celebrated English architect, who had master-minded the whole scheme. (Plates 29, 31) The church unveiled to the admiring crowds was scarcely recognisable as that which had existed up to 1871. In place of a dirty, straggling and precarious building, here was a pristine monument, the walls smooth and clean, the interior enhanced by splendid 'Gothic' furnishings; stained glass filled every window, and the tiled floors and marble columns glistened in the light provided by the new system of gas illumination. (Plates 2, 28) The old 'long choir', virtually half the cathedral, had vanished completely, to be replaced by a new east end, the design of which followed the layout of the original building of c.1200. The nave had been reconstructed on the model of the surviving thirteenth-century north wall and the whole building was now covered with stone vaults. The spirit of triumph that surrounded the opening ceremonies was marred only by a few discordant notes coming from a group of anti-ritualists, led by one of the canons of the cathedral, for whom Street's restoration was far too 'Romish' in character. But nothing could detract from the sense of achievement felt

---

1 Street & Seymour, p. 169.

by those involved, a feeling reflected in the pages of the huge volume, bound sumptuously in calf skin, that was published four years later to celebrate the event.[2]

The euphoria of the late nineteenth century did not, however, last all that long. By the middle years of the twentieth century Christ Church, like so much Victorian architecture, had fallen from grace, ignored or despised by the critics. The cathedral came to be regarded as little more than a Victorian construction, with George Edmund Street viewed as the destroyer rather than the saviour of the medieval fabric. Street would have been puzzled, and no doubt deeply offended, by such opinions, for he regarded himself as a cautious restorer, and was convinced that the quality of his work at Christ Church was unequalled in Europe.[3] What many recent observers tend to overlook is the condition of the building as it existed when Street arrived on the scene.

In 1868 Christ Church was not a particularly attractive piece of architecture, despite the efforts of local artists to romanticise its appearance. It was visually incoherent, a jumble of different architectural styles; it was structurally unsound, with the external stonework in a state of decay and the building propped up by miscellaneous buttresses and reinforcements; (Plates 23a, 24a) and it was ill-suited to the conduct of the contemporary liturgy: all services were held in the quire, which was isolated from the rest of the building. An article in the *Ecclesiologist* of 1852 described the cathedral in uncomplimentary terms as 'a worn and dingy building, grimed with smoke and dirt, and disfigured by modern mutilations and barbarous repairs'.[4] The mention of 'modern mutilations' was a pointed reference to an earlier restoration which had taken place between 1830 and 1833. Although poorly documented, this restoration was more extensive than is generally realised and it has a major bearing on what Street decided to do. It was occasioned by a frightening episode which took place on Sunday 9 November 1828, when 'strange noises' were heard during divine service, coming apparently from the fabric. According to the chapter minutes, 'extraordinary alarm' was shown by the congregation, and it threw the canons into a panic as well.[5] The crisis was the culmination of years of anxiety. Throughout the eighteenth century there had been worries about the structural condition of the cathedral and by 1829 the wall of the north transept was said to be overhanging the street outside by over two feet.[6] Dire warnings were given in 1821 by Edward Parke, the cathedral architect, who informed the chapter that their church was 'in a state of so much decay that although it will be safe for the present resort

---

2 See p. 372. The volume in question is Street & Seymour. 3 Street & Seymour, p. 156. 4 *Ecclesiologist*, xiii (1852), p. 169. 5 C6/1/7/11, pp 161–2. 6 C6/1/7/8, p. 7; C6/1/7/11, p. 140.

after no long time it must be rebuilt or fall into utter ruin'.[7] Other experts gave a similar diagnosis. The following year the chapter appointed a new architect, Matthew Price, assigning him the task of repairing and restoring the building. Price is an obscure figure in the annals of Dublin architecture;[8] he was evidently a relatively young man and it is far from clear how he qualified for the job.

Although the restoration of 1830-3 was prompted by fears of a collapse, most of Price's work was cosmetic rather than structural.[9] The exterior of the transepts was remodelled and the Romanesque doorway was transferred from the north to the south facade. (Plates 8, 24b) The demolition of houses in Skinners' Row and the removal of the last vestiges of the law courts had opened up the south side of the cathedral to public view, so Price was keen to enhance this part of the building. He added turrets at the corners of the transept, re-arranged the windows, and rebuilt the main gable. In the quire his intervention was even more drastic. He rebuilt the whole of the south aisle, added an extra doorway, elongated the pinnacles and remodelled all the parapets. (Plate 24) He also replaced the tracery in the windows. The details were all executed in the Perpendicular style, that final phase of English medieval architecture that appealed to architects in the early stages of the Gothic revival. In the context of Christ Church, however, the choice was anachronistic: Perpendicular had a negligible impact on Ireland and there are no ancient churches in the style anywhere in the country. The Perpendicular flavour of Price's work was especially obvious inside the quire, where he designed elaborate wooden panelling behind the choir stalls. (Plate 22) This was in fact a deceit, for the 'wooden' panelling was nothing more than plaster painted to look like oak. A similar technique was used on one of the arches, which in old photographs appears to be authentically Romanesque, but was in fact remodelled in plaster during the Price restoration. A new panelled ceiling was also inserted at this time. There is no reason to question Street's statement that, apart from a late Gothic piscina and the arches of the original late twelfth-century quire, no medieval features remained.

As knowledge of Gothic architecture increased, Price's work came in for criticism from ecclesiologically-minded observers. It was damned by the

---

7 C6/1/7/10, p. 145; Roger Stalley, 'Confronting the past: George Edmund Street at Christ Church cathedral, Dublin' in Frank Salmon (ed.), *Gothic and the Gothic revival, papers from the 26th annual symposium of the Society of Architectural Historians of Great Britain 1997* (London, 1999), pp 75–86. 8 C6/1/7/11, pp 217, 227. 9 The alterations are summarised in Street & Seymour, p. 71; Butler, *Measured drawings*, p. 8; Thomas Drew, letter to the *Irish Builder*, xxiii, no. 513 (1 May 1881), pp 140–1. For the pre-1830 state see *Dublin Penny Journal*, 3 October 1835; *Irish Builder*, xiii, no. 270 (15 March 1871), p. 71.

Ecclesiologist in 1852, as mentioned above, and it became the target of scathing criticism by Street himself: the work was 'mean and contemptible', the pews were 'of the worst sort'; every single detail of the quire was 'utterly wretched' and, he concluded, the most conservative of antiquaries could not object to its removal.[10] It is easy to understand why Street was hostile. In the high Victorian period 'Middle Pointed' or 'Early Pointed' rather than Perpendicular were the favoured styles, and the use of so much plaster must have seemed deeply dishonest. Street of course was scarcely an impartial witness and much of what he said was written in a spirit of self-justification. But he had plenty of supporters. Joining the chorus of disapproval, Thomas Drew solemnly declared that 'there was probably never so wholly despicable restoration perpetrated in the whole history of the Gothic revival'.[11] With such words, the reputation of Matthew Price was consigned to oblivion. In Price's defence, it should be remembered that, working on a limited budget, he was merely trying to bring Christ Church into line with the fashions of the time. Nor did he completely ignore the structural problems of the building: drawings made before 1830 show the south-east corner of the quire supported by timber props (Plate 23a) and the fragile condition of the fabric in this area explains why he decided to reconstruct the aisle.

In the years that followed the restoration of 1830–3, the chapter concerned itself only with routine repairs. Not until January 1868 were there signs that anything more ambitious was envisaged. Then, without any apparent warning, it was resolved on 8 January to ask George Edmund Street for a report on 'the present state' of the cathedral and the 'probable sum required to restore it'.[12] Street agreed to furnish a report either for £25 or for £50, the latter sum to be charged if no work was subsequently done, 'this on the understanding that if anything is done I am to be the Sole Architect'.[13] A major row ensued at the chapter meeting on 14 February 1868 when Street's conditions were discussed. Although it was agreed to commission the report, Dean West himself was strongly opposed, describing the proposal as 'an act of fruitless expenditure', which was 'manifestly improvident and wasteful' since there were 'no funds to carry out any work'.[14] One other canon supported the dean. Among those in favour of the resolution were William Lee, the archdeacon of Dublin, and Edward Seymour, who conducted the negotiations with Street.

Street submitted his report in less than seven weeks. The text was accompanied by plans and elevations of the proposed work. He outlined the history of the building, stressing its beauty and its archaeological interest. Keen

10 Street & Seymour, pp 69–70. 11 Drew, 'Christchurch'. 12 C6/1/7/13, p. 257. 13 Ibid., p. 258. 14 Ibid., p. 260. For West's alleged indifference to Christ Church, see p. 318 above.

to flatter his potential clients, he explained that 'ever since I have known Dublin, I have always regarded it as the greatest architectural treasure of the city'.[15] He described how he had explored the crypt and had established the plan of the original late Romanesque quire. Although he advocated the reconstruction of the quire, he admitted that, as it was not in urgent need of repair, it would be unwise to spend anything upon it.[16] Instead he recommended the restoration of the nave, which he estimated would cost £15,835. As this sum far exceeded the resources of the cathedral, the dean must have felt that his scepticism was justified. In fact the chapter forced Street to wait a year before paying for the report, and even indulged in a rather squalid argument over whether or not the fee of £50 included £9.50 for travelling expenses.[17]

The decision to contact Street was an enterprising move, and one that must have irritated the architectural profession in Ireland. While some of the leading Irish architects, J.J. McCarthy or G.C. Ashlin, for example, were too closely associated with Catholic clients, there was at least one obvious local candidate. This was T.N. Deane, who was responsible for the restoration of St Canice's, Kilkenny, and for the design of the new cathedral at Tuam. Having worked for Trinity College as well, Deane had all the credentials for an appointment at Christ Church. Instead, the chapter went directly to the forty-three year old Street, who had already built up a formidable reputation in England as an authority on Gothic architecture. A few months later he was to be awarded the commission for the design of the Law Courts in the Strand, and he had already designed (or restored) dozens of parish churches.[18] It is not clear who came up with the idea of contacting Street, though it is possible that the archbishop had something to do with it. Before returning to Ireland Richard Chevenix Trench had been dean of Westminster, where he was well acquainted with architectural developments in the English Church.[19] He was sympathetic to the aims of the Tractarian movement, having been for many years a close friend of Samuel Wilberforce, bishop of

15 Street, *Report, 1868*, p. 8.   16 Ibid., p. 15.   17 C6/1/7/13, p. 275.   18 For a summary of Street's career, see Joseph Kinnard, 'G.E. Street, the Law Courts and the Seventies' in Peter Ferriday (ed.), *Victorian architecture* (London, 1963), pp 221–34; Paul Joyce and John Hutchinson, *The architecture of George Edmund Street, R.A.* (Hull, 1981); David Brownlee, *The Law Courts: the architecture of George Edmund Street* (New York, Cambridge, Mass., and London, 1984); David Brownlee, 'Street, George Edmund' in *Macmillan Encyclopedia of Architects*, ed. A.K. Placzek (New York and London, [1982]); *R.I.B.A. Dictionary of British Architects 1834–1900* (London, 1993), pp 884–5 (with extensive bibliography); Peter Howell, 'Street, G(eorge) E(dmund)' in *The Macmillan Dictionary of Art* (London, 1997).   19 He must, for example, have been familiar with the church of St James the Less (1859) that Street designed near the abbey in Thorndike street, Stefan Muthesius, *The High Victorian movement in architecture 1850–1870* (London and Boston, 1972), pp 104–5.

Oxford. This was a crucial connection, for it was Wilberforce who was responsible for appointing Street as architect of the Oxford diocese in 1850. Street was firmly aligned to the high church party in England, and this, together with his reputation as an architect, must have made him the ideal candidate in the eyes of the archbishop. It is possible, perhaps even likely, that Street lobbied for the appointment. He had already visited Ireland on a number of occasions, having carried out commissions for Lord Bessborough,[20] and in 1866 he gave a public lecture in Dublin on the subject of thirteenth-century architecture. He chose this latter occasion to dwell on the 'exquisite' beauties of the nave of Christ Church, pointing out that 'St Patrick's never had any work quite so good as this', a comment which must have delighted Edward Seymour and his fellow canons.[21] No doubt plenty of chat ensued afterwards about the desirability of restoring the nave to its original thirteenth-century splendour. Street carefully prepared the ground for his subsequent appointment.

Whatever Street thought about the relative merits of the two Dublin cathedrals, the decay and dilapidation of Christ Church had become all the more noticeable after the restoration of St Patrick's in 1865. In April of that year the *Dublin Builder* carried an editorial urging the restoration of Christ Church, an operation which must have seemed essential to all who cared about the future of the cathedral.[22] Just as the initial building of St Patrick's in the thirteenth century had stirred Christ Church into action, so history was to repeat itself six hundred years later. The restoration of St Patrick's, however, was a highly controversial matter, thanks to the eccentricities of Sir Benjamin Lee Guinness, who insisted that no architect be involved. The work had been placed in the hands of a building company, Murphy and Son of Amiens Street, and their work incited the wrath of the architectural profession. They were denounced as vandals by J.J. McCarthy, and in England

20 A.E. Street, *Memoir of George Edmund Street R.A., 1824–1881* (London, 1888), p. 184. Street was sufficiently interested in Ireland in 1866 to attend a lecture at the Royal Institute of British Architects by T.N. Deane on the architecture of St Canice's, Kilkenny; his contribution at the end of the lecture made it clear that he had visited Kilkenny on more than one occasion, *Dublin Builder*, 1 April 1866, pp 81–3. Street designed the new parish church at Piltown (Kilkenny) for the earl of Bessborough, a building finished in 1863 and the church of St John the Evangelist at Ardamine (Wexford), consecrated in 1862, Jeremy Williams, *A companion guide to architecture in Ireland 1837–1921* (Dublin, 1994), pp 249–50, 374–5. I was informed of Street's work at Ardamine and Piltown by Paul Joyce, whom I would like to thank for generous advice in compiling this chapter. 21 G.E. Street, 'Architecture in the thirteenth century' in *The afternoon lectures on literature and art delivered in the theatre of the museum of industry, St Stephen's Green, Dublin in April and May, 1866* (London and Dublin, 1867), pp 3–45, especially pp 20–2, 31–2, 37–8. 22 *Dublin Builder*, vii, no. 128 (15 April 1865), pp 99–100.

the *Ecclesiologist* condemned 'the wilful blundering', sarcastically informing its readers that the builder had 'scarcely ever even seen, much less repaired, a mediaeval building'.[23] These disputes made it imperative for Christ Church to appoint a highly qualified architect with impeccable credentials. In the thirteenth century Christ Church had gone one better than St Patrick's in terms of design, and here was the chance to do the same again.

The late 1860s, however, was not an auspicious time for building, as the dean fully realised. There was much talk of disestablishment, and the royal commission of 1868 had even suggested that Christ Church be reduced to the rank of a parish church.[24] When William Butler was measuring the west door in 1870, he was taunted by 'a pack of ragged urchins' who predicted that Christ Church would soon become a Catholic chapel. This, he explained, was followed by a shower of stones and mud, which compelled him to take refuge inside the cathedral.[25] Christ Church was also threatened with a loss of its endowments, without which even routine repairs would be difficult. If there was to be just one cathedral in Dublin, there is no doubt that St Patrick's would be the preferred choice. Sir Benjamin Lee Guinness's bene-faction, together with the prospect of disestablishment and disendowment, had placed Christ Church in a vulnerable situation.

Having received Street's report in April 1868, the chapter dithered for two years, before the subject of restoration came back on the agenda. During this interval the passing of the Irish Church Act meant that from 1 January 1871 Christ Church would lose an annual income of £1,918 which it had hitherto received from its estates. Finding a sum of £15,835 to restore the nave was hopelessly unrealistic, so a much reduced scheme, designed to pre-vent the collapse of the north wall, was proposed by Street at an estimated cost of between £2,800 and £3,000. To raise the money the chapter decided in April 1870 to approach the Commissioners of Church Temporalities, enclosing a letter from Street describing his modified proposals.[26] A curt reply was received, the commissioners pointing out that the chapter still had an income of £1,918 for the current year, plus a balance in government stock of over £4,000. With some reluctance, therefore, the chapter agreed to use its own resources to repair the nave.[27] By the end of the year the prospect of financial help from the commissioners seems to have improved, and this encouraged the chapter to go ahead with the complete restoration of the nave as outlined in Street's original report of 1868. On 23 December a contract was agreed with a builder named John Butler to complete the works accord-ing to the specifications of Street in two years at a cost of £16,000.[28] All was

---

23 *Ecclesiologist*, xxvi (1865), pp 87–108.   24 See p. 321 above.   25 Butler, *Measured drawings*, p. 8.   26 C6/1/7/13, pp 284–5.   27 Ibid., pp 286–8.   28 Ibid., pp 302–6.

not well with the commissioners, however, and just seven days after signing the contract, Butler was ordered to stop work.[29]

Almost three years had now elapsed since the chapter first turned to Street for advice and the work of restoration was yet to begin. Despite the financial difficulties, lay friends of the cathedral harboured ambitions for a more comprehensive restoration on a par with that of St Patrick's. Early in 1871 the duke of Leinster invited Street to extend his proposals to include the quire, and to prepare plans for a synod hall beside the cathedral. It was at this point that Henry Roe of Mount Anville Park in Dundrum entered the scene. (Plate 29) On 31 March 1871 the archbishop received a remarkable letter, in which Henry Roe offered to pay for the complete restoration of the cathedral. He emphasised that the 'architectural beauties of the cathedral' were to be 'scrupulously preserved', and that the restoration should be placed under the control of George Edmund Street 'in whom the public will repose the fullest confidence'. He also specified the contractors, the 'experienced' building firm of Messrs Gilbert Cockburn and Son.[30] One week later Roe extended his offer to include the building of a synod hall.[31] After all the frustration of previous years, this act of generosity must have seemed almost unbelievable. It is unlikely that Roe had any inkling about the eventual cost: by 1878 he had expended £160,000 on the cathedral, with a further £60,000 on the synod hall.[32]

Street's second report was ready by 8 April 1871 and events then began to move rapidly. In the report Street outlined his intention of reconstructing the quire on the lines of the late Romanesque building and he explained how the synod hall could be built on the site of the medieval cloister. (Plate 32) The report was accompanied by a detailed plan, as well as a drawing of the cathedral from the south-east, showing the relationship with the proposed synod hall.[33] During the first year building work was restricted to the nave to allow services to continue in the quire, but on 10 June 1872 the architect requested permission 'to close the Choir of the cathedral in order that we may proceed to take it down'; services were suspended indefinitely.[34]

The reconstruction of the cathedral was a massive task, which involved some extraordinary pieces of engineering. The north wall of the nave, the one authentic section of medieval work in this part of the cathedral, leaned outwards to an alarming degree and the piers which supported it were badly ruptured. The obvious solution was to dismantle and rebuild, but, encour-

---

29 Ibid., p. 310.   30 The letter is printed in Street & Seymour, p. 54.   31 Street & Seymour, p. 55.   32 *Irish Builder*, xxxv, no. 793 (1 January 1893), pp 2–3; Drew, 'Christchurch'.   33 Street, Report, 1871.   34 C6/1/7/13, p. 328. There are various progress reports in the *Irish Builder*, xiii, no. 286 (15 Nov 1871), p. 299; xiv, no. 294 (15 April 1872), p. 119; xv, no. 320 (15 April 1873), p. 106. See also p. 321 above.

aged by Henry Roe, Street adopted a more risky strategy. The arches were supported on wooden baulks while the crumbling medieval piers were cut away and replaced with fresh stone.[35] The forest of timber used as a support is illustrated in a fine photograph by Millard and Robinson. (Plate 30a) This solution meant that the capitals and arcades, as well as the triforium, were largely untouched by the restorers. It also meant that the north wall retained its outward lean, a mixed blessing since the ancient wall, even with the piers renewed, was too fragile to permit the restoration of a stone vault. Street initially proposed a wooden vault as a means of reducing the stress,[36] but, with further support from Henry Roe, he began to devise ways of building the vaults in stone. The triforium passages were blocked, liquid cement was poured into every cavity, flying buttresses were constructed on the exterior, and hidden buttresses were erected under the aisle roof. While this involved compromises, it enabled Street to recreate a more convincing version of the thirteenth-century design. No such problems were encountered on the south side, the whole of which was built afresh from the level of the crypt upwards.

The reconstruction of the crossing was an equally risky undertaking. The existing piers dated from the sixteenth or early seventeenth century and in Street's view they were 'a complete eyesore', being 'rude and unsightly, plain, roughly dressed, and whitewashed'.[37] Moreover the arches they supported were ten feet lower than the projected vault of the nave, a situation which, if maintained, would ruin the spatial harmony of the building. (Plate 3) Street therefore set himself the task of remodelling the crossing without dismantling the tower above. The limestone piers were left in place but were dressed in situ with new mouldings by the nineteenth-century masons. Clusters of polished marble shafts, 104 of them altogether, were then placed in front.[38] (Plate 2) Brick arches were carefully inserted into the walls of the tower above the existing crossing arches, after which the masonry below was chopped away. New inner arches of cut stone were then erected under the brickwork. Street had used a similar method at Bristol cathedral, which, he felt, was less dangerous than shoring the tower with timber.[39] The whole operation was carried out to save the seventeenth-century tower.

The restoration of the transepts and quire was comparatively straightforward. Much of the north transept was dismantled, though the seventeenth-century roof timbers were somehow retained. The work in the south transept was less severe, but even here the clerestory walls and the whole of the south facade was reconstructed. Apart from the two late Romanesque arches beside the crossing, the quire and ambulatory were rebuilt in their entirety. The seven year programme of works appears to have gone relatively smoothly

35 Street & Seymour, pp 73, 118–9.   36 Street, *Report, 1868*, p. 18.   37 Street & Seymour, p. 128.   38 McVittie, *Restoration*, p. 80.   39 Street & Seymour, pp 128–9.

according to Robert McVittie, who gave a description of the operations, albeit one that was more romantic than plausible: 'one fact struck the attentive observer very forcibly', he wrote, 'namely the great decorum of the workmen; the total suppression of all noise, except what was perfectly unavoidable, suggesting more the idea that the men were at worship rather than at work; no uncouth roughness, no laughing, whistling or singing; but they pursued their allotted tasks as if under some potent spell'.[40] In return divine providence seems to have protected the labour force. As McVittie explains, 'during the entire work no accident to life or limb occurred worthy of note. One man only fell from a high scaffolding, and was taken up insensible. He was removed to Mercer's Hospital, and after a short time was able to resume his work in perfect health, no bone having been broken'.[41] The workmen were not quite as pious as McVittie imagined, for we know that progress was delayed on at least two occasions by strikes.

The reconstruction of Christ Church occupies a key position in the history of Victorian architecture. As well as being a successful practitioner, George Edmund Street was an influential writer and theorist, and his work in Dublin provides a clear statement of his approach to restoration, the most controversial architectural topic of the age. Early in his career, Street had been deeply impressed by the writings of John Ruskin, notably *The seven lamps of architecture* and *The stones of Venice*, works which encouraged him to travel in Italy and France. Like Ruskin he asserted that the 'marks of age' were an inherent part of the beauty and value of ancient buildings, and in 1857 he wrote a letter to the *Ecclesiologist* denouncing the destructive restorations that were taking place abroad, where 'building after building is sentenced to be recased because some of the stones are decayed'.[42] He was horrified at the proposed restoration of the sculptured porches at Chartres, insisting that it was better 'to let them go for the rest of time, as now, propped here and there with a heavy timber shore, than to let irreverent hands scrape off every weather stain, repair every damaged feature, and leave the whole as clean and new-looking as when it was first finished'.[43] Late in his career, Street still paid lip-service to this view, writing in the context of Christ Church that 'the marks of age on every stone ought to be held sacred', a comment worthy of Ruskin or William Morris.[44] In practice, however, he was more pragmatic, steering a careful path between the extreme views of the time. While he criticised the *needless* removal of old work (my italics), he asserted that restoration should not necessarily involve the preservation of every ancient stone.[45] Rather it was the task of the restorer to recover and

40 McVittie, *Restoration*, p. 6.   41 Ibid., p. 5.   42 *Ecclesiologist*, xviii (1857), pp 342–5. 43 Ibid., p. 342.   44 Street & Seymour, p. 85.   45 When addressing the Ecclesiological Society in 1865 he insisted that every piece of ancient work was so sacred that it should

recreate the intended design of the original architect, which at times required the sacrifice of later additions or alterations. The architect was the creative force in medieval building; he established the design, the workers merely following his directions; the design was the precious thing, not the actual fabric.[46] He attempted to draw a distinction between the sculptural adornment of buildings, which represented the artistic expression of individual craftsmen, and routine mouldings in which the masons merely carried out the instructions of the architect. In the latter case modern craftsmen were perfectly capable of replacing the works of their medieval forbears. He thus concluded, 'as long as the restorer is able to confine himself to such work as that which was originally done by numerous obedient workmen from the designs and orders of one man', he was doing a pious and laudable act.[47] Street was trying to get the best of all worlds and what he wrote is not always consistent. Moreover, there was often a gap between his rhetoric and his actions. Even his son admitted that he did not always display the greatest regard for old works and handle them in the most tender way.[48] When William Morris founded the Society for the Protection of Ancient Buildings in 1877, Street became a member, although its manifesto included several demands which were at odds with what had taken place in Dublin.

There are two important factors which need to be borne in mind when considering church restoration in Britain and Ireland. The first is that the churches were required to suit the needs of the Christian liturgy, as it was defined in the mid-Victorian age. The huge number of restorations that was carried out in the middle of the nineteenth century – some 7,000 churches in England were restored, rebuilt or enlarged between 1840 and 1875 – were not motivated simply by an enthusiasm for history;[49] it was rather that a resplendent church, whether new or restored, conferred dignity and authority on the services that were conducted within; restoration was an expression of Anglican reform. The point was neatly made by Street's son in the context of the new church which his father built at Holmbury St Mary: 'what the actual building has done for the outward beauty of the place has been equalled by the moral influence which has been exerted by the services'.[50] The whole point of restoration was the desire to enhance the architectural

---

not be touched; he then immediately went on to admit there were cases when 'destructive restoration' was unavoidable, *Ecclesiologist*, xxvi (1865), pp 242–5. 46 Street & Seymour, pp 74–5, 117–18; Seán O'Reilly, 'The arts of inference, presumption and invention: George Edmund Street rebuilds Christ Church' in Salmon, *Gothic and the Gothic revival*, pp 91–2. 47 Street & Seymour, p. 78. 48 Street, *Memoir*, p. 121. 49 Chris Miele, '"Their interest and habit": professionalism and the restoration of medieval churches, 1837–77' in C. Brooks and Andrew Saint (ed.), *The Victorian church* (Manchester and New York, 1995), p. 156. 50 Street, *Memoir*, p. 258.

setting of the liturgy. There was no point in presenting an inspiring ritual if it was invisible to the congregation, a particular problem at Christ Church, where the long quire was cut off from the rest of the building. (Plates 3, 5, 9b) Street himself argued in favour of short quires in which the altar was visible and accessible from the nave, as it was before the high middle ages. The re-instatement of the late twelfth-century quire at Christ Church provided not only 'an exact restoration' of the ancient building, but also 'a convenient and common sense arrangement of the interior'.[51] Thus in Dublin two different objectives, which could have been in conflict, were happily united. The argument is not quite as honest as it sounds, however, for Street's previous work as a church architect shows that he had already developed a preference for short chancels with apsidal terminations.

This brings us to the second factor: like almost all restoration architects, Street had an instinct to create and invent new forms, some of which were passed off under the guise of 'restoration'. Thomas Drew, who knew Street personally, believed that he was not a restorer by 'instinct or predilection'.[52] It is well known that restorations frequently reflect the attitudes of their own era rather than those of the period being restored. Street's personal imprint at Christ Church is very noticeable, particularly in the quire and crossing, where the prominence of the polished shafts under the tower (as well as their stout dimensions) is Victorian rather than medieval. (Plate 2) Moreover, while the plan of the east end as a whole was based on old foundations, the elevations are largely his invention. The detail is richer and heavier than would have been the case in the late twelfth century, and the linked triforium and clerestory, an arrangement copied from the early Gothic nave, was anachronistic. (Plate 6) Nor is there any historical evidence that the spandrels were covered in diaper and floral patterns.[53] Street must have been well aware of these points, but it did not prevent him from claiming that the quire was 'an exact reproduction of the original work', nor indulging in self congratulation for the 'recovery of an old design which has apparently been hopelessly lost'.[54] What he could justifiably have argued was that the details were 'correct' for the period c.1190–1220 and where possible individual motifs were based on

---

51 Street & Seymour, p. 86.   52 Thomas Drew, 'Street as a restorer: the discoveries at Christ Church cathedral' in *Dublin University Review*, 1 June 1886, p. 519.   53 In England the spandrels of Westminster abbey were treated with floral motifs but this did not occur until the middle years of the thirteenth century. A better precedent perhaps can be found in the Romanesque chapter house at Bristol (c.1150–70), which Street would have known well. Here the upper walls are covered with interlace and chevron patterns. Outside England, Street may have remembered the lavish surface ornament which fills the spandrels of the twelfth-century nave at Bayeux cathedral, a building he had visited in June 1855 (information from Paul Joyce).   54 Street & Seymour, p. 93.

old fragments, like the string course with Greek key ornament or the curious 'ice cream cornets' applied to some hood mouldings. But to argue that the whole design was an exact restoration was disingenuous. Street had no need to be so defensive, for his new scheme was highly effective. Had he followed the elevations of the transept, as strict adherence to historical veracity might have dictated, he would have been forced to produce a heavy and rather dull design at the focal point of the church. (Plate 9a) Propriety indicated that the area around the altar required something more elaborate. He was almost excessively anxious to provide historical justifications for the new design, and his knowledge of medieval architecture was such that few were in a position to doubt his word.

The ambulatory and eastern chapels are equally attractive pieces of architecture, with the irregular plan producing 'charming effects of perspective', as Street himself noted.[55] The outer walls were furnished with arcading, the arches themselves supported on polished marble shafts. Three different types of arch were employed and those in the north aisle were filled with coats of arms, some of them exquisitely carved. Wrought iron screens, designed by Street, separated the ambulatory from the sanctuary. The central chapel was lined with arcaded niches and provided with benches so that the chapter could meet there if occasion demanded; under each bench was a tiny trefoiled arcade, copied from an ancient fragment. The low walls flanking the side chapels were ornamented with Islamic-looking tiles, an imaginative idea, the designs being based on two Spanish majolica tiles found in the cathedral during the restoration.[56]

The exterior of the quire is a picturesque composition, though one inspired by Street's own predilections rather than any ancient remains. The bold combination of buttresses, turrets, corbels and battlements is characteristic of Street's work, so too the avoidance of fussy details. (Plate 1) The yellow dressings of Caen stone contrast attractively with the roughly hewn grey limestone used in the walls. The stepped battlements were extended around the whole church, although, as a feature of later medieval architecture in Ireland, they were not consistent with a late twelfth or early thirteenth-century design. The polygonal stair turrets, which disguise the junction between the eastern chapels and the ambulatory, could also be criticised on historical grounds. Street regarded them as authentic restorations, since he had found the remains of a spiral stair linking the crypt and the south aisle; this he believed must have been extended upwards as a turret.[57] The

55 Ibid., p. 97.   56 At the time Street wrote, shortly before his death in 1881, the three eastern chapels were not in fact furnished with altars, a point which Street appears to regret (Street & Seymour, p. 97). Paul Joyce informs me that the majolica tiles were made by F. Garrard of London, a former assistant in Street's office.   57 Street, *Report, 1868,*

evidence existed only on the south side, despite his assertion to the contrary. Street's arguments would sound more convincing if we did not know that he had already designed a somewhat similar stair turret in his church of St Philip and St James at Oxford (1859), where it fills the angle of the apse and transept.[58] This was not the only time that Street's preferences were fortuitously confirmed by supposed historical evidence. Canted walls, like those which defined the apse of Christ Church, were another part of the architect's existing repertoire.[59]

Elsewhere in the cathedral Street had less scope for invention. In the transepts he inserted a stone vault, though as he admitted, there was little evidence to go on. He decided to strip the walls of plaster, leaving the rough limestone exposed. There was evidently some dispute about this, and Street seemed to allow for the possibility that he might have been wrong.[60] On the outside he set about undoing the innovations of Matthew Price. Each transept was provided with square turrets, decorated with blind arches and capped by stone spires. (Plate 8) He claimed these were designed on the authority of 'old details', without specifying what they were. An old print was said to have provided the model for the windows in the south transept, although there are no prints that could have furnished the requisite level of detail.[61]

In the nave Street scrupulously followed the evidence provided by the surviving north elevation, rebuilding the south side as an exact replica (even repeating the minor changes in the final bay). The west facade, however, is entirely Street's work, though he did have one jamb of the original west window to guide him. (Plate 25) He was very proud of the fact that, having prepared a new west portal, the masons discovered, almost miraculously it seems, one original stone with a moulding identical to that which he had prescribed.[62] The most radical innovation in the nave was the addition of a baptistry. When the north aisle was being dismantled, the workmen discovered in the fourth bay from the east a trefoil-headed doorway opening into a narrow chamber, once vaulted in three bays. This gave Street the idea of constructing a somewhat larger building to serve as his baptistery. For various reasons this had to be erected one bay further west, and it was a far larger structure than the ruins uncovered by the workmen. Although Street tried to justify his work on the basis of the discoveries, it was in fact a completely new design. The six bays of vaulting are supported on a pair of clus-

pp 7–8; Ibid., *1871*, p. 7; Street & Seymour, p. 86 (where he refers to the remains of only one stair); Butler, *Measured drawings*, p. 5.   58 Muthesius, *High Victorian movement in architecture*, p. 107.   59 Employed for example at St Philip and St James, Oxford (1859), St Saviour, Eastbourne (1865–72), St John the Divine, Kennington (1871) and in the unsuccessful design for Edinburgh cathedral (1872).   60 Street & Seymour, p. 104.   61 Ibid., p. 100.   62 Ibid., p. 117.

tered marble piers, and Street was quite entitled to claim that the space 'adds much to the interest and beauty of the nave'.[63] His historical arguments are less convincing.

The reconstruction of the nave involved the demolition of the chapter room and vestry, for which an alternative site was now needed. Street sensibly decided to rebuild the schoolhouse, which had been fashioned out of the remains of the old Lady chapel. On the ground floor he designed a vestry and chapter room, in the centre of which is a single column supporting the floor above. The ceiling beams rest on powerfully moulded corbels, the wall being lined with cupboards and wooden panelling. A stone staircase leads to an upper chamber, designed to accommodate the choir school. This magnificent room is covered by an arched and panelled ceiling, the individual panels being filled with ornamental cusps and tracery patterns. As in the vestry, there is a monumental hooded fireplace.[64] The building was later extended to the east by Thomas Drew, who designed a facade based on his own reconstruction of the medieval chapter house. Drew also prepared the splendid table which now occupies the chapter room.[65]

The greatest scope for invention came with the design of the synod hall. Street's first project, published in 1871, contained many of the ingredients of the later scheme, including the two-storey hall surrounded by passages and lobbies.[66] It was carried out in a robust First Pointed style, with simple buttresses, circular turrets and plate tracery, but had it been erected, the south side of the nave would have been completely obscured.[67] (Plate 32) The decision to build on the site of St Michael's church, on the opposite side of St Michael's Hill, left the vista open, though it brought some awkward architectural problems.[68] The new site was irregular and Street had to incorporate a seventeenth-century tower. He rose to the occasion magnificently. The entrance hall, with its two arched screens supported on thick marble columns, leads to a theatrical stone stair that follows the contours of the site. The synod hall itself is covered by a remarkable multi-arched wooden roof. The external details of the building are quite sparse, but the arrangement of

63 Ibid., pp 122–3.   64 Described in McVittie, *Restoration*, pp 127–8.   65 There is a preparatory drawing in C6/4.   66 Street, *Report, 1871*, pp 15–18. The proposed synod hall would have blocked public access both to the doorway of the south transept and to the nave, so Street proposed transferring the late Romanesque doorway to the east side of the transept on the site of St Laurence O'Toole's chapel.   67 Opposition came from the *Irish Builder*, xiii, no. 275 (1 June 1871), pp 137–9. The site of St Michael's church was one of three suggested alternatives.   68 The church of St Michael and All Angels, which was dismissed by Street as a 'hideous modern structure', was erected to the design of J. Taylor in 1815 (H.A. Wheeler and M.J. Craig, *The Dublin city churches of the Church of Ireland* (Dublin, 1948), pp 27–8. For the decision to use the St Michael's site, see pp 323–4 above.

the different forms – gables, roofs, chimneys, and dormers – reach an impressive crescendo with the ancient tower. A final touch of genius was the Gothic bridge, Street's own version of the Venetian 'Bridge of Sighs'.[69] Linking the synod hall with the cathedral, it allowed ecclesiastical dignitaries to move in stately procession from one building to the other without venturing on to the public highway. The bridge was cleverly handled: from the outside one would never guess that it contains a descending staircase rather than a level passage.

Street was justifiably proud of what he achieved at Christ Church. While he may have overstated the degree to which his work was based on historical precedent, there was no other architect alive in Britain or Ireland who had his knowledge of medieval architecture. His analysis of the Romanesque and Gothic features of Christ Church, his views on chronology, and his conclusions about the likely models in the west of England, have never been seriously doubted.[70] Without the aid of photography, he acquired an astonishing grasp of early Gothic architecture. His proposals for the restoration of the cathedral were based on a scrupulous examination of the fabric, and he was determined that new stonework should be an exact match for the old. As the restoration proceeded, a careful record was made of every ancient moulding, each of which was transcribed into a large volume by those in charge of the works. This 'moulding book' contains over two hundred pages of drawings, each carefully marked 'ancient' or 'modern'.[71] (Plate 30b) Street's concern for accuracy is also reflected in the way that old capitals were copied. A number of moulded capitals of thirteenth-century date have a narrow vertical slit sawn through the stone. The slits were cut by the nineteenth-century masons, allowing a sheet of card or stiff paper to be inserted, so that the moulding could be copied with ease. (Plate 30c)

Although Street is remembered as an architect, his work at Christ Church embraced all the furnishings and fittings. He regarded church design as an all-encompassing task, which included responsibility for the smallest details.[72]

---

69 Street's bridge was designed in a First Pointed or early Gothic style, with relatively simple arcades lining the walls, a contrast to the Perpendicular tracery used in the famous bridge at St John's College, Cambridge. The covered bridge over New College Lane at Oxford was not built until 1913–14. Paul Joyce has pointed out that the Dublin bridge was a logical descendant of the series of bridges that Street had proposed in his Law Courts competition design of 1866–7. 70 Street & Seymour, pp 108–9. 71 C6/1/27/9. This is a commercially made volume, purchased from Joseph Dollard of Dame Street, Dublin. It measures 55.5 cms by 38 cms. As well as moulding profiles, a number of drawings by Street have been inserted. The function of the book is not entirely clear. The drawings were first made in pencil, with coloured washes added on the inside. The captions are by several different hands. 72 Joyce & Hutchinson, *Architecture of George Edmund Street*, p. 6.

At Christ Church he designed the choir stalls along with the archbishop's throne, the stone pulpit with its carvings of the four evangelists, the stone screen separating the nave from the quire, and the iron work of all the doors. The latter included the brass gates in the centre of the screen, the scintillating finish of which has not been diminished by a hundred years of enthusiastic polishing. (Plate 28b) The main motif is an openwork quatrefoil, and a wonderful touch is the minute billet ornament that surrounds the lock mechanism. In virtually every case the fittings were commissioned from established English firms known to Street: the oak choir stalls from Kett of Cambridge, the baptistry gates from James Leaver of Maidenhead, the light fittings, brass altar rails and the brass gates to the chancel from Potter of London, and the altar cloth from the sisters of St Margaret at East Grinstead. Even the figural capitals around the apse were carved by an English craftsman, a young sculptor called Taylerson who worked for Earp of London.[73] Street laid down a scheme for the stained glass, which was designed and manufactured by three different English firms.[74] The tiled pavement was also made to his design. During the restoration hundreds of medieval tiles were recovered from the nave, some of which were relaid in the south-east chapel of the quire. They included many designs found at other sites in Ireland, as well as the famous roundel showing a procession of foxes disguised as pilgrims.[75] Street recorded sixty-four different patterns, which he reused in his own scheme.[76] The new tiles, 83,360 altogether,[77] were made in England by Craven Dunnill of Jackfield, Ironbridge.[78] Unfortunately the medieval pavement was too damaged to recover the overall arrangement, and the present layout belongs entirely to Street. The floor was a dazzling achievement and it is a pity that much of it is now usually obscured by seating. Following a chance meeting with Henry Roe on the Holyhead boat, Street set about designing a new set of silver plate for the cathedral, paid for along with everything else by Henry Roe.[79] Almost all these furnishings and accessories have

---

73 McVittie, *Restoration*, p. 101.   74 Clayton and Bell, Hardman's of Birmingham, and James Bell (clerestory) of London, Street & Seymour, pp 140–5; see also Lesley Whiteside, *The stained glass of Christ Church cathedral Dublin* (Dublin, 1999). The windows in the baptistry were funded by Street in memory of his wife who died on 6 March 1876 while her husband was engaged on the restoration.   75 At one point Street stated that he had found sixty-three patterns, at another sixty-four. He also added that 'there may have been a few more of which I had no knowledge', Street & Seymour, pp 125, 145–7; see also E.S. Eames and Thomas Fanning, *Irish medieval tiles* (Dublin, 1988), p. 62.   76 On the day of the reopening of the cathedral, 1 May 1878, Edward Steele, director of the museum in Kildare Street, wrote to the chapter requesting as a gift or loan any tiles and ancient capitals that might be available, C6/1/7/13, pp 386–7. A few tiles subsequently found their way to the Ulster Museum.   77 The figure comes from McVittie, *Restoration*, p. 73n.   78 Butler, *Christ Church*, p. 27, mistakenly says Trowbridge not Ironbridge.   79 C6/1/7/13, p. 370.

survived to the present time, so that Christ Church has come down to us as a remarkably coherent example of High Victorian taste. The most obvious loss is a huge iron corona or candelabra which hung in the chancel, the design of which gave Street considerable satisfaction.[80]

Although the restoration of the cathedral did not excite the same hostility as that directed at St Patrick's, several aspects of the work proved contentious. 'Anti-restorationists' objected not just to the demolition of the 'long quire', but also to that of the sixteenth-century walls of the nave.[81] There was disquiet about the removal of the plaster in the transepts, as Street himself admitted. More serious was the charge that, failing to practice what he preached, he allowed far more ancient masonry to be removed than was strictly necessary. Over two thousand pieces of carved and moulded stone were later gathered together in the crypt, many of them almost undamaged; the very sight of them made it impossible to accept Street's declaration that 'not an ancient stone which could be retained in its old place' would be removed'.[82] William Butler, who surveyed the cathedral shortly before the restoration, pointed out that stones from windows in the north transept, which were kept in the crypt, 'proved that Mr Street was wrong in adopting the outlines' for their replacements. He added, 'the fact is, that Mr Street had to depend greatly upon his clerks of works for many of his facts, and these men were by no means reliable'.[83] Street was of course based in London, making only occasional visits to Dublin. Butler was also critical of the liberties that Street took with the north aisle of the nave, concluding: 'this "restoration" consisted in altering an ancient doorway into a window, putting a new archway where there had never been one before, blotting out a window, and erecting a new baptistery'.[84] The whole aisle was in fact dismantled and rebuilt anew in 1871–8. (Plate 30a)

Street – or perhaps his clerk of the works – was unwilling to tolerate some of the anomalies in the ancient building, which were ironed out in the interests of uniformity. The nave piers now have shaft rings at the mid-way point, but before 1871 they were absent in three places.[85] (Plates 14, 27) Butler was particularly upset that the old 'fount' stone, also known as the 'wishing' stone or 'bond' stone was removed from the third pier.[86] Victorian homogeneity

80 In his personal copy of Street & Seymour, Thomas Drew notes that the candlelabrum was transfered 'with general rejoicing' to the synod hall in 1895. Its present whereabouts are unknown. Other losses include the alabaster panels in the screen and one stained glass window, that in the St Laurence O'Toole chapel, which was replaced in 1964 with a design by Patrick Pollen.   81 *Irish Builder*, xxiii, no. 513 (1 May 1881), p. 140; Street, *Memoir*, p. 187.   82 Street & Seymour, p. 73.   83 Butler, *Christ Church*, p. 31. In the early years the clerk of works was a Mr Dooling.   84 Ibid., 20–1.   85 They were lacking on the east respond, and on piers three and four.   86 The stone was four feet eight inches above the

triumphed over medieval inconsistency, though in fairness to Street, one should add that many other irregularities in the building were retained, among which was the puzzling shaft with a 'growth' just below the capital, seen at the north-east corner of the north aisle.

Thomas Drew, who became architect of the cathedral in 1882, had a number of very specific criticisms of his own.[87] He disputed the design of the clerestory windows in the nave, where Street had installed a rather curious angular hood mould. Although Street insisted this was based on what he found, Drew was not convinced. Drew also ridiculed the addition of stepped battlements: Street was anxious, he explained, to include an Irish feature and having studied old photographs and illustrated works concluded that 'Irish "stepped" battlements to his parapets were just the thing'.[88] Drew did not seem to be bothered by a more obvious inconsistency, the addition of French style flying buttresses. (Plate 8) Instead he turned to Street's lack of understanding of the cloister, a criticism which was unfair since Drew had acquired additional knowledge from his own excavations. He made scathing remarks about Street's failure to appreciate the levels of the cloister walks and to realise the importance of the doorway at the east end of the nave. The latter had been converted into an entrance to the crypt and its relationship with the monastic cloister was obscured by a lean-to porch, an 'unfortunate little excrescence' to use the words of another observer.[89]

A more serious criticism, however, was Street's mistake over the origin of the freestone used in the medieval building, an error which was to prove very costly. Despite protests from local masons, Street 'without a moment's hesitation' pronounced it to be Caen stone from Normandy.[90] Caen stone is much softer than the oolitic limestone imported from Dundry, and Street's masonry decayed rapidly in the Dublin atmosphere. By 1908 a major programme of replacement was required.[91] Street's error is curious since he must have encountered the oolitic limestone from Somerset in many of his other projects. While he was worried about the use of Caen on the exterior and limited its use as best he could, he never admitted he was wrong.[92] His insistence on the use of French stone, however, does reflect his desire to use what he believed to be the authentic medieval material.

Most of these points would not have bothered the congregation of Christ Church, which was more concerned about the fate of the monuments and

floor level and had a flat surface, suggesting that it was not a stoup. It is just visible in the photograph of the nave by Millard and Robinson. 87 Drew, 'Street as a restorer', pp 519–31. 88 Ibid., p. 526. 89 Butler, *Christ Church*, p. 24. 90 Drew, 'Street as a restorer', p. 524; Butler, *Christ Church*, p. 44. 91 Thomas Drew, *Christchurch of the Holy Trinity, Dublin: report on the decay of stonework, 1908* (Dublin, 1908). Street used 3,944 tons of Caen stone according to McVittie, *Restoration*, p. 80n. 92 Street & Seymour, pp 97–8.

tombs. The cathedral contains a series of splendid neo-classical monuments, but these of course were out of keeping with the new Gothic interior. Almost all were despatched to the gloom of the crypt, some of them broken into sections as they were too tall for the space available, a fate that befell the monument to Sir John Bowes, the lord chancellor (d.1767). Following protests a few were later rescued, including Kirk's monument to Sir John Andrew Stevenson, the musician, which is now in the north aisle.[93]

A quite different protest marred the celebrations in May 1878. A small group of ultra-protestants, led by Dr Marrable, a canon of the cathedral, objected to some of the internal arrangements. The new choir screen, it was argued, needlessly separated the officiating clergy from the laity, and it was furnished with a cross and an image of the *agnus Dei*, both deeply offensive to Protestant sensibilities. (Plate 2) A crucifix was also visible in the stained glass of the east window (of the eastern chapel), where it could be seen immediately above the altar. Dr Marrable brought his protests to the chapter, where he declared: 'I object to all the aforesaid items as savouring of Romanism'.[94] He wrote to the newspapers, warning the public that 'distinct acts of idolatry' were taking place in the cathedral, and he organised a petition.[95] The fact that the cross above the screen was modelled on the Cross of Cong, one of the country's most celebrated ancient treasures, cut no ice with Dr Marrable and his supporters. Most of the controversy centred on the screen itself, which was said to have no practical use and ruined the beauty of the church. Street answered all the criticisms at great length, explaining the history of screens in the Christian church, and countering the various arguments one by one. He argued that his design minimised the obstruction, and demanded that his work be respected like that of an artist, insisting, somewhat petulantly, that if the screen was altered 'my work will be immensely damaged'.[96] The general synod of the Church of Ireland voted in favour of the screen and the *Irish Ecclesiastical Gazette* wrote an editorial in its defence.[97] But the arguments would not go away and in 1883 the carved alabaster panels which filled the lower section were replaced by metal grilles as a concession to the critics. This, it was maintained, would reduce the barrier and improve the acoustics.[98] By this time Street had been dead for two years.

---

93 *Irish Builder*, xx, no. 451 (1 October 1878), p. 287; *Irish Builder*, xx, no. 452 (15 October 1878), p. 302; Butler, *Christ Church*, pp 21–2. The Stevenson monument was brought up in 1896. Amongst the Drew papers in R.C.B. there are proposals for relocating the tombs, C6/5/8/26. For the fate of other monuments, see pp 326–7 above.   94 C6/1/7/13, pp 372–3.   95 Ibid., pp 421, 431.   96 Street & Seymour, p. 131; Street, *Memoir*, pp 194–5.   97 *Irish Ecclesiastical Gazette*, 1 May 1878, pp 129–30.   98 Ibid., 5 May 1883, p. 372 and 5 January 1884, p. 11. Thomas Drew seized the opportunity of re-using the alabaster panels as part of a reredos he was designing for Banbridge. For the 'ritualism' contro-

Although much admired by friends and pupils, Street was not held in much affection in certain circles in Dublin. Thomas Drew was scathing in some of his comments, claiming that Street was an arrogant, dogmatic man, with an unshakeable belief in his own judgement. (Plate 31) He went on to describe him as 'by temperament an active practical workman, aggressive, opinionated and intolerant of weaker and more questioning minds than his own'.[99] Street was certainly decisive and quick thinking, but had he been as unpleasant as Drew suggests, he would hardly have built up such an extensive band of clients and loyal friends. The Dublin architectural profession was no doubt unhappy that such a prestigious commission was awarded to an English architect over their heads, and the mistake over the identification of the stone provided ideal ammunition for local critics. Street's capacity for hard work was quite extraordinary, though he found it difficult to delegate, preparing every drawing himself.[100] He dashed around the country by train, often travelling overnight between Dublin and London. From his earliest days he spent his spare time 'ecclesiologising' and his wedding tour, after his marriage in 1852, consisted of visits to the French Gothic cathedrals. There was nobody who knew more about medieval architecture and, as Drew admitted in the context of Christ Church, it was unlikely that 'any other living architect would have acquitted himself in this peculiar task so well'.[101] The main cause of regret today is not what he actually did at the cathedral; rather the fact that no records were made of the medieval fabric as it was dismantled. The process of archaeological recording, however, still lay several decades in the future.

versy see also p. 326 above.   **99** Drew, 'Street as a restorer', p. 520.   **100** Kinnard, 'Street and the Law Courts', pp 228, 231.   **101** Drew, 'Street as a restorer', p. 523.

XVIII

Optimism and decline: music, 1870–*c*.1970

Barra Boydell

The century after disestablishment in 1871 initially saw choral services at Christ Church re-established on what appeared to be a secure and regular basis, but the social changes and the cathedral's declining financial position would eventually lead to a situation where radical changes had to be made to ensure the choir's very survival. Under the terms of the Irish Church Act which came into effect on 1 January 1871 the choir formally ceased to exist as it had for over three centuries. The vicars choral, stipendiaries and organist were, like the clergy, guaranteed their positions and incomes as an annuity during their working lifetimes, the capital from the sale of church property (including the former vicars' estates) being vested for this purpose in the commissioners of church temporalities in Ireland. The former choirmen, or annuitants, were encouraged to commute their interest for a lump sum estimated on the basis of their current income and life expectancy and this was entrusted to the Representative Church Body. The capital thus realised was invested and the annuitants' salaries paid out of the interest incurred. As the annuitants retired or died their places were filled by new appointees who would be paid directly by the cathedral. One of the more significant outcomes was that, as the annuitants (who had most often been members of both cathedral choirs) declined in number, the choirs of each cathedral came to be entirely separate, no longer sharing any of their singers as had been the case since at least the early seventeenth century.

While this arrangement provided in principle for the continuation of the cathedral's choral establishment along secure lines, had it not been for the generosity of Henry Roe, who was concerned not only to see the cathedral restored but also to ensure that its services matched the splendour of the new building, the future of music in the cathedral might have been very different. As it was, until the final decades of the twentieth century, the cathedral was to experience extreme difficulty in maintaining the choir. Without Henry Roe's contribution these difficulties would unquestionably have arisen even earlier on to the extent that recovery might not have been possible. Following the closure of the cathedral for rebuilding in 1872, Roe endowed £20,000 to provide for choral worship which was to be added to the fund held by the Representative Church Body representing the commuting value of the annuities paid to the organist, vicars and choirmen of Christ Church. Under the terms of the Roe endowment morning and evening prayer were to be celebrated chorally every Sunday and weekday in the year, as well as holy communion every Sunday and on Christmas and Ascension days, and the choir was established at twelve choirmen and at least twelve choirboys, in addition to the organist (in 1885 a reduction to ten choirmen was permitted due to the difficulties in finding twelve 'efficient' choirmen, but at one stage in the same year the number grew to fifteen).[1] Fulfilment of the terms of the endowment was to be certified annually by the archbishop. The full choir attended all services on Sundays, Christmas Day, Good Friday and the greater holy days, with a lesser number on weekdays (typically six choirmen, or half that number during July and August), the organist or his deputy attending every day.[2] Roe provided in 1878 a further £250 a year during his life for four additional choirmen to sing on Sunday afternoons and weekday services.[3] The service to mark the re-opening of the cathedral on 1 May 1878 started with a procession of about four hundred clergy, the choir singing Child's anthem 'Praise the Lord, O my soul'. R.P. Stewart's 'Te Deum' and 'Jubilate' in E flat for double choir and the holy communion setting for his service in G, the anthem being Boyce's 'I have surely built thee an house'. The service ended with Benjamin Rogers's recessional anthem 'Behold now, praise the Lord'. The elaborate nature and standard of the choral music on the occasion was described as surprising visitors and surpassing anything previously heard by those more familiar with the Dublin cathedral choirs.[4]

The increase in choral services led to problems with the annuitants who in 1878 challenged the authority of the dean and chapter to require them to attend services other than had been their duty prior to disestablishment. Disagreement rumbled on with recourse to legal opinion being sought by both sides, counsel eventually ruling in 1882 that the dean and chapter could not successfully take any action provided the annuitants performed their duties 'reasonably well'.[5] Such difficulties were essentially transient, new choirmen being appointed as the former vicars choral and stipendiaries retired or died. The new choirmen were paid on a 'by service' basis and provision for superannuation was established in 1889, the fund being substantially increased in 1903 by the Winstanley bequest of £500.[6] By the 1890s provi-

---

1 *Christ Church cathedral endowment* (Dublin, 1885), p. 13; C6/1/13/1, p. 407.   2 C6/1/22/2.   3 C6/1/13/1, p. 104.   4 Bumpus, 'Composers', pp 154–5; Vignoles, *Memoir*, p. 124.   5 C6/1/7/13, pp 396, 406–7, 410, 413, 424, 430, 434, 441; C6/1/7/14, pp 38–44, 47–50, 55–8.   6 C6/1/13/1, p. 504; C6/1/13/2, pp 64, 72, 75–6.

sion from the Roe endowment for the income of choir members was already beginning to decline in real terms. A pay increase with a return to a regular salary was sought in 1891 on the grounds of the extent of their duties, the cost of living, and comparison with English cathedrals. The board found that their singers were in fact paid higher than the English average, but their terms of leave were modified.[7] In 1902 the choirmen were granted one day off in the week and on Mondays both matins and evensong were thereafter sung by the boys only.[8] Unsuccessful requests for salary increases were to become all too regular a pattern as the new century progressed and proposed changes in choirmen's duties might be interpreted as a threat to the terms of the endowment. One solution was to celebrate weekday services with either choirmen or choirboys but not both, and the cessation of the last annuities paid under the Irish Church Act released additional capital for the running of the cathedral which provided some relief from 1909.[9] The board was aware of the choirmen's need to supplement their earnings outside the cathedral and the appointment of a competent deputy was agreed to in 1919 should any lay clerk have a definite offer of employment which would interfere with his weekday morning duties in the cathedral, but a request to give up choral weekday matins could not be granted.[10] A similar request by the lay vicars four years later was referred to the archbishop who now saw no problem under the terms of the endowment, all weekday matins henceforth being sung by the choristers alone with the organist.[11]

A choir fund established in 1932 provided small-scale funding beyond what was available from the endowment and the superannuation funds,[12] but the latter was insufficient to encourage retirement of older singers. In 1942 John Horan, then approaching fifty-nine years as a member of the choir, felt he could not afford to retire. In view of his exceptional service the board agreed to supplement his superannuation to ensure him a pension equivalent to his former salary (Horan was subsequently to bequeath £250 to the choir superannuation fund).[13] By the later 1940s as the value of their salaries continued to fall the choirmen questioned (unsuccessfully) the use of the Winstanley trust to provide pocket money for the choirboys rather than being used entirely for their own benefit, manifested their lack of morale through poor attendance and, with the support of the precentor, repeatedly but unsuccessfully sought a reduction in their duties.[14] The board was faced with making difficult choices between the terms of the Roe endowment which provided for most of what little was available for maintaining the choir, the

---

7 C6/1/13/1, pp 525, 527.   8 C6/1/13/2, p. 46.   9 Ibid., p. 150.   10 Ibid., p. 244. 11 Ibid., pp 280, 281; compare C6/1/22/5.   12 Ibid., pp 336, 337.   13 Ibid., 29 Jan. 1943, 28 Apr. 1950.   14 Ibid., 19 Dec. 1947, 30 Apr., 24 Sept., 29 Oct. 1948, 25 Feb., 27 May, 30 Sept. 1949, 24 Feb. 1950.

preservation of the choral services, and meeting the real needs of the choir members. The use of boys or part-time members to sing alto instead of replacing two vacant alto lay vicars was one solution reached in 1949, and in 1951 approval was given to the existing practice of only three lay vicars attending Saturday evensong, together with small increases in choir pay.[15] By the mid-1950s weekday choral services comprised matins sung daily by the choirboys and evensong sung on Mondays by the boys, on Tuesdays, Thursdays and Fridays by the boys with six gentlemen (on Friday there was no organ), and on Wednesdays and Saturdays by the gentlemen without the boys.[16] Increasing difficulty was experienced in attracting new singers as salaries became less attractive and weekday evensong at 3.00 p.m. conflicted with most jobs outside the cathedral. The position was exacerbated by comparison with St Patrick's which could afford to attract singers from English cathedrals (there was little or no musical contact with St Patrick's, a suggestion in 1954 that the two choirs might combine falling on deaf ears).[17] At Christ Church most singers had to hold other jobs, in some cases putting in deputies on weekdays as a matter of course, and resignations in favour of better-paid positions at St Patrick's were not infrequent. Changes in the time of evensong, first to 5.30 and then in 1963 to 6.00 pm, facilitated the choirmen, and in the same year Saturday evensong was abandoned.[18]

Difficult though the problems for the choirmen became, those of the boys and their schooling proved in the long run to be terminal. Growing financial problems were compounded by social and educational developments whose demands could not be met, resulting in the eventual closure of the school in 1972 and the replacement of the boys by women choir members. During the closure of the cathedral between 1872 and 1878 the choirboys were educated at the Erasmus Smith schools in Great Brunswick Street and the newly opened High School in Harcourt Street.[19] Following the reopening of the cathedral the term 'cathedral grammar school' came into use as teaching resumed on the cathedral premises.[20] As well as singing twice on Sundays and at both daily weekday services, the boys' schooling consisted of two hours of musical instruction and three of general education, until 1885 also on Saturdays. Later in 1878 it was decided to adjust the service times so that boys, who had no playground, would be kept occupied during their time at the cathedral and by 1882 a gymnasium had been provided.[21] In the light of the Roe endowment the board defined new parameters for the boys and their schooling for when the cathedral re-opened.[22] New choirboys,

15 Ibid., 30 Sept. 1949; C6/1/13/3, pp 5, 7, 9, 11; compare C6/1/22/8.   16 C6/1/13/3, p. 46; service sheets, 1954–6 (cathedral archives).   17 Ibid., p. 31.   18 Ibid., pp 74, 77, 78, 114, 115.   19 Ibid., p. 324.   20 C6/1/13/1, pp 20–3.   21 Ibid., pp 399–400, 296–7. 22 Ibid., pp 20–3.

selected by competition 'with due regard to the social position of parents or relations' when aged between seven and eight, were divided into six stipendiaries each receiving between £5 and £15 a year based on merit regardless of seniority, six probationers, and additional good singers as available known as supernumeraries. All current choristers were to be examined and replaced if unsuitable. The 'master of the choristers', who was also assistant organist, taught vocal and instrumental music including organ, and at least two pupils were articled to him to play the organ on weekdays in his absence. Richard Beatty, who had been music master since 1830, was granted retirement and John Horan, organist at Derry cathedral and later to become organist at Christ Church from 1894 to 1906, was appointed in his stead in May 1878. The number of boys in the choir would vary over the years according to the number of supernumerary boys available with suitable voices: at the re-opening of the cathedral there were fifteen, dropping to thirteen by the end of 1879, but the number would rise to sixteen in the mid-1880s and to over twenty by the 1920s.[23]

Until the end of the nineteenth century the average number of pupils in the school seldom surpassed twenty.[24] The roll book for 1890–5 indicates that there were three classes (all of which were taught by one teacher in one room), the emphasis in the lowest class (third) being on tables and English, though Latin, French, and English history were also taught. The boys in the first class (seniors) also learnt algebra, geometry, Irish history and German. The small size of the school was beginning to be recognised as a limiting factor both in the boys' education and in the attracting of new choristers to the cathedral.[25] With its larger grammar school, St Patrick's cathedral remained likely to attract the best potential choristers and pupils. A merger with the Merchant Tailors School discussed in 1878 and 1883 came to nothing, but the decision in principle in 1879 to take in private, fee-paying pupils would lay the grounds for the expansion of the school.[26] During the first decade of the century up to thirty boys attended the school, growing to forty-eight by 1920 and being taught by the headmaster with a full-time assistant and a part-time tutor for commercial classes.[27] The appointment as headmaster in 1936 of Revd Robert J. Ross, who had been assistant organist prior to his ordination in 1934 and was committed to the cathedral and its music, ushered in a period of growth and development,[28] including recognition in 1939 from the Department of Education as a secondary school (teaching up to Intermediate Certificate).

23 C6/1/23/8; C6/1/13/1, p. 407; C6/1/23/13.   24 School roll books, C6/1/25/1–3. 25 For a more detailed discussion of the cathedral school in the late nineteenth and twentieth centuries, Grindle, *Cathedral music*, pp 101–2, 123–6.   26 C6/1/13/1, pp 120, 171; C6/1/7/14, pp 71–2.   27 C6/1/25/1/3–6.   28 C6/1/13/2, p. 357.

When we consider the shortcomings of the manner in which the grammar school was housed we should not judge it by present-day standards. Few Irish secondary schools were well-housed until the latter part of the twentieth century. But perhaps Christ Church cathedral grammar school was worse off than most. Reinstated on the cathedral site in 1878, the school rapidly found itself, small though it was, seriously lacking in classroom accommodation, despite some improvements made to 'the large schoolroom' in 1908, when the windows overlooking St John's Lane were replaced.[29] Recreation grounds had always been lacking, a problem that was to some extent compensated for in 1902 when the cathedral board rented the play-ground attached to the adjacent St John's schools for the grammar school boys to play in.[30] In 1923 the premises of the former Fishamble Street Mission became available, and though somewhat out of repair and requiring costly maintenance, the boys' general education was transferred there, musical instruction taking place in the old school-room.[31] So dilapidated had the Fishamble Street building become by 1938 that parts of it were condemned and demolished, though the school remained where it was safe to do so.[32] In April 1939 the corporation refused permission for the re-building of the demolished premises on the basis that it had plans for the area that included the provision of a park and a bus station (leading, or misleading, Christ Church to hope that 'the cathedral will stand more conspicuous than ever'),[33] and offered a site in Castle Street instead. But when the cathedral learned that it would have to pay £250 for the Castle Street site it lost interest.[34] In 1941 the Fishamble Street rooms were vacated and set, and the school furniture either sold or moved to the music room which was brought back into service for general teaching.[35] Additional school accommodation was provided in 1942 by renting portion of the synod hall, a temporary arrangement again resorted to in 1958.[36]

The welfare of the pupils was undoubtedly a concern of the cathedral authorities. From 1903 to 1908 they were provided with a light lunch, in the latter year being given tram tickets to enable them to eat at home.[37] A troop of Boy Scouts was formed in 1914,[38] and in 1926 a Past Boys' Union got under way, having permission to play badminton (but not cards) in the music room once a month.[39] It lapsed, in the manner of all such organisations, only to be revived in the early 1940s, and in 1957 was called the 'Wynchester Society' after the choir's founder.[40] Contingency plans were made in 1941 to move the boys to Hollybrook, Bray, in case the government ordered evacuation. It never did.[41]

29 *Annual report 1908*, p. 9.   30 C6/1/13/2, p. 49.   31 Ibid., pp 285, 356; *Annual report 1926*, p. 7.   32 C6/1/13/2, pp 385–6.   33 Ibid., p. 410; *Year book 1940*.   34 C6/1/13/2, p. 455.   35 Ibid., p. 446.   36 C6/1/13/2, 18 Dec. 1942, C6/1/13/3, p. 72.   37 C6/1/13/2, p. 136.   38 *Annual report 1914*, p. 7.   39 C6/1/13/2, p. 300.   40 *Year book 1942–3*; *Year book 1957*, p. 23. Compare pp 237–8 above.   41 C6/1/13/2, p. 440.

The 1960s were however, to see vast changes in Irish education which had grave implications for small schools, small secondary schools in particular. The cathedral grammar school was one of the smallest, and was beset by staffing and accommodation difficulties. By 1963 the school's future was increasingly in doubt and rumours of closure were circulating. Fees had to be increased but the school was to continue for the time being.[42] A short-sighted decision to close the junior school in 1963 cut off the supply of potential choristers and it was reopened the following January.[43] A proposed merger with St Patrick's grammar school was rejected in 1970[44] and the following year, with numbers down to twenty-eight and the prospect of no more boys being available for the choir by 1973, the board recommended that the school should close as from September 1972.[45] And so the cathedral choir school, which had effectively existed since provision was made in 1480 for four boys to sing with the choir, ceased to exist. Choristers would now be educated at St Patrick's and receive their musical training at Christ Church but, despite the provision of free schooling and other incentives, the numbers of choir-boys continued to drop. Weekend services, financial assistance with fees introduced by the government in 1967, and the feeling that if boys were attending St Patrick's school they might as well sing in St Patrick's choir, all argued against joining a choir clearly in sharp decline.[46] As the number of boys fell the resulting lack of musical interest was causing choirmen to leave, four in as many weeks at the beginning of 1975, and weekday choral matins was discontinued in 1976, choral evensong having dropped to two days in the week the previous year.[47] The historic decision to introduce younger female singers at first met with some resistance, but in 1975 the first two girls joined the cathedral choir, although attempts to attract boys would continue until 1977.[48]

Telford was awarded the contract to re-erect the organ in the rebuilt cathedral using a new case designed by Street. He also added a fourth (solo) manual as well as dulciana and cornetto di basso stops, thus completing the work which had been interrupted in 1870.[49] The organ was now situated on a gallery in the north transept in an acoustically poor position: for the next hundred years, until it was replaced in 1984, the full organ would overwhelm the choir while the congregation at the west end could hardly hear it and the organist was out of sight of the choir. The eminent English organist Sir Henry Smart was engaged to report on the rebuilt instrument. He agreed that Telford had fulfilled the terms of his contract but considered that the

---

42 C6/1/13/3, pp 114, 115, 116, 117, 118.   43 Ibid., pp 117, 118, 120.   44 Ibid., pp 174, 176, 177.   45 Ibid., pp 174, 176, 177, 191, 194.   46 Ibid., pp 201, 226, 233, 239.   47 Ibid., pp 246, 260, 273.   48 Ibid., pp 246, 255, 275, 284, 287.   49 C6/1/13/1, pp 58, 60, 74, 82, 90.

organ was 'not on the whole a first-class or even very good instrument' and was unworthy of the newly rebuilt cathedral.[50] Telford responded by offering to add a new diapason at his own expense if the board paid for other additional stops to remedy Smart's criticisms, but the board declined to spend any additional money on the instrument.[51] Robert P. Stewart, who continued as organist until his death in 1894, was an unrelenting critic of Telford's organ which he described in 1881 as a 'saw-sharpener' which would 'stagger at every full chord ... for lack of wind'.[52] He urged both board and chapter to replace it but the financial implications put his suggestion beyond serious discussion.[53] Instead, Telford carried out work on the pedals in 1883 and, after much discussion by the board, further improvements in 1887, including provision of hydraulic power for the blower, improvements which met with Stewart's approval.[54] There were to be no significant complaints by Stewart's successors John Horan and then James Fitzgerald, who formally succeeded as organist in 1907, a role he had been filling for some years after Horan's final years were clouded by mental illness. Charles Kitson, appointed organist in 1913, reactivated moves for a new organ. An appeal was launched and an estimate agreed with Harrison and Harrison of Durham in 1916.[55] The first world war intervened however, and when Thomas Weaving became organist in 1920 most of the deposit paid to Harrisons was retrieved and Telfords were again asked to rebuild the organ using all existing pipes.[56] The work costing £1,635 included the addition of trumpet and Zauberflöte stops to the great organ and a tremulant to the swell, the replacement of tracker action by pneumatic action, and the installation of an electric blower. The choir organ was incorporated into the main case and the console set at right angles so that the organist could better see and hear the choir. The rebuilt organ was formally opened on 22 March 1923.[57]

Renovation of Telford's rebuilt 1857 organ began to be discussed in the early 1950s. Lack of funds prevented progress until 1956 when the organ of St Matthias's church in Adelaide Road, due to be demolished, was offered to Christ Church provided they organised and paid for its removal.[58] After it was safely stored in the cathedral an appeal was set up to raise the estimated £5,000 needed for a first-class rebuild incorporating the St Matthias's organ.[59] It was 1960 before a contract costing nearly £6,000 was agreed with Willis & Co. The rebuilt organ was dedicated with a recital by John Dykes

50 Henry Smart, *Report to the dean and chapter of Christ Church cathedral, Dublin, on the organ of the cathedral church* (Dublin, 1878).   51 C6/1/13/1, p. 140.   52 Letter to Canon Seymour, 26 Sept. 1881, quoted in Vignoles, *Memoir*, p. 130.   53 C6/1/13/1, p. 280; C6/1/7/14, p. 16.   54 Ibid., pp 447, 456, 457, 463, 468.   55 C6/1/13/2, pp 194, 197, 198, 218.   56 Ibid., pp 260, 262, 267, 268.   57 C6/6/4/1/18; C6/1/13/2, p. 281.   58 C6/1/13/3, pp 4, 21, 22, 56, 57.   59 Ibid., p. 68.

Bower, organist of St Paul's cathedral, on 26 October 1961, the outstanding balance of £3,000 eventually being cleared in 1965 with proceeds from the sale of the former Fishamble Street Mission building (which had been used for the choir school during the 1920s and 30s).[60] In addition to the main organ there were various smaller instruments in use. An organ belonging to the late Dr Morgan, the purchase of which (for the choir school) was discussed in 1876, may be the same instrument presented by Henry Roe in 1879.[61] In 1916 Mrs Ellis and Canon Hogan, the precentor, presented a small organ which was used while the cathedral organ was being rebuilt in 1922–3. The decision to sell it to the Royal Irish Academy of Music in 1948 came to nothing and it was advertised for sale in 1955, but again without result.[62] This instrument, a single-manual Telford organ, is now in the south transept.

Edward Seymour, appointed precentor in 1876, had previously demonstrated his interest in the cathedral's music.[63] He is credited with introducing choral communion into the Irish church and was largely responsible for the first *Church Hymnal Tune-book*.[64] By 1880 however the dean and chapter were accusing him of neglecting his duties, to which Seymour responded by publishing a booklet containing letters from leading churchmen, musicians and others praising the high standard of music.[65] While negative criticism would not be expected in such public testimonials, respected figures including R.P. Stewart, Joseph Robinson and John Stanford (father of the composer Charles V. Stanford) are uniformly positive and praise the boys in particular. Although Seymour appears to have silenced his critics, he resigned as precentor three years later.[66] Despite his high praise in 1880, Stewart wrote in 1885 that the choirboys were 'not generally good' and in 1890 that they had 'squalling bad voices' and that 'the slow tempi spoil the whole service'.[67] Seymour also appended to his booklet a list of anthems and services sung since 1878. Although he claims that 'every school of music was fairly represented', only four out of over 220 performances of anthems were of music from before 1660, composers of the later seventeenth and eighteenth centuries (to *c*.1775) accounting for 68 per cent of the music sung, the remainder being by more recent composers, Stevenson the most popular of all with six anthems

60 Ibid., pp 68, 97, 108, 136.   61 C6/1/13/1, p. 72; C6/1/7/13, p. 410.   62 C6/1/13/2, p. 287, 27 Feb. 1948; C6/1/13/3, pp 43, 45, 46; C6/6/4/2/9.   63 See Seymour, *Christ Church*, especially pp 71, 83; Edward Seymour, *The cathedral system* (Dublin 1870), pp 21–2.   64 Vignoles, *Memoir*, p. 190; music lists from 1846 and subsequent years do however list communion settings, 'Christ Church cathedral: course of services and anthems ...' (cathedral archives).   65 C6/1/7/13, pp 443, 445–6, 447, 449; Edward Seymour, *The choral services of Christ Church cathedral Dublin and their efficiency, during the first two years after the restoration of the cathedral* (Dublin, 1880).   66 C6/1/7/14, pp 60–1. See also p. 323 above.   67 Letters to Seymour quoted in Vignoles, *Memoir*, pp 132, 190.

sung a total of forty times. Both the repertoire of anthems and services and the amount of music by earlier composers had declined since 1849–50 when a complete year's music was first listed, but the emphasis on the late seventeenth and eighteenth centuries had changed little.[68] A book of anthem texts sung at the two Dublin cathedrals and published in 1880 tells a similar story:[69] Mendelssohn is the only nineteenth-century composer amongst the top five, the others being, as more than a century earlier, Greene, Croft, Handel and Boyce. More recent or living composers are however well represented, but Tudor and Stuart composers only account for between 4 and 5 per cent of the total. The most popular service settings in 1878–80 were Stewart in G followed by Aldrich in G which had topped the list in 1849–50. The cathedral's collection of music was not well cared for: Boyce's *Cathedral music* was stored in 1906 on chairs in the transept and three volumes had been lost.[70] The music was catalogued and partially rebound in 1949 and attention was focused on it in 1954 when what was thought at the time to be a unique copy of an anthem by Purcell was identified.[71]

The importance of music in attracting congregations, thus increasing income from collections, was recognised and an increasing emphasis on more recent music was blamed by the board in 1909 for a decrease in the numbers attending the cathedral, a view with which the organist Dr Fitzgerald disagreed.[72] Almost fifty years later the dean suggested that there was too much repetition of repertoire and insufficient practice (responsibility for selecting music had passed in 1946 from the precentor to the organist and choirmaster).[73] Musical standards had undoubtedly sunk very low in the course of the century. In order to earn an adequate living Thomas Weaving, organist from 1920 to 1950, also taught at the Royal Irish Academy of Music and examined for the Department of Education, entailing prolonged absences including Sundays, as well as conducting musical societies in Dublin. Billy (Edgar) Boucher, assistant organist in the 1940s and obliged to take on many of Weaving's duties in his absence, recalls that 'given that [Mr Weaving] was trying to do two jobs which were incompatible, and that the board were trying the impossible – running the school and daily services with insuffi-

68 'Christ Church cathedral: course of services and anthems ... 7 January 1849 [to] 6 Jan. 1850' (cathedral archives); in 1849–50 11 per cent of anthems dated from before 1660. 69 *Cathedral anthems published for the cathedrals of Christ Church, and St Patrick, Dublin* (London, 1880).   70 C6/1/13/2, pp 107–8.   71 Ibid., 25 Feb. 1949; C6/1/13/3, pp 38, 39, 40; the anthem 'Christ is risen' was subsequently found not to be by Purcell, but incomplete parts of another previously unidentified anthem by Purcell, 'Praise the Lord ye servants', have since been found in the libraries of St Patrick's and Christ Church cathedrals (information from Kerry Houston, St Patrick's cathedral).   72 C6/1/13/2, pp 157, 158, 161–2, 163. See also p. 331.   73 Ibid., 26 July 1946; C6/1/13/3, pp 44, 45.

cient money, with male singers not all of top class, with a loud but poor organ – it was inevitable that the standard was low'.[74] If anything, standards were to decline even further during the following decades. Around 1960, one former lay vicar recalls, the music was 'pretty awful', choir morale low, there was a feeling that the dean had no time for music, and the choir at times found itself on its own at weekday evensong with no clergy present. The musical repertoire was bound by tradition, certain anthems and services of little musical value being repeated 'because they had always been done'.[75] The use of the cathedral for a series of organ recitals given by Fred Tulan (U.S.A.), Nicholas Kynaston (Westminster cathedral), Kamiel D'Hooghe (Bruges) and Gerard Gillen (Dublin) in 1965 and the affiliation in the same year of the choir to the Royal School of Church Music suggest the beginnings of a more positive outlook for the cathedral and its music, an outlook encouraged by the use of the cathedral as a venue for a number of very successful performances by outside musicians.[76] But with the decreasing numbers of boys and the impending demise of the school it would be the 1980s before a significant turnaround would take place towards the flourishing musical life that distinguished Christ Church cathedral at the end of the twentieth century.

An aggrandisement of the cathedral bells in 1878 at the time of the restoration of Christ Church added new Murphy bells to make a ring of ten, with two semitones, making twelve ringing bells in all (that is, bells capable of being swung full-circle). An additional bell was hung 'dead' at the centre of the frame for the purpose of providing a necessary note for the operation of a tune-playing machine also provided at the time, all at the expense of Henry Roe.[77] When these new bells were first rung at the opening of the restored cathedral on 1 May 1878 the initial experience reflected, but with an absence of malice, what had happened to Murphy's bells for St Francis Xavier's church in Liverpool some years before: black lead had mistakenly been put in the pivots so that Murphy's new tenor proved difficult to ring.[78] One of the Rudhall bells cracked on Christmas Eve 1883 and, in the absence of Murphy, had to be re-cast and matched to the octave in 1885 by Taylor of Loughborough, Leicestershire, then for the first time rendering service to Christ Church.

74 Letter from Billy Boucher to the author, 28 June 1998.   75 Information from George Bannister, tenor lay clerk, 1958–63.   76 C6/1/13/3, pp 135, 137; notable performances at this time included Monteverdi's 'L'Orfeo' and John Blow's 'Venus and Adonis' directed by Eric Sweeney in 1974 and 1975, and concerts of early music by the Consort of St Sepulchre in 1976.   77 McVittie, *Restoration*.   78 Bell-ringer R. Wood's notebook (belfry records); compare pp 351–2 above.

Murphy's additions of 1878 included a tenor for the ten, found when it was checked in 1979 to weigh thirty-four cwts. In that year all the bells were taken out by Taylor and re-tuned, and the Murphy tenor, said to be fissured, was re-cast. The Taylor tenor weighs forty-five cwts and its note is B. It is inscribed 'The Gift of Fred Scott, A Former Bell Ringer'. Fred Scott in his will left funds for the repair of the bells. In 1936 the thirteenth bell, by Murphy, had been sold to Gillet and Johnston of London in part-payment for putting the bells on roller bearings, the tune-playing machine for which it was required having been sold in 1929 to St Patrick's.[79] Finally, its place was taken in 1997 by a bell of similar weight from St Andrew's church, Suffolk Street. This bell was made by Abraham Rudhall in 1756 and is inscribed 'Peace And Good Neighbourhood', a common motto on Rudhall bells made with no destination in mind, and a happy coincidence since it is now chimed daily for peace prayers.

There is very little information available as to how the bells were rung in earlier times, but we do know that in the twentieth century until the 1960s called-changes were preferred at Christ Church. From the 1960s method-ringing has been successfully practiced, while called-changes have also been rung. Notable achievements by Christ Church ringers have included the winning of an all-Ireland striking competition (in 1988)[80] ringing a method, Grandsire Triples, against teams ringing the easier called-changes, and an unprecedented sequence in the Irish context of high-quality ringing for services in the late 1990s with bands containing two double-handed ringers: that is, ringers ringing two bells each, both for called changes and in methods.[81] The cathedral tower rises not so far above the ground that the music of the bells is carried away and its immediate value lost. George Street's enlarging of the bell-chamber windows ensures that very little sound is wasted. In other words, physical properties, apart from the material of the bells themselves, contribute to a quality of sound which is distinctive and greatly admired. As to the range and versatility, sixteen can be rung at once, one fourteen also; three twelves, three tens, four eights, six sevens, seven fives – making a very large instrument for public music-making and for the teaching of a complicated art. The citizens today get what their ancestors wanted in 1670, when the lord mayor helped raise money in return for a guarantee of perpetual use of Christ Church bells to beat for the city's heart.

79 Letter in cathedral archives.   80 The team included two permitted 'outsiders' who were St Patrick's ringers, an echo of longstanding co-operation despite separation (*Irish Bell News*, 1988).   81 Christ Church ringers' attendance book (belfry records).

Postscript

In 1948 the general synod established the city and town parishes commission, a body charged with making recommendations as to how the parochial
system in urban areas might be reorganised in response to demographic
change.[1] In 1963 the operation of the statute was extended to allow the commission to include Christ Church cathedral within the scope of its activities.[2]
The cathedral community was informed in the 1967 *Year book* (published in
1966) that the archbishop had deferred the appointment of a successor to
Dean Emerson until the city and town parishes commissioners had completed
their report on the cathedral and its neighbouring parishes; in the interim,
Canon Ross would act as dean.

The diocesan councils of Dublin and Glendalough reported to the diocesan synod in 1966 that they had received from the city and town parishes
commission 'a scheme for the future of Christ Church, incorporating adjoining parishes' and further reported that the councils had agreed to talks with
representatives of St Patrick's cathedral on 'the possibility of a single cathedral unit.' This implied that one dean would serve both cathedrals, and in
view of the fact that the commissioners found Christ Church to be in a precarious financial position, with little or no commitment to it on the part of
the parishes (despite, as they were careful to add, the sterling efforts of recent
deans), inevitably the one dean would be, to all intents and purposes, the
dean of St Patrick's.[3] The diocesan council rejected the proposal that ensued,
although there were council members who had grave misgivings about doing
so, and early in 1967 Dean Salmon was appointed.[4]

Clearly, the new dean entered upon his duties in highly discouraging circumstances, and the fact that Christ Church seems not to have been enveloped
in a cloud of despondency owed much to his attitude and bearing, upheld as
he was by a profound spirituality, selfless conscientiousness and confidence in

1 Chapter 2 of 1948, 'Statute to provide for the union or grouping of parishes in cities,
towns and areas adjacent thereto'. 2 Chapter 7 of 1963, 'To extend the operation of the
statute of the general synod chapter 2 of 1948'. 3 *Report of the diocesan councils of Dublin
and Glendalough to the diocesan synods,1966*, p. 20; minutes of the diocesan council, 28
February 1966. 4 Interview with the Ven. R.G.F. Jenkins, former archdeacon of Dublin,
on 17 August 1994. Archdeacon Jenkins had no such misgivings.

the support of his archbishop. Dean Salmon's dedication inspired a similar dedication in others. As well as the cathedral clergy, he soon had around him a group of enthusiastic and hard-working laity whose enthusiasm expressed itself in many ways, and perhaps most spectacularly when Christ Church brought *son et lumière* to Dublin in 1967, scripted by Jack White, narrated by Micheál MacLiammóir and directed by Christian Ede who had devised similar performances at Canterbury, Durham and Winchester.[5]

But difficult decisions had to be faced, such as the restructuring of the choir and the consequent closing of the grammar school, described elsewhere. Nonetheless, the musical tradition survived, and was put at the service of the revised liturgy as contained in the *Alternative Prayer Book* of 1984, the dean believing it to be the cathedral's duty to support liturgical revision. Likewise he saw it as his duty to accept the added responsibilities that came with the initiation of what has come to be called the 'cathedral group of parishes'. For, while the commissioners' proposals for amalgamating the two cathedrals had been rejected, not all of their recommendations relative to Christ Church were abortive. General synod legislation of 1971,[6] based on the commission's work, initiated a complicated scheme whereby, eventually, the dean of Christ Church became incumbent (rector) of the parishes of St Andrew, St Werburgh, All Saints Grangegorman and the union of St Michan's, St Paul's and St Mary's. Another major undertaking in Dean Salmon's time was 'Safeguard Christ Church', an appeal for the sum of £500,000 to enable a vital restoration of the cathedral fabric to take place. Much of the success of the venture was due to the labours and generosity of Allen Figgis, the dean's trusty administrator, and a much-respected figure in Dublin's business and cultural life. But Figgis was the first to say that the high regard in which the dean was held in all quarters, and T.N.D.C. Salmon's unstinting giving of himself to the cause, were enormous attributes.

The ecclesiastical counterpart of liturgical revision was the burgeoning ecumenical movement that owed much to Vatican II. Dean Salmon had scarcely taken up his duties when he was invited to Áras an Uachtaráin by President de Valera, who expressed the wish that all the dean's hopes for Christ Church would come to pass,[7] and attended the Citizenship Service that year. The dean was already on friendly terms with Archbishop Ryan through biblical studies, and when in 1979 the Roman Catholic diocese made a pilgrimage to Eu in Normandy, the burial place of Laurence O'Toole, Dean

---

5 *Year book 1967.* 6 Chapter 9 of 1971, 'To provide for the grouping or union of certain parishes in the city and diocese of Dublin with the cathedral church of the Holy Trinity, commonly called Christ Church.' A similar arrangement exists at St Patrick's, where parishes are grouped under the incumbency of the dean of St Patrick's. 7 Interview with the Very Revd T.N.D.C. Salmon, 9 June 1999.

Salmon was invited to join the pilgrims, which he gladly did. Subsequently, Christ Church reciprocated that hospitality when a group of French pilgrims came to Christ Church and, led by Archbishop McAdoo and Archbishop Ryan, prayed in the chapel in the cathedral where St Laurence's heart is preserved. Dr Ryan's successor, Archbishop Connell, has attended services at Christ Church on several occasions., and has preached there.

Perhaps the most significant tribute that can be paid to Dean Salmon is that when he resigned in 1988 the appointment of a successor was never in doubt. John Thomas Farquhar Paterson, dean of Kildare, was made dean of Christ Church by Archbishop Caird, whose close interest and work for the cathedral was a strong encouragement to all those connected with it. Much of the credit for solving the long-standing problem of providing a deanery goes to the archbishop, who first saw the possibilities of converting the old school buildings in St Werburgh Street for that purpose. Dean Paterson came to Christ Church with wide experience and understanding of the Church of Ireland, enhanced by his years as an honorary secretary of the general synod. He also brought with him a keen liturgical sense and musical competence, valuable attributes given the major musical developments in Christ Church at this period.

By 1980 when Peter Sweeney was appointed organist and director of music there was only one boy left in the choir, and from March 1981 weekday choral evensong was only celebrated on Thursdays. Choir morale remained low, with considerable resentment amongst some of the older choirmen towards the introduction of women.[8] As older lay vicars resigned or retired the choir was gradually re-formed as a mixed chamber choir. It was Sweeney's conviction that the replacement of the old organ, by this stage only partially usable, would act as the catalyst for transforming the cathedral into a recognised centre of music, attracting good singers for the choir, and redefining the public's perception of cathedral music. The board responded positively and a new organ by Kenneth Jones was inaugurated in 1984 with a recital by the Japanese organist Kei Koito as part of the (now triennial) Dublin International Organ Festival for which Christ Church, now with the finest organ in Dublin, became the centre. The new organ was situated no longer in the north transept but free-standing below the north arch of the crossing, immediately behind and above the cantoris side of the choir. Suitable to accompany a much wider choral repertoire than the old instrument and situated closer to the choir with the organist in visual contact, the new organ reanimated the choir, while the growing acceptance of women choristers and the introduction of new, younger singers contributed to a significant rise in musical standards. Peter Sweeney also introduced the practice of the organist as choirmaster conducting from the chancel, the accompaniments being played by the assistant organist. A series of recitals on the new

8 See p. 380 above.

organ, together with the high international profile of the organ festival, encouraged public awareness of Christ Church as a centre for music.

When Peter Sweeney resigned in 1992 Mark Duley, a New Zealander, was appointed organist and choirmaster, and under his direction there was further dynamic expansion of the choir during the 1990s, most notably in the founding in 1995 of a girl's choir which sings evensong on Wednesdays. In the same year the lay vicars were reinstated, to provide a permanent nucleus to the choir, Christ Church being possibly the first Anglican cathedral to have women lay vicars. The ten lay vicars (four sopranos, two altos, two tenors, two basses) were supplemented by five choral scholars and up to fifteen other choir members who sang both Sunday services and Thursday evensong. With three weekday choral evensongs in addition to the two sung services on Sundays, the number of choral services in the cathedral was greater than had been the case since 1976, when sung matins was abandoned and choral evensong reduced to twice, subsequently once a week.

Today, the choir's repertoire is the largest of any cathedral in the country and includes recent commissions by composers from Ireland and abroad. A Guinness organ scholarship, established in 1995, not only provides valuable experience for younger organists but also helps in spreading the burden of the assistant organist's duties as the number of choral services has increased. The choir made its first tour to England in 1993, including on that occasion short residencies at Westminster abbey and Canterbury cathedral, the first time the choir had sung outside Ireland. Week-long residencies at English cathedrals have since become a regular part of the choir's activities, with tours to France (including Chartres cathedral) in 1998 and New Zealand in 1999, amongst more recent foreign visits. The choir broadcasts regularly both on RTÉ radio and television and on BBC, and has also made a number of commercial recordings. The development of music and the arts beyond the cathedral's liturgical context has included the establishment in 1998 with Arts Council funding of Christ Church Baroque, a developing period-instrument ensemble which performs both on its own and with the cathedral choir. Seven new bells at the lighter end of the scale were added to the cathedral ring by Taylor of Loughborough in 1999 giving Christ Church an even more impressive instrument. Six of these are inscribed with the opening words of psalms of praise, as follows: '*Confitebor Tibi*', '*In Domino Confido*', '*Exaltabo Te, Domine*', '*Exultate Deo*', '*Venite Exultemus*', '*Laudate Dominum*', and one quotes St Luke's gospel: '*Pax in Hominibus*'. Those inscribed with psalms have also the dean's name '*Johannes Paterson Decanus*',[9] while to the '*Pax*' bell is added '*Leslie Taylor, Magister*

9 Charles Cobbe, dean of Christ Church and bishop of Kildare, later archbishop of Dublin, is commemorated on the 1738 bells; Charles Lindsay, dean of Christ Church and bishop of Kildare, is commemorated on the bells of the 1840s.

Campanarum'. At the heart of this peal remain the marvellous and time-hon-
oured Rudhall-based eight with the Rudhall tenor of twenty-four cwts. So,
while the twentieth century saw the musical tradition at Christ Church decline
possibly to its lowest level within the five hundred years since boys joined the
monastic choir at the end of the fifteenth century, it has also seen that tradition reborn in the final decades of this century, with the cathedral becoming
one of Ireland's leading centres for music, both liturgical and public.

The past decade has seen renewed emphasis on other aspects of the cathedral's life. Its archives are for the most part under the professional care of the
Representative Church Body Library, and are receiving increased scholarly
attention, giving rise not only to this present work and its ancillary publications, but also to regular series of lunchtime lectures, offered to city and diocese. The annual Joe Coady lecture has been revived, commemorating the service he gave to Christ Church first as sexton, and then as dean's verger from
1959 until his death in 1987.[10] With the ordination of women to the priesthood
has come the appointment in 1996 of the first woman canon, the Revd Virginia
Kennerley. C.O.R.E (Christian Outreach through Renewal & Evangelism) now
a trustee church in its own right at the re-opened St Catherine's, began its life
at St Werburgh's, in the cathedral group of parishes. The inner-city carol service in aid of neighbouring charities is an expression of the cathedral's aspira-
tion to contribute increasingly to the welfare of its centre city location, as the
annual services of ordination and the Christmas carol service contribute to the
life of the diocese. *Ceiliúradh*, in June 2000, an international festival of liturgy,
past, present and future, marking the opening of the third millennium, is similarly intended to address issues that are central to the purposes of the church,
and to do so with the varied resources that the cathedral offers.

At the time of disestablishment, there were voices in the Church of
Ireland, as in the Church of England, expressing doubts as to the value of
cathedrals in the church's ministry. But now it is becoming apparent that
cathedrals are well placed to fulfil a distinctive ministry suited to a time of
rapidly accelerating change. It is inconceivable that the church's mode of
exercising its ministry should remain unchanged, and it must take account
of the positive as well as the negative mutations in society. Wealth, at home
and abroad, continues to be unequally divided, so undoubtedly there is a continuing need to stir consciences. Generations are increasingly questioning, so
there is an intellectual task to perform. At the same time, the arts are being
made more accessible to the public in general, so the cathedral 'as work of
art' can seek to evoke a response. For we are in danger of culpable neglect
of duty if we interpret present attitudes to Christianity as 'them' refusing to
respond to 'us'. The truth may well be vice versa.

10 *Year book 1959*, p. 27.

Priors and deans

PRIORS		DEANS	
Gervase	(?) c.1171	Robert Paynswick	1539
Columbanus	(?) c.1190	Thomas Lockwood	1543
Thomas	(?) c.1196	John Garvey	
H	(?) c.1201	(bp of Kilmore, 1585–9,	
Robert	c.1205	abp of Armagh, 1589–95)	1565
W	(?) c.1208	Jonas Wheeler	
Bernard	c.1220	(bp of Ossory, 1613–18)	1595
Roger	c.1225	Randolph (Ralph) Barlow	
Philip	(?) c.1235	(abp of Tuam, 1629–34)	1618
Robert de Stanford	c.1244	Henry Tilson	1634
[John]		James Margetson	1639
William de Gran	(?) c.1265	William Berrey	
Adam de la More	c.1279	(papal provision)	1644
John de Exeter	c.1292	Patrick Cahill (papal provision)	1644
Adam de Balsham	c.1296	Robert Mossom	1661
Henry de la Warre de Bristol	1301	John Parry	
John Pocock (Pocot)	1313	(bp of Ossory, 1672–7)	1666
Hugh de Sutton alias le Jeune	1320	William Moreton	
Robert de Gloucester	1326	(bp of Kildare, 1681–1705)	1677
Roger Goioun	1331	Alexius Stafford (appointed by	
Gilbert de Bolyniop	1337	James II, d. 1691)	1688
Simon de Ludegate	1343	Welbore Ellis (bp of Kildare)	1705
Robert de Hereforde	1346	Charles Cobbe (bp of Kildare)	1731
Stephen de Derby	1349	George Stone (bp of Kildare)	1743
Robert Lokynton	1382	Thomas Fletcher	
James de Redenesse	1397	(bp of Kildare)	1745
Nicholas Staunton	1409	Richard Robinson	
William Denys	1438	(bp of Kildare)	1761
William Lynton	1459	Charles Jackson	
Thomas Harrold	1474	(bp of Kildare)	1765
David Wynchester	1489	George Lewis Jones	
Richard Skyrrett	1499	(bp of Kildare)	1790
William Hassard	1519	Hon. Charles Dalrymple	
Robert Castle alias Paynswick	1537	Lindsay (bp of Kildare)	1804

(Kildare united to Dublin &
  Christ Church deanery united to
  St Patrick's)   *1846*
Hon. Henry Pakenham
  (dean of St Patrick's, 1846–63) 1846
John West
  (dean of St Patrick's, 1864–89) 1864
Richard Chenevix Trench
  (abp of Dublin, 1863–84)   1871
William Conyngham,
  Lord Plunket
  (abp of Dublin, 1884–87)   1884
(Abp Plunket resigned as dean,

appointing a canon of his
  cathedral)   *1887*
William Conyngham Greene   1887
James Hornidge Walsh   1908
Harry Vere White   1918
Herbert Brownlow Kennedy   1921
Ernest Henry Cornwall
  Lewis–Crosby   1938
Norman David Emerson   1962
Thomas Noel Desmond
  Cornwall Salmon   1967
John Thomas Farquhar
  Paterson   1989

(Compiled from Hand, 'Two cathedrals', pp 147–9 and Leslie, 'Fasti', pp 56–71)

Index

Abbot, Dr G., archbishop of Canterbury, 185
Abbott memorial, 327
account rolls, 12, 14–15
Act of Supremacy, 175
Act of Uniformity, 175
Act of Union, 2, 285, 291, 295, 339
Adam and Eve, chapel of, 292
admission charges, 328, 332
Adrian IV, pope, 43
Æthelnoth 'the Good', archbishop of Canterbury, 28
Æthelstan, king, 27
Æthelwig, abbot of Evesham, 34
Agar, Charles, archbishop of Dublin, 266n
Agard, Francis, 180
Agard, John, 201
Aix-la-Chapelle, treaty of, 300
Alcock, John, 311
Aldrich, H., 311–12, 383
Aldwin of Winchcombe, 35
ale-houses, 277
Alen, John, archbishop of Dublin, 31–2, 41, 162
All Hallows priory, 44, 90, 152, 161, 239
dissolution, 164
granted to corporation, 162
All Saints Grangegorman, 387
All Saints priory, 152
Alleyn, John, dean of St Patrick's, 18, 76, 152, 157
Allgood, Sara, 338
altar vessels, 92, 108, 126, 136, 156, 167–8, 197–8, 260n, 320
burial of, 275
donations of, 135–6
repairs, 324, 328
restoration, 369–70
returned from Chapel Royal, 333–4
'royal plate', 255
silver box, 108
transferred from St Patrick's, 168

altars, 100, 105, 134
after restoration, 326
Alternative Prayer Book, 387
Alton, Henry, 108
Alyngton, Henry, 249
Amlaíb Cúarán, king of Dublin, 27–9
Andrews, George, dean of Limerick, 194
Angelus ad Virginem, 145–6
Anglesey, 33
Anglicanism, 242
Anglo-Normans, 3, 26, 34–5, 37, 42
influence on Christ Church, 47–52
in Ireland, 45–6
annals, 37–8
Annals of Connacht, 164
Annals of Loch Cé, 164
annuitants, 323–5, 374, 375–6
Anselm, archbishop of Canterbury, 39
anthems, 300, 303, 339, 341, 343, 345, 349, 384
printed texts, 350–1, 382–3
recognition of, 298
17th c., 308–13
antiphonary, 130, 144
Archdall, M., 122–3
arches, 63
'abbreviated', 57–8
architecture. *See* cathedral building
archives, 8–10, 54, 78, 205
calendared, 14, 19, 21
deeds, 13–15
description of, 11–22
destruction, 10, 13
manuscript collection, 156–7
medieval, 12–17
moved to Dublin castle, 203
post-Reformation, 18–20
recovered, post-Restoration, 216
in T.C.D., 192
Ardee, County Louth, 108, 155
Ardfert cathedral, 3

Armagh diocese, 4–6, 39, 47, 93, 158, 184, 190, 205, 290, 316, 320
  church reform, 43
  primacy of, 29, 40–1, 43
Armagh cathedral, 308
  baculus Ihesu, 47, 93, 108, 132
Armagh monastery, 37
Arminianism, 198, 246
arms, searches for, 271
army
  billeting, 203, 278
  cess payment, 207
Arras cathedral, 72
Arrouasian canons, Christ Church, 44–5, 57, 121
  become secular clergy, 166
  buildings, 109–28
  community life, 77–9
  introduced, 129
  music used, 143–4
  no Irish admitted, 78–9
  robbery, 83
Arts Council, 389
Ashlin, G.C., 357
Assumption of the Blessed Virgin, feast of, 179
Aston, Arthur, 205
Áth Cliath, 1, 26
Athassel abbey, 102, 126
Atherton, John, sub-dean, bishop of Waterford and Lismore, 196–7, 199, 201
  choir discipline, 246–7
  execution, 202
Atkins, Revd Walter, 262
Auchmuty monument, 327
Auden, Andrew, 250n
Aughrim, battle of, 273
augmentation estate, 267, 298
Augustinians, 12, 52, 102, 109, 116, 122, 152, 161, 176, 237n. *See also* Arrouasian canons
  chapter houses, 121
  in Christ Church, 57
  community involvement, 157
  dissolutions, 162
  expelled, 50
  habit, 136–7, 171
  income, 161
  liturgy, 131–2
  music of, 146–7
  native Irish among, 154

  refectories, 126
  rule of, 15, 77–8, 155–6
  spread of, 43–4
Avignon papacy, 75

Back Lane, 194
baculus Ihesu, 3, 15, 65, 93–4, 99, 107, 157
  brought to Dublin, 37, 47, 108
  fate of, 164
  housing, 132
  oaths sworn on, 85, 159
  offerings, 137n, 160, 238
Bale, John, bishop of Ossory, 169
Balgriffin, County Dublin, 78, 161
Ball, Margaret, 179
Ball, Richard, sub-prior, 153, 163, 167, 172
Ball family, 154
Ballyboghil, County Dublin, 47
Ballymote, County Sligo, 214
Balscadden, County Dublin, 81, 159–1
Balytiper, County Dublin, 81, 81n; *see* Tipperstone
Bank of Ireland, 333
Bannister, George, 384n
Bannow, County Wexford, 273
baptisms, 20, 277, 338
baptistry, 366–7
Baptists, 212
barber surgeons' guild, 178
Barbers' chapel, 106
Barbor, Henry, 89
Barlow, Ralph, dean, archbishop of Tuam, 183, 193–4, 200
  resignation, 199
Barnard, J., 250
Barronstown, Armagh, 316
Bates, Mr, 296
Bateson, Thomas, 245, 247–8, 250
Bath, James, 179
Bath stone, 122
Battell, Richard, 306
Batten, A., 350
Battersby, Dr George, 326
Baugh, Thomas, 193
Bayeux cathedral, 364n
beadle, office of, 259, 279, 286, 328
Beaton Panels, 105n
Beatty, Richard, 344, 349, 378
Beaumaris, 224
Beauvais cathedral, 220

Becket, St Thomas, 46, 101, 179
Bedell, William, bishop of Kilmore, 192, 199, 249
Bedlow, James, 175
Begerin Island, 39
beggars, 91
Begge, John, 80
Belfast, 343
    Friends of cathedral, 337
Bell, George, 7
Bell, T., 95n, 98
bell-ringers, 189, 385
bells, 2, 107
    after restoration, 384–5
    civic celebrations, 178, 209, 269, 275, 304–5
    number increased, 303–4
    1999, 389–90
    repairs, 243–4, 351–2
    ringers' chamber, 232–3
    ringing styles, 304–5
Benedictines, 36, 41, 45, 152, 204
    chapter houses, 120
    in Christ Church, 56–7
    music, 146
Bennet, Thomas, 138, 237–8
Benson, William, 207
Bentinck, Cavendish, 320
bequests, 89
Berkeley, George, bishop of Cloyne, 327
Bernard, J.H., archbishop, 331; dean of St Patrick's, 5, 8
Bernard, Nicholas, 186
Berrey, William, 205
Berry, H.F., 5, 7
Bessborough, Lord, 358
Betagh, Richard, 168, 241
Betham, Sir William, 104n
Bethell, Denis, 35
Beza, Theodore, 185
Bicknor, Alexander, archbishop of Dublin, 30, 75, 91
Biggar, Scotland, 222n
Bilson, Thomas, bishop of Winchester, 193
Bindon abbey, 72n
Bird, Thomas, 189, 203
births, 277
Black Death, 97
Blackrock, County Dublin, 295
Bladen, Dr Thomas, 256–9, 273
Bladen, William, 256, 259n
Blayney, Lord, 259n

Blessed Mary, chapel of, 92, 138; *See* Lady chapel; Mary chapel; White Mary chapel
Blett, John, 309
Blow, John, 300, 310n, 311, 350, 384n
board
    boardroom table, 324, 367
    criticisms of restoration, 326
    established, 325
    minutes of, 21
    and organ, 381
    women members, 330
'bond' stone, 370
Book of Common Prayer, 175, 255, 257n, 298
    abolition proposed, 207–8
    revised, 1878, 325
'Book of obits', 12, 17, 19, 135, 152, 155, 164
    civic officials, 170, 238
    confraternity members, 91, 158
    description of, 16
    finishes, 1558, 177
    post-Reformation, 167
    printed edition, 8
    relic inventory, 15, 93, 133n
    in TCD, 192
    tenants, 159
'book of reformation', 168–9
Boswell, Dudley, 192, 208
Boucher, Billy (Edgar), 383–4
Bounell, merchant, 230
Bower, John Dykes, 381–2
Bowes, Sir John, 372
Boy Scouts, 379
Boyce, W., 310–12, 350, 383
Boydell, Barra, 198
Boyle abbey, 68, 68n, 122n
Boyne, battle of the, 275
Boys' Brigade, 334
Brabazon, Sir William, 170
Bradie, Thomas, 244
Bradley, John, 38, 42
Bradley, John, chancellor, 192
Bramhall, John, treasurer, bishop of Derry, 197–9, 201, 234
Bran mac Máel Morda, king of Leinster, 28
Brenaghe, John, 223–4, 228
Brene, mason, 227
Brereton, Sir William, 198, 234
brewhouse, 111, 126

Brewster, Nathaniel, 214
Brian Bórama, 55
bribery, 80, 84
Bridgeman, Henry, 199–200
Bridsall, Thomas, 214
Brigham, William, 206n
Brigid, St, 93
    veil of, 164
Bristol, 46, 59, 304
    cathedral, 361
    chapter house, 364n
Brodrick, Dr, archbishop of Cashel,
    287–9
Brookbank, John, precentor, 206, 208
Broughton, Hugh, 185, 193
Browne, George, archbishop of Dublin,
    163, 167, 170
    'book of reformation', 168–9
Bruce, Robert, 88
Bruce invasion, 119n
Bryan, Laurence, 184
Bulkeley, Lancelot, archbishop of Dublin,
    196, 208, 246
Bulkeley, William, archdeacon of Dublin,
    204
Bull, J., 308
Bullock, John, 112n, 182
Bull's Head inn, 296
Bumpus, John, 313
Bunting, Edward, 343
burials, 91, 136–7, 139, 190
    in chapter house, 120
    in cloister walks, 116
    confraternity members, 158
    costs of, 206, 263
    in Lady chapel, 107
    registers, 20
    skulls found, 226n
Burke, Edmund, 274
Bury, Mr, 215
Butler, John, 359
Butler, William, 5, 8, 63n, 69, 222n,
    260n, 359, 370
Byfield, John, 306
Byrd, W., 308, 311, 350
Byrne, Ellinor, 304
Byrne, Joseph, 274
Bysse, Christopher, 188

Cabra, Dublin, 230
Caen stone, 59n, 330, 332–3, 365, 371
Cahill, Patrick, 205

Caird, D., archbishop of Dublin, 388
Calvinism, 185, 195
Cambridge, 184–5
Campion, Edmund, 179
canons, 50, 154, 172
    biographies of, 153–5
Canterbury cathedral, 10–11, 18, 28–9,
    34, 36, 142, 387
    fire, 1174, 62, 101
    Friends of, 336
    Irish jurisdiction, 43
    music, 143
    reconstruction, 65
Cantok, Thomas, bishop of Emly, 90
Cantrell family, 154
Capper, Anne, 202
Carlingford castle, 227
Carlisle cathedral, 153, 161, 180
Carmody, W.P., 5
Carne, Edward, 109n
Carney, Edward, 189, 203
Carroll, John, 278
Carter, Charles Thomas, 313
Carter, Timothy, 313
Cartmel priory, Cumbria, 152, 161
Cartwright, Thomas, 193
Carville, William, 203
Cashel diocese, 39, 43, 50, 316
    synod, 1101, 39
    synod, 1171-2, 46, 129–30
Cashel cathedral, 3, 5, 102
Castle, Robert (Paynswick), prior, 154,
    163–4, 167, 169. See Paynswick, Robert
Castle Street, 27, 296, 379
Castleknock, County Dublin, 154–5, 158,
    230
catechising, 214
cathedral building, 9. See also sculpture
    1030-1250, 18, 30, 53–74
        rubble construction, 73–4, 219
        sequence of, 68–71
    1250-1530, 95–128
        chapter house, 115–24
        crossing tower, 102–3
        interior, 103–4
        'long quire', 95–102
        priory buildings, 109–28
    architectural style
        English comparisons, 61–2, 73–4
        French influence, 72
        Gothic, 48–9, 51, 59, 67–72, 101,
        105, 368

Gothic revival, 235, 356
Romanesque, 48, 57–8, 60–74, 95–6, 368
documentation, 20, 54, 70
foundations, 219
indulgences, 98
maintenance, 210, 263, 268, 293
after restoration, 332–3
rebuilding, 16th c., 223–31
rebuilding, 17th c., 230–1
17th c., 191
nave collapse and restoration, 218–36
plan, 1761, 110
Price restoration, 355–6
stone used, 59, 122
restoration, 371
12th c. rebuilding, 3
vault collapse, 180
cathedral grammar school, 377–80
cathedrals, 4–8, 10, 390
archive collections, 11
definition of, 26
future of, 320–1
music, 313, 339
secular, 165–6
Catherine, St, 108, 179
Catholic emancipation, 285, 292
Catholicism, 4, 195–6, 269, 305
1641 rebellion, 202, 205–6
detected in cathedral restoration, 325–6, 353, 372
Caulfield, Richard, 6
Ceiliúradh, 390
Cellach, archbishop of Armagh, 40–1
cellarer, 153
cellars, 111–12
Cely, John, bishop of Down, 107, 133n, 139
cess, 279
'Chain book', 137
Chambers, Elizabeth, 211
Champion, Arthur, 189, 203
chancellor, office of, 84, 167, 183–4, 257
house, 128, 277, 291
income, 184
chancery, 113
change-ringing, 304, 385
chantry chapels, 133–4
chantry endowments, 156
Chapel Royal, 259–60, 282, 285, 329, 333
choral performances, 340–1
organist, 343

Chapel Royal, St James's, 298, 300
Chapelizod, Dublin, 158
chapels, 104–6, 156, 158, 178
chaplains, 78
Chappel, William, bishop of Cork, 198–9
chapter, 294
1641 rebellion, 204–5
board representation, 325
clerk, 188, 197, 259
composition of, 183–5
17th c., 199–200
declining attendance, 187–8
disputes within, 288–9
English members, 256
established, 165–7
formal abolition, 209
under James II, 273
liberty management, 188–9, 275–6, 279
loss of liturgy, 207–8
under Mary, 172
minutes end, 1647, 208
number of meetings, 200
preachers, 261
proxies, 286–7
reconstituted
1220, 49–50
1660, 256–9
1872, 321–2
reform strategy, 17th c., 196–202
seal, 216, 288
Street restoration, 356–7, 359–60
and vicars choral, 240, 243, 250–1
chapter act book, 18, 21, 208, 216, 271–2, 290
begun, 176–7
dispute with archbishop, 282
house values, 291
offences recorded, 197
organist's contract, 248
proxies, 286–9
Chapter Court, 291
chapter house, 99, 112, 115, 116–24, 268, 332
demolished, 123–4
plan of, 121–2
size of, 120–1
chapter room, 222, 367
charitable activities, 177, 263–4, 266, 294, 331–2, 390
Charles I, king, 4, 174, 194–5, 204, 207, 255
execution commemorated, 260

Charles II, king, 216, 235, 259, 260, 275
  choral grant, 298, 314
  land grants, 265, 267
  liberty exemption, 278
charters, 9, 89
  1541, 167
  1604, 182
Chartres cathedral, 146, 389
Chaucer, Geoffrey, 145
Cheere, Henry, 105n, 327
Cheshire Cheese inn, 296
Chester, 199–200, 248
Chichester, Lord Deputy, 183, 190
Chichester, Revd Mr, 317
Chichester cathedral, 10, 65
Child, 310n, 312
choir, 148, 384, 387; see also vicars choral
  1480-1647, 237–51
  attendance books, 20
  choir-books, 240, 250, 310–13
  choirboys, 301–2, 343–4, 377–8
    care of, 263–4
  choral revival, 342
  discipline, 299, 342
  duties of, 240–1, 259, 349
  finances, 160, 293, 298, 314, 345
    in arrears, 250–1
    Bennet endowment, 138
    exchequer grant, 168
    state grant, 190
  girls' choir, 389
  grammar school, 377–80, 387
  joined with St Patrick's, 241, 244,
    298–9, 303, 314, 340–5
  lay clerks, 238–9
  liturgical changes, 241–2, 244–5
  masters, 156, 238, 242, 247–9, 302–3,
    344, 378
  modern repertoire, 389
  official cessation, 374
  outside performances, 161, 242, 300–1,
    340, 343
  overseas performances, 389
  rehearsals, 299, 300
  Roe endowment, 325, 374–7
  school, 238, 345–6, 377
    curriculum, 264
  size of, 244–5
  women in, 388
choir stalls, 299, 369
Christ Church Baroque, 389
Christ Church cathedral, 269. See also

cathedral building; finances; land
  endowments; restoration, 1868-78
Catholic deans appointed, 205–6
chapel royal, 259–60, 282
council, 1186, 49
dedication of, 29
Dublin chronicle, 37–8
functions of, 157–9
historiography, 6–10
history
  1660-1830, 255–97
  1641 rebellion, 202–4
  Anglo-Norman, 47–52
  cathedral status revived, 1660, 216–17
  constitution, 1872, 321–2
  Cromwellian congregation, 211–15
  disestablishment, 315–23
  foundation, 1, 13, 28–32, 35–6
  pre-Anglo-Norman, 29–46
  Reformation, 163–73
    1558-1625, 174–94
  re-opening, 1878, 375
monks expelled, 1100, 39
precincts, 54–5, 128, 201, 329
  dereliction, 291–2
  development committee, 295–6
  protection of, 336
public ceremonial, 84–6, 139–41, 171,
  177–8, 190, 260–1, 300
relations with city, 90–4, 157–9
rivalry with St Patrick's, 50–2, 74–7,
  139, 321
synod, 1186, 62, 130
visitation rights, 289–90
Christ Church Lane, 111, 113, 126, 291
  shingled, 296
  tenants, 290
Christ Church priory, 12, 28, 46, 48
  Anglo-Norman community, 47
  architecture, 56–7, 109–28
  archives, 12–18
  Augustinians introduced, 45
  Benedictines, 35
  campanile burnt, 1283, 52
  churches in care of, 160–1
  community life, 153–7
  foundation, 12–13
  liturgy, 129–41
  music, 142–8
  size of community, 120–1
'Christ Church' psalter, 12, 16–17, 102, 130
  description of, 143–4

Christ Church Yard, 123–4, 128, 189, 211
  exempt jurisdiction, 294
  houses in, 276
  tenants of, 278
Christchurch Place, 2, 27, 111, 329
Christian Outreach through Renewal & Evangelism (C.O.R.E.), 390
Christmas, 15, 335
  carol service, 390
Church, John, 310, 311
Church Act. See Irish Church Act
Church of Ireland, 174, 195, 213–14, 255–6, 293, 297, 325, 335, 388
  cathedrals, 4–6
  convention, 1870, 320–1
  disestablishment, 2, 7, 20, 315–23, 359, 390
  under James II, 269–75
  restored, 268–9
Church Temporalities Act. See Irish Church Temporalities Act
Church Temporalities Commissioners, 20, 319–20, 374
  Christ Church property vested in, 320
  and restoration project, 359–60
Cistercians, 39, 44, 114n, 161, 169, 229
  architecture, 58, 120
  community size, 153
cistern, 90, 127
'Cithuric, son of Absolea', 32
Citizenship Service, 2, 335, 387
city and town parishes commission, 386
civil war, English, 207–8
civil war, Irish, 334
Claregenet, John, 168, 241
Clarence, Lionel, duke of, 85
Clarke, John, 303
Cleaver, Dr E., archbishop of Dublin, 289
Clement III, pope, 48
clerestory, 58
cloisters, 112–16
  cloister walks, 113–15
  restoration, 371
Clondalkin, Dublin, 37
Clonenagh, 'old book' of, 39
Clonfert cathedral, 55
Clonkeen, 38, 42, 81, 88, 159, 160
  accounts, 15
Clonmacnois cathedral, 55–6, 68, 105
Clonmel, County Tipperary, 154

Clonskeagh, County Dublin, 229
Clontarf, County Dublin, 224, 226, 229
Cloyne cathedral, 11, 205
Cloyne diocese, 311
Coady, Joe, 390
Cobbe, Charles, dean, bishop of Kildare, archbishop of Dublin, 266, 389n
Cobh cathedral, 4
Cockburn, Gilbert, and Son, 360
Cole, Henry, seneschal, 295
College Green, Dublin, 295
Colley, W., 268
Collier, Thomas, 137
Colmcille, St, 164
Columba, St, 93
Columbanus, prior, 50
Comerford, Michael, 4
communion service
  in protestantism, 195, 197–8
composicio pacis, 13, 51–2, 75–6
confraternities, 3, 7, 170
  lay, 137–8, 158
Cong abbey, 116
Connacht, plantation of, 200
Connell, D., archbishop of Dublin, 388
Consort of St Sepulchre, 384n
constable, office of, 259, 279, 286, 293
Constantine, emperor, 55
Constantinople, fall of, 85
convenant, 211–12
Cook Street, 114
Cooke, 300
'Coolfabius', 124n, 125
Coote, Charles, 215–16
Copper Alley, 30
Corbet, Jane, 264
Corfe, 346
Cork, earl of, 192, 196
Cork cathedral, 205. See St Fin Barre's cathedral
Cork Hill, 329
coronation, 85–6, 131, 139, 159, 239
Corpus Christi Day, 137, 139–40
Corristown, County Kildare, 166
Cotton, Henry, treasurer, 5, 317–18
  pluralist, 286–7
court of chancery, 126, 296
court of common pleas, 128
court of exchequer, 241
court of king's bench, 113, 128
Covey, Tobias and William, 304–5
Cox, Samuel, 215

Cramer, 346
'Crede mihi', 14
Creighton, John, chancellor, 205, 208, 256
Cressy, Hugh, 204
Croft, William, 310, 311, 350, 383
Crofts, Phil, 304
Cromwell, Henry, 212–13, 215
Cromwell, Oliver, 213, 215, 259n, 269
Cromwell, Richard, 215
Cromwell, Thomas, 84, 90, 129, 165
Cromwellian government, 209–15
'crook chamber', 206
Crooke, Mary, 309n
cross, miraculous, 3, 15, 46, 85, 93,
    107–8, 133–4, 157
    fate of, 164
crossing tower, 223, 228, 236
    damaged, 102–3
    repairs, 224, 231–3
    restoration, 361, 364
Crosthwaite, John, 345, 351
Crosthwaite, J.C. and Todd, J.H., 8
Crowley, Matthias, 349
crusades, 85
crypt, 7, 36, 59, 63–7, 97, 128, 132
    archives in, 21
    date of, 60, 68–9
    monuments moved to, 326–7, 372
    pier reinforcement, 226
    plan of, 64
    rented space, 234
    stones moved to, 370
Cubius, St, 94
Culaght (Coillacht), 42n
Cumann Gaelach na hEaglaise, 330
Cumin, John, archbishop of Dublin, 31,
    49–50, 68–9, 109
    Christ Church construction, 62–3, 67
Curragh, John, 166
Curtis, E., 352
Curtis, R., 352
Curwen, Hugh, archbishop of Dublin,
    172
Cusack, Lady Joanna, 108
Cusack, lord chancellor, 169
Custom House, 291, 339
Cuvillie, John Baptist, 306

Dalkey, County Dublin, 292
Dame Street, 295
Dancer, Samuel, 309n
Darcy, Roger, knight, 114

Dardis, Nicholas, 174
d'Avaux, Count, 270
Davis, Edward, 278
Dawson, L.E., 331
Day, J., 250
Day, J.G. and Patton, H.E., 6
de Assheburne, Walter, 88
de Balsham, Adam, prior, 47, 51
de Bermingham, William, archbishop of
    Tuam, 102
de Clare, Isabel, 61
de Clare, Richard. See Strongbow
de Clifford, Brother William, 83
de Clontarf, Walter, 47
de Corbeil, William, archbishop of
    Canterbury, 40
de Derby, Stephen, prior, 130
de Grauntsete, John and Alice, 91
    endowment, 134–5
de Hotham, William, archbishop of
    Dublin, 51
de Jon, Francis, 185
de Kork, Henry, 47
de la Pulle, Walter, 25, 82
de Lokynton, Robert, 17
de Montmorency, H., 45
de Prendergast, M., 45
de Redenesse, James, prior, 17
de Sandford, Fulk, archbishop of Dublin,
    51
de St Paul, John, archbishop of Dublin, 104
    construction, 97–9, 101–2
de Sutton, Hugh, prior, 81–2. See le
    Jeune, Hugh
de Tureville, Geoffrey, bishop of Ossory,
    133
de Valera, Eamon, president, 335, 387
dead, masses for, 172
dean, office of, 183–4, 257
    archbishop as, 321–2
    archbishop resigns as, 329–30
    endowment fund, 329
    established, 165–6
    formal abolition, 209
    income, 183–4, 265, 267, 316
    post-Restoration, 257–9
    residence, 127, 277, 291, 297, 332
    role of, 21, 170, 276–7
    united with St Patrick's, 315, 317–18
Deane, T.N., 357, 358n
dean's kitchen, 126
dean's orchard, 295

dean's wood cellar, 111
deeds, 13–15, 19, 47–8
 witnesses, 156–7
Delahide, Richard, 152
Delamore, Adam, prior, 98
Delaney, Mrs, 300
Dermot, William, 183
Dermotstown, County Dublin, 81
Derry cathedral, 4, 6, 378
Derry monastery, 55
d'Escurs, Ralph, archbishop of
 Canterbury, 40
Desmond, earl of, 85
D'Hooghe, Kamiel, 384
Diarmait mac Máel na mBó, 32–4
Dickenson, Dr H.H., 329
'Dignitas decani', 11
diocesan system, 39, 43, 47–8
 development of, 2–3, 26
 Roman Catholic, 4
dissent, 195
Dixon, Richard, bishop of Cork, 175
Dobbin, Samuel, 341
Dodder valley, 228–30
Doddyr Wattyr, 226
Dodson, Mr, 304
Dollard, Joseph, 368n
Dominicans, 102
Domnall Gerrlámhach, 40
Domville, lord chief justice, 266
Donaghmore, St Patrick's, 186
Donelan, Edward, 193
Donnchad mac Domnaill Remair, 38, 42
Donngus, bishop of Dublin, 38
Dooling, Mr, 370n
Dopping, Dr A., bishop of Meath, 270
dormitory, 112, 125
Douglas, Robert, 267
Dowd, James, 5
Down and Connor diocese, 4
Down cathedral, 3, 5
Downham, George, bishop of Derry, 193,
 195–6, 198
Downpatrick monastery, 146
Doyle, Langrish, 302, 308, 348
drama, liturgical, 8, 15, 78, 239
Draycott's farm, 182
Drelincourt, Peter, precentor, 257
Drew, Sir Thomas, 7, 20, 54, 219, 279,
 324, 326, 364
 chapter house excavation, 116, 119–20,
 123
chapter room, 367
 on cloister, 112–15
 criticisms of restoration, 332–3, 371,
 373
 on crypt, 60
 school changes, 332
 on sewer, 125
 on west gate, 111–12
Drogheda, County Louth, 202, 205,
 231n
 parliament, 92
Drumcondra, Dublin, 42, 179
Druming, County Dublin, 42
Drumsallon, County Louth, 80
Drury, alderman, 266
Dublin, 54–5, 207, 285
 Anglo-Normans capture, 45–6
 Bruce attack, 88
 Christ Church property, 90, 159–60
 council, 1080, 37
 defence tax, 278–9
 episcopal seat, 29
 fire, 1283, 52
 liberties, 188–90
 monastic dissolutions, 165
 parochial system, 36–7
 population, 1778, 277
 population, 1800, 280
 property values, 291, 295
 public utilities, 294–5
 role of Christ Church in, 90–4
 urban development, 295–7, 335–6
 Viking rulers, 26–8, 32–3, 42, 46
Dublin, County, 42, 157, 184, 265
Dublin and Kingstown Railway, 293
Dublin diocese, 39–40, 320, 331
 absence of archbishop, 76
 administration of, 152
 Anglo-Norman bishops, 49–52
 archbishop as dean, 321–2
 archbishop to appoint dean, 338
 general synod, 321, 323, 386–7
 keeper of archiepiscopal cross, 76, 152
 licence to elect archbishop, 51–2,
 75–6
 parish contributions, 336
 relations with Christ Church, 279,
 281–4, 289–90, 333
 taxation, 50–1
 united with Kildare, 315–17
 visitations, 282–3, 289–90
Dublin Builder, 358

Dublin castle, 3, 83, 202, 260, 295, 301
 archives stored in, 205
 Catholic use of chapel, 270
 Chapel Royal, 260n, 285, 333, 340, 343
 and Christ Church, 82–7, 177–8,
  260–1
 dean of St Patrick's imprisoned, 269
 Independent administration, 209–15
 military coup, 1659, 215
 records moved to, 203
 Simnel banquet, 86
Dublin Chamber of Commerce, 334
Dublin corporation, 2, 77, 86, 92, 116n,
 176, 328, 379
 All Hallows grant to, 162
 archives, 12, 14
 chapter house leased to, 268
 grants from, 137–8, 179, 232
 monastic dissolutions, 165
 municipal reform, 290
 relations with Christ Church, 170,
  186–7, 279–80, 293–5
 liberties, 188–90, 276–81
 and religious houses, 90
 seat restored, 324
Dublin International Organ Festival, 388
Dublin Penny Journal, 222n, 224
Dublin Philharmonic Society, 349
'Dublin troper', 11, 144–5
Dublin University. *See* Trinity College,
 Dublin
Duffy, S., 36
Duiblinn, 1, 26–7, 29
Duleek, County Meath, 163
Duley, Mark, 389
Dúnán, bishop of Dublin, 15, 33, 35, 41,
 142
 first church, 28–31, 54–6
Duncan, Lilian, 330
Dundalk, County Louth, 165
Dundrum, Dublin, 158
Dundry stone, 59, 66n, 122, 371
Dungan's Hill, battle of, 210
Dunleary, County Dublin, 292
Dunne, Thomas, 278
Dunnill, Craven, 369
Dunsany, County Meath, 100
Dunsterville, Edward, 204
Dunton, John, 244, 260
Dupuis, T.S., 312
Durham cathedral, 11, 65, 339, 387
Dwyer, P., 5

Dyflinnarskiri, 42
Dyrre, John, 89

Easter, 140–1, 148, 260–1, 335
Ebdon, T., 350
ecclesiastical commissioners, 315–17
Ecclesiologist, 354–5, 359, 362
ecumenical movement, 387
Ede, Christian, 387
Edgecombe, Sir Richard, 86, 94
Edmund, king, 27
Education, Department of, 378, 383
Edward I, king, 12, 88
Edward II, king, 82, 87
Edward III, king, 82, 103
Edward IV, king, 100
Edward VI, king, 3, 19, 151, 168, 190
Egerton, John, 187, 192
electrification, 333
Eliot, John, 187n
Elizabeth I, queen, 3, 19, 174, 182–3, 241
Elliott, John, 344
Ellis, Mrs, 382
Ellis, Welbore, dean, 257, 262, 284
Ely cathedral, 101
Emerson, Norman David, dean, 330, 338,
 386
Emmet, Robert, 290
endowments. *See also* land endowments
 chantry, 156
 lay, 133–7
 liturgical recognition, 132–3
English, Thomas, 157
Énna mac Donnchad meic Murchada, 40,
 42, 44
Enniscorthy cathedral, 4
Enos, Richard, 233
episcopacy, revival of, 215–16
Erasmus Smith schools, 377
escheator, 77, 82
Esker, County Dublin, 184
Esmond, Simon, 206
estates, survey of, 20
Estrete, John, 94, 131, 138–9, 238
Ethelreda, St, 101
Eton choirbook, 239n
eucharist. *See* communion service
Eugenius III, pope, 43
Evesham monastery, 34
Exshaw, John, 16
External Affairs, Department of, 334
Eyre, Mr, 192

Fagan, Christopher, 179
Falkland, lord deputy, 190
Fallow, T.M., 6
Farmer, John, 247
Farnham, Humphrey, 191
Farrant, R., 311, 350
Fenn, Humphrey, 185–6
Ferdoghe, mason, 227
Ferguson, Sir Samuel, 14
Fermanagh, County, 189
Ferns, 43, 184, 187, 272
Fethard, County Wexford, 248
Fich, Geoffrey, dean of St Patrick's, 155, 163
Fich, Thomas, sub-prior, 13, 16, 151, 153–6
Fido, John, 247
Figgis, Allen, 387
finances, 48–9, 52, 77–8, 84, 159, 264–5, 386
    charitable donations, 263–4
    church collections, 329, 331
    disestablishment, 316, 328–32, 336–8
    economic problems, 250–1
        mid-17th c., 206–7
        1590s, 180
    income, 161
        1544, 166
        1616, 183–4
        1806, 293
        donations for repairs, 231–2
        fundraising, 387
        wartime losses, 88–9
    post-Restoration, 257–8
    public subscriptions, 178–9
    and reform, 200–2
    restoration project, 359–60
    state support, 168, 190–1, 233n
    subsidies to king, 87–8
    TCD support, 191–3
    wealth of priory, 81
Finell, Thomas, 307
Fingal, County Dublin, 38, 88
Finglas, Dublin, 202, 229
Finlayson, John, 7, 345
fire, 1283, 122–3
Fishamble Street, 27, 109, 277, 291–2, 296, 304
    dean's house, 332
    'Messiah' performed, 301
Fishamble Street Mission, 379, 382

fisheries
    rights of, 89–90
    tithes, 160, 201, 267
Fishers' Alley, 277
fitz Eustace, Maurice, 126
fitz Eustace, Robert, 94
Fitz Leon, Geoffrey, 133–4
Fitzgerald, Dr, 383
Fitzgerald, Gerald, 8th earl of Kildare, 85–6, 94, 132
    chantry chapel, 104–5, 107, 156
Fitzgerald, James, 381
Fitzgerald, John, archdeacon, 275
Fitzgerald, Nicholas, 209
Fitzgerald, Thomas Fitz John, earl of Kildare, 134
FitzGilbert, Richard, earl of Pembroke, 133
FitzRalph, Richard, archbishop of Armagh, 79
Fitzsimon, Henry, 187
Fitzsimon, Thomas, 225n
Fitzsimons, Nicholas, 224
FitzStephen, Robert, 45, 60
Fitzwilliam, Lord, 183
Fitzwilliam, lord deputy, 177
flags, 334
Flanders stone, 225n, 229
Fleetwood, lord deputy, 210
Fletcher, Alan, 29
Fletcher, Thomas, dean, 291
Fletcher, William, 19
Fletcher monument, 327
flying buttresses, 73, 220, 371
Foras feasa ar Eirean, 39
'form of the beads', 167
'fount' stone, 370
Four Courts, 111, 127, 266, 278
    moved from Christ Church, 290–1, 339
    moved to Christ Church, 112–13
    rent unpaid, 233
Foy, Nathaniel, bishop of Waterford, 274
France, 389
franchises, riding of, 293
Franciscans, 183, 292
Freemasons, 5
French, Thomas, 243
Frenchman, Thomas, 111n, 227
Friends of Christ Church, 336–7
Fulke, William, 193
Fuller, William, treasurer, bishop of Limerick, 256

furniture, 216, 255–6
  restoration, 368–9
Fyan, Richard, mayor, 244

Galloway, Peter, 6
Galvan, Richard, 248
Galway, 154, 256
Garrard, F., 365n
Garstin, J.R., 6
Garvey, John, dean, 176, 179, 183–4
Gascony, 52
gatehouse, 111–12, 296
gatekeeper, 328
gates, 109, 111–12
  'great gate', 111
  west gate, 111
Gaudry, Richard, 351
George III, king, 260, 288
George IV, king, 296
George V, king, 334
George's Lane, 295
George's Street, 291
Geree, John, 204
Gervase, prior, 47
Gervase of Canterbury, 18
Gibbons, O., 250, 308, 311, 350
Gilbert, Sir John, 7
Gilbert collection, 104–5
Giles, Nathaniel, 308
Gilla Meic Liac (Gelasius), archbishop of
  Armagh, 45
Gilla Pátraic, bishop of Dublin, 29, 34–8.
  See Pátraic
Gillen, Gerard, 384
Gillet and Johnston, 385
Giraldus Cambrensis, 46, 107, 109n, 133n
Gladstone, W.E., 319n
Glasnevin, Dublin, 15, 42, 275
  leases, 181–2
Glastonbury abbey, 61–2, 67
Glen Máma, battle of, 55
Glendalough diocese, 39–40, 43–4, 322
  cathedral, 55–6, 58, 68
  united with Dublin, 50, 315–16, 331,
    336
Glendie, John, 273
Glenmalure, County Wicklow, 158
Gloucester cathedral, 36, 66, 250
Godfrey, Thomas, 307, 313
Godfrid, 27
Gogh, John, 106n
Goioun, Roger, prior, 82

Goldbourne, John, 214
Gorman. See Grangegorman
Goshan, George, 247
Gough, Patrick, 226
'graces', 195
Graiguenamanagh, County Kilkenny,
  122n
grammar school, 177, 332, 377–80, 387
Grand Canal Company, 292
Grandsire Triples, 385
Grane, County Kildare, 162
Grange, manor of, 78
Grangegorman, 31–2, 87, 159, 230, 275
  accounts, 15
  alienated, 180, 182
  market jurisdiction, 276
  tithes, 201
granges, 31–2
Grave, Robert, 184n
Graves, Richard, dean of Ardagh, 287–9
Graves and Prim, 5
Gray, Enoch, 213, 215
Great Connell priory, Kildare, 154, 162
Greencastle, County Down, 227
Greene, Maurice, 310–12, 350, 383
Greene, William Conyngham, dean, 330
Gregory IX, pope, 48
Gregory VII, pope, 34
Gréne, bishop of Dublin, 15, 31, 35,
  40–5
Grey Abbey, County Down, 116
Grierson, George, 266
Grindle, Harry, 9
Grose, S., 123
Gruffudd ap Cynan, king of Gwynedd,
  32–3, 36, 42
guide-books, 8
Guildhall, 90
guilds, 3, 7, 92, 178, 280
  chantries, 145
  chapels, 132–3, 158, 170, 172
  endowments, 138
  and liberties, 189
Guinness, Sir Benjamin Lee, 358–9
gunpowder explosion, 180, 233
gunpowder plot, 1605, 210
Gwynn, Aubrey, 9, 13, 31, 35–6, 38, 40,
  56
Gylles, saddler, 244

Hackett, Sir Thomas, 269
Haghmon priory, Shropshire, 154

Hakett [Haketh], Robert, 81n, 88n
Hall, Fr, 274
Hall, Henry, precentor, 205, 257
Hamerton, William, 344
Hamlyn, Mathew, 244
Hancock, Laurence, 154
Hancock, Walter, prior of All Saints, 152
Hand, Geoffrey, 9–10
Handel, G.F., 300–1, 312, 383
Hanmer, Meredith, 187
Harcourt, Sir Simon, 204
Harding, John, chancellor, sub-dean, 184, 203–5
Harris, George, 305
Harris, John, 310
Harris, Renatus, 306, 308
Harrison, Thomas, 212–15
Harrison and Harrison, 381
Harrold, Walter, 182
Hassard, John, 157
Hassard, William, prior, 17, 151–5, 161, 239
   resignation, 162–3
Hatfield, Ridgely, 207
Hatten, John, 209
Hawkes, William, 9
Hawkshaw, John, 248, 299, 305, 307
Haydn, F.J., 343, 351
Hayes, Richard, 6
Hayes, William, 311, 350
hearth tax, 278
Henrietta Maria, queen, 204
Henris, mason, 224, 227–8
Henry I, king, 115n
Henry II, king, 43, 46–7, 49, 62, 99
Henry III, king, 70
Henry of London, archbishop of Dublin, 49, 50–1, 62n, 109, 133
Henry VII, king, 86, 161
Henry VIII, king, 19, 151, 165, 168, 171, 179
Hereford cathedral, 65, 123n, 247
Herman, John, 172, 176
Hetherington, John, 268
Heuet, Thomas, 157
Hewetson, Christopher, treasurer, 187, 193, 199
Hewitt, Esther, 285
Hewitt, James jnr, 285, 303, 344
Hewitt, James snr, 285
Hewitt, Jane, 285–6
Hewson, John, 211, 212, 213

Heydock, John, 251
Heyne, Richard, 157
Heyne family, 154
Heyward, Robert, 241–2, 247
Hibernian Catch Club, 301
Hiberno-Romanesque, 68
Higgins, Edward, 312
High School, 377
High Street, 265, 295
Highly, John, 154
Higley (Highly), Peter, 89, 154
Hill, Edward, 185n, 187, 192–3, 196
Hinde, Thomas, precentor, 257
Hitchcock, Walter, 303, 309
Hoadly, John, archbishop of Dublin, 284
Hodge, Robert, 310n
Hoey, James, 278
Hogan, Canon, 382
Hollister, Frederick, 346
Hollister, William Castles, 306
Holmbury St Mary, 363
Holmpatrick priory, 152
Holy Cross abbey, 114n
Holy Ghost chapel, 99n, 104, 156
Holy Thursday, 121
Holy Trinity chapel, 132, 138, 172
   repairs, 205
Holy Trinity guild, 92, 145
Holy Trinity priory. See Christ Church priory
Holywood, Rosina, 16
home rule movement, 4
Hooper, E., 311
Horan, James, 381
Horan, John, 376, 378
Hosier, Richard, 299, 303, 309
Hosier MS, 300, 303, 309–10
Hoskins, Mr, 245
Howard, Thomas, duke of Norfolk, 162
Howell, Thomas, 19, 203, 205, 211, 216, 285
Hull, William, 346
Humfrey, P., 300, 311
Hyde, Dr Douglas, 335
Hyde (Lyde?), John, 175
Hyde (Lyde?), Thomas, 172

Independency, 195, 209–10, 212
indulgences, 98, 130
Innocent III, pope, 43
Innocent VII, pope, 13
inquisition, 82

interdenominational services, 335
Irish Builder, 7, 367n
Irish Church Act, 1869, 20, 319–20, 328–9, 359, 376
  official cessation of choir, 374
Irish Church Temporalities Act, 1833, 20, 258, 290, 315–19, 329
Irish Committee for Historical Sciences, 338
Irish Ecclesiastical Gazette, 326, 372
Irish Free State, 333–4
Irish Guild of the Church, 330
Irish language, 330
Irish Municipal Reform Act, 1840, 295
Isaac(s), Bartholomew, 310, 313
Isaac, Peter, 307, 313
Isle of Man, 33, 36

jacobitism, 282
Jager, Robert, 340
James I, king, 182, 233n, 244, 275
James II, king, 258, 269–75, 305, 328
Jebb, John, 340, 342, 350
Jenkins, Ven. R.G.F., 386n
Jerome, Stephen, 192, 196, 204
Jesuits, 179, 187, 193–4
Jewett, James, 248n
Jewett, John, 248
Jewett, Randall (Randolph), 209, 248–9, 302, 307, 309
  anthems, 250
John, cook, 127
John, king, 13, 43, 89
John of Exeter, 83
John of St Paul, archbishop of Dublin, 76
Johnson, apothecary, 291
Johnson, Henry, 211
Johnston, Francis, 260n
Jones, Henry, bishop of Clogher, 210, 216; Meath, 203
Jones, Revd John, 262
Jones, Kenneth, 388
Jones, Michael, 207
Jones, Thomas, archbishop of Dublin, 191, 232
Jones, Thomas, verger, 286
jury of the manor, 293
jury service, 294–5
Jutland, battle of, 334

Kealdulek (Gorman), 29, 31–2. *See* Grangegorman

Keating, Geoffrey, 39
Keble, John, 315
Kells, 169
Kells abbey, 102
Kells-Mellifont, synod of, 1152, 31, 43–4
Kendyll, John, 155
Kennedy, dean, 336
Kennedy, George, 258
Kennedy, Herbert Brownlow, dean, 9, 330
Kennedy, Walter, 247
Kennerley, Revd Virginia, 390
Kent, James, 311–12
Kerdiff, John, 154–5, 172, 176, 240
Kerdiff, Sir John, 154
Kerdiff, Nicholas, 155
Kerdiff family, 154
Keting, John, 228
Kett of Cambridge, 369
Kilcullen, County Kildare, 77, 88, 161
Kildare, County, 27, 161, 265
Kildare, earls of, 160, 170
  Cheere memorial, 327
Kildare, marquess of, 323
Kildare cathedral, 3, 11, 205
Kildare diocese, 4, 43, 258
  united with Dublin, 315–17
Kilkenny, 43, 272
  confederation of, 205
  parliament, 79, 80
Kilkenny, County, 358n
Kilkenny cathedral. *See* St Canice's cathedral
Kill of the Grange. *See* Clonkeen
Killaloe cathedral, 3, 5
Killeen, County Meath, 100, 108
Killenaule, County Tipperary, 77
Kilmainham jail, 280
Kilmainham priory, 80, 162, 230
Kilmallock friary, 102
Kinch, Henry, 268
King, C., 312
King, John, 201
King, William, archbishop of Dublin, 20, 268, 271, 273–5
  dispute with cathedral, 281–3
  imprisoned, 269
King's College, Cambridge, 247
Kingstown, County Dublin, 295
Kinsaley, County Dublin, 42
Kirk, J., 372
Kitson, Charles, 381
knights, creation of, 85, 178

Knights Hospitallers, 162
'Knowd', the, 124n
Koito, Kei, 388
Kynaston, Nicholas, 384
Kyrcham, John, 243
Kyteler, Alice, 80

la Warr, Henry, archbishop of Dublin,
    12, 52
Lady chapel, 96, 98, 133–5, 139n, 345.
    See Blessed Mary chapel; Mary chapel;
    White Mary chapel
    converted to school, 367
    damaged, 227
    description of, 99
    history of, 106–7
    music, 237
Lamb, William, 303
Lambay Island, County Dublin, 31–3, 39,
    42
Lambkyn family, 154
land endowments, 38, 40, 44, 48–9, 77, 89
    1488, 94
    alienated, 201, 209
    within Dublin, 90, 159, 160
        sale of, 295–6
    extent of, 81
    Gréne's episcopate, 41–2
    management of, 166, 173, 180–3,
        200–1, 265–8
    Restoration settlement, 264–5
    statute of mortmain, 87
    types of property, 159–61
    valuations, 49
Lanfranc, archbishop of Canterbury,
    34–5, 38
Langrishe, Richard, 208n
latrine, 125
Laud, William, bishop of London; arch-
    bishop of Canterbury, 194–5, 199, 234,
    244, 249, 255
    church reform, 200
    execution, 201
    trial, 198
'Laudabiliter', 43, 47
law courts. See Four Courts
Lawlor, H.J., 5, 8–9, 260
Lawrence, Richard, archbishop of Cashel,
    286
lay clerks, 238–9
lay confraternity, 137–8, 158, 170
lay endowments, 237–8

lay vicars, 389
le Decer, John, 92
le Gros, Raymond, 45, 60
le Jeune (Joeven), Hugh; See de Sutton,
    Hugh
le Whyte, John son of Walter, 81
Leake, Revd Isaac, 264
Leaman, Henry, 346
Leary, Revd Fr, 273
leases, 19, 81, 166, 206, 209, 265, 299
    change of policy, 180–1
    dean's house, 291
    demand for, 181–2
    final renewals, 320
    fines, 266
    length of, 160, 265–6
    reversionary, 181, 201
    value of, 200–1
    to vicars choral, 242
Leaver, James, 369
Leche, John, archbishop of Dublin, 75
lectern, 216, 327
lectures, 390
Ledrede, Richard, bishop of Ossory, 80
Lee, William, archdeacon of Dublin, 320,
    356
Leeper, J.H. and Crosslé, Philip, 5
legal examinations, 159
Leiden university, 185
Leighlin diocese, 6, 43, 316
Leinster, duke of, 323, 327, 360
leper house, 176
Leslie, Charles, 275
Leslie, Henry, 194
Levet, Henry, 157
Lewet, Thomas, 154
Lewis, Sir Peter, precentor, 65n, 113,
    175, 179
    accounts for rebuilding, 223–31
Lewis-Crosby, Ernest Henry Cornwall,
    dean, 9, 330–3, 337–8
Leynam, Thomas, 228
'Liber albus', 8, 12–14, 16–17, 78
    description of, 13
    donated to T.C.D., 320
    rights of cathedral, 293
'Liber niger', 8–9, 28, 32, 52, 78, 157
    annals, 38
    belfry, 102–3
    construction, 54–6, 60–1, 66–7, 97–9
    description of, 12–13
    donated to T.C.D., 320

'Liber niger' (*continued*)
  foundation narrative, 30–1, 35–6
  Lady chapel, 106–7
  parliamentary session, 84
liberty, cathedral, 203, 266
  infringements on, 268
  law and order, 279
  management of, 276–81
  privileges of, 275–6
  riot, 1684, 280–1
  tenants, 198–9, 206–7, 277–8
library, 185, 193, 222
Lichfield cathedral, 72
Liffey, river
  fisheries, 89–90, 160
  fishery tithes, 201, 267
Lightburne, William, 256
Limerick cathedral. *See* St Mary's cathedral
Lincoln cathedral, 10, 62n, 65, 101, 192, 247, 256
  vaults collapse, 220
Lindsay, Charles, dean, bishop of Kildare, 285, 287–90, 316–17, 351, 389n
  monument, 326–7
Lisburn cathedral, 5
Lislaughtin friary, Kerry, 222n
literacy, 189
liturgy, 142, 285, 300, 340, 342, 364. *See also* service books
  1558–1625, 174–5, 177
  after disestablishment, 331
  bespoke, 132–9
  communion service, 255–6
    Independent, 214–15
    reform, 197
  international festival of, 390
  late medieval, 129–41
  loss of, 207–8
  post-Reformation, 167–8, 197–8
  post-Restoration, 262–3
  prestige, 139–41
  Reformation
    Edwardian reforms, 168–71
    Marian reforms, 171–4
  regular ('*cursus*'), 130–2
  revised, 1984, 387
  Roe endowment, 324–5
  use of choir, 148, 241–2, 244–5, 259, 342, 349–50, 376–7
  use of music, 249

Liverpool, 351–2, 384
Llandaff cathedral, 69n, 72n, 123n
Llanthony abbey, 72n, 152, 154, 162–3
local government reform, 275, 295
Lockwood, Thomas, dean, 169–71, 175, 218n, 241
  death, 176
Loftus, Adam, lord chancellor, 196
Loftus, Dr, archbishop of Dublin, 176n, 180, 184–5, 231
Loghan, John, 154
Loghan, N., 154
Loghan, William, sub-prior, 153–4
Longfield, John, 20
Longford cathedral, 4
Lord Edward Street, 329, 332
lord lieutenant, chaplains of, 256–7
lottery, 191, 233
Loughbracken, County Dublin, 157
Loughlinstown, County Dublin, 182
Louis XIV, king of France, 270–1
Louth, County, 161, 265
Lowe, Thomas, 203
Lucan, County Dublin, 200
Luke, archbishop of Dublin, 51, 62n, 74, 130
Lusk, County Dublin, 166
Luttrell, Simon, 201
Lyde (Hyde?), John, 175
Lyde (Hyde?), Robert, 172, 175
Lydon, James, 15
Lying-In Hospital, 292, 301
Lynton, William, 162
Lyon, John, 19, 21

Mac Lochlainn, Muirchertach, 43, 45
mac 'Meirboillan', 42
Mac Murchada, Diarmait, king of Leinster, 41, 43–6, 47, 129
Mac Torcaill, 43
Mac Torcaill, Aralt, 44
Mac Torcaill, Ascall, king of Dublin, 45–6. *See also* Ragnall mac Ragnaill
Mac Torcaill, Echmarcach, 44
Mac Torcaill, Hamund, 42, 46
Mac Torcaill, Sitriuc, 42
McAdoo, H.R., archbishop of Dublin, 388
McCarthy, J.J., 357–8
'Macdeardan Macduba', 32
McDowell, R.B., 289
McEnery, M.J., 14
McGlinn, Charles, 352

MacLiammóir, Micheál, 387
MacMahon, James, 333–4
Mac Murrough, 85
MacNichaill, Heneas, 158
McVittie, Robert, 7, 100, 219, 362
Máel Ísu, abbot of Armagh, 37
Máel Máedoc Ua Morgair. See Malachy
Máel Sechlainn, king, 37
Magee, William, archbishop of Dublin, 289–90
Maguire, Revd Fr, 273
Malachy, archbishop of Armagh, 43
Malahide, County Dublin, 158
Malmesbury abbey, 72n
Malone, Edmund, 187n
Malone, Richard, Baron Sunderlin, 343n
mandates controversy, 186–7
mandatum, 121
Mann, Isaac, 19
Mann, Peter, prior of Holmpatrick, 152
manorial courts, 290, 294–5
Mansion House Relief Fund, 124n
maps, 20
Margetson, James, dean, archbishop of Dublin, 199–200, 206, 208, 216
rebellion, 1641, 203
market cross, 90, 112
market jurisdictions, 276
'Marmacruadin', 42
Marrable, Dr William, 326, 372
marriage registers, 20
Marsh, Francis, archbishop of Dublin, 272, 281–2
Marsh, John, 313
Marsh, Narcissus, archbishop of Armagh, 281–2, 284
Marshall, William, earl of Leinster, 60–1
martello towers, 295n
martyrology, 8, 12, 17, 41, 133n
description of, 15–16
Irish saints, 47, 93
Mary chapel, 156. See Blessed Mary chapel; Lady chapel; White Mary chapel
Mary clerk, 244
Mary I, queen, 19, 151, 171–4, 241, 244
Mary II, queen, 275
Mason, John, 311
Mason, William Monck, 5, 10, 21, 339, 341
Master of the Egerton Genesis, 17
Mather, Samuel, 214
Mathews, John, 311
Matthew, archbishop of Ardagh, 103n

Matthews, John, 303n
Maxwell, Robert, 202
Mease, Revd C.W.O., 333
Meath, County, 154, 265
Meath, earl of, 266
liberty of, 275–6
Meath diocese, 85–6, 164
Meath Hospital, 301
Medcalf, Mrs Sarah, 277
Mellifont, County Louth, 120, 153, 169
Mendelssohn, Felix, 383
Mercer's Hospital, 362
Merchant Tailors School, 378
merchants' guild. See Trinity guild
Mercurius Publicus, 216–17
Merrion, Lord, 201
Merro, John, 250
Michan, St, 15
Millard and Robinson, 60, 361
Mills, Humphrey, 211
Mills, James, 7–8, 14–15
Mills, John, 268
Milltown, Dublin, 228–9
Milsanda, 77
'Minoreni', 32
Minot's tower, 236
Molyneaux, Thomas, 278
monasticism, 2–3, 37
architecture, 56–7
and bishops, 26
and cathedral chapters, 49–50
music, 143
royal commissioners, 164–5
suppression, 12, 16, 162, 165
Monkstown, County Dublin, 287
Monsell, Patrick, 157
Monsell, W.G., 318
Monteverdi, C., 384n
month's minds, 179
monuments, 7, 132, 337
after restoration, 326–7, 371–2
earl of Kildare, 104–5
Moore, George, 312
Moore, Mr, 273–4
morality plays, 8, 15, 78, 239
More, Christopher, 172, 175
More, Thomas, 172
Moreton, William, dean, bishop of Kildare, 257–8, 265, 273–4, 300, 309
dispute with archbishop, 279, 281–3
escape, 272
Morgan, Dr, 382

Morgan, Thomas, 307
Morris, William, 362–3
mortmain, statute of, 87
Morton, Thomas, 258
Morwylle, John, 136
Mos, John, 136n, 156, 167, 172
Mossom, Robert, dean, bishop of Derry,
  216, 256–8, 264, 276
  care of property, 267–8
Mothers' Union, 337
Motley, Walter, 123
Mulhuddart, County Dublin, 154
Mullingar priory, 4, 162
Murchad, king of Dublin, 32–3
Murcot, John, 212–13
Murphy, Revd Samuel, 302–3, 308,
  312–13, 350
Murphy and Son, 358–9
Murphy of Dublin, 305, 351–2, 384–5
music, 9. See also choir
  1480-1647, 237–51
  1660-1800, 298–314
  anthems, 245, 250
  choir books, 249–50
  'Christ Church' psalter, 17
  costs of, 325
  endowments, 138–9
  high church revival, 339, 342
  manuscript, 20
  in medieval priory, 142–8
  printing of, 309–13
  storage of, 383
  17th c. expansion, 198
  17th c. repertoire, 308–13
  19th c. repertoire, 339–52
  19th–20th c. repertoire, 374–85
musical instruments, 144, 249, 300
  makers of, 278
  taught, 240n, 245, 302, 346
Myles, Richard, 247

Naas, County Kildare, 39, 84
Nares, James, 311
National Museum of Ireland, 108, 334
nave, 68–74, 122, 175
  collapse, 1562, 218–36
    accounts for reconstruction, 223–31
    reasons for collapse, 219–21
  restoration, 366–7
Neale, William, 278
New Year's Eve, 2

New Zealand, 389
Newcastle, County Dublin, 214
Newcastle Mackynegan, County
  Wicklow, 88
Newcastle-Lyons priory, 17
Newman, John Henry, 315
Newtown Trim, County Meath, 121, 154
Neyland, Daniel, 257
Nic Donnchadha, Lil, 330
Nicholas, canon, 87–8
Nicholas III, pope, 51
Nobber, County Meath, 169
non-residence, 286–7
Norfolk, duke of, 162
Normandy, 387–8
Norragh, William, 78
North, John, 309n
Northwold, bishop of Ely, 101
Norwich cathedral, 10, 65
Notre-Dame-en-Vaux, 72
Nuremburg cathedral, 18

oak, gift of, 107n
oath of supremacy, 175–6, 186–7
obits. See 'Book of obits'
oblations, rights to, 51–2
O'Byrne, Feagh, 178
O'Casey, Seán, 338
Octavian, archbishop of Armagh, 85
O'Laverty, James, 4
Old Sarum cathedral, 65
O'Neill, Revd William Chichester, 347
Open Spaces Act, 1881, 328
ordinations, 169
organists, 209, 245, 247–9, 299, 303,
  307–8, 343, 348–9, 374, 381
  duties of, 302
  Roe endowment, 375–7
  salary, 206, 348
organs, 216, 248–9, 299, 308
  Byfield organ, 306, 346–8
  fund, 337
  Jones organ, 388–9
  music manuscripts, 20
  rebuilt, 1960, 381–2
  recitals, 384
  replaced, 1694, 305–7
  taught, 346, 348, 378
  Telford organ, 346–8, 380–1
Ormond, duke of, 203, 205, 207, 255–6,
  284
Ormond, earls of, 80, 152, 160

Orpen, R. Caufield, 20
Osborne, Charles jnr, 344–5
Osborne, Revd Charles, 303, 344–5
Ossory diocese, 152, 316
Ostmen, 41–2, 45–6
O'Toole, St Laurence. *See also* St
    Laurence O'Toole chapel; Ua Tuathail,
    St Lorcán
Ottar, of the Isles, 42
Our Lady's shrine, Trim, 164
Outlaw, Roger, prior of Kilmainham, 80
Overbury church, Tewkesbury, 72
Owen, John, 19
Owen, William, 154, 167
Owgan, Nicholas, 154
Oxford, 130, 156, 184, 281, 358
Oxford Movement, 315
Oxmantown, Dublin, 166, 266

Pächt, Otto, 17
'Paddy's opera', 341
paintings, 101
Pakenham, Henry, dean, 317–18, 346
Pale, the, 88, 151, 161
papal indulgences, 49
papal taxation, 49
Paparo, Cardinal John, 43
'*paraphonistae*', 138, 237
Parke, Edward, 235, 354–5
Parker, John, 208–9, 217, 257
parliament, Irish, 79, 83, 273
    attendance of prior, 80
    Christ Church funds, 191
    clerical subsidies, 87
    exemption granted by, 86–7
    guilds legislation, 92
    held in Christ Church, 52, 84, 157,
        175, 178
    petition on Book of Common Prayer,
        208
parliamentary commissioners, 207–10,
    212, 215
parochial system, 36–7
    churches, 160–1
    reorganisation, 386–7
Parry, Edward, treasurer, 198, 205, 208
Parry, John, dean, bishop of Ossory,
    257–8, 265, 304
Parsons, officer, 280
Parsons, Robert, SJ, 193
partridges, omen of, 90–1
Past Boys' Union, 379

Paterson, John Thomas Farquhar, dean,
    388–9
Patient, Thomas, 212
Pátraic, bishop of Dublin, 45, 67n, 109n.
    See Gilla Pátraic
    Benedictines, 56–7
    and construction, 66–7
    music, 143
Patrick, St, 13, 29, 35–6, 47, 66–7, 85,
    93
patronage, 183–4, 319
paving board, 294
Paynswick, Robert (Castle), prior. *See*
    Castle, Robert
Peace, John, 350
Pearce, Edward Lovett, 277, 332
Pease, Lancelot, 305, 307
penances, public, 175
pensions, 153
Perkins, William, 185
Perpendicular style, 355–6
Perrot, Sir John, 232
Pershore abbey, 66, 72, 72n
pews, 215–16, 279–80
    social order, 213
Philip II, king of Spain, 169
Philipstown, County Louth, 161
Phillips, W.A., 338
Phipps, Benjamin, chancellor, 257
pilgrimages, 3, 28, 86, 88, 93, 108, 132,
    157–8
    end, 166
    protection of, 92, 100
Piltown church, Kilkenny, 358n
plague, 194, 208
Platt, John, 216
Plunket, Lord, archbishop of Dublin,
    124n, 327, 329–30
Plunket, Thomas, 152
pluralism, 286–7
Pollen, Patrick, 370n
polyphony, 145–7, 237–41
    not used in Lent, 242
Portrane (Portracre), County Dublin, 29,
    31–3, 42
Potter of London, 369
Power, Patrick, 4
preachers' books, 20
preaching, 91, 185–6, 194, 217
    1641 rebellion, 204
    charity sermons, 301
    fund-raising sermons, 328–9

preaching (*continued*)
  Independents, 210, 212–15
  prebendaries, 261–2
  rota, 285
  under Stafford, 273–4
prebendaries, 258–9, 285, 293
  and diocesan visitation, 282–3
  property of, 267–8
  readers, 259
  right of succession, 319
precentor, office of, 153, 156, 167, 257, 288
  duties, 323
  house, 128, 277, 291
  income, 184
Presbyterians, 193, 213, 215
presbytery, 98
Preston, John, 207
Price, Matthew, 96, 107, 355–6, 366
'Pride of life, The,' 8, 15, 147–8
Prince of Wales, birth of, 269, 305
prior, office of
  apartments of, 127
  role of, 48, 79–80, 151–3
  royal rights during vacancy, 81–2
Prior, Thomas, 327
Prior's Land, 200
privy council, 178, 279
processionals, 130, 144–5, 148
proctor, office of, 84, 168, 320
  accounts, 18–19, 177, 180, 216, 281
    1806, 293
  protection of fabric, 223
  rent arrears, 268
psalter. *See* 'Christ Church' psalter
Public Record Office, 8, 10, 12–14
Purcell, Henry, 300, 310n, 311, 350, 383
Purdue, Roger and William, 304–5
puritanism, 184–6, 192–3, 199, 211

Quakers, 213
Queen's County (County Laois), 274
quire, 57, 61, 63, 101, 175, 221, 321
  alterations, 235
  layout, 65–6
  linkage of triforium and clerestory, 71–2
  'long quire', 95–102, 370
  organ loft replaced, 347
  public ceremonies, 178
  refurbishment, 198, 200, 227, 355
  restoration, 361–2, 364

radical sects, 213
Ragnald Godfridsson, king of York, 27
Ragnall mac Ragnaill meic Torcaill, 45
railways, 292–3
Ráith Bressail, synod of, 1111, 2, 31, 39–40
Ram, Thomas, precentor, bishop of Ferns, 184n, 185, 187, 195, 199, 200
Ramus, Peter, 193
Rathe, Christopher, 166, 168, 176, 244
'Rathkyllin', 44. *See* 'Realgeallyn'
Rathmichael, County Dublin, 171
Rathmines, battle of, 210
Rathoath, County Meath, 39
readers, 259
Reading, Thomas, 20, 110, 111, 113
  map of, 222n
Reading abbey, 115n
'Realgeallyn', 40, 44. *See* 'Rathkyllin'
rebellion, 1603, 186
rebellion, 1641, 4, 189, 202–4, 211, 260
rebellion, 1798, 290
rebellion, 1803, 290
rebellion, 1916, 334
Recra (Lambay), 29, 31
recusancy, 179, 186–8, 193–4
  St Anne's guild, 246
Reeves, 5
refectory, 112, 126
Reformation, 1, 3, 4, 15, 18, 77, 123, 127, 133, 204, 248, 304
  1558-1625, 174–94
  architectural effects on Christ Church, 105, 107
  initial effects of, 163–73
  music changes, 237
registers, 20
'Registrum novum', 13–14, 19, 21
relics, 3, 15, 47, 56, 65, 157, 173
  of Becket, 179
  description of, 93–4, 107–8
  display of, 101
  fate of, 164, 166
  holy stone, 135
  and liturgy, 132
  royal warrant, 86
  shrine for, 41
  testimony sworn on, 85
rents, 181, 182, 200, 206, 233, 265, 267, 299
  abatement sought, 274
  agent for, 268
  arrears, 201, 268

Reportorium Novum, 9
Representative Church Body, 320, 324, 329, 374–5
   Library, 21–2, 390
'reredorter', 125
Reresby, William, 256
restoration, 1868–78, 7, 20, 71, 219, 222, 318, 321, 348, 353–73
   accidents, 362
   Anglican reform, 363–4
   anomalies removed, 69–70
   cathedral closed, 322
   chapels, 104, 365
   choice of architect, 357–8
   criticisms of, 325–7, 353–4, 370–3
   crossing tower, 361
   dilapidation of building, 236, 356–7, 360
   engineering problems, 360–1
   exterior, 365–6
   nave, 366–7
   old material recovered, 53–4, 60
   quire, 361–2, 366
   re-opening, 325–6
   roof, 233
   stone used, 330, 332–3, 371
   use of imagination, 364–6
Restoration (monarchy), 216, 298
reversionary leases, 181, 201
Rheims cathedral, 72
Rich, Barnaby, 185, 188, 192
Richard II, king, 85
Richardson, John, bishop of Ardagh, 186
Richardson, Robert, 184n
riding the franchises, 293
Ripon cathedral, 197
robbery, 83–4
robe-keeper, 328
Robert of St Neots, brother, 125n
Robinson, Richard, archbishop, 290
Robinson, Francis, 344, 348–9
Robinson, J.L., 9
Robinson, John, 349
Robinson, Joseph, 341, 382
Robinson, Nicholas, chancellor, 187, 193
Robinson brothers, 341, 344
Rock, The, 326
Roe, George, and company, 321
Roe, Henry, 20, 236, 321, 323–4, 353, 360. *See also* restoration, 1868–78
   bells, 384
   cathedral income, 329

and monuments, 327
   organ, 382
Roe endowment, 322, 374–7
Roger, bishop of Salisbury, 40
Roger of Hoveden, 108
Rogers, Benjamin, 248–50, 309, 375
Rogers, Edward, 5
Rogers, George, 310
Rogers, John, 211–13
Rokeby, William, archbishop of Dublin, 152
Rome, 28
   appeal to, 51–2
   Sitriuc's visit, 55–6
Ronan, Myles, 5
rood screen, 175
roof, 227, 233
   repairs, 223–5, 228, 231, 233
Roscommon, County, 68
Roseingrave, Daniel, 307, 310
Roseingrave, Ralph, 308, 310, 312–13, 350
Ross, Revd Canon, Robert J., 378, 386
Ross cathedral, 6, 205
'*Rota versatilis*', 146–7
Rothe, William, 161
Rotunda Lying-In Hospital, 292, 301
Rouen cathedral, 18
Rourke, watchmaker, 290
Royal Canal Company, 292
Royal Dublin Society, 5, 327
Royal Exchange, 339
Royal Hospital, Kilmainham, 270
Royal Irish Academy of Music, 349, 382–3
Royal Irish Academy, 5, 7, 338
Royal School of Church Music, 384
Royal Society of Antiquaries of Ireland, 5, 7
Rudhall, Abraham, 305, 384–5, 390
Ruskin, John, 362
Rutland, duke of, 260
Ryan, Dermot, archbishop of Dublin, 387–8

sacrist, 153, 156
'Safeguard Christ Church', 387
St Andrews cathedral, Scotland, 153
St Andrew's church, Suffolk St, 385, 387
St Anne's guild, 3, 244
   recusancy, 246
St Ann's church, 351
St Anthony's Hospital, London, 237

St Audoen's, 3, 186, 209
  catechising, 214
  cess payment, 207
  organists, 247–9, 299n
  school, 332
  St Anne's guild, 246
  visitation, 282
St Bartholomew's, 326
St Bride's church, 46, 348
St Canice's cathedral, Kilkenny, 3, 5, 11,
  103n, 122n, 205, 357, 358n
  silver sold to, 197
St Catherine's church, 390
St Catherine's day, 179
St Colman's cathedral, Cloyne, 6
St Davids cathedral, 61, 63, 72n, 122n, 180
St Doulagh's church, 31
St Edmund, fraternity of, 92
St Edmund's chapel, 104, 138
St Edmund's guild, 133
St Fin Barre's cathedral, Cork, 6, 197n,
  198n, 200n
  archives, 11
St Finnan's convent, 28
St Francis Xavier's church, Liverpool,
  352n, 384
St Frideswide's, Oxford, 121
St George's day, 178
St George's parish, 292
St John of Jerusalem, 90
  plays, 239
St John the Evangelist, Ardamine, 358n
St John the Evangelist parish, 12, 130,
  164, 206, 267
  community residents, 207
  distribution of bread, 264
  manuscripts, 140, 144–5, 148
  music, 17
  parish clerk, 209
  prebendal, 182
  prebendaries, 187, 192–3, 208, 256–8,
    273
    residentiary canons, 322
  prebendary suspended, 283–4
  prebendary's house, 277
  rebellion, 1641, 203–4
  recusancy, 193
  schools, 332, 379
  synod meetings, 323–4
St John's College, Cambridge, 368n
St John's Lane, 65, 128, 234–5, 333, 379
  profit from stalls, 267

St Lasarian's cathedral, Leighlin, 6
St Laurence O'Toole, chapel of, 57–8,
  94, 99n, 104, 123n, 132, 367n
  Estrete mass endowment, 138
  music, 238
  refurnished, 337
  stained glass, 370n
St Leger, Sir Anthony, 166, 168, 170,
  227
St Margaret, sisters of, 369
St Mary Alba and St Laud, 104
St Mary's abbey, 90, 114, 121, 153, 169
  annals, 38–9
  dissolved, 179
  fishing rights, 89
  income, 161
  stone from, 229
St Mary's cathedral, Limerick, 5, 9, 205,
  306
St Mary's chapel, 268, 345
St Mary's parish church, 292
  appointments to, 316
  baptisms, 338
  parishes united, 387
  rectory of, 287
St Matthias's church, 381
St Michael's, 6, 30, 184, 267, 340, 367n
  built, 30–1
  post-Restoration, 256
  prebendal, 182
  prebendaries, 187, 192–3, 203, 205,
    256–7, 273, 287, 347
  choice of, 317
  residentiary canons, 322
  prebendary flees, 208
  prebendary's house, 277, 291–2
  recusancy, 193
  synod hall on site of, 367
  synod meetings, 323–4
St Michael's Hill, 125, 333, 367
St Michan's, 39, 89, 203, 267, 340
  divided, 292
  parishes united, 387
  prebendal, 182
  prebendaries, 183, 187, 208, 217, 257
    residentiary canons, 322
  prebendary's house, 277, 291–2
  recusancy, 193
St Nicholas Street, 1, 27
St Nicholas Within, 30
St Nicholas's chapel, 30, 106, 132
St Nicholas's church, Cork, 348

St Nicholas's parish, 181
St Patrick street, 89
St Patrick's cathedral, 1, 3, 18, 191, 221,
   228, 257, 262, 299, 305, 386
  architecture, 3, 58, 69–70, 74, 100n, 236
    rebuilding, 341, 370
    restoration, 358–9
  archives, 9, 11, 21
  augmentation estate, 267
  bell-ringers, 351, 385
  bells, 304, 351, 385
  cathedral status, 50–1, 173, 321
  chapter, 167, 183
  choir, 142, 148, 238–40, 245, 251, 309,
    312, 339, 377
    choirboys, 301–3
    combined with Christ Church,
      244–5, 298–9, 303, 314, 340–5
    grammar school, 378, 380
    harmonised responses, 350
    vicars choral, 339–40
  deanery, 5, 183, 224, 315, 317–18
  deans, 155, 157, 163, 256, 264, 323
  dean's liberty, 275
  diocesan administration, 152, 281–2
  dissolution, 166, 168–9, 241
  finances, 50–1, 87, 183–4, 293
    corporate assets removed, 320
  historiography, 8
  history, 5, 10
  liberty, 189, 277
  music, 142, 144, 310n
  organists, 248, 307–8, 349
  organs, 148, 306
  preachers, 186, 261–2
  precinct, 295–6
  Reformation, 163
  relations with government, 82–3, 85
  relations with Holy Trinity, 13
  restored status, 171
  rivalry with Christ Church, 50–2, 75–6,
    139, 321
  school, 214, 378, 380
  second dissolution proposed, 176
  spire, 236
  surrender of, 166
  vaults collapse, 220–1
  visitations, 289
St Patrick's College, Lisbon, 272
St Patrick's day, 50, 260
St Paul's cathedral, London, 10, 101,
   159, 203

  organist, 381–2
St Paul's chapel
  appointments to, 316
  parishes united, 387
St Peter's church, 26
St Philip and St James, Oxford, 366
St Remi cathedral, 72
St Sampson's, Balgriffin, 78
St Saviour's priory, 44
St Sepulchre's, 50, 109
  liberty, 275–6
St Stephen's leper house, 176
St Thomas's abbey, 90, 131n, 147, 152
  dissolution, 162
St Thomas's parish, 292
  appointments to, 316
  income, 161
St Werburgh Street, 27, 388
St Werburgh's, Chester, 152
St Werburgh's church, 155, 157, 387, 390
  accounts, 177
  school, 332, 388
St Wolstan's, 127, 162
saints, covenant of, 211–12
saints' days, 79, 93, 179
Salcock Wood, County Dublin, 230
Salisbury, bishop of, 317
Salisbury cathedral, 50, 130, 220, 307
Salmon, T.N.D.C., dean, 386–8
Samuel, bishop of Dublin, 38–9, 57
sanctuary, right of, 92
Sanderson, Nicholas, 303, 310
Sarum liturgy, 129–30, 142, 144, 146
Savage, John, 108, 156
schoolhouse, 107, 367
Scotland, 52, 63, 87
Scott, Fred, 385
screen, 326, 369, 372
scriptorium, 18
sculpture, 67–8, 71–2, 108, 328, 369
  billet ornament, 69
  capitals, 58–9, 67–9, 71–2, 115, 368–9
  chevron ornament, 57, 59, 61–2
  dog-tooth ornament, 122
  'English stiff leaf' capitals, 59
  Greek key ornament, 58
  running vine scroll ornament, 105
  scalloped ornament, 115
Seagrave, Christopher, 187n
Seagrave, Walter, 187n
Sedgwick, Revd Ralph, 262
Seele, Thomas, 264

Seggyrson, merchant, 230
Selyman, James, 91
Selyman, John, 116n
seneschal, office of, 279, 293–5
service books, 130, 250, 309–13, 382–3
sewers, 125, 296
sexton, 206, 208–9, 259, 283, 286, 390
  duties, 328
  income, 304
sextoness, 285
Seymour, Edward, precentor, 6–7, 110,
  323, 339, 341, 343, 356, 358, 382
Sheehy, Maurice, 9, 14
Shelton, John, 187n
Shelton, William, 187n
Shenton, Robert, 312–13, 350
Sherrard, Thomas, 296
Shillelagh oakwood, 107n
Ship Street, 209, 297
shops, 198–9, 234, 277–8, 296
shrines, 41, 164
Siadal, abbot and bishop, 26
Sidney, Sir Henry, 178, 180, 231, 242
Silos, Spain, 115n
Simmonscourt, Dublin, 183, 201
Simnel, Lambert, 85–6, 94, 139, 159, 239
simony, 258–9
Sinothe, Thomas, 107
Sitriuc Cáech, king of Dublin, 27
Sitriuc mac Amlaib, 36
Sitriuc macMurgh, 25
Sitriuc 'Silkbeard,' king of Dublin, 1, 13,
  27, 33, 42, 60
  cathedral foundation, 28–32, 54–5, 69
Skelton, Robert, 186
Skerret, Richard, prior, 151–2, 154
Skerret, Robert, 154–5
Skinners' Row, 111, 124, 167, 268, 274, 297
  demolitions, 355
slype, the, 125
Smallwood, Simon, 207
Smarmore, County Louth, 147
Smart, Sir Henry, 380–1
Smith, Bernard, 306
Smith, John, 289–90, 343, 350–1
Smith, John Stafford, 311
Smith, R.A.L., 9
Smith, Canon Richard Travers, 326
Smyth, Dr A., archbishop of Dublin, 236
social hierarchy, 213–15
Society for the Protection of Ancient
  Buildings, 363

Society of Ringers, 304, 351–2
son et lumière, 387
South, John, 276n
Southey, Henry, 191
Spain, 169, 195, 210
Spray, John, 303, 340, 343, 350
Stafford, Revd Alexius, dean, 272–4
Stagob, County Dublin, 201
Stalley, Roger, 9, 31, 51, 178
Stanford, Charles V., 382
Stanford, John, 382
Stanihurst, Richard, 179
Stanihurst family, 154
Stanley, Edward, 316
Staples, bishop of Meath, 167
Steele, Edward, 369n
steeple, 231, 236
  burnt, 1283, 122–3
  damaged, 1588, 179
Stephen of Derby, prior, 17, 102
Stevenson, Sir John, 312–13, 339, 342,
  343, 350, 382–3
  memorial, 327, 372
Stewart, Robert Prescott, 320, 340,
  347–9, 351, 375, 381–3
Stillorgan, County Dublin, 160
stipendiaries, 209, 240, 245, 251, 259,
  264, 289–90, 308
  duties of, 285
  income, 267, 298, 300–1, 314, 339–40
  right of succession, 319
  Roe Endowment, 374–7
Stokes, G.T., 279, 281
stone, 225n, 226, 227
  accidents, 228–9
  sources of, 229–30
Stone, George, dean, 291
storm, 1316, 102–3; 1461, 99, 108
Strafford, earl of, 107n, 190, 197–9, 200,
  235, 246
  removed, 201
  repairs, 234
Strasbourg cathedral, 18
Street, George Edmund, 20, 57–8, 73,
  115, 128, 232, 318, 353, 385. See also
  restoration, 1870s
  assessment of, 373
  criticism of Price, 356
  on crypt, 65
  English comparisons, 61–2
  on 'long quire', 95–6
  on nave collapse, 221
  synod hall, 323–4, 367–8

street lighting, 294
Strongbow, 42, 45–7, 107
    building attributed to, 60–1
    tomb, 178n, 218, 231
        after Street restoration, 327
Stubbs, J.W., 5
sub-dean, 322, 325
sub-priors, 153
Sussex, earl of, 171, 174, 175n, 178,
    218n, 241–2
Sweeney, Eric, 384n
Sweeney, Peter, 388–9
Swift, Jonathan, 262, 264
Swinfield, Ralph, 211
Swords, County Dublin, 42, 92n, 187,
    266
synod hall, 321, 323, 360, 370n, 379
    design of, 323–4, 367–8

Tadpole, John, 209, 266–7
Tady, slater, 223, 225, 227–8
tailors' guild, 189
Talbot, Richard, archbishop of Dublin,
    76, 136n, 137, 270
Tallant, Patrick, 277
Tallis, Thomas, 311, 350
Taney, Dublin, 42
taxation, 49–51
    dispute with city, 188–90, 278–9
    landgable, 90
    wartime, 87–8
Taylerson, sculptor, 369
Taylor, J., 367n
Taylor, Leslie, of Loughborough, 243n,
    305, 384–5, 389–90
'Te Deum laudamus', 148
Teate, Faithful, 204
Telford, William, 346–8, 380–2
tenants, 159–60, 274
    entry fines, 181
    liberty, 277–8
    recusancy among, 187
    state, 266, 278
Terell, Patrick, 224
theft, 228
Thistlewood, bell hanger, 351–2
Tholsel, 90, 112, 280
Thomas Court and Donore, liberty of,
    266, 275–6
Thomas Street, 321
Thomond, earl of, 178
Thomson, Nathaniel, 309n

Thornbury, Walter, 75
Tibradden, County Dublin, 42
Tilson, Henry, dean, bishop of Elphin,
    199, 201, 206
Tipper, 154
Tipperary, County, 154
Tipperstone, 88n. See Balytiper
Todd, J.H., 18
Tomkins, Thomas, 250
Torcall, 41
tourism, 6, 332
tower. See crossing tower
Tractarian movement, 342, 357–8
trade guilds, 79, 105–6
transepts, 57–9
    restoration, 361–2, 366
    vault, 59–60
treasurer, office of, 84, 291–2
    house, 277
treasury, 83, 119n
Tregury, Michael, archbishop of Dublin,
    76
Trench, Richard Chenevix, archbishop of
    Dublin, 318, 353
    dean, 321–2, 329
    monument, 327
    and restoration project, 357–8
Trim, County Meath, 164
Trinity chapel, 105–6, 123n, 178
    converted, 222, 268
Trinity College Dublin, 5, 8, 198, 204,
    214, 264, 281, 317, 357
    centenary, 300
    choral performances, 340–1
    Christ Church MS in, 16
    donations to, 320
    free education of choirboys, 346
    graduates in chapter, 184, 256, 287, 330
    historiography, 10
    land held by, 265
    music department, 248, 250, 303, 312,
        343, 349
    organists, 308, 349
    preachers, 185–6, 192–3
    relations with Christ Church, 191–3,
        279
    T.C.D. MS 79, 130
Trinity guild, 132, 138, 172, 174, 188
    chapel, 105–6, 158
    chapel repairs, 205
    goods seized by, 189
    seeks return of rights, 209

Trinity Lane, 90
Tristi, Richard, sub-prior, 103, 107
True Cross, 93, 133n
Tuam cathedral, 102, 357
Tuam diocese, 43, 266
Tucker, 310n
Tuke, Robert, 344
Tulan, Fred, 384
Tully, 42
Turrant, Mary, 211
Tye, 350
Tynan, 202
Tyrconnell, earl of, 269, 270

Ua Briain, Conchobar, 42
Ua Briain, Muirchertach, 33–40
Ua Briain, Toirrdelbach, 33
Ua Cáellaide, Aed, bishop of Louth, 44
Ua Conchobair, Conchobar, king of
    Dublin, 41
Ua Conchobair, Ruaidrí, 45
Ua Conchobair, Toirrdelbach, king of
    Connacht, 40–1, 45–7
Ua hÉnna, Domnall, bishop, 37–8
Ua Tuathail, Muirchertach, 44
Ua Tuathail, St Lorcán, archbishop of
    Dublin, 1, 15, 31, 44–7, 49, 52, 57, 77,
    129
  birthplace pilgrimage, 387–8
  building attributed to, 60–2
  fishing rights, 89
  miracle, 107
  and music, 145
  relic of, 328
  tower, 102–3
Uí Chennselaig, 33
Uí Dúnlainge, 26
Uí Fergusa, 26
Uí Lorcáin, 39
Uí Muiredaig, 44
Uí Rónáin, 37
Ulster, earl of, 85
Ulster Museum, 369n
United Irishmen, 290
University Choral Society, 349
University College Dublin, 9
urban development, 55, 295–7, 335–6
Urban II, pope, 13
Urban III, pope, 48, 275–6
Usher, Arland, 16
Ussher, Christopher, 156

Ussher, James, archbishop of Armagh,
    186, 192–4
Utrecht, treaty of, 300

Van Nost the younger, 327
Vatican II, 335, 387
Vaughan, Dr James, 256, 258n
vaults, 59–60
  collapse of, 73, 178, 180
  commercial space, 198–9
  dismantled, 234
  rebuilt, 235
verger, 209, 259, 285–6, 303, 344
vestments, 135, 156, 168, 185, 190
vestry, 330, 336, 367
  created, 325
vicars' brewhouse, 111, 126
vicars choral, 168, 172, 203, 209, 259,
    264, 283
  apartments of, 125, 277
  career routes, 183
  and choirboys, 303
  constitution, 244
  discipline, 197, 242–3, 246–7, 299
  duties of, 198
  established, 239–40
  finances, 293, 298, 314, 331, 339–40,
    345
    payment in arrears, 250–1
  leases to, 182
  marriages, 242
  members of chapter, 167
  national differences, 243
  oath of supremacy, 175–6
  property of, 267–8, 274, 299
  right of succession, 319
  Roe endowment, 374–7
  vacancies, 206
vicars' hall, 112
'Victime paschali laudes', 148
Victoria, queen, 334
Victorines, 131n. See also Augustinians
Vikings, 26–7
Visitatio sepulcri, 15, 141, 144, 147–8
visitations, 48, 79–80, 282–4, 289–90
voussoirs, 232

Wales, 36, 93, 180, 224
Walkelin, bishop of Winchester, 66
Walsh, George, 308
Walsh, James Hornidge, dean, 330, 332
Walsh, Richard, sub-prior, 153, 155

Walsh, William, 169
Walshe, George, 313
Walton, John, archbishop of Dublin, 76n
Wandesford, Christopher, 202
war memorials, 334–5
Ward, George, 278
Ward, Henry, 268
Ward, Samuel, 192
Ware, Sir James, 16–17, 25, 191, 197–8, 231n, 264
Ware, Robert, 213–15
warrant, royal, 86
Warren, William, 348–9, 351
Washington, Richard, precentor, 203
Water, Thomas, 157
water supply, 90, 127, 276
Waterford, 4, 30, 46–7
Waterford cathedral, 3, 6, 183, 210n
    archives, 11
Weaving, Thomas, 381, 383–4
Weber, Ferdinand, 302n, 306
Weelkes, T., 250
Wellesley, Walter, bishop of Kildare, 162
Wells cathedral, 62, 63, 67, 71, 220
Welsh, Henry, 186
Wentworth, Thomas, lord deputy. See
    Strafford, earl of
Werburgh Street, 27, 388
West, John, 207
West, John, dean, 318, 321, 323, 342
    opposed to restoration, 356
Westmeath, County, 343
Westminster abbey, 11, 318, 321, 357, 364n
Westminster cathedral, 384
Westoun, Thomas, 17–18
Wetenhall, Edward, precentor, bishop of
    Kilmore, 261–2, 264, 298–300, 306
    musical repertoire, 309
Wexford, County, 39, 41, 46, 224, 272–3, 358n
    timber from, 230
Weyman, David, 351
Weyrand, William, 243n
Whately, Richard, archbishop of Dublin, 290, 316–18
Wheeler, Jonas, dean, 182–3, 189, 192, 195
White, Harry Vere, dean, 330
White, Jack, 387
White, Richard, 76
White, Samuel, 212

White, Walter, precentor, 156, 163, 166, 172
    chancellor, 167
White Mary chapel, 104, 107, 133, 139n.
    See also Blessed Mary chapel; Lady
    chapel; Mary chapel
Wicklow, County, 42, 158, 202–3, 229
Wide Streets Commission, 295–7
Wilberforce, Samuel, bishop of Oxford, 357–8
Wilkes, Anthony, 245n
William III, of Orange, 255, 275, 305
William the Conqueror, 34
Williams, Mr, 216
Willis & Co., 381
Wilson, Nathanial, chancellor, 257
Winchcombe abbey, 34–5, 38
Winchester cathedral, 10–11, 34, 36, 387
    council, 1153, 43
    crypt, 66
    music, 143, 146
Winchester responses, 350
Winchester troper, 145
windows, 97–8, 107, 235
    damage to, 100
    east window, 326
    'switchline' tracery, 96–7
Windsor, treaty of, 47
Winetavern Street, 27, 90
Winstanley bequest, 375–6
Winter, Samuel, 209–10, 214–15
Winter, William, 309n
'wishing' stone, 370
witchcraft trial, 80
Witter, Daniel, 257
Wogan, John, 51
Wolfe, sub-verger, 271, 275
Wolsey, Cardinal Thomas, 162, 238n
women
    among community of saints, 211
    board members, 330
    in choir, 377, 380, 388
    as members of fraternity, 91n
    woman canon, 390
Wood, R., 384n
Wood, William, 208–9
Wood Quay, 54, 229
    explosion, 180, 233
Woodward, Richard jnr, 301–2, 308, 311–13, 350
Woodward, Richard snr, 308
Wooten, Henry, 210

Worcester cathedral, 11, 34–6, 38, 57, 72,
　247
　music, 143
Worcestershire, 71–2
work-house levy, 279
World War I, 334
World War II, 334–5, 379
Wulfstan, bishop, 34–5

Wynchester, David, prior, 13, 238
Wynchester Society, 379
Wyse Jackson, R., 6

Yago, St Patrick's, 169–70
Yeates, Robert, 352
Ymna, washerwoman, 127
York, 10, 26–7, 72, 197